CliffsAP®
World History

An American BookWorks Corporation Project

CliffsAP®

World History

An American BookWorks Corporation Project

Contributing Authors/Consultants

Todd Carney, Ph.D.

Charles A. Desnoyers, Ph.D.

Philip C. DiMare, Ph.D.

James Goodwin, Ph.D.

Shawndra Holderby, Ph.D.

Kathryn Jasper, M.A.

David Meier, Ph.D.

Judith-Rae Ross, Ph.D.

Ryan Wilkinson

Wiley Publishing, Inc.

Publisher's Acknowledgments

Editorial

Project Editor: Kelly D. Henthorne

Acquisitions Editor: Greg Tubach

Technical Editor: Moira Maguire

Production

Proofreader: Susan Sims

Wiley Publishing, Inc. Composition Services

CliffsAP® World History

Published by:
Wiley Publishing, Inc.
111 River Street
Hoboken, NJ 07030-5774
www.wiley.com

Copyright © 2006 Wiley, Hoboken, NJ

Published by Wiley, Hoboken, NJ
Published simultaneously in Canada

Library of Congress Cataloging-in-Publication data is available from the publisher upon request.

ISBN-13: 978-0-7645-9631-5

ISBN-10: 0-7645-9631-4

Printed in the United States of America

10 9 8 7 6 5 4 3 2 1

1B/RZ/QR/QW/IN

For general information on our other products and services or to obtain technical support please contact our Customer Care Department within the U.S. at 800-762-2974, outside the U.S. at 317-572-3993 or fax 317-572-4002.

Wiley also publishes its books in a variety of electronic formats. Some content that appears in print may not be available in electronic books. For more information about Wiley products, please visit our web site at www.wiley.com.

WILEY

Table of Contents

PART I: SUBJECT AREA REVIEWS

PART II: THREE FULL-LENGTH PRACTICE TESTS

Introduction

About the Exam

It's likely that at this point in your studies, you probably know about what information will be tested on the AP World History exam. However, it's important to know what to look forward to in terms of the type of test that you'll encounter, as well as how long it will last.

The exam will last 3 hours and 5 minutes and will include both a multiple-choice section and a free-response section. You will have 55 minutes in which to complete 70 multiple-choice questions, and you will have 130 minutes in which to complete the free-response section. The free responses are essays, which we will discuss shortly.

The multiple-choice section will encompass everything from 9000 BCE (BCE stands for "Before the Common Era" and is eventually expected to replace BC, which means "Before Christ") through the present, and the questions will be divided more or less equally among the following time periods and will cover the Common Era (CE) to topics indicated:

Foundations: c. 9000 BCE–600 CE

1. Locating world history in the environment and time
2. Developing agriculture and technology
3. Early civilizations in different environments: culture, state, and social structure
4. Classical civilizations
5. Major belief systems
6. Late Classical Period (200 CE– 600 CE)

600– 1450 CE

1. Periodization
2. The Islamic world
3. Interregional networks and contacts
4. China's internal and external expansion
5. Development in Europe
6. Social, cultural, economic, and political patterns in the Amerindian world
7. Demographic and environmental changes
8. Diverse interpretations

1450–1750 CE

1. Periodization
2. Changes in trade, technology, and global interactions
3. Knowledge of major empires and other political units and social systems
4. Slave systems and slave trade
5. Demographic and environmental changes
6. Cultural and intellectual developments
7. Diverse interpretations

1750–1914 CE

1. Periodization
2. Changes in global commerce, communications, and technology
3. Demographic and environmental changes
4. Changes in social and gender structure
5. Political revolutions and independence movements; new political ideas
6. Rise of Western dominance
7. Diverse interpretations

1914 CE–Present

1. Periodization
2. The World Wars, the Holocaust, the Cold War, nuclear weaponry, and international organizations and their impact on the global framework
3. New patterns of nationalism
4. Impact of major global economic developments
5. New forces of revolutions and other sources of political innovations
6. Social reform and social revolution
7. Globalization of science, technology, and culture
8. Demographic and environmental changes
9. Diverse interpretations

As you will see, this book is also divided into similar sections to help you focus on each area.

The Multiple-Choice Format

Most of the standardized tests that you've probably taken throughout your educational career have contained multiple-choice questions. For some reason, these types of questions give a large percentage of test-takers a difficult time. If you approach these questions carefully, they are easier than you think.

Let's analyze the concept of the multiple-choice question. Keep in mind that these questions are created to test your abilities to recognize the correct answer from five choices. This makes it a little more difficult than those with only four choices.

Questions are comprised of several parts.

1. The question stem
2. The correct choice
3. Distracters

As test-item writers create questions, they normally approach it as follows:

- One choice is absolutely correct.
- One or two choices are absolutely incorrect (distracters).
- One or two choices may be similar to the correct answer, but might contain some information that is not quite accurate or on target, or even might not answer the specific question (distracters).

How do you approach these questions? First, read the question and see whether you know the answer. If you know it automatically, then you can look at the choices and select the correct one. Let's look at a basic example.

> The main reason for the rise of the Nazis in Germany was
>
> **A.** Adolph Hitler.
> **B.** the Great Depression.
> **C.** the Treaty of Versailles.
> **D.** the breakdown of parliamentary democracy.
> **E.** the increase in production of fighter planes.

The correct choice is **B.** How did you do? Were you able to analyze the question in terms of the answer? First of all, you could have eliminated Choice **A.** Adolph Hitler certainly wasn't the main reason for the rise of the Nazi party. It began long before Hitler's rise to power. You should also have eliminated Choice **E.** An increase in weapons production is a *result* of the rise of the Nazis, not a cause. This is the time-honored approach of *process of elimination*.

You start by eliminating choices that do not seem logical, or those that you know immediately are incorrect. As we said, you can eliminate Choices **A** and **E.** This now leaves only three choices. You've reduced your odds of selecting the correct answer from one out of five (20 percent) to one out of three (33⅓ percent), which is a lot better.

After you've eliminated those two choices, move to the next choice. Let's look at The Treaty of Versailles. This treaty was extremely unpopular in Germany, and they tended to ignore it. This would not be a clear cause of the rise of fascism. So you can eliminate Choice **C.** Now you have only two choices left, and you've increased your odds to one out of two (50 percent).

Now, unless you know the correct answer, you can guess. However, in the AP World History test, random guessing can count against you, since one quarter (¼) of a point is deducted for incorrect answers. But on the other hand, you would have to answer four questions incorrectly in order to lose one point. So if you have some knowledge of the question and have used the process of elimination as described previously, you should take a chance on answering the question. At the same time, you don't lose anything by *not* answering a question—but unless you have no idea of the answer, no concept of which choices to eliminate—it's probably better to try to get points by taking a chance.

The correct answer, as we said previously, is Choice **B.** The main reason for the rise of fascism in Germany was the Great Depression, beginning in October 1929. The isolationist United States turned even further inward, and the shock to the world economy was severe. Germany was unable to meet their reparations payments and became open to the radical right with their black-and-white answers. Thus, fascism and the Nazis began their take over of Germany.

Pay attention to words like *always*, *never*, or *not*. Most things in the world are not *always* or *never*, and you should be careful if a question asks you to choose which of the choices is NOT. . . ! Watch the wording also on questions that state "All are correct EXCEPT . . . !"

It also might be helpful to go through the entire multiple-choice section as quickly as possible; answering all of the questions you can answer easily. Then go back and work on those that caused you more difficulty.

Free-Response Questions

The free-response section of the AP World History test includes three in-depth questions and is worth one-half (½) of your score on the overall test. Each of the free-response questions is scored equally, and, therefore, each of the three questions is worth 16.66 percent of the total grade (⅓ of 50 percent). You will have 130 minutes in which to complete this portion of the test.

Remember that these essays will be marked by teachers, not—as in the case of the multiple-choice questions—by machines, so you must follow some of the basics of writing a good essay.

Of course, the very first thing you must do is read the directions, make sure that you understand them, and then read the question. There are three different types of questions that comprise the free-response section, and we'll discuss them later in this introduction. Because there are three different types of question formats, it is vitally important that you understand the directions and the types of questions you'll encounter. Fortunately, we have provided you with samples in the tests at the end of the book, so you will be able to practice answering them.

Keep in mind the following points when composing an essay.

Whenever you write a paper analyzing, discussing, comparing, identifying causes or effects, or arguing a position, you should be able to write a *thesis statement*. You can refine and improve it as you go along, but try to begin with a one-sentence statement. A thesis statement can help you steer a straight course, avoiding the danger of digression.

Make your thesis statement say something. Don't be satisfied with weak generalities that fail to zero in on your main point. The following is an example of a pseudo-thesis statements:

> "People hold different opinions as to whether it is wise to impose sanctions on China because of their human rights violations."

You can see that this doesn't zero in on anything specific. What are their opinions? What is the majority opinion? What are the human rights violations?

Examine all of the parts of the questions. Make sure you understand how each of the items that are present have some sort of relationship. You will have to analyze the material before you can begin writing. You will be asked to form opinions and discuss the various sides, advantages, disadvantages, and so on, of the material. How are the items presented the same; how are they dissimilar?

Then you will have to discuss or compare the material in your writing. Do so clearly and concisely. Always keep in mind that someone will be reading this, and it is up to you to make sure the reader understands what you're trying to say. Divide the essays into logical paragraphs to make them easier to read and convey thoughts.

It is also necessary to write an ending that truly sums up what you were trying to say. Think of this ending as if you were a defense attorney making your summation to the jury, and that whatever you say will save your client's life if you win. It's an important part of any essay, and that last paragraph should bring together the major points that you dealt with in the body of the essay.

One other very important point that cannot be stressed too often is to write legibly. Regardless of how cogent your arguments may be, how well constructed your paragraphs, they're of no use if the scorer cannot read your essay. Since a good essay for AP World History should run a minimum of two pages (more is ideal), that's a lot for someone to read. It's up to you to make it as easy as possible for the reader, so he or she can get through it easily and understand what you've said.

There are three different types of questions on the free-response section: a document-based essay; a change-over-time essay; and a comparative essay. Let's take a look at each type of question.

Document-Based Essay Question

Nothing to get nervous about, this essay is based on 4 to 10 documents that will be part of the question. You will be asked to demonstrate your ability to analyze this material and then write a cogent essay based on these articles. You will have a 10-minute period in which to read the questions and accompanying articles, and then 40 minutes in which to write your essay.

The concepts to deal with here are "analysis" and "comparison." This is the focus of this type of question. You will be required to write your essay based on the question you're given and referring to documents that will accompany this question. You must use all (or all but one) of the documents, and you must discuss each of them within your essay. It is important to refer to them by name and/or author. You must be able to analyze these articles in regard to the question, and your writing should show that you understand all aspects of these documents. Further, you must be able to compare and contrast them within the context of the question. Some or all may be the same; some may differ in approach or ideas. It is up to you to demonstrate your comprehension of this material within the framework of world history and their chronology.

Change-Over-Time Essay Question

This essay will cover one of the chronological periods that make up the AP World History course outline (see previous) and will focus on at least one or more cultural areas. You will have 40 minutes in which to answer this question and write your essay. It should be clear from the title of this essay that you will be asked to demonstrate your knowledge of how things change over a period of time, dealing with technological issues, scientific areas, cultural topics, environmental changes, and so on. It is recommended that you spend the first 5 minutes going over the question, thinking about your approach, and outline your thoughts. If you had more time, you could follow the basics of "prewriting" your essay, which gives you a chance to do some editing. However, given the limited time, you don't have a chance to do that; some of it will have to be done in your head. Make some notes to yourself, and make sure that you demonstrate how the topic you are discussing relates to the big picture by thinking globally.

Comparative Essay Question

This is the last of the free-response questions, and it should be obvious that you will be asked to write an essay that will compare topics that you should have studied throughout the year. You will demonstrate your knowledge of how societies compare, their interactions with each other. Or, you will be asked to discuss major events throughout history, such as culture, world trade, technology, and so on. Like the other two essays, you'll have 40 minutes in which to write the essay. Again, take 5 minutes prior to writing to compose your thoughts, outline your answer, and start writing in your head.

And with all of these free-response questions, don't forget that all-important opening paragraph.

How to Use This book

There is a logic to the organization of this book. The first part deals with the major periods that comprise the AP World History framework. You should read through them. Much of this information should be familiar to you, since you're already enrolled in the course. But this is a *review* book, and that's what you'll be doing—reviewing the material. If you feel comfortable with the material, skim it. If not, take the time to read it more closely. Since the course covers an extremely wide period of time, there's a lot to know, and perhaps you are more knowledgeable about some of the time periods in the chronology. Others may require more studying, and it's on those that you should focus.

The second part of the book is the sample test section. We've provided three full-length exams. The purpose of the tests is two-fold. The first is to give you practice so that when you take the actual exam, you'll know the types of questions that you'll be asked. As you go through this book, take your time with the questions and answers within the chapters as well as on the tests. Try to analyze what you answered incorrectly and learn from the answers. Identify those questions where you were able to use the process of elimination. Check how well you did on those. How many did you just know and were able to answer? Don't worry just about how well or poorly you did. Take the time to do an analysis of your results. You're also learning and practicing the technique of answering multiple-choice questions.

The second purpose of these tests is to help you analyze your strengths and weaknesses in the subject matter. When you've completed the exams and checked your answers, look for a pattern that might show you those types of questions that gave you problems. Was it a specific time period? Were the questions pertaining to political topics? Economics? Religion? That's up to you to determine and might require you to do some further reading.

You will note that in the free-response questions, we did not provide you with actual essays. Instead, we've given you an outline of what should be included in *your* essay. This is a good way for you to understand how to answer these types of questions—to organize your thoughts, to outline them in your head, and then make sure that you've covered all of the points before beginning to write.

There are no secrets to being a successful test-taker. Obviously, you must be armed with an education and have the knowledge and skills to be able to take the test. You will also have a better chance if you practice the techniques of answering the multiple-choice questions that we've presented here in the sample tests. The real key to success is to practice as much as possible. The more you practice, the better you will do on the test. After reviewing all of the chapters in the book, take the practice exams. They are simulated exams, and it will be helpful if you time yourself, and take them in a quiet place, away from outside distractions. Use a stop watch, and you'll find that as you move from test to test, you will improve your ability to analyze and answer the questions.

When you've completed each exam, take a break and then check your answers. We've tried to provide clear explanations for each question, so that you'll learn something as you go along. If you have more questions, go back to the review chapters or ask your AP teacher for help. By the time you've finished this book, you'll be ready for the actual exam.

Good luck!

PART I

SUBJECT AREA REVIEWS

Foundations (c. 8000 BCE–600 CE)

First Contacts (600–1450 CE)

The Early Modern World (1450–1750 CE)

From Idealism to War—The World Coming Together (1750–1914 CE)

The Coming Together of One World—Is There a World Civilization? (1914–present)

Pre-Civilization

In *A Tale of Two Cities*, Charles Dickens points out how mid-nineteenth-century Victorian England and late eighteenth-century pre-revolutionary France resembled each other: Both were monarchies in need of political and tax reform; both countries were plagued with poverty, and both countries possessed an aristocracy that was interested only in its own welfare. Dickens' London readers needed to accept this assumption if they were to believe his premise, "Revolution in all its ferocity was about to break out in Piccadilly Circus, going thence to the Tower of London."

Dickens' work speaks to an urge to seek commonalities in previous times. The time periods deemed to be most like our own are often considered more relevant, which is why certain periods of history get more attention than others. We can think of some periods, such as the Victorian age as modern man in period costume. But those periods of history not readily resembling modern times get left on the historical scrap heap. What use are they; what have they to teach us? Too often the study of history is confined to those periods that most resemble modern times. Unfortunately, studying only the "relevant" historical material gives history a rough texture. This makes it impossible to see how certain intellectual movements, politics, and culture developed.

What do those periods that don't resemble the present have to teach us? Quite a lot! The first humans faced the same problems that haunt us today: securing food, shelter, clothing themselves and families, meeting their deadlines. Early humans were "hunters and gatherers." They survived by hunting game animals and gathering edible fruits and greens. This meant traveling to another place once food gave out. Pre-civilized humankind didn't concern themselves with flight schedules, but they understood leaving one area before winter or rain made travel impossible. Further deadlines also meant knowing when to gather wood and the length of time food would keep fresh. Pre-civilized humankind, like modern humankind, struggled to survive. But cave people lacked the blessings of modern technology; they weren't Fred and Wilma Flintstone with modern appliances made of stone.

Pre-civilization is defined as a pre-urban form of living in which all members are involved with the production of, or securing of, the food supply. The time period for a pre-civilized **society,** the group of people who live within and comprise a given pre-civilization or civilization, varies depending on the location and surrounding physical environment. Pre-civilized and civilized societies may co-exist. The earliest pre-civilized societies were the hunters and gatherers. These societies survived by hunting and eating wild animals, and gathering fruit and roots. Once the hunters and gatherers had exhausted the food supply, and/or the climate had become too warm or cold to support them, the hunters and gatherers moved to another location. They lived off the land and were totally dependent on nature for their food and water supply.

Pre-civilized societies have left clues as to their way of life. Burial practices suggest emotional ties between members of the village. Recent archaeological excavations suggest early humankind possessed beads and jewelry. This suggests aesthetic sense.

Pre-civilized societies, therefore, possessed the following:

- Tools and weapons
- Religious beliefs
- Aesthetic sense
- Emotional ties

These societies appear to have lacked the following:

- Writing
- Written mathematical skills
- Historical memory

Human life expectancy was approximately 20 years, although skeletons have been found of humans who were 40 years old at the time of death.

Understanding pre-historical times and pre-civilization sheds light on how humankind began its journey to the present. It's a long journey, but the first steps appear to have occurred when our biological ancestors climbed down from the trees.

For further information on homo sapiens' development, see *Human Evolution*, Columbia Encyclopedia, Sixth Edition, (www.bartleyby.com) 2001–05.

Environment's Role

Pre-civilized societies required certain environmental factors if they were to survive. These factors included

- Access to a fresh water supply
- Access to animals, a fresh meat supply
- Access to plants, a source of nutrition
- Flora and fauna to be used for fuel and tools
- Natural shelter from the elements
- Materials, if necessary, to construct shelter from the elements
- A climate to support these items

After the discovery of agriculture, pre-civilization's environmental needs expanded to include the following:

- Arable land
- Somewhat temperate climate
- Meadows (later) for domesticated farm animals

Early humankind had an adversarial relationship with the environment. Cave men were at the mercy of the weather and the water supply, not to mention saber-toothed tigers, mastodons, and megalodons.

Pre-civilized societies most likely formed to give humankind a fighting chance against mother nature—the first examples of the adage, "two heads are better than one." Those in search of historical commonalities may view the emergence of pre-civilization as the genesis of the corporate work group.

Hunters and gatherers' lives depended on the environment. Droughts or excessively wet weather not only threatened the food supply and water supply, but also triggered natural disasters, such as floods and fires. Worship of fire as the source of warmth and means of cooking meat may lay at the root of religious worship. But natural disasters weren't the only thing threatening the hunters and gatherers' way of life. Cave people were also prey for the animals that roamed earth. As mentioned, mastodons and saber-toothed tigers were hunters, as well as prey. Megalodons made fishing and swimming, especially at dawn and dusk, dangerous.

All of these environmental factors necessitated that the hunter and gatherer society work together. Survival depended on this. Life became even more precarious after the advent of the Ice Age, 125,000 to 28,000 BCE. Glacial temperatures threatened humankind, animals, and plants alike. While the Neanderthal human is often satirized, this species possessed a large brain cavity of 1600 cc, capable of coping with a freezing environment. Perhaps humankind inherited our will to survive from the Neanderthals.

Geographical Zones

The Earth is divided into five types of geographical zones in regards to human habitation. Pre-civilization most likely existed in two zones but could have existed in four of the five zones:

- **Tundra zones:** Areas of little growth or vegetation; cold climate; not conducive to human habitation
- **Agricultural zones:** Areas conducive to agriculture but not usually near trails or rivers; somewhat self-contained

- **Route zones:** Areas near water supplies with venues making it possible to travel to other points of the zone, possibly beyond the zone
- **Impact zones:** Zones lying at the borders of other zones; zones at which cultures meet; often points of recurring battles
- **Zones of refuge:** Zones conducive to human habitation but located far away from other geographical zones; zones used by humankind as a refuge from warring factions

Pre-civilization "habitation" was usually located in agricultural zones or, later, in route zones. Impact zones, zones in which frequent conflicts occurred, were the province of civilization. Conversely, zones of refuge suggest the presence of fighting usually associated with civilization.

Time before Civilization

Time measurement is a human invention; history, in part, is a record dependent on time. This raises interesting questions: How did pre-civilization societies view time, given that they didn't leave written records? By what means does modern society measure time when studying pre-civilization?

Cave men didn't wear Timex watches or fret about traffic jams making them late for work. Days began shortly after sunrise, probably ending shortly after sunset. Prior to the invention of agriculture, spring and fall were migration periods. As agriculture superseded nomadic life, spring became planting time, and fall became harvest time.

This left future historians with the problem of how to define eras. "Once upon a time" fails as an historical/scientific method to answer the question of when.

It may be that the telling of time to the minute and second first emerged during industrialization. But even agricultural societies before civilization's emergence understood that certain things—hunting, curing, gathering food supplies—had to be accomplished prior to the changes of the seasons, and the migration to winter or summer areas. Pre-civilized fishermen understood that certain fish had to be caught by a certain time. These were the essence of the first deadlines.

After civilization's advent, agricultural societies had to follow civilizations' timelines if they were to sell or barter their goods. Time played a role in each of the pre-civilized societies, even if early humankind did not read or tell time by the hour or minute.

In the latter nineteenth/early twentieth century, in the wake of Darwinian evolution theory, two means of telling time during pre-civilization came into use:

- Era definition
- Dating tools

Era definition of pre-civilization is based on archeological data. These eras include

- Paleolithic or old stone age, rudimentary tools: 2,500,000–120,000 BCE
- Mesolithic, transition age: 10,000 BCE–4000 BCE
- Neolithic, polished tools: 10,000–4500 BCE–Present
- Chalcolithic, stone and copper tools: 4400 BCE–Present
- Bronze Age, bronze and copper tools: 4000–3300 BCE–1000 BCE
- Iron Age, iron tools: 4000–1200 BCE–200 CE

Humankind probably evolved in Africa in the lower Pleistocene era, beginning close to two million years ago. The early hominid population lived in Africa. From Africa they migrated to the Middle East, Europe, and the Far East. The Neanderthals first emerged in present-day Germany.

Means of determining the approximate dates of pre-civilizations include the following:

- **Stratigraphy,** in cases of multiple layers of pre-civilization settlements; the older settlements lie at the bottom strata
- **Typology,** a measure in which implements at one site are compared with implements at another
- **Paleontology,** determining age by comparing human remains with animal remains of the times
- **Paleobotany,** determining the age of a pre-civilized society by comparing it to the plants found in the area

Means of precisely determining the dates of pre-civilization include the following:

- **Geochronology,** determining the age of pre-civilizations by counting the layers created by melts of water from a receding ice sheet.
- **Dendrochronology,** means of measuring climactic change by viewing the thickness in the layers in branches and around the trunks. Comparative dating of trees in pre-historic settlements has resulted in being able to date the ages of these pre-civilizations.
- **Carbon-14 dating,** determining the age of a pre-civilization by testing the decay of the carbon isotope 14 found in artifacts.

These means of determining the age of a pre-civilization work best when used in combination. Pre-civilizations did not emerge at precisely the same time, but they appear to progress through similar phases. By understanding the phases and comparing these societies with natural phenomena, it's possible to chart how pre-civilized societies evolved into civilized societies.

Practice Test Questions

1. Most pre-civilizations included all but one of the following:

   A. Religious beliefs
   B. Tools
   C. Sun dials
   D. Artwork

2. Most pre-civilizations excluded all but one of the following:

   A. Medicines
   B. History texts
   C. Bill of sale tablets
   D. Poetry

3. Pre-civilization would most likely exist in which zone?

   A. Agricultural
   B. Impact
   C. Tundra
   D. Route

4. What is the means for telling the differences between pre-civilized eras?

   A. Carbon dating
   B. DNA dating
   C. Types of materials used
   D. Tools

5. Which is not a means for precisely measuring time in pre-civilization?

   A. Carbon-14 dating
   B. Typology
   C. Dendrochronology
   D. Geochronology

Answers and Explanations

1. **C.** Pre-civilized humankind did not measure precise hours of the day. However pre-civilized society did possess tools, religious beliefs, and artwork, such as the cave paintings in modern-day Spain.

2. **A.** Pre-civilized humankind did practice medicine and surgery. There was one practitioner who performed successful brain surgery. The other three answers pre-suppose the existence of writing. Pre-civilized hunters and gatherers didn't write.

3. **D.** Route zones provided egress from one food-producing area to another.

4. **C.** While increasingly complex tools emerged with time, the materials used for those tools denoted the eras during pre-civilization.

5. **B.** Typology measures the advancement of one pre-civilized society against another by comparing the tools at both archeological sites. Carbon-14 dating measures the degree of decay of carbon in pre-civilization artifacts; Geochronology measures the imprint of layers of water left by the glaciers. Dendrology measures the climate by measuring the thickness of branches and tree trunks.

Agriculture and Its Impact on the Environment

Members of a pre-civilization society ultimately faced a big problem: how to feed their society when plants and animals became scarce. Perhaps their group packed whatever goods they possessed and left for the next valley. But constant wandering took its toll, and life became one big round of "will we make it over the next pass?"

Most pre-civilized social groups faced the same problem. Some groups joined together; others competed for whatever resources, food, or water remained. Either way, more humans meant scarcer resources. Perhaps necessity is the mother of invention. Maybe one of the cave men dropped a few seeds, and noticed they eventually produced new plants. Maybe another one noted that the calf they found in the snow grew to become a milk-producing cow. Maybe the discovery of metals made it easier to build, plant, and harvest. No one knows for sure how it occurred, but we certainly know that the discovery of agriculture changed life profoundly. **Agriculture** encompasses the ability to raise and cultivate grains, fruits, and vegetables; raise stock; and prepare these products to be used as food.

When it became feasible to produce enough food to feed society, wandering diminished, and **pastoral societies,** pre-civilized nomadic groups that kept and depended upon livestock for sustenance, developed. These groups migrated between pasturelands in order to feed their livestock. More grain meant healthier livestock. Healthier livestock, whether goats, cows, sheep, or oxen meant more milk, cheese, and butter. Healthier livestock also meant more calves, and, when the cows and bulls were too old to produce, more meat, and more clothing. Life was still precarious. Harvests failed; animals died. Disease, accidents, raids, and skirmishes remained fixtures in pre-civilized life.

The shift from hunting and gathering to agriculture and pastoralism meant less wandering and hunting, more food, and longer life expectancy. Pre-civilized societies gained their first senior citizens, most likely profiting and learning from their experiences.

Curiosity has always been humankind's hallmark. After society gained elders, even if elders were just over 30 years old, their stories not only helped keep society running, but also gave society identity and connections to the past. An unexpected outcome of agriculture's discovery was the birth of History. When pre-civilized society's seniors could recount their experiences, these experiences became part of the community's legacy. For example, elders' experiences helped develop strategies and procedures needed to cope with the problems of pre-civilized life. These also gave the community a unique identity. Listening and studying the elders' experience gave a flavor to life, connecting the community to its past.

Agriculture also affected the environment. As forests became fields, animals lost their nesting places, burrows, and homes. Land wore out if continually planted. All of this necessitated human migration and resettlement. Resettlement meant more land under cultivation and displacement. Perhaps the quest for food also drove humankind to populate every continent capable of providing food.

With the development of agriculture, humankind society changed dramatically. The Neolithic, or agricultural, revolution enabled pre-civilized societies to settle in one place, while still maintaining a food supply. Ultimately this resulted in the creation of villages, and as the villages grew, cities were created.

After cities came into being, society changed from pre-civilized to actual civilization. For more information, check *Neolithic Revolution* at Dictionary.com. The Neolithic revolution was the first step toward civilized life.

Africa

Agriculture's advent in Africa resulted in the Bantu Migration. The Bantu, a large group, arose in Africa c. 2000 BCE. As farmers and pastoralists, they soon discovered the difficulty of cultivating much of the land on the African continent.

The African topsoil layer was extremely thin and easily eroded. Planting was done by punching holes in the earth and then inserting the seeds. African land wore out quickly, necessitating frequent migration. Land ownership was not a problem. The Bantu believed that land was part of nature, like the sky, sun, or moon. Thus, only the use of the land could be bought or contracted. When the land became barren, it was a simple matter to pack up and leave.

The Bantu migrated south and east in Africa, forming farming settlements. When each settlement could no longer support its population, part of the group left to form a new settlement. It was a long and slow process. The Bantu often remained in their settlements until either the land wore out, or there was too large a population for the land to sustain the settlement. That's why the Bantu reached South Africa at the same time as Dutch explorers and settlers in the seventeenth century.

The Americas

The first humans who are now known as Native Americans probably walked from modern-day Siberia over the Bering Strait c. 20,000 BCE. They were hunters, following the animals, and seeking fresh food. By 7000 BCE the Native American migration reached the tip of South America. Like the Bantu, the Native-Americans came from another area; unlike the Bantu they didn't displace other humans or move because an area had become too populous. They were the Americas' first humans.

Native American settlement followed a pattern resembling that of the Bantu migration, moving in a south/southeast direction. Like the Bantu, the first Native Americans regarded land as a part of nature. It could neither be bought nor sold; only the right to use it was regulated.

As with the Bantu, food scarcity forced members of existing Native American settlements to migrate and found new settlements. Some Native American groups were nomadic, traveling to different areas with the change of the seasons. When the animals became scarce, nomadic patterns shifted, continuing settlement of the Americas.

But unlike the Bantus, the Native Americans settled in areas that were unfit for farming. Inuit (Eskimo) societies survived on fishing and hunting. Woodland Native American pre-civilized societies, such as the Iroquois, grew some crops but depended on forest game and plants for survival.

Some of these societies survived quite well, growing into civilizations. The Native Americans who built the Cahokia mounds of the American Midwest comprised an urban civilization, meaning that Native Americans lived in settlements that did not have to be solely concerned with food production. Other arts and trades flourished. In the southwest and northwest, seaboard towns emerged. These towns developed to the extent that wealth was generated in excess of subsistence levels. The Potlatch of the northwest coast who displayed their wealth by giving it to fellow villagers, revealed the extent of Native-American wealth.

Agriculture as a way of life in pre-civilized America emerged in Central and South America c. 2000 BCE. After the Native American societies in these regions learned how to plant and harvest food crops, such as maize (corn), c. 1500 BCE, it became possible to feed large populations. As it was no longer necessary for everyone to work at producing food, the groundwork was laid for civilizations to develop in Central and South America.

Southeast Asia

Agriculture in Southeast Asia—Vietnam, Cambodia, Laos, Thailand, and Indonesia—first emerged c. 2000 BCE during the Neolithic, (Iron Age) era. Unlike the Bantu and American migrations, the area supported native populations. Vast migrations didn't occur, nor was Southeast Asia settled by invaders.

The land supported rice cultivation. Fish was plentiful, as much of Southeast Asia is made up of islands or lies near the sea. In essence, Southeast Asia is a **route zone** in which the cultures of China and India blended; hence it was termed Indochina.

Spices attracted foreign interest in Southeast Asia. Initially, spices grew wild. After farmers discovered how spices enhanced food flavors, were useful as preservatives, and were believed to have curative powers, they were cultivated and sold.

Southeast Asia revealed how agriculture became the vehicle for the transformation of a pre-civilized society into an urban trading civilization. The development of an established food supply facilitated settlement of a larger population, some of whom could concentrate on trade, crafts, and manufactured articles, such as cloth, metal tools, and pottery.

Life in the Village

Agriculture changed life in pre-civilized society. With its invention, humankind ceased being largely nomadic, instead settling in small family groups that grew into tribes and clans. These settlements became villages. The village's existence suggests the first "giant leap" for humankind. Instead of accepting the natural environment, early humans moved out of the caves, cleared fields and pastures, and built dwellings. The village was humankind's first artifact that went beyond the creation of weapons. It was the first successful attempt for humankind to assert control over the natural environment as a community.

In villages, people lived in free-standing structures, not caves or lean-tos. The village included domesticated animals, such as cows, pigs, and fowl. These required enclosures and enclosed pastures. Grain required preparation before it could be eaten. The village possessed a milling system, as well as community ovens required for bread baking.

Village activities—farming, harvesting, milling, baking, animal husbandry, hunting, and foraging—required tools. The first villages possessed toolmakers and forges. In addition, someone in the village had charge of medicine, possibly combined with religious activities. This person required training, tools, and mixing materials.

In short, village life introduced a complex division of labor, which began a chain reaction. Division of labor resulted in more efficiency in the workplace. This, in turn, resulted in more time for nonfood-production activities. Extra time made it possible for village life to include the study and practice of medicine, the development of religion and art, and the creation of the teaching profession. The division of labor and the distribution of food, water, and material required agreed-upon distribution structures that would evolve into governments. Decision making had to be systematized and consolidated. The negotiations that resulted in these first political structures may well have been the first political activity.

Work began at dawn, when there was enough light to work. Most of those activities were related to agriculture. Food allotment and preparation were assigned to women, while activities related to hunting, herding, and tool making were assigned to men. Men most likely made the tools; women may well have been the doctors and religious interpreters. Children worked with parents. The work day ended when the sun set.

In addition to cultivating fields and herding domesticated animals, grain needed to be milled. Most likely this was accomplished at first by members of the village grinding the grain manually between stones. The first ovens might well have been hot stone slabs, requiring tending and reheating. Yeast, or leavening, might have been discovered by accident. It's possible that a flour and water mixture used for flat bread fermented, and the cooks noted its ability to make bread rise. Some yeast starter was passed from parents to children for generation in most pre-civilized societies that relied on wheat or corn for bread. This would most likely include Europe, Africa, South Asia, South America, North America, and Oceania.

Morning and evening meals most likely were communal. Perhaps this was when village business was decided or when that 30-something senior citizen told tales of the past. After the evening meal, members retired to bed, and then another day.

Although nuclear families, family units consisting solely of parents and children, emerged during the nineteenth and twentieth centuries, family groupings of brothers, sisters, spouses, aunts, and uncles probably lived together, resulting in the kinship that became the hallmark of families. The need to produce food made large family groups with defined activities a vital part of village society.

Life in the first villages might appear as drudgery. But more complex divisions of labor required more complex means of communications. Evolving farming technology required more complex oral communications. Longer life spans resulted in developing relationships. This, in turn, led to language that enabled village inhabitants to express emotions and to bind more closely. Perhaps the first person who said "I love you" lived in the pre-civilized village. Language facilitated closer friendships, and time around the nightly fire resulted in singing as well as stories.

Work in the village no doubt was arduous, whether hoeing fields, forging axes, or grinding grain. But survival aside, village life resulted in enhanced communications and, with that, creativity. This creativity might have led to the creation of the first music and entertainment. Early humankind's first music was thought to be percussive. If true, the drum's rhythms might have led to early dances. It would take millennia but Beethoven's Ninth Symphony might have had its distant origins around the evening fires at in pre-civilization's villages.

Use of Metals

Pre-civilization **technology,** the application of scientific knowledge to practical problems through the creation of more efficient processes and tools, primarily consisted of creating tools to better accomplish tasks at hand. It concentrated on building a mouse trap, rather than finding new ways to keep away the mice; creating sturdier farm implements, rather than working with different seeds and soil composition.

Metal implements played a large role in pre-civilization technologies. That's why pre-civilization is often divided roughly into three eras: the Stone Age, the Bronze Age, and the Iron Age. The Stone Age, lasting from humankind's appearance roughly 2,000,000 years ago until c. 6500 BCE, marked the time most pre-civilizations fashioned weapons and farm implements out of stone. The fabrication of tools from stone marked the first use of technology by humankind. As the Stone Age progressed, stone tools became both sharper and polished. But the discovery of metals led to a new age. Tools made of metals lasted longer than their stone counterparts, accomplishing tasks more efficiently and quickly. Bronze, an alloy of copper and tin, was more durable than stone and much easier to work. But bronze was not readily available, and its durability depended on the creation of the alloy. Too much copper, and bronze tools bent under pressure. Only the wealthier civilizations could readily afford bronze tools, which weren't much in evidence in early villages.

The Iron Age, lasting c. 2500 BCE to 500 CE affected civilizations and pre-civilizations alike. Iron wasn't an alloy and was readily available. The smelting process spread quickly through Asia, Africa, and Europe. After humankind learned how to mine iron, leaving enough carbon to keep the metal from cracking, iron tools and weapons gained popularity throughout the world, with the exception of the Americas.

Iron ploughs made it possible to sow seed deep in the soil, thereby ensuring larger harvests. Iron spears and arrow tips improved hunting efficiency, leading to increased meat consumption. Iron building materials and tools ensured longer lasting buildings, roads, and bridges.

As with all technology, iron was a double-edged sword, literally. Iron weapons and armor made war deadlier than it had been in the Stone and Bronze Ages. This might be the first case in which humankind realized that technology has the capacity to accomplish both good and evil.

But the Iron Age also resulted in more food and larger villages. Iron Age technology played a crucial role in transforming those first villages into an urban society. The bridge between pre-civilization and civilization was built from iron.

Practice Test Questions

1. The Bantu Migration and the Native American Migration are similar except

   A. both migrations took thousands of years.
   B. both migrations resulted from an invasion of their respective continents.
   C. both migrations created settlements, and when those settlements became too crowded, a group from the settlement set out to create a new settlement.
   D. both migrations believed that land could not be brought or sold.

2. Agricultural village life resulted in

   A. the birth of historical consciousness.
   B. the need for human or animal sacrifice to guarantee a large harvest.
   C. the scarecrow.
   D. village education systems.

17

3. The Iron Age

    A. preceded the Stone Age.

    B. preceded the Bronze Age.

    C. left few artifacts because iron was breakable.

    D. produced implements that were used by civilization and pre-civilization alike.

4. Bronze is

    A. a metal primarily used for making soldiers' helmet.

    B. a medal awarded the third place winner in the field-plowing contest.

    C. an alloy composed of copper and tin.

    D. a covering for sandals and other leather goods.

5. Southeast Asia was known for

    A. rice and yams.

    B. rice and lambs.

    C. rice and spice.

    D. rice and poi.

Answers and Explanations

1. B. The Bantu migration was not due to an invasion. The African topsoil layer was extremely thin and easily eroded. African land wore out quickly, necessitating frequent migration.

2. A. Besides being artifacts themselves, villages led to the development of language, music, art, and so on, all resulting in historical awareness.

3. D. The Iron Age lasted from 2500 BCE to 500 CE and left many artifacts because iron erodes slowly.

4. C. Bronze is an alloy, not a metal, and bronze tools were available to wealthier civilizations.

5. C. The land of Southeast Asia was perfect for cultivating rice, and spices grew wild. This area saw agriculture pave the way for urban trading and development.

The Emergence of Civilization

Civilization is defined as an urban way of living, but this definition sounds just plain wrong. Doesn't civilization signify the technological, artistic, literary, legal, and ethical accomplishments of any given advanced society? Are not museums, concert halls, libraries, and courtrooms the repositories of civilization? What do traffic, potholes, mass transit, small claims courts, blaring rap, screaming children, pickpockets, and rapists—all hallmarks of modern city living—have to do with civilization?

Each resulted from an urban way of living. Urban life occurs when many individuals dwell within a finite area, and the **society,** a group of people living within a given civilization, no longer depends on food production as "job one and only." Further, urban society requires a more complex governing structure than the village. In addition to an executive, sections of the city might require administrators and representation. Cities also require more complex waste and transit management. These structures make urban politics more complex than those in the village.

The first cities were more complex than the villages of pre-civilization. Larger populations living in smaller areas required multiple dwellings, shops, roads, and waste-disposal systems. Villages existed on only one level. They were single story, existing on a horizontal plane. City living often required people living in dwellings with more than one story. Civilization exists on vertical and horizontal planes. The ziggurats (tower dwellings) of Mesopotamia were the world's first skyscrapers, reaching upward of seven stories. Large populations living in close quarters also required regulation, government, laws, and the administration of each. These aspects of urban living necessitated record keeping, which, in turn, depended on some form of writing. The advent of civilization gave rise to a new profession, the **bureaucrat,** a nonelected official.

Urban societies include trade, commerce, and usually manufacturing. Such activities require an economy that relies on money and credit, rather than barter. If trade extends beyond the civilization's borders, economic agreements become necessary to protect merchants' safety and to agree on the exchange rate; hence another new profession emerged, the **diplomat,** an official charged with creating agreements between disparate peoples and nations and resolving conflicts with the least amount of unpleasantness.

Few economies are strong enough to support everyone working within them. Some members of society cannot live on their wages and must subsist or work for food, rather than money. Working for food alone is a form of slavery, since it makes the slave's actual survival dependent on the employer. Slavery, then, became a byproduct of the emergence of civilization. Slavery proved to be the solution to another problem created when villages turned into cities. Not every dispute between neighboring civilizations ended with handshakes and feasts. It was much more likely that civilizations would go to war to settle their differences.

But these wars weren't the grandparents' skirmishes to secure a larger share of the saber-tooth tiger. Civilized warfare required more than soldiers. When one city laid siege to another, the victor employed strategy to win, which relied upon arms and technology. Victory went to the side that best used its soldiers, capital, weapons, and technology to outwit the enemy. Sadly, modern warfare is a hallmark of civilization.

But modern warfare also provided the victor with an economic bonus. The losing civilization's army and able-bodied citizens became part of the conqueror's bounty and were brought back to work as slaves, enhancing the conqueror's labor force at little cost. Use of slave labor expanded the workforce without stressing the local economy.

Slavery, wars, hierarchy, writing, commerce, legal systems, and history all were facets of a unique way of life for each civilization—its **culture,** which is how the society lives within a given civilization. Writing made it possible for that culture to persist and facilitated passing on skills. Civilizations in some areas, such as South Asia and the Americas expanded without writing. But civilizations in the Americas used computations to keep their records. South Asians relied on oral tradition, but quickly inscribed their experience and knowledge with the advent of written Sanskrit.

With culture came a sense of communal and individual identity. After civilization established that identity, creativity took root. Civilized societies preserved their heritage in museums, expressed themselves through music, art, and literature and carved their identity in their architecture. Each was the face that given civilizations proudly showed the world. Cities might not be the cleanest, safest places. But that dirt, grime, and crime formed the ingredients from which humanity built its greatest legacies.

The Role of Religion in Early Civilization

Somewhere in pre-civilized times, humankind realized that there were forces beyond our control. This would have occurred at many times, such as during the aftermath of a flooded pasture, a burned settlement, an earthquake, or a tornado. The response to the unforeseen and uncontrollable was much the same whenever and wherever it happened: Humankind learned we couldn't control our destiny, necessitating the need to placate forces beyond our control.

Organized religion was born out of this fear of the uncontrollable. The first deities presided over and controlled nature's forces. Early man worshipped fertility goddesses and prayed to the gods of thunder and fire. The first priests and priestesses claimed to exert some control over nature, or they simply explained the reasons for untoward calamities.

Early man buried or burned their dead in hopes that they were going to an eternal life. They followed a rudimentary moral religious code, hoping to keep the deities appeased. Whether or not early civilizations viewed nature as divine forces or believed in some sort of afterlife, both civilized and pre-civilized humans understood there were forces in the universe they couldn't control. Showing respect and acting in a way not to make them angry were the first points of religion. Each of these functions expanded as pre-civilization evolved into early civilization.

Civilization required social hierarchy, government, and law. Religion legitimated government needed to regulate the civilization and the social hierarchies and laws it created. The government ruled because the deities sanctioned that it should rule. Similarly, religion legitimated the prevailing social structures. The deities demanded that society adhere to given familial structures so that the civilization could survive. Thus, religious belief justified laws and mores in early civilization. The high priests and priestesses played a significant role in dispensing justice. In Egypt and Mesoamerica, they formed the highest court.

Religion also explained the unexplainable to early civilizations. Religion specified how the deity/deities created the world, placing that civilization within its context. Thus, religion provided the basis for early civilization's history, hence its identity. Most important, religion explained the human condition. Some noted deities acted capriciously; others taught evil was the byproduct of sin; still others accepted evil as a part of living. Religion gave structure to a capricious universe.

Religion answered the scariest question of all: what happens after death. Life was short in the capricious universe of pre-civilization and early civilization. Early humankind gained both solace and strength knowing that earthly existence was simply the first step in a longer journey through the universe, or another step closer to merging with the cosmos, leaving earthly self, or reaching Nirvana.

Culture, State, and Environment

Mesopotamia means *land between two rivers*. Located in what is now modern Iraq, Mesopotamia is considered the oldest of the known world civilizations. The first Mesopotamian civilization was created by the Sumerians, c. 3200 BCE. Their civilization consisted of highly controlled city-states, in which the priests and councils of free men ruled. The monarch, or Lugar, appeared after city life became so complex that a united executive was needed.

City-states in Mesopotamia were sustained by complex irrigation systems. These states were also characterized by close economic and religious control and detailed written records. Mesopotamian cities were the first to exist on vertical as well as horizontal planes. The ziggurat, or tower, of Mesopotamia was the world's first skyscraper. Some of these rose seven stories. The Tower of Babel was a ziggurat.

The Mesopotamian civilizations were best known for the Code of Hammurabi (1728–1686 BCE). These laws were based on the premise that fear was a splendid tool to encourage respect for the law. Times haven't changed that much. The Code of Hammurabi protected the weak while providing the victim closure. This law code encompassed ancient consumer, religious, and domestic law. It was based on legal parity. Women were protected by anti-spousal abuse laws and allowed grounds for divorce. A person found guilty of a crime was punished by being forced to suffer the same injustice that he inflicted on the victim. Thus, a builder whose house collapsed and killed the owner, if found guilty, was condemned to death.

Egypt

Unlike Mesopotamia, Egypt was a united empire, rather than an empire comprised of sovereign city-states. Its main source of water was the Nile River. This river overflowed its banks once a year leaving behind a new layer of topsoil that fertilized the land for the remainder of the year.

Like Mesopotamia, Egypt possessed a ruling priest class. The priests acted as administrators and judges of the highest courts. Unlike Mesopotamia, Egypt was ruled by Pharaohs, kings with semi-divine status. Although a highly regulated society, women worked outside the home and enjoyed decision-making positions. For example, Hashepshet successfully ruled Egypt as Pharoah.

The Egyptians achieved technological miracles and are thought to have been the cultural leaders in the lands bordering the Mediterranean Sea. The Ebers Papyrus, describing medical ailments and treatments, is a model for medical cases. The pyramids remain masterpieces of architecture. The means of their creation remains a mystery. Some writers, such as Robert Von Donnigen even assert that they were built by extraterrestrials. Egyptian mummification processes continue to preserve the remains of Pharaohs and wealthy citizens thousands of years after their deaths.

The Egyptian civilization lasted 2,500 years, but eventually succumbed to the Roman Empire. What led to Egypt's decline? Was it because Rome was stronger? It's possible to blame Egypt's fall on the growing might of Augustus Caesar and his Roman Legions. But Egypt under Cleopatra had both the home court advantage and an alliance with Marc Anthony. A better general, or a more warlike queen, might have overcome Augustus Octavian.

It's also been argued that the Egyptians concentrated so much on the rites of death and mummification that they turned away from life. But if that were the case, there would have been a stronger emphasis on ending life. There's no record of mass suicides. Mummification was generally reserved for those wealthy enough to afford it. It's unlikely that there was a rush to suicide, or the embalmer.

Perhaps the reason for Egypt's demise lies in identity creation. The Egyptians created a complex writing system based on hieroglyphics. With that they were not only able to keep records of transactions, they were also able to create and chart a national identity. But just at the time the Romans began to create the empire, the Egyptians began losing the ability to read their own records. Lack of literacy led them to forget their historical identity. Fighting a war without a sense of self or purpose is futile. It appeared that the hieroglyphics became too detailed for most Egyptians and a slow loss of literacy occurred.

Successful civilizations foster a sense of history, coupled with a sense of identity. When that is forgotten, the civilization loses it, identity and reason to be. Alas, the Egyptians suffered from a terminal case of collective amnesia. It's not precisely known what caused this collective amnesia. Latin was becoming the language of the Mediterranean littoral; the Egyptians might have preferred Latin's simpler alphabet to the symbols of hieroglyphics. There is the possibility that the more vibrant, stronger economic culture will supersede an older culture. The brain interprets symbols and letters in different ways. When reading letters took precedence over reading symbols, it became increasingly difficult to read hieroglyphics. Sadly, Egypt suffered a crisis of confidence with continuing questions over the nature of Egyptian religion. The Pharoah Aknatan's attempt to transform Egyptian religion into a form of monotheism caused a stressful religious crisis. Collective amnesia may have been one of the reactions to stress.

Indus

The Indus River in India formed the basis for South Asian civilization. The first signs of civilization appeared c. 1500 BCE, with the cities of Mohenjo-Daro and Harrappa. Ruins of both cities reveal highly structured societies. Both cities are laid out on orderly grids, not winding lanes. In addition, some of the houses had hot and cold water, showers, and indoor plumbing. Sewage was pumped into the river. Artifacts remain that reveal the technological depth of Harrapan civilization.

In 1500 BCE the Arya (friends) or Aryans invaded India. This group co-opted the rigid social structures already in place, imposing the caste system. This system enabled the Aryans to sustain their conqueror's status within Hindu society. The caste system was based on purity and skin color. These divisions were known as varna. Whiter skin colors were considered more pure. Only the highest 20 percent of society were worthy of belonging to a caste. The remainder of the Hindu population was considered "untouchable." The imposition of the caste system was one of the first times in history that social distinctions were made based on skin color. The Aryans had lighter complexions than the Dravidians. Imposition of the caste system kept the Aryans in decision-making positions.

The castes were divided as follows:

Brahmin	priests
Kshatriyas	warrior princes
Vaisyas	merchants and artisans
Sudras	servants, poor farmers and artisans, original inhabitants
Untouchables	the remainder of society.

Hindus believe in reincarnation. Therefore, behavior in a former life influences caste placement in future lives. If an untouchable lived an exemplary life, he would be reincarnated into a higher caste. But if the untouchable person acted badly and died, he would lose castes, perhaps returning as an animal or a rock. This happened because his/her actions formed a sticky substance, karma, which prevented the person from joining a higher caste or merging with the oversoul.

Although most Hindus believe in one God, they also believe that God takes thousands of incarnations.

Shang

Civilization appeared in China 5000 BCE in northern China. Like Egypt and later India, China evolved into an empire, rather than a collection of city-states. The Hsia, 1994–1523 BCE were the first Chinese dynasty. They were followed by the Shang, 1600–1027 BCE. The Shang dynasty significantly influenced Chinese civilization until the mid-twentieth century. How was this accomplished? The Shang created the pictorial and ideographic writing system that China still employs today.

Chinese writing has several different types of letters and symbols. The oldest form of Chinese writing was questions written on animal bones. These questions were deciphered and answered by ancient Chinese priests. Ideographs consist of two pictures placed next to each other to form an abstract concept or thought. Phonograms, the equivalent of homonyms, were employed to represent words that sound alike but mean different things.

Each of these entered the writing system employed during the Shang dynasty. By the time the Shang dynasty was supplanted by the Chou dynasty (1027–256 BCE), the writing system had defined Chinese society. This definition occurred because the writing system was so complex. To be literate, according to the late Dr. Samuel Kung, it was necessary to know more than 70,000 letters, symbols, and combinations. Only the wealthiest Chinese could take the time needed to master the Chinese alphabet.

Those who mastered the Chinese alphabet and the rigors of Confucian doctrine studied to become members of the Chinese bureaucracy. This bureaucracy administered the Chinese government. They were civil servants, highly paid and highly respected. Technically anyone who qualified could study to join the Chinese bureaucracy. But the program took years to complete and was expensive. Sometimes a town would pay for one of its brightest children to enter school. But more often than not, training for the bureaucracy was limited to the wealthiest nobles and middle class.

The few Chinese who could afford an education controlled Chinese society. But only the wealthy could afford the luxury of education. All of this resulted in a hierarchical society that changed only when the world went to pieces during World War II.

Mesoamerica and Andean South America

The Americas faced a different set of problems than did civilizations in other parts of the world. America's civilizations were isolated from the world until the Spaniards and Portuguese arrived in the fifteenth century. Further, there were no humans on the North and South American continents until 25,000–50,000 years ago when the people who would become the first Americans wandered across the Bering Strait.

The Olmecs and the Tiwanacu exemplify Mesoamerican and Andean civilizations. The Olmec civilization began to flourish in 1500 BCE. As their food supply grew, so did their civilization. The Olmec lived on maize, eventually renamed corn. Although corn had to be replanted every year, it provided much of the needed nutrients for a civilization to grow.

Olmec society appears to have been led by a priestly class. Their towns had a similar typography. The Olmec Temple, shaped similarly to a pyramid, dominated the center of town. Like the other civilizations described here, the Olmec were polytheistic, their head deity being the jaguar. The population fanned out around the temple. It differed from Egyptian pyramids because the exterior formed a staircase to the altar at the temple's apex. According to Robert Garfield, the Olmec were farmers and traders.

Many civilizations become preoccupied with either philosophical or religious questions. The Olmec, according to Garfield, concerned themselves with the passage of time. They viewed time as cyclical and believed its passage to be part of a religious cycle. Their preoccupation with time suggested that the Olmecs placed emphasis on mathematics. The Olmecs didn't possess the wheel and might not have had domesticated animals for carrying foodstuffs and goods.

The Olmec left artifacts that today's archeologists puzzle over. The Olmec crafted a set of large stone heads, which they floated down rivers to new locations. What did these heads mean? Why were they transported? Were the Olmec attempting to celebrate, warn, or inform the world through these stone heads?

The Olmec civilization faded away, ultimately destroyed by war. But it might well have been the root of civilization for Mesoamerica. From the Olmecs until the Aztecs, Indian civilizations flourished in Mexico.

The South America Andes region was home to a different form of civilization. Like Mesoamerican civilizations, Andean civilizations thrived when food and water were plentiful. Plateaus and passes through the Andes were used for food cultivation and became way stations to civilizations higher in the mountains.

The altiplano plains in the high Andes framed the greatest Andean civilizations. In these plateaus, civilizations flourished. Tiwanacu became the major city/civilization in the area. Tiwanacu was ruled by priest/kings. The priestly classes were also the warrior classes, giving them the power to exact booty and taxes. The Tiwanacu also practiced human sacrifice. Warriors would return from battle with prisoners who became sacrificial victims. Sacrifices were thought to appease the gods who needed human blood for sustenance. Human sacrifice was practiced throughout Latin and South America.

The inhabitants of Tiwanacu lacked the tools to construct a stone city, something they accomplished with their hands alone. According to Garfield, buildings still stand that were fitted together without mortar.

Tiwanacu appears to have declined c. 1000 CE, and it collapsed by 1200 CE. The agricultural system collapse resulted in a simple; no food, no civilization. The collapse might have occurred because the climate changed.

Practice Test Questions

1. Culture is

   A. speaking correctly.
   B. how a civilization lives.
   C. eating with your pinky in the air.
   D. drinking absinthe or Crème de Menthe.

2. Which is not a hallmark of civilization?

   A. The economy
   B. War
   C. Equality
   D. Slavery

3. Which is a byproduct of civilization?

   A. Identity
   B. Styles
   C. Children
   D. Religion

4. Where in the ancient world could one be protected from spousal abuse?

   A. China
   B. India
   C. Mesopotamia
   D. Mesoamerica

5. In which ancient civilization would one get the best workout moving stone heads?

   A. Andean America
   B. Mesopotamia
   C. Mesoamerica
   D. China

Answers and Explanations

1. **B.** Each of the other choices are byproducts of culture or how a particular society lives.

2. **C.** War, and slavery are unfortunate byproducts in civilization. It takes time for equality to occur in civilized society. Most civilizations rarely achieve complete equality.

3. **A.** Civilizations develop their own unique identity. Styles and religion are part of civilization's culture. Pre-civilized and civilized societies require children to continue.

4. **C.** Mesopotamia.

5. **C.** Mesoamerica, the Olmec civilization.

Classical Civilizations

Classical civilizations lie at the roots of our modern culture—the way we live. Modern civilization evolved from classical civilization's roots; our political, social, and religious beliefs are based on the classical model. The triumphs of the classical civilizations lay at the roots of our triumphs; their disasters and declines foreshadow our own.

Modern civilizations share not only an intellectual bond to their classical forebears, but an emotional link as well. The early civilizations are the equivalent of our distant ancestors. Think of them as your great, great, great, . . . grandparents!

How Did the Classical Civilizations Differ from Earlier Civilizations?

Classical civilizations differed in complexity and social structure. Earlier civilizations were constrained by their primitive economic structures, in which the production of basic necessities such as food and water still loomed large.

Classical civilizations, however, usually had enough food to feed their populations. They refined the systems needed to sustain urban living. Earlier civilizations, before the rise of Greece and Rome, left fewer artifacts, writings, art, and music. Classical civilizations' artifacts remain. Earlier civilizations' belief systems shed little light on modern problems. Classical civilizations' beliefs lay at the root of our own.

We can imagine ourselves wearing a toga, discussing Confucius' *Analects,* meditating with the Buddha. How many of us can imagine ourselves preparing a mummy, arguing a case in a Babylonian court, or divining animal bones in China?

The belief and philosophical systems that played a major role in classical civilizations will be discussed in the next section as to how they relate to the individual classical civilizations. Detailed descriptions of the philosophical and belief systems will be explored in the next chapter.

The Mediterranean Littoral

Western classical civilizations began in the lands bordering on the Mediterranean Sea, known as the **Mediterranean Littoral.** These civilizations had several factors in common:

- Use of the Phoenician alphabet
- Interest in overseas trade
- Complex political structures which divided the decision-making process
- Interest in the metaphysical and concern about the human condition

The Egyptians developed hieroglyphics, a writing system based largely on pictures and symbols. But this system was difficult to learn, and, as the Egyptians discovered, difficult to remember. The Phoenicians created the use of letters forming the basis for words. These were easier to learn, and their writing system became accepted throughout the Mediterranean and eventually throughout much of the rest of the world. The Greeks translated the first two letters of the Phoenician alphabet as Alpha and Beta. The Greek word alphabet became the name for the letter system. The civilizations surrounding the Mediterranean discovered that the land wasn't good for farming. Lack of good farm lands made trade all the more important. The sea became the major route for goods, as well as food. But trading by sea presented a new set of problems: how to navigate the Mediterranean; how to propel the ship when there's no wind; how to house and feed the crew on long voyages. The Greeks and Phoenicians solved these problems, widening their world in the process. It was discovered that the stars and constellations made excellent points of reference for navigation. Sails were designed to better catch the wind to propel the ships. In addition, **galleys,** ships propelled by oars, requiring rows of sailors or galley slaves rowing in tandem, made it possible for ships to move, even when there was no wind. A sailor at the stern of the galley beat a drum continuously to keep the rowers synchronized. The Greek Trireme had three levels of oars. It also made an excellent warship. The rudder, or starboard, enhanced the ability to steer the ship.

All of this resulted in an influx of goods throughout Asia and the Mediterranean, and the understanding that the world was a large and interesting place. More than goods were exchanged. Ideas traveled between ports as well, and the civilizations around the littoral profited from those ideas. Aristotle's ideas on moderation resemble those of the Buddha; Confucius' *Analects* concerning loving your neighbor and treating others with respect resembled teachings in Judaism and early Christianity.

The Athenians, especially, created political structures that divided decision-making power between the executive and legislative branches. Citizens of the Greek peninsula created city-states known as **Polloi**. Each Polis developed is own unique form of government. But all of them, even Sparta, which was the most autocratic, had decision-making power delegated to its leading citizens. Although this should not be construed as universal suffrage, it revealed a belief that power didn't have to necessarily reside in the hands of one person. Only one-third of all Athenians had any rights to govern. There were no checks and balances. The Legislative branch would first be defined in writing in the American Constitution.

The Polloi inspired patriotism—the root of modern love of the state. An ancient example is seen when part of the Spartan army during war with Persia were trapped and boxed in at the pass at Thermopylae. They fought bravely but ultimately died defending the pass. The monument erected to their memory read as follows:

> "Go stranger to [Sparta] and there do tell
> Here according to our laws we fell."

The city or polis inspired patriotism because it both nurtured its citizens and gave them a sense of history, or something larger than the individual human. By providing laws and creating customs, the polis became a living entity, home, the end of a journey.

Athens is credited with creating democracy, equal rule by the citizens. Any citizen was eligible to participate in the legislative branch of the Council of 500.

American democracy is said to have Greek roots; it's more complicated. As with America, the Athenian citizens elected representatives to make decisions. But not every Athenian was a citizen. Athens at it strongest had a population of 225,000. Only 30 percent of the male population were citizens. In wartime, executive power was given to one man. But Athens at least paid lip service to the idea that citizens deserved input into the decision-making process. Because of this, Athens is considered the birthplace of democracy. Citizenship belonged to any male born in Athens of free parents who achieved an income large enough to allow the males to serve as citizens.

Not every polis was a democracy. In Sparta, the most militaristic of the Greek city-states, citizens participated in age-appropriate sets. Young boys learned weaponry and conduct; young men fought; senior citizen males made the policy. Those who were not citizens, the Helots, served the citizens. When their population increased, it became lawful to hunt the Helots as if they were jack rabbits or deer. The "herd" needed thinning. This was a male-centered society. Women were invisible, except as being mothers, mistresses, and silent advisors.

The city-states often declared war on each other. They united briefly to defeat the Persians in the fifth century, BCE. But after defeating the Persians, strains developed between Athens and Sparta. When relations finally collapsed in 431 BCE, Athens and Sparta declared war on each other.

The Peloponnesian War lasted 26 years, ending in 404 BCE with Sparta capturing Piraeus harbor and invading Athens. After their victory, Sparta became increasingly insular, withdrawing from international affairs. Greek political aspirations could have ended at that point, but the era of Greek philosophers, playwrights, and artists had really just begun.

The ancient Greek definition of the human condition, as reflected in their religious beliefs, resonates to this day. The Greek gods and goddesses were a capricious lot, who often toyed with their human subjects.

The gods reflected the human condition. Homer's *Iliad* reveals how the gods took sides in the siege of Troy. They even went to war, fighting each other. Life was capricious, a constant negotiation between a rock and a hard place (the modern version of Scylla and Charybdis, two sea monsters that Ulysses had to sail between). The Trojan War was the gods' creation. Had not Paris been awarded Helen, would the Greeks have sailed from Mycenae? Had Ulysses not sailed to Troy, would he have wandered over seven years?

The Greeks defined the human condition through the theatrical medium of tragedy. Many of the Greek tragedies and comedies were written to be recited at festivals honoring the gods. In a tragedy, the playwright created a no-win situation in which the protagonist must perish; there's no way out. But by facing doom bravely, the protagonist inspires the audience, thus, revealing humanity's nobility. Oedipus has no escape: He kills his father and marries his mother. But he faces the inevitable with courage, revealing humankind's strengths in the process, which is the essence of tragedy.

Literature also flourished during classical times. Homer's *Iliad* and *Odyssey* began as sung poems that were later written down. They, too, reflect the harshness of the human condition. While the gods and mortals fight for 10 years to defend or capture Troy, it's a foregone conclusion that the city will fall. According to the Greek Oracle, "Fate is the thing that no man born of woman, god or hero can escape."

The saga continued after Troy fell. Agamemnon, the expedition's leader, was forced to sacrifice his eldest daughter, Iphigenia, in order to obtain favorable sailing winds. Clytemnestra, Agamemnon's wife, vowed revenge; when Agamemnon was in Troy, she had an affair with Aegisthus. After Agamemnon returned, Clytemnestra assassinated him. Orestes, Agamemnon's son, avenged his father, killing Clytemnestra and Aegisthus. Hera avenged Clytemnestra by setting the harpies on Orestes. Orestes wandered Greece in torment, accompanied by his sister, Elektra, until arriving at Athena's temple in Athens, where Athena lifted the curse.

The study of history was another legacy of classical Greek civilization. The writing and study of history revealed the Greeks' development of a communal identity not too different from our own. Study of history also revealed that humankind was outgrowing simplistic explanations provided by ancient religions. Although each of those religions told a story of how the earth and humanity came into being, Herodotus wrote the first history of humankind. Herodotus related humankind's story as separate from religious roots. This enabled humankind to view itself as a noble species in its own right, rather than simply an offshoot of the divine. Herodotus viewed history as a series of events. In separating the mythical from the fact, his work mixes both while explaining what happened in human terms.

Thucydides took history to another level. An Athenian general during the Peloponnesian War, Thucydides wrote his history to explore why Athens lost the war. *The History of the Peloponnesian War* was the first work of analytical history. Thucydides contended Athens lost the war because the expedition to Sicily wasted precious resources and broke Athenian army morale. He concluded, "Having done what they did they suffered as men must."

What does this have to do with modern life? Thucydides words resonated during the Vietnam War, when America became involved in the struggle between Communist North Vietnam and South Vietnam. Ultimately the north won and united the country. America lost more than 58,000 men and women in a struggle that was not a threat to American security. In the process, so much distrust and hate between the generations grew that America still feels the impact of the Vietnam war.

Athens' loss of the Peloponnesian War sparked philosophical inquiry. Socrates questioned the state during the Peloponnesian War. He functioned as a gadfly, pressing question after question. What underlay this? Socrates may have been seeking a way for humans to form a more democratic polity. But the Athenian leaders weren't amused. Socrates was executed in 399 BCE for sedition. However, his method of questioning every supposition helped shape teaching methods widely in use today. They could not tolerate the philosopher's incessant questions. Some of Athens' leaders feared that his question would spark the overthrow of the government.

Socrates pupil, Plato, continued the search. In his *Republic*, Plato laid the groundwork for the model state. The republic was not a democracy, but a representative government. America followed this model. Americans elect their representatives to all governments, local, state, and national. But Plato was more than a theoretical political scientist; he worried about humankind's ability to perceive and understand reality. In Plato's allegory of the cave, the philosopher defined the human condition as seeing life as reflected off the wall of a cave, rather than life directly. How can humanity deal with the universe when it's impossible to see reality? Instead, humanity only sees reflections off the wall of a cave. Reflections cannot give the depth and proportions of reality. It's like seeing a hollow image, and assuming it represents the actual item.

Plato, in turn, tutored Aristotle. Aristotle believed that the secret of success was moderation, "the golden mean." Practicing moderation in all things would result in a balanced life and state. But Aristotle is better known for his most famous pupil, a mathematics prodigy, who didn't become a philosopher, but a conqueror. Aristotle tutored Alexander the Great, who conquered the known world, spreading Greek ideals and culture in his wake. It's possible that Aristotle's teachings laid the groundwork that made ancient Greece the cradle of modern civilization because Alexander spread these ideals throughout the known world.

Philosophy actually means "love of wisdom." It separated the search for wisdom from religious knowledge. Instead, it postulated that life could be understood through inquiry that would result in an orderly, peaceful world. Religion wasn't necessary. Interest in philosophy reflected humanity's dissatisfaction with a religious system based on caprice. It was another example of how humanity had progressed from being victims of nature to heroic survivors. Perhaps classical philosophy lies at the root of modern scientific inquiry. If knowledge is acquired by questioning the status quo, then science is the means of discovering answers by questioning and then discovering answers through experiments.

Art and architecture gave the world a physical manifestation of the ancient Greek life world view. The classical civilizations around the Mediterranean Littoral developed a sense of beauty that they communicated through their sculpture and architecture. Their art was characterized by simple lines and realistic depictions of the human form. Doric Greek pillars still grace government buildings. Greek sculptures recreated human forms. Praxiteles' *Market Woman* was old and wrinkled, yet beautiful in its realism. The *Discus Thrower* revealed the beauty of the human body. These weren't the first civilizations to prize beauty, but they may have been among the first to find beauty in humankind. This paralleled the confidence exhibited through the creation of historical study and philosophy.

India/South Asia

Alexander's conquest of India triggered the rise of classical civilization on the South Asian subcontinent. It united most of what is modern-day India, without imposing an onerous occupation. Nonetheless, any occupation results in questions about what creates a civilization and how a civilization can fall prey to a conqueror. It also facilitated the conquest of India by Chandragupta, the founder of the Mauryan dynasty.

Alexander died at the age of 33 in 323 BCE without naming a successor, leaving political chaos in his wake. Chandragupta's conquest of India restored needed order. However, it was Chandragupta's grandson, Asoka, who left the greatest legacy to Indian civilization, paving the way for Hindu classical culture. Like his father and grandfather, Asoka was a warrior. Battle didn't faze him until one particularly bloody battle turned him against war altogether. Asoka then embraced Buddhism, making it the religion of his empire.

Not every Hindu embraced Buddhism with Asoka's fervor, yet Buddhism's precepts blended with the asceticism and nonviolence found in the Hindu religion. The underlying principles of Buddhism intertwined with those of Hinduism. Buddhism taught that the world was filled with suffering and impermanence, that suffering is caused by desire, that squelching all desire is the only cure for suffering. This cure may be obtained by following Buddha's eightfold path, which stressed a forthright code of conduct. And it was this combination that underlay Hindu classical civilization.

After the Mauryan Empire collapsed around c.180 BCE, India fragmented into small warring states. This situation continued for close to 600 years until Chandragupta of the Gupta dynasty conquered India. As with the Mauryan Empire, Chandragupta established his capital at Patna. Samudra, his son, transformed the Gupta state into an empire. Under the rule of Chandragupta's grandson, Chandragupta II, the Mauryan Empire reached its summit. The achievements of the Gupta Empire, a classical civilization, resembled those of the classical civilizations of the Mediterranean Littoral:

1. International trade flourished.
2. The Gupta Empire fostered Sanskrit, and many Hindu religious works were committed to writing, which promoted literacy throughout the empire.
3. The Gupta Empire fostered education, especially mathematics.
4. Literature, art, and architecture flourished.

As a result of international trade, merchants from all over the world settled in India, further expanding Gupta culture. Many of these colonies have remained.

The spread of Sanskrit resulted in the creation of a body of Gupta literature. The greatest playwright and poet was Kalidasa, who can be compared to Aristophanes or Homer. Unlike Greek theater, Kalidasa's work always ended happily. Although this may appear artificial, it reflects a confident society that views the world as an ordered and just place.

Mathematics also flourished during the Gupta Empire. The Hindus were the first to use numerals instead of letters; they were the first to use zero as a numeral. Replacing letters with numerals enabled Gupta mathematicians to extend the discipline in practical as well as theoretical matters. It's no coincidence that Algebra was a Hindu invention.

Mathematics, of course, had a practical side. Astronomy flourished during the Gupta Empire. Hindu astronomer Aryabhata determined that the earth revolved around the sun and that the year was 365 days and eight hours long. In 499 CE a Hindu mapmaker pointed out that the world was round, not flat. Determining mathematical relationships between the earth, sun, and continents made it possible to map the known world.

This research reflects a confident outlook. Science didn't undermine religious belief. It didn't matter whether the world was round or traveled around the sun. Explaining the unexplainable and understanding the world weren't antithetical in the Gupta Empire. Knowledge didn't threaten the Indian deities.

But the Gupta Empire wasn't without hierarchies. The caste system ordered society, whether Hindu, Muslim, or Buddhist. While Guptian rules employed the dharma and Laws of Manu as laws of state, individual conduct determined caste, Moksha, or Nirvana. State and religion functioned on separate planes:

The Gupta civilization prized religious piety, regardless of religious belief. It fostered learning, holding curiosity as valuable rather than a threat to religion. Hence, it didn't impede learning or participating in affairs of state. Hindu epics celebrate the world's creation. Science was merely the study of that creation. This flexibility enabled Gupta culture to expand throughout Asia and the Middle East.

Why was Gupta civilization so enamored of education, literature, and science? The answer lay in the rise of a written tradition. Sanskrit became the means of communication between dominant religious cultures and the state. The transition from oral to written tradition stimulated questioning, unseen prior to writing. Questions form the first step to discovery. The growth of international trade gave a practical impetus to mathematics and science as it brought more ideas and an international merchant class in its wake.

The Gupta civilization may have lived in peace with its neighbors, but the influx of trade, written language, and Hindu and Buddhist teachings with their emphasis on impermanence and asceticism created an environment akin to a simmering cauldron. Add to that cauldron the order imposed by the caste system, an order that stipulated that 80 percent of the population was impure, and the cauldron's mixture boiled over, producing Classical Gupta civilization in the process.

Muslim conquest ended the Gupta Empire and with it classical Indian civilization. These conquerors could not blend their culture with the Gupta, and the modern strains between Hindus and Muslims had their beginnings in these conquests. South Asia would not be largely reunited until the Mughal dynasty. By that time Hindu and Muslim distrust was thoroughly ingrained in South Asian society.

China

"Yonder lays China, a sleeping giant.
Let her sleep. For when she awakes she
will shake the world."
—Napoleon Bonaparte

Until the mid-twentieth century China looked more like an enfeebled giant than a sleeping one. But Napoleon was right. Today, goods manufactured in China saturate world markets. China sits on the United Nations Security Council, playing a major role in world events. And the world has been shaking since the giant woke.

The roots of the sleeping giant's power lay in Chinese classical civilization, but this brings up another set of questions: When did Chinese classical civilization come into being? When did it end, and what is its legacy? Which dynasty(s) comprise Chinese classical civilization?

Some historians believe the Han and T'ang dynasties form Chinese classical civilization. Both are noted for their strides in government, art, and technology. The Chinese view the T'ang dynasty as a golden age. The Han rulers, according to Robert Garfield, engendered so much respect and love that the Chinese began referring to themselves as the Han. But the Han and T'ang dynasties brought to fruition ideas of an earlier dynasty; these ideas laid the groundwork that underlay Chinese success today.

Chinese classical civilization was born during the later Chou dynasty. The Chou dynasty ruled China from c. 1027–256 BCE. Chou rule is divided into two distinct eras: the early Chou dynasty, c. 1027–771 BCE and the later Chou dynasty 771–256 BCE. During the early Chou dynasty, the emperors moved away from directly administering the Chinese states. Instead they left the administration to trusted family members. The early Chou dynasty, thus, resorted to feudalism, a political system based on personal loyalty, usually employed when centralized government breaks down.

The later Chou dynasty became known as the era of the "Warring States." These wars lasted more than 500 years. Continuing battles destroyed food supplies, resulting in mass migrations to the cities. This, in turn, led to a shortage of farmers, and that made the food shortages worse. Famine stalked the land with disastrous consequences. The Chinese cities weren't ready for the influx of dispossessed farmers. Conditions akin to what occurred during the western European and American Industrial Revolution in the eighteenth to twentieth centuries first reared their head in the Chinese cities during the late Chou dynasty. Slums abounded. Urban life included starvation, disease, and crime. All of this led to more disorder. Society crumbled into near anarchy. Fear of impending anarchy resulted in the creation of three philosophical systems that have lain at the heart and root of Chinese life ever since: the Tao, Confucianism, and the School of Statecraft.

The Tao, "the road or path," was founded by Lao Tzu c. 600 BCE. He is believed to be the author of the Tao's text, the *Tao Te Ching*. It's this text that addressed the individual, the ideal state, the relationship of the individual to the state, and the attributes of a good leader. According to Lao Tzu, the individual was good, but individuals living in oppressively close proximity produced the chaos that characterized the later Chou dynasty.

Lao Tzu also believed that the universe depended on a set of balances between the **yin** and **yang**. The *yin* or feminine forces within the universe were cold, dark, and passive. The *yang* or masculine forces were active, hot, and light. For the universe to maintain equilibrium, the *yin* and *yang* needed to be equally balanced. These balances applied to everything from weather to meal preparation. Followers of the Tao concentrated on maintaining the balance between *yin* and *yang seeking that balance literally between hot and cold,* because a balanced universe guaranteed an end to the chaos of the later Chou dynasty.

But for Taoism to succeed someone had to make certain that the population received food, water, and shelter. Someone had to delay personal meditation to run the city while the inhabitants left for the country or meditated in their homes. Taoism did not address the needs of daily living. A century and one-half later, Confucius addressed those issues. Confucius, or Kung Fu-tzu, c. 551–c. 479 BCE was born into a poor noble family. He may have been powerfully built, as he excelled at archery, and excellence in this sport depended on wielding a 50-pound bow.

Because his family was poor, Confucius may not have had as extensive an education as most Chinese nobles. This may explain why Confucius sought to become the tutor in a noble family, but no noble family would hire him. Thus, Confucius settled for becoming a philosopher instead, gathering a set of loyal students to impart his teachings. Further, Confucius left no writings. He's remembered through his sayings and teachings, the *Analects*, compiled by those loyal students. Confucianism stressed the development of virtue. Humankind was capable of being educated to be virtuous. Virtue, the philosopher believed, could be developed through education, primarily the study of literature, history, and philosophy. These would inculcate the quality of virtue or *jen*. Education should be open to anyone, regardless of class. When society became educated and virtuous, stability would return.

Some characterize Confucius as an egalitarian because of his stance on education. But Confucius' stance on education probably resulted from the difficulty he had obtaining education, not a wish to radically restructure Chinese society. To the contrary, Confucius wanted to return to the virtues he saw in the early Chou dynasty, believing the woes of the later Chou dynasty to be the result of a breakdown in morality and a decline in religious observance. When humankind returned to a moral religious life, then and only then would the chaos of the late Chou dynasty dissipate. Education was simply the means to restore needed stability by teaching subjects that would instill virtue and morality.

Confucius believed that stability resulted from hierarchy. There were five hierarchical relationships that guaranteed stability:

1. Subject to emperor
2. Wife to husband
3. Eldest son to father
4. Younger brother to older brother
5. Friend to friend

Although the last relationship appears to be a relationship of equals, few friendships are based on equality. One friend usually dominates the relationship. Further, all members of society have specific roles or *li*. The *li* changes as the child grows to adulthood. Knowing and scrupulously adhering to one's *li* ensures stability by eliminating role stress.

Confucian society consisted of families led by a virtuous male. Each family member graciously accepted his/her role and submitted to the hierarchy. The head of the family led his family, urging the acceptance of virtue and reverence for religion and ancestors. The brightest, most virtuous men would form a bureaucracy that would assist the emperor in administering stable rule. This meritocracy came into being during the Han dynasty. Each family owed obedience to the emperor. The result was the achievement of stability at the expense of individuality.

The emperor in Confucius' system was the most virtuous leader. Being virtuous commanded the loyalty of the families in the realm. A century after Confucius's death, his disciple, Mencius, added a corollary to the *Analects*: All agreed that upon ascending the throne, the Emperor received the Mandate of Heaven. But the mandate was conditional. If the Emperor ruled capriciously and the Chinese people suffered as a result, then he would lose the mandate and could be replaced. The Emperor's rule also depended on virtue, living according to *li*, and maintaining stability and prosperity.

At first glance Confucianism and the Tao look like they're on opposite poles. Confucianism dealt with living within society; Taoism dealt with leaving the city behind, if only in meditation. But many Chinese observed Confucius' structure while following the Tao to achieve individual fulfillment.

The Tao laid out the way to individual fulfillment, balance, and peace; Confucianism provided a road toward stability and structure. Taken together they form a balance every bit as potent as the *yin* and *yang;* taken together, Confucianism and the Tao succeed in creating a balance between individual and societal needs.

Neither Confucianism nor the Tao ended the period of "Warring States" during the later Chou dynasty. It was the third philosophy, the School of Statecraft, with its emphasis on the philosophy of Legalism that finally ended the chaos—albeit at a very high price.

Followers of the School of Statecraft disagreed with the Tao's and Confucianism's tenet that humankind could improve through education or meditation. They believed stability depended on efficient administration of government institutions. China needed more efficient tax collectors, better police and army administration, and an efficient legal system, not virtuous leaders or good painters. With efficient government stability would return.

But it wasn't enough to make certain the roads were paved, taxes collected, and the army drilled. Underlying the need for efficiency was the philosophy of Legalism. This philosophy contended that humankind was evil, capricious, and lazy, making vigilance the price of stability.

It was necessary to make laws covering every facet of societal interaction and stating the punishment for violation of said law. Infractions must be vigorously punished. The School of Statecraft and Legalism believed stability could only be restored by use of fear. Punishment far exceeded the crime. The School of Statecraft and Legalism succeeded in ending the chaos of the later Chou dynasty. The dynasty fell to the Ch'in dynasty in 221 BCE. The Ch'in implemented the precepts of the School of Statecraft, and order was restored.

The Tao, Confucianism, and the School of Statecraft's tenets still resonate. Twenty-first century society still strives for balance, seeks peace and quiet away from urban settings, and yearns for wise leaders. What factors comprise the family is still open for debate, and that debate often becomes acrimonious. Even the modern status of women has roots in classic Chinese society. Modern society still struggles with equal pay for equal work and comparable worth of jobs held primarily by women versus those held mostly by males. The School of Statecraft also resonates in modern society. Do we lock up all convicted felons and literally throw away the key, or does society have the obligation to rehabilitate them?

Practice Test Questions

1. Classical Civilizations are

   A. civilizations studied in class.
   B. civilizations that lay at the roots of modern civilization.
   C. civilizations possessing more than one religion.
   D. civilizations with a musical tradition.

2. Greek civilization contributed _____ to future generations

   A. Greek salads
   B. layouts for country estates
   C. continuing daytime drama
   D. the alphabet

3. Greek tragedies inspire because

   A. the hero tugs at the heartstrings.
   B. they portray female characters in depth.
   C. the characters handle no-win situations courageously.
   D. the interaction between the chorus and characters gives insight.

4. One result of Indian international trade was that

   A. Hindus developed an interest in Chinese court customs.
   B. merchants from all over the world moved to India.
   C. colors began to appear in Hindu apparel.
   D. ivory became a world commodity.

5. Confucianism stresses

   A. education creates scholars.
   B. everyone should work to reach their potential.
   C. society must rely on virtue to be stable.
   D. the Emperor commands unconditional loyalty.

Answers and Explanations

1. **B.** Classical civilizations are the ancestors of modern civilization and culture.

2. **D.** The alphabet made writing and reading practical for the masses. The Greeks were an urban civilization. Greek salads and continuing daytime drama aren't considered major contributions.

3. **C.** Although the other answers may be true, we remember the courageous here, not the chorus.

4. **B.** The merchant colonies and villages remained. Some exist today.

5. **C.** Confucianism holds that education creates virtuous leaders. Women play a minor role in family relationships. Confucianism defines hierarchies. An Emperor who rules badly may be deposed, according to the Mencius corollary to the *Analects*.

Belief Systems from Their Inception to 600 CE

Belief systems are religious or philosophical doctrines that underlay individual and communal action within a given civilization. The individual accepts both religious and philosophic belief systems' tenets on faith. Often the system is inherited from previous generations and, thus, becomes tradition. Religious systems presuppose the presence of a deity or deities. Philosophical systems are based on a process of reason or logic without a deity or deities.

Religious and philosophical systems presuppose a world in which certain events lay beyond humankind's control. Both take note of evil's presence in daily life and strive to ameliorate its effects through adherence to their respective tenets; both promote creation of a stable society, minimize role stress, and justify sustaining societal hierarchies—a critical factor for gaining the support of individuals who are not members of a civilization's decision making elites.

Belief systems incorporate philosophic systems' emphasis on logic to enhance their credibility. Philosophical systems stress aspects of religious systems to gain more adherents and *gravitas*. Both rely on precedent to prove validity. Underlying both systems is the human need, the human yearning to end life's uncertainty and pain.

Ancient Religious and Philosophic Belief Systems

Some material tenets of religious and philosophical belief systems have already been discussed in Chapters 3 and 4. This section explores how belief and philosophical systems intertwine.

Religious Belief Systems

Polytheism is a religious belief system in which the world is ruled by more than one deity. Each deity controls an aspect of nature, reason, or emotion. These deities take either human or animal form—some combine both. Deities preside over both good and evil actions. Some deities, such as Ahriman and Lucifer, are evil incarnate.

From 1200 BCE to 500 CE deities evolved as civilizations became more complex. Gods and goddesses of fire, rain, and fertility played lesser roles than gods and goddesses of love, justice, reason, and war. Deities also developed personalities. The Greek deities had human weaknesses, which led to repercussions for humans. For example, humanity suffered as a result of the rivalries between Zeus and Hera. As mentioned in Chapter 4, the gods go to war in the later chapters of the *Iliad*.

Hinduism

The predominant religion in modern India is **Hinduism.** The roots of Hinduism remain a mystery because this religion's tenets were passed by oral tradition until the Gupta dynasty c. 320–500 CE. Hinduism may have been a mixture of faiths and customs that coalesced into one religion when the oral tradition was recorded. One of this religion's likely predecessors is Brahmin Ana, the teachings and later writings of the most holy priests.

Hinduism appears polytheistic. There are more than 3,000 gods, goddesses, and animals that take holy form. But Hindus believe these deities to be separate incarnations of the god Vishnu, "The Preserver of the World." In addition to Vishnu, the Hindus worship Shiva/Kali, "the destroyer of the world," and Shakti/Kali, the Earth mother and goddess of death.

Worship, traditionally, takes place both at home and in the Hindu temple. Prayers include visiting and leaving offerings at the deities' shrines, in addition to prayers and processions. Some Hindu families keep a shrine in their homes, offering daily prayers at that shrine. Home worship might also coincide with family milestones. Diwali, the Hindu New Year is one of the most important Hindu holidays, comparable to Rosh Hashanah, the Jewish New Year. Most religions have at least one holy book. Because Hinduism was passed on for centuries by oral tradition, the religion has no single holy written source; Hinduism has a set of holy literature.

The most sacred of Hindu scriptures, the *Veda*, is a collection of prayers, hymns, incantations, and services that were first handed down between 1500–1200 BCE. By the end of the Mauryan dynasty, the Sama Veda, Yajur Veda, and Arthava joined this body of holy literature. The Laws of Manu or Manava Dharma Shastra were also composed between 1500–1200 BCE. The latter, which comprises some of the holiest Hindu laws, was placed into writing between 100–200 CE.

In addition to the *Veda*, Hinduism included poems and epics. These might be another by-product of the oral tradition. Myths, family histories, and tales illustrate the history and laws of the Hindu faith in epic story form. The *Mahabharata*, "The Great Epic of the Aryans" chronicled both the Aryan conquest, while it gave a discourse on *dharma*, or "right conduct." The *Bhagavad-Gita*, "Song of the Lord," is an epic poem inserted in the *Mahabharata* in the form of a dialogue between Prince Arjuna and his chariot driver Krishna/Vishnu. The *Ramayana*, an epic poem describing the adventures of Prince Rama and his family is the vehicle for teaching right conduct and Hindu law.

The presence of these epics sheds light on how a major religion was formed from diverse customs and teachings. The Aryan invasion added another aspect to Hinduism, the caste system. One's caste determined the quality of life because it was the outward measure of the soul's or Atman's purity. The Brahmins, priests, were the highest caste; Kshatriyas, warriors and princes, were the second; Vaisyas, merchants, small landowners, were the third; shudras, landless peasants and artisans, were the fourth caste. Everyone else was considered untouchable. The caste system was in place by 500 BCE. Each caste followed certain rules of "right conduct" or *dharma*. The caste system in India was extremely rigid, with rules governing interactions between and amongst different castes; social mobility from one caste to another was virtually impossible.

The jati system reinforced the caste system. Jati derived from the word *Jat*, profession. Each member of a jati follows a proscribed profession. Members of each profession follow their *Dharma*. Since "right living" or *Dharma* required knowledge of an intricate system, it was impossible to learn the *Dharma* of an occupation outside the jati.

Each jati was an organized political and social group. Each group or subgroup was ruled by the *panchayat*, the head of the jati and his councilors. The *panchayat* enforced the *Dharma*. Like modern unions, it oversaw its members' welfare. But it also had the power to punish those who failed to follow the jati's *Dharma*. In extreme cases, it expelled wayward members, leaving them completely exiled, outside any social system. Hindu society, whether controlled by caste or jati, revealed the belief in structure and the order it imposed on daily life.

The caste and jati systems affected Hinduism's view of death and the afterlife. Unlike Christianity, or several polytheistic religions, there is no deity sitting in judgment after death. The *atman*, the Hindu equivalent of the soul yearns to return to the oversoul or *Brahma*. Hinduism also teaches that the universe is One; each thing a manifestation of the *Brahma*. Each carries the *atman* or scrap of divinity within.

Hinduism also stresses non-violence and the practice of asceticism. Asceticism is the process of actively avoiding things that bring pleasure. Avoidance of pleasurable things allows the soul or *atman* to remain free of *karma* and more quickly become one with the *Brahma*. Many Hindus view the cow as sacred, and refuse to eat meat or, in some cases, all animal products.

Jainism, an offshoot of Hinduism, takes the sacredness of all life to a higher level. Devout Jains refuse to kill any living entity and practice strict dietary laws. For many of them, life is so sacred they carry brooms to brush flies away from their paths. They refuse to farm because animal or insect life may be lost during the plowing. Mohandas Gandhi's mother followed Jainism, and it is believed that Mohandas Gandhi's respect for human life and his aesthetic way of life was influenced by this sect.

Followers of Hinduism practice cremation. This practice sheds light on gender status in Hinduism. Until recently, the widow of a deceased Hindu was expected to throw herself on her husband's funeral pyre. She would then be known as a *Sati*, virtuous woman. The word *Sati* has also been used to describe the sacrifice.

Women in ancient Hinduism gained their status by their relationship to men. A female was someone's daughter; a married women, someone's wife and mother. Female adultery was, and often still is, punished by burning. Perhaps by so doing the impurity was burned away.

Buddhism

Buddhism is one of the world's largest religions and is somewhat akin to Hinduism in that it can include reincarnation, and an extinction of self somewhat similar to Moksha. Buddhism came into being as one man's reaction to the differences between affluence and poverty prevalent at the same time in sixth century BCE India.

Siddhartha Gautama was born in northern India c. 570 BCE. The son of a wealthy prince, he lived in luxury. At age 30, 540 BCE, he saw a miserable beggar wandering in front of the castle; that beggar changed his life. Siddhartha was so shocked at the beggar's poverty that he left his wife and infant son, and all of his wealth behind to begin wandering as a holy man.

Siddhartha practiced asceticism, carrying it to an extreme level, but to no avail. He learned nothing by starving himself and wandering the land as a poor beggar. Finally, nearly starving and no closer to understanding the world, Siddhartha lay down under a fig tree and ate to keep from starving. At that point, he gained insight into why the world was so evil, why there was such extreme suffering and poverty, and what could be done to live well in this less-than-perfect world. In effect, Buddhism was born in the insights gained once Siddhartha had eaten under the shade of the fig tree. Siddhartha began preaching his insights and attracting students in the process. At this point, c. the late 530s BCE, he became known as Buddha, or the Enlightened One.

Buddhism addresses the question of the nature of suffering in the world, giving the reasons for suffering in the *Four Noble Truths*:

1. Suffering is universal.
2. Suffering is caused by desire.
3. The cure to suffering is eliminating all desire.
4. Following the *Noble Eightfold Path* will result in the elimination of all desire.

The *Noble Eightfold Path* stresses:

1. Right Knowledge, understanding suffering's causes
2. Right Aspirations, worthy goals and aspirations
3. Right Speech, speaking kindly, honestly, and truthfully
4. Right Conduct, pursuing honest, peaceful, and pure motives
5. Right Livelihood, earning a living in such a way that no harm comes to others
6. Right Effort, striving to eliminate desire
7. Right Mindfulness, keeping an alert mind and being open to new ideas
8. Right Meditation, praying, thinking, and acting in ways that will end all desire for things in the physical world

Like Hinduism, Buddhism pointed to desire as the reason for suffering and wrong behavior. Similarly, Hinduism and Buddhism stressed that *Karma* weighed the soul, or parts of the individual down, impacting the individual's place in the next life.

In Buddhism, the individual is made up of five components: body, feelings, perception, will, and consciousness. *Karma* may accrue to none, some, or all of these. The individual in her/his next life deals with the consequences, while continuing to strive to eliminate all desire.

Buddhist belief points to the extinction of all desires. Once achieved, the components that make up the individual no longer exist. This "self extinction" is called *Nirvana*. The ultimate goal of Buddhism is to extinguish all desire, and the self, in the process. Buddhism also differed from Hinduism as there is no need of caste, or priests. There is no afterlife.

It may appear that Buddhism is a philosophic belief system, a way of living that keeps suffering at lower levels. But as Buddhism spread, it divided into two general categories, which made Buddhism a religious belief system. *Theravada*, small wheel Buddhism, most closely follows the precepts of Siddhartha Gautama. He's regarded as a great prophet whose example will help his followers attain *Nirvana*. This form of Buddhism is practiced largely in Southeast Asia. It might have appealed to the Vietnamese because of its simplicity. Ancient Vietnamese society did not have gender biases to the same degree as Chinese or Indian society. Theravada Buddhism appealed to a society that sought examples of right conduct, rather than a deity to assist the individual.

Mahayana, or big wheel Buddhism, portrays Buddha as semi-divine, not too unlike Jesus. This form concentrates on reforming society. *Nirvana* can be achieved through conduct and prayer to Buddha Amitabha, the Buddha of the Western Heavens. This Buddha answers prayers and may shorten the process of attaining *Nirvana*, or granting *Nirvana* outright. This form of Buddhism is most often practiced in China, Japan, and the West. It is sometimes difficult to accept a system that appears philosophic. Chinese and Japanese Buddhism portrayed Buddha as divine in response for the need of a human/divine figure.

The Buddha's divinity varies from sect to sect. But the *Four Noble Truths* and the *Noble Eightfold Path* have taken on religious significance, regardless of sect. The prayer and meditation incorporated into Buddhism transformed it from a philosophic belief system to a religious belief system.

The Interplay between Philosophic and Religious Systems

Philosophy affected the two religious belief systems discussed previously. Each used philosophic ideas to help explain the human condition. It's tempting to stress that philosophic belief systems differed from religious belief systems because the latter possess deities; the deity in Buddhism remains unclear. It's possible that beliefs characterized as religious belief systems incorporate philosophy into some of their rituals, but the rituals and the mystic are vehicles to propagate the philosophies.

Just as religious belief systems incorporated philosophies, philosophic belief systems incorporated religion. Taoism and Confucianism came into being at the same time as Buddhism. Both Taoism and Confucianism were discussed in Chapter 4. What follows is an exploration of how they incorporated religious beliefs to make their points.

Philosophic Belief Systems

Taoism

In Chapter 3 Taoism was discussed as a response to the civil wars of the later Chou Dynasty. Stability and peace for the individual depended on maintaining balance in a chaotic universe between the yin and yang. This balance pertained to all aspects of life from food to thought. Taoism also called for a leader who would provide for everyone, thereby taking away the need for discontent. Discontent resulted in speculation, dissent, ultimately unrest, and war. Hence, Taoism stresses feeling and comfort over thought.

This philosophic system suggests that urban living is evil and that the Taoist should escape the city, meditate, and engage in something of beauty. Taoism, hence, addressed how individuals could survive well during stressful times. This was the case since Taoism's inception during the latter-Chou dynasty.

Not everyone could escape to the country when city living grew stressful; not everyone was capable of writing poetry or painting. Just as Hinduism and Buddhism blended philosophy with religion, Taoism blended religion into philosophy. Meditation became akin to prayer. Taoism urged the search for balance in the universe, the Yin and Yang. The Yin, the feminine aspect of the universe is cold and passive; the Yang, hot and active. The search for balance in the universe resulted in the search for blending the Yin and Yang. The universe assumed the proportions of a deity. The search for balance blended into a religious precept and way of life. Taoism incorporated religious needs into a philosophic belief system. This made Taoism more than an academic philosophy because it endowed it with religious trappings. All of this gave Taoism a universal appeal.

Taoism may have begun as a philosophy, as an answer to how an individual can survive in troubled times, but, through the incorporation of religious belief system of meditation, it expanded into a philosophic belief system that is very alive and well today.

Confucianism

Like Taoism, Confucianism is a philosophy originally constructed to bring stability during the later Chou dynasty. Confucianism, unlike Taoism, addressed how a society, not the individual, attains stability in the midst of civil war. Confucius stressed the need for hierarchies, education, virtue, and the family. Adherence to these would bring stability to the roots of society that would germinate and flow upward toward the decision makers.

Practicality runs through Confucianism. If everyone accepted their role in society, society would remain stable. As in the Tao, questioning and speculation result in unrest, and unrest in war. One of Confucius's sayings, or Analects, which were written down by his students, read "Let the father be a father and the son be a son." Confucius in this analect noted that each family member has a role, and if they practice this role well, life will become more stable.

None of this sounds religious. But Confucianism also stressed ancestor worship. Good followers of Confucius' philosophy set up shrines to their ancestors in their homes, worshipping there regularly. Confucius further stressed the need to follow the Chinese religion, a form of polytheism.

By stressing the need for religion, Confucius co-opted religion into his philosophy, thereby transforming it into a religious system as well. Some have argued that Confucianism cannot be a religion because it does not contain a deity per se. But it transformed ancestors into deities, and paid homage to the gods of nature. In time, Confucius, like the Buddha in Mahayana Buddhism, became the deity. Confucianism remained China's principal philosophic belief system until 1949. Aspects of Confucianism can still be seen in the modern Chinese bureaucracy.

The argument still continues whether or not Confucianism and Taoism are religious or philosophic belief systems because of the lack of deity. To some extent, the same question might be asked of Buddhism. In the Theravada sect, Buddha is human. Having made Nirvana, his example is all that remains. The examination of Buddhism, Taoism, and Confucianism raise an interesting question: Do religious belief systems require belief in one or more deities or is the fervent faith of their followers sufficient to be defined as religious belief systems?

Monotheistic Religious Belief Systems

Monotheistic belief systems possess an all-powerful, sometimes vengeful, sometimes merciful deity. Underlying each of these systems is faith that the deity takes an interest in each individual; each presupposes the need to understand this universe through worship of the deity. The deity decides the individual's fate, but the individual may mitigate that decision through prayer, conduct, and faith. There is usually belief in some form of afterlife, even when not explicitly spelled out.

How do philosophic belief systems impact monotheism? These religious belief systems may be more driven by causes or ideology, than philosophy. An examination and comparison of the two oldest monotheistic religious belief systems follow.

Judaism

The oldest monotheistic religion, Judaism never acquired a large following because it doesn't actively seek converts. Although a small group, Judaism has had a disproportionately large impact upon civilization. The laws set down in the Torah have become the basis of laws in Western states. Judaism is also the parent religion of Islam and Christianity. Thus, Jewish thought and precepts had a significant effect on Islam. Monotheism began with Judaism, and evolved from there.

Like Zoroastrianism, the religion of ancient Persia, Judaism originally had a male and female deity. That female deity, Shekhina, disappeared by the time the Torah, the *Five Books of Moses*, was completed. With the completion of the Talmud, a compendium of Jewish law, Judaism became male centered.

Worshipping one deity reflects a changed outlook of humankind's relationship to the universe. A world controlled by more than one deity was often a capricious place. Greek mythology abounds with one god's jealousy spelling misery for humanity. Worship of one God, *Yahweh*, suggests a purposeful universe. When evil struck, it struck for reasons humankind could either remedy or accept.

Humankind's position in the world rose with Judaism. God made a covenant with Judaism's founder, Abraham. In return for accepting God as the one true God, the Lord said He would protect the Jewish people as His Chosen. The presence of a contract with God suggested that humankind was capable of entering into contract with the Divine. Humans weren't merely pawns or victims anymore.

The emphasis on the Covenant informed Judaism's followers that they were the "Chosen People." To set themselves apart, Jews practiced strict dietary laws. Initially Jews practiced vegetarianism, but when they began eating meat, a code of dietary laws known as the kashrut appeared. Among other things, it's forbidden to mix dairy products and meat at one meal.

The first Jews settled in Canaan, the site of modern Israel. When Abraham's great-grandson, Joseph, became the Pharaoh's first minister, the Jewish population moved from Canaan to Egypt and became a powerful minority within the Egyptian government. The Hyksos invaded Egypt, 1674–1548 BCE, but retained Jewish bureaucrats within the Egyptian government. When the Hyksos were defeated, the Egyptians retaliated by enslaving the Jews. But, despite the change in the economic and social status of the Jews in Egypt, the Jewish slaves continued to flourish, and the Jewish population continued to grow. Pharaoh, fearful that the Jewish minority might reclaim power they had since Joseph, decided to destroy the Jews by killing all male Jewish babies.

That proved to be the last straw. Amram and Yokheved had a male child; Yokheved hid the baby in a basket, setting it afloat in the Nile near where Pharaoh's daughter was bathing. The Egyptian princess found the basket with the baby inside, brought the baby to court, naming him Moses, meaning, "I drew him forth." Moses was raised as an Egyptian and became well known, but he remembered his Jewish origin. In response to abuses against the Jews, Moses murdered a particularly harsh Egyptian guard and fled to Midian. It took ten plagues, including the death of Pharaoh's firstborn son and a tidal wave, but Moses succeeded in freeing the Jewish slaves, ultimately leading them back to the gates of Canaan, the Promised Land.

Achieving release from slavery was only a beginning. Learning how to live as a free people took time. It took 40 years until the generation that had been in Egyptian slavery died out, and new generations that understood freedom reached adulthood. Forty years of wandering cemented communal Jewish life. By the time these wanderers reached Canaan, they had coalesced into a community with a sense of communal obligation.

During their trek, Moses presented this Jewish community in transition with the Ten Commandments, which formed the foundation of Jewish life in the desert, and would become the basis of Western jurisprudence. The Ten Commandments were the first of 630 Mitzvoth, or good deeds. These cover the duties and actions of Jewish people to their religion and the community.

Freedom receives much attention in the third book of the Torah, *Leviticus*. Everyone, it's decreed, must wear clothes of free persons. Slaves must be freed every seven years. Those who choose to remain in slavery must be freed in the 49th or jubilee year. Emphasis on how to live made the Torah a guide to living. The Jewish people became known as the "people of the book." This lay at the root of Jewish historical memory, and the yearning for civilization free of persecution.

Passover affected individual identity as well. Moses's declaration to Pharaoh and the act of leaving Egypt reflect individual action. Slavery is an unacceptable way of living, and the individual has the right to contest it. This may be the first time in recorded history that individuals stood up to the establishment for a social cause. This may also be the first time a group announced they were too good to be slaves and they were leaving. Freedom was defined in their journey back to Canaan.

The Passover holiday was celebrated in ancient Israel, probably as soon as the Jews returned to Canaan. It commemorates how God's angel of death passed over the Jewish households to kill all Egyptian first-born children. But during the course of the *Seder* (order), or Passover dinner, the entire story of the Exodus is retold. Passover is celebrated for eight days. During that time no grain or yeast product is eaten. This occurred because the Jews had to leave Egypt so quickly that they did not have time to allow their bread to rise. Hence, on Passover, Jews abstain from eating wheat or grain.

Long before Jesus Christ, Jews were persecuted for being different. The Jews worshiped one God in polytheistic civilizations, and led lives that differed markedly from other members of society. That made them suspect, an easy target or scapegoat for any leader needing to solidify support.

But Passover set an historical precedent; the Jewish people fought back, and this precedent runs through Judaism like a *leitmotif*:

1. Hanukah celebrates the victory of Judah Maccabee over the Greeks in what may have been the first recorded guerilla war.
2. Purim celebrates Esther and Mordecai's victory over Haman, the evil Persian prime minister who plotted genocide against the Persian Jewish community.

Christianity

Christianity, the acceptance of Jesus as the Son of God and the way to salvation, evolved from Judaism. Christ's birth needs to be placed in historical perspective.

The Roman Empire conquered Israel, leaving the rule to King Herod (37–4 BCE). Herod, by all accounts, was paranoid, terribly afraid that his rule would be undermined by his Jewish subjects.

To further complicate matters, the Jewish community had divided into two groups: the Sadducees and the Pharisees. The Sadducees comprised the wealthier group of Jews in Jerusalem. They were priests and believed the *Five Books of Moses* alone formed the basis of Judaism. The Pharisees, largely middle class, believed the Jewish oral tradition to be important. The Sadducees allied with Herod: the Pharisees against. There was also at the same time a fringe group, the Essenes who prepared for the coming of the Messiah.

These were troubled times. Jesus was born in Bethlehem in either 10 or 4 BCE, in what may be considered miraculous circumstances. Mary and Joseph were called to give information for a Roman census in Bethlehem. When they arrived, there was no room at any of the local inns, and Mary was almost at the term of her pregnancy. They settled in a manger where Mary gave birth to Yehashua or Jesus.

During these troubled times, there was a popular belief throughout the Middle East that the coming of the Messiah was at hand. A supernova appeared in the skies over Bethlehem, and three kings, or Magi, Caspar, Melchior, and Balthazar, began their journey toward the nova, certain that it pointed the way to the Messiah. They reached Mary, Joseph, and Jesus when the child was three years old.

The rumor also reached the Romans, who decried that all male children in Judea/Israel three or younger were to be killed. Joseph, Mary, and Jesus fled to Egypt. During the sojourn in Egypt, Jesus developed a sense of his destiny. When he returned to Israel/Judea, he returned as the son of God and the Messiah, and began to attract disciples.

As with Moses, Jesus performed miracles. He fed the masses at Canae; walked on water; healed the sick by touch. Each of these was accepted as a sign that Jesus was indeed divine, as the Son of God, and the Messiah.

Jesus' comments reveal a pragmatic streak. 'Render onto Caesar what is Caesar's . . .' suggested that Jesus understood the dichotomy between religion and the Roman state, advising his followers on how to serve Rome and one's moral compass simultaneously.

Jesus also raised humanity's standard. "Love thy neighbor as thyself," and "Do onto others as you would have them do onto you," make human action divine. A call to social action resonates throughout Jesus' teachings. Underlying Judaism is the fight for individual and communal freedom, the right to make choices. Underlying Christianity is the fight for justice, regardless of economic class.

Jesus addresses this specifically on at least two occasions. "Blessed are the meek for they shall inherit the earth," and "It is harder for a rich man to get to heaven than for a camel to pass through the eye of a needle." These comments reveal a wish to restructure society on a more economically equal footing. While this wasn't socialism, Jesus understood that civilized society was inherently unequal. Comments, such as these challenged established Roman society. The more Jesus' brand of Judaism gathered followers, the more the Roman establishment got nervous. Religion was no longer legitimizing government. Something had to give.

It's possible that the road to Jesus' crucifixion and resurrection occurred exactly as written. It would not be the first time that a student betrayed the teacher for money, and perhaps status. After dying on earth the Son returned to the Father in Heaven. Questions remain. Mystery surrounds Judas Iscariot. Did he really exist? Was the betrayal part of some larger plan—a plan that went seriously awry? Was the crucifixion supposed to be staged so Jesus could get out of Roman clutches? What was the role of the community?

Some contend that Judas was a later invention to shift the blame from the Romans to the Jewish establishment. Early Christianity was viewed as just another sect of Judaism. Something was needed to make it unique; to separate it from the older religion in the strongest possible terms. Making Judaism Christianity's enemy served to forcefully separate both religions. It made their doctrines appear to be opposed, each rivaling the other.

Others believe that Jesus conspired with Judas on the betrayal. The crucifixion was to be a mock crucifixion to enable Jesus to escape Jerusalem and continue his work with one more very important miracle to sustain Him. But something went wrong. One of the Roman guards stabbed Jesus in the side with a spear, and he died on the cross. Some contend that loyal disciples spirited Jesus' body away, hence the legend of resurrection. Whether miracle, contrivance or failed plot, Passover melded with the Resurrection in Christianity. The Resurrection added new meaning to Christianity. Acceptance of Jesus as the Son of God guaranteed salvation.

Christians understood life was unfair. But if the poor accepted Jesus as the Son of God, they, because of their suffering, would be rewarded after death, just as Jesus was rewarded by returning to God the Father. Jesus' comments about the rich and heaven also suggested that the score would be evened out after death. Evil rich people would go to Hell.

The Resurrection strengthened these tenets of Christianity, making the new religion more attractive. Christianity placed the Divine on a human plane, and promised ultimate joy in an innately unfair world.

It took more than 200 years for Christianity to take root as a major religion. Saul of Tarsus, better known as St. Paul, spread Christianity among the populations surrounding the Mediterranean littoral. The religion had appeal, even if it became an underground faith, depending on whims of the Roman Emperors.

In 306 CE, the Emperor Constantine saw the image of the Cross in the sky on the evening before battle. Constantine vowed he'd convert to Christianity if God would only grant him victory. Constantine won and converted to Christianity. By the time of his death in 333 CE, Constantine declared Christianity to be the official religion of the Roman Empire.

Islam

Islam is the youngest of the monotheistic religions. Founded by Mohammad in 612 CE, Islam stressed the all-encompassing nature of Allah. Unlike the Christian belief that God included Father, Son, and Holy Spirit, Muslims believe that Allah is one and omnipotent. The angel Gabriel came to Mohammad and dictated Allah's word, the Q'uran, because both Judaism and Christianity had been corrupted. Islam accepted both the Jewish patriarchs and Jesus and the Apostles as holy because they were part of Islam's heritage. It's ironic that these three religions all stemming from a covenant between God and humankind have battled each other from medieval times until today. Maybe it's true: Familiarity breeds contempt. Perhaps, common roots result in the need to define and separate. Perhaps the time will soon come when the need to define will yield to the need to reconcile.

Note: Islam is discussed in detail in Chapter 8. For the history and doctrines of Islam, please see the opening sections of Chapter 8.

Concluding Thoughts on Monotheistic Belief Systems

Judaism and Christianity and Islam postulate a universe ruled by one God. Each believes humankind capable of reaching God. Humankind in these religious belief systems is not a victim or incapable of thought or action. All three religions energize their tenets with an activist ideology that is cause driven. But that's where the resemblances end.

Judaism values freedom and choice of destiny, which is the underlying thrust of Passover. God will watch over the community, ultimately aiding it in its struggle for freedom. Freedom, until the twentieth century, meant being able to live in peace as a community.

Early Christianity focused more on the individual's plight. Individual earthly suffering would be rewarded in heaven. Salvation rewards the earnest Christian, regardless of social standing. Passover, with its betrayal, melded with the Resurrection. God sent His human Son to minister to and dwell with humankind. When the time is right, Christ will return. Islam postulates the individual surrender him/herself to Allah, and, by following the laws set down in the Q'uran, will attain paradise.

The differences between Judaism and Christianity and Islam are somewhat analogous to the differences between Taoism and Confucianism. Both philosophic belief systems strive to bring humankind stability in troubled times. Taoism focuses on how the individual can attain stability; Confucianism centers on how a society can attain stability.

But there is one more very large difference in these these religions belief systems: Judaism doesn't actively seek converts; Christianity and Islam proselytize when both secular and religious leaders deem it necessary. Modern Judaism, like modern Christianity and modern Islam, has different sects. Not every one of these accepted the concept of a "Chosen or elected People." But all Jews agree that humankind has choices.

A significant number of Christians believe that acceptance of Jesus is the only way to salvation. Given that tenet, it's natural to work to bring more people into the fold. Not all Christians attempt to convert their neighbors and friends. But the certainty inherent in Christianity and Islam sometimes creates strains because non-Christians resent pressure. Monotheistic religious belief systems sustain themselves through their activist cores. But those same activist cores, bounding with idealism, have on more than one occasion led civilizations down a collision course . . . and innocent people perished. It's then that Thucydides' comments reecho: "Having done what they did, they suffered as men must."

Practice Test Questions

1. Greek polytheism often resulted in

   A. humankind being at the mercy of capricious deities.
   B. meeting deities in the Agora.
   C. picking a favorite god or goddess for special requests.
   D. extra Olympic Games.

2. Confucianism incorporated which precepts from religious belief systems?

   A. Buddhist shrines
   B. Ancestor worship
   C. Daily prayer services
   D. Religious education

3. Buddhism stressed which code of conduct?

   A. Following the Noble Eightfold Path
   B. Reaching Nirvana's eternal bliss
   C. Asceticism
   D. Transcendental meditation

4. Judaism

   A. sought converts to improve numbers.
   B. melded religious worship with a commitment to preserve freedom.
   C. worshipped God out of fear and terror.
   D. deified Moses.

5. Religious and philosophical belief systems

   A. combine each other's precepts.
   B. cannot coexist.
   C. must apply only to specific times.
   D. engage only an influential minority.

Answers and Explanations

1. **A.** The gods often sparred with each other, victimizing humankind in the process.

2. **B.** Ancestor worship created a sense of continuity in the family.

3. **A.** Following the Noble Eightfold Path enabled Buddhists to shed all desire and attain Nirvana, self extinction.

4. **B.** Judaism combined a monotheistic religious belief system with a commitment to freedom. Passover celebrates both God's help and freedom.

5. **A.** The successful religious or philosophic belief system must engage the individual on both emotional and intellectual planes. Therefore each combines elements of the other.

The Late Classical Period: 200–600 CE

What Differentiates the Late Classical Period from the Classical Period?

Later classical civilizations differ from their earlier counterparts in their worldview, economics, and belief systems. They're more technologically complex, more certain of their identity, and more hierarchical. They're less likely to accept new ideas or belief systems. They're less able to successfully go to war or defend themselves. This might be due to the fact that later classical civilizations became so confident in their ability to thrive that they lost the flexibility necessary to survive. Confidence sometimes breeds laxity.

The three civilizations examined in this chapter, the Gupta, Han, and Roman empires, although possessing different belief systems, had trade interaction, and declined at approximately the same time. This leads to two disturbing questions:

1. Did these civilizations go into decline for the same reasons?
2. Is there a modern lesson in their decline?

Empire's End

The Gupta Empire

During the Gupta age, 320-550 CE, art, literature, mathematics, and the sciences flourished under the aegis of the Gupta emperors. Education flourished, in part because of the extensive literature of Hinduism and Buddhism. The Gupta emperors created a large bureaucracy that managed both trade and agriculture. South Asia was both a trade and manufacturing hub. Trade, manufacturing, and education all point to a society comfortable enough with itself to be diverse and to tolerate diversity. The empire thrived on the synergism of ideas this diversity nourished.

What destroyed the Gupta Empire? The Gupta Empire, like the Roman and Chinese, was attacked by the Huns. The Gupta won, but it was a Pyrrhic victory—a victory that brought no benefits, while it drained the victor's resources. Skanda Gupta, the Gupta emperor, managed to confine the White Huns to what is today Pakistan and Afghanistan, but the Guptian economy buckled in the process. Trade was disrupted and the empire disintegrated. By the beginning of the sixth century CE, the Gupta Empire had crumbled into a group of warring states.

There's another parallel to the aftermath of the Roman Empire in Gupta history. From 606–648 CE, Harsha reunited South Asia, claiming to be the inheritor of the Gupta dynasty—a parallel to Charlemagne. But Harsha died without heirs, and the empire largely died with him.

It's an old maxim that outside invasion strengthens the home front. But this didn't apply in the late Gupta Empire. Subjects might have felt affection for the Emperor, but they had no such loyalties to the state bureaucracy. This disconnect proved fatal to the political and economic structure the Gupta emperors built.

Yet Gupta culture persisted. The arts, education, and architecture pioneered by the Gupta continued to flourish. The Gupta Empire defined South Asian culture, and continues to do so. It may be that political structures are fragile, but cultural structures endure, and these ultimately define an era and influence the future.

Han China: 202 BCE–220 CE

Like the Gupta Empire, the Han dynasty fostered education, arts, sciences, and technology. Also, the Han dynasty pursued an active trading policy. There are signs that women took part in society beyond the home, and that the Han emperors were well beloved because the times were prosperous and peaceful. Art pieces show women taking part in activities outside the home. Footbinding was not practiced until the Sung dynasty.

The Han created the government bureaucracy whose members entered college to train for their duties, based on academic merit, as advocated by Confucius. Confucius asserted that imperial government must function efficiently. That meant government functionaries had to acquire a vast education before entering the emperor's service.

A Han bureaucrat was expected to earn the equivalent of a Ph.D. The training was expensive, yet not every government functionary came from Chinese nobility. Sometimes a village sponsored a young, brilliant, but poor candidate. All of this should have pointed to a longer reigning dynasty. But in the beginning of the third century CE, the Han dynasty collapsed. What happened?

As with the Gupta Empire, the Han suffered invasion from the north by the Huns. As with the Gupta Empire, the Han economy buckled under the attacks. But the Gupta population felt little loyalty to the government, while the Chinese loved the Han.

The Han dynasty collapsed because well-loved emperors alone aren't enough to sustain a government. Chinese government during the Han dynasty relied on an early form of corporatism. Only designated groups of subjects had access to the Han emperor. **Corporatism** stipulates that the executive meet with representatives of particular classes, industries, and religious groups that form society. By meeting with groups, rather than disparate individuals, the executive charted policy for society.

Love of the emperor was insufficient in itself to hold the love of the populace. By the time the Han dynasty collapsed, most Chinese loved their Han emperors but hated the government established in their name. This dichotomy resulted in a disconnect. When the Huns challenged Han government, the populace felt little need to defend the government that it believed destroyed the small farmer . . . and the Han dynasty fell.

A period of wars between states followed. In 581/582 CE the Sui Dynasty ended these wars, re-establishing peace. But the Sui emperors were brutal rulers and were quickly displaced by the T'ang Dynasty. All of this was not lost on the T'ang. One of the first things the Emperor of the T'ang did was institute massive land reform. The land, especially in south China, was re-divided and returned to the small farmers.

Rome: 800 BCE–476 CE

Civic virtue loomed large in early Roman life. But like the Gupta and the Han, the Roman Empire declined and collapsed. It's a favorite historical pastime to search for the cause of the Western Roman Empire's demise. But before launching that examination, a discussion of Rome's history is in order.

Legend has it that Rome was founded by Romulus and Remus, twin orphans nursed by a she-wolf on the site of the city of Rome. Rome became part of the Etruscan kingdom, but, hating monarchy, it broke from the Etruscans and established itself as a republic.

These were also the virtues most prized by the Roman Republic. The Republic was divided into two social classes: the patricians and the plebeians. The patricians made the decisions for the good of the Roman Republic in the Senate. Plebeians voiced their concerns through two patricians, known as tribunes. The Senate combined legislative and executive functions. Only in times of national emergency did the Senate appoint a Consul with emergency executive powers. The Consul served no more that six months, and then returned to the Senate.

The Roman Republic, on the other hand, never created any long-term executive office. The fear and hatred of a king was just too great. Serving the state became an almost holy calling. For example, in 458 BCE, a military emergency necessitated appointing a consul, and the Senate elected a Patrician named Cincinnatus. It happened that Cincinnatus wasn't in Rome at the moment, but rather was at his farm outside the city.

A deputation left post haste, finding Cincinnatus covered with sweat, plowing his fields. The deputation eagerly began offering Cincinnatus the Consulship. But Cincinnatus stopped the ceremony, telling them to wait. The Senator refused to accept Rome's highest office drenched with sweat, and most likely nude or scantily clothed. Everything went on hold until Cincinnatus washed and had changed into his toga.

Why? Cincinnatus wasn't worried about the media or his looks. He believed the state had conferred its highest honor, and, out of reverence and respect, Cincinnatis needed to be dressed appropriately to receive it. Serving Rome in a virtuous manner became an article of faith. Cincinnatis' actions exemplified Roman virtue and respect for the State at its finest.

But lack of an executive group in government placed the Roman Republic in peril. The Roman Republic continued to grow, but lacked the ability to effectively govern new territories. As the Roman population swelled to 750,000, the Senate found it increasingly difficult to continue governing in an efficient manner.

It was only a matter of time before the Senate and the army moved into collision mode. Tyrants had attempted and failed to take over Rome before Julius Caesar. Caesar proved charismatic, but when he proclaimed himself Emperor, a cabal of Senators led by Brutus, eager to preserve the Republic, assassinated Caesar. A civil war between Marc Anthony's army and Octavian Caesar followed. Marc Anthony and his ally (and lover) Cleopatra lost to Octavian, who proclaimed himself Augustus Caesar, and the Roman Republic collapsed.

The Roman Empire rose from its ashes. The Roman Empire was an executive-based form of government with the decision-making apparatus resting in the head of the emperor. The emperor executed control through a bureaucracy; his was the final say. The transformation to a dictatorship was sudden, dramatic, and traumatic.

Why was the Roman Empire not greeted with massive rebellion? Augustus and most of the emperors that followed for the next 200 years brought order to a chaotic situation. During the era called the *Pax Romana,* life was orderly. Merchants traveled on well-kept roads. Functionaries carried out orders sent from Rome. Latin became the international language; Roman currency the international coin.

The state ran fairly efficiently during the Pax Romana, which lasted until 200 CE. Then things fell apart. Rome, or rather the Western Roman Empire, didn't collapse. Rather it went into a long slow decline . . . and that decline has remained the grist of history class term papers and academic speculation ever since. We will now consider the theories that have been advanced as causes of the Roman decline.

Theory 1: Christianity

Edward Gibbon in his work, *The Decline and Fall of the Roman Empire,* asserted that the Roman Empire declined and collapsed because its citizens embraced Christianity, waited for salvation and entrance into heaven, forsaking earthly cares, and earthly government, in the process. Gibbon went into minute detail about how most citizens disconnected so completely from everyday life that it became impossible for the Empire to continue.

Gibbon rightly pointed out a crisis of confidence in the late Roman Empire. But his arguments leave questions: What occurred as a result of Christianity becoming the religion of the Eastern Roman Empire? Why did the Eastern Empire continue to exist until 1453? Why did the early Roman Catholic Church take on the structure of the Roman Empire and thrive? Gibbon rightly noted the lack of confidence in the later Roman Empire. But it's possible that lack of confidence was a symptom of other structural flaws, rather than nascent Christianity.

Theory 2: Morality

One of the other casualties of the Roman Republic's destruction was the emphasis on Roman Republican virtue. The belief in holding to a moral code and sacrificing for the sake of the Republic was not present during the Roman Empire. As life grew increasingly chaotic after the Pax Romana, rigorous civic virtues ceased to exist. The Roman Empire lacked the moral fiber of the Roman Republic with serious consequences.

What was needed was some form of entertainment that would keep the good citizens happy, so they wouldn't notice the loss of their political power. The Roman Coliseum was built in 80 CE during Vespasian's reign. It became the home of gladiator games and animal circus attractions. The opening ran for three days, during which 1,800 people lost their lives in the name of mass entertainment. The games began in the morning. The first act would often be a battle between a man and a lion or tiger. Lions and tigers usually don't attack unless provoked, so their trainers would get them angry by teasing them with raw meat. By the time they came into the ring, the only thing on these large cats', minds was human food.

Some comic relief might follow. Two blind slaves would be let into the ring to fight to the death. This took time, the two had to find each other and handle their swords appropriately. Another animal act might follow. This time it might be an elephant walking on a tightrope or an ancient form of bear baiting. Some form of lunch would follow. Often the patron of the game distributed loaves of bread—hence the phrase, "bread and circuses."

Then the coliseum would be flooded for a reenactment of a sea battle. On occasion there would be fights between gladiators and alligators or sharks. This might continue until 9 PM. Then, once the field had dried a bit, the finale took place. Two gladiators would enter the ring, stand in front of the designated patron of that day's game, salute him, stating, "Those of us who are about to die salute you," and fight until one was at the point of killing the other.

Both would stop and look up at the designated patron. If the fight had been well executed the patron might make a sign with his thumb pointed upward. Both gladiators would live to fight another day. But most often the patron pointed his thumb down, whereupon the gladiator with the advantage killed his opponent.

The games were so popular that they were exported to other countries. They actually outlasted the Western Roman Empire by 74 years. The last game on record took place in 549 CE in Constantinople. It's valid to question "What is the effect of seeing a day of murder on the psyche? What happens to the civilization that promotes death as sport?" The games weren't the only form of interesting, somewhat sickening entertainment. The Roman orgy proved just as sickening but in a more literal way.

Guests came to banquets, ate themselves into a stupor, and then forced themselves to vomit. After recovering somewhat they ate again and repeated the cycle . . . all night. It's doubtful that these happy bulimics went to work in the morning. Sexual orgies also came into existence, a conduct not conducive to stable family life.

Not every Roman spent his/her days watching the lions or recovering from too much food. But these pastimes became popular enough that they point to a lack of work or movement in society. It's possible that these, like the disconnect factor described in the section on Christianity are symptoms of economic problems.

Theory 3: The Economy

Rome suffered two economic problems after 200 CE. The first, a decline in the currency value may well have resulted in the second, the demise of the small family farm. That demise had far-reaching effects on life in the empire.

Beginning with Augustus, when the Roman emperors needed money they tended to either clip metal out of the coinage or use a combination of silver and gold, electrum. After 200 CE, the cheaper coinage drove out the good coinage that remained, a process defined in a famous economic principle known as Gresham's Law. Prices went up, causing inflation.

Inflation made it impossible for many of the smaller farmers to keep their land. As with Han China, the smaller farmer sold their family plots to large estate owners, and became tenants on their former land. This practice in the later Roman Empire was called Patrocinium. Some consider this the forerunner of feudalism.

As with Han China, so many tenants working all the land resulted in less fertility. Many farmers abandoned their former homes, heading for the city. This new migration resulted in a new problem: urban unemployment.

Rome always had a large slave population. Slavery was an economic status, and slaves ranged from professionals to minors. Roman law permitted a slave to own up to four slaves. After the Spartacus rebellion failed, slavery continued to grow. But excess slave labor drove up unemployment. The new Roman resident, the disposed field migrant, could not find work. Slave labor made employment virtually impossible.

The games, the rise of Christianity, and the economy each could be tagged as the reason the Roman Empire fell. Each factor is interrelated. But each remains a symptom of something else.

Theory 4: Implosion

From the time Rome broke from the Etruscans, the city began to expand. It continued to expand until the Empire controlled all of Western Europe, the Middle East, and North Africa. Roman traders traveled as far as China. The expansion continued until 305 CE when Diocletian divided the empire, decreeing there would be no more expansion. The empire was at its height, so why expand any further? That decision, according to historian Alexander Butler, proved fatal to Rome. Somewhere in the empire's psyche was the need to expand. After the Empire ceased to expand, it began to collapse.

The Roman Empire resembled the shark. Just as the shark must constantly move forward, the empire could not function without growth. Problems intensified as the empire continued to contract. The contraction caused anther problem: the role of the legions. Roman soldiers were ill-equipped for civilian life. In addition, the Roman soldier had to accustom himself to a different pay schedule. Rome paid the army in salt, a salary. The soldier could trade the salt for goods. Money, inflated money, presented a scary challenge. When taken with all the other factors, the contraction buckled what was left of the economy, resulting in collapse.

What Really Caused the Roman Decline?

Only one problem was large enough to cause the empire to decline and fall. From its inception to Empire, Rome never developed a stable executive branch. The Romans hated the Etruscan monarchy, but could not function efficiently during the Republic. Julius Caesar established the Roman Empire.

The empire functioned relatively well until 200 CE. Some of the economic problems began to surface as early as Augustus' reign. But the string of incompetent emperors following the *Pax Romana,* 180 CE, made matters worse. The emperor Caligula ran a ludicrous, irrational government. He ordered his soldiers to attack the Mediterranean Sea, and then enrolled his horse as Pro Consul in the Senate. All of this was compounded by a debilitating plague.

The emperors during the Pax Romana each enjoyed fairly long reigns. The emperors during the third century CE had shorter reigns, some abruptly shortened by assassination. The weak executive resulted in the economic, moral, military, and confidence crisis described above. But it also resulted in one more factor, and this one delivered the *coup de grâce.*

The Final Blow

The Western Roman Empire didn't suffer a dramatic collapse; it simply withered away. All of the factors described above made living within the empire increasingly stressful. But very few citizens had any idea of the decline because it occurred gradually. Chronic unemployment, tempered by crowd-pleasing games, seemed to be the Roman way of life, not symptoms of trouble.

Why didn't the Roman citizenry see what lay in the future? According to medieval historian Eileen Power, Roman education failed its citizenry. In her essay *Precursors,* Power points out that Roman education failed to teach flexibility and insight, concentrating instead on the trivial. Ominous warning signs were present, but no one noticed.

The Western and Eastern Empire split in 264 CE. During the fourth century, Christianity became the religion of the empire, with its headquarters in Rome. The city itself was sacked by Germanic tribes led by Alaric. But still Rome persisted.

Then in 476 CE, the nine-year-old heir to the throne, Romulus Augustus, was deposed by the chief of the Visigoths. The chief informed the Eastern Emperor that a Western Emperor was no longer needed. No one thought anything of it initially. The idea of being part of Rome didn't end with the emperors. In the sixth century CE, Justinian ruled as emperor of Rome. In 800 CE, Charlemagne claimed he had reestablished the Roman Empire. It may have been that Europeans didn't realize the Roman Empire didn't collapse until feudalism waned, and a money economy took hold.

Practice Test Questions

1. The Gupta, Han, and Roman empires profited from

   A. international trade.
   B. trade in exotic animals.
   C. manufacture of fine cloth.
   D. slave trade.

2. Romans are best known for

   A. the dome, the vault, and the arch.
   B. their long-burning candles.
   C. weekly chariot races.
   D. three-tiered boats with many galley slaves.

3. What triggered the fall of the Han and Gupta empires?

   A. Poor emperors
   B. Imminent invasions by the Huns
   C. Too much child labor
   D. Too little food

4. What triggered the fall of the Western Roman Empire?

   A. The rise of Christianity
   B. Lax moral standards
   C. Lack of strong executive branch
   D. Crazed barbarians

5. What has threatened later classical civilizations and continues to threaten current modern civilizations?

   A. Global trade
   B. Slavery
   C. Survival games
   D. The Disconnect Factor

Answers and Explanations

1. **A.** The Gupta, Han, and Roman empires each profited from international trade.

2. **A.** The Romans were best known for their creation of the dome, vault, and arch.

3. **B.** The Han and Gupta empires were threatened by invasion by the Huns.

4. **C.** The Roman Empire fell because it lacked a strong executive branch.

5. **D.** The disconnect factor fatally weakened later classical civilization, and the alienation that results in disconnects threatens modern democracy.

A Question of Time

An era in history is considered to be a time span beginning with some starting point, which is characterized by a new and distinct order, and ending when that order either changes significantly or collapses. What makes 600 CE–1450 CE an era? The Roman, Han and Gupta Empires defined later classical civilization. Their cultures outlived their political systems. We see the beginnings of our modern cultures and mores in the civilizations of the later classical period.

But this time period is not remembered for the impact of its empires, cultures or economies. Quite the contrary! After the Gupta empire fell, South Asia would not be united again until the Mughal dynasty 1526–1858. Another period of "warring states" followed the fall of the Han dynasty in China. The period following the collapse of the Western Roman Empire resulted in total fragmentation. Western Europe almost completely re-forested as humankind in Western Europe nearly went extinct.

The people who lived during or immediately after this time period viewed it with disdain. Why? It's hard for people living in the twenty-first century world to understand feudal ties, cashless local economies, and serfdom. The era immediately following the Middle Ages called itself the Renaissance or "Rebirth" from an age of barbarity. Disdain for the Middle Ages lives on. In the twenty-first century we pride ourselves on our global reach, on our international economy. The Middle Ages appears to us to be quaint, at best; barbaric at worst. Yet this transition period forms the basis for many modern day political policies, hatreds and loyalties alike. Civilizations can define time periods. But transitions are equally important. They, too, define time periods, and form bases for the future.

Empire's Emergence

The governmental form that emerged after the fall of the late classical appears to contradict the introduction. The idea of empire continued. But these empires differed from the late classical empires in several ways:

1. Byzantium was based on a past evocation, rather than future vision.
2. The Muslim Empire was largely based on religious law, as interpreted at a local level.
3. China began a process of turning inward, away from the outside world. This process would be complete by 1450.
4. The Carolingian and Holy Roman Empire survived because of local, not national adhesion.

The outward form of empire-style government remained; its focus altered radically.

Byzantium

The Byzantines thought themselves to be the continuation of the Roman Empire. In reality they were a bridge to the differing customs of Eastern Europe. In part, Byzantium created these differing customs. The Byzantine Empire grew out of the Eastern Roman Empire. The Emperor Constantine is credited with being the first Byzantine Emperor, and the city of Byzantium renamed Constantinople in his honor. Constantine brought religious cohesion to the area. By his death in 337 CE, the emperor proclaimed Christianity the state religion. It was forbidden to observe any other faith, under penalty of death.

This shift to one recognized religion marks a major change from the older Roman Empire. Rome recognized all religions, placing the deities of each in the Pantheon, whose name means "[site of] all gods." Only religions that posed a threat to Rome were forbidden. Christians were initially persecuted, especially under the Roman Emperor Nero. After Constantine, Roman Christianity may have been the glue that held the later Roman Empire together.

Constantine also strengthened the role of the Emperor. Later Roman emperors were at the mercy of the Praetorian Guard. Many were assassinated shortly after assuming the throne. As emperor, Constantine added rituals to the office that transformed the human ruler into a human deity. Purple robes and the kissing of the robe's hem added to the Byzantine's Emperor's luster, keeping him safe from rebellious guards. By transforming the Emperor into a partial deity, regicide became a form of deicide. This kept the Emperor safe from rebellious guards. No guard wanted to be charged with the death of a semi-deity.

Language was the second shift. Romans spoke and wrote in Latin; Byzantines, Greek. Languages, in reality, are communication systems. Laws may remain unchanged, but differences between the means of communication—the languages— places each in a unique context. The medium was indeed the message. Why the switch to Greek? "Asia Minor," the area surrounding modern-day Turkey, was the area in which Alexander the Great spread Greek culture. Greek was the language of Constantinople. The shift to the Greek language also resulted in a shift in religious emphasis. Latin was the language of the Roman Catholic Church; Greek the language of the Greek Orthodox church. Byzantium, thus, looked to Greek Orthodoxy to legitimate its empire, rather than Catholicism. As the Greek Orthodox Church and the Roman Catholic Church drifted further apart, ultimately separating in 1054 CE, the Byzantine Empire and the Western European kingdoms also drifted apart. The axiom "East is east and west is west, and the two shall never twain" became a reality.

Civilizations require codes of law that are specific to the civilization's needs. Justinian, 527–565 CE, supplied the codes that became the basis of law in the Byzantine Empire. Justinian thought he was cataloging the Roman law when he issued *Corpus Juris Civilis,* or "Body of Civil Law."

Justinian's Code covered all aspects of Roman law, including the many details always present in civil law. The Code gave the Byzantine Empire the cohesiveness necessary for it to survive throughout this period. Finally, Justinian's actions enabled the Byzantine Empire to survive, rather than disintegrate into civil war. Like Constantine, Justinian sought to enhance the emperor's image through ritual and architecture. But new government building plans placed a tax burden on Constantinople's residents. This resulted in discontent. The discontent flared into riots when a fight at a chariot race got out of control. Subsequently the *Nika* riots turned Constantinople into a city in the throes of riots, and threatened Justinian's rule. Justinian prepared to flee the city, but his wife, Empress Theodora, shamed him into remaining. This enabled Justinian to quell the riots, after which the Emperor's throne remained solid until Constantinople fell to the Turks in 1453.

As mentioned, Byzantine Christianity differed significantly from Roman Catholicism. In 1054 CE, beliefs became so divergent that the Church in Byzantium split from the Roman Catholic Church, which is called the Great Schism.

The Great Schism occurred because differences emerged over the executive structure of the Church. Prior to the schism, five bishops or patriarchs, representing Alexandria, Antioch, Constantinople, Jerusalem, and Rome, the major cities throughout the Roman Empire, were supposed to act as an executive committee on church matters. But the Patriarch of Constantinople took on an added luster because he controlled church matters in the emperor's seat of residence. Western Europeans, on the other hand, looked increasingly to the Pope in Rome, the Holy See founded by St. Peter, for guidance.

Over the years, each of the bishops in the Byzantine Empire represented the ethnic mix of the church. Christianity regionalized in Byzantium because it focused on the individual bishop's rule of each individual ethnic group, rather than the leadership of one Bishop. Language became another divisive factor. Western Europeans became uncomfortable with Bibles written in Greek, a language they didn't understand. A Bible translated into Latin, called the *Vulgate* Bible, supplanted the Greek editions. Western and Eastern Europeans no longer read, or were read, the same text.

The issue of the Bishop's power finally split the church. Rome and Western Europe followed the Pope; Byzantium followed the Patriarchs. When the Pope, after many hundreds of years of meetings and councils that attempted to clarify if Christ held equal powers to those of God the Father failed to resolve this issue, single-handedly attempted to resolve whether or not Christ held equal powers to God the Father, a religious firestorm erupted. The Eastern Church withdrew, and the Christian Orthodox movement became a new branch of Christianity.

The Byzantine Empire survived for over 1,000 years. If it is viewed as the continuation of the Roman Empire, it survived for 1,700 years. But even empires with stable government become vulnerable when they underestimate the changes taking place around them. Byzantium valued stability so highly that it overlooked the changing political and diplomatic landscape. This oversight led to its downfall.

There had been border skirmishes between the Byzantines and Turks in the area of modern Anatolia for generations. The Byzantine Emperor Romanus decided to personally lead the army into Anatolia to drive out the Turks once and for all. Romanus was promised troops that never arrived, and his army was massacred in 1071 at Manzikert. That left a power void in Constantinople, which enabled the Turks to invade Anatolia and annex it.

Turkish power was growing rapidly in the Middle East, and Byzantium appealed to the West for help. This appeal resulted in the first Crusade in 1096. While the Crusaders were initially successful they kept any land liberated from the "infidel." Further, their unkempt appearance and perceived churlishness did not endear them to their Byzantine hosts. The help sent by the West proved the adage that sometimes the cure is worse than the disease. The Crusades were an amalgam of idealism combined with the lust for power. Peter the Hermit dreamt of Christ's return if the Holy Land was swept clean of infidels. Pope Urban VIII saw the perfect opportunity to serve God through liberating the Holy Land and re-asserting Papal power over Byzantium.

The Fourth Crusade in 1204 made matters worse yet. This Crusade was led by the Venetians, a growing mercantile power in the Mediterranean region. The Venetians were less interested in ridding the world of the infidel than they were in undercutting the economic power of the Byzantine Empire.

A dispute over some payments resulted in the Venetians sacking Constantinople in 1204. The Byzantines fought back, and, after years of fighting the Venetians and their allies, succeeded in restoring their empire in 1261.

Things were never the same. After 1261, many of the lands that were formerly Byzantine were now occupied by the Ottomans, who were Muslims. Venetian power in the Mediterranean was becoming increasingly important. The Byzantines were surrounded by aggressive neighbors, and they had lost much of their will to fight. On May 29, 1453, the Ottomans breached Constantinople's walls, ending the Byzantine Empire.

Perhaps empires have life cycles. Maybe it's a sign of terminal illness when an empire loses confidence in itself, and can no longer deal with a changing world. But maybe something else was afoot. During the Middle Ages, Byzantium set the world standard for culture, art, and literature, while during the same time Western Europe was a backwater. As time passed, the cultures of Western Europe and Byzantium diverged to the point they became antithetical to each other.

By the Great Schism in 1054, Byzantium and Western Europe were on a collision course. Byzantium survived the Venetians but the empire was terminally weakened in the process. The Byzantine Empire fell prey to the forces of a changing world, a world with which it was out of step.

Islam

It's generally believed that the Middle East was always almost exclusively Muslim. But Islam, the newest of the monotheistic religions, came into being in a very diverse area. This religion gained adherents because of the diplomatic skills and ardor of the "Seal of the prophets," Mohammad. When Mohammad died in 632, the question of succession imperiled the new religion's survival.

The tribal leaders met to choose a successor, as custom required. But rather than choosing Ali, Mohammad's son-in-law, the council chose Abu Bakr, Mohammad's close friend, first convert, and father of his second wife. Ali's rejection began a fight that resulted in the Sunni/Shi'a split.

Bakr became the caliph, or the "successor." He held Mohammad's secular power, and was also considered the *Amir al-Muminim*, Commander of the Faithful. The second title gave the Caliph a religious mandate, which solidified his secular position.

Bakr ruled for two years, during which time he solidified Mohammad's gains and extended Islam beyond Syria and Iraq. But Abu Bakr died in 634, whereupon the council or Umma met again—and again passed over Ali, instead choosing Umar of the Umayyad clan. Umar successfully continued Bakr's work, but rather than using diplomacy, he extended Islam by means of the sword. He did so swiftly. Syria fell in 635; Palestine, 638; Persia, 642. Byzantium relinquished Egypt that same year. But in 644 Umar was assassinated by one of his slaves.

The Umma met again and yet again passed over Ali, this time for Uthman, another member of the Umayyad clan. Much of North Africa, Afghanistan, and Pakistan became part of the Islamic empire under his rule. Uthman also consolidated the empire's gains by declaring Islam the sole religion of the Empire, as Constantine had done with regard to Christianity. Uthman also declared that all the population must convert to Islam on pain of death.

In addition, Uthman ordered the compilation of Mohammad's teachings and visions. This compilation, completed in the 650s, became the authorized and only copy of the Q'uran. This silenced further debate about the nature of Mohammad's revelations. But Uthman showed undue favoritism to the Umayyad clan, and in 656 was assassinated by one of his former supporters. The Umma met and, at last, chose Ali.

But Ali alienated many of his supporters by asserting that only a descendent of Mohammad could be Caliph. Nor was he a strong ruler, and one of his former supporters assassinated him in 661. At that point the Caliphate was seized by Muawiya, a cousin of Umar and a member of the Umayyad clan. This seizure of the Caliphate legitimized the Umayyad's claim to that office. Muawiya moved the capital from Medina, the site of the council that selected the Caliphs, to Damascus, in effect making the Caliphate hereditary.

Not every Muslim cheered. Followers of Ali believed that anyone was eligible to be Caliph. They also disagreed with Uthman's imposition of mandatory conversions. The Ummayads not only violated Muslim law, they usurped the Caliphate, making it their personal province.

The Shi'ite rose out of this dissention. They believed that the Caliph must be a descendant of Mohammad, and changed some of the prayer rituals. In 680 Ali's son, Hussain, journeyed to Iraq to lead his supporters to seize the Caliphate. He was ambushed and murdered at Kerbala.

The Ummayads declared the Shi'a illegal, resulting in the Shi'a becoming an underground movement. Ultimately, it became most popular in Iran, Iraq, and Afghanistan. The roots of the Sunni/Shi'a split that dominates the Mideast today began in the seventh century.

The Ummayads faced opposition beyond the Shi'a. Other Muslims resented the Umayyads' lavish life style in Damascus, as well as their policy of forcible conversion. The Abbassid dynasty staked a claim on the Caliphate, stating they were descendants of Mohammad's uncle, Abbas. This clan overwhelmed the Umayyads in the 740s.

Dissention or no, the Muslim empire kept expanding. The Muslims completed the conquest of North Africa in 699; Spain, 711; eastern India and central Asia in the 720s. These conquests brought new problems to the Ummayads and Abbassid Caliphate in the form of large non-Muslim populations. The Abbasids allowed other religions in the empire, provided they pay an extra tax, the *Jizya*. Many non-Muslims converted to avoid this tax.

Conquest and unrest over the throne resulted in a movement toward monarchy. The Abbasids copied the Persian monarchy, imitating the styles present before their conquest. They lived in splendor, away from their subjects. Turkish underlings did the actual administration and ruling. This led to the introduction of the Sultan, Grand Vizier, and the Shaykhs or Sheiks into the government. The idea of councils gradually withered away.

In theory, the Abbasids presided over a world extending from the Atlantic to central Asia. But conquest was one matter; ruling another. The area broke up into small kingdoms, ruled in name only by the Abbasids. In reality each was a small kingdom. Spain was ruled by a descendant of the Ummayads. The military toppled the government in Iraq during the 930s. Then, in 958 the Mongols under Genghis Khan captured Baghdad, and the Caliphate crumbled. Many of the provinces became separate kingdoms. The tradition of republican government with leaders chosen by councils was not revived until Lawrence of Arabia's attempt to hold a council in 1918.

The Islamic Empire may never have been a genuinely cohesive empire. What seemed to hold it together was a way of life, a clear set of laws, the Shariah, and at least a grudging tolerance for other religions within its borders. Like the Han and Gupta Empire, the political boundaries disappeared but the culture persisted, and continues today.

China

Note: The dynasties described below never ruled China in its entirety; the area was too large to be controlled by a single dynasty. These dynasties are described as ruling dynasties simply because they dominated other, smaller houses.

The later Chou Dynasty, which began in 771 BCE, fell in 221 BCE, to be replaced by the Qin. This dynasty focused on the Chinese philosophy of law. The School of Legalism and Statecraft postulated that humankind was frivolous and given to temptation. That was one of the reasons that China suffered under the Chou. Hence, the law was applied rigorously; infractions were punished in ways that served as intimidating examples of what would befall the lawbreaker. It was up to the accused to prove his/her innocence; the state did not have to prove guilt. The Qin dynasty lasted only

19 years. Its rule was so rigorous that it alienated most of the Chinese population. But the Qin had one lasting accomplishment: it gave China a national identity. After the Qin dynasty the area became known as China.

The Qin ruled so harshly that the Han looked wonderful in comparison. The Han dynasty created the Confucian curriculum and school for Chinese bureaucrats. Art and education flourished. Much of the Chinese government system came into being during the Han dynasty. That's why it lasted over 400 years. Han government structure is still present in China in some measure today. An era of civil wars, known as the "Warring States," followed the Han dynasty collapse in 220. The civil wars continued until 589 when the Sui ended the internal fighting. But like the Qin, the Sui ruled so harshly they were considered oppressive. Their rule lasted 29 years. In 618 they were displaced by the T'ang dynasty.

The first act of this dynasty was to re-divide the landholdings in China, thereby creating a class of smaller landowners. This ensured the dynasty's popularity. In addition, the T'ang, like the Han, fostered education, art, and poetry. They re-built the capital Chang-an. Chinese culture flourished, and, with it, Chinese identity. That's why the T'ang dynasty lasted over 300 years.

The T'ang also employed and fostered technological development. During their rule, the Chinese developed printing, gun powder, fireworks, more advanced herbalogy, and medicine. The technology made the T'ang one of the richest societies in the world.

In time the problems that dogged the Han dynasty resurfaced, cutting short T'ang rule. The T'ang fell into the trap of enhancing their glory through edifices. Palaces cost money, as did the T'ang imperial lifestyle. In addition, as the ties between the royal families and the rich strengthened many wealthy Chinese used their connections to evade taxes. As the trappings of empire became more and more extravagant, wealthier citizens, in their attempt to ape the court, persistently evaded tax obligations. This shifted the tax burden to the middle and lower classes. The gulf between wealthy and poor widened, with the middle class becoming increasingly squeezed.

As in the later Roman Empire and the later Han dynasty, small farmers who no longer could afford to pay their taxes either sold their lands to larger landowners (becoming tenants on the land they formerly owned), or moved to the city to join the urban poor. To complicate matters further, China was threatened from the north by the same nomads that had threatened the Han. These nomads forced the T'ang to spend increasingly on the military, which worsened the economic situation. Northern China on several occasions was actually ruled by these nomads. Only the nomads' lack of governmental structure kept the northern Chinese provinces from permanently breaking away from China and forming a separate state.

The T'ang dynasty collapsed in 960, to be replaced by the Sung dynasty. The T'ang began their rule by re-dividing land-holdings; the Sung restructured the economy by restructuring the gender roles. During the Han and T'ang dynasties, women took an active role in economic and civic affairs. The best example of this occurred during the T'ang dynasty, when from 655–705 China was ruled, semi-officially, and ultimately officially, by the Empress Wu.

This changed during the Sung dynasty. With the advent of female footbinding, movement beyond the home became almost impossible. But footbinding served another purpose. It removed females from any decision-making capacities in society. The well-bred young woman often had to lean on a man in order to walk, in effect confining her to her home. With women out of society, there was less competition in the Chinese economy. Mutilation became a way to enforce hierarchy. But it should be noted that Confucianism inveighed against mutilation.

The Sung also struggled against nomadic tribes in the north. Ultimately, the Khitan Mongols took over northern China, ruling from 907–1127. These tribes employed many of the Chinese government structures but never inspired the loyalty that would have solidified their conquests.

Economic problems persisted. Ultimately, the combination of economic and military problems proved too much for the Sung. In 1279 the Sung fell to the Mongol invaders under the leadership of Genghis Khan, who created the Yuan dynasty.

Like the Khitan Mongols, the Yuan made use of Chinese institutions to solidify their rule. They also employed foreign advisors. European trade had begun under the later Sung dynasty, and the Yuan encouraged the dialogue between China and Europe. Marco Polo's journeys and service to Kublai Khan exemplify this.

But the Chinese chafed under Yuan rule. The institutions created in the previous dynasties created a national identity. The continual warfare in the Northern provinces created a loathing for strangers. It was perceived they brought chaos and conquest. In 1368, 89 years after the Mongol invasion, the Yuan were displaced by the Ming, or "brilliant" dynasty. The Ming solidified Chinese institutions and rule, and extended Chinese power throughout the known world.

From 1405–1435 the Chinese treasure ships sailed from China to Africa. One scholar believes they reached America and sailed around the world. That may be the stuff of fiction. But under the command of Cheng Ho, the Chinese treasure fleet defeated the pirates situated around the straits of Malacca, and spread Chinese influence throughout the known world. It's believed the largest fleet had 27,800 sailors.

In 1435 the voyages abruptly ended; ships rotted at the dock. A subsequent law made it illegal to build a ship with more than two sails. What happened? The urge to trade and exchange cultural values clashed with Confucian teaching that the Chinese shouldn't travel too far from China, but instead concentrate instead on tending their lands. It's understandable. The Chinese possessed a brilliant culture filled with art, music, architecture, technology, and medicine which they thought was clearly superior to Europe, India, or Africa.

Further, the Chinese had created government bureaucracies that ensured stability, a hard-won stability. Contact with foreigners, it was believed, would endanger their culture, the Chinese way of life. Exploration and trade had to end to preserve Chinese culture. More compelling reasons for insularity emerged later in the Ming dynasty. In the sixteenth century the Jesuits came to China, eager to create schools to bring the Middle Kingdom into the Catholic fold. These schools became quite popular.

China turned inward to preserve the Chinese way of life. It seemed a sound decision. China had already achieved stability, and possessed both a vibrant culture and technology. Pleased at achieving what was believed to be the pinnacle of success, China turned away from the rest of the world. During the Ming dynasty, China became the "sleeping giant." But when awakened she discovered to her horror that the world had changed dramatically, and like it or not she had a choice: change or be conquered.

Charlemagne's Europe

After the collapse of the Western Roman Empire, Europe was ruled by various Germanic tribes. Internecine warfare characterized the aftermath of the Western Roman Empire. One tribe ultimately took control over the others, setting the tone for European relationships until the present. That Germanic tribe was called the Franks.

What separated the Franks from other Germanic tribes was their organization. The first Frankish king, Clovis, took control of all the clans, reigning from 481–511. Before the Battle of Vouille, Clovis, like Constantine before him, vowed that if he was victorious, to convert and order his army to convert to Christianity. Clovis won, whereupon Clovis and his army converted to Roman Catholicism. In one move they went from being just another tribe to a much-needed and respected ally of the Pope. The new alliance required learning Latin. The Latin language, combined with the Frank's language, became the basis for French. Hence the Franks are considered the progenitors of the French, even though their holdings largely centered in what is modern Germany.

But Clovis' conquests didn't last. Like Rome, land upon death was divided equally between sons, and Clovis had four sons. Civil war broke out, and the fighting continued every time a son or grandson died. It appeared that the early Franks or Merovingians were headed for the same fate as the Visigoths.

What changed? During Merovingian times the administration of the kingdom was performed by the Mayor of the Palace. Pepin d'Heristal, 670–714, succeeded in making the office hereditary. His son, Charles Martel (or Charles the Hammer), 715–741, ruled with unquestioned authority. He controlled the military, stopping the Muslim invasion of Europe in 732 at the Battle of Tours. He started the Carolingian dynasty or Charles' dynasty.

Charles was succeeded by his son Pepin the Short, 741–768, who succeeded in getting himself declared King in 750 by Pope Stephen II. Pepin repaid Pope Stephen by clearing Italy of the Lombards, and granting Pope Stephen land that would become known as the Papal States. Pepin died in 768. During the next three years a struggle ensued over who would be the next king. In 771 one of the brothers died and Pepin's son Charles, better known as Charlemagne, took the throne.

Charlemagne, 742–814, continued his conquests. By the close of the eighth century, Frankish holdings included Germany plus parts of Italy, Spain, and France. An engineer by training, Charlemagne worked to create roads, irrigation channels, and bridges. Interestingly, his palace at Aachen may have been the first in recorded history to contain an indoor swimming pool.

It's undisputed that he was one of the greatest rulers Europe ever produced. Charlemagne encouraged learning, dealt fairly with minorities, and protected Jewish populations. Charlemagne also supported the church, bequeathing a tithe of 10 percent for church upkeep. In addition, he divided the kingdom into counties to facilitate the keeping of records. The officials involved in keeping censuses became known as Margraves or "March counts."

The king had a close relationship with the man who became Pope Leo III in 796. Some factions in Rome didn't trust or like him because Leo wasn't noble, and they believed the Pope had to be noble. They attempted to end Leo's Papacy by attacking Leo and attempting to mutilate him. A requirement for spiritual and temporal rule during the Middle Ages was that rulers possess no physical defects when ascending the throne.

Leo fled to Charlemagne for protection. Charlemagne saw to it that Leo had medical attention, then escorted him back to Rome. A court of inquiry was held November 24, 800, on whether or not Leo had acted improperly because he wasn't noble, in which Charlemagne heard the charges against Leo. Leo swore before that court the charges were false, was acquitted, and Leo resumed the Papacy.

On Christmas Day, 800, Leo crowned Charlemagne King of the Romans, Charles Augustus. It appeared the Roman Empire had been restored. The late art historian Edward Janssen believed Charlemagne's ascension heralded the beginning of the Renaissance.

Charlemagne died in 814 and, according to custom, divided his kingdom between his three sons, resulting in civil war. Much of Charlemagne's work was destroyed during the warfare. But stability dies hard. In 1155 Emperor Frederick Barbarossa declared the outlines of much of Charlemagne's kingdom, which became known as the Holy Roman Empire. This empire fell to Napoleon's armies in 1806, but was resurrected as the Austro-Hungarian Empire in the wake of Waterloo.

Practice Test Questions

1. Justinian is best remembered for

    A. marrying Theodora.
    B. imposing heavy taxes.
    C. wearing purple.
    D. compiling and codifying Roman law.

2. The Islamic Empire did away with which institution?

    A. Roman gladiator games
    B. Women's landowning rights
    C. The tribal council
    D. The feast after Ramadan

3. The Shi'a believed

    A. that Allah would come to earth when everyone became Muslims.
    B. that all Caliphs should be related to Mohammad.
    C. that Baghdad should be the center of Islam.
    D. that females must be given equal access to education.

4. Charlemagne

    A. preferred a simple life and introduced vegetable farming.
    B. fathered 18 children and invented the carol.
    C. ruled over a united Europe, which he organized into counties.
    D. wrote the *Song of Roland* and fought the Vikings.

5. Each of these empires collapsed because of

    A. increased warfare.
    B. the inability to tolerate change.
    C. repeated famines.
    D. repeated regicides.

Answers and Explanations

1. **D.** Although Theodora was a remarkable Empress, Justinian is most remembered for compiling and codifying the Roman law.

2. **C.** Tribal councils were replaced by hereditary monarchies. They re-emerged during World War I.

3. **B.** All Caliphs should be related to Mohammad. They were angered over the Caliphate being passed to the Umayyads.

4. **C.** Charlemagne ruled over a united Europe, which he organized into counties. It was widely believed that Charlemagne had recreated the Western Roman Empire.

5. **B.** Each of the empires described in this chapter collapsed because it couldn't tolerate change. Rome's collapse left a deep-seeded fear of instability.

The Islamic World

Islam, the youngest of the monotheistic religions, was founded by Mohammad in the seventh century CE. It emerged during the confusion and political void left by the collapse of the Western Roman Empire. Like Abraham and the Buddha, Mohammad was human and is believed to be a great prophet. He was chosen as Allah's messenger to bring Islam to the world.

Mohammad was born in 570 in Mecca. His father died before his birth; his mother died in 576. Mohammad was raised first by his grandfather and then by his uncle. Some sources suggest Mohammad's family made and sold idols; others suggest Mohammad's uncle was a merchant. Mohammad's education specialized in management, including the mathematics needed to become a merchant. He never learned to read.

At 15, Mohammad managed the flocks of the newly widowed Khadija. They married when Mohammad was 25 and Khadija 40. It was a happy marriage. The couple had six children: two sons who died and four daughters. Mohammad was meditating in a cave in 610 when the angel Gabriel appeared to him with an astounding message: God, Allah, had appointed him to be the bearer of the message of a new religion. According to the angel Gabriel, Allah asserted that both Judaism and Christianity had been corrupted. Using Mohammad as the medium, and the last or "seal" of the prophets, Gabriel would deliver Allah's uncorrupted word.

Mohammad found all of this quite troubling, so he returned home and confided his feelings to Khadija. According to some sources, Khadija took Mohammad to her brother, an expert in Torah. This leads to an interesting question: Was Khadija Jewish? The brother examined Mohammad in detail, reporting that the vision was real, and that Mohammad was, indeed, the Prophet. Having been pronounced sane, Mohammad returned to the cave to hear Allah's word.

After Mohammad's death, Islam split into two major sects: the Sunni and the Shi'a. The Shi'a make up a sizable part of the population in both Iran and Iraq. They questioned why Allah chose Mohammad, who was illiterate. Perhaps it had something to do with the fact that illiterate people often have prodigious memories. Mohammad succeeded in memorizing large amounts of what would become the *Qur'an* (the Koran in English), the holy book of Islam, and then dictated them to the scribes Khadija hired. In this way the final word of Allah was transmitted and recorded.

But it took more than the completed *Qur'an* to convince the peoples living in the Middle East. The elders in Mecca dismissed the young prophet in 613, viewing him as the poor cousin who married the rich widow. Mohammad and his new religion were brushed aside.

Then in 622 the city of Yathrib experienced unrest. The city had become ungovernable, and the elders asked Mohammad to move there and settle all disputes. Mohammad agreed to come, making the journey later in 622. That move is known as the *Hegira*. Mohammad restored order to Yathrib by imposing Islamic law. Islam not only provided a cohesive belief system, but a way of life. The religion was based on the *Five Pillars of Faith*.

The Pillars include the following:

1. Shahada or affirmation: "There is nothing worthy of worship but Allah, and Mohammad is the Messenger of God."
2. Salat prayer: a devout Muslim prays five times a day.
3. Zakat or alms to the poor: The poor by right of their existence deserve compassion and care. If able, Muslims pledge $\frac{1}{40}$ of their net worth to the poor.
4. Siyam or observing the Fast of Ramadan.
5. Haj Pilgrimage to Mecca.

Mohammad renamed the city of Yathrib, Medina. During his tenure, the city of Mecca attacked Medina, but Mohammad staved off the attacks. As word of Mohammad's peaceful and prosperous rule under the tenets of Islam spread, the new religion attracted more and more converts in the area surrounding Medina. By 630 the city of Mecca invited Mohammad to return. After returning and clearing away all the other idols in the q'uaba, Mecca's religious shrine in which all tolerated religions placed their idols, the equivalent of the Roman Pantheon, Mohammad returned to Medina. He made one last pilgrimage to Mecca in 632, then returned to Medina. He died in June, 632.

Mohammad's death created a crisis in Islam. "The Seal of the Prophet" left no written instructions. Who was going to define doctrine? Mohammad was both political and religious ruler. But the religious title was granted by Allah, not the city or priesthood. This left the question of religious leadership open. To further complicate matters, Mohammad's position as political leader was legitimated by his religious stature. The question facing Islam was how does one perpetuate a religious government without the humans designated by the deity to rule the government?

The religious issues created by Mohammad's death actually may have been the simpler problem. Mohammad's decisions regarding definitions of the laws were compiled as **Sunna,** or Mohammad's sayings as written down by his students. These were collected in much the same way Confucius's students recorded the **Analects**. The Sunna became critically important immediately after Mohammad's death because these made it possible to chart how Mohammad might have reacted to a given situation. They provided guideposts for this new religion, and were derived from the Hadith.

The Hadith were Mohammad's interpretations of particular problems. The first part would detail the problem; the second, Mohammad's comments and opinions on how the problem should be solved; the final part, the solution as based on Mohammad's interpretation of the problem. Some Hadith were complex, others simple. Some scholars have noted that different Hadith take on more or less relevance as times change. But both Sunna and Hadith made it possible for Islamic religious law to be interpreted according to Mohammad's teachings and rulings.

The Shariah were the laws set down in the *Qur'an*. There are actually four sets of laws, and these were standardized after Caliph Uthman oversaw the re-editing of the *Qur'an*, discussed later in this chapter. These laws formed the basis of civil law in all Islam-ruled kingdoms. Thus, it was possible to travel from North Africa to Pakistan and be subject to the same set of laws. This made Islam much cohesion.

However, the political solution decided upon after Mohammad's death did not work nearly as well. Separate family factions feuded over political power, which ultimately resulted in a religious split that resonates today. Just as Mohammad left no clear-cut instructions on how Islam would continue as a religious, he left even less instruction as to how the political rule of Islam would continue.

The question remained: Who should rule? A compromise was reached which involved the creation of the Caliph or "successor." This person, chosen by a council of clans, would rule according to Islamic law, and the Imams or teachers would maintain, interpret, and foster Islam. The split between the Sunni and Shi'a occurred because of the disagreements between factions over who would be appointed successor.

When Mohammed died in 632, much of the population believed his son-in-law, Ali would be appointed Caliph. Abu Bakr, Mohammed's best friend, and father of Mohammad's last wife was appointed instead. Abu Bakr reigned for 2 years, dying in 634. Ali again was, in thought, to be named Caliph. But Umar, a representative of the Ummayad clan, was appointed Caliph, and under his rule Islam began conquests that, in the next century, would expand Islam from the Middle East into North Africa, India, Spain, and Eastern Europe. Umar's armies conquered Syria in 635, Palestine in 638, and Persia by 642. Egypt surrendered to Umar in 644. After Umar was assassinated in 644, Ali was again passed over for another member of the Ummayad clad, Uthman.

Uthman consolidated Ummayad rule. He continued the conquests. Much of modern-day Pakistan, Afghanistan, and a significant part of North Africa fell under Uthman's rule. In addition, Uthman decreed that only Muslims could live in Arabia. All others were to convert or face death. His decree resembled Roman Emperor Constantine's decree making Christianity the religion of the Roman Empire. Uthman's decree, when enforced, gave Islam cultural conesiveness. But Uthman didn't stop with religious enforcement. He ordered a compilation and translation of the *Qur'an*. This standardized the *Qur'an*, and created the edition used today. Uthman ordered all previous sources destroyed.

Uthman's measures should have both standardized Islam and created a stable succession in the Ummayad clan. Instead it created bitterness. Many resented Uthman's partiality to his clan, as well as his overseeing the re-editing of the *Qur'an*. This resulted Uthman's assassination in 656. Ali, finally, was chosen as Caliph. But Ali was a negotiator, and because of that was perceived as a weak Caliph. He was assassinated in 661 by a former supporter. Muawiya, Syria's governor seized power, declaring that the Ummayad family were the hereditary caliphs.

This was the beginning of the split between the Sunni and the Shi'a. While the first four Caliphs, Abu Bakr, Umar, Uthman, and Ali were regarded as the "right-guided" Caliphs, Ali's supporters believed that the Ummayad clan had corrupted Islam.

They pointed out that Mohammad believed no person should be forced to convert to Islam. They also contended that any Caliphs after Ali were "illegitimate." Finally, they insisted that only descendents of Ali and his wife, Mohammad's daughter Fatima, were eligible to be Caliphs.

The split crystallized in 680 after Ali's son, Hussain, journeyed from Medina to Iraq to lead a group that had offered him the office of Caliph. Hussain and his troops were ambushed and killed at modern-day Kerbala in Iraq, and ended Mohammad's direct descendents. The Shi'a (sect) went underground, working with any group who worked against the Ummayads. They're still an active religious sect of Islam in Iran and Iraq.

The Shi'a may have been driven underground, but this didn't end opposition to the Ummayad clan. Many became disgusted with the Ummayad's decadent lifestyle and misuse of power. A group rose in Persia called the Abbasids, who claimed descent from Mohammad's uncle Abbas. The Abbasids first took control of Persia, then marched on Damascus. By 740 CE Damascus fell, ending Ummayad rule and establishing the Abbasid dynasty. At this point, the Abbasids worked to make the office of Caliph hereditary to their family. This resulted in their moving the capital from Damascus to a new capital city in Iraq on the Tigris river, and finally to Baghdad in 762, The Abbasid Caliphs also accepted non-Muslims in Arabia, but imposed a tax, the Jizya, as the price for practicing their faith. Ultimately, many non-Muslims converted to Islam, becoming known as the Muwalis. While the Sunni's objected to these newer Muslims being treated as equals, the Abbasids insisted that, according to Mohammad, all Muslims were equal.

The Abbasid dynasty was short-lived, as it could not rely on either religious or political cohesion. While each Abbasid ruler attempted to secure succession for a member of his family, intrigue among factions arose after each Abbasid Caliph's death. The land was too large to be administered well by one Caliph. Leaders rose in many of the Abbasid lands who called themselves Caliph and didn't acknowledge Baghdad. The Ummayad family fled to Spain and established a Caliphate in 755, and North Africa split into several kingdoms during the ninth century. Egypt was taken over by a family during the tenth century that claimed descent from Mohammad's daughter, Fatima. By the eleventh century, the Islamic empire was in reality a group of loosely divided kingdoms or monarchies that called themselves Caliphates. The Mongol invasion of 1258 CE ended the Abbasid Caliphate.

But while Islam, in reality, remained a set of separate Caliphates, the legal system based on Shariah gave Islamic kingdoms the appearance of being one culture or state. Thus the term Dar Al Islam, "world of Islam," had meaning for Muslims whether in North Africa, Europe, South Asia, or the Middle East. Each of these lands followed the laws set down in the Qur'an. The belief of a united Islamic empire, thus, took root. The concept of Dar Al Islam made Islam more than another invading group, but rather a whole way of life. This led to the idea that Arabia was always one land. For additional information please see Robert Garfield's, Portraits of Civilization, Vol 1.

The Role of Dar Al Islam in Eurasia and Africa

As noted, the Islamic empire was too large to actually be ruled by one administration. But all areas conquered by either the Ummayad or Abbasid rulers followed Shariah, which facilitated trade and communication. Good trade and communication resulted in prosperity. All of this was conducive to the creation of universities, which flourished through Spain, North Africa, and Egypt. Under the Abbasids, and the Caliphates that were established during their dynasty, minorities lived with some security. By the ninth century, Dar Al Islam, the conception that all areas ruled by Muslim Caliphs belonged to a larger Islamic world included North Africa, Spain, and Egypt. Islamic conquest went as far west as Paris, to be halted by the Merovingians under Charles Martel, as a result of the Battle of Tours in 732 CE.

The greater Arabian empire was, in reality, a set of kingdoms ruled more or less by the same set of laws. Islam didn't interfere with commerce or local customs, as long as these didn't challenge Islamic rule. The political situation resulted in the rise of scientific and medical advances. Medicine especially prospered in North Africa. Islamic doctors concentrated on the anatomy of the human body and careful diagnosis. With the rise of the universities came a teaching faculty in the universities. Medicine became an academic discipline. Scientific fields also flourished, including astronomy and mathematics. The study of medicine revealed how to treat and understand the human body; science sought to reveal the world created by Allah. Neither impinged on the revealed word of the Qur'an.

The split between the Sunni and Shi'a wasn't the only religious question appearing after Mohammad's death. Islam fostered a mystic movement as well. The Sufis believed that Allah could be reached through movement and song. The term "whirling dervish" originated with the Sufis. The Sufis emerged in the ninth century CE as a reaction to the legalism engendered by the study of Shariah. The word Sufi derived from wool because many Sufis owned only one simple wool garment. After 1200 CE many Sufis belonged to brotherhoods, or Tariqas. These organizations provided both security and economic help to their Sufi members. The emergence of the Sufis was a symptom of a larger question. Was Islam a religion based on Shariah or the individual's relation to Allah? While the Sufis helped increase conversions to Islam, its mystical nature kept it from becoming a sect equal in importance to Sunni Islam. Islam remained a religion practiced through the Shariah written in the *Qur'an*.

Practice Test Questions

1. Mohammad was considered

- A. the God of Islam.
- B. the Seal of the Prophets.
- C. the writer of the *Qur'an*.
- D. the first caliph.

2. The caliphate is

- A. the area around a mosque.
- B. the area surrounding a Middle Eastern city.
- C. a Muslim kingdom after the death of Mohammad.
- D. a section of the *Qur'an*.

3. The Hegira is

- A. the rite of Islamic marriage.
- B. Mohammad's flight to Yathrib.
- C. Mohammad's return to Mecca.
- D. the opening section of the *Qur'an*.

4. Shariah is

- A. Islamic philosophy.
- B. Islamic mathematics.
- C. Islamic prayer.
- D. Islamic law.

5. Dar al Islam means

- A. community of the faithful.
- B. the full title for the city of Mecca.
- C. world of Islam.
- D. task of Islam.

Answers and Explanations

1. B. The Seal of the Prophets. Mohammad was human, not divine. He was illiterate. Caliphs were created after Mohammad's death.

2. C. A Muslim kingdom after the death of Mohammad. Caliph means "successor"; Caliphate means "kingdom".

3. B. Mohammad's flight to Yathrib. By bringing peace to Yathrib and administering it under Muslim law, Mohammad transformed Islam into a so-called "respectable" religion. Islam after the Hegira gained so many adherents that the elders in Mecca asked Mohammad to return to that city and convert it to Islam.

4. D. Islamic law. Mathematics, philosophy, and prayer either follow the precepts of Shariah or are encouraged by it.

5. C. World of Islam. The term refers to areas under Muslim rule. While Islam was divided into many kingdoms, use of the Shariah as Muslim law in each made the term "world of Islam" an apt term. The use of a single legal system made it possible for Muslims to see themselves as belonging to one state.

First Steps toward Globalization: Positives and Negatives

Globalization is commonly thought to be a modern phenomenon associated with outsourcing, tariffs, and multinational corporations. In fact, globalization is any process that brings disparate parts of the world together in some way. Globalization processes can be seen as far back as the later Middle Ages. Most globalization processes seem to be double-edged swords; not everyone profits from distant contacts. That was true even in the later Middle Ages. This chapter examines both the positives and the negatives.

Major Trade Routes

Trade is an economic relationship in which one nation exchanges goods, usually for money but sometimes for other goods, with another nation. Long-distance trading implies an agreed-upon currency exchange, relatively secure roads or sea routes, and the technology to travel said routes. Globalization began with the securing of three major trade routes, each of which brought the goods and cultures of the world closer together.

Trans-Sahara

This trade route extended from the North African Muslim states through the Sahara Desert to sub-Saharan Africa. Through this route, goods from the Mediterranean Littoral were traded for Benin jewelry, Ashanti cloth, or Asian goods.

Once through the Sahara, goods were moved from village to village and city to city through African markets. These markets were generally run by women who set rates and moved goods throughout the continent, 10 to 12 miles at a time. But through the markets and through the Saharan caravans, the African continental civilizations received and traded goods from China to the Americas—long before the first Europeans set foot in Africa. This trade flourished through the fourteenth century.

However, with the defeat of the Muslims in Spain and the Portuguese conquest of the Swahili cities, Africa became increasingly isolated. Trade in goods gave way to a surge in the slave trade, with disastrous results.

Indian Ocean

The Indian ocean became a sea route that facilitated trade between civilizations in Africa, India, China, and the Spice Islands. This was the major artery for the non-western world.

Cases in point: Jewelry from China has been found in the Great Zimbabwe; spices traveled into Africa, thence to Europe via the Indian Ocean; China used the Indian Ocean to extend its influence throughout Asia.

From 1405–1433, the Ming Dynasty equipped a fleet that included at least 60 large ships and 350 smaller vessels. It's estimated that the crews for these fleets numbered close to 30,000. Under the command of Cheng Ho, a six-foot-tall eunuch, the **gift ships,** or ships bearing gifts to be presented to those nations that accepted Chinese superiority, sailed throughout the Indian Ocean.

These fleets reached India and Africa. Cheng Ho demanded allegiance to the Emperor; in return he presented the new "conquests" with many valuable presents, including silks, porcelain, and jade. These were offers no city could refuse; the gifts were too good to pass up.

The voyages ended suddenly in 1433. Perhaps this signifies the need to defend northern China from **invasion,** the forcible takeover of one civilization by another, often accompanied by the forcible imposition of one culture on another. Or, perhaps the merchant class that favored trade and contact lost influence at court.

But it's possible the sudden end to the voyages was a reaction against globalization. Just as China was expanding its influence through trade, contact with other cultures was affecting China. Ethnocentrism triumphed over business. China remained secluded from the rest of the world until the 1840s. The rationale for this seclusion was that contact with the rest of the world would only dilute Chinese culture and threaten Chinese religious practices. Napoleon once described China as a "sleeping giant," who would shake the world upon awakening. In the 1840s, England, eager for access into China and trade concessions from the Chinese government, launched the Opium Wars. Much of the Chinese peasantry became hooked on opium, and to keep the country from being conquered, China acceded to English demands and opened her cities to Europeans. Years of economic subjugation followed as China was forced to rejoin the modern world on Europe's terms. It would take over 150 years before China, "the Sleeping Giant," resumed its place as a world power.

Portuguese explorers under Vasco da Gama sailed around the Cape of Good Hope in 1498, and, following exploration, they became conquerors. They overcame the Swahili cities by 1511, and then moved to conquer the cities that comprised the Indian Ocean's trade centers.

For a short time this made Portugal a world power. It controlled major trade routes to the east. But trade advantages proved the mother of invention. Columbus, in his quest to find an alternate route to India and China, fortuitously sailed into the Americas. Other explorers followed, discovering riches beyond their wildest dreams. These, in turn, resulted in more rivalries and newer technologies. By 1521 the Magellan expedition succeeded in sailing around the world. Globalization was in full swing.

The Silk Road

This is the oldest of the trade routes which came into being during the late Classical period. Not just one road, it's a network of roads that wind over the mountains and around the deserts that surround China.

The route carried far more than silk. It was the major conduit between China and the west until the fifteenth century. The road began in Western Europe, continued through Eastern Europe, and led to Asia. It was the sole road to China throughout the earlier Middle Ages, reaching its highest popularity in the mid-eighth century.

In addition to trade goods, Buddhism traveled to China via the Silk Road. Thus, this route became the means for diverse cultures and religions to enter China. By Marco Polo's time, travelers had the option of sailing to the Levant via the Italian Levantine fleet, then proceeding overland. The Yuan, or Mongol, Dynasty encouraged contacts with European traders, the Silk Road being the route of choice.

The Yuan Dynasty lasted only one century, to be supplanted by the Ming. The Chinese, viewing the former as interlopers, may have disdained the European trade brought in through that route. That disdain may also explain the shift to the large expeditions cited above.

But culture doesn't travel only on dry land. Ideas also run by sea. Hence the end to all foreign trade in China, as previously mentioned, until the mid 1840s.

Missionary Outreach

More than goods traveled the trade routes. Religion traveled with the goods, influencing the cultures contacted. Religion shaped both policy and culture, perhaps more than the goods traded along all routes.

Islam

Islam initially appeared in Spain and North Africa through conquest, but flourished because of its law and trade policies. Muslim trade was governed by the laws set down in the Q'uran. It was a uniform set of laws, observed wherever Muslims lived and worked. The laws regarding trade underlay the expansion of Islam.

In addition, Islam spread to the Spice Islands through the Indian Ocean routes. It became a world religion. Today most of the world's Muslims live in Indonesia, rather than the Middle East.

Buddhism

As noted above, Buddhism moved from India into China and Japan via the Silk Road. It also proceeded from the Silk Road into Southeast Asia, Afghanistan, and Nepal through the trade routes.

But Buddhism lost some of its uniformity in the process. Chinese Buddhism and Japanese Mahayana Buddhism emphasize a semi-divine Buddha who can personally help the believer achieve Nirvana. Japanese Free Land Buddhism views the Buddha as a divine figure similar to Christ, who is the key to salvation. Vietnamese Theravada Buddhism emphasizes Buddha's example, rather than his personal divinity. Followers of the Dalai Lama regard him as the direct descendant of Buddha, hence a semi-divine leader.

Buddhism never attempted to forcibly supplant other religions in the region. In the area between India and China, Buddhism and Hinduism blended into something of a meld between both. In Japan it was not unusual for the Shinto and Buddhist monks to guard each other's shrines.

Thus trade affected shifts in culture.

Christianity

Spreading Christianity became an integral part of conquest. Two examples: Britain and Spain combined missionary zeal with conquest. When the Spanish conquered Latin America, they destroyed much of the Indian culture, replacing it with Christianity. The mission system forced the Indians to work on mission land and adopt Christianity as a condition for food. Subsequent to the Spanish conquest, the majority of Latin American Indians died of diseases brought by the Spaniards. Those who survived either fled to the forests or converted to Christianity. Much of the Latin American Indian culture is being researched today, some of it by means of archeology.

The British also exported Christianity as they settled throughout the world. They viewed part of their trade and exploration as a means of "civilizing" the peoples under their control. Rudyard Kipling's poem, "White Man's Burden", exhorted the British to bring Christianity to those nations, "half sullen and half child."

What impulse resulted in European attempts to convert those peoples who fell under European control? It may have been the belief that Christianity guaranteed salvation. More likely, the Europeans and Americans were spurred on by a confidence bred from technology, industry, science, and implicit racism. Part of their success, it was reasoned, was they were the fittest, and Christianity was one of the factors that made western nations superior. The adage claims "pride goes before a fall." Missionary zeal gave way to economic disparity, distrust, and hatred . . . And Jesus had nothing to do with this.

The Crusades

As discussed in Chapter 8, the Crusades traumatized the Levantine countries. While the kingdoms established by the Crusaders lasted less than 200 years, the trauma created by their invasion ingrained itself on Middle-Eastern Muslim communal memory.

The Crusades, however, also profoundly changed life in Europe. Europeans developed a taste for all things Middle Eastern. Architecture changed. The square-shaped castles of northern Europe, such as the castle in Oidunk, Belgium, sported minarets atop their towers.

Underclothes and pajamas also returned with the Crusaders. Europeans developed a taste for silk and scarves. Clothing lines became more fluid. More colors entered the European wardrobe.

The spice trade boomed. Ginger and cinnamon were used both as flavorings and medicine. Opium entered European markets. It became the most sought-after painkiller. It's ironic that drugs capable of causing addiction and death entered the west through a religious movement.

Why didn't the Crusades succeed? Unlike the spread of Islam or Buddhism, the Crusaders never succeeded in blending their culture with the cultures in the Middle East. According to Alfred Crosby's *Ecological Imperialism,* the Crusaders remained aloof from the cultures they found in the Holy Land. That included the Latin Christians. Societies that succeed in conquests create enduring political, social, and economic structures that affect all concerned. Such structures may be intended to favor the conquerors, but they allow upward movement for the conquered.

The Crusaders remained "strangers in a strange land," eventually seen as trespassers, and finally ejected by natives as unwanted guests.

The Mongol Invasions

The Mongols may have ruled the largest empire ever acquired by one people. Beginning their conquests in the early thirteenth century under Temujin, the Mongols conquered Persia, China, Russia, India, and much of the Middle East.

They attacked on horseback, literally riding down and crushing all in their path. There are recurring tales, such as recounted in James Michener's *Caravans*, of a Mongol conquest in Afghanistan in which civilians hid in a merchant's way station. The Mongol force discovered them, bound them hand and foot and piled their prisoners one on top of the other. After a few days they poured concrete over them to create a ghastly pillar. Mongol law required beatings for every infraction. The worse the crime, the more savage the beating.

The Mongol empire grew too large to be ruled by one person. It split into four khanates. Each was ruled by a descendant of Temujin. The most famous ruler was Kublai Khan of China. The Mughal Dynasty in India was Mongol, and during this dynasty India may have been the wealthiest nation in the world.

Russia was also ruled as a separate kingdom. Textbook author Anthony Esler suggests that the autocratic rule of the Russian Mongols, the Tartars, resulted directly in the autocratic rule of the Tsars.

Who drove out the Mongols? There was no great confrontation or defeat. The Yuan dynasty gave way to the Ming. The Mughal dynasty declined. The Tartars gave way, ultimately, to the Romanovs. The Mongols assimilated into the cultures they conquered, and then were themselves conquered in the normal scheme of things.

Today they remain the primary residents of Mongolia. Recently they were the main attraction at the Barnum and Bailey Circus, earning this honor because of their horsemanship.

But the Mongols left their mark on the places they conquered. Kublai Khan's openness to outside trade may have contributed to China's turn inward during the Ming dynasty. The authoritarian influence of the Tartars in Russia may have contributed to Russia's autocratic tsarist government, and even more autocratic Stalinist regime. The void left by the collapse of the Mughal Dynasty created a political void that may have left South Asia vulnerable to the British. The Mongols earned a place in communal memory as a terrifying conqueror.

The Mongols assimilated and vanished, but the authoritarian stamp they placed on the conquered in many of the areas they ruled still resonates.

An Additional Invasion—The Bubonic Plague

The Bubonic Plague appears to have originated in Mongolia, traveled west to Constantinople in 1334, then to the Levant where diseased rats climbed on board a ship going from Messina to Genoa. The captain, having discovered plague on the ship, sank the ship rather than let it enter Genoa harbor. But the rats swam ashore, leading to the deaths of 25–30 million people in 1347–1348.

The Bubonic Plague traveled from Mongolia to Europe in the mid-fourteenth century, following the trade routes created by invasions as well as commerce. The plague had visited Europe before—perhaps, according to Dr. Frederick Cartwright, as early as the sixth century.

Each visitation brought misery and chaos in its wake, probably more than most invading armies.

The plague, however, also was an agent for cultural and social change. Satirical poetry, opera, the development of the concept of the individual, parliamentary government, and religious reformation each owed their origins to the plague.

No one can make the plague "warm and fuzzy." But it should be noted that disease is an invader that affects civilization profoundly. It results from globalization, and perhaps is the greatest agent of all for change.

Practice Test Questions

1. Globalization is

   A. a plot to take over America by the United Nations.
   B. a process of bringing the world together begun in the later Middle Ages.
   C. the practice of shifting work overseas.
   D. China's economic policy.

2. Trade is

   A. the process whereby one society exchanges goods with another.
   B. the means of shifting one baseball player in a slump to another team.
   C. the agreement between Lucifer and an aging depressed physician.
   D. attempting to achieve the better part of a deal.

3. The oldest trade route is

   A. the road to Mandalay.
   B. the Trans-Sahara route.
   C. the Indian Ocean sea lanes.
   D. the Silk Road.

4. The Trans-Sahara Route extends

   A. from Benin to Suez.
   B. through Ethiopia to the Swahili Cities.
   C. from North Africa south through the Sahara Desert.
   D. from Egypt to Gibraltar.

5. The Mongols conquered

   A. Asia and Africa.
   B. Asia, South Asia, Russia, and much of the Middle East.
   C. Africa and India.
   D. Mongolia and China.

Answers and Explanations

1. **B.** The process of bringing civilizations together begun in the later Middle-Ages.

2. **A.** The process by which one society exchanges goods with another society. While the other answers noted here are technically correct, they do not pertain to globalization.

3. **D.** The Silk Road.

4. **C.** Through North Africa south through the Sahara Desert to Sub-Saharan Africa.

5. **B.** Asia, South Asia, Russia, and much of the Middle East.

From T'ang to Ming China: Perfecting Society and Culture

The Cultural Impact of the T'ang Dynasty

After the breakup of the Han Empire in 220 CE, China, like the Western Roman Empire, went through a prolonged period of regional kingdoms, many founded by nomadic peoples such as the Toba from Central Asia and various Turkic-speaking groups. After taking power, however, these peoples tended to settle down, assimilate to Chinese civilization, and intermarry with local people, establishing a pattern that would be repeated by later migrant conquerors. In 589, a remarkable leader named Yangdi united nearly all of the old Han lands and called his new dynasty, the Sui. Bent on expansion into northern Korea and northern Vietnam, however, Yangdi's campaigns led to a brief dynastic struggle in which a sixteen-year-old commander named Li Shimin put his father on the throne as the Emperor Gaozi in 618 and ruled from behind the scenes until deposing him and ruling outright as Emperor Taizong in 627. The new dynasty was called the **T'ang** and lasted until 907. From Chang'an, the old Qin and Han capital, the T'ang pushed its control of the Silk Road deep into Central Asia, giving the T'ang state the shape of a barbell. By controlling the caravan routes, hosting refugees and visitors from abroad, and becoming the center of the Mahayana Buddhist world, T'ang China is often considered by scholars to be China's most outgoing and cosmopolitan dynasty until modern times.

Two important factors help account for the outward-looking worldview of T'ang China, and in return, its expansive economy. The first was the position of the capital, Chang'an, at one end of the Silk Road. Its strategic placement connected it to the vast caravan trails that extended through Central Asia to Persia and the Mediterranean—with branches into India. Thus, all of the goods that came from North Africa, the Byzantine Empire, and the expanding Muslim world had to pass through this point. From Chang'an, one of the best transportation networks in the world distributed these goods by river, canal, and coastal shipping to China's cities and to Korea, Southeast Asia, and Japan. Thus, Chang'an was both a capital and an important trade city, which at its height was—with Baghdad and Constantinople—one of the world's largest cities, with a population of over a million. It may also be considered one of the world's most tolerant cities in that it created special quarters for merchants and religious practitioners of Nestorian Christianity, Judaism, Islam, and Zoroastrianism, in addition to having substantial numbers of Buddhists of many schools and Daoists. It created, imported, and exported practical and luxury items and fashions in clothing, literature, and even music. For example, beautiful, dynamic, realistic figurines with tan and jade color glazes form a distinctive T'ang style of near-porcelain ware that was exported all over Eurasia and North Africa. Toward the end of the seventh century, the imperial court at Chang'an welcomed the family of the last of the Persian Sassanid rulers, who had been driven out by Arab invaders. They brought with them entirely new art traditions in silver, glass, music, and clothing that became characteristic of Chinese art during the T'ang era. China's first silver artwork comes from this period and its designs and even inscriptions reflect its Persian influences.

A second powerful impact of the T'ang came from its position as a world center of Buddhism. Although Chinese influence over the Korean kingdoms and northern Vietnam had come as a result of earlier military campaigns, the growing influence of Mahayana Buddhism in China provided a powerful cultural bond and a means to spread other aspects of Chinese culture abroad. As will be noted in more detail in following sections, Buddhist monks from Korea came to Japan in the 500s and brought with them the written language, theories of government, philosophy, and the entire cultural production of the mainland. Chinese Buddhist monks also wandered the length of the Silk Road setting up monasteries, hostels, trading posts, and way stations for travelers—thus facilitating trade as well as religion. As China became a center of Buddhist culture during the T'ang period, it was increasingly a site for pilgrimages and a place from which pilgrims traveled to holy sites in India, Central Asia, Sri Lanka, Southeast Asia, Korea, and Japan. The most famous of these travelers was Xuan zang, who spent sixteen years in India searching for authentic ancient Buddhist scriptures. In 645 he returned to Chang'an and was presented by the emperor with a position at the Wild Goose Pagoda just outside the modern city of X'ian; many of the original books he brought back, written on palm leaves, are still housed there today. As with the constant travel to and from Mecca in the Islamic world, this ongoing exchange of people, goods, and ideas vastly enhanced China's trade economy and created colonies of Chinese merchants from Southeast Asia to Korea.

Perhaps the peak of Buddhist influence in China came during the reign of one of China's handful of women rulers, Wu Zitian, the famous Empress Wu, who ruled from 684 to 705. The daughter of a public works official, she spent time as a

Buddhist nun before coming to court as an imperial servant, where she caught the eye of the emperor's son. Beautiful, highly educated, and an able leader, she ruled as Empress Dowager and regent following her husband's death in 684. In 690 she announced the founding of a new dynasty and in 693 took the Buddhist title of "Divine Empress Who Rules the Universe," in effect creating a Buddhist state. These moves provoked a brief rebellion, which she handily suppressed before finally passing away of natural causes in 705.

In the half century following the reign of Empress Wu, T'ang power reached its greatest extent and began to quickly ebb. Expansion along the Silk Road ended with defeat at the hands of the Arabs at the Battle of Talas in 751, quickly following setbacks at the hands of the Tibetans and rebellions in Manchuria, Korea, and southern China. From 755 to 762 a widespread revolt by a disaffected T'ang general, An Lushan, devastated a large portion of the empire. Heavy taxes were imposed in its wake, adding to the already chronic problems of rural poverty, a shrinking revenue base, and provisioning the capital. T'ang China's rural economics were heavily skewed toward the more productive rice lands of the central and southern areas, which held about 70 percent of the population and produced nearly 90percent of the tax revenue. Yet political power still resided in the north, and the elaborate infrastructure of roads, canals, and coastal and inland ports necessary to move goods around the empire cost ever more to maintain.

Despite a degree of recovery during the empire's last century, its economic woes helped spark increasing unease about the political and cultural direction of the regime. Confucianists in particular stepped up their longstanding critique of Buddhism, as supported by the court, which was viewed as a "foreign" religion: Its practices such as celibacy and monasticism went against hallowed Confucian concepts of the vital importance of the family; while its elaborate cosmology went against the Confucian emphasis on a morally perfectible order in the here and now. The actions of Empress Wu had also alienated many who considered her a usurper for attempting to found a new—and avowedly Buddhist—dynasty. On a more practical level, the many tax-exempt Buddhist holdings in the empire were increasingly tempting targets for the cash-strapped court. In 845 the government seized all the Buddhist monasteries, though it continued to tolerate the faith. For the last fifty years of the dynasty, however, sporadic civil war plagued the regime until its collapse in 906.

Gunpowder, Printing, and Porcelain: The Impact of the Sung Dynasty

If the T'ang set the standard of wealth and taste for later Chinese dynasties, the Sung in many ways refined this lifestyle to the highest degree found anywhere in the world. In science and technology— which yielded such developments as gunpowder, rockets, printed books, the compass, porcelain, and a host of nautical devices hundreds of years before Europe—in urban living, in banking and commerce, and in agriculture, Sung China equaled or surpassed the rest of the world. In its intellectual life, a reaction against the influence of Buddhism as a foreign religion helped foster the rise of **Neo-confucianism**, a revival of the ethical and political ideas of the Confucian school with cosmological concepts borrowed from Buddhism and Daoism. With relatively minor changes, Neo-Confucianism would remain the official ideology of all remaining Chinese dynasties until the end of the Qing in 1912.

The Sung era is usually divided into two periods:

- Northern Sung (960–1126). This early part of the dynasty reigned over a reduced territory inherited from the T'ang and several minor rulers during the intervening period from 907 to 960. The Sung capital during this time was Kaifeng, which grew to more than a million people. Increasing pressure from northern nomads ultimately forced the dynasty to abandon the capital and move south.

- Southern Sung (1127–1279). Semi-nomadic peoples along the northern borders, some of whom, like the Qitan and Jurchens, had set up regional states of their own, were being threatened by the rising power of the Mongols. By the early 1200s the Mongols had brought down one of these states, that of the Jin, which had pushed the Sung southward. From the Southern Sung capital at Hangzhou, which Marco Polo found so appealing, the Sung forces fought a long and ultimately losing struggle against Kubalai Khan, the grandson of Jenghis Khan (Gengis Khan), who ultimately defeated them and proclaimed a new Chinese dynasty in 1280—the Yuan (1280–1368).

The advances in technology and material culture that marked the Sung Dynasty helped set the pace for China's long-standing position as a dominant exporter of luxury goods. In addition to established items like silk, the first true porcelain appeared during the Sung period and became a coveted domestic and export item. Laquerware, jade, wooden furniture, and decorative art items also proved popular as exports. Chinese merchants remained active in nearby areas such as Japan, Southeast Asia, and Korea, and Indian and Arab intermediaries carried their goods to North Africa and, increasingly, to the East African ports. Even today, the houses of the well-to-do in such East African cities as Malindi and Mogadishu often have antique Chinese porcelains prominently displayed.

China's internal economy also prospered. Two of the three major river systems in the empire, the Huang He (Yellow River) and Yangtze, were now connected by the Grand Canal. This proved vital in supplying the northern cities with rice and other provisions during times of scarcity and provided the main north/south artery of the empire. Indeed, the capitals of Kaifeng and Hangzhou grew rich and populous largely because of their strategic positions along the river and canal systems. The introduction of new food crops, particularly faster growing and ripening strains of rice, also aided in the general prosperity and helped the regional trade centers and market towns develop. Elaborate commercial networks serviced by merchant guilds and traveling sales representatives in silk and tea helped develop early modern banking and credit institutions and the use of checks and paper money. Strategic industries, such as salt and iron, remained tightly controlled by the government, but advances in metallurgy and the use of coal-fired furnaces brought iron making and even some steel production to the highest pre-industrial levels anywhere in the world. In fact, China produced more iron than the rest of the world combined until about 1700.

In cultural terms, the Sung refined many of the amenities of urban life developed during the T'ang to the highest levels in the pre-modern world. Printing, which had been developed under the T'ang, became a major industry in China, Japan, and Korea, and helped to spread functional literacy to the highest rates in the world until the eighteenth century. While Buddhist subjects retained considerable popularity, the new Confucian concepts of Zhu Xi (1130–1200) increasingly dominated the intellectual climate. These Neo-Confucian ideas—involving more consistent interpretations of the Confucian canon and emphasizing the union of ethics and theories of knowledge contained within them, with a strong insistence on service—also exercised a lasting influence on politics. The system of official examinations established during the Han and revived during the T'ang was also reinstituted under the Sung. From this period on, a highly organized, graded system of tests based on an understanding of the Confucian classics became the only sure route to government office and the wealth and prestige that went with it. It was also a system that was open, in theory at least, to males from all segments of society and remained an important avenue of social mobility throughout the imperial era.

Given the "modernity" of so much of Sung society, one paradoxical development was the beginning and spread of the practice of footbinding. While women from wealthy families were often highly educated and accomplished, and a few, like the poet Li Qingzhao (1084–1160), were able to live life largely on their own terms, women were on the whole increasingly relegated to the "inner quarters," and sequestered in the home. At the same time, as if to emphasize this condition, the fashion of tightly wrapping the feet of young girls in order to reduce them to "lilybuds" of three or four inches in length came into vogue and remained so off and on until well into the twentieth century. The process was painful and resulted in largely hobbling the women on whom it was practiced; at the same time it was considered the height of female beauty and daintiness by generations of Chinese men. Thus, especially among the well-to-do and those aspiring to upward mobility through marriage, it was considered by many a vital part of a young woman's "development."

Despite advances on so many fronts, in terms of politics, the Sung were slowly ground down by the increasing power of the northern border peoples. As the threat to the Northern Sung grew, the government fielded larger and larger armies, but their new technology of gunpowder weapons and rockets was soon picked up by their more mobile enemies. By the time of the Southern Sung, the huge but unwieldy armies of over a million men were increasingly replaced by aggressive use of the world's most modern navy along the river systems and in coastal regions. Again, however, despite the firepower of the Sung ships, their cities fell one by one to advanced Mongol siege machinery and explosives, while the Mongol's mass cavalry tactics repeatedly bested the remaining Sung field armies. Finally, in 1280, having driven the last Sung pretender into the sea, the Mongol Kubalai Khan proclaimed the Yuan Dynasty (1280–1368) and adopted the reign name of Shizu.

Turning Outward and Inward under the Ming Dynasty

The brief period of the Yuan Dynasty (See chapter 9) had linked China to nearly all of Eurasia from Korea to Poland and the Mediterranean through Mongol control of caravan routes. Scholars are somewhat divided as to how the Yuan Dynasty should be viewed: On the one hand, Mongol sponsorship of trade and commerce helped to spread novel ideas and inventions across much of the world, although some areas notably prospered more than others. On the other hand, rule by the "barbarian" Mongols, who consciously avoided being assimilated into Chinese culture, was widely resented by many Chinese. The Confucian scholar-bureaucrats who had run the government especially resented the Mongol's use of foreigners in the highest government positions, and it was decades before the Confucian tests were reinstated for government jobs. High taxes and ruthless reprisals against opponents also inspired resentment. Finally, the outbreak of the Bubonic Plague, traveling east and west along major trade routes, devastated China to a similar degree that it did Europe and the Middle East: By some estimates, China's population by the mid-fourteenth century had declined by a third. In the 1360s, therefore, accumulated frustration with Mongol rule accompanied by growing Mongol weakness resulted in a successful rebellion by the warrior-monk Zhu Yuanzhang, who took the name Taizi (1368–1398) and named his new dynasty **Ming** (meaning brilliant). The Ming Dynasty would last from 1368 to1644.

Once the new regime had consolidated its power, its rulers set about streamlining and centralizing the system of imperial government. More than in any other dynasty since the Qin, power was put in the hands of the emperor, with the ministries and provincial officials in a strict hierarchy that recruited the best candidates from the Confucian exams. By the early sixteenth century, a number of problems related to land ownership and tenure, and especially the bewildering number of taxes that had accrued over the decades, resulted in a sweeping tax reform nicknamed "the single whip." The older customary dues were bundled together into a single tax payable in silver by installments set up to make payment more convenient to the peasants. The measure also eliminated government labor dues by peasants. In order to keep watch on villagers and bypass the power of the local gentry, the government also devised a system of individuals and families to take responsibility for each other and to be held accountable for wrongdoing. Every ten families would have one family held responsible for their behavior; of every ten of those families, one would then be held responsible, and so on. With variations, this system lasted through the nineteenth century.

The first decades of the Ming period continued the outward orientation that had characterized that of the Yuan. In fact, the high point of China's naval and commercial power came during the years 1405 to 1430. Fearful that usurpers to the throne might have escaped overseas, and anxious to gain more of a strategic understanding of the outside world, the Emperor Yongle (r. 1403–25) sent his servant, the eunuch Zhenghe (Cheng Ho) on a series of expeditions to Indonesia, India, Arabia, and the East African ports. With huge fleets of the largest ships ever assembled up to that time—some more than 400 feet long—and 20,000–30,000 men, the Ming set up trade relations with a host of states throughout the region. Had they kept on going, they might well have met the Portuguese working their way east around Africa. By 1430, however, the new emperor, Renzong, concluded that not only were there no threats to Chinese interests in these areas, but that such expeditions were too expensive to continue for the relatively small benefit they generated. Instead, China grew increasingly insular, and such overseas expeditions were discontinued. Politically, the government concentrated on eliminating the renewed threat overland of the Mongols; in terms of diplomacy and trade, they set up a system—sometimes, though erroneously, called the Tribute System—in which representatives from countries interested in doing business in China came every three years, presented themselves at court, and received certificates allowing them to trade.

The Impact of China on its Neighbors

Like the Greco-Roman world in western Eurasia, imperial China had far-reaching effects on its immediate neighbors in a variety of ways. At various times, all of them faced the threat of invasion; Korea and northern Vietnam were in fact under Chinese occupation for long periods. More lasting were the political, economic, social, and cultural institutions exported by China to these regions. The Chinese writing system, the Confucian canon, systems of dating, bureaucratic institutions, various schools of Buddhism, and genres of literature, art, and architecture all established themselves firmly on the empire's periphery. Even today, they form the core of much of the individual traditions of these countries.

Korea

Because of the proximity of Korea to the ancient Chinese states of the Zhou period (1122–256 BCE) as well as to the imperial dynasties, Chinese influence in Korea goes back a long time. The technology of bronze making diffused across the North China Plain into what is now Manchuria and northern Korea certainly no later than about 1000 BCE. At that time, an ancestral Korean state called Choson held sway over the northern Korean Peninsula and southern Manchuria, and power and influence has ever since gone back and forth across the Yalu River dividing these regions. Chinese influence also came with refugees from the Warring States period in China (403–221 BCE) and especially with the unification of China by the Qin after 221 BCE. It is at this point that the first written records of Korea appear in Chinese. Nearly every Chinese imperial dynasty attempted to extend its rule into the peninsula. Most notably, the Han Emperor Wudi occupied northern Korea in 108 BCE, and the Chinese did not leave until the collapse of the Han three centuries later. During this time, the Chinese writing system, ideas of government, philosophy, and literature were firmly rooted and spread to various degrees to the three major Korean kingdoms that formed over the next thousand years.

The most directly affected state was Koguryo (37 BCE–668 CE), which, owing to its location in the north bore the greatest influx of Chinese culture and settlers. Further south, Paekche (18 BCE–660 CE) and Silla (57 BCE–935 CE), the most long-lived of the three, were less influenced by China and had close ties to the tribal societies and Yamato state of Japan, especially after the Japanese colony of Kaya was set up there in 42 CE. In the power vacuum following the fall of the Han, Korguryo pushed northward into Manchuria, and over the next few centuries, made itself over into a Chinese-style state with a Confucian bureaucracy, imperial court, and, by the sixth century, the adoption of Buddhism. Chinese re-invasions of the north under the Sui and T'ang ultimately eliminated the Japanese enclave of Kaya and the state of Paekche, and a T'ang alliance with Silla left that kingdom in control of the southern peninsula. Koguryo was finally dissolved in 668. Of these Three Kingdoms (Korguryo, Paekche, and Silla) of Korea, Silla remained the most unaffected by Chinese influence, setting up a Buddhist monarchy in the sixth century. In the north, a new state called Parhae, founded on the ruins of Koguryo, again occupied the borderland on both sides of the Yalu until conquered by the Qitans in 935.

The T'ang collapse allowed a new kingdom called Koryo—the source of the name Korea—to be formed, again heavily modeled on Chinese institutions, until it was absorbed by the Mongols from 1259–1368. The fall of the Mongols and the ascent of the new Ming Dynasty in China threatened yet another invasion of Korea. This time, however, the new Yi Dynasty, which would rule Korea until 1910, formed a second state of Choson and entered into an agreement with the Ming under which they would retain their independence and become part of the new so-called tribute system of trade and diplomacy described previously. As was the case with Japan, the Chinese writing system was not a terribly good fit with the Korean written language, and in one of the great cultural reforms of the era, the Yi king Sejong (r. 1418–1450) devised a phonetic writing system called **Hangul** as an aid to mass literacy in his kingdom. It is essentially the same system still used in Korea today.

Japan

Ancient Japanese history is usually divided into the **Jomon** period, lasting from the last Ice Age to perhaps the third century BCE, the **Yayoi** period, from perhaps 250 BCE to the third century CE, and the **Yamato** period, from about 250 CE to the end of the sixth century. During the Jomon era, some of the world's earliest clay pottery was produced by a people whose origins might have been on the Asian mainland, but about whom scholars still know very little. They lived in matrilineal clan societies—in which family lineage is traced through the mother's side—based on fishing villages, and, they had domesticated a few local plants. The Yayoi era marked a crucial transition during which influences from the Chinese states and the Qin empire began to find their way to the islands via the Korean Peninsula. The cultivation of rice was introduced, soon followed by the art of bronze making introduced by refugees from Chinese attempts to dominate the early Korean kingdoms. By the third century CE, the area around the Kanto Plain on the central island of Honshu had become the site of the expansion of the Yamato clan into the beginnings of a state. Even today, the region is marked by large keyhole-shaped burial mounds indicating the newfound wealth and prestige of the Yamato leaders.

552 CE is traditionally thought to be the year in which Korean Buddhist missionaries arrived in earnest and began to convert the Yamato and other clans to the new faith. Although there was initial conflict with the native **Shinto** priests, the two faiths ultimately found common ground within a few decades. Along with Buddhism came the Chinese written language, Confucian ideas of government and ethics, and large numbers of craftsmen, artisans, and assorted advisors. During these years, disturbances on the Korean Peninsula often resulted in an influx of refugees, thus renewing the mainland influence on the islands. For the Yamato, the power of an established world religion and the notion of universal rule promoted by

Chinese emperors was absorbed and turned to their own purposes. After a period of sporadic absorption, the Yamato rulers ordained the Great Reform (**Taika**) in 645: The government would be completely revamped along T'ang Chinese lines, complete with a Confucian/Buddhist civil service, ministries, conscription, protocol, and a permanent capital. The new capital was erected first at Nara from 710 to 794; it was then moved to a grander location called Heian-kyo, the origin of the modern city of Kyoto.

In many ways, the Heian period, from 794 to 1185, was the greatest age of Chinese influence on Japan. The capital itself was laid out as an exact replica of T'ang-era Chang'an; court protocol mimicked that of the T'ang; the Japanese calendar and court histories were put together based on Chinese models; and the Buddhist schools within the Mahayana branch flourished. But in many ways, as with Korea and Vietnam, the transition was relatively complete at court and superficial at best in the provinces. One problem was that, as with Korean, spoken Japanese was a poor fit for the Chinese written language. By the Heian period, Japanese writers had developed the syllable-based **kana** system, which used variations of simple Chinese characters to represent the 50 sounds of the Japanese spoken language. For centuries, classical Chinese remained the language of men, but educated women now wrote in kana, and by the eleventh century, the efforts of a court woman known as Murasaki Shikibu had produced the world's first novel, *The Tale of Genji*.

Other problems sprang from Japan's clan traditions. In the countryside, people tended to obey their clan elders rather than the new bureaucrats sent from the capital. In addition, tax revenues declined after the mid-eighth century when the islands were decimated by smallpox. Buddhist monasteries and estates carved out of land taken from Japan's aboriginal peoples, whom they called the Ainu, were tax exempt. By the twelfth century, court disputes over regencies for emperors and the power of the provinces forced the creation of the office of **shogun**—the emperor's chief military and political officer—with headquarters in the town of Kamakura. By the fourteenth century, nearly all power was in the hands of the shogun, and the emperor was relegated to his court in Kyoto as a mere figurehead. In the mid 1330s, one emperor, Go-Daigo attempted to regain power, but after considerable intrigue, he was deposed by the new shogun, who moved his headquarters to the capital. This Ashikaga Shogunate marked a period when the Chinese influences at court—including skill at painting, poetry, and calligraphy, merged with the warrior ethic of the **daimyo** and **samurai** (feudal lords and retainers) to help spread a host of cultural practices, including Zen Buddhism and the tea ceremony, that are today firmly identified as Japanese.

Rival claimants for the title of shogun plunged Japan into civil war in 1467, and for nearly a century chaos plagued the country. In the midst of this conflict, the first Europeans landed in Japan, provided the opposing daimyo with the new technology of firearms, and converted thousands of Japanese to Christianity. By the 1560s the warlord Oda Nobunaga had made a strong beginning toward reuniting Japan. Following his assassination in 1582, Toyotomi Hideyoshi finished the process, and in 1592 launched an incredibly ambitious invasion of Korea with a view to ultimately conquering China. In 1598 he tried again but died while campaigning, and in the resulting battle for supremacy, the Tokugawa family claimed the title of shogun in 1603. For the next 264 years, the shogunate would be the hereditary possession of the Tokugawas. Along the way, they attempted to freeze Japan in the state of peace that had finally been achieved. All foreigners except the Dutch were expelled after 1637; Christianity and firearms were banned; and the samurai and daimyo became Confucian officials with the power of life and death over all commoners. Because the Tokugawa mistrusted the lords who had opposed them, an elaborate system of holding their families hostage and requiring them to reside in the capital in alternate years ensured compliance with the new order. The constant traffic on the roads to the capital helped the domestic economy to expand, and the capital itself, called Edo, grew to a city of a million people. After 1868 the capital became known as Tokyo.

Vietnam

Like Korea, Southeast Asia was, to some degree, a battleground of competing cultures. In Vietnam, particularly in the north, Chinese influence predominated; in the southern and western areas, the cultures of India and its offshoots exercised a strong influence. But from ancient times, the people of the region have stubbornly asserted their independence. As early as 8000 BCE, the area might have seen the first domestication of fowl; Dongsan culture, which can be dated from approximately 4500 BCE, might have been the source of the first bronzes produced in Asia and some of the earliest produced anywhere. Throughout the earliest Chinese dynasties, the Xia, Shang, and Zhou, the area of southern China and northern Vietnam was known to the Chinese as Yue, and the villages and clans there appear to have been matrilineal—their lineages were traced through the mother. By the second century BCE, Theravada Buddhism had made its way to Southeast Asia through the missionary efforts of the rulers of Ceylon.

In 221 BCE, the Qin emperor drove south in his bid to complete the unification of China by subduing Yue. In the process, he pushed into northern Vietnam and began a continuing historical pattern of Chinese occupation of the area. As in other places along the Chinese periphery, with the military forces came a cultural invasion. Chinese writing, literature, governmental systems and institutions were all planted in northern Vietnam over the coming centuries. Vietnamese elites thus gained admission into the world of cosmopolitan China and the Buddhist cultural and religious sphere centered there. At its height, from the seventh to the tenth centuries, this world stretched from Central Asia and modern Afghanistan to Korea and Japan, and south from Ceylon to modern Indonesia. These connections, and the position of Southeast Asia, made its ports important trade centers and stimulated the region's people to be entrepreneurial and outward looking.

As it had with Korea, invasion also helped create an early sense of national identity among the Vietnamese. The collapse of the Qin allowed for a successful revolt against the local Chinese officials of **Nam Viet**, "the Far South" as the Chinese had called their new southern province. In less than a century, however, the Han emperor Wudi reoccupied northern Vietnam (111 BCE) and, as he had in Korea, brought with him the full apparatus of Chinese culture and statecraft. Han attempts at imposing Chinese values and institutions prompted conflicts between the new Chinese-influenced elites in the larger towns and valleys and those living in more remote areas. In 39 BCE a conflict arose that is celebrated even today as one of the milestones on the path to Vietnamese nationhood. When Chinese authorities executed a popular local leader, his widow, Trung Trac, and her sister, Trung Nhi, swiftly organized a revolt, and their militia drove the Han garrison out of the region. In two years, however, the Chinese came back and overwhelmed the forces of the Trung sisters, who drowned themselves rather than be taken alive. It would be nearly a thousand years before Vietnam would be independent again.

The best opportunity came in the years following the breakup of the Han Empire in 220 CE. But although northern Vietnam was able to keep direct Chinese control at arm's length, a growing cultural allegiance among their elites forced them to place themselves under the suzerainty of various neighboring Chinese states until the empire was reunified under the Sui in 589. Meanwhile, the north set about conquering the southern Indian-influenced Buddhist kingdoms. By the high point of the T'ang Dynasty in the early 700s, the north had been fully reincorporated into imperial China, and the dominant division of East Asian Buddhism, Mahayana, had been firmly planted in Vietnam as well. With the fall of the T'ang in 907, the 50-year power vacuum before the ascendancy of the Sung finally allowed the Vietnamese to create an independent state.

The Sung had accorded the new state tributary status, but their continual troubles with the nomadic peoples on their own northern borders kept them from pursuing another invasion and occupation. In the meantime, the unifier of Vietnam, **Dinh Bo Linh,** solidified his control in 968. Within a half century, the new Li Dynasty had adopted the Neo-Confucian bureaucratic system of the Sung and expanded its state building efforts by systematically driving south from 1010 to 1225. The successors to the Li, the Tran Dynasty (1225–1400), were shortly confronted with no less than three attempted Mongol invasions from 1257 to 1287. The Vietnamese proved to be among the handful of peoples able to throw the Mongols back, and the Tran were thus able to keep the throne throughout the Mongol era.

At the same time, the imperial Vietnam of the north continued its drive south. Earlier, Vietnamese pressure on the state of Champa had diverted that state's expansion toward its rival, Funan. As early as the 600s, the chams and the Khmers had jointly eliminated Funan. South of the two main divisions of Vietnam, **Tonkin** and **Annam**, lay the revived state of Champa, representing not just a political rival to the north but, within its Indian-influenced, Sanskrit, Hindu, and Theravada Buddhist state, a cultural one as well. Hence, in 1471, Vietnamese forces defeated the Chams, who fled to modern Cambodia (Kampuchea.) This state was ultimately absorbed by Vietnam in 1720.

A new dynasty, the Le, was founded in 1428 following Ming efforts to re-impose Chinese rule on the area and lasted until 1789. The founder, **Le Loi,** who styled himself ruler of **Dai Viet,** or "Great Viet," and like his contemporaries, the Yi, in Korea, imposed yet another Chinese-style regime on his new state. In another interesting parallel to the situation in Korea, literary Chinese was adopted for use in a Chinese style bureaucracy; Confucian exams were held; and Confucian law codes, Chinese style historiography, and dress codes were all adopted. The new capital was set up at Hanoi, but by the early 1500s civil war had erupted between rival families. In 1527, the Chinese-backed faction took over in Hanoi, while the Le and Nguyen families established their own regime in Hue to the south. By 1592, however, the Le family had taken power again in Hanoi. Civil conflict would erupt once more with the Nguyen family in 1674. By 1740, the last remaining stronghold of the Khmers had fallen, and Vietnam was now recognized by the Qing Dynasty in China as "the lesser dragon." Like Korea, it was an independent state, but one operating within a hierarchical system based upon shared assumptions of Qing seniority; in Confucian terms, a younger brother state.

Practice Test Questions

1. The T'ang Dynasty in China is noteworthy for being

   A. insular.
   B. cosmopolitan.
   C. racist.
   D. Islamic.
   E. All of the above.

2. Among the most significant Sung developments were

   A. the use of printing, gunpowder, and porcelain.
   B. the invention of steam-powered looms.
   C. the launching of trans-Pacific voyages.
   D. the conquest of the Mongols.
   E. contact with the Portuguese.

3. One of the most important accomplishments of the Korean king Sejong was

   A. the conquest of Northern China and Manchuria.
   B. the invention of the Han-g'ul system of writing.
   C. the enlargement of the Yi empire.
   D. the expulsion of all foreign merchants.
   E. the destruction of the state of Silla.

4. The Trung sisters were famous as

   A. Vietnamese Buddhist nuns.
   B. Chinese generals who invaded Vietnam in 39 BCE.
   C. Korean Buddhist missionaries to Japan.
   D. leaders of a rebellion against Chinese occupation of Vietnam.
   E. the founders of Mahayana Buddhism.

5. The tribute system of the Ming Dynasty was

   A. a Confucian model for managing diplomacy and foreign affairs.
   B. designed to attract foreign traders and missionaries.
   C. sometimes called "the single whip" tax system.
   D. designed to facilitate the posting of Chinese ambassadors abroad.
   E. set up to collect back taxes from Chinese living abroad.

Answers and Explanations

1. **B.** Choice **A** is clearly opposite; **C** and **D** are patently false.

2. **A.** The other choices are either anachronistic or did not take place in China.

3. **B.** Choices **A, C, D,** and **E** are false or anachronistic.

4. **D.** The other choices rely on possible associations students might make with Buddhism or with the Chinese invasion of Vietnam.

5. **A.** Obviously, the word tribute might be associated with taxes as in Choices **C** or **E**; the rest run counter to the general pattern of China becoming more insular and making traders and diplomats come to them.

Western Europe after the Fall of the Western Roman Empire

By the time it had reached its zenith during the second century of the Common Era, the Roman Empire had developed into one of the greatest civilizations the ancient world had ever known. Cities scattered across an imperial region that stretched from the North Sea to the Red Sea had flourished under a well-ordered governing body housed in Rome. These regional centers stood unfortified in the countryside, while armies stationed along the Rhine, the Danube, and the Euphrates sustained the *Pax Romana*, or Roman Peace. By the beginning of the third century, however, the empire was in the midst of crisis. Indeed, over the course of this century, internal anarchy and foreign invasion would so radically transform the great Roman realm that during the fourth century it was ultimately spilt in two. Although the prominence of Rome would be re-established in the eastern part of the empire during the early fourth-century reign of Constantine, as the fifth century began, it became increasingly clear that the western part of the empire could no longer be sustained. What led to this gradual collapse of the Western Roman Empire? And further, how did what we call Western Europe emerge out of the crumbling expanse that was the Roman imperial West? To attempt to answer these questions, we must begin by examining how the Roman Empire was originally established.

The Establishment of the Roman Empire

Although the Roman Golden Era is generally understood by historians as extending from the reign of Trajan through that of Marcus Aurelius, the essential character of this age began to be defined during the reign of Octavian, who ruled as Roman Emperor from 27 BCE until his death in 14 CE. Octavian rose to power out of the internecine struggle that ensued following the murder of Julius Caesar. The enemies of Caesar, chaffing under what they felt was his dismantling of republican rule, had seized on every opportunity to accuse him of seeking to make Rome into a dictatorial monarchy. Eventually a senatorial conspiracy of some 60 individuals developed under the influence of Gaius Cassius Longinus and Marcus Junius Brutus, and when the imperious Caesar entered the Senate on March 15, 44 BCE, characteristically without a bodyguard, he was stabbed to death. While the assassins saw themselves as heroes who had cleansed Rome of the tyrannical Caesar, their actions ultimately left Rome in a state of political chaos. Having failed to define a clear-cut plan by which the Roman Republic could be restored, the conspiratorial senators created the conditions for 13 years of bloody civil war.[1]

Although Caesar's death had left open the possibility that the very capable Mark Antony would succeed him, the ill-fated ruler had designated his 18-year-old grandnephew, Gaius Octavius, as his heir, leaving him three-quarters of his incredible wealth. Even though Octavius was rather sickly, and certainly inexperienced, he surprised many by coming to Rome to claim his legacy. Once there, he was able to win the support of many of Caesar's followers and to gather a formidable army around him. The Senate, attempting to retain as much power as possible, sought to hold on to imperial power by setting Octavius against Mark Antony. Seeking to solidify his own power, Octavius requested that the Senate make him one of Rome's two chief consuls, or magistrates of the state. When the Senate refused, Octavius led his army on a march on Rome, where, in 43 BCE, he finally secured the position of consul he so desperately desired. He also declared the assassins of Caesar criminals and took the name C. Julius Caesar Octavianus, although modern historians identify him as Octavian during this period of his career.

Brutus and Cassius, although being branded outlaws by Octavian, possessed an army of their own, and so had little to fear from the newly constituted ruler when he initially came to power. After Octavian formed an alliance with Mark Antony and M. Aemilius Lepidus, however, everything changed in Rome. These three figures took control of the empire and had themselves appointed triumvirs to put the republic in order. Ironically, this Second Triumvirate eventually became so powerful that it was able to rule almost dictatorially. Greed and a seemingly constant struggle for power afflicted the Triumvirate from the very beginning. In order to control the republic, and each other, Octavian, Antony, and Lepidus began to impose oppressive prohibitions on their people. They also defeated the army of Brutus and Cassius, virtually ensuring that republican rule would never return to Rome. Each of the members of the Triumvirate received a command: Lepidus, the least powerful among the three, was given Africa; Antony took control of the rich and inviting east; and Octavian received the west.[2]

Octavian was forced to deal with a number of difficult political and social issues in the west. Realizing that it would be all but impossible to control even the western territories he presently commanded without the counsel of others, he now began to develop alliances with a small number of talented and loyal advisors. One of his key consultants and diplomatic agents during and after the time he was a member of the Second Triumvirate was Gaius Maecenas, an ally of Etruscan noble descent who helped Octavian negotiate the precarious relationships he shared with Lepidus, Antony, and different, sometimes dangerous, political factions that surrounded him. He was also wise enough to become a patron of the arts, counting among his clients both Virgil and Horace. The latter two were particularly important to Octavian, as they were able to paint him as a "restorer of traditional Roman values, as a man of Roman virtues, and as the culmination of Roman destiny." Increasingly, Octavian became associated with Italy and the west, as well as with order, justice, and virtue.[3]

While Octavian was dealing with issues in the west, Mark Antony was spending most of his time in Alexandria with Cleopatra, the queen of Egypt. When he made the ill-advised decision to attack Parthia (in the Persian east) in 36 BCE, Octavian promised to send troops from the west in order to aid Antony's campaign. When the struggle with Parthia began to produce disastrous results, and no troops were forthcoming from Octavian, Mark Antony was forced to turn to the east for assistance. This basically meant increasingly allying himself, both politically and militarily, with Cleopatra. Octavian took this opportunity to characterize himself as the true representative of the west, while identifying Antony as a man of the east and a mere dupe of Cleopatra, who, he claimed, was trying both to render Alexandria the center of the Roman empire and to install herself as its ruler. Antony, of course, resisted this characterization of both himself and of his relationship with Cleopatra, although he did not help his cause when he agreed to a ceremonial festival in Alexandria during which he and Cleopatra sat on golden thrones and proclaimed her "Queen of Kings" and her son by Julius Caesar, "King of Kings."[4]

Having displaced Lepidus, Antony and Octavian realized that they alone were now locked in a struggle for the soul of the empire, one, it seemed, that must inevitably end in violence. The issue was settled at the famous Battle of Actium in 31 BCE, where Agrippa, Octavian's best general and future son-in-law, managed to flank the eastern enemy on both land and sea, finally compelling and winning a decisive naval battle.[5] Although Antony and Cleopatra escaped to Egypt, Octavian tracked them to Alexandria, where the star-crossed lovers took their own lives. Having survived the brutal struggle for power with the other members of the Second Triumvirate, Octavian, at 32, became master of the entire Mediterranean world. But although his power was now enormous, he still faced great difficulties: "He had to restore peace, prosperity, and confidence. All of these required establishing a constitution that would reflect the new realities without offending unduly the traditional republican prejudices that still had so firm a grip on Rome and Italy."[6]

In 27 BCE, having bided his time for four years, Octavian was able to consolidate his power by shrewdly coming before the Senate and claiming that he wanted to give up his imperial authority. The Senate, in what was certainly a well-rehearsed, complicitous response, pleaded with him to reconsider his decision. Bowing to their wishes, Octavian agreed only to keep control over the provinces of Spain, Gaul, and Syria, to preserve his position as proconsul with authority over the military, and to retain his administrative consulship in Rome. The other provinces in the empire would continued to be governed by the Senate, although because those that were controlled by Octavian were border provinces, and also because they contained 20 of Rome's 26 legions, his power remained undiminished. The well-trained members of the Senate, however, reacting with almost hysterical gratitude to Octavian's purported acquiescence to their dominance, granted him even more extensive honors, among them the semi-religious name of Augustus, a title that carried implications of veneration, majesty, and holiness.

From this point forward, historians identify Augustus as Rome's first emperor and his administration as the *Principate*, a designation that many scholars believe Octavian would have appreciated as it successfully covers over the "unrepublican nature of the regime and the naked power on which it rested." Augustus made significant changes in the empire, drastically reducing its inefficiency and corruption, which protected the realm from the maneuverings of overly ambitious individuals. He also purged the Senate of those he felt were unscrupulous and began to recruit new members from wealthy men who were thought to be of good character; and even though he ultimately possessed overwhelming power, Augustus continued to treat the Senate with respect and honor. In regard to the city of Rome itself, he divided it into wards that carried with them elected officials; gave it its first public fire department and rudimentary police force; created organizations to ensure that the city possessed an adequate water supply; and instituted policies to ensure that grain distribution to the poor was closely monitored and controlled.

Christ Is Born

It was, of course, during the rule of Augustus that Jesus was born. Raised in a Jewish community in Nazareth, in the northern part of what is today Israel, Jesus was baptized and began preaching at some point during the late 20s of the first century. After a relatively short ministry, he was crucified by the Roman procurator Pontius Pilate, sometime between 30 and 33 CE. The most important accounts of the life of Jesus are found in the four Gospels (good news) of the Christian New Testament. Although attributed to the figures Matthew, Mark, Luke, and John, the true authors of these narratives are unknown, as the texts originally circulated anonymously until names were appended to them by second-century church fathers. The first of the Gospels to be written was that attributed to Mark, who probably composed it sometime between 67 and 70 CE. The Gospels of Matthew and Luke (who also wrote the Book of Acts, a companion piece to his Gospel) followed that of Mark; Matthew's probably being written during the late 70s or early 80s, Luke's during the mid-to-late 80s. The last of the four Gospels, attributed to John, was probably written sometime during the 90s, as the first century came to a close. Although none of the Gospel writers was a direct disciple of Jesus, all of their texts being written long after his death, they provide us with narratives clearly produced by men of faith. Whether or not they thought that Jesus was the incarnate Son of God, it seems certain that all four believed that he had come into the world in order to redeem humanity and to offer immortality to those who accepted him as lord and savior.

Significantly, Jesus was born into a Jewish world that was deeply influenced by the idea of *messianic expectation.* The Jewish notion of the Messiah, which is very different from that of Christianity, traces its scriptural roots back to an Old Testament account presented in 2 Samuel. Here God promises the great King David that a future salvific figure will come in his line in order to usher in a period of peace and stability for Israel.

In the Jewish tradition, this figure, the messiah, or anointed one, is not thought to be divine in any way, as according to Judaism, this latter, Christian notion of messiahship represents a perversion of the glory and uniqueness of God. By the time Luke's Gospel was written during the 80s, however, the followers of Jesus had begun to think of him as a different kind of messianic figure. Identified by Luke as a heavenly savior, Jesus began to be known in the early Christian community as Christ, or *Christos*, the Greek word that translates the Jewish term *mashiah*, but one which now indicated that Jesus as the Christ was a divine messianic figure. This powerful belief in Jesus's divine messiahship would have profound implications for the burgeoning Roman Empire.

Jesus himself had little influence on anyone outside of the comparatively small circle of Jews to whom he preached during his lifetime. By the end of the first century of the Common Era, however, his message was beginning to attract an increasing number of followers. One of the issues that hindered the spread of Christianity was whether or not this fledgling movement was actually something different from Judaism, or simply another of the various sects of the latter, long-established monotheistic tradition. Jesus himself had given no indication that he had come into the world in order to define a new religious tradition; in fact in the Gospels he says quite clearly that his message was meant for the Jews and not for the gentiles. After his death, however, a former Pharisaic Jew, Saul of Tarsus, who became the most vocal and surely the most important disciple of Christianity after his life-changing epiphany (appearance to him of the crucified Christ) on the road to Damascus, began to spread the message of Jesus as the Christ far beyond the Jewish community.

Paul Spreads the Word

A Roman citizen whose powerful New Testament letters, or *Epistles,* were addressed to cities such as Corinth, Galatia, and Ephesus, Saul, who would come to be known by his Greco-Roman name Paul, was able to travel and spread the message of Jesus to people throughout the many regions of the empire because of the peace and prosperity that existed there during the first century. His extremely inclusive notion of Jesus as the crucified and resurrected savior of the world was especially appealing to non-Jews across the empire, for, as Paul made clear, the salvific message of Jesus was offered to everyone and it did not require gentiles, regardless of who they were, to convert to Judaism in order to become Christians. Central to Paul's understanding of Christianity was the idea that the followers of Jesus must be evangelists, or messengers, who should spread the good news of God's gracious gift of his crucified Son. He also taught that Jesus would return for an apocalyptic Day of Judgment. This *parousia*, or Second Coming, would occur when least expected, suddenly, in the twinkling of an eye, as Paul wrote in his first Letter to the Corinthians (1 Corinthians 15: 51–53).[7]

Although Paul was executed in Rome sometime around 60 CE, his evangelism, and that of his followers, allowed Christianity to spread across the Roman Empire, especially within the cities and among the poor and enslaved. The religious rites of early Christianity were probably restricted to a simple celebration of a communal meal, the *agape*, or "love feast," followed by a Eucharistic ceremony during which the Lord's Supper was re-enacted by way of the consumption of unleavened bread and unfermented wine. There were, most probably, also prayers, hymns, and readings from both the Jewish Scriptures and, ultimately, from the Gospels, Acts, and Letters of the New Testament. Although the Christian message was particularly appealing to the most disaffected members of the empire, not all of the followers of Jesus were marginal members of the community. Indeed, many Christians were part of what we might understand today as the middle class, and some were quite wealthy. Because of this, it became customary for those of means to provide for the poor so that the latter could continue to participate in communal worship services. These benevolent acts of common love brought Christian communities together in a way that allowed them to focus their attention on the plight of the weak, the sick, and the unprotected. This show of concern for others who were less fortunate distinguished Christianity as a movement that offered *all* people of the world, even those who were poor, enslaved, or female, the possibility of experiencing a sense of communal compassion. Because the movement was based on these foundational charitable principles, Christianity stood in marked contrast to both the civil religion of Rome and to the pagan cult religions that had flourished throughout the empire. It was also different from those other, more established movements in that it claimed that salvation was open to everyone, that God cared about each and every human soul, and that a spiritual equality existed among those who practiced the faith.[8]

Church versus State

As Christianity evolved during the second century, it was necessary for it to develop some kind of organizational structure. Gradually, the increasingly complex affairs of the early churches were placed in the hands of presbyters, or elders, and deacons, or those who served. Upon this foundation, individual churches began to build up an episcopal structure consisting of bishops (*episkopoi*) who were initially elected by their congregations to oversee worship and to supervise the gathering of funds, but who eventually began to extend their authority to outlying villages and towns. Ultimately, the ever-increasing power of the bishops was supported by the doctrine of Apostolic Succession, which "asserted that the powers Jesus had given his original disciples were passed on from bishop to bishop by ordination." By the second century, these bishops began to define what would become the universal or *catholic* nature of the Church by developing an ideology of doctrinal orthodoxy (right belief) and orthopraxis (right practice) among the various Christian communities of the empire. They also acted as intermediaries between the civil and religious worlds, and eventually began to gather together in councils in order to reconcile difficult ecclesiastical issues, to establish theological standards, and even to expel as heretics those who would not accept their opinions.[9]

Ironically, Christianity's second-century push toward catholicism evoked a sense of distrust and even animosity from both the pagan world and the imperial government. Because Christianity had been understood by the imperial authorities of the first century as merely another Jewish sect, its followers, like other Jews, were protected under Roman law. But as this increasingly radical movement became more and more popular, and more and more organized, it became clear that it was quite different from Judaism. Christianity was understood by Roman administrators as a mysterious and dangerous movement, one whose followers not only denied the existence of the pagan gods but also refused to worship the emperor, a practice that was deemed treasonous. Further, their love feasts were reported to be scandalous scenes of sexual depravity, while their "alarming doctrine of the actual presence of Jesus' body in the Eucharist was distorted into an accusation of cannibalism." Suspicious of the "privacy and secrecy that marked Christian life," which Roman administrators felt was a violation of their traditional rejection of "any private association, especially any of a religious nature," Claudius expelled the Christians from Rome, while Nero sought to make them scapegoats for the tragic fire that struck the city in 64 CE. Indeed, by the end of the first century, Christianity came to be understood as such a threat to the internal stability of the empire that leaders in Rome made it a crime to practice the faith.[10]

Roman Expansionism, Imperial Crisis, and the World of Constantine

After the death of Augustus, his successors finally dispensed with the republican illusion he had created. The ruler came to be called *imperator*—thus, Emperor—as well as Caesar; the former title indicated the ruler's control of the military, the latter his connection to the imperial house. Although Augustus, because his power was ostensibly voted to him by the Senate, could not legally designate a successor, he made it clear whom he felt should follow him by bestowing favors upon certain individuals and allowing them to share in imperial power and responsibility. As the emperorship passed through the most important members of the *Julio-Claudian Dynasty*, Tiberius (r. 14–37 CE), Gaius (Caligula, r. 37–41 CE), Claudius (r. 41–54 CE), and Nero (r. 54–68 CE), the monarchical and hereditary structure of the regime became obvious. Perhaps even more significantly, the naked military nature of imperial rule became clear after the death of Gaius in 41 CE, when the Praetorian Guard pulled a shaking, terrified Claudius from behind a curtain and forcibly installed him as emperor. By 68 CE, when the incompetent and hugely unpopular Nero died, the realm had reached a point of political chaos. The next year would see no fewer than four men become emperor, as the members of different Roman armies succeeded in placing their respective commanders on the throne.[11]

By the time Augustus died in 14 CE, the Roman Empire was already vast, extending as it did across all of Europe, most of northern Africa, and into Asia Minor. Although the very size of the realm made it difficult to rule, the ingenuity of Rome's military and administrative ideas allowed it to keep the empire in check. Although under Augustus the army was reduced from 60 legions to just 28, the imperial forces, which were primarily responsible for holding the empire together, nevertheless became truly professional. During the previous era of the Roman Republic, generals had usually recruited armies, not only providing them with weapons but also paying them. Fearing that one such general might become a threat to his rule, Augustus established a central military treasury from which he drew funds in order to pay the members of his legions. Although enlistment required a commitment of 20 years, the legionnaires were pleased to receive a steady income instead of having to rely for their income on booty taken during war. Under imperial rule, they were paid well and occasionally received bonuses; they even had what might be considered a retirement plan, which assured them a pension, most often consisting of parcels of land.

As powerful and efficient as the imperial military was, however, it was barely able to protect the empire from the forces massed along its borders. The origins of this problem with foreign peoples can be traced to the early imperial period and the reign of Augustus. After the civil wars ended and Augustus came to power, he involved himself in quelling tribal uprisings in the western part of the empire between Italy and France. He also worked to pacify Spain, while in 12 CE his stepson Drusus (Nero Claudias Drusus Germanicus) conquered Germany. Despite its obvious successes, though, Rome's early imperial conquests did not come without difficulties. Spread across their wide-ranging borders, the legions of Rome were often stretched extremely thin.

Imperial Defense

Although Rome would continue to grow its empire through a practice of offensive expansionism for a century after the death of Augustus in 14 CE, during the course of the second century it began to rely more and more on an imperial policy that was defensive in character. This was certainly the case in regard to the political and military policy decisions made by Hadrian, the third of the five good emperors. Upon coming to power, Hadrian immediately abandoned the eastern territories that had been taken by his predecessor Trajan. Determining that it would be beyond the capability of Rome's armies to maintain permanent frontier borders as far away as the Persian Gulf, Hadrian withdrew his forces from that part of the world and reestablished the eastern imperial frontier at the Euphrates.[12]

Perhaps what was most notable about Hadrian's reign is that he spent half of it outside of Italy. Part of this was due to his unquenchable curiosity about the world, one that led him to explore the far reaches of the empire. Of greater importance, though, was his desire to learn more about how better to administer to and defend the empire. The latter of these concerns was of particular import for Hadrian, and thus he spent a good deal of his time away from Italy involving himself in the inspection, maintenance, and improvement of the Roman army. Significantly, as historian Michael Grant points out, "one of the first fruits of this active military policy, following upon a minor reverse on the British frontier, was the best preserved of all the fortifications of the empire, Hadrian's Wall from Tyne to Solway, manned by fifteen thousand auxiliaries watching over the bare brown hills that rolled away to the still unconquered north."[13]

The construction of this important Roman fortification came about after Hadrian and his engineers surveyed the 73-mile span across the width of northern Britain and then designed a stone wall that could stretch across the entire distance, linking together sixteen forts and numerous smaller guard posts and watchtowers. The wall was meant not only to demonstrate Rome's military might even on its far northern frontier, but also to separate out undesirable peoples who might attempt to make their way within the imperial borders. From the end point of Hadrian's British Isle fortification in Solway, the Roman line of defense now extended eastward along the North Sea, and then, in a chain of additional frontier towns and forts, down the Rhine and the Danube Rivers to the Black Sea. From there, it "ran south from the Black Sea coast, down the valleys of the Tigris and Euphrates Rivers, and turned west across Palestine, Arabia, Egypt, and North Africa, all the way to Morocco on the North African Atlantic coast."[14]

After Marcus Aurelius' untimely death in a military camp on the Danube, his dysfunctional son Commodus (r. 180–192) became Emperor. Although Commodus was able to end the conflicts on the Danube, he did so by offering the invaders an overly generous and lenient treaty, an act that, ironically, generated even more interest on the part of foreign peoples in waging war on Rome. In regard to the empire itself, Commodus displayed utter indifference toward provincial administrators and the military, successfully breaking down much of the communal good will that had been built up by the four good emperors who had preceded him.

Civil War and Economic Decline

After Commodus was strangled to death in 192 CE, civil war ensued for the next year, until the Severan dynasty (193–235 CE) was finally established in 193 CE. As was the case with the *Principate* after the death of Augustus, however, the members of the Severan dynasty tended to fear the military; thus, during this time, the governance of Rome was basically left in the hands of warring armies. After the last Severan emperor was murdered by his own troops in 235, 50 years of bloody civil war, invasions, and the rise of new foreign threats followed. The period proved to be so anarchic and dangerous, in fact, that of the 50 men who became emperor during this span, only one died a natural death.

Adding to the chaotic state of the empire during this problematic period was the long economic decline that Rome experienced as it struggle through the third century. Although economic vulnerability had always been a part of the Roman Empire, it appears that during the third century, Rome's fiscal liabilities became even more acute, especially after it stopped plundering newly conquered people. In addition to this, Rome was struck with a devastating third- and fourth-century outbreak of bubonic plague, one that effectively reduced the population of the empire by as much as 20 percent between 250 and 400 CE. This resulted in shrinking markets, a reduction in the volume of trade, and diminished international exchange, which in turn acted to weaken the relationship of various parts of the empire. As Norman Cantor suggests, the economy also suffered for other reasons, most notably because of Rome's "failure to develop an industrial technology."[15] This lack of industrialization created an economically stagnant situation across the empire, one which was characterized by a lack of specialized production and an increase in the dominance of the *latifundia*, the great cash crop plantations that were owned by wealthy Romans.

Because Roman administrators during the third century were consumed by external threats, they did little to address the destructive conditions that haunted the empire. The much-needed reconstruction of the empire would have to await the rise to power of Diocletian (r. 284–305), a rough-hewn soldier and shrewd administrator. Realizing that the empire had grown too large for one man to control, Diocletian decreed that Rome would now be ruled by a *tetrarchy*, four men with power divided among them. Diocletian and Maximian would share the title of Augustus, and Galerius and Constantius would each bear the lesser title of Caesar. This administrative system, which allowed each man control over his own geographical territory, appeared not only to offer a solution to the military problems that had plagued the empire for more than 50 years, but also seemed to ensure the possibility of a peaceful imperial succession. Diocletian would reign as the senior Augustus, controlling the provinces of Thrace, Asia, and Egypt, or the Prefecture of the east; while Maximian would reign as the junior Augustus, controlling Italy, Africa, and Spain, or the Prefecture of Italy. As one Caesar, Galerius would be in charge of the Danube frontier and the Balkans, or the Prefecture of Illyricum; while Constantius, as the other Caesar, would control Britain and Gaul, or the Prefecture of Gaul. The two Caesars were designated as successors to the western and eastern parts of the empire, and their "loyalty was enhanced by marriages to daughters of the Augusti."

In 305 CE, Diocletian unexpectedly retired, also compelling Maximian to step down from his position as co-emperor. However, Diocletian's vision of a smooth succession, with Galerius and Constantius now becoming the new Augusti, failed miserably, as bitter civil war immediately ensued. Indeed, by 310 CE three generals were vying for control of the empire: Licinius in the east; Maxentius in Italy; and Constantine, whose power base was in Gaul and Britain, the poorest and least populated region of the Roman world. Although he was badly outnumbered by the forces of Maxentius, Constantine threw caution to the wind and proceeded to march over the Alps and upon Rome. At the famous battle of the Milvian Bridge near Rome, he defeated and killed his enemy, making him ruler over the western part of the empire. From 312 until 324 he shared the rule of the empire with Licinius, at which point he defeated and deposed his eastern rival and became sole ruler of the Roman world.

Although it is unclear what really happened at the momentous battle of the Milvian Bridge, that Constantine deemed Christianity acceptable as a religion within the Roman Empire is certain. Where Diocletian had persecuted Christians, doing his best to rid the realm of this ever-expanding movement, Constantine made the practice of Christianity legal in the empire by issuing his Edict of Milan in 313 CE. Ironically, once the religion was made legal within the Roman Empire, a great struggle over the question of Christian orthodoxy ensued. As heresies emerged (beliefs contrary to those of the Catholic Church) and began to threaten the unity of an empire that was now Christian, they took on a political character and inevitably involved the emperor and the powers of the state.[16]

This was especially true in regard to what was termed the *Arian Controversy*. Named after the Alexandrian priest Arius (c. 280–336 CE), Arianism concerned the relationship of God the Father to God the Son. Arius argued that although the Father was eternal, Jesus as the Son was a created being, and thus did not share the substance of God. As Arius himself said, "The Son has a beginning, but God is without beginning." For Arius, then, "Jesus was neither fully man nor fully God, but something in between." His position, argued Arius, did away with the difficult doctrine of the Trinity, the idea that God was somehow three persons, Father, Son, and Holy Spirit, but still one substance and essence. Although much less complex and much more philosophically defensible than the doctrine of the Trinity, for the major adversary of Arius, the future bishop of Alexandria, Anthanasius, the Arian position was seriously flawed. In particularly, Anthanasius argued, it undercut the Christian notion of salvation that was predicated on the salvific event of Christ crucified and resurrected. Only if Jesus were fully human and fully God, said Anthanasius, could "the transformation of humanity to divinity have taken place in him and be transmitted by him to his disciples." According to Anthanasius, "Christ was made man that we might be made divine."

In order to address this growing controversy, which had literally split the Church, Constantine called a council of Christian bishops in the city of Nicaea in 325. Gathering in this city not far from Constantinople, the bishops argued over a point of orthodoxy, which for Constantine was merely political, but for them concerned salvation itself. They finally came down on the side of Anthanasius, embodying the priest's ideas on the matter in the Nicene Creed. Arianism did not die out, however, as many bishops and some future emperors were Arians. Indeed, as we shall see, this controversy would remain an issue even after the collapse of the empire in the west.

The Fall of the Western Roman Empire and the Rise of Western Europe

In moving the Roman capital to the city of Byzantium, Constantine ensured the continuation of the empire in the more stable eastern part of the realm. In fact, during the fourth and fifth centuries, the eastern part of the empire, with its prosperous cities, strong commercial economy, productive peasantry, and larger population, thrived. But as historian Edward Peters makes clear, unlike in the east, the western regions of the empire "felt the consequences of having fewer people, less productive and fewer cities, [and] a less-developed economy."[17] In addition to this, extending what had begun to occur during Rome's "third-century crisis," the western peasantry now became even more oppressed by the wealthy land owners of the *latifundia*.

The declining conditions in the west left the northern and western frontier regions of this part of the empire increasingly open to attacks by members of so-called Germanic tribes, such as the Burgundians, Vandals, Franks, Angles, Saxons, Lombards and Goths. These peoples of *Germania*, as the Romans called the area beyond the frontiers of the Rhine and the Danube, were often referred to with the rather derogatory label of barbarians. Just who were these barbarians of *Germania*? This is an extremely difficult question to answer, as the term barbarian, and indeed the designation *Germanic tribes* itself, was used to identify the members of extremely diverse groups of peoples. First of all, it is necessary to point out that the Romans referred in a general sense to people who existed beyond their imperial borders as *externae gentes*, the "people living outside." They broke down this overarching category of *externae gentes* further after comparing the cultures of non-Roman peoples to the elite culture and social organizations of Rome. Within the framework of this system of subclassification, a foreign people might be understood as a *populus*, "virtually identical to Roman standards; a *gens*, not yet culturally developed or politically organized; or a *natio* . . . a 'horde,' a body of individuals supposedly related by common descent, but lacking the technical and intellectual culture or sociopolitical organization of a *gens*."[18]

These Roman divisions were, in a certain sense, related back to the Greek classification for foreign peoples. For the Greeks, foreigners who could learn to speak and read Greek were considered potentially respectable members of the *oikumene* (the Greek term for the "known world"); those who were unable to master Greek were considered *barbaroi*, or barbarians, peoples whose languages, to the ears of the Greeks, were nothing more than a jumble of incomprehensible noise. The Romans borrowed this Greek term, *barbaroi*, Latinizing it as *barbari* and applied it to the *externae gentes* in general, and, in particular, to the *nationes*, the hordes who existed beyond the frontiers of the empire.

During the third century CE, the most aggressive of the German tribes had been the Goths, a people who ultimately split into two great kingdoms, the western Visigoths and the eastern Ostrogoths. The Goths had initially made their way from their ancestral home near the Baltic Sea into an area in southern Russia. By the middle of the third century of the Common Era they began to put pressure on the northern Danube frontiers of the Roman Empire. In roughly 250 CE, they were able to break through the Roman defenses and overrun the Balkan provinces. In order to meet this threat, and that of the Persian Sassanids in the east, the Romans took the calculated risk of pulling some of their legions away from the western frontiers. Unfortunately, this weakening of defenses in the west led other Germanic peoples, particularly the Franks and the Alemanni, to attack and overrun the borders in those regions.

By the fourth century, different groups of Germanic peoples had been fixtures on the frontiers of the Roman Empire for hundreds of years. Although, as we have just seen, some of these groups had attacked the border regions of the empire, the interaction between the Romans and the Germans had been relatively peaceful throughout the first two centuries of the Common Era. The Romans had even imported some of these people into the empire as domestics, slaves, and soldiers. Interestingly, some of these barbarian soldiers rose to positions of leadership in the Roman legions, even becoming famous throughout the empire. By the end of the fourth century, however, the relationship between the Romans and the Germans began to change radically as a great influx of Visigoths swept toward the western frontiers of the empire.

The Visigoths were expert horsemen and fierce warriors, who had themselves been pushed to the borders of the Roman Empire by the vicious Huns, who stemmed from what is today Mongolia. They originally made their way to southern Gaul and Spain, and once there, they entered into a political and military contract with the Roman emperor Valens (r. 364–378), agreeing to act as his *foederati*, or special allies, who would protect the eastern frontier of the empire. Instead of being regarded as valued members of the empire, though, the Visigoths received harsh treatment from Valens. They finally rebelled against the emperor, defeating him and his forces at the Battle of Adrianople in 378.

Disturbed by defeats like that at Adrianople and sensing the growing weakness of the west, Rome rather passively began to allow the settlement of German tribes in the very heart of the western empire. In large part because of this attitude, in 406 CE the Vandals were able to cross over the Rhine and within a mere 30 years control much of North Africa and a good deal of the Mediterranean. Following after the Vandals, the Burgundians eventually settled in southern Gaul, while the most important group in regard to the early history of Western Europe, the Franks, settled northern and central Gaul; the Salian Franks along the seacoast and the Ripuarian Franks along the Rhine, the Seine, and the Loire Rivers.

Although the settlement of these barbarians within imperial borders was clearly a major blow to both the pride and status of the Romans, perhaps what was even more devastating was the series of attacks leveled against the eternal city of Rome itself. In 410 CE the Visigoths, led by Alaric (c. 370–410 CE), revolted and sacked Rome; in 452 CE the Huns, led by Attila, invaded Italy; and in 455 CE, the former capital city was overrun by the Vandals. As a result of all of this, by the middle of the fifth century power in the western empire passed decisively from the Roman emperors to barbarian chieftains. By the end of the fifth century, barbarians had completely overwhelmed the western empire, with the Ostrogoths in Italy, the Franks in northern Gaul, the Burgundians in Provence, the Vandals in Africa and the western Mediterranean, and the Angles and Saxons in England. As scholars are quick to point out, this shift in power from the Romans to the different barbarian groups that now commanded the western region of the empire did not make Western Europe into a savage land. The Germanic peoples who now controlled the western empire were willing, and even anxious to adopt the culture of the people that they had conquered. Indeed, with the exception of Britain and northern Gaul, across the west, Roman language, law, and government mingled together with Germanic institutions. Much of this had to do with the fact that the Visigoths, the Ostrogoths, and the Vandals were already Christian when they arrived in the west. They were, however, Arians, as the bishops who had converted them to Christianity had been followers of Arius. This gave rise to an intense hostility against the barbarians among Roman Christians, who believed Arianism to be heretical. Despite this, though, the German peoples were great admirers of Roman culture and had no desire to see it disappear. Ultimately, around 500 CE, the Franks, under their powerful king, Clovis, and supported by bishops in Rome, converted to the post-Nicaea, Catholic form of Christianity. As Roman Christians, the Franks were instrumental in conquering and converting the Goths and other barbarians in Western Europe to orthodox Christianity.

The church had become increasingly important in the west as this part of the empire began to crumble. After Christianity had been made legal by Constantine, and especially after it had become the state religion under Theodosius (r. 379–395) at the end of the fourth century, the political structure of the church had mirrored that of the imperial government. Church government was centralized and formed into a hierarchy, with bishops in the major cities around the empire all looking for spiritual guidance from the bishop of Rome, the *papa*, or father, who eventually become the Pope. As the western empire declined, Roman governors left the cities and their populations began to migrate to the countryside, where the "resulting vacuum of authority was filled by local bishops and cathedral chapters." The local cathedral, especially in this tenuous time, became the center of urban life, while the local bishop filled the role of governing authority. Although the church, like the royal government, was challenged by the decline of the western empire, it was able to survive the period of both Germanic and Islamic invasions and remain a "potent civilizing and unifying force."

The Catholic Church would ultimately follow the path of the empire and split apart into western and eastern halves. Although much of this had to do with the linguistic and cultural differences that marked the eastern Greek and western Latin parts of the empire, there were also important ecclesiastical differences between the churches of the west and the east. Like the administrative structure of its western cousin, the structure of the Eastern Church also reflected that of the secular state. Denying the authority of the Pope, however, the Eastern Church appointed a patriarch, who tended to be tightly controlled by the Roman emperors. This Patriarch oversaw archbishops serving in key cities, who in turn were responsible for the local clergy. Unlike the Roman church, which did not allow its clergy to marry, the Eastern Church permitted the marriage of priests, but forbid bishops to marry. Further diverging from the Roman church, the Eastern Church allowed its laity to divorce and it used vernacular languages in its worship services.

Beyond these ecclesiastical differences, there were also three other major issues that separated the churches of the east and west. First, was the issue of doctrinal authority. The church in the east put more stress on the authority of the Bible and on "ecumenical" (empire-wide) councils rather than on the decrees of the bishop of Rome. The Eastern Church rejected the Roman bishop's claim that he had special authority based on Peter's commission from Jesus found in the Gospel of Matthew. The second issue had to do with the Roman church's addition of the so-called *filioque* phrase to the Nicene Creed, an anti-Arian clause that stated that the Holy Spirit proceeds "also from the Son" (*filioque*) as well as the Father. Because the Eastern Church tended to compromise doctrinally with the still-powerful Arian Christians, this creedal addition was problematic for them. The third issue concerned what came to be called the *iconoclastic controversy*. In 725 the eastern Emperor, Leo III, banned the use of images in Eastern Churches, claming that they subverted the power and majesty of God. Leo ran into heavy opposition in attempting to enforce the ban in the west, as the members of the Western Church cherished their religious iconography. In order to punish the west for refusing to follow his decree, Leo confiscated papal lands in Sicily and Calabria, placing them under control of Constantinople. Because these papal lands brought in a substantial amount of revenue, the Roman church "could not but view the emperor's action as a declaration of war."[19]

Pressured not only by this confrontation with Leo, but also by a renewed threat from the Lombards of northern Italy, the Roman church seemed as if it might go under. The Western Church, however, had long been safeguarded by the Franks; and now, during the time of this new crisis, it once again turned to these protectors. Sealing one of the most significant political alliances of the Middle Ages, Pope Stephen II (r. 752–757) called upon the Franks and their ruler, Pepin III, not only to defend the church against the threat of the Lombards, but also to act as a counterweight to the Eastern emperor. In the end, this "marriage of religion and politics created a new Western Church and empire; it also determined much of the course of Western history into our time."[20]

Clovis (c. 466–511), the king under whom the Franks had converted to the Catholic form of Christianity in 500 CE, was the man who founded the first Frankish dynasty, the Merovingian, called after Merovich, an early leader of one branch of the Franks. He and his Merovingian successors were not only able to unite the Salian and Ripuarian Franks, but, as was already mentioned, were also able to bring the Burgundians and the Visigoths under control. They eventually established the kingdom of the Franks in ancient Gaul, "making the Franks and the Merovingian kings a significant force in Western Europe." Ironically, the Merovingian rulers had a difficult time managing their sprawling kingdoms, as they found themselves in a constant struggle to define a centralized government that commanded *transregional loyalty* while "powerful local magnates strove to preserve their regional autonomy and traditions." The Merovingian kings sought to deal with this issue by entering into pacts of alliance with the landed nobility and by creating the royal office of *count*.[21]

By the seventh century, the king of the Franks was a ruler in name only, as the real power in the realm became concentrated in the office of the *mayor of the palace*, the spokesperson for the great land holders of the three large areas into which the Frankish kingdom had been divided: Neustria, Austrasia, and Burgundy. It was through this office that the second great Frankish dynasty, the Carolingians, came to power. The Carolingians controlled the office of the mayor of the palace from the time of the ascent to that position of Pepin I (d. 639) of Austrasia until 751 CE, when, with the help of the pope, they seized the Frankish crown. Pepin I, or Pepin the Elder, was a wealthy and powerful land owner who served the Merovingian king Clotaire II as mayor of the palace of Austriasia from 584 to 629 CE. His grandson, Pepin of Herstal, although he too served the Merovingian king and held only the mayor's position, became the true ruler of the Frankish kingdom in 687 CE. Pepin of Herstal was succeeded by his illegitimate son, Charles Martel, after whom the dynasty is called, as the name Carolingian comes from the Latin word for Charles, *Carolus*.[22]

Significantly, Charles Martel was able to build up a large cavalry by granting lands to powerful noblemen as *benefices*, or fiefs, in return for their promise to serve as the king's army. These lands that Charles so benevolently bestowed upon the nobility were taken from the church, which by this time, as we have seen, had grown more and more dependent upon the protection of the Franks against the Eastern emperor and the Lombards. When Charles demanded that their lands be turned over to the nobles, the church was forced to acquiesce and surrender these properties. By establishing in this way a relatively strong relationship with the landed aristocracy, Charles and the Carolingians were able to succeed politically where the Merovingians had failed. Where the Merovingians had sought to counteract the power of the nobility by elevating the weak, the Carolingians strengthened their realms by soothing the egos of the nobles instead of by challenging them.

The church also played a role in the Carolingian rise to power. Charles Martel and his successor, his grandson Pepin III, or Pepin the Short, used the church to placate disgruntled tribes that had been conquered by the Carolingians: the Frisians, Thüringians, Bavarians, and in particular, their long-time enemies, the Saxons. Eventually, conversion to the Nicene form of Christianity became an integral part of the successful annexation of conquered lands and people. This arrangement benefited not only the Carolingian kings, but also the Roman Church, as Christian bishops in the west who served in missionary districts were appointed lords and accorded all the privileges of this office. The church did not only assist in Carolingian expansion, however, as Pope Zacharias (r. 741–752) also "sanctioned Pepin the Short's termination of the vestigial Merovingian dynasty and supported the Carolingian accession to outright kingship of the Franks." With the blessing of the pope, Pepin was "proclaimed king by the nobility in council in 751."[23]

Charles the Great, or Charlemagne, the son of Pepin the Short, carried on his father's tradition of the Carolingian king acting as the papal protector of Italy. Having convincingly defeated King Desiderius and the Lombards in northern Italy in 774, Charlemagne now proclaimed himself King of the Lombards and proceeded to expand his realm by subjugating surrounding pagan tribes, especially the Saxons, whom the Franks brutally Christianized and then scattered in small groups across their vast territory. The Muslims, who had been repelled by Charles Martel, were now pushed back beyond the Pyrenees, while the Avars, a vicious tribe related to the Huns, were thoroughly destroyed. By the time the great Charlemagne died in 814, his kingdom "embraced modern France, Belgium, Holland, Switzerland, almost the whole of western Germany, much of Italy, a portion of Spain, and the island of Corsica."[24]

Charlemagne, it seems, had notions of becoming more than just the king of the Franks. Encouraged by his ambitious advisors, he began to envision himself as an imperial ruler reigning over both the state and the church. Although cautious not to offend the emperors of the east by making his desires too explicit, he nevertheless had his sacred palace city of Aachen (Aix-la-Chapelle) constructed in the manner of the great cities of the ancient Roman and contemporary emperors of the east. In regard to the church, although he did grant it a certain amount of independence, he watched over it as an ever-vigilant parent. As Charles Martel and Pepin III had successfully done before him, Charlemagne used the church to maintain social stability and hierarchical order within the realm. Hand-in-hand with the papacy he was ultimately able to create a Frankish Christian Empire.

It was, perhaps, on Christmas Day, 800, that Charlemagne's imperial dreams were fulfilled, as it was then that Pope Leo III (r. 795–816) crowned him emperor. Although the coronation was an attempt by the pope to increase the power of the church and to gain some leverage over the headstrong king, after the event, Charlemagne's control over both church and state remained undiminished. As was the political custom, Charlemagne ruled his kingdom through the use of the royal office of the count. Under his rule, there were as many as 250 of these royal appointees who were strategically assigned to the administrative districts into which the kingdom had been divided. The Carolingian count was usually a local magnate who already possessed an armed force and in whose self-interest it was to serve the king. The count had three basic responsibilities: "to maintain a local army loyal to the king, to collect tribute and dues, and to administer justice throughout his district."

As has already been pointed out, even the Carolingians struggled to maintain an effective centralized government during the Middle Ages. This was so because at this time the western world was characterized by the threat of famine, disease, and invasion. Beyond this, the districts of the different kingdoms were spread over an expansive area, and the men who ruled them, even under strong kings like Charlemagne, often became a law unto themselves. Subject to these conditions, the weak sought out the strong for protection. This process of placing oneself under the protection of a stronger individual traces its origins to the problems that emerged within Merovingian society. Because the Merovingian kings were never able to command loyalty from either the nobles or the counts they had put in place, it became customary during the sixth and seventh centuries for weaker *freemen* who feared for their lives to seek out other, stronger freemen to protect them. This system was mutually beneficial, as the latter were able to build up armies and become local *magnates*, or men of influence, while the former were able to resolve the problem of simple survival. The freemen who gave themselves over to these other, stronger freemen were referred to as *ingenui in obsequio*, or "freemen in a contractual relation of dependence." Men who gave themselves to the king in this way were called *antrustiones*. All of those who functioned within this system were called *vassals*, or those who serve, from which evolved the term *vassalage*, meaning the placement of oneself in the personal service of another who promises protection in return.[25]

The feudal practice of vassalage obviously placed a great deal of power in the hands of the lords. Indeed, as Cantor makes clear, "lordship [was] the indispensable element in feudalism." The economic power of the lords came primarily from their control of large estates and a *dependent peasantry*.[26] It is here, in regard to the lord's economic power, that we may come to understand the manorial agrarian system that was mentioned earlier. Manors varied in size from one locale to another. A small manor could consist of as few as a dozen households, each with an allotment of land of roughly 30 acres. The smallest manors, then, probably had approximately 350 acres of arable land, not counting forests, common meadows, and the *demesne*, land set aside exclusively for the lord's use. On the other extreme, a large manor might have consisted of up to 50 households spread across as many as 5,000 acres.

In return for laboring on the lord's *demesne*, peasants were allotted parcels of arable land under the open-field system, where the fields were subdivided into strips. They were allowed to graze animals in the common areas and to gather dead wood from the forests, but had many restrictions placed on them by the lord of the manor. In general, peasants were treated according to their personal status and the size of their tenements. A freeman who possessed a small parcel of land not subject to the claims of the lord could become a serf by surrendering his property to a wealthier landowner in exchange for his protection. The freeman would then receive his land back from the lord under a contractual agreement. Although he no longer owned his property, "he had full possession and use of it, and the number of services and amount of goods he was so supply to the lord were carefully spelled out." Those peasants who placed themselves under the protection of the lord, but who possessed very little property, became unfree serfs. Unlike free serfs, who retained some control over their own lives, unfree serfs were subject to the dictates of their manorial overseers, spending as many as three days per week working the land of the lord. Peasants who came to the lord with absolutely nothing "had the lowest status and were the least protected from the excessive demands on their labor."[27]

Although the economic power of the lords came from their control of large estates, their political and military power stemmed from the control they had over freeman soldiers and the decentralized governmental and legal institutions characteristic of the Middle Ages. Indeed, by the time of the Frankish kingdoms, lordship became the basic social and political institution of the medieval world. This can be seen in the structure of the *comitatus*, or "war band" of the German tribes, which was based on the ideal of the loyalty of warriors to their chieftain in return for his protection and generosity with the spoils of conflict. The vassalage system of the sixth and seventh centuries, then, may be understood as an extension of the German *comitatus*, with freemen willingly putting themselves at the disposal of their lord or king. As Cantor points out, though, initially these military vassals were nothing more than "gangs of thugs" who fought on behalf of their warlord. They were far removed from the glorious chivalric knights who were depicted in the great *chansons de geste* (songs of great deeds) of the twelfth and thirteenth centuries.[28]

Although political and military vassalage is often thought to be associated with the notion of land grants given for heroic deeds, most vassals before the eighth century were landless. It was only after the superiority of the mounted cavalry became evident, and more enlightened warlords began to build their armies around the *mailed and mounted soldier*, that vassalage truely began to be connected to land ownership. This was so because even though the *chevalier*, or knight was superior to the foot soldier, his equipment was extraordinarily expensive. If a warlord wanted an army of knights among his vassals, he found it to his advantage to invest his *chevaliers* with manorial estates, from which they could draw an income in order to outfit themselves for battle. The growing association of vassalage with the fief eventually began to raise the social status of the vassal. Less and less a mercenary thug, the vassal himself was now becoming a local lord, often controlling one, or sometimes more than one, manor.[29]

In the final stage of the development of feudalism, governmental and legal authority was gradually passed from the state into the hands of the king's great feudal vassals. Characteristic of the ninth century, this late stage of feudalism

84

was the result of the last Carolingian kings' inability to control their own lords. Although wealthy land owners had always had power over the dependant peasantry within the feudal system, the passing of public power into private hands in the ninth century represented a radical reconfiguration of feudal society. The feudal lords had now wrested from the ever more feeble monarchy the authority to collect taxes, to hold courts to hear important pleas, and to hang criminals in their duchies and counties. As the tenth century unfolded in France, the great powers that had once been possessed by the Carolingian kings were "swallowed up in the private feudal courts, which exercised overlapping and conflicting jurisdictions in a crazy patchwork of decentralized authority."[30]

End Notes

1. Donald Kagan, Steven Ozment, and Frank M.Turner, *The Western Heritage: Volume 1, To 1740* (Upper Saddle River: Prentice Hall, 2004), pp. 136–140. Other excellent introductory texts on this material include: Roy T. Matthews and F. Dewitt Platt, *The Western Humanities: Volume 1, Beginnings through the Renaissance* (Mountain View: Mayfield Publishing Company, 1998); Palmira Brummett, et al., *Civilization, Past and Present: Volume 1, To 1650* (New York: Addison-Wesley Educational Publishers, Inc., 2000); Janetta Rebold Benton and Robert DiYanni, *Arts and Culture: An Introduction to the Humanities, Volume 1* (Upper Saddle River: Prentice Hall, 1998).

2. Michael Grant, *History of Rome* (New York: History Book Club, 1978), pp. 242–246.

3. *The Western Heritage*, p. 142.

4. *The Western Heritage*, p. 142. See also, "Augustus," *History of Rome*, pp. 242–273.

5. *History of Rome*, p. 245.

6. *The Western Heritage*, p. 142.

7. See "From Judaism to Christianity," Norman Cantor, *The Civilization of the Middle Ages* (New York: Harper Collins Publishers, pp. 29–40); "The Jews, Jesus, and Paul," in, *History of Rome*, pp. 334–348; "Religion and Society in Antiquity," in, *Europe and the Middle Ages* (Upper Saddle River: Prentice Hall, 1997), pp. 25–53.

8. *The Civilization of the Middle Ages*, pp. 37–38.

9. *The Civilization of the Middle Ages*, pp. 38–40.

10. *The Western Heritage*, pp. 168–169.

11. *The Western Heritage*, pp. 154–155.

12. *History of Rome*, pp. 302–304.

13. *History of Rome*, pp. 302-303.

14. *Europe and the Middle Ages*, pp. 10–11.

15. *The Civilization of the Middle Ages*, p. 42.

16. *The Civilization of the Middle Ages*, pp. 48–52.

17. *Europe and the Middle Ages*, p. 20.

18. *Europe and the Middle Ages*, p. 11.

19. *The Western Heritage*, pp. 208–209.

20. *The Western Heritage*, p. 210.

21. *The Western Heritage*, p. 211. See also *Civilization in the Middle Ages*, pp. 111–120.

22. *Europe and the Middle Ages*, pp. 143–148.

23. *The Western Heritage*, p. 212.

24. *The Western Heritage*, p. 212.

25. *The Western Heritage*, pp. 221–222.

26. *The Civilization of the Middle Ages*, pp. 196–197.

27. *The Western Heritage*, p. 216.

28. *The Civilization of the Middle Ages*, pp. 197–198.

29. *The Civilization of the Middle Ages*, pp. 198–199.

30. *The Civilization of the Middle Ages*, p. 200.

Practice Test Questions

1. The Second Triumvirate was made of which three men?

   A. Octavian, Mark Antony, Trajan
   B. Octavian, Mark Antony, Lepidus
   C. Mark Antony, Lepidus, Trajan
   D. Octavian, Mark Antony, Nero

2. The figure that spread the message of Jesus to the gentiles was

   A. Paul.
   B. Peter.
   C. John.
   D. Augustine.

3. The great Roman fortification that stretched across Britain was built under whose reign?

   A. Octavian
   B. Marcus Aurelius
   C. Commodus
   D. Hadrian

4. The Visigoths, Ostrogoths, and Vandals were members of which religious tradition when they originally came to power in the west during the fourth century?

   A. Judaism
   B. Islam
   C. Arian Christianity
   D. Paganism

5. Those that filled the office of count under the Merovingians were

   A. wealthy nobles.
   B. unpropertied.
   C. barbarians.
   D. warriors.

Answers and Explanations

1. **B.** The very important Second Triumvirate was made up of Octavian, Mark Antony, and Lepidus. Lepidus was never really the equal in power of Octavian and Antony, and thus the latter two were rivals for sole control of the Roman realm. Octavian finally defeated the forces of Antony and Cleopatra, who ultimately committed suicide, leaving Octavian in control of the empire. Trajan and Nero were later emperors.

2. **A.** After the death of Jesus, tension arose between Paul and Peter over who would be considered Jesus' privileged disciple. The two reached a compromise, agreeing that Peter would continue to preach to the Jews, while Paul would spread the "good news" to the gentiles. John was one of the disciples of Jesus who allied himself with Peter on this issue. Augustine was a Christian church father who lived between 354 and 430, well after the "word" had been spread throughout the Roman Empire.

3. **D.** Although Marcus Aurelius would deal with his own issues concerning the fortification of the empire, the great Wall in northern Britain was built under Hadrian, whose reign preceded that of Marcus Aurelius. Commodus, the son of Marcus Aurelius, was an ineffective ruler who succeeded his father. Octavian was long dead by the time Hadrian's Wall was built.

4. **C.** All three of these groups had been converted to Arian Christianity before they were converted to the Roman, or Nicene form, of Christianity. The Arian controversy, which dealt with the issue of Jesus as a created being, neither fully human nor fully God, split the Church during the fourth century. This controversy would be one of the issues taken up by the bishops who were called together by Constantine at Nicaea.

5. **B.** Hoping both to marginalize the nobles and to curry favor from the new lords they were appointing, the Merovingian kings filled the position of the "office of count" with men who were unpropertied. Along with their appointment came a grant of land from the king. Unfortunately for the Merovingian kings, the new lords proved as disloyal as the propertied nobles.

The Mythic Origins of the Mesoamerican and Andean Worlds

During the sixteenth century CE, *conquistadors* from Spain toppled two of the greatest cultures in the western world, the Aztec and the Inca. By the time Hernán Cortez and his troops arrived in the great Aztec capital of Tenochtitlán in 1519, extraordinary pre-Columbian Empires, including the Olmec, the Maya, the Toltec, and finally the Aztec, had controlled most of what is now known as Mesoamerica for some 3,000 years. Today this sprawling area includes the central valley region of Mexico, the southern Mexican and Pacific Coast states of Puebla, Guerrero, Oaxaca and Chiapas, the Yucatán Peninsula states of Yucatán, Quintana Roo, and Belize, the Gulf Coast region of Mexico, and the Central American countries of Guatemala, Honduras, and El Salvador. A decade after the collapse of the Aztec Empire in 1521, Spanish troops led by Francisco Pizarro overcame the forces of the Incas. By the time of this second major Spanish invasion in the Americas in 1532, the influence of the incredible Inca Empire stretched across what is today Peru, and parts of Ecuador, Brazil, Bolivia, Chile, and Argentina. Given that the Aztec and Inca empires were both so vast and so powerful, how was it that the Spanish *conquistadors* were so easily able to conquer them? This is a question that cannot be answered without examining in detail the histories of the peoples of the Amerindian world, an examination that properly begins with a discussion of the mythic origins of the Mesoamerican and Andean worlds.

Between the fall of the great city of Teotihuacán, somewhere around 600 BCE, and the rise of the amazing Aztec Empire, toward the end of the fourteenth century of the Common Era, groups of fierce warriors swept down from the northern reaches of Mesoamerica into the Valley of Mexico. Loosely divided into diverse assemblies of tribal peoples, these invaders from the north were collectively known as *Chichimecs*, literally "People of Dog Lineage," a title that was meant to define both their skill in fighting and their barbarism. Foremost among these groups was the Tolteca-Chichimeca, or Toltecs, a tenth-century society, legend tells us, led by the ferocious warrior and gifted leader Mixcóatl, or Cloud Serpent. Swiftly subduing his opponents, Mixcóatl eventually established his capital at Culhuacán. A victim of familial jealousy, Mixcóatl was soon assassinated by his brother, who assumed leadership of the Toltecs for himself. Fearing for her life, and for the life of her unborn child, the slain king's widow fled into exile, where in due course she gave birth to a son, Ce Acatl Topiltzin. During his adolescence, the boy became a devotee of the god Quetzalcóatl. After establishing himself as the high priest of the cult of the deity, Topiltzin ultimately took the name of this Feathered Serpent god, becoming Topiltzin-Quetzalcóatl.

Upon reaching manhood, Topiltzin-Quetzalcóatl, seeking to avenge his father's death, killed his uncle in single combat and made himself ruler of the Toltecs. He eventually moved his capital from Culhuacán to an area some fifty miles northwest of what would become the Aztec city of Tenochtitlán, located in what is present-day Mexico City. There, probably around 968 CE, he founded the extraordinary city of Tula, the most important Mesoamerican capital developed between the fall of Teotihuacán and the rise of Tenochtitlán. From Tula the Toltecs extended their authority throughout the valley region until they became the greatest power in central Mexico. Although their empire lasted for little more than two centuries, they would continue to maintain an almost mythical hold on Mesoamerican consciousness for some 500 years after their collapse.[1] Of particular significance for later Mesoamerican cultures was the effect that the Toltec legends would have on the Aztecs themselves. For the Aztecs, the magnificent city of Tula was understood as a paradise on earth. Its palace interiors were said to have been adorned with brilliantly colored feathers of exotic birds and lined with sheets of gold, jewels, and rare seashells; its fields were described as bursting with produce of gigantic proportions. Perhaps of even more importance to the Aztecs, though, were the stories surrounding Topiltzin and the Feathered Serpent god, Quetzalcóatl. Topiltzin, after all, had been the wise and benevolent leader who was reputed to have given his people the gift of writing, the ritual calendar, and the ability to produce the architectural wonders of Tula; while Quetzalcóatl had been the powerful yet compassionate god who had been satisfied with sacrifices of butterflies, birds, and snakes, and offerings of jade, incense, and even tortillas.

There was, then, much to be admired about Topiltzin and Quetzalcóatl in the eyes of the Aztecs. Among their own Toltec peoples, however, it appears that even the divine gifts of these two generous figures could not prevent the emergence of rebellious factions within the capital city. Scholars believe that the insurgent groups that emerged in Tula most probably arose from the ranks of both the unassimilated tribes living in the city and from indigenous peoples who were adherents of the invisible, unpredictable god Tezcatlipoca. The latter peoples are thought to have been particularly troublesome, as they came to resent the exaltation of Topiltzin's god, Quetzalcóatl, and thus the king himself. These followers of Tezcatlipoca ultimately sought to discredit Topiltzin, who, it must be remembered, was not only their king but the high priest of Quetzalcóatl, as well. According to one particularly telling story regarding the political intrigue that ensued in Tula and finally led to the downfall of Topiltzin, one night Tezcatlipoca disguised himself and stole into the house of the king, where he offered the ailing monarch what he said was a strong medicinal mixture, but which was really *pulque*, a distilled cactus juice. Although Topiltzin initially refused to partake of the mixture, in the end he was convinced by Tezcatlipoca to take a sip of the special drink. Finding it pleasing to the tongue, the king preceded to consume five cupfuls, finally becoming drunk and passing out. When he awoke the next morning, his sister was found lying beside him on his royal sleeping mat. Outraged, the people of the empire accused their king of breaking his priestly vows and disgracing himself by indulging in drunkenness and incest. After almost twenty years of enlightened rule, Topiltzin was forced into exile.

Although his rule ended in disgrace, the great king of Tula did not disappear from Mesoamerican history. According to one particularly important account, as Topiltzin and his partisans left Tula they fired arrows through saplings in order to mark their way, creating cross-like directional signs. Once in exile, the light-skinned, bearded Topiltzin sent word that he would return in the year Ce Acatl, the fifty-second anniversary of his birth year, and reclaim his rightful throne. Five centuries later, great floating mountains with bellowing white clouds appeared on the waters of the eastern horizon of the Aztec Empire. These enormous ships, the like of which had never been seen in this region, were carrying Spaniards who were white, bearded, and wearing crosses. The year was 1519, Ce Acatl.

The arrival of the Spanish would also affect the Andean neighbors of the Aztecs, the South American Incas of Peru. A decade after the fall of Tenochtitlán and the Aztec Empire, on November 15, 1532, a small force of Spanish conquistadors made their way into the very heart of what was perhaps the most powerful empire in the Americas. Led by Francisco Pizarro, the group entered the plaza of Cajamarca, an important Inca center in the Peruvian highlands, and demanded to see the king. Nearby, surrounded by what is said to have been an army of some 80,000 warriors, the prince Atawallpa was completing a ritual fast and enjoying his military victory over his brother, Prince Waskhar, a victory that had made him ruler of the Incas. Refusing to be taken away from his sacred duties, Atawallpa declined to meet his unwanted guests, but agreed to see them the next day. Astonishingly, by the following evening he was the prisoner of Pizarro. Over the next eight months, Pizarro would extract some $50 million worth of treasure as a ransom for Atawallpa. Once he had collected all that he could from the Inca people, Pizarro ordered that their ruler should be tried and executed. By July of 1533, Atawallpa was dead and the monumental Inca Empire was in decline.

Creating the Foundations of Mesoamerica: The Olmecs, the Maya, and the Toltecs

Urban, organized societies appeared in Mesoamerica long before the Spanish arrived in 1519, emerging over the course of the 3,000 year period that stretched from roughly 1500 BCE to the point at which the Aztec Empire was overthrown in 1521 CE. As with cultures in other parts of the world that started out as smallish tribal bands and family groups before finally evolving into advanced societies, the ancestral cultures of Mesoamerica began as hunters and gatherers, pursuing deer and other small game, fishing in lakes and streams, and foraging for such things as fruits, seeds, and wild roots. Anthropologists believe that sometime around 7000 BCE certain of these ancestral Mesoamericans "discovered" agriculture, coming to understand that seeds and roots could be planted in order to produce foodstuffs. Over the course of hundreds of years, these early agriculturalists slowly domesticated several plants, including squash, beans, chile peppers, and, most importantly, maize, or corn.

In due course, the development of more and more sophisticated agricultural practices allowed some nomadic tribes to break free from their constant search for food, which in turn permitted them to settle into increasingly sedentary village communities. The peoples of these nascent farming communities were able to develop larger tracts of cultivable land by burning off underbrush and jungle areas, terracing slopes, and draining and filling unsuitable wetlands, all of which led to the production of greater surpluses of food. Gradually, advances in agriculture, population growth, and the complexification of village life led naturally to the creation of political and social systems, law codes, and, of particular significance, religious systems.

Built on the foundational elements of polytheistic pantheons, pyramid temple structures, and rituals carried out by communal priests, or "shamans," the religious systems of ancestral Mesoamerican peoples became central components of their cultures. Properly performed under the leadership of the priests, religious rituals were thought to bind together human beings and the gods, ultimately guaranteeing the stability of the community. Priests were considered holy persons in these communities, as they filled the vastly important role of a special being that was able to move back and forth between the human and spiritual realms of existence. Because of the unique abilities possessed by the priests, they were responsible both for keeping the rulers and other people of their villages safe, as well as for ensuring that the many gods and goddesses of the various Mesoamerican pantheons looked favorably upon their respective communities. Toward this end, priests developed and performed sacred rituals, including human sacrifice, by which they sought to placate the gods and goddesses of such things as the sun, the moon, the annual harvest, rain, fertility, and war. They also presided over important community ceremonies related to birth, illness, and death, and were instrumental in guiding the construction of flat-top, pyramid-shaped structures that were considered sacred and served as centers for the worship of the gods.

Archeologists and historians generally divide pre-Columbian Mesoamerican cultures into three distinct periods of development: the Pre-Classic, or Formative period, extending from approximately 2000 BCE to100 CE; the Classic period, extending from 100-200 CE to approximately 900 CE; and the Post-Classic period, extending from 900 CE until the overthrow of the Aztec Empire in 1521. Although the different cultures that emerged in Mesoamerica during the Pre-Classic period all had distinctive features, they also had many things in common. All of these cultures, for instance, depended on maize as a food staple, as Mexicans still do today. They also cultivated agave plants for fiber and in order to produce a beer-like drink called *octli* or *pulque*; they developed religious systems that were polytheistic, with gods and goddesses that were generally connected to nature; they built truncated mound or step-pyramids that served as platforms for their temples; they had dual calendars; they developed highly stylized art and architecture; and most of them had outside "ball courts."

The oldest of the "civilized" Mesoamerican cultures is known as the Olmec, a somewhat mysterious people often understood as a sort of "parent" society for those that came after. Archeologists had long known about hundreds of small jade figurines that were characterized by a distinctive carved style emphasizing what appear to be infants with snarling, jaguar-like features, perhaps depicting the union between a primal woman and an earthly animal. These exquisite pieces were linked to the Olmeca, or "rubber people," who were said by the Aztecs to have inhabited the Gulf Coast regions of what is today southern Vera Cruz and neighboring Tabasco.

Although it is difficult to determine the exact date at which Olmec culture emerged, historians and archeologists believe that by the twelfth century BCE the area around San Lorenzo, Vera Cruz, was civilized by these enigmatic peoples. Emerging out of a village culture that was probably settled around 1700 BCE by Mixe-Zoqueans, but which had become thoroughly Olmec by 1500 BCE, the San Lorenzo community eventually grew into a sort of "state society" that included an administrative hierarchy, a standing army, calendar and writing systems, markets, and a large population of peasants who allowed the community to grow. Beyond the creation of the small, delicate figurines that were already mentioned, the Olmecs are probably best known as carvers of massive stone pieces, such as stelae (commemorative slabs or pillars), altars, and colossal heads, some of which were produced in San Lorenzo. The last of these, the colossal stone heads for which the Olmecs are perhaps most famous, are thought to be likenesses of certain rulers. Standing over nine feet high, the largest of these massive stone works weighs in excess of 40 tons.

By 900 BCE the San Lorenzo site was eclipsed by the one at La Venta, Tabasco. Here, while the Olmecs continued to create their superb carvings, they also began to produce a style of massive architecture. Of note in regard to this Olmec architectural style is La Venta's huge clay pyramid. Stretching to 110 feet, the mound-like structure was originally thought to have been built as a reflection of the nearby volcanic mountains. However, further archeological research has shown that the edifice was in fact initially a rectangular pyramid with stepped sides and inset corners. That this soaring pyramid was produced at this time, the largest to that point in Mesoamerican history, is significant, as it appears to indicate that the Olmec people were seeking to raise their temples to the sky in order to get nearer to the gods.

Emerging in relation to the Olmec cultures was the extremely advanced civilization of the Maya. The Maya envisioned themselves as existing within the latest of a vast number of historical time cycles. According to scholars, it is difficult to determine precisely when the unique "high culture" of the Maya began to emerge, as during the Late Pre-Classic Period the Maya were heavily influenced not only by the Olmecs but also by other cultures that existed at this point in Mesoamerican history. One of these was the Izapan, a people who are characterized by historians as occupying a sort of "middle ground in time and space" between the Pre-Classic Olmec and the Early Classic Maya. The creative hallmarks of the Izapan people included the production of more than 80 temple mounds at their capital city of Izapa and the development of an elaborate style of art, examples of which have been found spread over a wide-ranging area from Tres Zapotes on the Vera Cruz coast to the Pacific plain regions of Chiapas and Guatemala.

In examining Pre-Classic cultures like those of the Olmecs and the Izapans, it becomes apparent that the Mayan civilization did not arise in a vacuum, as it was clearly influenced by the ideas of other peoples. By the end of the Late Pre-Classic Period, however, during the second and third centuries CE, Mayan culture was on the threshold of what would become the Classic Mayan civilization. As we have seen, by this point the Maya were already making use of writing. In addition, they had already produced great temples and pyramids, involved themselves in tomb building, and begun to create frescoes and carvings with naturalistic subjects. The zenith of Mayan civilization, though, would be achieved during the Classic Period, roughly between 250 CE and 900 CE.

Within the vast geographical area occupied by the Maya, archeologists distinguish three regions where relatively diverse yet related cultures existed. In the "highlands" of central Guatemala, El Salvador, and Honduras, the Maya found fertile soil, a gentle climate, and sufficient resources to support a large population. The "low-lying" areas of the Yucatán peninsula, although a tropical plain that was virtually treeless and suffered from low soil deposits and little rainfall, still had enough sub-surface water and natural wells to make cultivation possible. Between the highlands and the Yucatan lies the third Mayan region, the central lowlands with its Petén jungle core and the adjacent upland area of Chiapas. This last area, seemingly the least hospitable for human settlement, as it is mostly covered by tropical forests interspersed with rivers and swamps and subject to heavy rainfall and humidity, turned out to be the area where Mayan civilization flourished.

We are fortunate enough to have a consistently dated archeological record of the Mayan civilization, inscribed on stelae and other monuments, spanning the Classic Period. It was during this period that the Maya built the great ceremonial centers at sites such as Bonampak, Copán, Palenque, Piedras Negras, and Tikal. Archeologists point to an elaborate series of causeways that connected some of these sites, facilitating the collection of tribute and allowing for trade. Significantly, these "cities" were not merely urban communities, but instead functioned as "civic-religious centers." Mayan societies were hierarchical, with a small group of elite hereditary nobility, made up of priests and ranking officials and their families, at the top; the majority of the population, consisting of craftsmen, commoners, and peasant farmers, in the middle; and at the bottom, a large contingent of slaves, which was made up of convicted criminals, prisoners of war, or sometimes people who had sold themselves into servitude.

There is still debate among scholars as to whether Mayan societies were theocratic, in other words, controlled by officials, usually priests, who were thought to be divinely inspired by the gods. Although there may have been a secular ruler and a high priest who served him, there was certainly a privileged hierarchy of priests within these societies whose responsibilities included prophesy, medicine, the education of candidates for the priesthood, and the performance of religious rituals. The last, the performance of religious rituals, was particularly important, as Mayan civilization gave expression to a fully developed pantheon of gods and goddesses who needed to be placated in order to assure the safety and stability of the community. As with earlier Mesoamerican cultures, the Mayan pantheon was dominated by nature divinities. The most ubiquitous of these were the Rain God, which some scholars believe may have been a transformation of one of the Olmec were-jaguars, and his consort, the Water Goddess. There was also a creator divinity, who was often depicted as an ancient Fire God, or sometimes as an old man and woman. In addition, there were the Sun God, the Moon Goddess, Ix Chill, and the Feathered Serpent, who would come to be known among the Aztecs as Quetzalcóatl.

Perhaps the greatness of Mayan civilization is most profoundly expressed in the construction of their city sites during the Classic Period. Of particular note at these Classic sites are the soaring pyramids that most often served as bases for temples, the cut-stone buildings that were probably used as civic headquarters and residences for officials, and the ball courts, plazas, stelae, and water-reservoirs, all of which were produced without metal tools. It is interesting to note the evolutionary variations in construction among the sites that were produced by the Maya over the span of this period. When speaking about the Classic Period in regard to the Maya, historians and archeologists generally divide this time span into two shorter periods: the Early Period, running roughly from 300 to 600 CE; and the Late Period, running from 600 to 900. The major difference between these two Classic Mayan "mini-periods," scholars suggest, is that during the first, the Mayan peoples of the eastern regions of Mesoamerica were profoundly influenced by the peoples of the extraordinary central valley culture of Teotihuacán.

As scholars point out, no other site of the early Classic Period, not even those of the Maya, rivaled the influence of the great capital city of Teotihuacán. Located some 40 miles northeast of Tenochtitlán, the ruins of Teotihuacán became a vastly important pilgrimage site for Aztec kings. This was because Teotihuacán played an important part in the creation myths of the Aztecs. Understanding that they were clearly not the first peoples to have occupied the central valley region, the Aztecs believed that they and the peoples who had come to Mexico before them traced their heritage to the mystical, primal land of Tamoanchan, a paradisiacal place inhabited by the gods and the ancestors of humans. The original civilization of Tamoanchan, the Aztecs believed, was ultimately transferred to Teotihuacán, where the gods met to determine which of them would sacrifice himself in order to become the new, Fifth Sun. The most humble of the gods, Nanahuatzin, was said to have cast himself into the cosmic flames, becoming the sun. For some reason, though, the heavens did not move, requiring all of the gods to sacrifice themselves as a gift to human kind so that the era of the Fifth Sun could begin.

The Aztecs ultimately found the ruins of what was the fully urbanized capital city of Teotihuacán when they arrived in the central valley of Mexico. The city had emerged in the first century CE as the largest site in the pre-Columbian world. Covering some eight square miles, Teotihuacán was split by a major axis known as the Avenue of the Dead. Today, a two-mile long avenue extends from the Pyramid of the Moon at the northern end of the site, past the monumental Pyramid of the Sun lying to the east of the avenue, all the way to the Ciudadela ("Citadel") complex dominated by the Temple of Quetzalcóatl at the southern end of the site. Scholars now know that this main avenue originally extended up to four miles and was bisected in front of the Ciudadela complex by an east-west avenue of equal length, creating a city structure that, like the Aztec capital of Tenochtitlán, was laid out in quarters.

Although much smaller than the Pyramids of the Moon and the Sun, the Temple of Quetzalcóatl is of particular significance in relation to the Maya due to its architectural style and the lavish façade decoration that adorns its seven-tiered step-pyramid exterior. The Temple itself is built in a stepped platform style with the typical *talud-tablero* motif (a rectangular, inset panel, the *tablero*, placed over a low, sloped wall, the *talud*). Carved around the tiers of the structure are Feathered Serpents that carry mosaic headdresses, which in other places in Teotihuacán are shown on the heads of warriors. Seashells are also carved into the background of the tiers, suggesting that the scene is taking place in a watery environment, perhaps a primal ocean in which the Temple's opposing serpents, one representing life, greenness, and peace, the other, heat, the desert, and war, frolic and converse with each other.

From the capital city site in the central valley of Mexico, Teotihuacán influence radiated out into the Early Classic Mayan areas of Mesoamerica. Scholars suggest that shortly after 400 CE, for example, the Mayan highlands fell under the control of peoples from Teotihuacán. Most probably, a powerful group of intruders from the central Mexico city overwhelmed the Mayan site of Kaminaljuyú and there built a scaled-down version of their own capital. Interestingly, the elite central valley rulers that administered to the captive Mayan population in Kaminaljuyú were eventually "swayed by native cultural tastes and traditions," becoming "Mayanized" to the point where they began to import pottery and other wares back to the central valley in order to stock their tombs at Teotihuacán. Yet this "hybrid" culture, controlled by Teotihuacáns and known as the Esperanza, produced temple complexes in Kaminaljuyú that were not in the least typical of what would become the unique Mayan architectural style. These Esperanzan structures are reflective of the stepped temple platforms of Teotihuacán, with a *talud-tablero* motif. A single stairway ran up the front of the structure, while the temple sanctuary on top carried either a thatched roof or more often the flat-beamed-and-mortar construction characteristic of Teotihuacán.

In the central Petén area, the Mayan civilization was in full bloom by the Early Classic Period. Here, archeologists have found enormous ceremonial centers filled with masonry temples and "palaces" that look out on to plazas covered with white stucco; stelae and altars that are inscribed with dates and embellished with images of men and what appear to be gods; and polychrome pottery emphasizing Mayan style images of cranes, parrots, or men on bowls with a "kind of apron" encircling the lower part. Along with these purely Mayan ceramics, though, are vessels that are marked by the imprint of Teotihuacán: the cylindrical vase, supported by three legs, and the small spouted jug. In Tikal, a major center in the Petén area, a great Mayan conquest during the Early Classic Period was celebrated by the construction of what archeologists point out is a very "non-Mayan structure." Here, once again, there is an altar-platform in the purest Teotihuacán style, complete with the *talud-tablero*.

All of this would begin to change for the Mayan civilization with the mysterious fall of Teotihuacán sometime around 600 CE. Scholars are still unsure what caused the collapse of this great capital city, but at some point the city was deliberately burned, the blaze destroying mainly the temples and palaces along the Avenue of the Dead. Perhaps internal crises, or disruption of trade and tribute routes, or what historians suggest may have been a "long-term political and economic malaise," caused the collapse of this important central valley site. Whatever the cause, though, scholars believe that by the early seventh century CE, "almost all Teotihuacán influence over the rest of Mesoamerica ceases."[2]

The fall of Teotihuacán would have important implications for the development of Late Classic period Mayan civilization.

Lying at the foot of a chain of low hills and covered with a tall rain forest, Palenque is considered by some as the most beautiful of the Mayan sites. Visiting the site today, one finds brightly colored macaws and parrots in the high trees, and on rainy days one may be treated to the strange roar of howler monkeys near the ruins. Of the temple-pyramids built at the site, those dedicated to the Sun, the Cross, and the Foliated Cross are of particular note. These structures are arranged around a plaza on the eastern side of the site, each resting on a stepped platform with a frontal stairway and an inner and outer vaulted room. In the rear of each of the inner vaulted rooms is a low relief tablet inscribed with long hieroglyphic texts and carved in the same motif: "two Mayan men, one taller than the other, facing each other on either side of a ceremonial object." In the Temple of the Sun, "the most perfect of Mayan buildings," the centrally placed object is the mask of the Jaguar God of the Underworld, "the sun in its night aspect, before two crossed spears."[3]

One more of the uniquely Mayan structures of the Late Classic Period located at Palenque is the incredible palace that graces the site. This palace is a labyrinthine structure, extending some 300 feet in length and 240 feet in width, and consisting of a series of "vaulted galleries and rooms arranged about interior courtyards or patios," which are dominated by a "unique four-story square tower with an interior stairway." Of particular significance in regard to this ruin are the "grotesque reliefs" that are arranged along the sides of the palace's two patios. These reliefs bear the images of prisoners showing submission to their captives in the usual way, one hand raised to the opposite shoulder, indicating that the palace may have been the place to which captives were taken to be tortured and sacrificed.

Of the discoveries in the Mayan area, few can rank with the murals that were found at the site at Bonampak. The site was revealed to non-Mayan eyes only in 1946, when two "American adventurers" were taken there by Lacandón Indians with whom they had been living. A short time later, a photographer named Giles Healey was taken to the site by another group of Natives, becoming the first "outsider" to view the extraordinary paintings that adorn three of the walls of one of the center's structures. As scholars point out, the Bonampak murals, which, based on Long Count inscriptions and stylistic considerations, can be dated to approximately 800 CE, give expression to a single narrative: "a story of battle, its aftermath, and the victory celebrations."

Ironically, although Mayan civilization in the Central area reached its greatest heights during the eighth century, the causes of its collapse must already have been apparent during this period. For in "the hundred or more years that followed," all of the area's magnificent cities had declined sharply and were ultimately abandoned. This was not the case in all areas, as during this period the Maya exerted an incredible influence over the Gulf Coast, an influence that even spread into the central highlands of Mexico. Interestingly, in the northern Mayan regions, cities achieved a "remarkable florescence" during this period, finally falling only to foreign invasion. The period from 800 CE to roughly 925, then, proved to be a era of both "tragedy and triumph," an era in which "thrones toppled in the south as a new political order took shape in the north, in which southern cities fell into the dust as northern ones flourished." Ultimately, this would be a time of the widespread movements of peoples; a time during which the fate of Mesoamerica and the Mayan areas was determined, setting the stage for the rise of the next great power in Mexico, the Toltecs.[4]

In many ways, the Toltec Empire binds together the cultures of the Classic Period with those of the Post-Classic, and in particular with the Aztec Empire. Not a great deal is known about who the Toltecs actually were, for although we have some archeological evidence and legendary historical information about these peoples, the myths about them tend to be inextricably woven through what has come down to us as their "history." The creation of this mytho-history, unfortunately, has left us with conflicting accounts about the Toltecs, some of which appear to have been borrowed from other cultures. In addition, a number of the Toltec leaders bore the same name, a problem that is further complicated because as priest-kings, many of them took the name of the god they served and whose attributes they assumed. This makes it difficult to distinguish between actual historical figures, some of whom were deified after their deaths, and figures that existed for the Toltecs only as transcendent beings.

As was mentioned in the introduction, between the fall of Teotihuacán and the rise of the Aztec Empire, bands of warriors known as *Chichimecs* swept down from the northern sections of Mexico into the central valley region. Foremost among these nomadic peoples were the Toltec-Chichimec, or the Toltecs, who originally settled in Culhuacán. Under their enlightened and peaceful king Topiltzin, they relocated their capital city to Tula, a site about 50 miles north of what would become Tenochtitlán and not far from the ruins of Teotihuacán. Scholars believe that with the rise to power of the more militant factions in Tula, which again were comprised mainly of the followers of Tezcatlipoca, who, as we have seen, eventually toppled the monarchy of Topiltzin, the Toltecs became much more fearsome in character. This new sense of Toltec ferocity was given expression in both the bas-relief friezes depicting the military orders of the jaguar and the eagle that adorned their pyramids, and in the towering statues of impassive yet frightening warriors that were mounted on top of these pyramids.

It is probably under the bloody rule of the Tezcatlipoca party in Tula that the Toltecs experienced their greatest period of expansion, ultimately creating a tributary empire that stretched across most of central Mexico. Historians and archeologists point to the years between CE 950 and 1150 as the time during which the capital city, which was certainly one of the largest, if not the largest in Mesoamerica at the time, experienced its principal occupation, and when the construction of the monumental civic-religious center called Tula Grande was carried out. At some point during the twelfth century, scholars believe, Tula seems to have suffered a series of catastrophic events leading to the dispersal of many of its inhabitants and the decline and eventual collapse of its imperial power. It is not clear what these destructive events were, although we do know that the ceremonial halls of the city were burned to the ground and that its great Serpent Wall was toppled. Perhaps the death of the city was due to invasion and conquest by one or more of the bands of Chichimecs who were again pushing down from the northwest. Whatever happened at Tula, the Toltecs finally fell, giving rise to an extended period of bloody conflict, one that did not end until the Aztecs brought together one of the world's most powerful confederacies during the fifteenth century.

The Aztecs

The accounts provided to us by Aztec historians depict the initial stages of a nation that are so "humble and obscure," with a culture only a few generations removed from "abject barbarism," that it is difficult to understand how these people eventually came to dominate most of Mexico. Although the origins of the Aztec rise to power are still not clear, scholars generally agree on the broad outlines of the narrative. With the fall of Tula, a power vacuum was created in the central valley region of Mexico. Nahuatl-speaking *Chichimecas* from the north poured into the valley, creating an extremely populous region in which invading groups attempted to stake their claim to particular territorial areas. The invading *Chichimecas* probably settled in urban areas that initially had been settled by Toltec peoples who had been dispersed after the collapse of Tula, but who had kept their cultural heritage alive. As has happened over and over, the nomadic groups were gradually assimilated into the culture of the more advanced and sedentary peoples they encountered.

Of these *Chichimec* groups that made their way south into the valley of Mexico, one, of course, concerns us above all others. Calling themselves the "Mexica" (pronounced Meheeka), this nomadic assembly came to be known as the Aztecs. Latecomers on this turbulent scene, the Aztecs were the last important group to enter the valley. Although they began to be recognized as a significant people some 200 years before the Spanish arrived, their real rise to power did not occur until the century before the invasion of Cortez in 1519.

As with the Toltecs before them, it is difficult to tease apart the "history" of the Aztecs from the mythology that has grown up around them. Some of this is due to the unreliability of the historical legends that were created about the Aztecs beginning during the years immediately following the Spanish conquest. Much of it, though, is due to the Aztecs rewriting their own history once they became secure in the central valley. This was done in order to depict themselves in a more favorable light in regard to their conquest of other peoples, as well as in an attempt to define a dynastic line that linked the Aztecs back to the Toltecs.

Aztec historians tell us that the earthly roots of the Mexica can be traced back to the mythical land of Aztlán (Place of Reeds), which was said to exist somewhere on the northwestern coast of Mexico. In the year 1111 CE, spurred on by the terrible god of the sun and war, Huitzilopochtli (Hummingbird of the Left, or Hummingbird of the South), who claimed that they would ultimately subdue all others and conquer the world, the Aztecs left Aztlán and began to make their way down toward the valley of Mexico. Their arrival in the central valley proved less than auspicious, as by the time the

Aztecs appeared there in the late thirteenth century, the entire region had already been carved up and claimed by other groups. The new band of wanderers was perceived by those who had previously settled the area as a group of uncultured squatters, and they were urged to move on. Particularly disturbing to the much more refined inhabitants of the valley area were the Aztec practices of stealing the wives of their neighbors and, especially, the bloody human sacrifices they performed in order to placate their god Huitzilopochtli.

However repulsed the inhabitants of the valley were by the Aztec intruders, they eventually came to respect them, if only because they were forced to by these young, militant people. From the last third of the thirteenth century until 1319, the Aztecs existed on the margins of Mexican society, occupying the hill of Chapultepec, which is today a park in Mexico City. Continuing their fierce practices, they finally angered the leaders of several of the surrounding towns, leading them to form a coalition of forces that was used to drive the intruders from Chapultepec. To ensure that they understood completely that they were no longer welcome in the area, the Aztec chieftain and his daughter were executed. The survivors of the coalition attack hid themselves in the rushes along the shores of the lakes that dotted the valley region, where they remained until it was safe to emerge.

Upon emerging from their hiding places, the Aztecs found themselves subject to the rule of Coxcox, the king of Culhuacán. Displaying his beneficence, Coxcox gave them the dubious gift of a dusty, rattlesnake-infested plot of land on which to settle. Legend has it that the Aztecs were undaunted by this turn of events, actually enjoying the rattlesnake meat that the area provided. Biding their time, they waited for an opportune moment to assert themselves. This moment came when Coxcox promised them their freedom and better land if they assisted him in subduing the rival city of Xochimilco. The Aztecs proved how valuable they could be, and how frightening, when they presented a much disturbed Coxcox with sacks containing the ears of 8,000 Xochimilcas.

Making good on his promise after Xochimilco was defeated, the king promptly freed the Aztecs and gave them better land to settle. Pressing their newly won advantage, the Aztecs prevailed upon Coxcox to give them his daughter. She would become the Aztec queen, they said, and be made into a goddess. Coxcox agreed and his daughter was given over to his new allies. Seeking to demonstrate their independence, though, the Aztecs sacrificed and flayed the princess. To the horror of her father, he found himself at a celebratory banquet, given in his honor, at which the entertainment included the dance of a priest who presented himself to the king dressed in the skin of his slain daughter.

The outraged Coxcox raised an army and attacked the Aztecs. Defeated and dispersed, the Aztecs again proved resilient, once more hiding themselves in the reeds that bordered the central valley lakes. This time, though, they took advantage of their situation. Realizing that no one paid much attention to them in their marshy lakeside abode, the Aztecs sustained themselves by way of the abundant fish, fowl, and other game that populated the region. Unmolested, they finally claimed a small island area at the southwestern edge of Lake Texcoco in 1325. Through trade, they quickly started to acquire the materials needed to expand their tiny, burgeoning empire. Dredging the lake bottom in order to provide more surface soil and building causeways that stretched to the mainland, the Aztecs now began to put down the foundations of what would become the glorious city of Tenochtitlán.

The development of the Aztec island, no matter how humble, eventually drew the attention of Tezozómoc, the ruler of Anáhuac. Concerned by the activity of the Aztecs, he brought them under his control and used them as mercenaries. Although he made unreasonable tribute demands on the Aztecs, Tezozómoc was wise enough not to push these dangerous people beyond their limits. Gradually the Aztecs were accepted as minor partners, and were finally given permission by Tezozómoc to establish a "royal dynasty." In 1376, Acamapichtli became the first ruler of the Aztecs, and until the death of Tezozómoc in 1426, the two groups maintained a peaceful, if cautious relationship.

By the time of Tezozómoc's death, the Aztecs were prospering, and it was around this time that they elected the powerful Itzcóatl as their ruler. Although his strong leadership led to Aztec independence and the expansion of trade, a power struggle ensued among the central valley communities, ultimately necessitating the establishment of a triple alliance among the cities of Tenochtitlán, Texcoco, and the weakest of the three, Tlacopan. Together, the cities of Tenochtitlán, Texcoco, and Tlacopan would come to control all of central Mexico. Although for a time Texcoco proved to be powerful enough to maintain a position of equality with Tenochtitlán, in the end, the Aztecs would finally come to dominate the alliance. Indeed, from their capital city of Tenochtitlán, they would eventually expand their influence over most of Mexico. Of particular importance in regard to this expansion was the rise to power of Moctezuma I, who became the ruler of his people after Itzcóatl's death in 1440. Even before he began his 28-year rule as king, Moctezuma I had already won the respect of his people, for as a ferocious general, he had won a series of devastating victories as the Aztecs extended their imperial control to the south and northeast of Tenochtitlán. Once he became king, Moctezuma I was also instrumental in pushing the Aztecs toward becoming a cohesive, formalized state society.

By the beginning of the sixteenth century, the densely populated island site of Tenochtitlán covered roughly five square miles, occupying most of what is today the center of Mexico City. Alive with activity, the city had numerous market-places, which historians believe accommodated up to 60,000 people every day. It was also home to a vast *zócalo*, or square, where daily, thousands gathered to barter or simply to visit with each other. The square bordered the *Templo Mayor*, the extremely important double pyramid dedicated to Huitzilopochtli and Tláloc. When the Spanish arrived in Tenochtitlán they were both mesmerized by the lavish temples of the gods and the royal palaces of the nobles and horri-fied at the sight of the *tzompantli*, the giant stone rack on which thousands of human skulls were displayed.

From the central district of Tenochtitlán the city extended out to the residences of the nobles. The rulers of the Empire, as well as their families, were naturally part of the noble class, which existed at the highest level of the Aztec state society. Royal offspring were numerous, as the leading nobles often took many wives and produced many children. The wives of royals were considered privileged persons in the community and their advice was taken seriously and appreciated at court. Emperors were always chosen from the royal family, although unlike most monarchies, it was not always the king's son who became the next ruler, but the best male candidate, a policy in keeping with the Aztec notion of the "recognition of merit over birth."

The vast majority of the Aztec population was identified with the community's huge middle class, which was principally made up of farmers, laborers, minor craftsmen, and servants. These middle-class Aztecs were divided up into wards or districts called *calpullis*—what the Spanish called *barrios*—which consisted of several thousand households and a local temple dedicated to the patron deity of the community. Each *calpulli* represented a close-knit unit that lived, fought, and worshipped together. The unit was responsible for portioning out commonly held land to family heads for their use, as well as for choosing a "captain" who served as both an administrative leader and a military commander and who was responsi-ble for keeping the order and maintaining the safety of those who lived in the district. Below these commoners on the socioeconomic scale were the slaves. Slavery in Aztec culture was different from that which marked the United States, as slaves in the Aztec world had certain rights, one of those being that their servitude was not passed down from generation to generation. In fact, some slaves entered into contractual agreements with their masters, much like the system of indentured servitude that characterized colonial America, allowing them to serve for a certain length of time before they were freed. In the end, most forms of Aztec slavery did not lead those who served, or their children, to be stigmatized; a prime example of this was the rise to power of Itzcóatl, a king who was born to a mother who had once been a slave.

A different category of servitude existed for those who were captured in battle and destined for sacrifice. As we have seen, human sacrifice was certainly not unique to the Aztecs, as a number of other Mesoamerican cultures had involved themselves in this practice long before the Mexica arrived on the scene. But again, even as the Aztecs were making their way to what would become Tenochtitlán, they sacrificed humans to their god Huitzilopochtli in order to ensure their safety. The mythology that produced this practice is interesting. First, the Aztecs understood the beginning of their cycle of the Fifth Sun to have been brought about by the beneficent gift of the cosmic sacrifice of the gods. If the gods were willing to sacrifice themselves for the people, they reasoned, how could the people not be willing to sacrifice themselves for the gods? Second, it should be remembered that the Aztecs believed that the cycles of the four Suns that had proceeded the age of the Fifth Sun had ended in cataclysmic moments during which the entire universe was destroyed. The recreated universe of the Fifth Sun was destined to suffer its own traumatic end, an event that could only be delayed by way of the intervention of the gods. Human sacrifice, then, was necessary in order to appease powerful divinities such as Huitzilopochtli, Tláloc, Tezcatlipoca and Quetzalcóatl, and to keep them on the side of the Aztecs in the great cosmic war that was being waged over the Fifth Sun.

Significantly, the rapid growth of the Aztec Empire had been checked during the middle of the fifteenth century by natural disasters that caused a "catastrophic famine." Believing that their lack of food was a result of divine wrath, the Aztecs expanded their practice of human sacrifice in order to placate the gods. When the situation did not abate, and in fact became worse as desperate animals came down out of the mountains and began to feed on humans, people went so far as to sell themselves as slaves to the Totonacs of the Gulf Coast, an area that had not been affected by the famine. The increasingly desperate plight of the Aztecs led the priests to perform still greater numbers of human sacrifice. Once the famine ended, the priests attributed the community's reversal of fortunes to their own sacred sacrificial practices.

Having defined the sacrifice of humans as a foundational element of their communal and even cosmic existence, it is not surprising that the Aztecs came to believe that sacrificial blood was necessary in order to carry out their imperial expansion. This was especially the case as Aztec rule passed through three of the sons of Moctezuma I, Axayácatl, Tizoc, and Ahuítzotl. The last of these, Ahuítzotl, who came to power in 1486, was a particularly fierce ruler. Leading a series of wide-ranging military expeditions, he stormed into and conquered the valley of Oaxaca, drove down the Pacific coast to Guatemala, and finally forced his way into the Gulf Coast region of Mexico. His merciless rule allowed the Aztecs not only to expand the area that they controlled, but also to extract greater tribute payments from those who had been conquered.

By the time Ahuítzotl died in 1502, Aztec rule extended over several hundred city-states or "ethnic kingdoms." Interestingly, while the peoples of a city state, or *altepetl*, paid tribute to their Aztec rulers, Aztec imperialism was really a system of "conquest without consolidation." As historians Geoffrey Conrad and Arthur Demarest point out:

> . . . the "Aztec Empire" was not really an "empire" at all, at least not in the usual sense of the term. Rather, it was a loose hegemony of city-states pledging obedience and tribute to [Tenochtitlán]. After defeating the armies of a region, the Mexica would take hundreds or thousands of the foreign warriors as captives to be sacrificed at Tenochtitlán. Then they would install a ruler—often of the very dynasty they had just defeated—on the throne of the subjugated province. No real attempt was made to assimilate the conquered peoples, either culturally or politically. The only real change in the vanquished state would be the onerous periodic tribute payments that had to be paid. . . . By leaving the local leadership structure intact, the Aztecs minimized their administrative problems, but they also increased the possibility of rebellion. Indeed, such insurrections, usually initiated by murdering the local Aztec tribute collectors, were common occurrences. Previously subjugated regions had to be reconquered again and again.[5]

When the ill-fated Moctezuma II came to power after the death of Ahuítzotl in 1502, he ruled over a vast, but relatively unstable imperial region, one which consisted of the modern states of Mexico, Morelos, Puebla, Hidalgo, most of Vera Cruz, much of Oaxaca and Guerrero, and the coastal areas of Chiapas. If, as some historians and archeologists believe, the "empire" of Moctezuma II consisted of a population of nearly 30 million people, it means that he ruled over a country that was larger than any in Europe at the beginning of the sixteenth century, as France at this time had only 20 million people and Spain probably not more than 10 million. His enormous power and prestige allowed him to lead a lifestyle that can only be described as perversely luxurious. Three thousand servants attended him in his huge palace; and although it is said that when he ate, he "ate sparingly," taking his meals alone and behind a screen, each day he was presented with 100 different dishes from which to choose. He also had his choice of women, and for his pleasure, he was entertained by dwarfs, jesters, tumblers, acrobats, musicians, and dancers. His subjects were not allowed to look directly at him, nor could they turn their backs on him.

Heralded for his bravery in leading successful military campaigns into Mixtec and Mayan areas, Moctezuma II was also highly respected for his comprehensive knowledge of Mexican history. Ironically, although it was admirable that the king was so well informed in regard to his people's past, possessing the particulars of this historical narrative may have proved troubling for Moctezuma II. After all, knowing what he knew, the king must have been well aware both that the cataclysmic destruction of the Fifth Sun was inevitable and also that the great Quetzalcóatl had promised that he would one day return to reclaim his rightful throne. Strange phenomenon, interpreted by his priests as "evil portents," must have also disturbed the king: "Lightning, unaccompanied by thunder, 'like a blow from the sun,' damaged a temple; a strange bird was found with a 'mirror in its head,' in which Moctezuma saw a host of foreign warriors. In 1517 a comet appeared 'like a flaming ear of corn . . . it seemed to bleed fire, drop by drop, like a wound in the sky." Most chillingly, Moctezuma's agents reported seeing "towers or small mountains floating on the waves of the sea." Then, in 1519, the Aztec year of Ce Acatl, Moctezuma experienced a profound sense of dread when "a courier arrived bearing ominous paintings—they depicted the encampment on Aztec shores of bearded white men with crosses."[6]

The Incas

The southern neighbors of the Aztecs, the mighty Incas, trace their roots back to peoples who found their way to the rugged regions of western South America thousands of years before the Common Era. Wandering along the Pacific coast, certain of these peoples finally settled in the Andes mountain region of what is today Peru. It was here that the Incas would ultimately build their great capital city of Cuzco. Like the ancestral peoples of the Aztecs, the ancestors of the

Incas initially formed into family groups and tribal bands of nomadic hunters and gatherers, and, as with the peoples of Mesoamerica, those who wandered in and around the Andean region of Peru gradually became agricultural.

Historians and archeologists divide Andean history across an evolutionary chronology that is similar to that which they use to define the early history of Mesoamerica. This Andean chronology is defined in relation to the following, sometimes roughly dated periods: the Preceramic, extending from 2500–1800 BCE; the Initial, extending from 1800–800 BCE; the Early Horizon, extending from 800 BCE into the first century CE; the Early Intermediate, extending from 100–700 CE; the Middle Horizon, extending from 700–1000 CE; the Late Intermediate, extending from 1000–1400/1500 CE; the Late Horizon, extending from 1500–1532 CE; and the Colonial, after 1532 CE.

Somewhere around 2500 BCE, at the beginning of the Preceramic Period, nomadic groups in the Andean region were increasingly settled into more and more complex village communities. As early as this Preceramic Period, the peoples of western South America had domesticated crops, created Chiefdom-ruled political organizations, and constructed their first "monumental" architectural structures, such as small pyramids.

Not long after this, during the Initial Period, between 1800 and 800 BCE, certain groups settled the inland parts of Andean valleys and began to create incredibly elaborate ceremonial complexes, in addition to developing the agricultural systems that would eventually feed the huge populations of the Inca Empire. Significantly, similarities in design among as many as 45 of these ceremonial centers indicate that the architects and builders of the structures on these sites shared a certain homogeneous understanding of the cosmos. As scholars point out, the "visual imagery of the pyramids was truly imposing," displaying "pillared entrances, stairwells, brilliant friezes," and, at the site of Cerro Sechín, a "gruesome parade of warriors and dismembered human bodies." From examples such as that at Cerro Sechín, scholars conclude that even before the beginning of the Common Era, war and human sacrifice were important elements in solidifying political power across the Andean region.[7]

The Early Horizon Period, stretching over the last centuries before the Common Era from roughly 800 BCE to 100 CE, was marked by the creation of religious iconography, now increasingly oriented around sacred cults, as well as by a significant growth in craft technology, including advances in the production of ornately modeled and incised pieces and the development of metallurgy that allowed for soldering, and silver-gold alloying. It was also during this period, some suggest, that the most dazzling of the Andean textiles were produced.

As Andean cultures evolved from the Early Horizon to the Early Intermediate Period, the first true state and urban communities appear. A number of unique "state societies" emerge during this era, among them those at Nasca on the southern coast of Peru, at Recuay in the northern highlands, and in particular, at Moche on the northern coast. Archeological evidence from Moche suggests that here priestly, political, military, and social roles were woven together without the people of the community defining distinct administrative positions. Moche was also home to the greatest adobe pyramid ever raised in the native Americas, containing as it did 143 million bricks. Pyramid structures like that at Moche were extremely important in Andean communities, as they represented some of the most elaborate burial sites found in South America.

That unique cultures, such as those at Moche, Wari, and Tiwanaku, developed in the Andean world during the first thousand years of the Common Era is significant in relation to the Incas. As scholars point out, by 1000 CE the political environment in the region was extremely fragmented and diverse, and as late as 1200 CE, war raged from southern Ecuador to Argentina. In order to protect themselves from these conflicts, many peoples in the region settled in isolated villages well above the best valley farmlands. A number of the most powerful of these societies, such as the Lopaqa and the Qolla, established themselves in the areas around Lake Titicaca. Although these peoples reported to the Spanish that their rulers were kings, it is doubtful that these societies ever attained a "state" level of organization. Groups that settled in the populous region of the Peruvian sierra may have produced village communities with as many as 4,500 domiciles, housing up to 10,000 people. Most of the villages in the area of the southern Andes probably contained no more than 1,000 residents, with the largest, regional centers consisting of perhaps 20,000 people. Interestingly, by 1200 CE the area around what would become the capital city of Cuzco may already have been integrated into an organized state society, setting the scene for the meteoric rise of the Inca.

Scholars have had a difficult time establishing an historical timeline in regard to the Incas. Reasons include the lack of an indigenous writing system, the reconstruction of history for political reasons, and the way that the Andean peoples envisioned time. Even so, most scholars believe that the reign of the Inca, for all its magnificence, was a short-lived phenomenon, extending for no more than a century between the 1430s CE and the 1532 Spanish invasion. Most authorities point to the 1586 chronicle of the cleric Miguel de Cabello Valboa to substantiate this claim. Valboa suggested that Inca imperial rule began in 1438 when the Incas repelled an attack by the Chankas, a group that lived in the areas around Cuzco. He calculated that the next three Inca successions occurred in 1471, 1493, and 1526. Although the sources used by Valboa are not known, there is independent corroboration of his dates, as other chroniclers reported that Inca rule extended from the reign of Pachakuti Inka Yupanki beginning in 1438, through that of Thupa Inka Yupanki beginning in 1471 and Wayna Qhapaq beginning in 1493, to the period of the civil war between Wayna Qhapaq's sons, Atawallpa and Waskhar, somewhere around the time of the Spanish invasion.

With D'Altroy's caveat in mind, then, one turns to the history of the Incas cautiously. The Inca literally divided their world into four parts (*suyu*), with the political and social center at Cuzco. Indeed, the Inca name for their realm, *Tawantinsuyu*, means the "four parts." The upper level of the Inca political structure was comprised of four "lords" who ruled over the respective divisions of the empire and who acted as advisors to the emperor in Cuzco. The most populous of the four parts of the Inca realm was *Chinchaysuyu*, which was named after the highly respected Chincha *etnía*, or ethnic group, of the south-central region of Peru, an area that stretched across the Peruvian coast, the adjacent highlands, and the northern Andes. *Antisuyu*, which was named for the "warm forests of the montaña, known in Hispanic form as the *Andes*," was located to the northeast of Cuzco. *Kollasuyu*, which extended from Peru's southern highlands "through the antiplano all the way to central Chile and adjacent Argentina," represented the largest geographical part of the empire. The smallest part of the realm was *Cuntisuyu*, which claimed only a small stretch of land extending from Cuzco to the Pacific.

Beyond the basic political units of the monarch and his lords, the Inca world was defined by a complex hierarchical system that "fused Inca kinship and ancestor worship with ethnicity and a rigid class structure." Interestingly, in the Inca realm, both mummies of "long-dead kings and queens" and "oracular idols" participated in communal activities by way of cults formed by their descendents. Although the Spanish would point to this practice as a clear example of the "handiwork of the Devil," the Incas understood it as perfectly natural, as the world was certainly "shared by the living, the dead, the gods, and the spirits." As with the Aztecs, the king, along with his royal family, was granted a position at the apex of the Inca social order. Although two classes of "aristocratic Inca kin" and an "honorary class of Inca nobility" existed alongside the royal leader, the king was considered not only to be the absolute ruler of the Inca state, but also to be a divine being that possessed a heavenly mandate to govern the world. Yet even though accorded this special status, each of the all-too-human Inca rulers was forced to rely heavily on his advisors and to work closely with what proved to be a "contentious aristocracy" in order to maintain control of his realm.

Unlike the Aztecs, the Incas drew no distinction among positions of power, and thus the king generally "melded political, social, military and sacred leadership in a single person." For the Incas, the ideal ruler would pass through three stages during his lifetime: initially he would prove himself to be a brave warrior, earning the respect and support of the "noble kin" of Cuzco; once he had been anointed the "Sun to rule the land," he would be revered as a god who had been blessed with powers greater than those of any other being who "walked the earth"; finally, in death, he would be exalted as a being with "great vitality," one who "feasted and conversed with the quick and the dead by day and retired to his quarters for repose at night." Again, from his "sanctified plane," an Inca emperor who had died continued to participate in his community's political and social activities, a point that will be discussed momentarily. The mummies of rulers, although for a time stored in specially constructed chapels, were ultimately kept either in the houses of their descendents or in "sanctuaries on royal estates."

By the time the Spanish arrived in 1532, the High Priest of the Sun was probably the second-most-powerful person in the Inca community. According to several chroniclers, the position was elevated during the reign of Pachakuti. Although part of the power of the High Priest came from his role in selecting the next king, the priests of both Atawallpa and Manqo Inka were also "field marshals in the last dynastic war and the neo-Inca era, respectively." Again, although the king was the absolute ruler of the Inca realm, he was surrounded by royal kin groups, or *panaqa*. Because the *panaqa* were also instrumental in choosing the next ruler, they possessed a great deal of power in Inca society. Significantly, the highest ranking of these aristocratic Incas were those who were kin to the current king, not kin to the most ancient ruler.

The vast majority of the Inca population, as many as 95–98 percent, consisted of peasant families living in towns and villages. This group was made up of farmers, herders, fishermen, and artisans. Again, above the level of the basic family unit, the people of the community were divided into kin groups known as *ayllu*. Generally, the *ayllu* was a group of people that traced its line of descent to a particular common ancestor. The men of the kin group were arranged "patrilineally," the women "matrilineally," and there were certain marriage taboos that defined the *ayllu*. In addition to defining Inca kin groups, the term *ayllu* was also used to describe basic landholding groups in the community. Each *ayllu* owned a designated tract of land and members of individual families within the group cultivated as much of this land as they needed to sustain themselves. The members of each *ayllu* maintained a series of "reciprocal obligations," which they were required to honor. These included helping other members of the group build houses and cultivate land, and also providing communal support for the elderly, the infirm, widows, and orphans.

Of particular significance in regard to the *ayllu* was the responsibility that its members bore for cultivating land in order to provide food both for sacrifices and to support the group's shrines and deities. In an interesting way, these "sacred" uses of property reveal an important connection that the members of Inca *ayllus* had to the pan-Andean practice of ancestor worship. Most typically, when an individual died in Andean cultures, some of his or her property was burned and some was buried with the deceased. After the burial ceremony, descendants of the deceased visited the tomb in order to renew offerings of food, drink, and clothing. The bodies of the deceased were taken from the tombs so that these revered beings could participate in the processions and festivals for the dead. A kin group that ignored these rituals would risk angering the ancestors, possibly bringing harm upon the community. This was certainly the case in regard to the Inca *ayllus*, as these kin groups were responsible for supporting the ancestors by designating for cultivation certain parcels of land "inherited" from the deceased in order to support the dead. This practice, termed "split inheritance," was especially important in relation to the property rights of kings after they died. Because Inca rulers were thought to be divine beings, they possessed vast amounts of personal wealth, which split inheritance allowed them to retain even after they were dead. When a king died, his "principal heir," a son or another qualified family member, would take over his governmental position and all of the duties that went with it, but would acquire no "material legacy from his predecessor." Rather, the ruler's personal wealth would be given over to his "secondary heirs," the members of his royal kin group, or *panaqa*, not as their own, but in "trust" where it remained vested in the dead king.

Again, when the Spanish entered Cuzco in 1532, they found mummified kings still occupying their palaces. This, it may be said, can be understood as a literal expression of both the Inca practice of ancestor worship and of split inheritance, as the dead king was still thought to be a "living," and vital member of the community who needed to be supported in death as he was in life. The Spanish found this practice so strange that they spent a good deal of time describing it in their reports and diaries.

The significance of this communal treatment of dead kings as sacred beings cannot be overstated in regard to understanding the Inca. Indeed, it has everything to do with what may be considered the "great integrating concept of Inca religion," the notion of *huaca*, or "embodied holiness." Understood in its most specific sense, the term *huaca* refers to a person, place, or thing with sacred or supernatural connections. In a more generally way, though, the concept was used to identify almost anything that was considered odd or abnormal. Because of this, the number of *huaca* in the Inca world was staggering. All *huaca*, whether people, alive or dead, shrines, or sites in nature, were considered to possess "oracular powers," and they were "worshipped with prayers and sacrifices."

As one might expect, the notion of *huaca* was inextricably bound to the Inca vision of the gods. By the time the Inca imperial world began to be defined in the fifteenth century, these peoples had come to believe that their rulers and their culture in general had descended from a divine being named Inti. Spanish chronicles identify Inti as the Sun God, but contemporary scholars believe that the Inca idea of divinity did not necessarily distinguish discrete deities. Rather, the Inca pantheon was conceived of as a complex group of overlapping, interrelated divine beings. Thus, although the Spanish tended to identify three powerful and unique members of an Inca divine trinity, which consisted of the Creator God, Wiraqocha, the Sun God, Inti, and the Thunder God, Inti-Illapa, this was clearly an imposition of the Christian notion of Father, Son, and Holy Spirit upon the Inca pantheon.

Because the sun, particularly as some formulation of the Sun God Inti, was understood as the "founding father of the Inca dynasty," the cult dedicated to this deity was particularly important in Inca culture. This became obvious to the Spanish almost immediately when they arrived in Cuzco, as it was clear to them that the most important temple complex in the city was the *Qorikancha*, or Golden Enclosure, commonly identified as the Temple of the Sun. Although the designation "Temple of the Sun" is a bit of a misnomer, as all of the major Inca deities, in all their complex manifestations, were worshipped there, and although the structure housed many different images of the multifaceted Inca gods, the most important statue to be found there was clearly that of Punchao, the image of the Sun itself.

These references to the cult of the Sun bring us naturally to the place of the Inca practice of human sacrifice. Although the numbers of persons sacrificed by these Andean peoples never reached the extraordinary levels attained by their northern imperial neighbors the Aztecs, the Incas nevertheless did involve themselves in this ritual activity. Their victims were usually boys or girls, chosen for their beauty from throughout the empire, and sometimes captives who were taken in battle. As one would expect, the Incas paid homage to the Sun, seeking to assure his ascendancy and general well-being, by offering this deity human sacrifices. They also offered up the "ultimate sacrifice" during times of great calamity, such as earthquakes, eclipses, and epidemics.

End Notes

1. Michael C. Myers, William L. Sherman, Susan M. Deeds, *The Course of Mexican History* (New York: Oxford University Press, 2003), pp. 36–40.

2. Michael Coe and Rex Koontz, *Mexico: From the Olmecs to the Aztecs* (London: Thames & Hudson, 2002), p. 120.

3. Michael Coe, *The Maya* (New York: Thames & Hudson, 1993), p. 108.

4. *The Maya*, p. 127.

5. Geoffrey W. Conrad and Arthur A. Demarest, *Religion and Empire: The Dynamics of Aztec and Inca Expansionism* (New York: Cambridge University Press, 1994), p. 53.

6. *The Course of Mexican History,* pp. 84–87.

7. Terence N. D'Altroy, *The Incas* (Oxford: Blackwell Publishing, 2004), pp. 36–44.

Practice Test Questions

1. The oldest of the so-called "civilized cultures" in Mesoamerica was

   A. the Aztec.
   B. the Inca.
   C. the Olmec.
   D. the Toltec.

2. The Early Classic Period of Mayan civilization was influenced by the culture of what great Mesoamerican capital city?

   A. Teotihuacán
   B. Tenochtitlán
   C. Tres Zapotes
   D. Culhuacán

3. The Aztecs ascended to a position of supremacy within the political space of the power vacuum that emerged after the collapse of what great central valley culture?

   A. The Maya
   B. The Toltecs
   C. The Incas
   D. The Olmecs

4. When the Aztecs first came to power they existed as

   A. an independent empire.
   B. a partner of the Toltecs.
   C. a member of a triple alliance.
   D. None of the above.

5. Scholars have had a difficult time establishing an historical timeline for the Incas due to

   A. the lack of an indigenous writing system.
   B. the Inca's rewriting of their own history.
   C. the peculiarities of the Andean vision of time.
   D. All of the above.

Answers and Explanations

1. **C.** It is important to remember that Mesoamerican cultures did not arise in a vacuum; they built on the foundations that were laid out by previous cultures. Thus, the Olmecs, considered by scholars to be the oldest Mesoamerican culture, provided the foundation upon which the Toltec and Aztec civilizations were built. The Inca were members of an Andean culture in South America, and thus were not part of the Mesoamerican world.

2. **A.** The city of Teotihuacán, located just north of what would become Tenochtitlán, extended its influence over most of Mesoamerica before its mysterious decline and fall. The Mayan cultures of the Early Classic Period were cultural groups that were heavily influenced by this amazing civilization.

3. **B.** Although many people believe that the Aztecs were the only significant Mesoamerican culture, this great civilization was really the last in a long line of important cultures that emerged in this area of the world. The Olmec, the Maya, and the Toltec cultures preceded them. The Aztecs filled the power vacuum created by the collapse of the Toltecs.

4. **C.** When the Aztecs first emerged as an imperial power they were initially members of a powerful "triple alliance" with the cities of Texcoco and Tlacopan. It was only later that the Aztecs became the independent empire that ruled throughout Mesoamerica.

5. **D.** Unlike their northern cousins, the Aztecs, the Incas had no system of writing, which has made it difficult for scholars to trace their history. In addition to this, after the Incas came to power in the Andean world, they "reimagined" their history within their own peculiar understanding of time. This allowed them to think of themselves as having always existing as the central power in the region.

Demographics and Environment

Looking at diverse civilizations makes each of them appear to exist in a void. They have certain things in common, such as their rise, success, decline, and fall. But all civilizations are influenced by the environment and their **demographics**—the study of the characteristics of a population or population segment, including age, sex, economics, and religion. The environment and the demographics function as the unique setting for each civilization's movement on history's stage. Studying these factors sheds light on civilizations' development.

Environment frames civilization. It is both catalyst and definer of what each civilization holds sacred. Necessity may be the mother of invention; environment is its grandmother.

Civilizations respond to their environment. Civilizations blessed with resources are less likely to covet their neighbors' resources, less likely to go to war, but more likely to need to defend themselves from neighbors with fewer resources. Civilizations that contend with harsh climates may, out of necessity, develop technological solutions to concerns over food and shelter. Civilizations located in remote areas become self-sufficient and may be wary of outside influence. Civilizations that grow up along trade routes tend to possess flexibility because they're exposed to different ideas.

But environment also acted as a spur, pushing peoples to move from one area to another. As such, the environment created the conditions resulting in massive migrations. These will be examined in this chapter.

Nomad Migrations

A **migration** is the mass movement of a given people from one area to another. This movement often takes two forms: nomadic migration or the continuous movement of a pre-agricultural people seeking land for their flocks and food; and agricultural migration, the movement of a people seeking lands to farm. The migrations described here possess commonalities. Nomads, tribal peoples, either became integral parts of existing civilizations or learned how to use the strengths of neighboring civilizations to their benefit. Each of these nomadic migrations dramatically changed the areas they invaded, and the history that followed.

The environment frames the migrations described in this chapter. The need for food and resources set in motion each of the migrations described below. Migrations take place in both civilized and pre-civilized societies.

Arabs

The Middle East prior to Islam's advent was composed of various Arab peoples—some Nomadic, others urban. Islam's advent provided the cohesive element needed to make these diverse peoples conquerors. While, as discussed in Chapter 8, Muslims disagreed and the religion wasn't monolithic, the Sunni version, within 100 years, provided cohesiveness to Muslim conquest and migration. These conquests facilitated the worldwide spread of Islam.

But the environment also spurred Muslim conquests. By the seventh century, the Middle East was no longer the land of the fertile crescent. The need for water, fertile land, and resources spurred the conquests and movement of Islam. Expanded power meant expanded trade. Thus, arid soil and the lack of water, coupled with a growing population and need of resources, fueled the Muslim conquest/migration.

By the seventh century, the Arabs invaded North Africa, Spain, and southern modern-day Pakistan. The North African and Spanish conquests gave the Muslims control of the Mediterranean and African trade. These conquests resulted in groups of Muslim kingdoms, rather than one empire. But Islam provided the cohesion that resulted in kingdoms exhibiting similar cultures. As also mentioned in Chapter 8, Islamic thought proved the catalyst for the study of medicine, astronomy, and mathematics. Through Islamic universities, learning flourished. During the eighth and ninth centuries, Muslim invaders had conquered Afghanistan and the Punjab as well. This spread Islam throughout the northern part of South Asia. Through trade contacts, Islam also spread through the islands of Southeast Asia, especially modern-day Indonesia. Government based on the Q'uran facilitated the creation of stable societies in the areas conquered.

But conquest also affected the practice of Hinduism. It spurred Hinduism to crystallize and to discover ways of living with this newest invader. The caste system expanded to include Muslims. But these conquests had a longer-lasting effect. An increasing number of Muslims settled in the northern portions of South Asia, today known as Pakistan, Nepal, and Bangladesh. Toward the end of the Mughal dynasty in the seventeenth century, Muslims were increasingly persecuted by their rulers. Great Britain had little use for either Hindus or Muslims, exploiting South Asia for its resources. This tension between Hindu and Muslim erupted into civil war after the British left South Asia in 1947. Over a million people were killed, the most famous victim, Mohandas Gandhi. Some of these tensions have begun to fade. Indians and Pakistanis have begun to discuss their disputes, including control over the province of Kashmir. But the tensions remaining after the Mughals still resonate.

The Turks

The Turks conquered many of the areas initially ruled by the Arabs. Originally Asian nomads, many Turkish males became mercenary soldiers in Muslim armies, converting to Islam in the process. They also became the administrators for the various Caliphates in the Middle East. As they gained power, the tradition of Arab councils declined. Kingship replaced councils. The Sultan, head of the Turkish army, became the ruler. The Turks controlled the Abbasid Caliphs by the tenth century. They drove the Byzantines out of Anatolia in 1071, permanently weakening the Byzantine Empire. By 1453 the Ottoman Turks conquered Constantinople, thereby ending the Byzantine Empire.

Prior to the Turks' rise as a civilization, this group was nomadic, providing soldiers to the civilizations in the area. But like the Arabs before them, the Turks required water and resources. Once they held the military power it was not difficult conquering the civilizations in the area and expanding their hold on power.

The need for food proved a powerful spur. The term "military" originally meant those who served and were paid in the grain millet, rather than money. This revealed how much food supplies motivated migration and conquest.

In their quest for more land, the Turks also moved into South Asia, from the Punjab area to much of modern-day Pakistan in the late tenth century. This invasion largely converted most of the northern part of South Asia to Islam, and led to such instability that the northern part of South Asia became, as Robert Garfield described it, "The wild east." As such it was a place that Muslims, whatever their nationality, could make their fortunes. But the Turks went further. They created the Sultanate of Delhi, which lasted 300 years. All of these lands then fell to another Turkish conqueror, Timur, or Tamerlane. He conquered the northern part of South Asia in 1398-99. His rule left northern South Asia in chaos.

The Turks also conquered the Middle East. They were superseded by the Ottomans, a Turkish tribe that made its living raiding. By the fifteenth century the Ottomans occupied Anatolia and the Balkans, and by the mid-fifteenth century, conquered the Byzantine Empire. The Ottomans held much of the Middle East until the end of World War I. The present state of Turkey is the last vestige of the empires created by Turkish/Ottoman tribes.

The Mongols

The Mongols originally were a tribe in the northern part of China. Northern China had few resources, and the Mongols survived as shepherds with no legacy or talent. They were considered by the Chinese to be one of a group of "barbarian" tribes that threatened the Chinese Empire. By the thirteenth century those threats became reality. The Mongols began their conquests and their search for more land under the leadership of Temujin, later called Ghenghis Khan. Temujin rose to leadership among the Mongolian tribes, creating a cavalry so powerful that it seemed undefeatable. The Mongols were known for their ruthlessness and their discipline. However, Ghenghis was loyal to his family, and a brilliant administrator. When he died in 1226 he had provided for a stable succession.

Under Temujin's leadership the Mongols first began a conquest of China, ultimately establishing the Yuan dynasty in 1279. Under Kublai Khan, the first Yuan emperor, China re-opened the Silk Road, making overtures to the west. Marco Polo, a member of a Venetian merchant family that specialized in the saffron trade traveled to China as a young man during the Khan's reign. He served Kublai Khan as an ambassador and envoy for 24 years before returning to Venice. Captured in a battle between Venice and Genoa, Polo dictated his adventures in China while a prisoner in Genoa. The book became an international bestseller, but few believed it was more than an exaggerated tale, and Polo became something of a laughingstock. Marco Polo died in 1324, stating that he'd not even begun to tell of all he had seen.

The Chinese conquest was only one prong of the Mongol conquests. During the mid-thirteenth century the Mongols conquered Russia, Hungary, and Poland. They even conquered Baghdad, ending the Caliphate. They also attempted to conquer Southeast Asia. Burma fell to the Mongols but they were defeated by the Vietnamese. In India the later Mughal dynasty was an offshoot of the Mongol empire.

The empire was too large to be governed by one ruler. Hence, it was divided into five Khanates, the Khan of each subject to the Khakhan or Great Khan. The Blue and White Khanate, or Russia, became known as the Golden Horde. Il-Khanate comprised Persia and much of the Middle East, the Yuan Dynasty was China, and the Changhadai Khanate comprised western China and parts of South Asia. After Kublai Khan's death the office of the Khakhan was abolished, and the Empire fragmented, although it was still considered the Mongol Empire. Ultimately each Khanate was re-conquered, and the Mongols, to this day, remain in Mongolia.

It should be noted that under Mongol rule trade flourished, ideas circulated, and diverse cultures existed side by side, exchanging ideas in the process. The Mongol world was a cosmopolitan one that allowed for the free flow of ideas, and was tolerant of all religions—as long as tribute was paid on time!

But the savagery of the Mongol conquest, coupled with the efficiency of the Mongol government, left another mark. As mentioned in Chapter 9, Mongolian rule facilitated the growth of autocracy in Russia. Reaction to the Mongol rule contributed to China's withdrawal from the world during the Ming dynasty. After the defeat of the Il-Khanate by Tamerlane the Middle East was left vulnerable to western European forces. By the early seventeenth century the Turks and Arabs were driven out of the Mediterranean . . . and the Mongols whose thirst for more land and wealth formed the second largest empire in history remained an unpleasant memory.

The Vikings

The Vikings or Norsemen differ somewhat from the other nomadic migrations and conquest already described. Unlike the Arabs, Turks, and Mongols who began migrations and conquests from the Middle and Far East, the Vikings came from Northern Europe: Denmark, Sweden, and Norway. They farmed, but traveled to other lands by sea. Their voyages may not qualify as migrations, but they had a lasting impact on both eastern and western Europe. What fueled the Viking voyages? Like the Arabs, Turks, and Mongols, the Vikings sought food. The Viking lands weren't conducive to farming, and the climate was cold. During the winter there was little light; during the summer the sun never set. Hunger drove these warriors.

Viking ships from the sixth to the eleventh centuries navigated both rivers and oceans. Shaped like large serpents, these ships moved both by sail and by oars. The Norsemen rowed from Northern Europe to Iceland, Greenland, and ultimately northern Canada, reaching the Americas 500 years before the Nina, Pinta, and Santa Maria. Some note that Viking architecture can be found in America as far south as Kansas. The only reason the Vikings failed to colonize North America lay in the distances. The supply lines were too long, especially in the very stormy North Atlantic.

But the distances to eastern and western Europe posed no problems, and their ships spread terror whenever they came into port. Europeans who lived near the Atlantic or the larger river routes added a prayer to the Sunday morning church service, "Heaven deliver us from the fury of the Norsemen." Vikings combined trade with piracy, in the case of the latter leaving few survivors. Often having long red hair, Norsemen warriors were called "Berserkers" because of their ferocity. It seemed they almost went mad during battle. The word "berserk" lives on today as a description of someone who has gone completely mad and is throwing a fit.

If a Viking ship rowed into port with a white sail, inhabitants knew the Vikings wished to trade, not pillage. If, however, the sail was red, the Vikings had piracy and pillage, not trade, on their minds. No one was certain of Viking intentions until the Viking ship was in clear view, too late to do much preparation for war.

The Vikings did not confine their ships to western Europe. The riches of the Slavic states and Russians also attracted their attention. In the early ninth century the Vikings, or Varangians as they were called in eastern Europe, attacked Constantinople, nearly conquering the city. They attacked Constantinople several more times, but never succeeded in conquering that city. The pattern of trade and piracy worked as well in Russia and the Slavic states as it did in western Europe.

Unlike the other migrations the Vikings didn't vanish as the result of lost battles. Instead, they settled in Northern Europe and the province of Normandy in modern-day France. Always good administrators, they urbanized with the rest of western Europe. But they didn't entirely stop their conquests.

Duke William of Normandy invaded and deposed King Harold, the Saxon who ruled much of England in 1066. King William established a regime that enabled England to become a nation-state, and a world power by the end of the six-teenth century. William I's famous descendent, Henry II, also had Viking long red hair.

Sweden remained a world power until the mid-seventeenth century. Delaware was originally a Swedish colony. When the Vikings stopped raiding it was because they had developed their own well-governed nation-states. Once in posses-sion of resources the Vikings evolved into a peaceful society. They're the original Danes, Norwegians, and Swedes, all among the most progressive nations in the world.

The Vikings also left their mark on European culture. The Niebelungleid was in part a Viking tale, and the worship of Thor and Odin, Viking gods, continued into the sixteenth century, according to Denise Garfield. Richard Wagner mod-ernized the Niebelungleid in his Ring opera cycle. These tell of the forming of a ring of gold that has the power to con-trol the world to the downfall of the Norse gods in Gotterdammerung.

The Aztecs

The Aztec migration resembles the Turkish migration. The Aztecs originally were a group of tribes in what today is Mexico. Like the Turks, the Aztecs originally acted as mercenary soldiers in the armies of other civilizations in modern-day Mexico. Like the Turks, the need for land, food, and resources drove them to settle and conquer modern-day Mexico.

By 1200 the Aztecs began fighting their way north into the Valley of Mexico. At this point they began calling them-selves Mexicans. Densely populated, the Aztecs, like the Turks, volunteered their services as mercenaries. They were rewarded by receiving land on a hillside called Chapultepec. By 1300, they had moved down the hillside, captured the lakes in the valley and established the city of Tenochtitlán, today Mexico City.

Tenochtitlan was built on a set of lakes and canals. It had a sewage system, food supply, and, thanks to a set of fields, actually anchored in the lakes. Aztec technology extended to medicine. The Aztecs successfully performed certain types of brain surgery. Life expectancy was upwards of 60 years old.

This was a highly rigid but lawful society. Crimes were punished with amputation and death. As a result Aztec homes didn't have doors. There was no need as the climate was warm, and lawlessness was so unmercifully punished that doors were unnecessary. No one would ever enter an Aztec home without permission.

Tenochtitlan formed the heart of the Aztec Empire. Texcoco and Tlacopan, also Aztec cities, kept order over the empire. All subjects were granted religious and cultural freedom. The only thing the Aztecs required were taxes and humans for sacrifice.

The latter contributed to the Aztecs' fall. The Aztec belief that their gods required human blood meant that a supply of humans was always needed for sacrifice. Often these sacrifices were public spectacles. Prisoners stood in line at the base of a pyramid, advancing step by step upward until they reached the top. Once at the top the prisoner's heart would be cut out by the priests, and held up while still beating. The heart would be thrown in the fire and the body over the top of the pyramid.

But the ritual sacrifice didn't end. After the sacrifices were completed, the populace practiced ritual cannibalism. Men ate the brains; women the liver and other organs. Sacrifice and ritual cannibalism resulted in strained relations between the Aztecs and their subjects. No one wants to be a sacrifice. Further, the eating of one's own species results in kuru, the human equivalent of Mad Cow Disease. The Aztecs weakened themselves biologically, just as much as they did strategically.

Another factor, psychological in nature also contributed to the Aztecs' fall. The Aztecs believed that time was cyclical, each cycle lasting 56 years. Moctezuma II, the Aztecs' king, believed the empire was in its last cycle, and that Hernan Cortez was the god who would end the last cycle. Moctezuma, thus, was at a distinct disadvantage. He believed that it was ordained that Cortez would be victorious. Cortez noted Moctezuma's manner and, by refusing to eat, drink or sleep, gave Moctezuma the impression that his visitor was sent by the gods to conquer. Those who do not believe they can win usually lose.

The Aztec Empire collapsed in 1520, defeated by Cortez and his forces. Cortez's victory has been traditionally ascribed to superior firearms—800 Europeans defeated over 100,000 Aztecs. But other factors were at work. The Europeans had assistance from the Aztec tributary states; Moctezuma II believed the battle lost before it was fought; Cortez burned his ships. His men knew they had no choice but to win, or they would be sacrificed en masse in the center square.

While much of the Aztec culture was thought to have been destroyed, many traditions continue, such as the holiday in November known as the Day of the Dead. Additional details about the Aztec language and new artifacts are still being rediscovered.

Agricultural Migrations

Unlike nomadic migrations, agricultural migrations didn't involve conquest. Rather, they were slower movements of peoples across areas seeking farmland. These peoples didn't destroy or necessarily displace other peoples. They settled down with them, influencing the cultures they came into contact with, and were influenced by those cultures. Agricultural migrations may be considered evolutionary rather than revolutionary. Thus agricultural migrations appear more benign than nomadic migrations.

The Bantu Migration

This migration has already been discussed in Chapter 2. The Bantu began moving through Africa 2000 years BCE. They moved in small groups, setting up farms and agricultural villages. When the land could no longer support the group, some moved on, creating new agricultural villages. Technology helped each group become more productive. Two thousand years ago the Bantu could not farm in the forested areas. Once the Bantu learned how to construct and use iron tools they became more adept at farming, using land previously impossible to farm.

The Bantu weren't the only peoples in Africa. The Khoisan, Bushmen, and the Mbuti, Pygmies, also lived in Africa. But both tribes were hunters and gatherers, either assimilating into the Bantu or following the animals into those parts of the forests the Bantu could not farm.

The Bantu migration reached South Africa at the same time as the Dutch explorers. This ended the long migration from North to South Africa. Because both the Bantu and the Dutch reached South Africa at the same time, the Dutch claimed the land to be rightfully theirs, subjugating the Bantu in the process. During the nineteenth century, after the discovery of quinine as an effective treatment of malaria, European nations settled, conquered, and exploited all of Africa. This settlement was so rapid that it resembled a feeding frenzy. In 1884–85 the Berlin Conference, the meeting of European states, divided Africa into over 50 states, thus effectively ending the Bantu migration.

Dividing Africa into smaller states also placed Africans in conflict with both Europe and itself. France's carving of Burundi and Rwanda into separate states set the stage for the massacres in the early 1990s. South Africa is still attempting to come to terms with the affects of apartheid. The division of Africa without regard to existing civilizations and borders resulted in mass poverty and war. It's an interesting question: What would have happened if the Bantu migration continued unimpeded?

Assarting

Assarting, the migration which took place in Europe shortly after 1000 CE in which many Europeans moved from western to central and eastern Europe, isn't well known today, but it had a far-reaching impact on Europe. Shortly after 1000 CE, Polish lords offered free land to anyone willing to migrate to eastern Europe. According to historian Frederick Heer, a migration took place much like the American movement westward in the nineteenth century. Western European serfs left the manor to become landowning peasants in eastern Europe. The migration across Europe also contributed to trade and spread diverse cultures. The influx of western Europeans may also explain why much of eastern Europe remained Catholic rather than Orthodox.

Assarting also changed life in western Europe. It was the first death knell of Manorialism, the relationship of lord and serf. Serfdom was a state of the absence of freedom. The serf was bound to the land. Leaving the manor for ownership in another area meant that the contracts between lord and serf needed re-negotiation. By 1200 most serfs in western Europe had left serfdom to become peasants. Landownership became a means to enter the upper classes. Fear of the re-imposition of feudalism was one of the factors that led to the French Revolution.

Feudalism was a political system based on the mutual bond of loyalties. These loyalties ran from lord to serf and vassal, and from vassal and serf to lord. Once those loyalties became breakable, feudalism declined. But Assarting wasn't the only cause of feudalism's demise. It was just one symptom.

The Rise of the Cities

As mentioned in Chapter 3, civilization is an urban way of living. After the western Roman Empire's demise there was very little urban living in early Medieval Europe. But that changed after 1000 CE. The cities that came into being during the late Middle Ages looked nothing like modern cities. Medieval cities were trade centers, rather than hubs of finance or industry. They were also seen as refuges from feudalism, and the catalyst for free living. The English, American, and French Revolutions began as urban movements. In its way the medieval city was the focus of migration. Anyone seeking a better living, and not being at the mercy of a feudal lord, fled to the city. If he/she remained free of the lord for a year and a day, all feudal bonds were null and void. The Medieval city was also considered the place to make a fortune. Many tales begin with the story of a poor person fleeing a manor to become a rich merchant in a city. Thus the Medieval city was a point of migration.

Once western Europeans realized that Christ wasn't coming back, money and credit began playing a larger role in the European economy. Goods were traded and bought at fairs held at the same times and places every year. The fairs resulted in the creation of communes, groups of merchants and artisans who were free from feudal influence, sometimes under royal protection, and who concentrated on protecting their citizens and promoting commerce. Some of these communes grew into cities. In addition, many established market towns also transformed into actual cities again.

Cities led to the rise of the middle class. This class, neither peasant nor noble, consisted of merchants, manufacturers, artisans, and members of the professions. These groups were the first capitalists. They made money, money that bought both consumer goods and weapons. In addition, the cities extended the culture. Trade made it possible to obtain goods from cities as far away as China.

Because cities facilitated trade and brought diverse peoples together in that process, new ideas also entered late Medieval European culture. This diversity of ideas in part resulted in the creation of universities, interest in the ancient world, and interest in the world beyond. Thus the re-emergence of the city acerbated the end of feudalism, ushering in the modern world in the process.

But before assuming that Europe was blessed with multiple real versions of the Emerald City, L. Frank Baum's wondrous city at the end of the yellow brick road in the *Wizard of Oz*, it's prudent to remember that western European cities were built without sewage systems. Live sewage often ran along the street. City dwellers often threw garbage out the window. Streets in western Europe were often no more than five feet wide. Refrigeration was simply storing perishables on the window sill, a technique that didn't work well in summer. Rooms were overcrowded; privacy unknown. The poor often slept in the streets. Everyone, except the very rich lived in close quarters. An unwanted spark could destroy an entire section of the city. Bad rainstorms and blizzards still paralyze modern cities. Think of what these could have done in the thirteenth or fourteenth centuries.

The Plague Redux

The advent of the plague in 1348 was discussed in Chapter 9. This pandemic may be the partial result of the migrations and growth discussed in this chapter. The plague traveled the same routes as the merchants and the conquerors. It came to Europe on a merchant ship, then moved from Italy to Scandinavia along the trade routes.

Cities with close quarters and lack of sanitation provided an ideal venue for spreading disease. The only means of controlling it that was known to medicine in the fourteenth century was designating the house as a plague house by placing a red cross on the doorpost, and confining its inhabitants within. This sentenced entire families to death.

The pandemic brought out the best and worst of human behavior. According to Barbara Tuchman, many Christian Germans blamed the plague on their Jewish neighbors, claiming the Jews had poisoned the wells. So many Jews were murdered or burned alive as a result of these accusations that Tuchman claimed there was "hardly a Jew left in Germany" after the plague's visitation.

In England the plague proved to be a catalyst to Parliament's development. Lack of labor, coupled with rising prices, resulted in dissatisfaction with the crown and aristocracy. In 1381 the peasants and artisans revolted over the economy. King Richard II saved his throne by riding to the head of the rebels, offering to be their leader. Because of the chaos left by the plague and the War of Roses from 1435-1485, Parliament was able to whittle down the royal prerogative. The rights ultimately gained by the middle classes in England form the traditions underlying the American Constitution. These traditions had their roots in the plague. There were also cases of neighbors nursing neighbors and families banding together in times of trouble. As with the present, disasters bring out the best and worst in people.

The plague also affected religion. Questions about the role of the individual and God arose as families mourned their dead, and questioned why this had happened. These questions ultimately resulted in questions concerning the priesthood, faith, and the individual's relation to God. The Reformations of the sixteenth century also had their roots in the anguish and questioning caused by the plague.

Bubonic Plague also affected western musical development. In 1348 groups of men called flagellants wandered through European cities flogging themselves while singing. Their choruses became increasingly harmonic and elaborate. These choruses evolved into operatic choruses by the beginning of the seventeenth century. Thus modern opera had its beginnings with the plague.

The plague subsided in Europe in the beginning of the eighteenth century. No one really knows why. Some note that one species of rat, the species thought to carry the plague, declined. Maybe better sanitation and medical techniques stalled the pandemic. But perhaps the plague is cyclical. A cure for the plague was discovered in the beginning of the twentieth century, and there are broad-spectrum antibiotics that successfully treat plague. Nonetheless, it's still possible this oldest of diseases, as historian of disease, Frederick Cartwright notes, may reappear sometime in the future with the same catastrophic results.

Practice Test Questions

1. The Arabs used what means to extend their empire?

   A. The battering ram
   B. Greek fire
   C. Islam
   D. Tricking the leadership

2. The Turks increased their empire by

   A. first creating a structure within Arab governments.
   B. giving large gifts to all countries that accepted Turkish rule.
   C. threatening to wipe out everyone who did not accept Turkish rule.
   D. creating markets for Turkish goods.

3. The Mongols conquered by

   A. getting the better of their adversaries through negotiations.
   B. having an outstanding and quickly-moving cavalry.
   C. getting control of the food supply.
   D. scaring their opponents.

4. The Aztecs resemble which other nomadic people in their means of conquest?

   A. The Vikings
   B. The Mongols
   C. The Arabs
   D. The Turks

5. The Vikings ceased their conquests because

    A. they couldn't live in America.

    B. they became excellent administrators and created stable societies.

    C. they went berserk.

    D. they began manufacturing ships for the English.

Answers and Explanations

1. **C.** Islam. Islam provided a universal set of laws for the Arabs, and as mentioned in Chapter 8, gave each conquered area a cohesive organization.

2. **A.** First creating a structure within Arab governments. The Turks served as mercenaries within Arab governments. Ultimately they became the administrators as well.

3. **B.** Possessing a powerful and mobile cavalry. Mongol charges were feared throughout Europe and Asia. However, the advance of the cavalry sent fear through the target, therefore making fear of the Mongols a powerful weapon.

4. **D.** The Turks. Like the Turks, the Aztecs served as mercenaries for other civilizations.

5. **B.** They became excellent administrators and created stable societies. Once they could sustain themselves, they ceased their conquests. Sweden became a world power in the seventeenth century.

The mid-fourteenth century is generally considered the beginning of a transition between the medieval and modern worlds. The transition was characterized by a renewed interest in ideas from the Greek and Roman period and is referred to as the *Renaissance*, French for rebirth. The movement began in the city-states of Italy and encompassed almost all facets of life including politics, thought, and art. The Renaissance began in the Italian city-states for a number of reasons including the large amount of wealth that Venice had accumulated as they transported goods and people between the east and the west during the medieval period. The Italian city-states also had easy access to ancient Roman artifacts and documents, which served as a constant reminder of the past glories of Rome. The main contributors to the Renaissance recognized their efforts as different from those that came before them in the medieval period. They tended to classify the medieval period as slow and dark, a time of little education or innovation. They viewed the medieval period as an interruption of culture between the classical world of Greece and Rome and themselves.

The medieval period had not been an easy time for many people. They faced real threats from famine, disease, and warfare. These dangers tended to foster a a less independent style of life. Many people who lived in the medieval period found themselves dependent on others within the community in areas such as work and religion. For instance, a medieval craftsman belonged to a guild. The guild determined how he would run his business; how long his apprenticeship was; how long he was a journeyman; when he could become a master; and how much he could charge for his work. He could not charge more or less than the others in his guild. The idea was that all should make a good living, but no one craftsman should do substantially better than the rest. Because the dangers were so real in the medieval world, risk was often shared among a number of people, in this case, the craftsmen in the guild. Medieval people also tended to rely heavily on religion. In this period in western Europe, the Catholic Church was the only Christian church. But again, religion was more of a collective activity. Most of the parishioners in any given church did not understand the mass, which was delivered in Latin, and they certainly could not read the Bible. The Catholic Church was still using the Vulgate Bible, which was written in Latin. Religion was an important part of people's lives in the medieval period, but it was not the personal kind of religion that would become important later in the period, when reformers such as Martin Luther and John Calvin questioned the church and its practices. Medieval religion tended to rely heavily on ceremony and tradition. This allowed people who did not understand Latin to participate in the religious services. Although the medieval period was characterized by the idea of community, the Renaissance, on the other hand, stressed the importance of the individual and the importance of individual talents. This idea, known as individualism, is apparent in the philosophy and art of the period.

Scholars during the Renaissance period began to look at ancient Greek and Roman documents and early Christian documents differently than their medieval predecessors. As scholars improved their ability to read Greek and Latin, they began to study documents from the ancient period, such as the writings of Plato and Cicero among others. While medieval scholars had studied the documents to see what they could learn about God and Christianity, Renaissance scholars studied them with an eye to discovering more about human nature. This new interpretation was known as humanism. The Renaissance scholars were Christians just as the medieval scholars had been, but the scholars during the period of the Renaissance had a different priority when studying the documents. Francesco Petrarch (1304–1374) is known as the father of humanism. Petrarch admired the ancient Roman writers and adopted their style in his own poetry. His poetry and sonnets reflect the importance that Romans placed on the natural world. Petrarch's writings mark a shift from the spiritual emphasis of the medieval world to the secular emphasis of the Renaissance writers. The new emphasis can also be seen in *The Prince,* written by Niccolo Machiavelli. This work, which is considered to be one of the most important works on politics, instructs a new prince on the correct ways to gain and maintain power. *The Prince* is basically an instruction manual that explains how a prince should treat his subjects, run a war, and conduct diplomacy with other countries. Machiavelli tells his readers that morals and principals have no place in politics. Whether or not a prince is moral makes no difference in his ability to reign effectively. He must only appear to be moral. In Machiavelli's world, appearance and not substance is what counts.

The new philosophical interest in human nature can also be seen in the art of the period. While medieval art was meant to teach a lesson, perhaps a story from the Bible to an illiterate peasantry, Renaissance art, although often still reflecting a religious theme, now glorified the humanity of the individuals being portrayed. In order to achieve this, artists such as Leonardo da Vinci (1452–1519) and Michelangelo (1475–1564) studied anatomy so that the individuals portrayed in the art seemed more lifelike and more realistic. One of da Vinci's most famous works, the *Mona Lisa,* shows his expert knowledge of anatomy in the precise and delicate structure of the woman's hands in the painting. Statues, such as Michangelo's *David* recall the idealized portrayal of the human body found in ancient Greek sculptures. Medieval statutes tended to be of saints carved on the pillars of gothic Cathedrals, such as those on the Cathedral at Chartres in France. These statues appear very unnatural. There was no attempt to make them reflect the individuals they represented. Because of Michelangelo's knowledge of anatomy, *David* appears to be caught right at the moment before he is about to move. No longer are statutes frozen images of piety, now they appear to be lifelike and ready for action.

The Renaissance elevated artists such as da Vinci and Michelangelo to the position of artistic geniuses. They created their art for their patrons, who paid them well. The Vatican was one of the greatest patrons to artists such as Michelangelo, who painted the Sistine Chapel for Pope Julius II. Other patrons included the leading families of the Italian city-states such as the De Medici family of Florence and the Sforza family of Milan. Renaissance artists kept their art works exclusive by creating them on commission for their patrons. The Renaissance that started in the Italian city-states eventually spread to Northern Europe, where it took on a decidedly different flavor.

The Northern Renaissance

As Northern European scholars became influenced by the ideas of the Renaissance, they began to study the ancient Greek and Roman classics and the Christian fathers as well. While Italian humanists had been concerned with political and social ideas, Northern European Renaissance scholars, sometimes referred to as Christian humanists, focused on the ideas of individual piety and morality. One of the most important of the Christian humanists was Desiderius Erasmus (1466–1536). He was a prolific writer who criticized the morality of society and the corruption of the clergy and church. He wrote a new Latin translation of the New Testament from the original Greek. Martin Luther later used this translation when he translated the New Testament into German. Erasmus called for a simple religion that was free of what he saw as the empty medieval rituals of the church. He did not call for any kind of break or schism within the church and after the Protestant Reformation began he repeatedly called for Christian unity instead of division within the church.

The Reformation

The Protestant Reformation that began when Martin Luther nailed his 95 theses to the church door in Wittenberg had a long history. Beginning in the late medieval period, the Catholic Church had begun to take on a much more secular tone. Clergy, from the parish priests to the pope, had begun to be distracted from their church duties by the outside world. An increasingly educated laity developed a number of complaints about the way the clergy behaved and how the church was being run. Complaints about plurality, simony, and benefit of clergy centered around the special privileges that clergy members enjoyed. Plurality was the practice of clergy members holding more than one church office at the same time. This often resulted in the clergy member failing to uphold the responsibilities of all the offices he held. It also often resulted in the problem of absenteeism. Since the clergy member could not physically be in two or more places at once, he often had to rely on other less qualified clergy members to hold mass and deal with the business of his different church offices.

The laity was also concerned that many of the positions within the church were not rewarded to the best-qualified person, but instead were given to the person who could pay for the position. The selling of church offices, called simony, resulted in the enrichment of the higher clergy and the Pope. The practice known as benefit of clergy caused many people to resent the church. This practice allowed clergy members who had committed crimes to escape secular punishment. Instead, they were tried by a church court and punished in a church prison. They generally served very short sentences even for very serious crimes.

The laity was also concerned over the seeming ignorance and immoral behavior of the clergy. As the laity became more educated, it became apparent to many that the priests were not qualified. A number of the clergy could not speak or read Latin. This was a real problem since the mass was held in Latin. Some began to questions what happened if the Latin was mispronounced during the mass. Did the people still benefit from the blessing? The issue of clerical morality also caused the laity to question the conduct of the clergy. Since the early medieval period, the clergy was supposed to follow the rule of celibacy. This was notoriously difficult to enforce. Ultimately the responsibility for enforcing the celibacy of the priests fell to the bishops, many of whom were not following the rule themselves. In fact, a number of popes beginning in the medieval period had multiple mistresses and a number of children. Clergy members were also

111

accused of drunken brawling and gambling. While all of the above were important issues that the church needed to address, the selling of indulgences would bring the problem of clerical and church abuses to a head. Indulgences allowed people remission from temporal punishment for sin. Instead of making a pilgrimage or fasting, a person could buy an indulgence. Since the Catholic Church held that anyone who failed to finish their temporal punishment would be punished after death in purgatory, the indulgences effectively reduced the time that a person would spend working off their sins in Purgatory. (Purgatory was the place between heaven and hell, where people went to work off their sins. After they had spent a required but varying time in purgatory they could then proceed to heaven.) A living person could use the indulgence or it could be purchased and used for a relative who had already died.

The fact that the church sold the indulgences, using them as a sort of fundraiser, bothered many people, including Martin Luther, who felt the need to speak out against their use. Martin Luther (1483–1546) was an Augustinian Monk, who held a doctorate of theology and taught at the University in Wittenberg. Luther was extremely devout, but began to suffer from a crisis of faith. He wondered how he could be sure that he was going to go heaven when he died. He performed the required "good works"—praying, fasting, and confession, that the church required, but still he was not sure. Being a religious scholar, Luther returned to the Bible for guidance; there he found in the letter from Paul to the Romans the passage that "the just shall live by faith." Luther realized that all the good works that the church demanded were not required for salvation and he began to preach the idea of faith alone.

When Luther learned of the selling of indulgences in Saxony, he felt obliged to speak out about the practice. The indulgences were being sold by a monk named John Tetzel for the benefit of Albrecht of Brandenburg, the Archbishop of Mainz and to help Pope Leo X fund the building of the basilica in Rome. Tetzel was a very good salesman. He had a song to help sell the indulgences, "When coin in coffer rings, a soul from purgatory springs." He also used voices to imitate the pleas of a person's loved one begging them to buy the indulgence and relieve their suffering in purgatory. Luther objected to the selling of indulgences because he believed that Tetzel was playing on the fears and emotions of people and forcing them to spend more than they could really afford. Luther also believed that the people buying the indulgences did not really understand that they were still required to repent for their sins. He was afraid that people would just buy the indulgences, never repent, and believe that they had done enough to be forgiven by God. Luther wrote up his concerns in the form of 95 complaints against the church, including the selling of indulgences, known as the 95 theses and posted them on the church door at Wittenberg. Luther was not calling for a break with the Catholic Church at this point; he was calling for a public debate on the Church practices, which he felt did not correspond with the guideline in the Bible. Luther debated another theology professor, John Eck, in Leipzig. During the debate, Luther challenged the idea that the pope was infallible. Luther believed that only faith was needed for salvation. He believed that the traditions of the church that had developed throughout the medieval period, such as indulgences and good works, were not based on scripture and therefore played no role in salvation.

Luther also called for the Bible to be translated into the vernacular, making it accessible for all literate people, not just those who could read Latin. This dependence on faith and scripture meant that the ceremonies of the church and the reliance on the priests to interpret the Bible were no longer needed. This was a direct threat to the Catholic Church and its clergy. Luther also wrote three pamphlets appealing mainly to the secular princes of Germany in hopes of persuading them to reform the church within their territories. Although the pope had not considered Luther anything more than a disobedient clergy member in the beginning, this was going too far, and the pope would have to act against Luther. The pope acted by issuing a papal bull demanding that Luther publicly recant his views within two months or face excommunication from the church. To a devout Christian, excommunication was serious business. If a Christian found himself excommunicated he could not receive the rites of church including communion or last rites if he should die. This would condemn his soul to hell for eternity. By this point, Luther had begun to question whether or not there should even be a pope. When he received the papal bull, Luther had decided that since the Bible did not specifically call for a pope to rule over the church, the pope was not needed. To show that he did not recognize the role or authority of the pope, Luther publicly burned the pope's papal bull. Charles V, Holy Roman Emperor, demanded that Luther present himself at the Diet of Worms, in order to explain his actions and recant. Although Luther did go to the Diet of Worms, he refused to recant and Charles V declared Luther to be an outlaw. This was dangerous; it meant that anyone could capture or even kill Luther.

Luther found a protector in Frederick the Wise, Elector of Saxony. Frederick was willing to hide and protect Luther in defiance of the Holy Roman Emperor's order because Frederick wanted to show Charles V that he did not have political power over Saxony. Luther was fortunate that many of the rulers in the Holy Roman Empire were willing to stand up to Charles V and the pope. This was a period of rising political power within the varying German territories; some exercised their power by defying the Holy Roman Emperor, and others sided with them. While in hiding, Luther translated the New Testament from Latin to German. Luther's popularity suffered among the lower classes when he failed to support the Peasant's Revolt in 1524–1525. Luther did not support social revolution. He urged the peasants to end the revolt, and he supported the German rulers' actions when they crushed the revolt violently. A temporary settlement surrounding the reformation was reached in 1555 following a war between Catholic forces and Protestant forces. The Peace of Augsburg recognized Lutheranism and allowed the princes of each territory within the Holy Roman Empire to choose for themselves and their people whether they would practice Catholicism or Lutheranism. Although the Protestant Reformation began with a theology professor in Wittenberg, with the help of the printing press and the growing feelings of anticlericalism, the reform movement soon spread throughout Europe.

Calvinism

John Calvin, a lawyer turned religious reform leader, brought the reformation to Geneva. Although Calvin agreed with many of Luther's reforms, he was most interested in extending the morality and discipline of the church to the secular government. Sins against the church, such as adultery, gambling, and gossiping were tried and punished in secular courts in Calvin's Geneva. The concept of predestination was also important to Calvin's Protestantism. Calvin believed that God had determined who would be saved and who would not be saved at the beginning of time. A person's actions had no effect on whether or not he would be saved. Calvin's interpretation of Protestantism proved to be very popular in a time of religious uncertainty. People believed that they were among the chosen and would be saved. Calvinism spread throughout western Europe including Scotland, England, Germany, the Dutch Netherlands, and even appeared in the New World with the Puritans.

English Reformation

England was a very unlikely place for the Protestant Reformation to appear in the early sixteenth century. A strong Catholic king, Henry VIII held the throne. He had even been given the title "Defender of the Faith" by the pope for an essay he wrote condemning Luther and the Protestant faith. At the beginning of the sixteenth century, events would evolve that would lead Henry to make the decision to break with the Catholic Church. The trouble began in 1527, when Henry VIII publicly announced that he would seek a divorce from his first wife, Catherine of Aragon, in order to marry another woman, Anne Boleyn. Henry needed a divorce and a new wife in order to produce a male heir. Henry had been married to Catherine of Aragon, the daughter of Ferdinand and Isabella, for 18 years. The couple had managed to produce only one surviving child, a daughter, the future Mary I. Henry, who was only one generation removed from the aristocratic conflict over the English throne known as the Wars of the Roses, became concerned over the continuation of his dynasty and the security of the throne. While there was no law prohibiting women from taking the throne, there had only been one woman, Mathilda, who had ruled England prior to the mid-sixteenth century. Matilda had attempted to rule England following the death of her father, Henry I, but she lost the throne to a male cousin and plunged England into an aristocratic civil war. With this kind of history, it was no wonder that Henry VIII was concerned over his daughter's ability to hold the throne and continue the Tudor dynasty. Henry, who was a devout Catholic, decided that there most be some reason that God was punishing him by denying him a son. Henry's answer came from Leviticus, in the Bible. Henry had not been Catherine's first husband. She had been married to Henry's older brother Arthur. Arthur had died shortly after the marriage took place and Catherine had sworn to the pope that the marriage had not been consummated. Because Leviticus prohibits a man from marrying his brother's wife, Henry and Catherine had been granted special permission from the pope to marry. Henry believed that the permission should never have been granted and that God was punishing him by withholding a son. Although divorce was not available within the Catholic Church, it was possible for Henry and Catherine to receive an annulment from the Pope. Annulments were granted when there was some reason that the two people should never have been legally married. Henry believed that when the new pope, Clement VII, realized the mistake, he would declare the marriage null and void and Henry would be able to find a new wife. Since the new marriage would not be in violation of the passage from Leviticus, Henry would get his son. Due to the timing of the request, Henry would not be able to get his annulment. First of all, in order for the new pope to grant the annulment on the grounds of Leviticus, he would have to say that the previous pope had made a mistake in allowing the marriage. This would mean that the pope was fallible. The new pope could not say this without risking the questioning of all the past rulings of all the previous popes. The other problem was a political one; the pope was under the control of the Holy Roman Emperor, Charles V. Charles V was Catherine of Aragon's nephew and he did not want the pope to grant the divorce. Charles V threatened to invade the Papal States if Pope Clement VII granted the divorce. The pope chose to delay.

Back in England, Henry could not afford a delay. Henry had become infatuated with one of Catherine's ladies-in-waiting, Anne Boleyn. By January of 1533, Anne had become pregnant. It was imperative that Henry divorce Catherine and marry Anne before the child was born, since only legitimate children could inherit the throne. Realizing that the divorce would never come from Rome, Henry chose to separate the church in England from Rome. He played on the anti-clerical feelings of the controlling classes in England, who were all too willing to keep tithes and other traditional moneys in England instead of sending them to Rome. The new Church of England with Henry at the head granted the divorce from Catherine in the spring of 1533, allowing Henry to marry Anne. All Henry had to do then was wait for the birth of his hoped-for son. Anne gave birth in September of 1533 to a daughter, the future Elizabeth I. Henry was upset but sure that sons would come soon. He had to secure his control over the church. He formally made himself head of the church. He also nationalized all church land within England and closed the monasteries and nunneries. He used this land to reward those members of the aristocracy who had supported his break from the church. The rest was sold to finance Henry's continuing wars with France and Scotland. It is important to remember that Henry VIII was not a Protestant in the real sense of the word. Throughout the rest of his reign, which lasted until 1547, Henry punished Protestants. Henry believed himself to be a good Catholic whom the Pope had wronged. Because of this, Henry did almost nothing to alter the church. The real Protestant Reformation would happen under his children. The longed-for son, Edward VI ruled from 1547–1553. Under Edward's reign, England became a haven for radical Protestantism. After his death, Mary I ruled from 1553–1558 and attempted to return England to Catholicism. She earned the nickname Bloody Mary for the execution of 287 Protestants, including men, women and children. After Mary's death, Elizabeth I ruled England for 45 years. Elizabeth established and presided over a moderate Protestant Church of England.

Catholic Reformation

Following the Protestant Reformation, the Catholic Church answered with a reformation of its own. The Catholic or Counter Reformation was an attempt by the Catholic Church to reform itself and reaffirm its theology in the face of the Protestant challenge. In 1545, Pope Paul III called a general church council to meet in Trent for the purpose of reasserting its doctrine and reforming itself. The Council of Trent met off and on for the next 17 years and shaped the Catholic Church for the next 400 years until Vatican II in the 1960s. The council both reaffirmed Catholic doctrine and called for changes that would reform the church and answer some of the criticisms that had resulted in the Protestant split. First of all, the council affirmed the importance of good works along with faith in providing salvation for individuals. They also affirmed the supremacy of the clergy in all religious matters, especially communion. The Council also reasserted the importance of the seven sacraments to Christian theology. Luther had claimed that there were in fact only two sacraments, baptism and communion. The council answered the critique of papal ignorance by calling for seminaries to be established in every diocese that would be responsible for ensuring that the clergy was fluent in Latin and understood Catholic theology. Bishops, who were now required to live in their dioceses, were charged with overseeing the education of the clergy at these new seminaries.

Although not a direct result of the Council of Trent, but certainly inspired it, Ignatius of Loyola founded the Society of Jesus to defend Catholicism and the pope throughout Europe. The Jesuits, as they came to be known, were organized more as a military operation than a religious order. They worked to defend the principles of Catholicism in Catholic countries and to reconvert people to Catholicism in Protestant countries. Jesuit missionaries were especially important in spreading Catholicism to the New World in both North and South America.

Witchcraft

The Early Modern Period also saw the eruption of the witchcraft trials throughout Europe. Historians disagree as to exactly what caused the outbreak, and it is fairly unlikely that there was one single cause. The period before the outbreak of the witch trials was racked with uncertainty brought on by the Protestant Reformation, wars, and disease. One thing that does seem to be certain is that during this period, there was a shift in the belief and understanding of magic. The belief in magic had existed for a long time. It was not uncommon for people to say charms as they planted their crops or to see the local wise man or woman for a love charm to make someone fall in love with them. The church also used magic in its rituals. In the Early Modern Period the use of some magic, harmful magic known as malificium, became associated with the devil. In an attempt to root out the devil from their communities, people began to arrest, try, and, in some cases, execute those they suspected of being witches.

The witch-hunts lasted from 1400 to 1700 and resulted in the deaths of 70,000-100,000 people. People believed that witches caused illness, crop failure, infertility, famine, and drought by casting spells. In fact, almost any misfortune that befell a community could be blamed on witchcraft. Witches were believed to worship the devil at witches' sabbats where they performed sexual rituals and engaged in cannibalism by eating Christian children. Witches reached the sabbat by flying.

Women were accused of practicing witchcraft more often than men throughout most of Europe, with 80 percent of those accused being women. Some historians believe that the witch-hunts exposed a hatred of women, and, as a result, the hunts were a direct attack on them, but it is very likely that women were accused for the simple reason that they had very little political or social power in this period. Women accused of witchcraft tended to be single and between the ages of 45 and 60. Many had been widowed and found themselves and their children dependent on the community for food and other assistance to survive. For those members of the community who resented having to help support these women, they became easy targets for accusations of witchcraft. One group of women that often found themselves in a precarious position was midwives. Because they might find themselves presiding over a birth where the mother and or the child did not survive they could find themselves accused of witchcraft. It is important to remember that some midwives cooperated with the authorities and assisted in examining accused witches for the devil's mark, a third nipple where the devil's familiar could suck blood. As the witch-hunts developed into witch crazes others, including men and children, began to be accused and condemned as witches. Historians continue to debate why the witch-hunts increased in number during this period. While women were accused, tried, and executed in both Catholic and Protestant areas, the demonization of the use of magic by the Catholic Church for things such as using holy water for blessings may have played a part.

The witch-hunts drew to a close in most parts of Europe as society began to accept a more scientific worldview. Judges and other officials, who had been drawn into the hunt for witches, began to question whether witches ever existed at all. Prosecutions for witchcraft fell dramatically after the beginning of the eighteenth century in Europe.

Practice Test Questions

1. One of the reasons the Renaissance began in the Italian city-states is

   A. they had easy access to ancient Roman artifacts.
   B. Italy had not experienced the medieval period.
   C. the pope commanded that all of Italy support the Renaissance artists.
   D. the Italian city-states were controlled by Muslim forces for most of the medieval period.

2. Luther believed that salvation could only be achieved by

   A. faith and good works.
   B. faith alone.
   C. following all seven sacraments.
   D. the purchase of indulgences.

3. The Catholic Reformation

   A. accepted most of the Protestant theology.
   B. refused to reform itself under any circumstances.
   C. reaffirmed its theology but refused to reform its education of the clergy.
   D. reaffirmed its theology and took steps to reform the education of the clergy.

4. Who was most responsible for making England a Protestant country?

   A. Henry VIII
   B. Pope Clement VII
   C. Mary I
   D. Edward VI and Elizabeth I

5. The witch trials in Europe represented

   A. the general uneasiness and stress over the events of the period.
   B. a general hatred of women during the period.
   C. a belief the population growth should be controlled by judicial means.
   D. the belief that only children could be witches.

Answers and Explanations

1. A. People in the Italian city-states had daily access to the buildings and much of the artwork of Ancient Rome. This encouraged them to rediscover the ideas of Ancient Rome.

2. B. After his crisis of faith, Luther studied the Bible, and, through a study of Paul's letters, came to the conclusion that faith alone was needed for salvation.

3. D. At the Council of Trent, the Catholic Church reaffirmed its theology including the need for faith and good works for salvation, and the seven sacraments. The Council also put bishops in charge of seminaries in their dioceses, giving them the responsibility for the education of the clergy.

4. D. Henry VIII remained a Catholic all his life. He believed that the Pope had wronged him. Mary I tried to return England to Catholicism. Edward VI and Elizabeth both ruled as Protestant monarchs.

5. A. The witch trials in Europe occurred during a time of religious and social uncertainty. Although women do seem to have been the main target of the trials, it is very likely that they became targets due to factors other than just their gender.

Trade, Technology, and Global Interactions

Beginning in the late fifteenth century, European nations began to turn their attention away from the concerns of the continent and became interested in the prospects offered by a control of the trade with the East, such as China. Europe had been trading with the East since the time of Ancient Rome when traders followed the Silk Road. Europeans had developed an appetite for eastern spices, silks, and porcelains that were delivered to Europe via the Muslim traders of the Ottoman Empire. Europeans hoped to reduce their costs and increase their own profits by cutting out the Muslim middlemen and finding their own route to the riches of the East. Portugal and Spain were the first to venture out on this quest, but the Dutch, English, and French followed them within half a century, each claiming a part of the newly explored territory. This European expansion resulted in a revolutionary interaction amongst people from almost every continent. European explorers, conquerors, missionaries, and colonists had a profound impact on the everyday lives of the people living in these territories as they forced them to accept, or at least live within, a European social system that was often imposed on the conquered peoples around the globe.

European Explorers

The Portuguese, hoping to open direct trading relations with India and China, opened the period of European exploration. Portuguese sailors, backed financially by Prince Henry the Navigator, took an eastern route along the coast of Africa to reach China and the riches of the East. The various voyages allowed mapmakers to gain a clearer idea of the outline of the African continent, allowing them to make their maps more accurate. The explorers Bartholomeu Dias and Vasco da Gama were able to round Africa at the Cape of Good Hope and open Eastern Africa and the East to the Portuguese traders. The Portuguese were never really interested in setting up permanent settler colonies during this period. They did not have the large amount of resources necessary to set up permanent colonies in Africa and the East. Instead, they set up trading posts and reprovisioning posts along the African and Indian coasts. Although the Portuguese were the first to venture away from Europe, they would have difficulty holding on to much of their territory once others, including the Dutch, challenged them.

The Spanish also participated in the early exploration of the period. Christopher Columbus, who was backed financially by Queen Isabella of Castile, set sail from Spain in 1492, convinced that he could find an alternative route to China by sailing west. Columbus estimated that China was well within sailing distance from Spain. Whether he made a mistake or intentionally underestimated the distance in order to receive funding, it is impossible to know. Although Columbus believed until his dying day that he had in fact found China, he had instead run into the Caribbean island known as the Bahamas. After further explorations by Vasco Nunez de Balboa, who saw the vast expanse of the Pacific Ocean from the western shore of the Isthmus of Panama, and the expedition led by Ferdinand Magellan that rounded the tip of South Africa and circumnavigated the globe, it became apparent that unless a short cut through the North or South American continents was found, the journey westward from Europe to China was simply too long and dangerous. (Although Magellan was killed after reaching the Philippines, his officer Juan Sebastian del Cano completed the voyage by returning to Spain three years after the expedition began.) Spain would have to be content with extracting the natural resources from the Caribbean, Mexico, and South American continent.

The quest for that shortcut through the Americas did not disappear; explorers just moved their quest to the North American continent. The search for the Northwest Passage began in the sixteenth century and centered on the Canadian Arctic. English explorers such as Martin Frobisher and Henry Hudson explored Canadian waterways in the late sixteenth and early seventeenth centuries in hopes of finding a passage to the East. It wasn't until the mid-nineteenth century that Robert McClure led an expedition that found the Northwest Passage, completing it by ship and sled. He had actually been on a search mission for a previous expedition led by Sir John Franklin. The disappearance of the Franklin expedition captured the imaginations of many would-be explorers and a number of search parties were launched. Historians disagree about how the Franklin party met their deaths. Historical theories included starvation, scurvy, lead poisoning, and cannibalism among the sailors. The Northwest Passage was not completed entirely by sea until 1906 when Norwegian explorer Roald Amundsen completed the trip. It took him three years to complete the passage. Amundsen's route, although successful, proved impractical for shipping due to the time requirements and the near impossibility of moving large ships along the shallow waterways along his route.

The Conquest of the Americas

Faced with the loss of a quick passage to the East, Spain focused its colonial resources on the islands of the Caribbean and the South American continent. Although Spain was the first European power to reach the Western Hemisphere, Portugal also claimed territory on the South American continent. Pope Alexander VI negotiated the Treaty of Tordesillas with the two powers. The treaty drew an imaginary line running north and south roughly 1,100 miles west of the Cape Verde Islands. Everything west of the line belonged to Spain and everything east of the line belonged to Portugal. Because the tip of Brazil was over the line and a Portuguese explorer, Pedro Alvarez Cabral landed on Brazil in 1500 and named it Tierra da Vera Cruz, which translates as Land of the True Cross, Portugal received control of Brazil and gained a foothold on the South American continent.

The Spanish set up colonies on a number of the islands in the Caribbean. These colonies grew sugar cane and tobacco, which proved to be valuable commodities back in Europe. But the Spanish were not content with the profits from these crops; they had heard stories of civilizations in Mexico and on the South American continent that had enormous amounts of gold, silver and other precious metals. The result was an invasion of the continent by conquistadors looking to conquer these civilizations and enrich themselves and Spain. In 1519, Hernan Cortes sailed from Cuba and landed on the Mexican coast. Leading 550 soldiers, Cortes planned to attack and conquer the Aztec Empire. Although Cortes led a relatively small group of soldiers, disgruntled native Amerindians, who were unhappy with their treatment under the Aztec ruler, aided him. Cortes captured the Aztec capital Tenochtitlan, claimed the area for Spain, naming it New Spain and within two years the entire area was under the control of the Holy Roman Emperor, Charles V. Technological superiority and disease also helped Cortes' efforts. The Aztec fighters still used Stone Age weapons, which were simply no match for Cortes's firepower. Disease may have been the most lethal and unintentional weapon that Cortes and his men brought to bear on the Aztec Empire. Because the Amerindian populations had been separated from Europe, they did not experience the same diseases and therefore had no natural immunity to those diseases common in Europe. The soldiers infected the native population with smallpox, measles, and other diseases that proved to be incredibly fatal to the population of the Aztec Empire. There is a lot of controversy among historians about the exact pre-Columbian native populations of the Caribbean islands and both continents of the Americas. The population of the Aztec Empire and the surrounding area, before Cortes's invasion, was most likely 25-28 million people. Disease and adverse working conditions decimated the native population and within a century the population had been reduced to 1-2 million people. These same diseases had already killed a high number of the Caribbean population and would later be brought by other Europeans to the North American continent with similar results.

In 1532, the Incan Empire located in the Andes Mountains in Peru suffered a fate similar to that of the Aztecs. Francisco Pizarro led 170 soldiers into the Andes. Tales of incredible wealth and large stashes of gold had lured him there. At the time of the invasion, the Incan Empire ruled over a vast territory, which included Peru, Ecuador, Bolivia, and the northern part of Chile. Just as in the Aztec Empire, many of the subject peoples were unhappy with their treatment and were willing to help the European force. By 1533, Pizarro had control of the entire empire and the Spanish made Lima the administrative capital of the region.

Catholic missionaries followed the conquistadors into the Spanish-controlled areas of the Caribbean and South America. The missionaries, who were made up of Franciscans, Dominicans and Jesuits, hoped to convert the native populations to Catholicism. They generally demonized the native ways of life, including religion, and pressured the natives to convert. Although some of the missionaries, such as Bartolome de Las Casas, objected to the harsh treatment of the natives by the Europeans, most tended to support the Spanish administration as a means for allowing the conversion of the natives.

The Spanish exploited the land and the peoples of the region in order to enrich themselves. The Spanish instituted a number of economic systems in order to help them force the native population to work both in the fields and the silver mines that the Spanish now controlled. Silver mines like the one in Potosi in Bolivia required a large number of workers to labor in very dangerous conditions. In order to get workers, the Spanish relied on two different methods. The first, **encomienda** was a practice where the Spanish king granted to a Spaniard or other European the right to force natives to work for him in the mines or in his fields doing agricultural work. The second, **repartimiento** was a revamping of an Incan practice known as the *mita*, which required all adult males to work for a set period of time in service to the government. Both of these systems gave the Spanish a pool of native workers to do the most dangerous work in the mines. Because both systems put a time limit on the length of service, native workers were often exploited and abused. The working conditions and the spread of European diseases among the native workers often resulted in their deaths.

With the native working population depleted so severely, the Spanish would have to look for a new workforce they could exploit. They found that work force in African slaves, which they began to import to work in both agricultural and mining operations. We will discuss African slavery and its impact in the New World and Africa in more detail in "Demographic and Environmental Changes" later in this book.

By the seventeenth century, Spain and Portugal had become very wealthy from their colonies, which enticed other European countries to join in the quest for gold and wealth in the new world. Although there had been attempts to settle in Canada by the French as early as the mid-sixteenth century, an incredibly harsh winter resulted in deadly cases of scurvy among many of those who attempted to winter in Canada. European fishermen, fishing the Newfoundland Banks, and trappers continued to set up summer camps in North America, but fearing the hard winters, generally returned to Europe before winter set in. In 1587, the English made their first attempt at a permanent settlement on Roanoke Island, Virginia (today, North Carolina). The colony was low on supplies, so the governor of the colony, John White, returned to England for supplies. Although he had hoped to return quickly, he was delayed due to the Spanish Armada's attack on England. He did not return to the colony until 1590. When he reached Roanoke, he found it deserted. His only clue to the whereabouts of the colonists was the word "Croatoan," which had been carved into a post. Many believe that the message meant that the colonists had gone to join the Croatoans, a friendly Indian tribe. But White was concerned because the message lacked the cross, which had been the agreed-on symbol for distress. Bad weather forced White to return to England before he could search for the colonists with the Croatoans. Although others searched for the colonists, no trace of the colonists was ever found. The Lost Colony of Roanoke remains one of history's most intriguing mysteries. After the failure in Canada and Roanoke, permanent settlements would not appear in North America until the next century.

The possibility of trade with the native North Americans drew Europeans back by the beginning of the seventeenth century. At first they were mostly interested in setting up trading posts along the coast. The Swedish set up a trading post at Fort Nassau, today Port Albany in New York. The Dutch followed, and by 1624 had built a trading post on Manhattan Island. These forts allowed the Europeans to trade with the native North Americans for fish and fur pelts. The beaver pelt was especially valued since beaver hats had become the height of fashion for European men at this time. Relationships with the Native Americans tended to be good at this point; because Europeans were really only interested in trading, they did not try to subject the natives to European social codes or laws. They also tended to be content to control only the land immediately surrounding the trading post. The infringement on native lands would come later with the more permanent settlements of the French and English.

Samuel de Champlain, a French explorer, founded the first successful French colony at Quebec in 1608. The first winter almost ended the colony. Of the 38 colonists who started the winter, only 8 were still alive when spring finally came to Quebec. The colonists died from scurvy and smallpox. The colony survived due to Champlain's belief in the importance of a French presence on the St. Lawrence and his excellent recruiting skills. He spent the majority of the rest of his life in Quebec, often serving as its governor. He died in Quebec in 1635.

The first successful English colony was established in Jamestown in 1607. The colony was made possible through the use of a joint-stock company. Joint-stock companies, which had become very popular in Europe, allowed for the financing of a number of different ventures through a number of investors pitching in a small amount of money. If the company did well, the investors would receive a return on their investment in proportion to the amount of their initial investment without risking total bankruptcy if the company failed. In 1606, King James I of England granted a charter to a joint-stock company called the Virginia Company to establish a colony in the Chesapeake Bay region. King James I had granted the colonists the rights to mine for gold, silver, and other precious metals in the region. James I would receive a percentage of all the precious metals found by the colonists. The colonists named their colony Jamestown after the king. The Jamestown settlement represented a new kind of colony in North America. While the earlier European settlements had focused around trading posts, Jamestown was a more permanent type of settlement with colonists who would need land to farm. This need for large amounts of land would put the colonists into direct confrontation with native peoples who did not want the colonists encroaching onto their land. The colony at Jamestown would experience on-again off-again difficulties with the native Algonquian in the area.

Although recent evidence has shown that most of the colonists worked hard to make the colony succeed, the colony continued to struggle to survive for a number of years. Following the departure of Captain John Smith in 1609, the colony went through a particularly hard winter, known as the "starving time" in which less than a third of the original settlers survived. While many of the Jamestown settlers had planned on becoming wealthy by finding gold and silver in Virginia, it soon became apparent that Virginia was not Mexico and no such easy riches would be found. Instead, many

119

of Virginia's settlers would become wealthy by growing tobacco and exporting it back to Europe. John Rolfe imported tobacco seeds from the Caribbean in 1611 and by 1613 sent his first crop back to England. Tobacco became a highly successful cash crop for Virginia farmers, who were sending 1.5 million pounds of tobacco back to Europe by the 1620s. As crops such as tobacco and, later, cotton became profitable for Virginians to grow and export, the necessity of a large labor force also became important. Slaves from Africa would be used to work the tobacco and cotton fields, keeping the labor costs low and the profits high for farmers.

Religion also played a part in the settlement of Europeans in North America. While colonies such as Virginia were founded as economic ventures, other colonies were founded to allow the colonists to follow their conscious and practice their own forms of religion. It is important to remember that for the most part, we are not talking about true religious freedom. Many of the colonies refused to let dissenters, those who followed a different religion, worship in the colony. The Massachusetts Bay Colony, which was set up by Puritans, did not allow women to preach. Anne Hutchinson was exiled from the colony for her beliefs, which challenged the ruling Puritans, and for conducting church services within her home.

Mercantilism

Regardless of why a colony was established or which European country established it, all colonies had an economic relationship with their mother countries. In the early modern period, an economic theory known as mercantilism developed. Basically, mercantilism is a theory used during the period to understand wealth and the trading relationships of European countries and their colonies. First of all, the theory explains that wealth is finite. That is, in order for one country to become wealthier, another country must become poorer. This set up a great deal of competition among the European countries. During this period, wealth was measured in gold and silver bullion. The more bullion a country possessed, the wealthier it was under this theory. Countries gained more bullion by having a favorable trade balance with other nations. In order to achieve this, European countries instituted a number of economic policies related to their colonies throughout the world. Generally, it was important to have high tariffs on imported manufactured goods and low tariffs on imported raw materials. In this way, a country could discourage its people from buying foreign manufactured goods by artificially inflating the price and thus keeping the valuable bullion in the country. The tariff on imported raw materials should remain low in order to keep manufacturing costs low. This allowed the manufacturer to sell the product at a lower rate within the country and also to enjoy a larger profit when the product was sold overseas. European colonies throughout the world were important in making this theory work. Colonies helped the mother countries on both ends of this process. Colonies supplied the raw materials that were needed to manufacture the product and they served as a captive market to buy the manufactured goods from the mother country.

When dealing with the American colonies, the English Parliament passed a series of laws known as the Navigation Acts to help secure England's continued wealth. The laws put four basic principles in place that supported the mercantilist interpretation of trade between the mother country and the colonies.

1. Only English or colonial merchants could trade within the colonies. This made certain that the prized gold or silver bullion could not pass to another country.

2. Highly desired American items, such as tobacco, sugar, and furs could only be sold to English merchants.

3. Any foreign goods that were imported into the colonies had to be transported on English ships and had to pay English import duties.

4. No manufactured colonial goods could be made that would compete with those produced in the mother country.

In order to compete, all European countries placed similar restrictions and regulations on their own colonies and the products they produced.

Although mercantilism was the commonly accepted economic theory of the period, it did not always function well in the real world. For instance, mother countries often could not produce enough goods for their colonies, forcing the colonies to trade secretly with other countries and colonies. Many colonies resented having to trade exclusively with their mother countries, especially when they could get the items for a cheaper price by trading directly with someone else. The result of this resentment was a great deal of smuggling among the colonies in this period. Although smuggling was illegal in all the colonies and smugglers who were caught were punished, it was almost impossible to control the miles of shoreline in each colony, and smuggling continued during this period.

Shifts in Global Interactions

As Europe expanded and set up colonies throughout the world, interactions between these areas changed forever. The transatlantic trade that developed is an example of this shift in relationships between Europe, Africa, and the Americas. The slave trade that developed in Africa represents the key to this trading system. The American colonies supplied raw materials such as cotton and furs, as well as luxury items such as sugar, tobacco, and coffee to Europe. The raw materials, once in Europe, were manufactured into goods, which could be sold back to the colonies or traded in Africa for slaves, ivory, timber, and gold. Slaves from Africa were then transported to the Americas, where they supplied the labor to produce the goods that the American colonies sent to Europe. European expansion and the resulting trading network locked these areas into a dependent relationship, which centered on the African slave trade.

Another example of the shifting in global interactions can be seen in the changes in South Africa in the mid-seventeenth century. In 1652, the Dutch founded Africa's first permanent European settlement at Table Bay. By this period, the Dutch had taken over most of the old reprovisioning stations that had been set up earlier by the Portuguese. The desire to provide fresh fruits and other foods in the ports led to the development of farming in South Africa. The farmers, who called themselves Boers or Afrikaners, were Calvinists from the Netherlands and France. They used slave labor on the farms to grow the food. As would happen later with other European colonies in other parts of Africa and India, a strict racial division developed. Europeans placed themselves at the top of this division, controlling government and land. Black Africans were kept in a strictly subordinate position with almost no rights or privileges. In South Africa this practice became known as Apartheid and existed until the late twentieth century.

Practice Test Questions

1. Europeans began looking for a new trading route with the East because

   A. the old trading route had been destroyed by an earthquake.
   B. they hoped to reestablish a trading relationship with the East that had been lost after the Barbarian invasions of the Roman Empire.
   C. Europeans hoped to cut out the Ottomans who had been serving as middlemen and thus lower the cost of eastern goods.
   D. the Ottomans had stopped trading with Europeans, preferring to trade only with the Chinese.

2. The Northwest Passage was finally completed by sea in 1906 by Roald Amundsen. Why was the passage not used for shipping?

   A. Jealousy. After looking for so long, Amundsen refused to reveal how he did it.
   B. It was too long and impractical for shipping.
   C. By this time, a number of Northwest Passages had been discovered throughout the United States.
   D. Shipping was no longer important and the passage was not needed.

3. All of the following helped Cortes and Pizarro defeat the native empires except

   A. disease.
   B. superior technology.
   C. native aid.
   D. help of French soldiers.

4. Catholic missionaries who followed the conquistadors generally

   A. helped the native population resist Spanish control.
   B. supported the Spanish administration.
   C. called on the native populations to revolt against Spanish control.
   D. failed to convert any natives to Catholicism.

5. Mercantilism

   A. was used to explain the trading relationship between colonies and mother countries.
   B. was used to replace the risk of joint-stock companies.
   C. was a theory that said all of a country's resources belonged to the king.
   D. resulted in the Lost Colony of Roanoke.

Answers and Explanations

1. **C.** Europeans wanted to lower the cost and increase their own profits on goods from China.

2. **B.** Amundsen took three years to complete the voyage and much of the route was in water too shallow for large ships to pass.

3. **D.** Disease, superior technology, and native aid helped Cortes defeat the Aztec Empire. He did not receive help from any other European power.

4. **B.** Although a few Catholic missionaries spoke about the abuse and exploitation of native workers, most supported the Spanish administration, believing it was the only way to convert the natives to Catholicism.

5. **A.** In the Early Modern Period many economists supported the mercantilism theory and it was used to explain how countries should run their colonies.

Empires

The Early Modern Period witnessed the consolidation of power and the expansion of certain civilizations throughout the world. The nation-states, which developed in Europe and the empires, as well as in Asia and Africa allowed for the consolidation of power under one ruler. The major exception to this trend was England, which developed a form of constitutional monarchy, that included a monarch and a parliament, both of which, at least theoretically, shared power. As you read through the discussion of the development of nation-states and empires, it is interesting to consider what they have in common and how they are different.

The Development of European Nation-States

Power in the Middle Ages tended to be divided between three often competing elements: the monarchy, the nobility, and the Church in Europe. The Early Modern Period, on the other hand, saw the rise of a number of powerful monarchs who were able to consolidate power and, thus, weaken the nobility and the church in Europe. Nation-states, no matter where they exist, tend to have a number of features in common. First, the state must have fixed boundaries that can be identified on a map. This does not mean that the borders cannot expand and contract over time, but they will generally stay fairly close to the original borders. Second, the people within the borders must identify and buy into the idea of the state. This is sometimes referred to as **nationalism.** The people share a belief that they are unique from the people on the other side of the borders. In order to achieve this, the people tend to share a common language, religion, heritage, and culture. These can be real or created as long as the people involved accept the ideas as their own.

Nation-states tend to work best with people who are similar and believe that they share all of these traits. People who are too different from each other and who do not accept a shared identity or belief often find it very difficult to exist within a nation-state. Yugoslavia was a nation-state with diverse peoples who were not able to find a common ground, and the result was internal warfare and finally the breaking apart of the state. Third, the government of the nation-state must hold military power. It is impossible for a ruler to hold supreme power if someone else within the state can threaten him militarily. Finally, the people within the nation-state must accept the ruler and the legitimacy of his rule.

Absolutism in France

By the seventeenth century, countries such as France and England had begun to develop systems of government that would lead to the development of strong nation-states. Over the course of two monarchies, France developed into an absolutist state in which the ruler, in this case the king, controlled all facets of government. Although absolutism began under Louis XIII (1610–1643) and his chief minister, Cardinal Richelieu (d. 1642), it was under the rule of Louis XIV that France became a true absolutist government. Louis XIV consolidated his power over the nobility by allowing them to keep their noble titles and privileges, but removing them from any real control within the government. Louis XIV built a palace at Versailles and made it the seat of his government. The nobility moved to Versailles, where Louis made certain they were entertained and kept busy with trivial matters. This allowed him to run the government and removed the threat of any noble attempt to regain their power through revolt. Louis XIV created a system of professional bureaucrats who were drawn from the educated upper middle class and ran the government of France. Since these men owed their rank to Louis and not to an inherited title, they remained loyal to Louis and the state.

In 1685, Louis revoked the Edict of Nantes that had been granted to French Protestants known as Huguenots by Henry IV in 1598. The protection afforded the Huguenots under the edict had become increasingly unpopular through the years. Although Louis was aware of the unpopularity of the edict, he ordered its removal because he believed that a country needed religious unity in order to succeed. When the edict was revoked, all French Huguenots were required to accept the Catholic faith. Huguenots responded in one of three ways to the end of their protections and special privileges. Some truly converted to Catholicism, some outwardly converted but continued to practice Protestantism in secret, and a large number left France, relocating to Protestant areas including territories within the Holy Roman Empire, England, and Protestant colonies in North America.

Louis XIV also used his newly developed army to attempt to expand his territory and increase the power of France in Europe. For the most part, Louis was unsuccessful in his goals. Other nations resisted Louis' attempts at expansion by banding together to preserve the balance of power on the continent. Louis was able to attempt this expansion due to the development of his new state army. Prior to the Early Modern Period, armies were supplied and led by noblemen who might or might not prove loyal to the king. Many battles were decided because a king placed his faith in the wrong nobleman, who, on the day of the battle, showed up with his forces on the opposite side of the battlefield. Louis created a state army, which was loyal to him and therefore France. The soldiers were paid and supplies were provided by the state, not a member of the nobility.

Louis also standardized the rank system throughout his army and, thus, created a firm chain of command with himself at the top. Louis XIV created a state in which he was the absolute power. He was known as the Sun King and his emblem of the sun was reproduced on buildings and used throughout the décor of Versailles. Louis believed that just as everything revolved around the Sun, all of France revolved around him. By the time of his death in 1715, France was the leading country in Europe. Monarchs of lesser countries strove to emulate Louis XIV with varying degrees of success, by learning French, building their own palaces in the image of Versailles and, most importantly, attempting to control those who vied for their power by implementing the principles of absolutism within their own territories.

Constitutionalism in England

Although the English monarchs would have liked to follow France's example and create an absolutist government in England, the Scottish Stuart monarchs were not adept at working with the English Parliament and failed to consolidate power under themselves. James I, who became the king of England following the death of the last Tudor monarch, Elizabeth I, in 1603, believed in the idea of divine right monarchy, which stated that a monarch owed his power and position to the will of God alone. Under this system, God determines who will rule and there is no place for the consent of the governed or any type of election. Divine right monarchs believed that they were above the law and answerable to no one but God.

This belief did not sit well with the English Parliament, which believed itself to be a sort of partner to the king in the ruling of England. The English Parliament, which originated in the medieval period, had developed into an advisory body with a real role in the law making and tax collecting in England. For instance, by the sixteenth century, only Parliament could approve new taxes for the kingdom and although it met at the monarch's pleasure, enjoyed a fairly regular schedule under the Tudor monarchs. Because of disputes over increased taxes and James I's belief that he did not have to answer to Parliament, the relationship between them was often strained. James excluded Parliament from a role in government and the Parliament retaliated by refusing to grant James additional revenue through increased taxation.

James I's son, Charles I, also attempted to rule as an absolutist or divine right monarch when he took the throne in 1625 by attempting to force Parliament to recognize his rule as the supreme head of state. Desperate for money, early in his reign, Charles signed the Petition of Right, which formally recognized the role of Parliament in the areas of taxation and therefore curtailed royal power, in exchange for money. Although Charles had signed the petition, he quickly changed his mind and refused to accept the conditions within it. When Parliament pushed the issue, Charles responded by dismissing them and ruled without calling Parliament for the next 11 years. By 1639, Charles was forced to return to Parliament in hopes of getting funds to put down a rebellion in Scotland. Charles, who was king of both England and Scotland, had attempted to force the Anglican Church of England on the Calvinist Scottish, who responded by revolting. Parliament, sensing Charles' desperation, attempted to push him to accept the Petition of Right and acknowledge their role in England's government. Charles' continued reluctance and Parliament's continued insistence resulted in the English Civil War, which broke out in 1642 and ended with the capture and execution by beheading of Charles I in 1649.

The victorious Parliamentary forces had been led by Oliver Cromwell and following the capture of Charles I, he set up a commonwealth government in England. Although claiming to be a republic, Cromwell's government was in fact a military state. Throughout his rule, Cromwell had continual problems with the Parliament who did not appreciate Cromwell's absolutism any more than they had appreciate the absolutism of the Stuart monarchs. After Cromwell's death, the parliament invited Charles I's son, Charles II, to return as their king. Partly due to the fact that he had been invited by Parliament and partly due to the fact that Charles II did not want to end up with his father's fate, he backed away from the absolutist and divine right ideals of his father and grandfather.

While Charles II was able to reconcile his monarchy with the participatory role of Parliament, he faced additional problems in the area of religion. Since the time of Elizabeth I, England had been a Protestant nation. During Elizabeth's reign, Philip II and the Pope had attempted to force the return of England to Catholicism through the failed invasion attempt of the Spanish Armada and the use of Jesuit missionaries in England. Knowing that English Protestants continued to fear attempts to return them to Catholicism, Charles II kept his Catholicism a secret and only confessed on his deathbed.

The problem for English Protestants centered around Charles II's heir, his brother, James II, who was not only a Catholic, but unlike his brother, saw no reason to keep it a secret. In the period before Charles II's death, Parliament debated about whether or not to allow an openly Catholic monarch to take the throne of England. In the end, Parliament decided that James II could take the throne. By this period he was getting old and his two heirs, adult daughters Mary and Ann were Protestants. Mary, in fact, was married to the leader of Protestant Europe, William of Orange, who ruled the Dutch Republic. Unfortunately for Parliament, James did not behave after he took the throne. He not only flaunted his Catholicism, he also chose to ignore the laws that restrict the promotion of Catholics to high offices in the government and the military. The most troubling action, though, was his marriage to a young Italian and Catholic princess. This union quickly produced a male heir, which bumped James's Protestant daughters from their place in the succession and replaced them with a new male Catholic heir to the English throne. Parliament decided to act and in doing so claimed the ability to determine who would be the monarch of England.

Secretly, Parliament negotiated with James' eldest daughter Mary and her husband, William of Orange, to take the throne of England. In 1688, William landed in England with a small force. James fled to France with his wife and son to raise an army and take back his throne. Parliament claimed that by fleeing to France, James had abandoned the throne and proclaimed William and Mary to be coregents of England. This bloodless transfer of power is known as the Glorious Revolution and firmly established the role of Parliament in the governing of England. As part of the deal, William and Mary accepted the Bill of Rights, which outlined the civil rights of the English people and described the powers of Parliament. Although the early Stuart monarchs had attempted to establish the English government along the lines of absolutism, the later Stuart monarchs secured the throne by recognizing the traditional power of Parliament and agreeing to share the rule of England.

What developed during this period and later in England was a constitutional monarchy. Under this system, the monarch is controlled by the legislative branch of government, which represents the will of at least some of the people. In this period, that representation is limited to the nobility, but England's Industrial Revolution and expanding empire would shortly expand the influence of the other lower classes in England.

The Rise of Absolutism in Russia

For much of the medieval and Early Modern Period, Russia's experiences differed from those of the rest of Europe. Controlled until about 1480 by Mongol Khans, Russia's orientation had been to the East with only very limited contact with western culture or political systems. One exception was the Christian Orthodox Church in Constantinople. When the Turks finally succeeded in capturing Constantinople in 1453, the Russian tsars claimed to be the successors of the Byzantine Church and the protectors of Orthodox Christians in the world.

This claim was strengthened after Ivan III married the last Byzantine emperor's niece and took the Byzantine emperor's seal of the double-headed eagle as his own. Both Ivan III and Ivan IV, known as Ivan the Terrible, were able to add vast tracts of land to their growing Muscovite Empire through military victories against failing khanates in the North and East. Although Ivan IV tried to add land in the West, he failed to defeat the Polish and Lithuanian factions, resulting in a long drawn-out 25-year war. In internal matters, both Ivan III and Ivan IV worked to control the traditional nobility, the Boyars. Ivan IV, who came to the throne at three years of age, seems to have suffered under boyar power as a child when different factions competed to control him and those the Muscovite state. After his failed attempt to take control of territory in the West, Ivan IV blamed the boyars and sent out killing squads to murder the boyars and their families. Although he did not kill all the boyars, their power was significantly reduced. What developed was a service nobility, which was appointed by the ruler, had limited powers, and served the state in the army and bureaucracy.

The tradition of expansion and autocratic rule, which began in the Muscovite state, continued under the rule of the Romanov dynasty, which began in 1613 with the rule of Michael Romanov. The Romanov dynasty controlled Russia until 1917. Although Michael Romanov, who was Ivan IV's grandnephew, was heavily supported by the Russian aristocracy, who believed he could bring about an end to the internal strife and conflict known as the Time of Troubles, his influence proved to be short lived and his immediate successors struggled to contain the explosive forces within Russia. Peter the Great, who ruled Russia from 1682 until 1725, instituted a number of changes within Russia, which allowed for the development of an absolutist-style government and an increase in the territory controlled by the Russian Empire. Peter had two very significant goals when he took power: He wanted to make Russia a player on the European stage, and he wanted to expand Russian territory in order to acquire a warm-water port. At the bottom of both of these goals was a desire by Peter to increase his power both within the state and over the territories surrounding Russia.

Shortly after becoming Tsar, Peter took an extensive tour of Western Europe. He was most interested in the advanced technology of the West and planned to apply what he learned to the modernization of Russia. After he returned, Peter began a policy of westernization and instituted a number of reforms mainly among the Russian nobility. Peter forbade nobles to wear long beards at court and anyone who defied Peter was very likely to have his beard cut off publicly. Peter required that his nobles become more western. They were required to wear western dress, send their sons away for western schooling, and they were ordered to eat and socialize with women.

Most of Peter's reforms were not permanent. They proved to be very unpopular and most were turned back by his successors. One area where Peter's reforms remained was his redesign of the army. While in Europe, Peter had met with the Prussian king and admired his professional and well-trained army. Once he returned, Peter was determined to have a bigger and better army in Russia.

In order to make his army better, Peter had to initiate a number of reforms. First of all, he needed to change his semi-professional part-time army into a real fighting machine. He did this by creating stability in the army by requiring all nobles to serve in the army for life. He also instituted a draft for the peasantry, who were also drafted for life. By the time he was finished, Peter had a standing army of 200,000 professional soldiers who were well trained, well armed, and serving for life. Peter realized that a standing army was incrediblly expensive, so he instituted taxes and raised existing taxes to pay for his new army.

Once his army was in place, Peter wasted little time in testing it. In the Great Northern War, Peter's larger army proved successful against Sweden's much smaller army, and Peter added Estonia, Latvia, and part of Finland to his empire. Under Peter the Great, Russia became the dominant power in the Baltic and he moved his capital from Moscow to St. Petersburg, which he called, his "window on the west." By the end of Peter the Great's reign, Russia was a major European power, controlling a large amount of land in Eastern Europe and on the Baltic. Although Peter was unable to add the warm-water port to his empire, that would be achieved by Catherine the Great, who ruled Russia from 1762–1796. Peter continued the legacy of his Muscovite predecessors by continuing to consolidate his own power within Russia and to expand the Russian Empire by taking control of neighboring lands and expanding Russian influence and control.

Empires

Although empires have existed throughout history, the Early Modern Period saw the development of a number of empires throughout the world. An empire is different from a nation-state in that it usually exists over a much larger territory and encompasses people of very different cultures. Like the nation-state, a strong single authority controls the empire, but there is no requirement that the leader possess the consent of the people that he governs. In most cases, hereditary rulers who pass their title from father to son ruled the empires of the Early Modern Period. Just as in the ancient world of empires, there is always the possibility that the hereditary ruler could be usurped and replaced by a distant family member or someone outside of the family.

Empires, whether they exist in the ancient world or the Early Modern Period, faced a number of challenges, including the effective control of a large amount of territory, the systematic collection of taxes, and the ability to assemble an army. In all of the cases discussed below, the emperors managed to meet these challenges through effective use of their resources. In most cases, empires are built through warfare; just as Peter the Great used his army to expand the territory controlled by the Russian Empire, other emperors throughout the world used military force to extend their authority. Although the strict control of empires tended to break down over time, during the zenith of their power, most emperors provided their people with long periods of internal peace. These periods often resulted in great works of art and architecture, which were generally funded by the emperor himself.

Asian Empires

During the Early Modern Period, a number of empires ruled various lands throughout Asia. While most have long histories that extended at least to the medieval period, others were formed during this period.

Ottoman Empire

The Ottoman Empire, which was founded by a Turkish Emir, Osman I, in 1299, proved to be one of the longest lived of the Asian Empires. Because of its location to the south of Europe, the Ottoman Empire came into contact with various European countries throughout its existence and was even drawn into a number of its conflicts through alliances with European powers. The early history of the Ottoman Empire throughout the medieval period and the Early Modern Period is one of expansion through conflict. By 1320, the emperors, or Sultans, controlled all of Anatolia and later emperors added territory in the Balkans and parts of Greece. One of the reasons that the Ottoman military proved to be so effective was due to its use of professional soldiers that had been raised within the military system. These soldiers, known as the Janissary Troops, consisted of male children that had been taken from Christian territories under the sultan's rule. These children were converted to Islam, received military training, and became a military force with loyalty to no one other than the sultan and the Ottoman Empire. At the height of its power, the Ottoman Empire extended from the Danube River in Europe to the Euphrates River in present-day Iraq.

As the Ottoman Empire expanded it took control of areas with Muslims, Christians, and Jews. Following the dictates of the Koran, the Ottoman Empire protected the "people of the book" and allowed them to continue to worship as either Christians or Jews. Although European propaganda often accused the Ottomans of forcing Christians and Jews to convert to Islam, forced conversion was only practiced on those still following pagan religions. When Medmed II succeeded in conquering Constantinople in 1453 after an almost two-month siege, many within the city welcomed the Islamic conquerors and the liberal religious policy of the Ottomans. As with almost all empires throughout history, Mehmed II had to ensure that the primary functions of empire were fulfilled. He set up a system for the collection of taxes and instituted a bureaucracy that could oversee the day-to-day functioning of the empire. The Ottoman Empire continued to exist, although with a number of problems, until the end of the First World War. Often referred to as the "sick man of Europe" by European powers, the empire finally succumbed to nationalism and broke apart following its defeat in 1918.

Mughal Empire

The Mughal Empire, which existed in India from 1524 until 1857, had lost any real power with the coming of the British in 1760. The last empire was not removed from power by the British until 1857. Babur, a ruler of a petty kingdom in Central Asia, seized control of Afghanistan and then expanded his control over Northern India. Just as an innovation in military training aided the Ottomans in expansion, Babur was also able to expand his empire due to improved technology, in this case guns and cannons. With the defeat of the King of Delhi, Babur became the Emperor of Hindustan. Although he was eager to continue his expansion within India, his death in 1530 prevented that. After the disastrous rule of Babur's son, who lost a great deal of the territory that his father had conquered, Babur's grandson, Akbar, began the process of regaining the family's territory and prestige. Again through warfare, Akbar was able to regain the family's lost territory and add to his kingdom.

Since the Mughal Empire was a foreign rule imposed on India, it was important that Akbar have complete control of the government. He set up an absolutist-style government. Akbar controlled all facets of government, and the Koran and Islamic tradition were his only restraints in ruling his empire. Although it was not absolutely necessary, Akbar realized that his rule and the future rule of his successors would proceed more smoothly if he could reconcile the two religions within his empire. Akbar extended opportunities in government to some of his Hindu subjects. He did not authorize any forced conversions and attempted to include both his Muslim and Hindu subjects in positions in government. He even encouraged intermarriage between the two groups. Although a number of intermarriages did take place, including Akbar himself, the two groups never really accepted each other. Later Mughal rulers would fail to follow Akbar's example and religious differences would continue to plague the empire. By 1760, the Mughal Empire was in serious trouble due to a series of invasions, ineffective leadership, and religious differences. This period of internal difficulty is referred to as the Great Anarchy and was only ended by the British when they extended their control over India through the British East India Company.

Tokugawa Empire

By the time that Tokugawa Ieyasu took the title of Shogun in 1603, setting up the Tokugawa Shogunate, a hereditary military dictatorship, Japan had been under the control of an emperor for roughly 400 years. Tokugawa extended his control of Japan by first defeating rival forces and usurping the throne of the rightful infant heir. But once he was in control, it was important to keep it and he set up a number of policies to ensure that he and his successors would be able to control Japan. The Japanese nobility, daimyo, of which Tokugawa had been a part, had enjoyed a large amount of freedom under the previous ruler. Tokugawa needed to put an end to that, so, like Louis XIV, he created a new capital city where the nobility was required to spend at least part of their time. The new capital at Edo, present-day Tokyo, became a sort of trap for the nobility. Families of noblemen were required to stay at the capital permanently and the noblemen themselves were required to spend every other year at Edo. Since it was a new capital, Tokugawa encouraged the nobility to spend vast amounts of money building new houses that would allow them to live in luxury. Most of the nobility could not afford the huge amounts of money they spent in Edo, thus insuring that they would be distracted by their finances and less likely to present any real challenge to Tokugawa's rule. In order to ensure that his nobility was not plotting against him, Tokugawa created a secret police that watched the activities of the nobility and the peasantry.

Unlike other empires in Asia, Tokugawa also forced Japan into a period of isolation. Christian missionaries in Japan had grown increasingly successful at converting the Japanese away from the traditional religions to Christianity. Because of the missionaries' failure to accept religions other than Christianity, Tokugawa feared that these new Christians might begin to question his control over the empire. As a result of this fear, Tokugawa expelled all missionaries and banned Christianity throughout Japan. Christianity disappeared from Japan fairly quickly after the missionaries left. After Tokugawa's death, his successors would expel all foreigners, including European traders and forbade all Japanese from traveling abroad. Tokugawa's descendants ruled Japan until 1868. Although Japan experienced isolation from the western world during the Tokugawa period, they did experience relative peace, resulting in a flourishing culture at the royal court.

African Empires

From the late medieval period to the coming of the Europeans, Africa experienced a period of empire in which rulers consolidated their power and expanded their territories. Most of the empires had become wealthy from the gold or salt trade and used that wealth as a means of expansion. Although some kingdoms, such as the Benin, increased their wealth due to the trans-Atlantic slave trade, most kingdoms found it difficult to survive when faced with the European demand for ever-increasing numbers of slaves. One of the most striking features of these African empires is there expert artistic work in ivory, gold, and bronze.

Songhay Empire

The Songhay Empire, which developed in Africa around the middle of the fifteenth century, was located in West Africa along the Niger River. The empire, which was founded by Sunni Ali, was built on the remnants of the older Mali kingdom. The empire, which controlled access to the gold trade in Western Africa, became very wealthy. Ali followed a policy of expansion using a navy and highly trained cavalry; he quickly took control of neighboring Jenne and Timbuktu. In order to make his territory easier to control, Ali like many other emperors, divided his territory into districts and appointed trusted officials to oversee the running of the provinces. Under his successors, the Songhay Empire developed into one of the most important empires in Africa. The empire stretched from just short of the Atlantic coast in the west, to the Sahara in the north and to central Sudan in the east. Although Sunni Ali followed the traditional African religion, his successors converted to Islam and remade the state to reflect its new Islamic focus. The empire reached its height under Muhammad the Great, who encouraged education and brought in Muslim advisors and judges to help with the adoption of Islam within the empire. Although the empire itself lasted until about the 1600s, it finally collapsed under the continued pressure of the European slave trade.

Benin Empire

The Benin Empire, which developed as early as the 1300s, became the most powerful kingdom in West Africa. The kingdom extended from Lagos to the Niger River and was one of the first African kingdoms to come into contact with the European traders. The most important king, King Euware, took power in the 1500s and set about expanding his territory and consolidating his rule within the empire. Traditionally, a king, or oba, was believed to be at least partly divine and extremely powerful. The king was so powerful in fact that his health was seen as a reflection of the health of the kingdom. King Euware instituted a system where he had ultimate authority over the entire empire and used his army to expand the empire. By the seventeenth century, the Benin Empire possessed land from the southern Niger Delta to at least the eastern edge of the neighboring Ijebu territory.

Oral tradition within the Benin Empire claims that Benin conquered and controlled the Ijebu, but the Ijebu oral tradition disputes this claim. Slavery existed within the empire, but historians consider it to be a more humane system than was practiced during the trans-Atlantic slave trade that developed a little later. The Benin Empire cooperated with the European trans-Atlantic slave trade and increased its wealth. Just as in the empires in other places around the world, the Benin emperors took great pride in supporting the arts within the empire. When a new oba took the throne, he commissioned artists to make beautiful and intricate bronze heads to represent and honor his immediate predecessors. While it is true that each head represented a particular oba, they were not portraits in the truest sense of the word; instead, those who study the heads today believe that they reflect particular attributes that a king must possess in order to be successful.

Practice Test Questions

1. Louis XIV established Versailles

    A. as a vacation spot where he could get away from the stresses of running France.

    B. as a royal palace where he could run the government outside of Paris.

    C. as an example of neo-classical architecture.

    D. Versailles was built after the death of Louis XIV.

2. Following the fall of Constantinople, Russia

    A. became an Islamic state.

    B. attacked the Ottoman Empire.

    C. claimed to be the new protector of the Orthodox Church.

    D. claimed Constantinople for itself.

3. One of the most important aspects of Benin culture was

    A. its law code.

    B. its highly detailed and beautiful bronze artwork.

    C. it ability to capture and control the entire continent of Africa.

    D. its acceptance and spreading of Christianity over the entire continent of Africa.

4. Akbar strengthened his rule over India by

    A. sheer force of arms.

    B. marrying into the old royal family.

    C. allowing Hindus as well as Muslims to hold state offices.

    D. forcibly relocating all Hindus outside the borders of his empire.

5. Jews and Christians within the Ottoman Empire

    A. experienced horrific living conditions.

    B. were enslaved.

    C. were forced to leave the empire.

    D. were protected and allowed to worship freely as "people of the book."

Answers and Explanations

1. **B.** Louis XIV believed that he could better control the monarchy and therefore ran the government from Versailles. Louis had had difficulty controlling the nobility who had attempted to gain power during his minority. Running the government from Versailles put Louis firmly in control by cutting the aristocracy off from their traditional power base in Paris.

2. **C.** Russia claimed to be the heir of the Byzantine Empire and the protector of Orthodox Christians After the fall of Constantinople to the Turks, Ivan III strengthened his claim that Russia was the heir to the Byzantine Empire by marrying the niece of the last Byzantine Empire.

3. **B.** The Benin emperors supported the court artists who produced bronze sculptures. Benin emperors took great pride in supporting the arts. Artists often made bronze sculptures that reflected the characteristics of the emperors.

4. **C.** Akbar attempted to stabilize his empire by allowing both Hindus and Muslims to participate in government.

5. **D.** Following the Koran, the Ottoman Empire allowed Jews and Christians to worship freely. The Koran considers Jews and Christians to be people of the book and allows them to worship with very few restrictions.

Slave Systems and the Slave Trade

The practice of slavery has existed throughout most of human history. The practice of slavery has been identified in Mayan, Aztec, Egyptian, Greek, and Roman civilizations. When a person or group of people was forced to work for another group without being reimbursed in money or goods, that was slavery. The practice of slavery was a brutal form of human interaction. Slaves were considered the property of their owners. Slaves often had very few rights and were at the bottom of every social hierarchy. They could not choose to leave their work for another job. Slaves were often brutalized, and in many cases an owner could beat or even kill his slaves with no legal repercussions. Slaves could sometimes be freed by their owner, but that depended on the time and place in which the slaves found themselves. For instance, an owner could free a slave in the Roman Empire. Some slaves were even permitted to work and earn money to buy their freedom. In some cases, ancient Hebrew law required that a slave be freed if his owner brutalized him. On the other hand, a slave in Sparta could never be freed. Since the slaves were essential to the effective running of Spartan society, the slaves were state owned—that is, not owned by individuals but the government as a whole—and the government forbid the freeing of any slaves in Sparta.

The ancient world practiced slavery, and in many places, including the Roman Empire, the economy was dependent on the work performed by slaves. For instance, the Roman Empire would not have been able to survive as long as it did if slave labor had not been available to them. Slavery is also discussed in both the Bible and the Koran. Although there are a number of examples of slavery in the ancient world, it is important to remember that the slavery practiced in places like Greece and Roman was different from the slavery that developed in the New World during the early modern period. In the ancient world, a person found him or herself in slavery under certain circumstances:

1. To settle a debt. A person could sell himself into slavery to settle a debt he had incurred. He could sell his children into slavery to settle the debt, or his debtors could decide that they were not going to wait any longer for repayment and sell the person into slavery to settle the debt themselves and thus recoup their money. Although it is not always true, when a person sold his children into slavery, he often sold his daughters, who were considered much less valuable to the family.

2. A person could be captured during a war and find himself a slave in the country of the victor. There are a number of examples of defeated peoples being sold into slavery by those who had defeated them. In 416 BC during the Peloponnesian War, Athens defeated the island of Melos. The Athenians killed all the men on the island and sold the women and children into slavery. As Rome expanded during the late republic and empire periods, many defeated peoples, such as those in Gaul and Briton were sent back to Rome as slaves.

3. A person could be born into slavery. If his parents were slaves, then he was also a slave.

It is important to remember, that slavery in the ancient world was not race based. Slaves and masters often looked very much alike. This could prove a problem for owners and often made it easier for slaves in the ancient world to escape and blend in. But it also allowed the descendants of freed slaves, called freedmen, to assimilate into society much easier and faster than if they had been identifiably different. In Rome, children of freedmen had all the rights of a Roman citizen and could even run for public office. Slavery also existed within Europe, concentrated in Spain and Italy, during the High Middle Ages. Poor economic conditions in central and eastern Europe resulted in a number of people being enslaved from that region. Since a large number of those enslaved during that period were of Slavic origin, the word slave most likely evolved from its origin meaning of an unfree person of Slavic origin to include all people held in bondage, regardless of their ethnic background. Although it is true that African slaves began to appear in large numbers throughout Europe in the sixteenth century, slaves were not popular in most of Europe. This unpopularity is most likely due to the large number of poor European workers that were available, making slavery in Europe unnecessary. It may also have been due to the continued use of serf labor in places such as eastern Europe. Although the use of serfs no longer existed in western Europe by this period, it did continue in eastern Europe and Russia until the eighteenth and nineteenth centuries.

Slavery in the Early Modern Period

When Europeans found themselves short on labor due to the deaths of the native populations in the Caribbean and the Americas, both from disease and overwork, they began to forcibly import African slaves to work in their mines and fields. This slavery was different in a number of ways than the slavery that had existed in the ancient world. The most important difference being that this slave trade was race based and generationally perpetual—that is, always passed from parent to child. Europeans believed themselves to be superior to people of color, especially Africans, in every way, including culturally, socially, politically, and intellectually. This feeling of superiority was based primarily on skin color. Slavery in the Caribbean and the Americas was for the most part race based. This meant that slaves were identifiably different. This made it easier to identify who were slaves and who were not slaves in the European colonies. The use of slaves made the European plantations much more profitable and added to the desirability of using African slaves. The use of slaves in the Caribbean made the practice of imperialism more profitable for Europeans in the Caribbean and Europe. While it is true that Europeans thought of themselves as superior to people of color throughout the world, that is not the only reason that the Europeans looked to Africa to supply slaves for their plantations. In fact, Europeans took advantage of a slavery system that was already operating in Africa. Africa experienced the slave trade on a number of different levels. Prior to the beginning of the trans-Atlantic slave trade, slavery existed within Africa and slaves were exported to the Islamic Middle East. The internal slave trade in Africa was much like the older pre-modern model of slavery. Slaves tended to be captured in war. Slavery was not race based. Slaves worked in a number of fields including as soldiers, sailors, agricultural workers, and domestic workers. There is a fair amount of controversy surrounding the conditions under which the African slave trade existed within Africa. Some historians have argued that slavery within Africa was less brutal than the slave trade outside of Africa. While historians have not been able to come to a conclusion, it is important to remember that slaves within Africa were slaves and therefore not free to live their lives as they wished.

The Oriental Slave Trade

Europeans did not originate the African slave trade. In fact, slaves had been exported from Africa to Islamic countries in the East at least a century before the Atlantic slave trade began. The slave trade from Africa to the East is called the Oriental slave trade. Slaves were mostly taken from the eastern part of Africa and the African Horn. Slaves exported to the East were often servants to the sultanates of the Middle East. They worked as sailors, soldiers, agricultural workers, and domestics. A large number of young African women were taken as slaves and forced to become concubines and sex slaves. Because eunuchs brought a high price in the oriental slave trade, the young boys who were captured as slaves were often castrated before they were sold. While it is true that Oriental slave trade never exported the large number of slaves that the Atlantic slave trade exported, it has been estimated that close to 10,000 slaves left Africa each year as a result of the oriental trade. Although it has been argued that the Oriental trade was not race based because slaves of every color could be found in Islamic countries, it is possible that racism did play a part. Recently historians have found that although the institution of slavery was not limited to people of a certain color, African slaves do seem to have been considered less valuable than other slaves due to their skin color. The oriental slave trade, which began before the Atlantic slave trade, lasted much longer. Saudi Arabia abolished slavery in the 1960s only after a great deal of pressure from western countries such as Great Britain and France. Slavery still exists in a handful of Islamic countries today.

The Occidental Slave Trade

Historians generally refer to the slave trade that developed in the fifteenth century between Africa and the New World as the Occidental slave trade. Europeans had originally relied on the native populations to work on the plantations, but as the native population succumbed to the European diseases and the brutality of the forced labor practices, Europeans were forced to find a new source of labor. Europeans turned to the already well-established slave trade operating in Africa. Since Europeans imported slaves mainly for agricultural work, they tended to import more male slaves, unlike the Muslims, who tended to import more female slaves.

This slave trade centered on the needs of the plantation economy that developed in the European colonies of the New World. In the beginning, African slaves were needed to work on the labor-intensive sugar plantations in the Caribbean. By the mid-sixteenth century, large numbers of African slaves were being brought to Brazil to work the large and incredibly profitable sugar plantations. Sugar plantations required large amounts of land and large amounts of workers. The only way to keep the profits high was to use unpaid labor, in this case slave labor from Africa. African slaves proved to be better able to handle the heat than European workers and they were more resistant to European diseases than the native populations had been and therefore they made ideal workers on the European plantations. The plantation system developed by the

Portuguese was adapted to tobacco, rice, and cotton and used throughout the Caribbean and the Americas. The acquisition of slaves to work on the plantations became the most valuable part of the trans-Atlantic trading system in the late sixteenth century.

Although Europeans, first the Dutch, then the Portuguese, the British, and the Americans all participated in the transfer of slaves across the Atlantic, they could not capture the slaves for themselves. The interior of Africa harbored a number of deadly diseases for which the Europeans and later Americans had no immunities, so they had to rely on the Africans to capture the slaves and transport them to the coast where they could be picked up and loaded on board ships bound for the New World. Those, including some African rulers such as the ruler of Dahomey, who cooperated with the European slave traders, prospered and became very wealthy. Most of the slaves were captured in raids by warring tribes, although as the prices for slaves increased, some found themselves enslaved for even minor transgressions, which were punished by enslavement in the New World.

Captured Africans from the interior were forced to march long distances to the coast where they could be traded for manufactured goods, including guns, and taken to the New World. Due to the long distances, little time for rest, and little or no food, as many as half of the captives died before they reached the coast. Captives were held at the coast in slave factories for up to a year in horrible conditions before they boarded a ship that would cross the Atlantic and take them to the New World.

The trip across the Atlantic from Africa to the New World is generally referred to as the middle passage. It gained this name from the system of Triangular Trade, which described the trans-Atlantic trade as a triangle going from Europe to Africa, from Africa to the New World, and then back to Europe. Europeans traded guns and other manufactured goods for the slaves that they then transported to the New World. Once they reached the Caribbean or the Americas, the traders sold the slaves and return to Europe with raw materials to be processed in Europe, as well as the products grown with slave labor including sugar, cotton, and tobacco. Although historians rarely refer to the trans-Atlantic trade as the Triangular Trade, the trade was much more complex, but the term middle passage has remained to describe the journey and horrible experiences of the slaves being transported across the Atlantic.

Slave ships carried anywhere from 200–600 slaves who were packed closely together on the ships in order to allow the maximum number of slaves to make the journey and thus increase the slaver's profit once he reached the New World. Slaves had very little room and male slaves were shackled together to prevent them from revolting while onboard the ship. Since the crews had little fear of women and children they were often not shackled together although they had no more room than male slaves. Female slaves also faced the real possibility that the ship's crew would sexually exploit them during the voyage. The journey could take anywhere from five weeks to three months depending on the time of year and the weather in the Atlantic. Slaves were kept below deck for much of the journey. As long as the weather was good, slaves were allowed to be on deck, still shackled together, for a short period of time every day. For at least part of their time on deck they were forced to "dance" to the beat of a drum. This was the only exercise they received during the voyage.

Because the slaves were packed so closely together on the ship, there were often sanitation problems; people were forced to lie in the feces, urine, or vomit of the slaves shackled next to them. Because of the lack of sanitary conditions on the ships disease often broke out among the slaves and quickly infected the crews. Diseases such as small pox, typhoid, and Opthalmia, which causes blindness, often raged aboard slave ships. Some captains, in an attempt to avoid a full-fledged epidemic, would order that any slave showing any signs of illness be thrown overboard. Captains felt they could do this since the cargo, slaves, was insured should it be swept overboard. Therefore, the European investors would receive compensation for any slave lost at sea. Sometimes this worked, but insurance companies were hesitant to pay and fought it whenever they could.

Slaves did not always die from disease aboard ship; some slaves committed suicide by jumping overboard or refusing to eat, choosing to die rather than becoming slaves. Historians estimate that up to 20 percent of slaves died during the middle passage from disease, brutality, or suicide. Because of the unsanitary conditions and the resulting horrible smell aboard slave ships, it was said that a person on land could smell the ship before it docked at port. Some port cities, fearing disease, refused to allow slaving ships to come into port and instead forced them to unload their cargo in smaller ships to bring them ashore. The plantations of the Caribbean and Brazil received the largest number of slaves during the early modern period.

Slavery in the New World

The cultivation of sugar, tobacco, rice, and cotton on a large scale required the use of plantations and a plantation labor system. Slaves who survived the middle passage were then sold at auction to work on the large plantations. Because plantations required a great deal of land, slaves often found themselves in isolated rural areas far from the next plantation. Since slaves came from throughout Africa, it was entirely possible that the slave would not speak the same language as other slaves on the plantation, adding to his/her isolation. One of the reasons that native slaves had been unsuccessful in the Caribbean and Americas was because they had knowledge of the area and a place to run back to if they escaped. African slaves, who were far from home and family, had no idea of the surrounding countryside and no hope of returning to their home and family. While it is true that the treatment a slave received depended on which colony he lived in, it is important to remember that slavery was a brutal system no matter where in the New World it was practiced. Slaves were considered to be property in most instances and a slave owner almost always had complete control over whether a slave lived or died. Although a slave owner would be reluctant to kill a slave and thus lose his investment, slaves were often beaten severely for even minor infractions. Since a plantation owner wanted to maximize his profits, slaves often had little to eat, lived in substandard housing and had minimal clothing. Slaves brought to the plantations worked mainly as agricultural workers on the labor-intensive cash crops (sugar, rice, cotton, and tobacco) that were exported back to Europe at great profits for the plantation owners. Some slaves worked as domestics, especially women slaves who cooked the meals, cleaned the house, and looked after the children of the plantation owners.

Although fictional stories about the slave plantations, especially in the southern colonies of North America, such as *Gone With the Wind* by Margaret Mitchell, often portray slaves as compliant and even happy to serve their white owners, this is pure fiction. Africans were never happy to live as slaves and resisted whenever possible. While slave revolts were the most dramatic and had the greatest impact on the white population, causing them to live in fear of their or their neighbors' slaves, they were relatively rare events. Slave codes, which restricted where slaves could meet, what they could be taught, and how they could be treated, existed in most areas with slave populations in an attempt to prevent slave revolts. Instead of revolting, many slaves turned to less violent but effective means of resistance. Field slaves often deliberately worked only as hard and as fast as they had to in order to avoid being disciplined. They also intentionally trampled crops as they worked in the fields. Women slaves practiced birth control in order to reduce the number of children and, therefore, future slaves that they produced.

Slaves were also converted to Christianity while on the plantations. Slaves followed the religion of their plantation owner, so slaves in the Caribbean and South America converted to Roman Catholic Christianity, while slaves in the English colonies tended to convert to Protestantism. While it was possible for the slaves to retain some of their African culture and religion, they almost always had to disguise it under the practice of Christianity. Voodoo, which is still practiced both in Africa and throughout the Caribbean and parts of the Americas today is an example of this blending of religions. Voodoo or Vodon, as it is known in Africa, is a very ancient religion that originated in West Africa and came to the New World with the slaves. Once in the New World, the slaves, especially in Haiti, combined their old religion with Roman Catholicism to make it acceptable to their owners. Over time, the religion also combined elements of the native Taino population. The Voodoo that developed in the New World was a true blending of African, European, and Indian cultures.

The Cost of Slavery to Africa

The big loser in the slave trade, whether it was the oriental or the Occidental trade was Africa itself. The slave trade, which promised profits for Africans who captured and sold slaves, promoted internal warfare among the tribes. The slave trades also created a vicious circle as those Africans who cooperated with the Europeans had to capture more and more slaves in order to keep their European customers happy. The European guns became necessary not only in the capture of their fellow Africans, but also to protect themselves from those who would capture and enslave them. Historians do not agree on the number of Africans forcibly relocated to the New World in the early modern period. Conservative estimates range from about 10-12 million, although some historians put that number much higher. The number of slaves who died in transit either in Africa or during the middle passage is even more controversial. Many historians believe that for every African that made the voyage and became a slave one died at some point in transit. This would put the number of Africans directly affected by the trans-Atlantic slave trade at between 20-24 million, if we use the more conservative numbers. It is also important to remember that a number of people died trying to defend their villages from raids by the slavers. In the oriental trade for instance, slavers would attack villages, killing as many of the men and older women as possible, making it easier for them to capture the more highly priced young women and young boys in the village. There is really no way to calculate how many people died in these kinds of raids or other internal wars, which were a direct result of the slave trades in both the East and West. Historians estimate that Africa lost close to half of its population as a result of all aspects of the slave trade during the early modern period.

Practice Test Questions

1. The middle passage refers to

   A. the crossing of the Atlantic ocean by slave ships.

   B. the time period that slaves were held on the coast before they were loaded on to slave ships.

   C. the period of time that they remained on the slave ships before they went to the slave auctions.

   D. None of the above.

2. In order to avoid an outbreak of disease aboard a slave ship, a captain might

   A. refuse to transport any slave that looked weak.

   B. feed the slaves well and keep their area of the ship clean.

   C. throw all ill slaves overboard.

   D. reduce the number of slaves transported to keep the ship sanitary.

3. The plantation system was developed by the

   A. Portuguese.

   B. Dutch.

   C. English.

   D. Spanish.

4. What percentage of slaves are estimated to have died during the middle passage?

   A. 15 percent

   B. 50 percent

   C. 25 percent

   D. 20 percent

5. Europeans turned to African slaves to work their fields because

   A. the native populations had been too susceptible to European diseases.

   B. only Africans knew how to make crops grow in the colonies in the Caribbean.

   C. Africans were used to the plantation style of agriculture practiced in the Caribbean.

   D. All of the above.

Answers and Explanations

1. A. The middle passage refers to the second or middle leg of the journey for trading ships. They sailed from Europe to Africa, Africa to the New World and then back to Europe. This refers to the middle leg of the Triangular Trade.

2. C. In order to protect his crew and his cargo, a captain would order sick slaves to be thrown overboard. Because he was interested in maximizing his profits, he would always load as many slaves as possible regardless of sanitary concerns.

3. A. The plantation system was developed in the sugar fields of Portuguese plantations in Brazil. Because the plantation system was so successful and profitable for European plantation owners, the system was adopted by other European powers throughout the Caribbean and the Americas.

4. D. Historians believe that about 20 percent of slaves died from disease, brutality, and suicide during the middle passage. The crossing was incredibly difficult for the slaves, who were held in cramped quarters and given very little food.

5. A. Europeans turned to African slaves after the deaths of large number of natives in the Caribbean and the Americas. Although in the early years of colonization, Europeans used native populations, they often proved too susceptible to European disease, and Europeans were forced to import other workers from Africa.

Demographic and Environmental Changes

African Diaspora

Originally applied to the historical scattering of the Jews after the Roman-Jewish war of 66–70 CE, the Greek word, *diaspora*, has come to refer to the redistribution of a people, often by force, from one place to other places.

The African Diaspora was the result of the forced migration of millions of slaves, mostly from West Africa, and mostly to North and South America during the sixteenth, seventeenth, eighteenth, and into the nineteenth centuries. With the diaspora of people came the diaspora of their culture, food traditions, and languages.

Biota

The plant and animal species indigenous to a given place or region. Since human intervention is always occurring in the natural world, biotas change over time. In the context of early modern history, the colonization of the Americas by Europeans resulted in a mixing of the biota of Eurasia, Africa, and the Americas. See "Columbian Exchange" and "Virgin Soil Epidemic" later in this chapter.

Columbian Exchange

The European "discovery" of the New World resulted in an exchange (sometimes unknowingly) of plant, animal, and microorganism species (biota) between Eurasia, Africa, and the Americas (previously isolated by two oceans). Prominent among the list of species imported into Europe was the potato, the tomato, cacao (chocolate), maize ("corn"), and squash.

Demographic Transition

At various times in their history, a people or even an entire civilization goes through changes in their population growth (or decline). These are usually characterized in terms of birth and death rates. A people who experience a high birth (HB) rate and a high death (HD) rate are said to be in phase I of the demographic transition. A HB/HD phase usually results in little or no population growth. This phase characterizes most of the Middle Ages in Europe and around the World.

Phase II begins when birth rates are still high but when death rates decline (DD). In a population with HB/DD, population (and usually the economy) begins to grow and change. In Europe, this phase began during the sixteenth century and continued well into the nineteenth.

Phase III is characterized as HB/LD, and by rapid population growth. This was Europe and its "Frontier"—the United States and other European satellites—in the eighteenth and nineteenth centuries.

Phase IV is best described as low birth and low death (LB/LD)—the industrialized world in the twentieth century.

Enclosures

This is the conversion and fencing in of common pastures and other tenant-farmed lands beginning in the sixteenth century, displacing tenant farm families in the drive by landlords for greater profits from their lands.

In England and in other places in Western Europe, the result of enclosures was homelessness and vagrancy—serious social problems solved only partly by emigration to overseas colonies. In Latin America and India, the establishment of *latifundia*—great landed estates—similarly broke up traditional communities and the family-oriented use of lands. This, too, resulted in long-term dependence and poverty for indigenous peoples.

Mestiso/Métis

Mestiso is the Spanish word for a person of part Indian, part Spanish ancestry. In French, the similar word is *métis*. In those regions of North America colonized by the French, the Spanish, and the Portuguese—all Catholic— there was frequent intermarriage between Europeans and Native Americans, though the ethnic mixing was more extensive and therefore more significant among the Spanish and the Indians.

It can be said that Latin American culture is *mestiso* culture. After the large-scale introduction of West African peoples, the interethnic makeup of Latin America became more complex.

Such intermarriage was rare among, and was scorned by, the Protestant English and Dutch.

Virgin Soil Epidemic

When a disease is first introduced to a place or region in which it had not been previously known, the people indigenous to that place have little or no acquired immunity to that disease. Without previous exposure, the human immune system can be overwhelmed by vigorous diseases such as measles and smallpox.

Even though such diseases usually did not kill a healthy European, virgin soil epidemics of these diseases among Native Americans killed, by some estimates, at least 90 percent of the native population between 1500 and 1700.

As pockets of native peoples were exposed as late as the 1830s, similar decimating (reducing to a tenth) epidemics could strike. More than any other reason, virgin soil epidemics allowed Europeans to dominate the world after 1500.

Population Shifts

The Early Modern era (1450–1750) was a period of rapid and extensive changes in the World's population. The various regions of the World experienced these changes in different ways and to varying degrees, and some were more dynamic than others. The following begins with the region that experienced the least population change and ends with greatest.

Asia

After the fall of the Chinese Ming dynasty in the 1640s, Manchus from recently-united Manchuria took advantage of Chinese weakness and began to move in a flood south of the Great Wall. Manchu rulers established the Qing dynasty, with Beijing as its capital. Though recurring plagues took their toll on Qing China, between 1500 and 1600 the Chinese population rose from 100 million to about 160 million. War and famine brought about a decline by 1650, but by 1750 China's population stood at about 225 million, a 60 percent increase in a 100 years.

Similar growth was experienced in Japan. During the first century of the early modern period, Japan was embroiled in prolonged civil war. In 1600, the shogun Tokugawa managed to stabilize Japanese government and society, in part by carefully controlling outside influences. This stability helped the Japanese economy and agriculture. By 1700, farm production had increased two-fold, and this resulted in long-term population growth. But after 1700, various non-economic factors worked to limit growth.

Between 1700 and 1850, Japan went through a demographic transition in which contraception, late marriage, abortion, and infanticide (killing or allowing newborn infants to die) limited growth. The usual explanation is that Japan was running out of land and this transition was the response.

Africa

Between 1500 and 1700, the population of sub-Saharan Africa went from about 34 million to over 52 million. In part, the increase was due to new foodstuffs such as maize, manioc (a cereal grain), and peanuts coming from the Americas. In particular, manioc bread became a staple of the West African diet by the 1700s. Better-fed populations are usually better able to reproduce and to rear more children to maturity. But one must keep in mind that this population increase was accompanied by, and was in spite of, the forced emigration of around 11 million slaves between 1600 and 1870, the great era of the *African Diaspora*.

Historians estimate that as many as an additional four million died before they could be sold "on the block" in the Americas.

Europe

At the beginning of the early modern period, Europe's population was somewhere between one-third and one-half of what it had been before the plagues of the fourteenth century. In the Middle Ages, high birth and death rates caused Europe's population to remain fairly stable (phase I of the Demographic Transition). The new economic and social realities of the post-plague and post-Renaissance era pushed Europe into Phase II, and the population numbers began to rise. This was true especially in northwestern Europe. In a few regions such as Germany, population actually declined during the seventeenth century, mostly because of the wars of the Protestant Reformation.

Some estimates are that Germany lost as much as 40 percent of its population during the Thirty Years War (1618–1648). There were, however, significant migrations of German speakers from the traditional center of German settlement in central and Western Europe to Eastern Europe and Russian lands.

The introduction of new foodstuffs from the Americas (most notably the potato), along with improvements in farming practices, helped to make for a declining death rate while the birth rate remained high. Thus, Europe entered Phase II of the Demographic Transition. At the same time, the population of Western Europe (including England) was becoming more urbanized as trade and manufacturing became more important.

Moreover, in England as in many other places in Europe, lands that had traditionally been farmed by peasants and tenants were increasingly being converted to pasture ("enclosed") for the greater profits that returned to landowners. Many western Europeans who emigrated to the Americas before 1750 did so because they had been dislocated by these enclosures.

Those who stayed in Europe drifted into the new trade and industrial towns and cities such as Manchester in England, to Flanders (in the modern-day Nethlerlands), and to Lyon in France. Trade, manufacturing, and the growing centralization of nation-states made port and capital cities much more important than they had been during the Middle Ages.

As the economy and population began to shift from the countryside to the city, so did the traditional social and power structures of European society. Land-owning aristocrats, with their base of power and influence over local and even national affairs traditionally rooted in the country, would now have to compete with newly-important merchants, bankers, and bureaucrats—all centered in the towns and cities. The Early Modern Era, then, would see the rise of the *bourgeoisie*, the middle-class urbanite who, over the next three centuries, would eventually triumph over an aristocracy that had ruled for more than a thousand years.

Perhaps the most historically momentous of the European population shifts of the Early Modern era was the development of an Atlantic regional system that linked Africa, the Americas, and Europe. This "Atlantic Revolution" replaced the old Europe dominated by the Mediterranean. Between 1450 and 1800, various circuits of trade were established in slaves, sugar, rum, and agricultural products grown in the European colonies of the New World. The so-called "Triangle Trade" (Carribbean molasses to New England, New England rum made from the molasses to Africa, and slaves from Africa to the Carribbean) was actually more complicated, but it illustrates how new trade networks emerged in the trans-Atlantic World.

Americas

The accidental "discovery" of the Western Hemisphere by Columbus and subsequent explorers touched off one of the biggest and longest-lasting migrations of population in the history of the world. Between 1492 and today, a period of more than 500 years, tens of millions of people left (or were taken from) ancestral home lands and settled in the Americas (including the Caribbean Islands).

These millions came from all the world's continents. The mixing and mingling, and the cultural interaction, that took place between these peoples and those who were already present in the Americas resulted in the pluralism that is characteristic of life in the Western Hemisphere. But it must not be assumed that life and population was static in the Americas before the arrival of Europeans. It is clear that the indigenous peoples of the Western Hemisphere were like all people everywhere: dynamic and always on the move.

A language map of the Americas would, in fact, tell an interesting story of migration and movement. Speakers of languages of the Athabaskan group mentioned above can be found all along the Alaskan and Pacific Coasts of North America, with the largest number of present-day speakers in Arizona and New Mexico.

Likewise, Uto-Aztecan, Shishonian, Iroquoian, and Algonquian languages can be scattered all over the continent. This scattering can only be explained in terms of migration, sometimes voluntary, sometimes not. In 1492, linguists estimate there were as many as 500 mutually-unintelligible native languages in North America, representing several dozen language groups.

As varied and as mobile as native peoples were, it is clear the arrival of Europeans would force enormous change on most of Native America over the five centuries since the Columbian discovery. The most significant population changes came as a result of virgin soil epidemics of measles and smallpox, decimating Native populations almost everywhere.

Other consequences of European encroachment and settlement depended upon which of the European nationalities and empires was involved. The Catholic Spanish, Portuguese, and French were more interested in economic exploitation, in missionary work, and in strategic advantage than in settling large numbers of their countrymen in the New World. Indeed, it was often difficult to entice Spanish or French peasants to migrate, owing mostly to the still-feudal nature of their land laws.

The English, however, had developed through its Common Law a more liberal land-owning system in which small landowners need not be beholden to a superior landlord. He (or she) could own land outright, in *fee simple*. Given the liberal English law and the large number of landless vagrants in England, the English in America proved to be perpetually land hungry, and for Native Americans, this meant struggle and displacement.

Environmental Changes

In discussing environmental change in history, two realities should be kept in mind. The first is that any human habitation results in environmental change, however subtle and hard to detect. Just the presence of humans (or any other life form, for that matter) brings about significant change. The second reality is that the "environment" is not a static thing to be either changed or left alone by humans. Even without human habitation, "nature" is always changing. Properly seen, human activity should be understood as just one of many factors that bring about change.

However, there is no doubt that *anthropogenic* (human-caused) environmental change began to accelerate in the world beginning around 1500, and the principal cause was global population growth. In regions of the world that had experienced rapid population growth, including South and East Asia and the Americas, greater population pressure would strain traditional land use and other resources. Depleted soils and over-logged forests were often the result of too many people and too few resources. As Europeans came to dominate the World's landscapes, many changes were forced on the environment.

The landscape of most of the major Caribbean islands was virtually transformed by the introduction of sugar cane and sugar-growing plantations worked by slave labor brought from Africa. In the Americas, large tracts of once-forested lands were cleared for cultivation, echoing the same deforestation that had taken place in Europe, China, and many other regions of the world in previous centuries.

139

Recently, the historian John F. Richards identified four global developments that intensified after 1500. The first of these was the significant increase of human impact in settlement "frontiers"—zones where population had been very thin or virtually non-existent but now inhabited by new settlers. This impact would be most significant when the way in which newcomers used the land was markedly different from those few who had been using it.

The second global development involved what Richards called "biological invasions." Sometimes new plants or animals were introduced into a place intentionally, and sometimes accidentally. Many of the noxious weeds that infest both cultivated and "wild" lands around the world were introduced inadvertently. This was certainly the case with diseases such as smallpox and syphilis.

The third global development was the rise of commercial hunting of wildlife, most notably various species of whale (for the oil contained in their blubber), the North American beaver (for hats and other felt products), and the American bison (for their hides and for mounted heads). Where these animals played important roles in the ecology of their natural ranges, over-hunting (in some cases close to extinction) would radically change the natural environment.

The fourth development identified by Richards as having global impact involved the problems of energy scarcity. During the early modern period, this meant the growing scarcity of firewood in world regions long occupied and settled—in Europe, Asia, and Africa. In the Americas, the vast woodlands and rain forests would scarcely be touched during this period—one of the reasons why emigration to America was so attractive to so many.

Diseases

The extension and elaboration of trade networks around the world beginning in the late Middle Ages helped to break the long-standing isolation common in earlier times, but this cosmopolitanism came at a price. Various strains of the bubonic plague were brought into Europe and North Africa from India and Southeast Asia in the fourteenth and fifteenth centuries. It is very clear that European diseases like smallpox and measles killed very large numbers of Native Americans after the Columbian expeditions. No factor was more significant in the Europeanization of the Americas since 1500.

Evidence is less clear that syphilis was brought into Europe by Europeans returning from the Americas, beginning with the return of the Nina, Pinta, and Santa Maria. If it was, it was not a fair exchange because the European diseases killed tens of millions of American Indians, and syphilis very few Europeans.

Certain long-term exposure to disease during this era was actually beneficial to many slave owners in the West Indies and the American mainland colonies as they found that West Africans had significant natural (and hereditary) immunity to diseases such as malaria and yellow fever, diseases that disabled or killed large numbers of white Western Europeans laboring as indentured servants in New World during the seventeenth century.

Animals

Over a period of several hundred years, the landscape of much of the Americas would be transformed by the introduction of large numbers of animals that had long been domesticated in the Old World but were unknown in New World until the arrival of Europeans: cattle, sheep, horses, chickens, and the honeybee (for honey production), to name a few.

In many cases these animals would bring about significant environmental changes. In both North and South America, large native land mammals such as the bison and the antelope were displaced on the broad grasslands of both continents by domestic cattle and sheep.

The introduction of privately owned herds of cattle and sheep would, over the centuries, result in extensive damage from overgrazing, actually killing much of the grass and opening the soil to the introduction of opportunistic and invasive plants such as sagebrush that had no value as animal forage.

The introduction of the horse to North America would significantly change the way of life of many native peoples, and it would often alter long-standing balances of power between competing native nations. Additionally, feral (domestic animals gone wild) herds of horses competed on the rangelands with native land mammals. The introduction of the chicken might have made few direct changes in the American environment, but the honeybee would alter natural patterns of pollenization, often benefiting domesticated fruits and vegetables more than native species.

New Crops

It would be in the exchange of new crops between the New and the Old World that the greatest environmental and historical changes would result. By 1750, maize (corn), potatoes, squash, peppers, and tomatoes had become very important staples of the European diet, helping to make possible the rise of the European nations as world powers.

The potato was the most important of these. Though often maligned by modern-day diet "experts," the potato is very rich in vitamins and minerals, and it grows in a wide variety of soils without being labor intensive. The potato transformed the diet of Europe, making it virtually famine-proof and helping to increase its population and enlarge its economy. Similarly, the introduction of manioc (especially in the form of bread), helped to touch off a sustained rise in population in western Africa.

From Europe, settlers brought wheat, rye, rice (by way of Africa), and other cereals previously unknown in North or South America. Large amounts of cultivated land were given over to these imported crops. Two foreign crops in particular—sugar cane and rice—helped to drive the growing slave plantation economy of both South and North America.

Practice Test Questions

1. One significant outcome of the African Diaspora was the

   A. rise of Muslim empires in East Africa.
   B. mixing and mingling of African with European and American cultures.
   C. decline of the importance of Africa in the new Atlantic system.
   D. general increase of African population.
   E. None of the above

2. Which of the following is an example of a virgin soil epidemic during the Early Modern Era?

   A. Malaria
   B. Cholera
   C. Gastroenteritis
   D. Smallpox
   E. All of the above

3. Which of the following is an example of anthropogenic change in the world's environment before 1750?

   A. Recurring draught
   B. Massive inceases in "greenhouse" gases
   C. Deforestation
   D. Increase in the population of cod and other commercial fisheries
   E. All of the above

4. Of the following elements of the Columbian Exchange, which was most closely related to the development of plantation slavery in the Americas?

   A. Sugar cane
   B. Millet
   C. The tomato
   D. The potato
   E. All of the above

5. Of the American plants introduced into Europe after 1492, which of the following was the most historically significant?

   A. Tomato
   B. Potato
   C. Maize ("corn")
   D. Tobacco
   E. None of the above

Answers and Explanations

1. **B.** One significant outcome of the African Diaspora was the mixing and mingling of African with European and American cultures. Option **A** is incorrect because the Diaspora actually brought about a decline in the African kingdoms and empires. Option **C** is not a good choice because the Diaspora made Africa more important in the Atlantic system, and Option **D** might seem right, because African population increased steadily, even during the Diaspora. However, the increase was in spite of the Diaspora rather than because of it.

2. **D.** The only example of a virgin soil epidemic in the list of options was smallpox. The other options, malaria (**A**), cholera (**B**), and gastroenteritis (**C**) could and did breakout in epidemics, but they are diseases that were known globally and for centuries. A virgin soil epidemic is one that is new to a place or region, brought by outsiders making significant and repeated contact for the first time.

3. **C.** Deforestation (Option **C**) is an example of anthropogenic change in the World's environment before 1750. Draught (Option **A**) occurred off and on around the World during this period (and all periods), but it is not anthropogenic—man made. It is the result of complex global and atmospheric interactions completely outside of human control. Option **B**, massive increases in "greenhouse" gases, might be true of the period 1750 to the present, but not before 1750. Increases in the population of commercial fisheries (Option **D**) did not happen at all during the period. If anything, the increases in World population put increased pressure on the fisheries.

4. **A.** Sugar cane (Option **A**) was the element of the Columbian Exchange most closely related to the development of plantation slavery in the Americas. Though millet (Option **B**), the tomato (Option **C**), and the potato (Option **D**) were important foodstuffs brought to Europe from the Americas, they were adopted within the subsistence-farming system of Europe and were not grown on American plantations using slave labor. Sugar, tobacco, rice, and indigo were among the major staple crops produced on American plantations.

5. **B.** Of the American plants introduced into Europe after 1492, the most historically significant was the potato (Option **B**). The lowly potato (called an "earth apple" in French) revolutionized the food supply of Europe. It is easily grown and high yielding even in poor soils and under adverse conditions, and it is an excellent and nearly complete human food—high in vitamins, minerals, and with an ideal proportion of proteins (amino acids) and starch (used by the body as an energy source). The potato made Europe virtually famine proof by the turn of the eighteenth century. This resulted in a Europe with a well-fed and vigorous population that enjoyed a dynamic and progressive economy.

Cultural and Intellectual Developments

In both Europe and in Asia, cultural and intellectual movements were underway that would lead, in both places but in different ways, to the momentous transformations of the modern era. In both places, a more scientific and therefore mechanical world view would emerge that would come to replace the spiritual and "superstitious" dualism that had dominated for centuries between mind and matter, and between the spirit and the body.

Causes and Impact of Cultural Change

One useful way of getting at this question of cultural change in the early-modern world (1450–1750) is to look briefly at a few parts of the modern (Western) world view and compare them to those of past eras. Here are three common assumptions of the modern Westerner:

1. "Today, things will be better than, or at least different from, yesterday."
2. "No one is superior to me without my consent."
3. "The central project of my life is self-fulfillment."

One of the hardest things to do in historical analysis is to put oneself into the mind—the mentality—of those in the past. In the medieval mind, these three assumptions would have been blasphemous nonsense. Even to most Europeans well into the nineteenth century, these assumptions would have been mostly foreign. In the rest of the world until quite recently, these assumptions would also have been poorly received. There are still many societies in which tradition clashes with these "liberal" Western ideas.

How did these concepts, so rich as they are with philosophical and political meaning, come to develop in Western Europe, and in the modern era (since 1750), sweep across the world, transforming nearly everything in their path? To answer this question, we have to look to the Enlightenment and the **Scientific Revolution**—the change in thought that began during the Renaissance in Europe that resulted, ultimately, in the replacement of a religious world view with one derived from observation of the real world, along with reasoned analysis of how the world works at a natural system. Instead of God (or the gods) magically controlling it, the Scientific Revolution resulted in an understanding of nature as a system—the clock was a favorite metaphor—that could be studied and understood. Closely related to the developments of the Scientific Revolution, the **Enlightenment** took the world view of science—that true knowledge comes from observation and reason rather than from "revealed" truth from churches or scripture. Just as the new "scientists" (known as **natural philosophers** until late in the eighteenth century) would study nature, Enlightenment thinkers would study humankind and its social, political, economic, and cultural characteristics. The most important consequences of Enlightenment thinking came from political analysis and thought during the eighteenth century. Many Enlightenment ideas provided the philosophical basis for the American and French Revolutions.

Both the Scientific Revolution and the Enlightenment had their roots in the rediscovery of the learning of the ancient Greeks and Romans during the so-called Renaissance. Ancient philosophy and mathematics—all created and written by polytheistic pagans and not Christians—reminded many thinkers in the fifteenth and sixteenth centuries that truth and knowledge can come from many sources, not just the church and the Bible. And the careful and meticulous (even tedious) reasoning used by the ancients became a model for thought in the early modern era.

By the sixteenth century, a philosophical movement known as Humanism emerged among leading thinkers in Western Europe, and it was heavily influenced by the ancient Greek notion, expressed in many ways, that "man is the measure of all things." Humanism, though it did not overthrow Christian religion, nevertheless took the edge off the Christian notion that mankind had "fallen," and that humans were hopelessly depraved sinners, all but worthless in the eyes of God. One very important outcome of humanistic thought was the idea that one need not take the world or anything in it as a "given," created by God and unchangeable.

This humanistic idea that change was both possible and sometimes desirable extended even into religion and the dominant institution of Western European Christianity—the Roman Catholic Church. Humanist thinkers began to suggest in the late fifteenth century that the church should be reformed and shed of corruption and non-biblical teachings and practices. By the early sixteenth century, led by reformers from within the church such as Martin Luther, reformist criticism had become the Protestant Reformation, and large portions of the church broke away from Rome, especially in Germany and Western Europe.

Beginning in 1517, Luther had argued that the church was not only corrupt, but that many of its core assumptions were flawed. First of all, he claimed, the church taught a false doctrine of salvation, the way in which a fallen person (and that meant everybody) could be "saved" and return again to God in eternal life. According to the church, salvation came from both faith and from performing specific works known as "sacraments"—baptism, marriage, confession, and the like. These sacraments could only be performed by priests within the authority of the church and the bishops, archbishops, and popes. But according to the Bible, Luther argued, salvation was a free gift given to all who had faith in Jesus Christ. Sacraments, and therefore most of the structure of the church, were not based on scripture.

This criticism related to greater critique that a church was not to stand as an intercessor between God and humanity. A person needed no "go-between" in his or her relationship with God. A church should simply be an institution that promotes teaching and practice of true religion and faith, and not an intercessor. It certainly should not be an arm of the government, with police powers and special privileges.

The Protestant idea that the individual stands alone with nothing and no one between him and God had profound cultural and political implications. If Luther was right, what authority could the church or kings claim? If you don't need a church, do you need a government? If you did need a government, how should it relate to the individual? If all—even kings— stand naked, as it were, before God, then aren't all equal?

Care must be taken not to assume that the cultural and political implications of the Reformation were quickly realized. Traditional notions of deference and respect for authority remained strong well into the twentieth century. What did happen, though, was that the critique of the Reformation, combined with the drift toward naturalism and humanism, begun during the Renaissance, would fuel the later ideological and cultural developments of the Scientific Revolution and the Enlightenment.

Historians do not always agree on when or what started the Scientific Revolution, but most would agree that the Polish priest-professor, Nicolas Copernicus, inadvertently set the revolution in motion, so to speak, when he published a book titled (in Latin) *De Revolutionibus* in 1530, in which he posited that the earth rotated on an axis once a day and that this accounted for the perception of the rising and setting sun, and that Earth and the other planets revolved around the sun once every year. This was the first time in history that a theory of a *heliocentric* (sun-centered) "universe" had been published.

The classical model had been, since ancient times, of a *geocentric* system, with Earth at the center and all the heavenly bodies in orbit about it. This had been the teachings the ancient Alexandrian Claudius Ptolemy, and his conception had been endorsed by the Church. After all, the Judeo-Christian story of creation seems to make Earth the center of God's creation, and mankind the highest creation on Earth. That a pagan had come up with the idea only made the truth seem more certain.

Copernicus died decades before his book was to receive public attention. It got that attention when an Italian mathematics professor, Galileo Galilei, published another book in 1630 that repeated Copernicus's assertion, but also backed it up with concrete and carefully made observations. This book touched off a firestorm of resistance and reaction from the church in Rome. Much had happened since 1530 (such as the bloodiest of the consequences of the Protestant Reformation), and this was not the first time Galileo had challenged the church's official position on the universe.

In 1611, Galileo had constructed a simple telescope, one of the first ever built, and turned it on the sun, the moon, the stars, and the planets. What he found astonished him and the rest of the Western world. He found, for instance, that the sun had spots, and that these changed over time. The church had taught that the sun and the other heavenly bodies were perfect and featureless spheres. Seeing a magnified moon through his telescope revealed mountain ranges and craters—a landscape not unlike Earth's—again disproving "revealed" truth. Seeing the so-called Milky Way, he could see through his scope that it was made up of millions of individual stars.

The most impressive of Galileo's discoveries occurred when he looked at the planets through his telescope. He found that Venus had "phases" like those of Earth's moon. These could be explained only if Venus orbited the sun, not Earth. Most interesting of all was the discovery of the rings of Saturn, and that both Saturn and Jupiter had moons in orbit around them—so not everything orbited Earth. Galileo soon published his findings and became a famous man overnight, and since these discoveries came during the papacy of a sympathetic and "liberal" pope, the church did not openly object.

The phases of Venus, and the apparent backtracking of the paths of the planets in the night sky (known as retrograde motion and never convincingly explained in terms of a geocentric model), were not explainable by Ptolemy's universe, but could be by Copernicus'. Saying so got Galileo into deep trouble with the Inquisition.

But the significance of the Galileo story is not that he was punished for publishing against the teaching of the Chruch, but that he was doing *science*—making careful observations of real-world phenomina, and then applying reason to the results of the observations. The old Ptolemeic model did not fit the observations, the Copernican model did. It would be foolish to argue that this was the first time the so-called scientific method had ever been applied, but Galileo's evidence against a geocentric model of what we now call the solar system is an especially clear and early example the method as it was emerging in early modern Europe.

Other important scientists—natural philosophers, and as they were called then—picked up where Galileo left off. Perhaps the most important of these in the study of physics was Isaac Newton, an English mathematician (mathematics was the key to the study of physics). As the inventor of calculus, and the first to identify and quantify gravity as a force, Newton made more impact than any other scientist until Darwin.

Again, his method was observation and reason, though many of his "discoveries" had come from his taking of raw numeric data from the tentative works of others and drawing new and important conclusions from them. It was in this way that his famous law of gravity was devised: that the force of gravity changed according to the product of the masses of two bodies and inversely as the square of the distance between them. In the twentieth century, scientists were able to predict down to a meter the path of an orbiting satellite or other craft using nothing other that Newton's law and methods of calculaton (and some very precise measuring instrucments that Newton did not have).

What Galileo, Newton, and many others did to advance the Scientific Revolution, John Locke and subsequent philosophers did for the intellectual movement known as the Enlightenment. Locke was among the first to apply observation and reason to the study of human nature—how humans behave, how they think—in short, what they are. He concluded that humans are born *tabula rasa*—a blank slate (blackboard). They have no nature at all at birth, except animal needs and appetites. Everything that a person becomes thereafter is the result of things that get written on the "slate"—culture, feelings, attitudes—all acquired from one's surrounding family, community, and society, from one's environment.

Naturally, any number of things are written on that slate, and some are good while others are harmful to the individual and to society. But Locke chose his metaphors carefully. He didn't say that humans are born a blank stone on which things are chistled, but rather a blank slate, and what has been written on a blackboard can be erased and replaced with something of one's choosing, something coherent and beneficial to replace the random and sometimes harmful writings from the environment.

Considering the implications of this idea is not easy task, for they are profound. The blank-slate concept essentially means that:

1. all persons are equal (equally blank) at birth.
2. a person can improve his nature (and even eventually perfect it) by rewriting what is on his slate.
3. society can be changed as well, one slate at a time.

In addition to its egalitarian implications, Locke's blank-slate theory was profoundly optimistic—a prominent characteristic of Enlightenment thinking—and one would not have to think too hard to imagine some of its political and social implications. Locke and other Enlightenment thinkers also advanced the idea that societies—even ones ruled by kings and emperors—were formed and kept together on the basis of the "social contract." In order to protect their lives and their property (and property was seen as essential to the preservation of life), people voluntarily submitted themselves to some kind of government to which they surrendered some of their natural freedoms. Among those freedoms, Locke wrote, were "life, liberty, and property," a phrase that would be paraphrased decades later in the American Declaration of Independence (a virtual display piece of eighteenth-century Enlightenment thinking).

Jean Jacques Rousseau and other French philosophers advanced similar ideas. But not all Englightenment thinkers were satisfied with Locke's blank-slate notion. A countervailing strain of the thought sometimes known as the "Common Sense School" promoted the notion that everyone was born, by nature, with certain sensibilities. Thomas Hutcheson, for instance, would argue that all are born with a moral sense, and that even those who have never been taught morals still know right from wrong. David Hume promoted the idea that everyone is born with a natural sense of politics—what is or is not correct in terms of policy or political questions.

Perhaps the most influencial of these Common Sense philosophers—was Adam Smith. He argued that all are born with a common sense of economics. Like Hutcheson and Hume, Smith argued that people were born with inate sensibilities and that they had a natural understanding of their place in the world. Smith would apply this idea to a person's behavior in the "marketplace."

According to Smith (and easily observed at almost all times and places), people had two essential characteristics: They were naturally selfish and self-interested, and they were rational. Together, this meant that people had an inate sense of what would or would not be good for them in any marketplace transaction. Setting aside questions of fraud, misrepresentation, or mistakes in fact, no one would knowingly engage in a transaction that was not in his or her best interests. No one had to teach them this. Their selfishness and their rationality was sufficient to warn them away from a bad "deal."

For this reason, government intervention was not really necessary, either to help the individual avoid foolish mistakes or to allocate economic resources rationally and fairly—these functions could best be provided by the "marketplace." Within the free and open market, Smith argued, the individual should be allowed to pursue his or her self-interests rationally, without undue interference from government. Each person would act in his best interests, and in the "marketplace" wherein all were thus freely acting, each in his or her self-interest, needs and wants would be balanced naturally, as if by some "invisible hand." Smith's use of the term "invisible hand" was reminiscent of the Enlightenment term so much in circulation among the American and French Revolutionaries: "nature's God." Smith was looking for, and believed he had found, the natural laws of economics and human behavior.

For Smith and for other thinkers, the best feature of what would come to be called "capitalism" was that it was based on human nature—selfish and self-interested. If left alone, selfishness creates wealth, and the natural discipline of the marketplace—free and open competition—would keep selfishness in check, and the whole process would lead to the greatest wealth for the greatest number of people. Thus, by a happy twist of nature, the private vice of selfishness was transformed into a public good.

The common threads of all these long-term developments—the Reformation, the Scientific Revolution, and the Enlightenment—were these: All three promoted the value of careful observation and reason, all three advanced the idea of human equality, and all three (even the Reformation) moved the Western mind away from religion and toward a fully naturalistic and secular world view. This would take centuries, though by the nineteenth century, the process would accelerate, sometimes seemingly out of control.

Changes in Confucianism

In East Asia, the most significant cultural and intellectual development during this period was the elaboration and official endorsement of Neo-Confuscianism. Emerging around 1100 CE, this movement was in many ways backward-looking. It sought to recover a "purer" form of Confucianism to replace the mixture of Buddhist and Taoist elements that had crept in over the centuries (mostly from "foreign" sources in India).

In contrast to Buddhists and Taoists, neo-Confucians did not believe in dual universe—the touchable world of "matter" and the spiritual world beyond. For this reason, Neo-Confucians usually rejected ideas associated with such mystical notions as reincarnation and karma.

Nevertheless, Neo-Confucians were especially anxious to reconcile the classic concepts of Confucianism with Buddhist teachings. Though the Neo-Confucians rejected dualism (the separation of the physical from the spiritual world), they nevertheless promoted the idea that *li*, pure principals or ideals, were often corrupted in the company of *qi*, the material world. The only proper response to this corruption was action aimed at "purifying" both the *qi* and the *li*.

Neo-Confucians had differing ideas for what kind of action was most useful in the pursuit of purity. One prominent strain of Neo-Confucian thought held that the "Investigation of Things," more or less a kind of academic observational science, was the key to peace and happiness. Along with what would now be called a scientific approach would come the Neo-Confucian ideal of order, best implemented in the imperial and other government bureaucracies in China and Japan (after 1600).

Neo-Confucianism became the accepted state philosophy by the Ming Dynasty (1368–1644), and continued in this way through the Qing Dynasty (1644–1912). For this reason, it is sometimes assumed that Neo-Confucianism is essentially authoritarian inasmuch as it seemed to enhance the power of the state system. But the essential element of Neo-Confuscianism is not authority but rather order and a purified *li*. In addition to statecraft, many elements of Chinese culture were influenced by Neo-Confucian thought such as visual art, traditional Chinese medicine, and martial arts.

Perhaps the clearest example of the application of Neo-Confucian philosophy would come in Japan with the establishment of the Tokugawa shogunate. As a way of bringing order to a Japanese society scrambled by generations of civil war, and as a means of keeping the daimyo (feudal lords) under control, Tokugawa Ieyasu adopted Neo-Confuciansism as the official state philosophy of Japan. Following Neo-Confucian principle, Tokugawa built an elaborate bureaucracy using the Chinese as an example. With this bureaucracy, and with the control of the daimyo, came over two and a half centuries of domestic tranquility in Japan. In the minds of some historical observers, the virtue of Neo-Confucianism was that it was secular, and that it emphasized the rational understanding of both the physical world and the human worlds.

The most significant influence of Neo-Confucianism on Japanese culture was the creation of "bushido" or "the way of the warrior" during the seventeenth century. For centuries, the samurai (warriors) had constituted a separate class within the larger Japanese society (similar to the Knights of Western Europe in the Middle Ages). With the establishment of the Tokugawa shogunate, though, Japan was at peace and there was no war. This essentially meant that the warrior class was idle, and some thought this was a menace to the peace that had been so hard won.

An additional consideration with regard to the samurai was that by giving them a prominent (though peaceful) place in the rigid class system of Japan, the Tokugawa shoguns could use the samurai to cement that class system in place. Also, by giving the samurai the special and exclusive privilege of bearing arms, the peasants were prevented from arming themselves and rebelling against official authority. It also meant that no local daimyo could raise an army of peasants to challenge the government of the shogun.

But, in order to keep this privileged and highly armed samurai class on a "short leash," a new culture and code of conduct had to be invented for them. According to its founders, the role of a samurai was to serve as a model for others in society. Employing the Neo-Confucian ideal of action, this meant that an adherent of the bushido code had to be a person who actually acted for good in society.

The first thing the samurai would have to do was to become educated—as warriors, they had had no need of education. They would also have to follow a strict moral code that included temperance, self-sacrifice, and fearlessness. Above all other moral virtues was devotion to authority and obedience. Added to the moral qualities to the samurai was the obligation to develop themselves intellectually, cultural, and politically (making them into a sort of armed version of the Catholic Jesuits!). The purpose of the bushido code was clear; it was to turn a class of what had been essentially just hard-fighting thugs into the natural leaders of the new Japan.

In both China and Japan, Neo-Confucianism was a movement away from religion and the spiritual and toward modern science and secularism. With its Neo-Confucian world view, after centuries of isolation, Japan would modernize faster than any other nation of that era, beginning in the middle of the nineteenth century. By the twentieth century, Japan was a World power, and its Neo-Confucian code of the bushido would help propel Japan's expansionism in that century.

147

Practice Test Questions

1. As an intellectual movement, Humanism

   A. was opposed to Christian religion.
   B. was open to new ideas.
   C. resisted the changes of the Reformation.
   D. argued against the notion of original sin.
   E. All of the above.

2. Galileo ran afoul of church authorities when he promoted the idea that

   A. observation and reason were superior to other scientific methods.
   B. direct observation of the natural world was the only source of human knowledge.
   C. Ptolemy, and not Copernicus, had the correct heliocentric model.
   D. Earth was not the center of God's creation.
   E. All of the above.

3. Among the implications of John Locke's "blank slate" metaphor were

   A. all persons are essentially equal at birth.
   B. a person can improve or even perfect his nature.
   C. perfect individuals could lead to a perfected society.
   D. All of the above are correct.
   E. Only A and C are correct.

4. Neo-Confucian thinkers sought to reconcile the corrupting nature of the material world by

   A. returning to the old Confucian texts for inspiration.
   B. adopting Taoist dualism.
   C. means of the Investigation of Things (observational science).
   D. avoiding direct action in favor of meditation.
   E. All of the above.

5. Among the accomplishments of the Tokugawa shogunate was the

   A. decentralization of power into the hands of the daimyo.
   B. reimposition of traditional Confucianism into Japanese life.
   C. rationalization and organization of a Japanese bureaucracy.
   D. All of the above are correct.
   E. None of the above.

Answers and Explanations

1. **B.** As an intellectual movement, Humanism was open to new ideas (Option **B**). None of the Humanist thinkers were openly opposed to religion (Option **A**), or even to the Roman church. Though Humanists may not have been enthusiastic about the idea of original sin (Option **D**), a criticism of it was not part of their writings. They certainly did not oppose the Reformation (Option **C**), at least not on the grounds that the church and its doctrines were in no need of reform.

2. **D.** Galileo ran afoul of church authorities when he promoted the idea that Earth was not the center of God's creation (Option **D**). Option **A**, "observation and reason were superior to other scientific methods," is a nonsense answer, as is Option **C**, "Ptolemy, and not Copernacus, had the correct heliocentric model" (Ptolemy's model was *geocentric*). Option **B**, "direct observation of the natural world was the only source of human knowledge" was not an idea advanced by Galileo, in spite of his attachment to what we now call the scientific method.

3. D. Among the implications of John Locke's "blank slate" metaphor were all of the following: all persons are essentially equal at birth (Option A), a person can improve or even perfect his nature (Option **B**), and perfect individuals could lead to a perfected society (Option **C**). The correct answer is Option **D**, "all of the above."

4. C. Neo-Confucian thinkers sought to reconcile the corrupting nature of the material world by means of the Investigation of Things, a kind of observational science (Option **C**). Option **A**, returning to old texts, makes no sense with the "neo" prefix before "Confucian." Option **B**, "adopting Taoist dualism," might be tempting, but Neo-Confucianists only sought to rationalize both Buddhist and Taoist dualism with secular Confucian philosophies and not to "incorporate" them. Neo-Confucianism was, in fact, a reaction to excessive dualism in Chinese thought. Option **D**, "avoiding direct action in favor of meditation," would have been anathema (or its secular equivalent, "foolishness") to Neo-Confucians.

5. C. Among the accomplishments of the Tokugawa shogunate was the rationalization and organization of a Japanese bureaucracy (Option **C**). Since Tokugawa explicitly adopted Neo-Confucianism as part of his long-term strategy for the stabilization of Japan after generations of civil war, Option **B**, "reimposition of traditional Confucianism into Japanese life," makes no sense at all, nor does Option **A**, the decentralization of power into the hands of the daimyo." It was to keep the feudal lords under control that the shogun created a Neo-Confucian bureaucracy.

1750 to 1914: From Enlightenment to the Modern World

Perhaps the most momentous changes in world history since the founding of the first cities took place in little more than a century and a half from the middle of the eighteenth century to the outbreak of World War I. During this time nearly all of the features commonly associated with our modern world—the expectation of progress, market economics, liberal democracy, urbanization, open-ended technological innovation; in short, the transition from agrarian to scientific-industrial society—were created. These changes came with dizzying, and to contemporaries, often unsettling, speed. Thus, during nearly every major transition, lawmakers and reformers, intellectuals and opinion makers struggled to make sense of the changes and alleviate their excesses. In the end, the tensions created by these changes in terms of wealth, power, and national prestige on a worldwide scale would lead to a war that would inflict unprecedented destruction on Europe and affect nearly all of the world's people in some way.

1750–1914: How Does This Period Differ from the Early Modern World?

Although students of world history have recently begun to put the dividing line between the "early modern" world and the "modern world" in the middle part of the eighteenth century, the older periodization of European specialists tended to see the entire century as the "Enlightenment" or the "Age of Reason." And indeed, there is considerable continuity and intensification of key "Enlightenment" concepts both before and after 1750. There are, however, several important reasons for such a division, which will become clearer as the following chapters unfold.

First, in the realm of intellectual history, and at that crucial place where ideas are translated into action, the latter part of the century was the proving ground for many key Enlightenment concepts. This was the age of the American and French Revolutions, in which many of the ideas that have come to define the modern world—human rights and freedoms, equality before the law, and representative government, to name but a few—were taken from the realm of theory to that of practice. **Further, the idea of revolution itself as a means of reconstructing society surfaces for the first time during this period.** A related intellectual movement that began at about this time was also a revolt of sorts: A desire to move away from the supremacy of reason in human affairs and to put oneself in tune with nature and with "natural" spontaneous expressions of human behavior—the Romantic movement. In this, the writings of Jean Jacques Rousseau, spanning the middle of the century, were crucial in arguing that civilization corrupts and that nature cures. Rousseau's political writings, especially *The Social Contract* (1762) would **also** have a profound influence on the direction of the French Revolution decades later. The Romantic movement itself dominated literature and the arts in the West over the course of several decades in the beginning of the nineteenth century.

Second, the period around 1750 marks the opening of the time in which a unique matrix of technology, institutions, and practices created the beginnings of the Industrial Revolution and the infrastructure of the modern world. As we shall see, these events first take shape in eighteenth-century England, where an improved agriculture, a vigorous trade and business environment, a need for improvements in cotton spinning, and a number of relatively simple technical innovations led to the beginnings of the factory system and mass production. By the opening of the nineteenth century, the growing application of the steam engine and the mushrooming demand for technical improvements in a host of related industries made Great Britain the "workshop of the world" by 1850 and forced competitors in the United States and Europe to embark on their own industrial revolutions. Thus our present modern world, with its faith in the power of technology and science, and its expectations of constant progress had its roots during the period after 1750.

Third, the "twin revolutions"—industrial and political—as the English historian Eric Hobsbawm has called them, in jointly creating the modern world unleashed a third force, imperialism, as their troubled stepchild. Despite the fact that Great Britain lost its American colonies at the end of the eighteenth century, the period after 1750 may nonetheless be seen as significant in this regard because it marks the beginning of Britain's involvement in earnest with India and, within a few decades, with China and parts of Southeast Asia, with France and other Western countries eventually following in its wake. While the most dramatic phase of this process, dubbed by historians the "New Imperialism," takes place in the final quarter of the nineteenth century, in many ways its seeds had already been sown by the end of the eighteenth. From this period until the outbreak of the first World War in 1914, the power of nationalism and military and industrial technology made possible conquest on an unheard-of scale. The legacy of imperialism and the struggles of its subjects for independence are still central in world politics today and have played a primary role in forming the present worldviews of many, if not most, of the former Western colonies in Asia, Africa, and the Middle East.

What Causes Changes and Breaks within This Period?

As implied above, the problem of **periodization** is a difficult and often-contested one for historians. To a great extent, it is determined by the particular set of historical problems under consideration. Because of the complexity of forces and events in any historical era, however, there are bound to be contradictory or ambiguous trends within such periods as well. Hence, all attempts to label historical periods are, to some degree, convenient fictions for historians; a kind of shorthand used to identify large trends or to convey elements of the "character" of an era. In looking at the three main topics in this part—political revolution, industrial revolution, and imperialism—one therefore finds that the most intense periods of each of these, though somewhat separate from each other, do overlap to a considerable extent; and also, that each contains elements that contradict the premise of the periodization.

For example, the "Age of Revolutions" is often considered to be from 1776, the year of the American Declaration of Independence, to 1848, the year marked by the last widespread attempts at revolution across Europe. During this time, we find the American, French, Haitian, and Latin American revolutions, the latter made possible by the Napoleonic conquests that swept away many of the monarchies of Europe and briefly planted the ideals and institutions of the French Revolution in their place. Within this revolutionary period, however, there was also the so-called "Age of Reaction" from 1815 until 1848: With Napoleon defeated, European monarchs attempted to reimpose their wills on their former kingdoms and even reclaim their newly independent colonies in the Americas. But within France, Poland, Russia, Austria, and the German and Italian states, the ideals of nationalism and self-government from the Napoleonic period developed and spread below the surface, resulting in a renewed revolution in France in 1830 and in France and much of the rest of Europe in 1848.

Although labor unrest and poor harvests also played a role in the upheavals of 1848, political historians use it as a convenient year to mark the beginning of an "Age of Nationalism" that would last until 1914 and the outbreak of World War I. The potent idea that people sharing ties of ethnicity, language, religion, long-time occupation of territory, and shared oppression—even a common mythology— should have their own state had already gathered considerable momentum since the French Revolution in 1789. After 1848, however, we begin to see more and more states actually organizing themselves according to this principle. Because the older empires and monarchies in Europe, Asia, and Africa were often made up of many different groups, they tended to resist the trend toward creating nation-states for fear it would destroy their empires. Thus, Austria opposed the unification of Germany under the lead of Prussia (1871), as well as the unification of Italy (1870). The Ottoman Empire fought throughout the century against the struggles for independent nationhood of Greece, Egypt, and the Balkan states, as did Russia with Poland and the Baltic states. The desire to gain nationhood, the need for protective alliances, and the maneuverings of the most powerful states all contributed, along with the international arms race and the competition for colonies, to the outbreak of World War I.

Within the Industrial Revolution, historians usually distinguish between the first stage, from roughly 1750 through 1850, and the Second Industrial Revolution from 1850 through 1914. In the first stage, simple improvements in existing machines and consolidation of processes involved in textile production reached a take-off point by the 1780s and early 1790s. Here the development of practical steam power and the cotton gin in the American south allowed for the sustainable mass production of textiles. The need of coal for fuel, improved iron, and the demand for moving ever-larger amounts of bulk goods led to the application of steam power to transportation in the early decades of the nineteenth century. From these early experiments at building steamships and railroads, the application of steam power to an ever-increasing number of industrial processes took off. By 1850, England, as the pioneer in this movement, was called "the workshop of the world," and the use of machines had spread to the United States and northern Europe.

Some disagreement among historians exists about when to properly date the Second Industrial Revolution. The period immediately after 1850, when new methods were developed for mass-producing steel, is seen by some as properly beginning a new age of heavy industry. Others begin the period somewhat later in the 1870 with the growing use of oil, the development of electricity, and the expanding need for exotic raw materials such as rubber.

Finally, most historians date the Age of Imperialism, sometimes called the New Imperialism, variously from anywhere between 1870 and 1884 until 1914. As noted, the idea of creating overseas empires or colonies was not new during this period. What *was* new was the rationale for it and the means with which to carry it out. Though as we noted above, England's encroachment on India had begun as early as the 1750's, most of the more powerful countries of Europe tended to view overseas colonies as burdensome. Instead, for much of the first half of the nineteenth century, they preferred to force countries like China, Japan, Vietnam, and the Ottoman Empire into granting favorable trade concessions and small pieces of strategic territory.

By the 1870s, however, the demand for materials and markets, the control of strategic areas like the Suez Canal (opened in 1869), and the host of new weapons emerging from the Second Industrial Revolution made it both possible and desirable to create empires. Increasingly, such conquests were backed by the application of Charles Darwin's ideas of natural selection to human society by Social Darwinists, who argued that the weaker nations must be subdued by the strong if the human race is to progress. Matters came to a head in 1884 when a conference in Berlin agreed to a partition of Africa among the European powers, thus inaugurating the so called "Scramble for Africa." By 1914, Africa had been reduced to a set of European colonies. Indeed, by 1900, in addition to Africa, China was on the verge of collapse and partition; Southeast Asia was under French control; nearly every Pacific island had a European or American claim on it; and most recently, a newly industrialized and westernized Japan had established control over Korea, Taiwan, and claimed large areas of Manchuria. The frenzy for colonies, the race for alliances as nations sought protection from the powerful in blocs, and the arms and naval competition of all against all, particularly between England and Germany, would prove to be the major catalysts of World War I.

Revolution on a Global Scale

As is evident from the discussion above, the one overriding theme of this period from 1750–1914 is revolution: From the American Revolution and French Revolutions, which shaped the most dynamic political movements of the era in Europe and the Americas; through the Industrial Revolution, which created unprecedented abilities to mass produce goods, to transport them more quickly than ever before across land and sea, and to communicate instantly across oceans and continents, it was an age in which change seemed to be the order of the day—itself a revolutionary concept. For people in Europe or the United States, and by the end of the century, Japan or India, it must have indeed seemed that "Time's Winged Chariot," in the words of the seventeenth-century poet Andrew Marvell, was surely "hurrying near."

For people in many places in Asia, Africa, and Oceania, however, the chariot came with guns and soldiers. The "twin revolutions," as we have seen, had also resulted in the explosive growth of imperialism: the competition among the industrially advanced nations to create world-wide empires from the 1870s to 1914. The swiftness of this third revolution is astonishing. In 1800, Europeans controlled 35 percent of the Earth's surface; in 1914, 84 percent. Nowhere was this more dramatic than in Africa, where between 1884 and 1914 only Liberia and Ethiopia remained in the hands of Africans. These changes were so swift and all-encompassing that historian Theodore Von Laue has called them collectively "The World Revolution of Westernization."

As we will see in the following chapters, the reasons for empire building were many and varied. Industrial nations constantly sought raw materials and reliable markets for manufactured goods; as new industries were created, more exotic materials were needed for them, and governments and companies pushed farther and farther into more remote places. Competition and national pride spurred countries on. Trading nations needed islands for coaling stations and naval bases; canals in Suez and Panama made trade routes shorter, and competition for railroad and telegraph lines spurred further expansion. Countries that came late to the competition found they had to fight aggressively for colonies and concessions: In the 1890s, Germany and the United States both seized territory in the Pacific. By 1900, those nations that had not joined the imperial club were increasingly seen as bypassed by history and thus in decline.

Such empire building naturally created resistance among those subjected to it. But by the 1880s, the successive waves of the Industrial Revolution had created a divide that those nations that did not have a developing industrial base would find nearly impossible to bridge. To cite just one example, throughout the eighteenth century, the practice of trading firearms for slaves had saturated a large area of West Africa with guns. Local blacksmiths soon learned to make effective copies of these weapons, multiplying their numbers even more. The possibility of heavy resistance, combined with lack of European immunity to such diseases as malaria, effectively prevented any large-scale foreign penetration of the area. By the end of the nineteenth century, however, treatments for malaria and other tropical diseases allowed Europeans to survive in tropical environments. More tellingly, breakthroughs in manufacturing precision parts brought on by the Industrial Revolution now allowed the production of machine guns, repeating rifles, and a host of military hardware that no village blacksmith, no matter how skilled, could hope to copy. For the first time, small numbers of men armed with these weapons could subdue very large numbers of men without them.

Even before this, European pressure on the Ottoman Empire, India and South Asia, China, Japan, Korea, and Southeast Asia had produced crisis conditions for the governments of these places. Different factions asked questions that still echo down to the present: Do we fight these forces from the outside with what we have? Do we bide our time and try to imitate the weapons and innovations of the newcomers? And by the beginning of the new century it was increasingly asked: Will nothing else save us but revolution and completely new institutions?

The Spirit of the Age: Emancipation

Though the promise and practice of revolution often turned out to be two very different things, "the spirit of the age," to borrow a phrase from the philosopher G.W.F. Hegel, that animated it more than any other force was the hope of **emancipation**. The most basic definition of emancipation is "to free from bondage." Enlightenment thinkers such as Voltaire, Diderot, and Rousseau argued that European institutions of absolute monarchy and established churches held their subjects in bondage and that true freedom could only come with the end of both. Thus, the rise of representative government in the United States and during the French Revolution, and animating the revolutions of Haiti and Latin America, represented for their advocates the fulfillment of the promise of emancipation.

But for those who did not benefit from these movements, the goal of emancipation would, in some cases, remain elusive throughout the nineteenth century and beyond. For many in Europe, the questions would revolve largely around the idea of the nation-state: that the political boundaries of state should encompass the people who have tangible links to each other by language, religion, ethnicity, and shared history—"blood and soil." Thus, nationalism and the drive to form nation-states either by separation from larger empires or joining together smaller states, remained a powerful force throughout the period.

Of equal importance was the drive to remove barriers to full participation *within* different societies. The most dramatic of these was the gradual elimination of the slave trade during the late eighteenth and first decades of the nineteenth century, and the emancipation of slaves in the United States, Cuba, Brazil, and, eventually, much of Africa. The emancipation of serfs in Russia and periodic attempts at eliminating different trades in contract labor were also part of this general trend.

Religious dissenters of all sorts also sought, and in many places achieved, emancipation through the elimination of legal barriers to participatory citizenship. But the largest emancipation movement, and one still vital today, is that of women. From Mary Wollstonecraft's *Vindication of the Rights of Women* (1792) in the late eighteenth century, through suffragette movements in the nineteenth and twentieth centuries, women campaigned for equal rights in marriage, in the workplace, in owning property, in child custody, and in voting—and still today in some places even in such matters as forced female circumcision.

Practice Test Questions

1. The period 1750–1914 differs most from the previous period because of
   - A. the growth of feudalism.
   - B. the importance of revolution and nationalism.
   - C. the two World Wars.
   - D. the rise of the Gunpowder Empires.
   - E. the decline of the Catholic Church.

2. What historians have called the "twin revolutions" of the period are
   - A. the English and French.
   - B. the Mexican and French.
   - C. the Industrial and Political.
   - D. the Reactionary and American.
   - E. the Latin American and French.

3. The term emancipation is most closely associated with which of the following during this period?

    A. Serfs and slaves

    B. Migrant workers

    C. Indentured servants

    D. Children and single mothers

    E. The Catholic Church

4. Those nations that benefited most from the development of industrialism, nationalism, and the political revolutions of the nineteenth century were generally in

    A. Europe and the Middle East.

    B. South and East Asia.

    C. North America and Europe.

    D. South America and Africa.

    E. North and South America.

5. Improved communications from 1750–1914 had which of the following effects?

    A. More people than ever before listened to radio programs.

    B. Transatlantic voyages were reduced to three months.

    C. News of the French Revolution was telegraphed around the world.

    D. Merchants and businessmen could react more quickly to market changes.

    E. Most people in industrialized countries owned automobiles.

Answers and Explanations

1. B. None of the other choices take place during the period. The decline of the church is usually associated with Protestantism in the sixteenth century.

2. C. All the other choices are combinations of political revolutions. Reactionary is in opposition to revolution.

3. A. All the other choices involve groups either already or not fully emancipated, even in the most politically advanced countries; the Church did not generally take the lead in advocating emancipation for different groups during this time.

4. C. The other choices have at least one place where all these elements were not in evidence or did not benefit directly from them.

5. D. All the other choices are anachronistic for the period. Although radios and cars had been invented, radio programs were not yet broadcast, and relatively few people owned cars.

Global Commerce, Communications, Technology, and World Trade

According to the *American Heritage Dictionary*, one definition of "work" would be "the means by which one makes a living; an occupation." But the means by which many people made a living changed radically from 1750 to 1914. In 1750, the great majority of the world's people were engaged in subsistence agriculture. In the Caribbean, Brazil, and the British American colonies, institutions of slavery also engaged several million people in the production of cash crops for export such as tobacco, indigo, and, especially, sugar. Other prominent cash crops grown in various places in the world included tea, cocoa, and coffee. But with the exception of those crops grown on large plantations by forced labor, the work habits of the greater portion of the world's people were dictated by the rhythms of their regional agricultural cycles. That is, nuclear and extended families tended to work together on small plots and live in rural villages, and their working days revolved around when particular crops had to be planted, cultivated, and harvested.

The rise of greater crop variety, and expanding export markets made available by faster modes of transportation, increased the pace of farm work and also tended to extend it throughout the year during the nineteenth century. The explosion in the development and use of a vast array of farm machinery also transformed agriculture in Europe, North America, and, by 1914, Japan and some regions of India and China, from a *subsistence* activity—in which families raised what they needed with perhaps a bit of surplus for the local market—into a *commercial* activity in which crops are raised more specifically for sale at regional, national, even international markets, and foodstuffs are increasingly bought rather than raised by individual farmers. In short, *peasant agriculture* was being transformed into *farming*.

Other changes in the nature of work were becoming evident in the cities and towns of the nineteenth-century world as well. The last part of the eighteenth century saw the beginning of a process of urbanization that continues to the present. Not only did people migrate from marginal lands to cities looking for employment, but the nature of the cities themselves changed in purpose as well as size. As the Industrial Revolution proceeded, entire towns sprang up around the new factories and became magnets for those seeking work. Manchester in the English Midlands, for example, grew from a modest town of 35,000 in the late eighteenth century to over 200,000 by 1850—and more than doubled again by 1900. It was in these new industrial cities and mill towns that the most fundamental changes in the nature of work were to be found.

The most dramatic change was in the lives of rural people used to traditional work patterns who now came to work in the new factories. They were transformed from being masters in large part of their own work time to becoming "hands": those who tended the new factory machines according to hours of work demanded by factory owners and forced to keep up with the speed of the machines themselves. Artisans, skilled craftsmen, small producers involved in different stages of textile production, and so on also had their work patterns transformed as their jobs were increasingly taken over by machines. By the 1830s men, women, and children could be found working in factories for 14–16 hours a day, six days a week for set wages. Those who had been accustomed to seeing the fruits of their work—seamstresses, weavers, spinners, cobblers—were increasingly relegated to being anonymous cogs in the expanding factory system. In short, between 1750 and 1914 the world was being transformed from being fundamentally agricultural into one increasingly industrial and urbanized, in which men increasingly went to work outside the home and women and children did the household chores and/or went to school.

Industrial Revolution

While machines have been made by peoples all over the world since ancient times, historians have given the collective developments seen for the first time in England in the later eighteenth century the title of *Industrial Revolution*. Although scholars have come up with numerous definitions for this phenomenon, most agree that it is characterized by the following points:

- The *sustained* ability to mass-produce goods by the use of machines.
- The expansion of machine-driven mass production into an increasing variety of fields.
- The expanding ability of this mode of production to create its own infrastructure.
- The ability of such mass-produced goods to create their own demand and markets in addition to simply satisfying an existing demand.
- An ultimate transformation to a *mass society*.

While other countries were arguably richer or better endowed with natural resources, Great Britain in 1750 was particularly well suited to all of the requirements for a transition to factory-based machine production. As Europe's leading trading nation, Britain had a vigorous merchant class and a growing middle class actively looking for outlets for investment. The practice of enclosing land for raising sheep had already begun to drive large numbers of rural people into the cities, where they constituted a potential labor force. There was already a high concentration of skilled mechanics and artisans who could improve the efficiency of existing machines for producing different items. Finally, there was an industry in need of increased efficiency in order to compete in the world market: cotton textiles.

British cotton "factors"—brokers, traders, and merchant's representatives—found themselves at a disadvantage in trying to undersell cotton cloth imported from India. One reason for this was that the factors were required to bring the cotton to skilled and semi-skilled workers to complete each successive stage of production. Different trades undertook the combing, spinning, weaving, dying, cutting, and tailoring involved in making a cotton garment. All these workers charged their own prices for their work and taking the goods to their homes or shops required considerable leg work for the factor. By the last part of the eighteenth century, therefore, the factors were attempting to bring those involved in the steps of cloth making into large buildings that came to be called *factories*.

While this lowered the cost of production considerably, the wages of skilled workers were still high and the different speeds at which they could work often created delays and bottlenecks. A series of machines developed around mid-century—the "spinning jenny," which could spin up to ten threads at a time; the flying shuttle and water frame, which multiplied weaving productivity; and by 1780 the "mule" which combined spinning and weaving into one machine—now allowed productivity to reach the point where British cotton cloth could compete with the Indian types. By the 1780s as well, improvements made by James Watt and Matthew Boulton in the steam engine added an untiring and portable source of power to factory production. Since the machines were simple to operate and watch over, skilled labor was no longer necessary to the production process and the lowest possible wages could be paid to the unskilled "hands"—increasingly women and children.

By the opening of the nineteenth century, the machine-driven textile industry had reached the point where it was no longer a novelty and had become self-sustaining. In addition, the need for iron and coal to build and run the machines stimulated improvements in mining and associated industries. The need to transport bulk cargoes resulted in putting steam engines in boats and ships and, by the 1820s, creating the first steam locomotives and rail lines. The list of multiplying technologies growing out of this process is far too long to list here. Among the most important, however, were the gas and chemical industries growing from coal tar derivatives, the development of large scale steel production by the end of the 1850, and the stringing of telegraph wires from experiments with electricity in the 1830s and 1840s.

Global Commerce and World Trade

The Industrial Revolution caused profound changes in the speed with which goods could be traded, in the changing patterns of the *world systems* of trade, and finally in the nature of the goods most avidly sought by different countries.

In terms of the speed of trade, an important development up to roughly 1870 was the refinement of nautical technology in sailing ships, especially the development of the famous "clipper ship." Designed as merchant vessels for long sea voyages, the wooden- (and later, iron-) hulled clippers with their beautiful lines, complex arrays of sails, and great speed dominated runs where fast transportation was the most important consideration: racing to bring the first tea cargoes to England from China or getting gold seekers to California or Australia. By the 1870s, however, their limited cargo capacity led to their demise as the technology of steamships continued to improve.

In increasing the speed and scope of world trade, the two most important innovations were the rise of the railroad and the steamship. The railroad sprang from the fortunate combination of steam engines used to pump water from deep mines and the longtime use of wooden and iron rails for mining carts. By the early nineteenth century it was a short step to extend the rails from mine heads to canals or river ports to make coal and iron transport easier. By the 1820s in Britain and the United States, experiments were underway in which the steam engine itself was mounted on a carriage in order to pull a line of freight cars on rails. In 1829 the first passenger line, the Liverpool and Manchester Railway, was opened in England and the railroad boom was on.

The 1840s saw an explosion of railroad building in England as the relatively short distances involved and the growing amount of freight and passenger demand made the new technology a favorite investment for entrepreneurs. The following decade saw an even greater railroad boom in the United States, where the lines from the Midwest to the cities of the East made the region the breadbasket of the country, and rail hubs like the new city of Chicago grew at a frenzied pace. By 1860 the United States had more railroad trackage than the rest of the world combined. The Civil War pushed the overall industrial pace of both North and South to even greater heights. With the completion of the transcontinental railroad in 1869, the vast territory of the United States was increasingly knit together by the world's most advanced railroad network.

As the railroad was transforming land transport, the development of the steamship and the growth of cargo and passenger lines completely altered maritime trade. Steam engines had been used experimentally as a means to propel small boats as early as 1787. By the early part of the nineteenth century, successful use of such engines in riverboats made it possible for craft of all sizes to move independently of wind and current. Shallow draft paddle-wheel steamboats became the favored means of transporting people and goods on all the navigable rivers of the Americas and Western Europe, and their introduction soon followed in South and East Asia.

For a variety of reasons, the use of oceangoing steamers lagged somewhat behind that of riverboats. The limitations of the technology were such that for decades after the first Atlantic crossing by a steamer in 1827, sails continued to be used for auxiliary power. The engines were inefficient and burned so much fuel that little space was left for cargo. In addition the paddle-wheels proved unreliable on long ocean voyages. The development of the screw propeller, the advent of more powerful and safer engines, and the increasing use of iron in hull construction made for bigger and faster ships. By the 1870s the steamers had become fast and efficient enough so that crossings of the major oceans took only a fraction of their former time.

Such potential for speedy transportation and projection of power lent itself to the creation of what the sociologist Immanuel Wallerstein has called *world systems*: systems of trade in which trading partners, treaty ports, colonies, and so forth—*the peripheral areas*—are guided by the needs and wants of the *core* or *metropole*—the "mother country."

Here the British Empire is the foremost example. Trade policy was guided by government ministries that saw their duty as safeguarding and expanding British trade. Those engaged in the trade, in turn, relied on the influence of the British government and the power of the British Navy for support. Where possible, they wanted to have favorable conditions to conduct trade with as little competition as possible. Hence, they imposed the "unequal treaties" on China with the view of expanding British trade there and forcing the Chinese to conduct such trade on British terms. The control of colonies and dependencies was also part of this world system, as it gave an automatically favored position to British merchants and goods. Finally, the British argued for Free Trade (lowering or abolishing of protective tariffs by other countries) for much of the century because they believed that given a level playing field, they could out-compete local manufacturers and open other countries to British goods. Thus, they tried with limited success to open China to cheap British textiles. Their trade relations with the American south, in which they sold manufactured goods in return for American cotton, created intense regional conflict because the industrial states sought tariff protection for American manufactured goods, while southern states wanted to lower or abolish U.S. tariffs. In the case of the outright British possessions, they got the best of both worlds: cheap raw materials and captive markets for finished goods.

The demand for wider markets was driven in part by the changing demands of the industrial *core* of the British Isles during the Second Industrial Revolution. Though well-supplied with coal and iron, the new industries demanded increasingly exotic materials like petroleum, copper, rare earths, manganese, rubber, and nitrates. As was also the case with other imperial powers, these were for the most part not available domestically and thus had to be obtained through trade. Since many of these items came from tropical areas like Africa, the Middle East, and Southeast Asia, interest in these commodities helped spur imperial competition to obtain them and control their supply.

As we will also see at the beginning of the following chapter, changes in the nature of the food supply and the ability of the new railroads and steamships to carry it quickly greatly raised the level of foodstuffs as trade items. By the 1870s for example, Great Britain had not only become the first country to have a larger urban than rural population, but that population was now so large that it had to be sustained by food imports. Thus, the United States and Argentina supplied wheat, beef, and pork as trade items, while the British dependencies of Australia, New Zealand, and Canada also did so within a tighter trading sphere. Japan, too, struggled with the problem of supplying a booming, increasingly urban population with enough food. Subsidies to farmers at home and colonization ventures in Korea, Taiwan, and Manchuria were undertaken to alleviate the situation.

157

Communications

The increasing speed of transportation was accompanied by breathtaking advances in the speed of communication. Steamships and railroads vastly increased the speed and decreased the price of postal transport. The ability of people to keep in regular touch over vast distances undoubtedly made the world seem a much smaller place and facilitated financial and commercial transactions. But the most spectacular advance in communication was the development and rapid spread of telegraphic systems. By the 1840s a number of experimenters had developed signaling systems powered by electricity sent over metal wires. As the simplest and most reliable of these, the system of Samuel F.B. Morse in the United States soon became the international standard. The telegraph quickly spread through Europe and the Americas by the 1850s. The need to string miles of wire to poles made it a natural accompaniment to new rail lines, and these two items became prominent features of the landscape on nearly every continent by the 1860s. Constant improvements and systems for sending multiple messages on the same line came into use in the 1860s and 1870s.

Once messages could be instantaneously sent across continents, the idea of laying undersea telegraphic cables naturally suggested itself. Here, the obstacles were more challenging. Still, by 1868 the first transatlantic cable had been laid and by the end of the century, the major continents were linked by undersea telegraph lines. They would soon be followed by the telephone, developed in 1876, and the wireless telegraph (1893). By the eve of World War I, the major systems of landline communication were in place and the rudiments of radio communication, developed by Marconi and improved by DeForest were gaining ground. It was now possible for ships to communicate with each other at sea, and by the early post-war period, the first commercial radio stations would be set up.

The advantages of instantaneous communication were profound. News of disasters or emergencies could be rapidly transmitted and help could come by rail or ship far faster than ever before. Voting results, governmental decrees, and official business could now be sent to remote places, vastly aiding the centralizing efforts of national governments. Long-distance diplomacy could also be conducted, cutting down on miscommunications among governments. In this case, however, governments soon learned how to manipulate the system: Clever editing of a telegram by the Prussian chancellor, Otto Von Bismarck, helped provoke the French Emperor Napoleon III into war in 1870; while the British interception of the secret German Zimmermann telegram helped push the United States into World War I.

Two other means of communication are also worth mentioning because of the role they played in fostering what historians sometimes call "mass society." The first is the rapid rise of the newspaper industry. While gazettes, notices, broadsides, and so on had been in use for hundreds of years in Europe and Asia, the development during the mid-nineteenth century of the high-speed rotary printing press and the mass production of wood pulp paper vastly increased the capacity of newspapers to cheaply print large daily editions. The new mail and telegraphic systems allowed the rapid acquisition of news from around the world, and so people from all walks of life now had the opportunity to be better informed than ever before. The papers thus helped popularize the need for literacy and also proved central to the shaping of public opinion.

Finally, another key to the immediacy of communication was the development of photography. The first systems for capturing light and shadow on chemically treated glass plates were developed in France in the 1830s. By the early 1840s the technology had spread to the Americas, England, and much of Europe. The clumsiness of the process, and the requirement that subjects sit for some time while the image was set, restricted it at first to a portrait and landscape medium. But its potential for exact recording of historical personages and events soon broadened its use, while improvements over the following decades made the equipment more reliable and portable.

By the end of the century, still more technical developments created the first moving pictures and the small, convenient Kodak box camera that made amateur photography a popular pastime around the world. Thus, by 1914, people from all walks of life could see photographs from all over the world printed in newspapers, postcards, and in "movie" form in the local theater. As with the other communications media examined above, photography contributed to a perception that the world was rapidly shrinking.

Technology

As should be obvious by now, the seemingly endless number of new technologies produced during the Industrial Revolution is far too large for us to even touch on here. Still, at least two major trends emerge for examination. The first is that the proliferation of machines in different fields created the basis for societies that were increasingly reliant on technology. For example, England held the first world's fair, the Great Exhibition, in 1851 and was proclaimed "the Workshop of the World." They were followed by France in 1867, Austria in 1873, and the United States in 1876. All of these countries by roughly mid-century had reached a threshold at which they not only were reliant on existing technologies, but national welfare and even survival increasingly depended on their keeping up with technological competitors. While the development of the early technologies in England had been the result of individual entrepreneurs, by the 1840s governments on the continent were increasingly inaugurating national programs to foster railroad and telegraph systems. Even in the United States, the government made immense amounts of cheap land available to railroad companies, while generous patent and copyright laws fostered technological development.

A second major trend is that by the latter part of the nineteenth century, new technologies were increasingly coming from the joint work of scientists and engineers rather than from the experiments of inspired tinkerers. Thomas Edison, for example, although starting out as a gifted mechanic who designed improvements in telegraph systems, created one of the first genuine research laboratories at Menlo Park, New Jersey. In a real sense, it was a kind of invention factory wherein devices such as the electric light bulb, phonograph, designs for electrical generation and transmission, and moving pictures were developed. In fact, all over the industrializing world, technical schools, research institutes, and engineering colleges proliferated. In all these places, the enormous complexity of refining existing technologies and creating new ones was increasingly the province of professionals. In short, the Industrial Revolution had been firmly institutionalized. Those countries that had been late to embrace the new order found themselves further and further behind as they desperately sought to create their own industrial bases.

How Did the Industrial Revolution Affect Culture and World Society?

In this chapter we have already had some glimpses into the ways in which the Industrial Revolution affected culture and world society. To summarize briefly, it did this in two major ways:

- The wealth, power, and influence it gave those who embraced it earliest and longest (Great Britain, Western Europe, the United States) allowed them to project their cultures directly and indirectly in innumerable ways wherever their interests took them. In other words, as the muscle behind the imperial and economic expansion of the industrial powers, it allowed them to transplant and/or impose certain aspects of their culture onto their possessions and trading partners.

- By creating entirely new media, social conditions, and institutions, it altered the cultural outlook of the countries in which it developed and those who later adopted it. Because certain consequences of industrialism were common to all those places that adopted it, cultural differences among the major industrial countries were reduced to a considerable degree.

One can see a number of instances of the first process at work in British India. In the eighteenth century, the merchants of the British East India Company generally had no thought of imposing British institutions on the Indians. In fact, they often dressed in Indian clothes and took Indian wives while they made their fortunes trading Indian goods. By the mid-1850s this had changed radically. British attempts at reform of Indian institutions, railroad building, attempts to set up industrial enterprises, and missionary activity had profoundly alienated many Indians. Matters came to a head in 1857 when British introduction of the new Enfield rifle to their Sepoy (Indian) soldiers, the bullets of which were said to be greased with pork and beef fat (thus violating the food restrictions of Muslims and Hindus), sparked the Great Rebellion (sometimes called the Great Mutiny). In the following decades, the British created an entirely new civil service staffed by British-educated Indians. Perhaps the most famous figure to emerge from the new education system was Mohandas Gandhi, trained in India and England as a lawyer.

In other places, transformations of culture took place as a consequence of decisions to adopt aspects of Western military modernization and the industrial base to support it. Thus, one sees the adoption of European-style political reforms and the setting up of technical schools in the Ottoman Empire during the 1870s; the sending of students abroad and the "Self-Strengthening Movement" in China; and, most dramatically of all, the wholesale adoption of European and American political, educational, military, and industrial institutions in Japan. All of these places saw deep resistance to the imposition or adoption of such practices. Their arguments, examined in more detail in Chapter 25, usually centered on the idea that to adopt foreign technical institutions was to unavoidably be influenced by foreign culture and thus lose some or all of their identity. Even Japan, which did this in the most thoroughgoing and successful way, faced a bloody rebellion over these issues by disaffected samurai in 1877.

By 1914, the results of the second point above were also evident. The modern districts of the world's major cities had all begun to share common features: railroad stations, telegraph and telephone lines, electricity and gas, trolleys, the first reinforced concrete and steel buildings, even primitive automobiles. In China, Japan, India, Turkey, and Egypt, one could also find universities, technical institutions, and factories. The industrial workers first found in England in the early nineteenth century now grew in numbers on every continent, as did the mass media and, increasingly, mass entertainment. As we will also see in Chapter 25, mass movements for the betterment of workers and assorted Socialist organizations would be found in all these places by the eve of World War I.

Cultural transmission, however, was, at least for some, a two-way street. While Western influence was growing in non-Western countries, interest in "exotic" cultures grew in Europe and the United States. The paintings of Delacroix, for example, with their subjects of Arab men, imagined details of harem life, and romantic vision of the "Orient" fascinated viewers, as did the first photographs to be taken in Asia and Africa. From the 1870s on, Chinese and Japanese art motifs became extremely popular. The vibrant colors and stylized views of Japanese decorative arts found their way into the work of Impressionist painters. Travel accounts of remote areas of Asia and Africa became staples of popular culture, while the founding of geographical societies helped to spread more accurate information on such places on a mass scale. In all, despite considerable violence and cultural conflict, a kind of global fusion of cultures was beginning to take place and continues in ever more intensified form today.

Practice Test Questions

1. By 1850, the most advanced industrial nation was

    A. Great Britain.
    B. France.
    C. Germany.
    D. Russia.
    E. Japan.

2. The growing use of which of the following did the most to speed global trade in the nineteenth century?

    A. Stagecoach
    B. Steamship
    C. Riverboat
    D. Keel boat
    E. Schooner

3. The key development in rapid communication until 1876 was

    A. the telephone.
    B. the wireless.
    C. the telegraph.
    D. the semaphore system.
    E. the vacuum tube.

4. By the latter half of the nineteenth century, technological development was increasingly carried out by

    A. mechanics.
    B. factory hands.
    C. mathematicians.
    D. scientists and engineers.
    E. land grant colleges.

5. Of the following groups, which ones benefited most from the early Industrial Revolution?

    A. Manufacturers

    B. Women

    C. Children

    D. Skilled workers

    E. Slaves

Answers and Explanations

1. A. France had not caught up to Britain; Germany was not yet a united country; Russia had barely begun building modern industry; Japan was still secluded from foreign contact.

2. B. Stagecoaches were used only on land, riverboats and keel boats on inland waters, and schooners were small sailing ships.

3. C. Semaphore systems had been around for centuries; the telephone, invented in 1876 was not in widespread use until the turn of the century; the wireless and vacuum tubes were factors only after the turn of the century.

4. D. Mechanics can be credited with many of the breakthroughs of the *early* Industrial Revolution; factory hands operated machines but seldom invented them; mathematicians were increasingly confined to theory; land grant colleges tended at first to concentrate on agricultural and practical mechanical subjects.

5. A. All the rest may be classed at some level as being "victims" of the early Industrial Revolution. In the case of slavery, it took on new life in the American South because of the demand of the mills for cotton.

Demographics and the Environment

In addition to the immense changes brought about by the political and industrial revolutions, the period from 1750 to 1914 was marked by the greatest demographic transition and consequent impact on the environment that the world had yet seen. Unprecedented population increases took place on every continent, most dramatically in Europe, Asia, and especially North America, and vast areas of lightly or uninhabited land were brought under human cultivation. Several interrelated factors may be seen as contributing to this growth. First, there was a vast increase in the food supply: Growing speed and reliability of world trade in foodstuffs and the successful spread of such staple crops as corn (maize), potatoes, and assorted grains allowed more people to be fed more efficiently than ever before. After 1750 this process was abetted by advances in agronomy and animal husbandry in Europe and North America. Second, even with the ending of the slave trade, the period was marked by a great surge of immigration, particularly from Europe to North America, which peaked during the opening decade of the twentieth century. As the immigrants settled into their new environment, they not only added to the population of the new country by their own numbers, but their families expanded the population ever more rapidly. Here, the advances in communication and transportation of the Industrial Revolution played a pivotal role in making it possible for immigration on such a scale. Finally, increased urbanization, scientific and medical advances, and the growing wealth and power of the middle classes in the industrialized countries all contributed to significant changes in birth patterns and increased life expectancy. These have been steadily spreading throughout the world down to the present.

Food Supply

The eighteenth and nineteenth centuries saw a number of changes in the relationship between human groups and the means by which they raised, transported, and stored food. In general such means were vastly improved, but the improvement was uneven and the era still saw a lack of food supply, leading to starvation and famine in a number of places. On the other hand, improvements in the food supply also sustained an enormous increase in the populations of Europe and the Americas—Europe's population multiplied threefold between 1800 and 1900, while the U.S. population soared from 4 million in 1790 to near 100 million by the beginning of the new century. In other places, however, the supply barely kept pace, as in China and India, which both saw their populations double during this time.

The reasons for a near doubling of the world's population from 900 million in 1800 to 1.6 billion in 1900 are many. Urbanization, mass efforts and new techniques to improve hygiene, a vastly improved understanding of disease, and a drop in the death rate all played important roles. But keeping the food supply adequate was central to all of these. The English thinker Thomas Malthus (1766-1834) had predicted in his 1798 *Essay on the Principle of Population* that human populations would always vastly outpace their food supplies unless slowed by such "natural checks" as war, disease, and famine. Yet for the most part this did not happen.

Several factors may be seen as responsible for this. First, the beginnings of scientific agronomy pioneered in England, France, and the Low Countries during the second half of the eighteenth century allowed for more varied crops and large increases in livestock production. Clover, for example, as both a forage crop for animals and as a means of returning nutrients to the soil was a key innovation in this regard. Second, the fruits of the "Columbian Exchange"—the huge movement of new crops to and from the Americas—began to have an increasingly large impact in both places. Such crops as maize/corn, potatoes, beans, tomatoes, peanuts, and so on allowed marginal lands in many areas of the world to be cultivated, while increasing areas of the United States, Argentina, and Russia were given over to wheat production, now made possible on a vast scale by the development of improved plows and mechanical harvesters. The Americas, Australia, and New Zealand also became centers for raising pigs, sheep, cattle, and horses—the staples of Eurasia—on a previously unheard-of scale. Finally, revolutions in transportation by clipper ship, steamer, and railroads allowed foodstuffs to be shipped at unprecedented speed. By the end of the century, the widespread use of canning and the advent of mechanical refrigeration would allow food to be shipped virtually anywhere in the world and remain fresh. Perhaps more important, rapid communication by mail, telegraph, undersea cable, and telephone allowed warnings of famine or natural disasters to be transmitted and emergency supplies shipped to alleviate the sufferings of the people.

Mass Migrations

A migration occurs when people move from one place to another. A mass migration is when they move in large numbers. Such migrations may be voluntary or involuntary, and are often prompted by natural or human-made disasters. For example, the United States was the site of one of the longest and largest mass migrations in world history as millions of people **emigrated**—left one country to settle in another—there from the 1840s through the early decades of the twentieth century. Different groups, however, were moved by different motivations. The early waves of Irish **immigrants**—people who move to and settle in a foreign country—in the late 1840s and 1850s were driven in large part because a deadly blight attacked the potato crop on which most Irish peasants had come to depend. The resulting famine and mass starvation caused millions to come to America to make a new start. Later waves of Irish, however, came for the opportunities the new land afforded rather than to avoid starvation. The failure of most of the European revolutions of 1848 likewise pushed many Germans and Central Europeans to move overseas in the hope of political freedom and economic opportunity. Similarly, the *pogroms* against Jews in Russia in the late nineteenth and early twentieth centuries induced many to move out of that empire. The eviction of the Native American peoples in the 1830s from the eastern United States to the Indian Territory of Oklahoma provides a particularly dramatic example of a forced mass migration.

Just as mass migrations have been the result of people being *pushed*, so have they occurred because something attractive *pulled* them. In this, hope of better economic conditions has often played a leading role. The discovery of gold in California, Australia, South Africa, and Alaska all moved people from different places around the world to try their luck at striking it rich. Likewise, the hope of cheap land stimulated immigration as did the demand for labor. Thus, in the nineteenth and early twentieth centuries, such places as the Chinese territory of Manchuria were sites for Japanese and Russian immigration; the British territories of South Africa and Australia attracted Europeans, Chinese, and South Asians; and, most spectacularly, the United States became the favored destination for millions of Europeans and, until 1882, hundreds of thousands of Chinese. In fact, it was the need for labor in various capacities that stimulated perhaps the largest forced mass migration of all: the slave trade, which reached its peak by the final decades of the eighteenth century. In the following century, following the abolition of the Slave Trade, various schemes were hatched to ship Chinese, Japanese, Indian, and Indonesian contract laborers—treated in many cases like slaves—to places in the British Empire and the Americas—particularly Cuba and Peru—to work in the sugar, mining, and *guano* industries.

Mass Migration and the End of the Slave Trade

The situation of the slave trade deserves a special mention in this section on mass migration because on the one hand, it was the largest migration of any kind for nearly half the period in question, and on the other, its end represented a significant victory for the champions of the new modern values of human rights and emancipation. Here, the end of the Slave Trade is defined as the end of the Atlantic Slave Trade: The shipping of slaves obtained from West African ports through European, Arab, and African brokers and shipped by European and American traders across the Atlantic Ocean (the brutal and dangerous middle passage), to buyers in North America, the Caribbean, and South America. That the process subjected vast numbers of people to the evils of forced separation, imprisonment, brutal punishments, and, in all stages of their voyage, an extremely high death rate from confinement, disease, execution, and shipwreck was recognized from the beginning. It was, however, usually justified by arguments of economic necessity and, often, by claiming that the process helped to civilize and Christianize the slaves.

By the eighteenth century, as we have seen, the majority of Enlightenment *philosophes* had come to condemn the trade as a violation of basic human rights. Thus the high point of the trade was seen toward the middle of the eighteenth century. It slowly declined in North America as the northern states of the new American republic banned slavery by 1804, and the relatively moderate climate of the upper south allowed the slave population to survive above the replacement rate. While the new constitution postponed any discussion of abolishing the trade until 1808, the horrors of it were sufficient to convince Congress to ban it that very year. It should be noted, however, that up to the Civil War, illegal traders attempted to get around the law and the American and British navies played active roles in attempting to suppress them. It must also be said that a vigorous and expanding *internal* slave trade flourished in the American South as the demand for cotton continued to soar up to 1861.

As in the American South, British sugar and indigo planters in the Caribbean, and the large number of slave traders serving them, continued to do a brisk business into the early years of the nineteenth century. The moral force of the abolitionist argument, however, had more immediate impact there than in the United States. The chief influence in this regard was the Evangelical philanthropist William Wilberforce (1759-1833). For 20 years, from 1787 to 1807 he had campaigned in Parliament for the abolition of the British slave trade, finally succeeding in the year before the American ban. His appeal to "practical Christianity" and his championing of the spread of anti-slavery societies kept the pressure on Parliament for another two and a half decades. Finally, three days before Wilberforce's death in 1833, slavery was banned in the British Empire and the British Navy redoubled its efforts to patrol the African coast in order to suppress the trade.

With the end of slavery in the Americas by 1888 (in Brazil), efforts were stepped up to stop it in East Africa, where it continued to flourish in various African and Arab territories. Ironically, one of the arguments used by the advocates of imperialism in Africa was the final abolition of the slave trade there. Even today, however, there are still remote places in Africa, the Middle East, and South Asia where forms of involuntary servitude survive.

New Birth Rate Patterns

One of the most momentous changes of the period 1750-1914 was that of both a decreasing death rate and, primarily among the urban and town-dwelling middle classes, a decline in the birth rate. With all but a small percentage of their people involved in agricultural work, the older agrarian societies had been characterized by both high birth rates and high death rates. At a time when whole societies could be ravaged by bubonic plague, smallpox, or cholera, and subsistence economies left people vulnerable to malnutrition and the diseases that sprang from it, women tended to have as many children as possible because they could expect that perhaps half would die before reaching adulthood. In addition, each child provided an additional farm laborer, so it made economic sense to have a large family.

By the 1850s however, the trends were already in place to change these practices. First, the food supplies in Europe and the United States were growing and the world trade in foodstuffs helped ensure against famine. Thus, the Irish potato famine of the 1840s was the last widespread such event in Western Europe. Second, with urban sanitation improved and the risk of epidemics and childhood diseases reduced, the death rate came down rapidly and the growing number of middle-class families could afford to have fewer children. Relieved of having to use children as labor on the farm, such urban families could invest much more emotionally and economically in each child. Children could therefore get a head start on education through their mothers before they entered school, which became compulsory in many countries as the century progressed. Thus, among the wealthy, the growing numbers of the middle class, and even the members of the upper working class, the desire to limit the family to a manageable size began to outstrip the traditional desire to have as many children as possible. Children came to be seen more as dependants than potential laborers.

Paradoxically, even though this trend spread as countries became more urbanized, overall population continued to soar. One reason for this is that people lived longer. With better diets came increased health and resistance to disease. As public and private sanitation improved and vaccination became more widespread, the rate of disease went down. The increased availability and knowledge of doctors also cut down markedly on the death of women during childbirth. With more women and children surviving, the number of mothers increased even as the size of their families went down. This aided in popularizing the Victorian nuclear family-centered "cult of domesticity." Finally, the last of Malthus' "natural checks" also went down dramatically in nineteenth century Europe: warfare. Although limited wars were fought in Europe, there were no mass campaigns on the scale of the Napoleonic Wars for a century until the outbreak of World War I.

Thus, the increasingly healthy, urbanized, and industrialized nations saw the largest proportional population increases in the world. This was also true of the United States, with its enormous level of immigration boosting the population even more dramatically. But it was also true outside of the Euro-American world: Japan, joining the ranks of industrialized nations by the turn of the twentieth century, saw its population more than double in the space of a few decades. Population pressures provided an important rationale for Japanese expansion onto the Asian mainland until the end of World War II. It should be mentioned also that the old agrarian lands of China and India, while not experiencing these new birth and urbanization patterns to a very great extent at this point, still saw their populations expand in absolute terms. Then, as now, they were the two most populous places on earth.

Practice Test Questions

1. Which of the following would *not* be considered an immigrant?

    A. A Cherokee born in Oklahoma Indian Territory

    B. A Japanese worker landing in Brazil

    C. An Indian merchant getting off a ship in Trinidad

    D. An Italian stonemason arriving at Ellis Island

    E. An African slave bound for St. Dominque

2. Which of the following was a nineteenth-century mass migration?

    A. Polynesians to Hawaii

    B. Irish to the United States

    C. Manchus to China

    D. Bantu-speaking peoples to Southern Africa

    E. Patagonians to Antarctica

3. American participation in the Slave Trade did not end until 1808 in part because

    A. the U.S. Constitution would not allow action to be taken until then.

    B. slaves were only considered to be three-fifths of a person.

    C. four of the first five U.S. presidents were slave owners.

    D. the Southern states threatened to secede from the Union.

    E. mobs threatened violence against abolitionists.

4. The great crusader against slavery in the British Empire was

    A. Cecil Rhodes.

    B. James Watt.

    C. George III.

    D. William Wilberforce.

    E. Thomas B. Macaulay.

5. The British thinker Thomas Malthus predicted that

    A. population would always outstrip food supplies.

    B. population would level off as countries became richer.

    C. population growth would be guided by an "unseen hand."

    D. famine would be eliminated in his lifetime.

    E. urbanization would gradually alleviate population pressures.

Answers and Explanations

1. A. The Cherokee was *born* in Oklahoma and is therefore not an immigrant. All of the other choices provide examples of immigrants.

2. B. The key words in the question are "nineteenth century." Choices **A, C,** and **D** all took place before this time; as for Choice **E,** it is completely false as no group has ever migrated to Antarctica.

3. A. As soon as the Constitution's 20-year moratorium on discussing it was up in 1808, Congress banned the slave trade. The other choices are essentially true but not relevant to the issue at the time.

4. D. Of the other choices, Rhodes was an imperialist, Watt an inventor, George a king, and Macaulay a parliamentary reformer.

5. A. Malthus did not predict these other things; the "unseen hand" is a concept popularized by Adam Smith in economics.

Social Change: 1750–1914

Perhaps more than any other event in modern human history, the Industrial Revolution upended old assumptions about social roles. Within the space of about a century, much of the world was transformed from societies that saw the basic function of their institutions as conserving tried-and-true methods of maintaining a stable *corporate* or *organic* society— one in which each group was part of the larger whole and had a specific, well-defined role to play—into societies that considered *dynamism*—rapid, open-ended change—as the means for creating a just, fair, and perfectible order.

In the following sections, we will examine effects of the Industrial Revolution on specific groups—serfs, slaves, women, and children—but will first consider its effects on an entirely new class: industrial wage workers. It is the creation of this new class and the attempts of reformers and revolutionaries to help it that defined much of the social struggle of the era. The patterns set during this time and their consequences influenced notions of class and class struggle down to the present.

The New Class: The Industrial Revolution and Wage Workers

As we have seen, the long hours and often brutal conditions of the early factories frequently subjected workers to physical danger, in addition to the low wages offered as factory owners struggled to wring a profit from their pioneering enterprises. In addition, however, the legacy of older feudal relations between employer and employee resulted in factory workers suffering from a number of legal disabilities. Because of the need for labor and the desire to reduce the numbers of the indigent, men in England and in other places were *required* to work; to refuse an offer of employment could bring imprisonment or time in the "workhouse." In addition, the tradition of the small artisan or craftsman was kept alive in laws that required the employer and employee to decide for themselves the wages and other conditions of work: Laws strictly banned collective bargaining. Finally, with machines putting laborers with newly outmoded skills increasingly out of work, they often found themselves becoming "hands" and taking ever-lower wages. Thus, from 1800 to 1830, factory wages actually went down in England.

At the same time, however, the period saw growing protest movements among laborers. As we noted earlier, as early as the mid-eighteenth century, a mob of angry spinners burned early models of the "spinning jenny" because they sensed its implications for their livelihoods. By the early years of the nineteenth century, bands of workers called Luddites— from a mythical character named Ned Ludd—roamed the countryside attacking mills and machines. In France, the common act of throwing wooden shoes called *sabots* into the machinery gave us the word *sabotage*. Sporadic acts of violence against the machines themselves soon gave way to attempts at worker organization. Following the infamous Peterloo Massacre in the industrial city of Manchester in 1819, pressure mounted in Great Britain to repeal the laws, called the Combination Acts, that banned labor organizing, which was effected in 1824. As industrialization became more pervasive, individual and regional labor movements coalesced into the nationwide Chartist cause: Huge petitions, ultimately with more than a million signatures, were presented repeatedly to the throne demanding various reforms. By the 1850s, their demands had largely been granted and the movement died out, to be replaced by a growing emphasis on specific kinds of trade unions.

At the same time, there were those outside the new working class who attempted to devise ways to make the new system more humane. The most famous of these were called, derisively, the Utopian Socialists. Two of them, the Frenchmen Comte de St. Simon and Charles Fourier, devised entire systems of political and industrial organization that, although visionary, proved impractical and suffered from lack of funding. The third, Robert Owen (1771–1858), was more successful. Owen had worked in a factory as a boy in the 1780s and early 1790s, and his drive and skill allowed him to advance to factory manager. He remembered the hard life he had endured, and by trial and error, created a factory system in New Lanark, Scotland, that incorporated a number of novel features: high wages, comfortable housing for workers, shortened hours, factory safety improvements, workman's compensation insurance, an infirmary, and even a school for the children. New Lanark was not only a model of paternalistic labor relations but made a good profit as well. Owen tirelessly tried to convince others of the viability of his ideas but with only limited success. In 1825 he led a group to set up an even more ambitious factory town in New Harmony, Indiana. After several years, the experiment collapsed and Owen spent the rest of his life championing the rights of workers and supporting the growing movement in England for recognition of trade unions.

For some, the chief drawback to such visionary schemes was that they did not get at the root of the problem, which was that the new industrial society was the inevitable product of laws of history and economics. By far the most important thinkers in this regard were Karl Marx (1818–1883) and Friedrich Engels (1820–1895). Marx had been an intellectual and agitator during the 1840s when he met Engels, who had inherited a factory in Manchester and had already written an important study of working conditions in Great Britain. In 1848 they produced a short work called *The Communist Manifesto* that has remained among the most influential books in the world ever since.

"The history of all hitherto existing societies," said Marx, "is the history of class struggle." Borrowing the idea of "dialectics" (opposing forces or ideas) that propel the process of history forward, Marx said that it is the struggle of economic classes throughout history that has dictated the character of the government and institutions of each historical period. Most recently, the French Revolution and its aftermath produced "bourgeois society"—one in which the capitalist class owns the means of production (factories) and is locked in struggle with the "proletariat" (wage workers). The government in the most industrially advanced countries, said Marx, consists of constitutions guaranteeing property rights, property qualifications for the vote, and encouragement of industry that spring from the dominant role of the bourgeoisie as an economic class.

The Rise of the Industrial Middle Class and Mass Society

Nearly as dramatic as the creation of the industrial working class was the transformation of the middle class from a commercial and professional class to one in which the factory and machine production become increasingly central. Though far less numerous than the working and agricultural classes, who still numbered perhaps 80 percent of the population, they nevertheless accounted for much of the economic and political dynamism of the era. Moreover, their collective tastes in manners, family life, leisure activities, religious observance, and the arts put its stamp on the period as the "Victorian Era." The qualities they espoused—thrift, sobriety, self-discipline, hard work, education, and moral earnestness—led the sociologist Max Weber to associate their attitudes with religious Calvinism in his study, *The Protestant Ethic and the Spirit of Capitalism*.

The mushrooming of new industries, particularly during the Second Industrial Revolution of the last decades of the nineteenth century, created vastly enhanced middle-class employment opportunities while helping to create subdivisions within the class itself. For those at the top, the leading industrialists, mine, and railroad magnates, their vast wealth often led to receiving titles of nobility and becoming part of the aristocracy; or for men like Andrew Carnegie and John D. Rockefeller, wielding enormous power as private citizens. Smaller industrialists and new specialists such as scientists and engineers, along with the more traditional elite merchants, bankers, professional classes such as lawyers and doctors, occupied the realms of the middle and upper-middle classes. One should also include the well-to-do farmers and ranchers here. On the lower rungs were the small business owners, shopkeepers, lower civil servants, clerks, secretaries, typists, and those who did white-collar work for the lowest salaries. By the end of the nineteenth century, with wages rising and the array of consumer goods rapidly multiplying, a growing number of working-class families also found themselves essentially living at a middle-class income level and developing the tastes for opportunity and advancement typical of their new status.

Indeed, the growing wealth and influence of the middle class as a whole had played a major role in creating what historians have termed "mass society" by the end of the century. The ability to mass produce consumer goods sparked parallel endeavors in other areas aimed at middle-class and, in some cases, working class consumers. The growing emphasis on literacy spurred the publishing industry in printing everything from novels and scientific works to a wide variety of self-help literature. Successful writers like Charles Dickens, Harriet Beecher Stowe, and Mark Twain could become wealthy from their efforts and achieve international celebrity. On a more mundane level, the period from mid-century on was the great age of the mass circulation newspapers and magazines, which aided and reinforced the need for literacy and education.

The Industrial Revolution's Impact on Demographics

The Industrial Revolution had a profound influence on the rise of populations in industrializing countries and often in determining where the greatest concentrations of population would be. This can be seen dramatically in the following statistics:

- In 1800, there were perhaps a half dozen cities with populations of 500,000 or more. Four of these, Constantinople, Edo (the future Tokyo), Beijing, and Guangzhou (Canton) were in Asia or the Middle East.
- In 1900, there were more than 80 cities between 250,000 and 500,000; only about 20 percent of these were in Asia. Moreover, the world's largest cities, with two million or more, were largely concentrated in Europe and the United States: London, New York, Paris, Vienna, Chicago, and Philadelphia.

What had happened during this century to so completely alter the demographic landscape? Why had the momentum of human population growth swung so completely away from the old agrarian empires and toward the upstart industrial states? As we have noted, one clue can be traced to the increased efficiencies created by the so-called eighteenth-century agrarian revolution. Clover as an animal fodder and soil regenerator; turnips as winter forage and food crops; the use of water meadows to keep grass green during winter for feeding livestock; the scientific selection of new seed and crop varieties from around the world—maize/corn, potatoes, tomatoes, peanuts, beans, peppers, and so on—all supplemented more traditional fare such as wheat and barley. Climatologists tell us that the Little Ice Age of 1300–1700 had also begun to abate, with the result that countries in the northern temperate zones gradually expanded their growing seasons.

More significant, however, was the rise and then the fall of the urban death rate. During the first decades of the eighteenth century, despite mounting immigration from the countryside, London's population actually declined. London became the first modern city with a large body of urban poor—peasants just in from the rural areas, mostly without marketable skills; increasingly crowded into makeshift housing in the most disease-prone areas of the expanding city. Hygiene was rudimentary in terms of finding clean water and disposing of human waste. Compounding the miseries of the poor was the wild proliferation of distilled spirits—especially gin. By some estimates, as many as one third of the buildings in London were gin shops or home distilleries. The satirical painting by William Hogarth called "Gin Lane"—in which a comically horrifying spectacle of disaster is depicted because of the drink—is indicative of how widespread the problem had become.

By the second half of the eighteenth century, however, the situation had been greatly improved. Government regulation of gin shops from the 1750s on and some genuine attempts at improved sanitation and charity works had lowered the deadly effects of London living. By this time too, markets carrying the new and improved crops made food cheaper and more plentiful, while Britain's growing domination of maritime trade created more employment opportunities. By 1800, London had surpassed the million mark; by the 1830s, it had become the world's largest city.

In addition to more and better food, steps toward modern sanitation, and attempts at reform, the impact of the new Industrial Revolution was just beginning to be felt. Despite the low wages, dangerous conditions, and depressing living circumstances in the new mill towns and industrial areas, they proved relatively attractive to the rural poor with few other prospects. Moreover, each new technology created increased demand in related fields and multiplied employment possibilities. Thus, Manchester, as we have seen earlier, grew at a fantastic pace during its rise as a center of the textile trade but so did all of those transportation, communication, mining, and financial areas of the economy needed to keep it going. As whole new industrial towns and cities sprang up, people flocked to them hoping to better themselves. By the second part of the nineteenth century, with industrial reform taking root and the formation of unions and labor-based political movements, working conditions improved in most of the established industries. The associated scientific establishment, struggling to improve urban hygiene and sanitation, made enormous strides in spurring the technical developments that ultimately yielded reliable urban water and wastewater systems, drained low areas, cleaned streets, and thus helped to drastically cut down on contagious diseases. All of these elements lowered the death rate and, with increased medical knowledge to help women during labor and childbirth, dramatically raised the survival rate of children during their early years.

A final indicator of the influence of the Industrial Revolution on population may be seen in East Asia. China's population had doubled to over 300 million between 1750 and 1850. But most of this had been due to the influence of the growing world traffic in new crops, which, as they had elsewhere, allowed increasingly marginal lands to be opened up.

Many historians believe that China had now reached the limits of the land to support the population of an agrarian society. Over time, abetted by the disaster of the Taiping Rebellion, China's rural areas became increasingly impoverished by their population pressures.

The real growth from this time, however, took place in the burgeoning port cities and, after the turn of the century, in cities that slowly grew into industrial centers. For example, Beijing, which had a population of about a million in 1800, had grown only slightly larger by 1900. Shanghai, on the other hand, as the country's leading port, and one with the most advanced industries, grew from a relative backwater to China's largest and most cosmopolitan city—the "Paris of the East."

The most rapid growth took place in the region's most industrialized country, Japan. Japan had maintained an extremely low rate of population growth during the Tokugawa Shogunate (1603-1867) because of the limitations of the land in supporting a large population. In 1850, Japan had perhaps 25-30 million people. With the opening of the country and its rapid industrialization, however, the population had doubled by the turn of the century and overcrowding formed a large part of the rationale for imperial expansion into more sparsely populated and resource-abundant regions such as Manchuria.

The Industrial Revolution's Impact on Serfs

By the first decades of the nineteenth century, it was widely recognized that serfdom was an archaic and inefficient institution. The great explosion of revolutionary fervor that accompanied Napoleon's conquests saw serfdom as a medieval system from which its victims needed emancipation. Thus, in all the French-held areas up to 1815, the abolition of serfdom was proclaimed. In addition, the inefficiencies of the system, which locked serfs into producing what their lords desired, discouraged innovation and, at best, kept the cultivators at a subsistence level. During the Middle Ages, such a system appeared to make sense because of the need for a stable, self-contained economic system. With the political goals of universal suffrage, representative government, and reward for merit all coming to the fore, however, and the need for more efficient agricultural production to satisfy the demands of industrial cities and towns, the old system had essentially disappeared by the 1850s in Western Europe and was preserved only in Imperial Russia.

It was the Russian Tsars who most enthusiastically embraced the idea of a Holy Alliance against political and social change during the period of reaction in post-Napoleonic Europe. Even within their domains, however, dissident intellectuals, or "Westernizers," were advocating the kinds of political liberalization and industrialism then moving forward in England and France. The 1830 and 1848 revolutions in Western and Central Europe also had their echoes in the Russian empire, particularly in Poland, further adding to the agitation for change. By the mid-1850s, Russia's disastrous showing in the Crimean War against the growing industrial powers of Great Britain and France added fuel to the desire for social reform and modernization. With the advent of the Tsar Alexander II (reigned 1855-1881), the decision was made to emancipate the serfs, compensate their lords, and distribute holdings with low-interest loans to former serfs in 1861. Such a move, it was argued, would help modernize Russian agriculture by supporting small-scale land ownership and profit incentives for individual families.

The Industrial Revolution's Impact on Slavery

Like serfdom, slavery was an institution that was widely seen as being incompatible with societies groping toward equality, representative government, and the recognition of merit. That the institution itself was inherently evil, and that its only real advantages derived from the economics of semi-tropical and tropical plantation crops, were also widely recognized by the end of the eighteenth century. Still, the regional economies that had been built upon the institution such as the tobacco, indigo, and rice areas of the American south, and the sugar-producing islands of the Caribbean, were unwilling to risk emancipation. In addition to fear for the economic vitality of their regions and the fear of the revenge of the formerly enslaved, they had developed elaborate justifications for keeping Africans in bondage over the centuries, which had, by the early nineteenth century, developed into a full-blown ideology of racism and black inferiority.

Nonetheless, with the rapid spread of American and French revolutionary ideas, it was widely considered that the institution was outmoded and would soon die out. Indeed, the independence of Haiti (despite Napoleon's attempts to re-conquer it) seemed to signal the beginning of the end. Ironically, however, it would be the voracious demands of the Industrial Revolution that would prolong the institution's life for another six to eight decades.

169

As the early British textile factories boomed in the 1790s, they required more and more raw cotton. The price and quality of Indian and Egyptian varieties proved inferior to the longer stranded American bolls. The problem, however, was "ginning" the seeds out of it efficiently. The development of the cotton gin to perform this task—usually credited to the inventor and future industrialist Eli Whitney—quickly raised the demand for American cotton. Since cotton could only be efficiently grown in the south on large plantations, it created an upsurge in the demand for slave labor and a new lease on life for "the peculiar institution." Moreover, since cotton wore the land out quickly, investors, fortune seekers, and settlers constantly moved west in search of cotton lands; by 1848 cotton had become "king" from the Carolinas to Texas and was by far the largest American export item. Along the way, the economics of cotton had pushed slavery from being seen as "a necessary evil" to "a positive good" by its most ardent supporters.

Ultimately, of course, the southern states seceded and the long and bloody American Civil war was fought and won by the Union. Against the backdrop of saving the Union, abolitionist pressure and the desire by free blacks to fight for the Union cause, Abraham Lincoln (1809-1865) issued the Emancipation Proclamation, freeing all slaves in the states currently rebelling, which went into effect on January 1, 1863. After the war's end, the Thirteenth, Fourteenth, and Fifteenth Amendments freed all slaves, made them citizens, and enfranchised them.

The Industrial Revolution's Impact on Women

Despite some promising intellectual notions during the late eighteenth century, the Industrial Revolution in many ways worsened the condition of women and children until at least the mid-nineteenth century. In the drive to squeeze the last ounce of profit from the new factories, mill owners quickly found that they could hire unskilled workers to run the machines on the cheap, and could hire women even more cheaply. The work was long, monotonous, often dangerous, and carried out with virtually no safety regulations. Fourteen- to sixteen-hour days were the norm, with a break for lunch, six days a week. The mills were choked with flammable cotton dust and their chimneys spewed high-sulfur coal smoke into the air of the mill towns. Women and children, in addition, were used in other dangerous and degrading kinds of work, most notoriously mining, where they could squeeze into small coal seams to dig. Sometimes, they were actually hitched to carts like animals to pull coal within low, narrow shafts.

By the 1830s and 40s a series of British parliamentary investigations resulted in a series of Factory Acts that began the long process of improving basic safety conditions, restricting hours, and curtailing women and child labor. Yet the impact of these acts also reduced the earning power of many working class women and, along with the growing influence of middle-class notions of the home as the proper sphere for women, helped to foster the idea of women as dependent. Thus historians have not reached a consensus on how these reforms should be interpreted: Should they be seen as "progressive" and placed alongside other kinds of factory legislation like minimum wage laws and the right of collective bargaining, or should they be seen as leading toward restricting women's agency? Regardless of the intent of these reforms, it should be noted that women still accounted for 30-40 percent of factory workers by the last quarter of the century.

Women with the means and the education to do so also frequently formed groups and societies to agitate for various social reforms. In the United States, for example, women were prominent in the abolition movement, and many of the same leaders shifted increasingly to campaigns for women's rights after the Civil War. In both England and America, strong movements for women's voting and office-holding rights gained momentum through the turn of the century and eventually resulted in their suffrage after World War I, and in France and Japan after World War II.

The Industrial Revolution's Impact on Children

Like women, the roles of children changed radically during the course of the Industrial Revolution. Families tended to work together during the eighteenth century on small farms, in various trades, or in shops. Children seldom attended school, but generally started with small tasks to learn the ropes of their parent's trade or were apprenticed outside the home. With the coming of the factory, however, these older practices were gradually pushed aside as children increasingly were put to work in the mills. As was the case with women, children worked long hours for short pay, often under appalling conditions in the mines and factories. In addition, they suffered from lack of supervision and were frequently subject to physical and even sexual abuse from the older workers and supervisors.

The furor over such conditions exposed by government investigations led, as with women, to increasing restrictions on child labor hours, improvement of the worst conditions, and as part of more general efforts at reform, a movement toward compulsory education. By the turn of the century, all the industrialized countries (including Japan) had instituted systems of free, state-financed compulsory primary education. Some also opened up the possibility for higher education for graduates and, increasingly, for women. In fact, the proliferation of state and normal schools by century's end placed woman in dominant positions as teachers in primary schools in many places—two-thirds in the United States—thus creating the stereotype of the strict but loving "schoolmarm" of the American west.

The reasons for the growth of public education involve the growing influence of middle-class values, but also the needs of increasingly sophisticated new industries and the process of state centralization. As we have seen, the new middle classes propagated an unshakable belief in the power of education to better one's condition. Thus, knowledge in and of itself was a powerful tool for social improvement, as was the need for the proper credentials in an increasingly scientific and technically oriented world. The new industries needed more engineers and technicians, the new research institutions needed more scientists, and the expanding university systems needed professors in all fields. Moreover, the burgeoning empires of the powers needed trained administrators, lawyers, and civil servants, as well as a host of technical specialists. Thus, the needs of industry and the state coincided conveniently.

Practice Test Questions

1. The Luddites were famous for

   A. championing the use of steam power.
   B. destroying factory machinery.
   C. manufacturing the spinning jenny.
   D. leading the Chartist movement.
   E. attacking the workers during the Peterloo Massacre.

2. The beliefs popularized by the new industrial middle classes included

   A. a return to serfdom for peasants.
   B. thrift, sobriety, and education.
   C. making slavery permanent.
   D. women taking jobs outside the home.
   E. free university education for women.

3. One reason the Industrial Revolution encouraged population increases was that

   A. the death rate decreased because of new factory safety regulations.
   B. it was accompanied by improved urban sanitation and waste removal.
   C. mothers had twice as many children as in the Middle Ages.
   D. overcrowded rural countries deported their excess population to industrialized areas.
   E. the non-working poor in Great Britain were subject to abortion and euthanasia.

4. Although it ultimately helped cause its demise, slavery was actually helped for a time by the Industrial Revolution because

   A. American cotton was needed for English factories.
   B. Egypt edged the United States out of the cotton market during the American Civil War.
   C. New areas for cotton plantations were opened up in the African interior.
   D. Chinese exclusion laws banned contract laborers from the United States.
   E. Indian laborers migrated in large numbers to Trinidad.

5. Marx and Engels' *Communist Manifesto* stated that

   A. class conflict and economics move history forward.
   B. peasants are the backbone of the revolution.
   C. history will end with bourgeois control of the means of production.
   D. each country's clash of roles will be different.
   E. revolution will take place first in the most primitive societies.

Answers and Explanations

1. **B.** Answers **A, C,** and **E** suggest actions in favor of the new machines or industries; **D** involves peaceful protest several decades later.

2. **B.** Choices **A** and **C** are fundamentally against middle-class values, though some middle-class members in England and the American south might have hoped for a continuing supply of slave-produced cotton. **D** goes against the middle class "cult of domesticity" for women, as does **E.**

3. **B.** Choice **A** is wrong because such improvements would not be widespread enough to account for vast population increases; **C** and **D** are factually incorrect; **E** is a vague play on Swift's *A Modest Proposal* in which he suggests tongue-in-cheek that the Irish poor be eaten by the well-to-do as a way to solve the population problem.

4. **A.** The voracious appetite of English (and New England) textile mills were largely responsible for making cotton "king" in the American south and expanding the slave system westward. **B, D,** and **E** are factually correct but irrelevant; **C** is simply incorrect.

5. **A.** As for **B,** Marx saw peasants as conservative; in **C,** Marx and Engels felt history would end with the proletariat overthrowing the bourgeoisie; **D** and **E** are directly opposite to the ideas of the *Manifesto*.

Revolutions, Reform, and Democracy

Comparative Views of Revolutions

Before the latter part of the eighteenth century, the term **revolution** suggested a cycle of familiar political change in which a decadent ruler might be ousted in a palace revolt and replaced with a more able one. From the period of the American Revolution on, however, and especially after the French Revolution, the term came to mean not just the replacement of one ruler or government with another, but a radical change in the structure of government as well. Indeed, with the French Revolution, the goals of the most radical leaders went even further and attempted to change society itself at the most basic level.

The United States

The Seven Years War (1756–1763), in many ways the first true "world war," ended with Great Britain among the winners and France among the defeated. Fighting had taken place in Europe, on the high seas, in India, and especially in North America, where it was known as the French and Indian War. The British had pushed the French out of India, thus beginning the growth of British control there; they had also taken over most of the French territory in North America. The cost of the war had been heavy, and the vastly expanded territories of the British Empire now demanded more efficient organization and tighter political and economic control. Both of these factors played a major role in causing the American Revolution.

The 13 British colonies, though formally under the control of the Parliament and royal officials, had been used to a much higher degree of self-government than their countrymen across the Atlantic. The vastness of the colonial territory, the great distances separating it from the homeland, and English concentration on European matters had left the colonies largely to themselves. Accordingly, they had developed their own local institutions. In many cases, as with the Puritans in New England and the Quakers in Pennsylvania, many colonists were also religious dissenters who had fled persecution by the state and the established church. For all of these reasons, any attempts at increased control from the home country were likely to be unpopular.

In 1765, the British government attempted to impose a tax on official stamps used in various transactions as a means to make the colonist pay a share of the war debt. This Stamp Act provoked riots and protests and so was repealed the following year. It was soon followed, however, by a steady stream of other taxes and escalating restrictions through the 1760s aimed at keeping the trade of the colonies firmly in British hands, and even providing for the stationing of British soldiers in private homes. Tensions continued to mount, exploding in the Boston Massacre of 1770, when panicked soldiers fired into an angry mob. The cycle of provocation, protest, and repression continued for several more years, culminating in the most famous incident of the period: Incensed at the double-taxing of tea, colonists, loosely disguised as Indians, broke into the holds of anchored merchant ships and threw their chests of tea into Boston harbor in 1773—an event remembered ever after as the Boston Tea Party. The British responded by closing the harbor and through the so-called "Intolerable Acts" sought to intimidate the colonists from engaging in similar acts of resistance. In response, colonial representatives met in the first Continental Congress in 1774 to form a plan of action.

In 1775, matters escalated into open warfare. Colonial militias fired on British troops attempting to seize caches of arms at Lexington and Concord, Massachusetts; after being repulsed with considerable losses at Bunker Hill, the British went on to occupy Boston. Last-minute attempts to reach a compromise with the crown failed, and by the spring of 1776, a growing number of members of the Continental Congress had come to the conclusion that the colonies must become independent. In July, a Declaration of Independence was issued in Philadelphia, and a continental army under the command of George Washington was formed to contest the British—who were now systematically attempting to seize the major ports of the colonies and suppress the rebellion before it could gain momentum.

The position of the new United States was difficult at best. It faced a power with the world's best navy, immense wealth, and a large, well-trained army. Moreover, at this point, only a minority of the colonists actually favored independence; a sizeable number remained Loyalists, and many more decided to see how the war would go before committing themselves. The sponsors of the Declaration had written it in part to attract diplomatic recognition of the new government and, it was hoped, military and financial support. In this, they pinned their hopes on France, which they realized would be alert for any opportunity to recoup its losses against Britain. But the French would not help without some sign that the new state could survive. Here, Washington's morale-building victories at Trenton and Princeton, New Jersey during the winter of 1776 kept colonial hopes alive during the British occupation of Philadelphia. During this time as well, foreign advisors such as Lafayette, Von Steuben, and Kosciusko, attracted by the cause of the colonists, helped to train American forces in European-style drill, tactics, and especially bayonet fighting. With the decisive American victory at Saratoga, New York, in 1777, frequently cited as a pivotal event in the war, the French were moved to a aid the colonists in force. For their part, the British now chose to concentrate their efforts more in the south, where they calculated that Loyalist sentiment ran deeper. This move, however, provoked some of the bloodiest fighting of the war. Charlotte, North Carolina, became famous as the "Hornet's Nest" as British forces, Loyalist militias, and patriot forces fought a savage guerilla war in which no quarter was asked and none given. By 1780, with Washington's continental army now larger and better trained, the war had moved into a stalemate and the British, faced with growing anti-war sentiment at home, were growing increasingly weary of it. Finally, in 1781, a combination of American and French troops under Washington sealed up the main British force on the Yorktown Peninsula of Virginia, while the French navy held off the British relief force. The British surrendered to the Americans and, after two more years of negotiations, agreed to American independence at the Treaty of Paris in 1783.

But the American War for Independence marked only the first step in what was to be revolutionary about what one historian has called "the first new nation." In arguing that it was "self-evident that all men are created equal, and that they are endowed by their Creator with certain inalienable rights," Thomas Jefferson, Benjamin Franklin, and the other contributors to the Declaration of Independence drew from a wide array of Enlightenment ideas, especially those of the English thinker John Locke. Governments were not meant to be ruled by kings appointed by "divine right" but instead "derive their just powers from the consent of the governed." Not only that; if any government becomes oppressive, it is the "right and the duty" of the people to "alter or abolish it." Thus, in theory at least, the nationhood of the United States was not created so much by ties of ethnicity or religion or even shared history—as with the theories of nationalism developed in nineteenth-century Europe; it was instead created by this idea of government by, for, and through the people.

But what should such a government look like? During the war, the Continental Congress had essentially functioned as the government and had drawn up "Articles of Confederation" as its initial attempt to create a structure for it. But because the Articles were largely a response to perceived abuses of the British, and because the newly independent states jealously guarded their hard-won rights, the central government was scarcely able to function. In effect, the 13 states were like small countries: each minted its own money, collected its own tariffs and taxes, maintained its own militia, and barely acknowledged that there *was* a central government.

By 1787, all of these problems prompted the convening of a convention in Philadelphia, the new nation's largest city, to revise the Articles into a more workable basic law for the country. Under the leadership of James Madison, the Articles were quickly scrapped, and work began on a constitution which would completely redefine the structure of the government. In the end, the new constitution's aim was "to form a more perfect union," which it did by strictly outlining the function, rights, and duties of the new central government, and setting them over and above those reserved for the states. Concern about certain basic rights left undefined in the new Constitution led to a series of ten amendments called the Bill of Rights attached to it in the spring of 1789.

While the Constitution gave the new republic a sound framework in which to govern and expand, it was not without its problems. The most serious of these grew out of compromises made between delegates from the slave-holding states and the non-slave states. While only men could vote, a state's entire population was counted during each census (every ten years from 1790) to determine the number of representatives to which it was entitled. The more populous northern states argued that because slaves were not allowed to vote, they should not be counted as part of the population for purposes of determining representation in Congress. The slave-holding states argued just the opposite—that slaves should be counted. The compromise reached was that three-fifths of the slave population would be counted and proved to be divisive right up to the Civil War (1861–1865). Similarly, the delegates agreed not to enact any legislation respecting the slave trade until 1808 (twenty years after the provision was adopted), under the assumption that slavery might well die out by that time of its own accord.

The French Revolution

The conditions in France that led to its much longer and fiercer revolution—and later revolutions in 1830 and 1848—were quite different than those in colonial North America. Unlike the British colonies, which collectively enjoyed one of the highest standards of living in the eighteenth-century world, France was a country of vast differences in wealth. While the French court at Versailles had arguably the greatest concentration of riches in the world, a sizeable portion of the French peasantry was poor enough to be on the edge of famine when harvests were inadequate.

Such disparities were evident in other areas as well. The middle classes in the British colonies had already gained a degree of local political power and influence, as epitomized by the self-made inventor and printer, Benjamin Franklin, or lawyers like John Adams. The French middle classes, or *bourgeoisie*, had become powerful economically but were mostly shut out of political power by the nobles and the royal bureaucracy. Indeed, the French monarchy had clung to the concept of *absolute* monarchy from the reign of Louis XIV (1643–1715), through those of his descendants Louis XV (1715–1774) and Louis XVI (1774–1792). As we have seen, under this system, the monarch dictated virtually everything from law, to religion, to taxes, to even fashion and design. The overall goal was to have a strong, unified, rich country, without the infighting among the nobility and their supporters that had marked France in the sixteenth and early seventeenth centuries.

Ironically, it was amidst such repressive circumstances that many of the most famous of the *philosophes* flourished—though often only with the intercession of powerful friends at court. Such champions of free thought as Voltaire, Montesquieu, Diderot, Rousseau, and the Physiocrats in economics, had made France the center of the Enlightenment. But while their ideas had vast repercussions elsewhere, they made little headway in changing the politics and society of France. While their ideas caused a sensation in the *salons* of the privileged, no provision was made in France to introduce them into the government or social institutions and perfect them by trial and error.

For the *philosophes* of Europe, the events in America therefore assumed immense importance. Here for the first time leaders were actually attempting to create a country and government from scratch using the most modern ideas of the age. Some young French idealists like the Marquis de Lafayette (1757–1834) came to fight for "liberty." Others were fascinated by American representatives like Franklin, whose plain dress and obvious genius contrasted so markedly with the decadent French nobility. In the forces the French sent to America, many young men would carry back the ideals they learned fighting alongside the American colonists.

Though France emerged from the Treaty of Paris in 1783 on the winning side, the debt that had built up throughout the preceding century continued to snowball. Taxes, heavy and varied already, could only be raised so much. In addition, the privileged position of the nobility, who did not pay taxes, meant that all of the revenues had to come from the peasants and middle classes. As the debt crisis grew worse, various remedies were tried, but the government was neither able to raise the funds nor borrow its way out of its predicament. In desperation, the king called delegates to Paris for a meeting of the Estates General in the spring of 1789—a move to which French kings had not resorted since 1614, further underscoring the severity of the situation.

The Estates General was made up of representatives from the three "estates" or classes of the people that had been recognized since the Middle Ages: The First Estate consisted of the clergy, whose role it was to pray for the country; the Second Estate was made up of the nobility, whose job had originally been to fight for the country; and the Third Estate comprised everyone else—peasants, artisans, lawyers, merchants, bankers, etc. But as in 1614, the representatives were to deliberate and vote on issues by Estate, thus ensuring that the first two estates could always outvote the third, which represented about 98 percent of the population. As excitement grew and the unfairness of the estate system increasingly raised resentment, the Abbe de Sieyes, a member of the First Estate, wrote a pamphlet titled, "Who is the Third Estate?" His answer was, "the people." In June, 1789, therefore, the Third Estate delegates, accompanied by sympathetic members of the other two estates, met in a local tennis court and constituted themselves as a National Assembly, swearing that they would not disband until they had written a constitution for France.

Events now turned violent. While the king mulled over developments at Versailles, street orators of every political persuasion harangued mobs of Parisians. On July 14, they attacked the Bastille prison, hated as a symbol of royal political repression, freed its few remaining prisoners, and killed and mutilated the defenders. Similar uprisings began to break out around the country, and by the end of July, the rural areas were gripped by what became known as the Great Fear.

Amid the quickening pace of events, the National Assembly on August 26 produced the central document of the French Revolution, and a model for many later political movements: "The Declaration of the Rights of Man and the Citizen."

Like the Declaration of Independence, the "Rights of Man" was meant as a statement of the aims of its framers, but also as a summary of the new rights of "the French people." As such, it was also seen as a kind of universal declaration of human rights. Among other things it stated that, "men are born and remain free and equal in rights . . ."; these include "liberty, property, security, and resistance to oppression." It went on to assert that "the law is an expression of the general will . . ." as opposed to the will of the king; that all persons are guaranteed due legal process, security against arbitrary search and seizure of property, that taxation could not be imposed except by the general will for the good of the nation; and that in order to guarantee these rights, a national constitution was necessary. With the tide of public opinion running strongly against him and the army now of uncertain loyalty, the king agreed to these items and was forced to return with his family to Paris by a large force of armed women.

Between 1790 and 1793, the new regime disbanded the French Catholic Church, created and abolished a constitutional monarchy, formed an enormous national army, created a new calendar from scratch, a new system of weights and measures (the metric system), inaugurated a new civil religion, and, ultimately, executed Louis XVI and his wife, Marie Antoinette (1775–1793). During the most radical phase of the revolution, the years 1793 and 1794, the ruling National Convention was largely in the hands of its Committee of Public Safety under Maximilien Robespierre (1758–1794). While the French army, now at war with much of Europe, successfully defended the revolution, Robespierre imposed the Reign of Terror on the country. Tens of thousands of suspected counter-revolutionaries were denounced to the authorities and most received long prison sentences or execution. The emblematic means of execution was the *guillotine*— originally devised as a more reliable, and thus humane, way of beheading the condemned by means of a weighted blade sliding down a track—instead of by an axe wielded by a headsman. In Paris, the almost daily executions became a popular public spectacle.

By July, or Thermidor, as it was called in the new French calendar, a coalition of Convention deputies managed to depose Robespierre and send him to the guillotine. From this point on, often referred to by historians as the "Thermidorian Reaction," the revolution turned more conservative. A group of deputies called the Directory took over the running of the country, but could do little because of infighting among various factions ranging from the remaining *Jacobins* to those who wanted to bring back the monarchy. In addition, the finances of the government were in trouble and the war dragged on with no sign of victory on either side. After drifting for five years in this manner, a young officer named Napoleon Bonaparte (1769–1821) seized control of the government and forced the Convention to give him complete executive power as First Consul in 1799.

Napoleon quickly moved to consolidate his power. He had already shown his prowess on the battlefield and now moved quickly through a combination of force and compromise to bring order to the internal matters of France. In 1801, he allowed the Catholic Church to re-establish itself in France in return for dropping its opposition to the republic. He created a new civil code that revoked the most radical measures of the 1790s but ensured that merit in both military and civilian life would be rewarded. He created a new conscript army that went on to conquer most of Europe; at the same time, he was often arbitrary in the rights he chose to curtail, such as freedom of the press.

Mexico

In the three centuries of Spanish rule up to the beginning of the nineteenth century, the social and economic structure of Mexico, like the rest of Spanish America, changed very little. The economy was dependent on providing raw materials and precious metals to Spain in return for finished goods, while the landed classes held enormous estates worked by the descendants of the Aztecs and Mayas. African slavery had also been introduced, and through intermarriage, the population included classes of *mestizo* (Spanish and Indian) and *mulatto* (Spanish and African) people. The tiny elites consisted of *creoles* (Spanish, born in Mexico) and *peninsulars* (from the Iberian Peninsula; Spanish born in Spain). The Catholic Church, while at times championing the cause of the Indians and the poor, was also a major landholder and tended to identify more with the powerful.

As it had in so many other areas, the French Revolution had a profound effect on Spain's possessions in the Americas. In addition to the transmission of the revolutionary values to the Spanish colonies, the removal of the Spanish monarchy by Napoleon provided an opportunity to declare independence. Resentment at Spanish mistreatment of native peoples had always been present; for the upper classes, however, there was also extreme dissatisfaction with the monarchy's and

Bonaparte's efforts to tighten control of trade. On September 16, 1810, celebrated ever after as Mexico's Independence Day, a priest named Miguel Hidalgo y Costilla inspired a small group of poorly armed Indians and laborers to attempt a revolution. This was quickly put down and resulted in Hidalgo's execution.

The role of class leadership soon asserted itself in Mexico, as it had in the American colonies and in France. Frightened of a genuine mass revolution, the creole and peninsular leaders mounted their own revolution and created an independent Mexico under Augustin de Iturbide in 1821. Potentially wealthy and with a sparse population, the new government encouraged immigration to its northern areas, especially Texas. Land-hungry Americans emigrated by the thousands, and, with the local population, soon contemplated secession. In addition to latent loyalty to the United States, many of the settlers brought slaves, and slavery had been abolished by the Mexican government. By 1836, the general Antonio Lopez de Santa Anna led Mexican troops to quell the rebels, but after a brief war and the capture of Santa Anna, Texas was able to break away.

As the strong man of Mexico until 1855, Santa Anna also presided over the Mexican War with the United States from 1846-48. Here the nation lost nearly a third of its remaining territory, including California and the future states of Arizona and New Mexico. As if to add insult to injury, gold was discovered in California the following year. By the 1860s American preoccupation with its Civil War allowed the French to install the Austrian Prince Maximilian as Emperor of Mexico from 1864–67. He was soon deposed and executed by revolutionaries. In the 1870s, Mexico finally entered a period of relative peace. Under the dictator Porfirio Diaz (r. 1876–1910), the poorest witnessed scant improvement and political liberalism made little progress. However, a small middle class gained a foothold and foreign investment by the British and Americans saw the building of modest industries, rails, telegraphs, and other kinds of infrastructure.

In 1910, the more liberal Francisco Madero ousted Diaz and in the chaotic political climate that followed, the first modern attempts at mass revolution followed. During the period from 1910 to 1920, a bitter three-way struggle wore on among Madero, Emiliano Zapata, who organized the native peoples of southern Mexico, and Venustiano Carranza. In 1917 a new, more liberal constitution was adopted and a process of land reform begun. With the ousting and execution of Carranza in 1920, a process of breaking the political power of the landed elites was continued and political power was vested firmly in the hands of the largely middle-class Institutional Revolutionary Party, where it would remain for most of the twentieth century after being brought to fruition by Lazaro Cardenas during his presidency from 1934–1940.

China

Like the two other great Eurasian empires, Russia and Ottoman Turkey, Qing China was in a state of relative decline by the beginning of the nineteenth century. Arguably at the height of its power during the reign of the Qianlong emperor (1736–1795), smoldering rebellion and increased foreign efforts to pull the empire into the new world systems of European trade put China into an increasingly weakened position. The rapidly increasing illicit opium trade, controlled largely by British merchants, disrupted the older system of licensed Chinese traders and their counterparts from the East India companies of the British, French, and Dutch. Moreover, the increase in legitimate trade in tea, porcelain, lacquer ware, and other luxury goods put increasing pressure on the Qing to open more ports to trade beyond Guangzhou (Canton). Increased trade also brought pressure to bear on Chinese authorities to allow foreign missionary activity and to find new methods of establishing common legal ground for settling disputes. Hovering over all of these problems was that of diplomatic recognition: The European and American governments insisted that China institute embassies and consulates along Western lines, while the Qing preferred to deal with foreigners within the traditional tributary system.

Matters came to a head in 1839. The opium trade had grown to such a size that it was the largest revenue producer in British India, where it was grown for export. In southern China, opium use had increased to epidemic proportions and a special imperial commissioner, Lin Zexu, had been sent to root out and destroy it. Lin forced the opium merchants to give up thousands of chests of the drug, which he destroyed, and the British merchants appealed to their government for reimbursement. The British government decided to take advantage of the incident to settle their other outstanding disputes with the Qing. When they sent their fleet to force the issue, the First Opium War began and lasted until 1842. With the advantages of the world's biggest navy and the new technologies of the young Industrial Revolution, the British were able to compel the Qing to sue for peace in 1842. The resulting Treaty of Nanjing (Nanking), in demanding the island of Hong Kong, compensation for the cost of the war, and the opening of additional ports and consulates, set the pattern for the remainder of a century of "unequal treaties."

Numerous diplomatic crises and three additional wars with Great Britain and France (1856–1860), France (1884–1885), and Japan (1894–1895) increasingly weakened the empire, despite a series of attempts at adopting Western technology and institutions. Such attempts were not sustained, however, and were constantly subject to factionalism among Confucian officials and members of the court. Far more costly, however, was the potential for rebellion, which was never far from the surface. The humiliation of defeat in the First Opium War raised the level of anti-Qing sentiment in South China, while severe economic problems from the rerouting of trade to the newly opened ports helped spawn the epic Taiping Rebellion (1851–1864). Led by a failed Confucian exam candidate who, during a nervous breakdown, believed he had been appointed to be the younger brother of Jesus Christ, the Taipings launched a war not only against the Qing but against Confucian society itself. The Taipings called for equality for all—including women—the banning of footbinding, gambling, opium smoking, and private property, in addition to the adoption of this Chinese version of Christianity. The rebellion, which some historians insist was, in fact, a revolution, was the bloodiest human conflict until World War II, with an estimated 20 to 30 million people killed, and vast areas of China devastated for decades. While the Qing ultimately quelled the revolt, it left the government weak and desperate to hold on to its dynastic power by any means available.

The Chinese defeat by Japan in the Sino-Japanese War of 1894–95 effectively ended realistic hopes of reform from within. More immediately, it opened up a period of intensified foreign encroachment by Japan, Russia, Germany, France, and Britain almost to the point of the empire's collapse. At least in part because of foreign imperialism, 1900 saw the outbreak of the anti-foreign Boxer Rebellion. At first attempting to crush the revolt, the Qing court switched sides and joined the Boxers by declaring war on all the foreign powers in China. By August 1900, a multinational force took Beijing and the major cities in northern China, drove the government from the capital, and bloodily suppressed the rebels. The indemnities forced on the Qing forced the regime into bankruptcy and partial occupation by the treaty powers.

Despite final belated attempts at reform aimed at making China a constitutional monarchy from 1903 through 1911, a growing number of Chinese began to see revolution as the only hope of creating a strong China. The most important of these was Sun Yat-sen (1866–1925), widely traveled and trained as a medical doctor. Sun borrowed extensively from British, French, German, American, and even Japanese ideas of representative government. Convinced that the first necessity was the removal of the Manchus, the people who had conquered China and imposed the Qing Dynasty in 1644, he attempted a series of unsuccessful revolts from 1896 until 1911. Along the way, he forged ties with Chinese secret societies and dissident groups, attempted to create a revolutionary army, and, perhaps most importantly, create an ideology for his movement.

Sun's ideas were distilled into the easily understood and remembered "Three People's Principles": *Sovereignty*, in which the Manchus were to be expelled and Chinese territory taken back from the foreign powers; *Democracy*, in which the people would rule themselves. But China had no experience with self-government, said Sun, so his party would have to rule during a period during which one or two generations of Chinese learn the practices and institutions of democracy. The third principle was *The People's Livelihood*, sometimes translated as "socialism": Sun believed that land reform and redistribution was crucial to alleviating the poverty of China's tens of millions of peasants, and so borrowed ideas as diverse as Confucian economic tradition and the theories of the American economist Henry George.

On October 10, 1911, a revolt broke out in an army barracks, and within a few months the revolution was finally ignited and gaining strength. By February, 1912, the boy Qing emperor abdicated and the new Republic of China was recognized by the United States and the European powers. But China's revolution was destined to continue through foreign invasion and civil war until 1949. Sun was driven into exile within a year of the "Double-Ten" revolution, the former Qing minister Yuan Shikai became president, and in the chaos that followed Yuan's death in 1916, China descended into a decade of rule by feuding warlords. Sun, meanwhile would revamp his party, now called the Nationalist Party, with help from the new Bolshevik state in Russia, and was on the verge of making a second bid for power when he died of cancer in 1925.

While the five revolutions outlined above are widely separated in time, space, and culture, they all share certain common features. In a way, this is not surprising because the two earliest revolutions, especially that of the French, were widely seen as models to be emulated. Thus, all of them had at their core certain Enlightenment ideas, such as the right to revolt against unjust government, the idea that sovereignty should reside with the people rather than with a divinely anointed king or emperor, the idea of the nation-state, and the idea that government and social institutions could be created anew by reason and thus radically improve the lives of all citizens.

But as we have also seen, the results of these ideas varied widely according to culture and historical circumstances. The American Revolutionaries, for example, were motivated at first by a desire to *regain* certain rights that they felt were being taken away from them. As time went on and both sides found it impossible to back down, the more radical idea of national independence began to take hold. While historians disagree on the precise measure of radicalism in the American Revolution, all agree that the social institutions of the new republic were altered far less than was the case in Haiti, France, or Mexico.

While the American Revolution formed the model for national independence, the French Revolution inspired an entire spectrum of radical political and social reform. The idea that ancient traditions could be overturned and entirely new, rational institutions created has been a powerful one down to the present. Indeed, from Karl Marx through Vladimir Lenin, Mao Zedong, and nearly all of the twentieth-century revolutionaries, the French Revolution remained not just an inspiration in the ideals that it represented, but as the universal model for *how* revolutions start and progress. But its failures also suggested the need for repeated revolution, which France underwent through much of the nineteenth century, and Mexico through the first decades of the twentieth. Historians of China have argued that, similarly, the Chinese Revolution did not end with the abdication of the Qing, but with the victory of the Communists in 1949; indeed, many argue that the Chinese social revolution, so turbulent during the Maoist years up to 1976, is still going on in the twenty-first century. Even the United States, it is sometimes said, did not actually complete its revolution until the end of the Civil War.

What about social revolution, then? Over time, all of our examples resulted in emancipation for a large percentage of the population. In France, the re-imposition of the monarchy after 1815 held the gains of the 1790s back, in some cases, until the formation of the Third Republic in 1870. In Haiti, the abolition of slavery emancipated almost the entire population, but the political unrest and economic stagnation did tragically little to raise the quality of life for the people. Similarly, in the American south, while the slaves were finally freed, the premature ending of Reconstruction in 1877, and the imposition of legal segregation tended to negate their freedom. The early stages of the Chinese Revolution that we examined did little to change the existing traditions and leftover Confucian institutions in the new Chinese Republic. Real change would not be evident until the 1920s; the old social order would not die until the 1950s. Genuine social changes would, however, be seen in Mexico during the 1920s and 1930s, where the middle classes would finally oust the landed elites and at least some measure of political participation given to the masses. It should be noted that the largest social group in each of these places—women—would not achieve political power until the twentieth century.

Latin American Independence Movements

As with their contemporaries in Mexico, the disruptions of the Napoleonic era and its aftermath provided an opportunity to fight for independence in the Spanish and Portuguese territories of South and Central America. In the case of Brazil, the largest of these colonies, the Portuguese court fled to Rio de Janeiro during the French invasion of the Iberian Peninsula. When the court was restored in 1815, Prince Pedro insisted on staying and set up a joint kingdom with Portugal in Brazil. Shortly thereafter, in 1822, with the cry, "Independence or Death!" he declared an independent Brazilian kingdom. Though initially inclined to end slavery, Dom Pedro was force to retain it at the insistence of the sugar planters, with the result that under his son, Dom Pedro II, Brazil was the last country in the Americas to abolish slavery, in 1888.

The same Iberian invasion gave rise to the desire for independence in the Spanish territories. As we saw in the case of Mexico, the continuation of *mercantilism* by the Spanish and Napoleonic governments, and efforts by the British to break into the Latin American trading sphere caused tension among the elites. Some of the upper classes had also been influenced by radical and liberal ideas of the Enlightenment and French Revolution and were anxious about the possibility of being overtaken by mass revolts. Thus a liberal movement soon began in Argentina in 1810 but had lapsed into dictatorship by mid-century. Other governments were set up at the same time in Chile, Columbia, and Venezuela. Spanish attempts to regain power were ultimately crushed between 1818 and 1824 under the leadership of Jose de San Martin (1778–1850) of Argentina and Simon Bolivar of Venezuela (1783–1830). Thus the independence of all of the Spanish territories in South America was effected by 1824.

In their effort to restore the old balance of power in Europe, the European monarchs contemplated assisting the Spanish in an effort to retake the colonies. The United States, however, felt its political freedom and new trade relations with the independent South America threatened by such action. The British, too, had benefited from the breaking of the old,

179

closed Spanish trade system. In 1823, the American president James Monroe issued the famous Monroe Doctrine, in which the United States pledged resistance to any outside power attempting to impose its will on the Americas. The British sided with the Americans, and the potential of the combined American and British navies proved sufficient to discourage any further attempts at re-colonization.

Reform Movements

In addition to being an age of revolutions, the nineteenth century was also a great age of reform. Given the spread of Enlightenment and revolutionary values, this is not surprising. On the one hand, the incompleteness of the political rights and emancipation of women, slaves, and certain ethnic groups as a result of revolution left great numbers of people with aroused expectations of what was possible. On the other hand, places that experienced no political revolution but feared creating the conditions for one ultimately saw reform as a necessity.

For example, state reforms expanding voting rights took place throughout the first part of the nineteenth century in the United States, creating virtual white adult male suffrage by the Civil War. Great Britain was somewhat slower, but nevertheless passed sweeping Reform Acts in 1832 and 1867, expanding the opportunity to serve in Parliament to the middle classes and essentially abolishing property qualifications to vote. A similar broadening of the franchise was accomplished through the Revolutions of 1830 and 1848 in France; the franchise also came with formation of the German and Italian states.

At the same time, as we have also seen in previous chapters, the early nineteenth century saw the rise of abolition movements in both Great Britain and the United States, which finally outlawed slavery in 1833 and 1863–1865, respectively. Similarly, from Mary Wollstonecraft's call for the rights of women in 1792 through the actions of suffragettes in England and, following the Seneca Falls movement in 1848, the United States, agitation for women's voting rights continued right into the twentieth century. Similarly, the new structures of the Victorian family at once tended to place middle-class women more firmly in the home, yet allowed them to create powerful positions for themselves as arbiters of etiquette, behavior, and new forms of work such as writing for publication and teaching as countries adopted the concept of compulsory education.

Finally, the concept of reform may also be seen at work in the influence of the "twin revolutions" on the non-Euro-American world. In British India, for example, the same reforming impulse that was at work in the British Isles was busily creating English-style schools, recasting Indian land tenure and tax collection, and after the Great Rebellion (Mutiny) of 1857, the creation of an India Civil Service. In other cases, reform was undertaken from fear of foreign conquest. Thus in the Ottoman Empire, repeated attempts were made to modernize the military, revamp traditional institutions, reinvigorate the bureaucracy, and even create a constitutional sultanate in 1876. Less successfully, as we previously noted, Chinese officials attempted the idea of "self-strengthening," by using new foreign technologies under the slogan "Chinese studies for the essence; Western studies for practical application." It was in Japan, however, that such reforms took place in the most dramatic form. From 1868, the unification of the country under the emperor Meiji was completed, the old Tokugawa Shogunate deposed, and a wholesale program of military and institutional modernization was begun. It was, in effect, a revolution from the top down in response to foreign attempts to impose unequal treaties. By the end of the century, Japan itself was able to join the imperial powers.

Democracy, Advantages, and Limitations

As should be evident from this chapter, the changes created by the revolutions of the eighteenth and nineteenth centuries completely altered the political landscape of Europe, North America, and to, a lesser extent, South America and Asia. The forces unleashed by the spread of nationalism, representative government, and European Enlightenment values would continue to gather force right through the twentieth century; even before this, they would play a major role in the events leading to the outbreak of World War I. But as the sections on the different national and regional revolutions and reform movements revealed, they were in all cases incomplete to some degree. Here, their main limitations most often revolved around the twin obstacles of the place of women and the meaning and implications of race in their respective societies—problems with which most of the world's nations are still wrestling today.

The advent of representative government and democracy in Europe and the United States at first seemed to hold considerable promise for greater gender equality. One of the ironies of the eighteenth century, however, is that for aristocratic women, their limited numbers and influence at court and in salons made them in some respects more powerful than they would be during much of the nineteenth century. Moreover, the nature of peasant labor made it fundamentally a family affair with a somewhat equal sharing of tasks among men, women, and children. Among the artisans and small shop owners, women were also prominent in such trades as the "putting-out system" of textile production and running taverns. Thus, though most men and women lacked political power, they held a surprising amount of economic power.

The age of political reform, coming as it did with the Industrial Revolution, made women's demands for political equality more insistent on the one hand, but on the other, tended to chain poor women and children to factory and mine work, while confining their middle class sisters increasingly to "the domestic sphere." The pressures of reform aimed at freeing women and children from backbreaking and dangerous mill work also tended to move them more into the home as the century progressed. It is also the case that those who now held political power were generally reluctant to share with potential competitors. Thus women found themselves increasingly adopting new techniques of correspondence, organization, and agitation to try to convince the male electorate of their ability to hold the franchise. We can therefore say that, in terms of economic diversity and contribution to the family economy, the nineteenth century was a difficult time for women and that democracy was something that would be hard won. The only way to win it, however, was through the democratic means of persuasion, agitation, and political pressure.

Race

The role of race in the development of nineteenth-century democracy was similar in many respects to that of gender. But while women were held to be subordinate to men during the early modern period, the negotiation of relationships between men and women had taken place throughout history and was regarded as eternal no matter what form it might take at any given time. The pervasiveness of slavery, however, had created elaborate justifications that grew into more developed theories of racism. That is, from the seventeenth century well into the twentieth, the idea of African, Indian, and, generally, non-Euro-American inferiority was used to justify their exploitation and second-class status. Despite Enlightenment condemnation of slavery and abuse of Amerindians, and the development of abolitionism, ever more hotly defended theories of African and Indian inferiority were circulated to justify their respective conditions. By the late nineteenth and early twentieth centuries, despite the freeing of slaves in the Americas, new pseudo-scientific ideas of Social Darwinism were used to bolster segregation—even lynching in the United States—and the New Imperialism abroad.

What, then, were the advantages and limits of democracy in terms of race? Given the different ways that slaves were emancipated in the United States and serfs in Imperial Russia, this is a thought-provoking question. On the one hand, a reform-minded absolute monarch such as Tsar Alexander II could, by his will alone, free millions of people, despite what the rest of the country might think. In America, on the other hand, it took a half-century of demands and compromises among the contending democratic forces before the issue was finally settled on the battlefields of the Civil War. Even then, for another century, democratic forces fought to keep the freed slaves and their descendants from full participation. Here, we must say that although the democratic tide ultimately ran in favor of equality, it was a long hard slog, with the tools of democracy often being used to keep it from being extended to all.

Practice Test Questions

1. The turning point of the American Revolution usually cited by historians is the

   A. Battle of Bunker Hill.
   B. Battle of the Brandywine.
   C. Battle of Germantown.
   D. Battle of Saratoga.
   E. Battle of Trenton.

2. Perhaps the most influential document of the early French Revolution was

   A. the Code Napoleon.
   B. Concordat of Worms.
   C. The Declaration of the Rights of Man and the Citizen.
   D. The Treaty of Utrecht.
   E. The Rosetta Stone.

3. The Mexican revolutionary who organized the native peoples of the south was

   A. Emiliano Zapata.
   B. General Lopez de Santa Anna.
   C. Emperor Maximilian.
   D. Dom Pedro.
   E. Pancho Villa.

4. The revolutionary program of Dr. Sun Yat-sen in China was called

   A. self-strengthening.
   B. the Boxer Protocols.
   C. spheres of influence.
   D. the Three People's Principles.
   E. the Constitution of 1889.

5. Two men most commonly associated with conservative and radical positions on the French Revolution are

   A. Edmund Burke and Thomas Paine.
   B. Immanuel Kant and G.W. F. Hegel.
   C. George Eliot and Georges Sand.
   D. Lord Byron and William Godwin.
   E. Thomas Jefferson and John C. Calhoun.

Answers and Explanations

1. **D.** **A, B,** and **C** were British victories; **E** was important but did not result in French recognition of the United States, which ultimately played a key role in the Americans winning the war.

2. **C.** **A** came a decade and a half after the Rights of Man; **B** was an agreement between the Holy Roman Emperor and the Papacy in the Middle Ages; **D** was a treaty of 1712; **E** enabled scholars to decipher Egyptian hieroglyphs.

3. **A.** Zapata and Villa are associated with each other but Zapata is the better choice; Santa Anna and Maximilian were not revolutionaries though they were rulers; Dom Pedro was the emperor of Brazil.

4. **D.** **A, B,** and **C** are associated with late Qing Chinese history but not with Sun; **E** was the Japanese Constitution under Emperor Meiji.

5. **A.** **B** are German philosophers; **C** are actually women; **D** and **E,** though no doubt on opposite sides on many issues, did not make themselves famous with this one.

Globalization and the Rise of the West

As we indicated in the overview to this section, the immense changes brought about through the industrial and political revolutions of the eighteenth and nineteenth century were accompanied by—and in many ways made possible—a new and thoroughgoing globalization. A primary stimulus for this was the so-called New Imperialism of the latter decades of the nineteenth century. A number of factors—the drive for markets and raw materials; technical advances in transportation, communications, and weapons; intensifying nationalist competition; and the development of ideologies of domination, such as Social Darwinism—all played significant roles in this vast transformation. By 1914, the power of the West—the Great Powers of Europe and the United States, had become paramount, while in East Asia, a rapidly industrializing Japan had moved to the forefront of the regional stage.

Impact of World Expansion

The impact of world expansion may be seen in several areas. The first is that overseas empires and their supporting structures were able to be created in a far more extensive way than had ever been possible before. The older European empires, with the exception of the colonies in the Americas, were fundamentally trade empires. With few exceptions, the European maritime powers in the sixteenth, seventeenth, and eighteenth centuries were not interested in outright conquest, and in most cases were not capable of it. With the vast advances in steamship technology, the advent of steel warships, and the rapid communication of telegraphs and undersea cables, however, keeping in touch with the home country and administrative tasks could be carried out far more swiftly and efficiently.

The means of maintaining these empires also increased the imperialists' domination of them. That is, shipping lanes needed to be guarded against pirates and competitors; naval bases, along with supply and coaling stations on far-flung islands and territories needed to be set up as well. Finally, as the pace of colonial competition increased, the strategic position of empires became increasingly important. For example, following the Sino-Japanese War of 1894-95, Japan seized a part of the Chinese mainland. Fearful that Japan would gain a key advantage against a weakened China, Germany, Russia, and France forced the Japanese to give the territory back in the so-called Triple Intervention. Russia then turned around and leased the area from China, helping to set the stage for the Russo-Japanese War (1904–1905). Meanwhile, Germany leased its own naval base to counter that of Russia, Britain augmented its position by leasing the Kowloon territory adjacent to Hong Kong, and the so-called Race for Concessions was on. An important reason that the United States annexed the Philippines in 1899 after acquiring it from Spain was the fear of one of the other powers forcing concessions there from an independent, but weak, Filipino government.

Imperialism and Colonialism

Imperialism and colonialism were the main processes by which new systems of domination were created and extended throughout the world during the nineteenth century. In this, they can be considered principal drivers of world expansion. Literally, **imperialism** is the act of building an empire. More precisely, it refers to a period in the late nineteenth century when a number of industrializing countries—mostly in Europe, but by 1914 also including the United States, Russia, and Japan—created global empires. By 1914 the British Empire alone controlled a quarter of the world's people, and 80 percent of the globe was under some form of European control. The reasons for this so-called New Imperialism are varied, but for the most part may be grouped under the following categories:

- **A need to constantly expand trade.** This was the primary motivation for the creation of treaty ports and favored status for certain countries' merchants in the Ottoman Empire and especially in China and East Asia.
- **A desire for captive markets.** Overseas territories guaranteed favorable markets for the home country's products because competitors could be shut out.

- **The ever-increasing need for raw materials.** The Second Industrial Revolution, which, roughly speaking, coincided with the New Imperialism, required a number of exotic tropical resources for its industries. Oil, copper for electrical devices and wire, rubber, nickel, manganese, and other minerals not found in the industrial states themselves pushed them to look abroad for these items. Along with gold and diamonds, these were increasingly found in Africa and the (then) Dutch East Indies.

- **Changing politics and ideology.** The scientific and technological advances of the Industrial Revolution, combined with the push for nationalism, more representative government, and the democratization of culture, helped create a worldview among these states that they were the leaders of world civilization. It followed that those who were left behind in the race were inferior or in decline. On the one hand, then, there were those who believed that it was the duty of the "advanced" nations to export scientific-industrial civilization to the less fortunate—forcibly, if need be. On the other hand, the biological theories of natural selection and "survival of the fittest" espoused by Charles Darwin (1809-1882) were taken up by Social Darwinists: those who believed that nations, ethnic groups, and races were governed by these biological laws. Thus, if humanity was to evolve, only the "fittest" peoples should rule or even be allowed to survive.

- **Intensified nationalism.** The changing political climate bred heated rivalries as nations came to see their prestige bound up in empire building. France, for example, after suffering a humiliating defeat at the hands of Prussia/Germany in 1870, saw empire building as a way to rebuild its reputation as a great power. Germany, which concentrated on consolidating its territories in Europe during the 1870s and 1880s, decided in the 1890s that it needed "its place in the sun" to enhance its prestige on the world stage. Even the United States, content for the most part to build its power in North America, came to join the club of imperial powers by forming an overseas empire in Hawaii and the Philippines in the 1890s. By 1914 it was considered a given among policy makers that a country without overseas possessions was a second-rate power at best.

- **Advances in medicine and technology.** Finally, by the end of the nineteenth century, the Second Industrial Revolution had created the means by which its beneficiaries could go out and conquer large overseas empires. Advances in medicine for the first time allowed outsiders to penetrate the African and other tropical forests without being wiped out by the host of deadly diseases and parasites native to these areas. Equally important, the astonishing power of new weapons such as the Maxim machine gun, the repeating rifle, and rapid-fire artillery allowed small numbers of men armed with these weapons to repeatedly defeat large numbers of men without them.

Closely tied to the phenomenon of imperialism is **Colonialism**—the practice of setting up colonies. The terms "imperialism" and "colonialism" are sometimes used interchangeably though they are not exactly the same. They are, however, associated with each other during the era of the New Imperialism because many of the territories of these empires were seen as places to be colonized by settlers from the home country. Thus we usually find the term used in two ways:

- Colonialism can refer to an imperial system in which the territories outside the home country are controlled in a clearly subordinate manner. Generally, this use of the term implies some level of exploitation. In this sense, India, although relatively few people from Great Britain moved there to settle, was often referred to as a colony—especially by Indians struggling for independence—because of the way it was governed by the British. In fact, in India today there is an entire academic and literary genre called "postcolonial."

- Colonialism can also refer to the setting up of imperial territories as places for settlers from the home country. This was the case in Canada, Australia, South Africa, Kenya, and French Algeria, where eventually more than two million outsiders settled between 1830 and 1962.

The same forces brought to bear in exercising dominance in imperialism may be seen in colonialism as well. In colonies where large numbers of settlers came, however, the conflicts were often more violent. Whatever the predisposition of colonial administrators might have been regarding reform or imposing culture on local people, their first duty was to attempt to keep the peace. In this situation, the settlers were frequently a destabilizing factor. Just as constant pressure from settlers to open up lands of Native Americans sparked constant reneging on treaties by the U.S. government, settlers in the colonies often started trouble with local people by taking their land and then expecting the colonial government to back them up.

Responses to World Expansion and Imperialism

The impact of the expanding West presented the societies of nearly every place that encountered it with a crisis of some degree and an array of choices of how to deal with the intrusion. These choices may be grouped under the headings discussed in this section: reform, rebellion, resistance, and later, nationalism. By and large, the path of reform tended to be tried by the larger and better-organized societies of the Ottoman Empire and East Asia. We should keep in mind, however, that sometimes more than one of these choices was tried, and sometimes more than one tried at once. Thus, in addition to provoking a crisis of how to react to imperialism, partisans of different approaches sometimes fought each other.

Reform

For most of the nineteenth and early twentieth centuries, the chief problems that faced reformers centered on fears of the religious, cultural, and social effects that the introduction of European technologies and institutions might bring. Was it possible, for example, to *really* have "Chinese studies for the essence and Western studies for practical application" as Chinese reformers argued, or would the introduction of these things change forever the most vital parts of what made Chinese civilization "Chinese?" Echoes of this question could be found nearly everywhere such reforms were contemplated. Nevertheless, by the 1890s reforms were in various stages of being implemented in the following places:

- **The Ottoman Empire.** The modernization of the military and governing institutions inaugurated by the Ottoman governor of Egypt, Muhammad Ali and his successor, the Khedive Ismail, encouraged similar attempts by reformers in Istanbul. In the process of this, their efforts were given added urgency: Like Russia, Turkey witnessed firsthand the degree to which the Industrial Revolution had vastly improved the military power of France and England during the Crimean War. Thus, reform was seen by many as a necessity for the survival of the empire. Following the destruction of the old warrior class of *Janissaries* in 1826, a series of reforms, starting in 1839 and spread over four decades known as the *Tanzimat,* was inaugurated, culminating in 1876 with a constitutional monarchy. These were seen by the Europeans as encouraging steps, but the opposition of entrenched Muslim clerical institutions forced a repudiation of the constitution in 1877 and ushered in a period of bloody repression of minorities and Balkan independence movements. At the Congress of Berlin in 1878, much of the empire's outlying territory was given to Austria-Hungary and Russia, while Serbia, Montenegro, Rumania, and part of Bulgaria were given their independence. Like Russia, Turkey would enter World War I woefully unprepared for modern total warfare. Also like Russia, the empire would be dismantled at war's end.

- **Qing China.** The humiliation of the Opium War and unequal treaties set off policy debates among Chinese officials from the 1840's right through the nineteenth century. Following the Second Opium War (1856–1860) and the devastating carnage of the Taiping Rebellion (1851–1864), a decade of normalized relations with the treaty powers in China allowed reformers like Li Hongzhang (1823–1901) to sponsor promising experiments in building modern arsenals and shipyards, creating Western-style commercial and shipping companies, opening mines, sending students abroad, and, in later decades, building railroads, telegraphs, and ironclad warships. Such reforms were always hampered by officials who feared that the Chinese "essence" would become westernized by such innovations and by the political infighting around two successive child emperors. By 1894, the spottiness of such reforms and the corruption surrounding them were revealed by the ease with which Japan humiliated China and imposed its own unequal treaties on the Qing. Chinese weakness then encouraged more Western intrusion, climaxing in the Boxer Rebellion of 1900, in which a large foreign coalition drove the Qing from Beijing and imposed the last and most severe of the treaties on the Qing. Taking their cue from the successful reforms of Japan, the Qing belatedly attempted to set up sweeping reforms—many of which had been briefly tried in the abortive Hundred Days of Reform in 1898—and turn China into a constitutional monarchy. While in the midst of this transition, the revolution of 1911 forced the Qing from the throne in early 1912.

- **Japan.** Of all the non-European and American countries, Japan not only successfully resisted imperialism, but turned the tables and became an imperial power itself. At first, it appeared as if the Tokugawa Shogunate, which had ruled Japan since 1603, would end up much like the Qing. The Tokugawa signed unequal treaties with the United States, Great Britain, France, and other European nations in the 1850's, and these in turn set up concessions in several Japanese ports. Japan's samurai warrior class, however, challenged this situation from the beginning, and by 1863 dissident *daimyo* (feudal lords) launched a civil war to reunite Japan under the emperor, who

185

had been relegated to being a ceremonial and religious leader since the twelfth century. By 1867 they had driven the Tokugawa from power and in 1868 the new emperor, Meiji (r. 1868–1912), immediately gathered about him an extraordinarily gifted set of advisors, who set about imposing on Japan the most thorough set of reforms of the era. In a way, it was almost a revolution from the top down. Under the slogans "Eastern ethics, Western science," "Enrich the country, strengthen the military," and "Civilization and Enlightenment," the Meiji government systematically borrowed what it considered to be the best of European and American education, science and technology, created a constitutional monarchy, and built the strongest army and navy in East Asia. From 1895 to 1914 they created an empire that included Taiwan, the Ryukyu Islands, Korea, and areas of Manchuria. At the beginning of World War I, they also seized Germany's East Asian territories.

- **Thailand and Ethiopia.** In the imperial struggle for control of Southeast Asia, Thailand, or Siam, managed to borrow heavily from British and French institutions in the effort to reform its government and act as a buffer between the French colonies in Indochina and the British in Burma and Malaya. The chief architects of these reforms were the kings Mongkut and his son Chulalongkorn, whose tutor Anna Leonowens wrote an account of her time at court in the early 1860's that became the source for the musical "The King and I." In the case of Ethiopia, astute purchases of modern weapons and European advisors allowed the army of Emperor Menelik II to defeat an Italian colonial force at the Battle of Adowa in 1896—a defeat which Fascist Italy under Mussolini was bent on avenging forty years later.

Rebellion

In charting the history of rebellion in the nineteenth century, scholars are sometimes at odds over which revolts were caused directly by imperialism and which ones might have been provoked by anger at foreign intrusion but were also fueled by other grievances against the existing government. Among the most important were:

- **The Taiping Rebellion.** This upheaval against the Qing government from 1851 to 1864—with smaller accompanying rebellions continuing until 1867—was the largest human conflict in history until World War II. The death toll is variously estimated at 20-30 million people and it gravely wounded the dynasty, which barely hung on for another four decades. (A dynasty that "hung on for another four decades" hardly seems to have been "fatally wounded.") It is also a good example of a rebellion that included many grievances against nineteenth-century Confucian society that had nothing specific to do with the foreign presence in China, but was precipitated by an odd coincidence of Western influence. The grievances stemmed in part from simmering resentment at rule by the northern Manchus in southern China, ethnic conflict between the Hakkas and Puntis, anger at Qing inability to stop foreign intrusion, and worsening economic conditions as trade that formerly went through Canton was siphoned off to the newly opened ports to the north. These conflicts exploded with the introduction of the Taiping ideology: a bizarre amalgam of Protestant Christianity and ancient Chinese religious ideas. Its leader, Hong Xiuquan, who collapsed in a nervous breakdown after failing his official examinations, announced on awakening that he had been taken up into the Christian heaven and had been anointed as Jesus' younger brother. Preaching his message, he slowly gained a following of the discontented of south China and along the way created a new vision of society: equality among all believers, abolition of private property, no opium use, no gambling, no footbinding, and members would let their hair grow in front and cut their queues (braids), the sign of submission to the Qing. By 1853 the movement was so powerful that it nearly drove the Qing from Beijing. Settling in and around the walled city of Nanking, they made it their capital until the Qing finally retook it in 1864. Ultimately, the Qing put together powerful regional armies, bought large amounts of modern armaments, and even hired Western advisors to help train troops. The suppression of the movement, as devastating as it was, also marks the first instance of cooperation between the Qing and the treaty powers, and China's "Self-Strengthening" reform movement is usually dated from this time (1860–1895).

- **Boxers.** The Boxer Rebellion (1899–1900) in many ways marked the low ebb of the Qing Dynasty. As with the Taipings, Boxer grievances arose from resentment at the Manchu's inability to safeguard the empire from foreign intrusion, now greatly intensified by China's humiliation at the hands of Japan. A secret society with a history of resistance to Manchu rule, the Boxer rites involved a complicated series of *taiji* exercises and martial arts moves that believers were convinced conveyed invulnerability to bullets. Provoked by the aggressive German intrusion into Shandong province, the Boxers attacked missionaries and Chinese Christians. The foreign community put pressure on the Qing government to suppress the Boxers, but maneuvering at court convinced the Empress Dowager Cixi (Tzu Hsi) to covertly support the movement. Matters came to a head in June 1900, when the murder of the German ambassador prompted the Qing to declare war on all the foreign powers in China. While officials in most parts of the empire awaited events in the capital, northern China became a killing field for foreigners and their sympathizers. The foreign legations in Beijing were besieged for 45 days before a multinational relief force drove the Boxers and the government from the capital. In the pacification that followed, coalition forces wiped out thousands of villagers in their search for Boxers. When negotiations finally began, the foreign powers imposed indemnities so severe that the Qing had to borrow money from foreign banks to pay them. Foreign troops were now posted in the capital and major cities and the Empress Dowager, her hand forced by events, finally sanctioned widespread reforms that led ultimately to a brief constitutional monarchy before being overthrown by the revolution.

- **Samurai.** The accession of the Meiji government in 1868 saw the disbanding of the samurai as a class in Japan. They were pensioned off by the government, some becoming schoolmasters, a number becoming entrepreneurs, but many retreating to their rural homes dissatisfied with the direction the new regime seemed to be taking. Their disappointment was made keener by the creation of a new Western-style professional army with its own officer training programs and French and German advisors. Since the samurai were the retainers of the feudal lords, or *daimyo,* during the Tokugawa period, the Meiji government had acted quickly to undercut their resistance to the sweeping away of the old order. For those with no stake in the new order, however, it only multiplied their resentment. Their grievances were personified in the hulking general and statesman Saigo Takamori. Saigo had initially fought to install the new government. In the early 1870s he advocated opening Korea to Japanese influence the way the Americans had "opened" Japan. But the new government felt such a move would be premature and would alienate the foreign powers Japan needed to help its reform programs. In 1877, samurai discontent exploded into outright rebellion and Saigo was convinced to lend his prestige to the movement. In a sense, it was the last attempt of the old order to turn the clock back to the era of the shoguns. It was also emblematic of the way such last-ditch attempts by conservative elements tended to fail. Their initial success against militia units convinced the samurai that their skill and valor would win out over the new weapons of their enemies. In the end they were tragically mistaken, as the repeating arms and Gatling guns of the regular army utterly routed them. Saigo himself committed suicide, but is still considered a hero of the samurai spirit in Japan today.

- **Sepoys.** The Sepoy Rebellion (variously called "The Sepoy Mutiny," "the Great Mutiny," or the "Great Rebellion"), though it took place in India 20 years earlier, came about for many of the same reasons as that of the samurai in Japan. The sepoys were Indian troops originally employed by the British East India Company and officered by the English as a protective force for the company's trading posts. Following the spread of British power in northern India after the Seven Years War (1756–1763), they became the most powerful armed presence in the region. By the early nineteenth century, however, the Company's less intrusive presence in Indian society was being replaced by administrators who sought to reform Indian institutions along British lines. In addition to technical improvements like railroads and telegraphs, tax reform for reasons of efficiency broke down old systems of payment in kind and land tenure. Missionary schools were also set up, violating the cultural and religious sensibilities of Hindus and Muslims alike. The company's system of indirect rule also relied on a strategy of divide and conquer: Caste was pitted against caste, religion against religion, region against region, in an attempt to minimize resistance. The simmering discontent at the increasingly intrusive British presence exploded in 1857 at a military barracks in northern India. In the incident recounted in an earlier chapter, a rumor spread that the paper cartridges to be used in the newly issued Enfield rifle were greased with both cow and pig fat, which would break the food restrictions of both Hindus and Muslims. Having been violated this way, the Sepoy troops believed, they would then be open to conversion to Christianity. They thus took over the barracks, contacted troops and like-minded supporters across northern India and made one last attempt to expel the British. With their pent-up rage came frightful atrocities against foreigners and their supporters. The leaders found the last descendant of the old Mughal Dynasty and enthroned him as rightful ruler of India. The British, caught unawares and vastly outnumbered, diverted troops from fighting the Second Opium War in China and by 1858 had crushed the rebellion. In so doing they committed frightful atrocities of their own: The characteristic method of execution of rebels was to rope them to the mouths of cannons and blow them to bits while the troops watched. In the end, the British completely revamped their government in India: The East India Company was dissolved; British government administrators were sent; a civil service including Indians was created, and India would now be ruled directly.

Resistance

In addition to rebellion against longstanding governments, the imperial period also saw widespread resistance to initial foreign intrusions. Below are three prominent instances of such resistance:

- **Ghost Dance.** The history of Europeans in North America was written largely in terms of struggle between various groups of Native Americans and the rapidly expanding numbers of settlers. By the 1870s the last groups of these peoples, the Plains Indians launched their last attempt to stave off the settling of the west. Though they achieved spectacular success at the Battle of the Little Bighorn, in a pattern that would become familiar in widely separated areas of the world, they would ultimately be ruthlessly subdued. By the mid-1880s all of the major Indian groups had been decimated by war and disease and were confined to reservations. But the new life of farming and sheep-raising encouraged by the government was not congenial to many, and the efforts of agents and missionaries to spread Christianity and suppress native languages was also seen as a form of cultural imperialism. By the late 1880s an indigenous religious revival was being spread among the western reservations by a shaman called Wovoka, who preached the practice of the Ghost Dance. Like the Boxers a few years later, the Ghost Dancers believed that if the dance was performed properly, the special Ghost Dance shirts worn would protect them from bullets. Indeed, it was believed that with enough followers dancing correctly the new order would vanish and the buffalo would return. The U.S. government, alarmed at the speed with which the movement spread and its subversive potential, acted quickly to suppress it. The dance was banned on all reservations, but a large gathering at Wounded Knee, South Dakota, in 1890 was surrounded by troops, who slaughtered hundreds in the winter freeze. With them died the last real hopes for any kind of Native independence or autonomy.

- **Wahhabis.** In 1882, the British government moved into Egypt in response to the Khedive's inability to make good on the Suez Canal bonds owned by the British. The British from this point essentially controlled Egypt and, as the major investors in the Canal, assumed responsibility for defending it as their lifeline to India. The Egyptians had long attempted to bring Sudan under their control and had moved into the city of Khartoum as an advance post. In the Sudan, however, a conservative Muslim sect, the Wahhabis, had rallied around a Muhammad Ahmad, who called himself the Mahdi, and resolved to not only resist the Egyptians but to launch a holy war against modernizing Egypt itself. The Anglo-Egyptian government sent an army under Charles George Gordon, who had achieved fame as the leader of the Qing Dynasty's "Ever Victorious Army" during the Taiping years, to guard Khartoum and stop the Mahdi's forces. Despite superior weaponry and sound defensive works at Khartoum, the Mahdi's forces wiped out Gordon's force and beheaded him in 1885. For the next decade, central and southern Sudan remained under the control of the Wahhabis, while the British press agitated for a punitive expedition. Finally, in 1898, a much larger force lead by General Kitchener of World War I fame, and containing a young officer named Winston Churchill, faced the Mahdi's successor, Khalifa, at Omdurman. The repeating rifles, automatic pistols, machine guns, and field artillery of the British forces made such complete work of the opposition that Churchill later commented on how sick it made him to contemplate such utter slaughter of the enemy.

- **Zulus.** A similar sequence of initial success followed by complete devastation was seen in southern Africa. The early Dutch settlers of the Cape Colony had encountered relatively little resistance from the Koi-San people, because their diseases and guns had rapidly depopulated the area. As the settlers moved farther north in the 1830s, however, they encountered the large Zulu nation expanding southward. Unlike the Koi-san, the Zulus had a degree of immunity to the European diseases, and their warrior culture and large population made them formidable opponents. After a signal victory over a Zulu force in 1838, settler expansion continued and they set up their own republics, the Transvaal and the Orange Free State. By the 1870s, British expeditions were sent to subdue the Zulus. The British, overconfident of their weapons and abilities, were at first routed in early 1879 at Isandlwana, losing more than 1,300 men in a battle the Zulus called "the washing of the spears." Like their compatriots in the north, however, they mounted renewed expeditions and eventually broke the power of the Zulus in the region. In the end, the British-controlled Cape Colony would also subdue the Boer (Dutch-descended settlers) territories of Transvaal and the Orange Free State in a bloody and draining conflict from 1899–1902, ultimately creating the Union of South Africa.

World Expansion, Imperialism, and Racism

Racism is the belief that humankind is divided into specific groups defined by physical features such as skin color, and that there is a hierarchy of superior and inferior races. In the European and American historical experience the legacy of African slavery and nineteenth-century imperialism has made the term synonymous with "white racism." That is, the ideology of race in the late nineteenth century centered chiefly on the idea that the northern European "Anglo-Saxon races" were superior to the Celts, Mediterranean peoples, Slavs, and other Europeans, and in turn superior to all peoples with dark skin. It should be noted that this idea was closely bound up in the beliefs of Social Darwinism. It should also be noted that although white racism was the predominant type, other peoples practiced their own forms of racism and/or ethnocentrism—belief in the superiority of one's ethnic group—as well. Finally, while ideas of race and empire building were closely bound together, racism was not the sole factor in imperialism, particularly regarding expansion in Australia, New Zealand, and Canada—though it was certainly not absent in European colonists dealings with the original inhabitants of these places.

In addition to the factors mentioned previously that contributed to the development of racism, the imperial experience itself added a good deal. For their part, native peoples who resisted with traditional means and weapons were generally seen as "savage" or "barbaric" and not susceptible to the kinds of diplomacy and negotiation conducted by "civilized" peoples. It followed, then, that force was "the only language these people understand," and consequently the imperial powers were far less inhibited about using it in the colonies than at home. Contempt of the colonized by the colonizer was widespread: These were the "savage wars of peace" Rudyard Kipling wrote of in his poem, "The White Man's Burden." Thus while American leaders at home referred to the Filipinos as "little brown brothers," American soldiers fighting Philippine insurgents sang "Damn, damn, damn the Filipino, civilize him with a Krag (a brand of rifle)." Such contempt for the inhabitants of the new empires was not limited to Europeans or Americans: The Japanese also scorned the Chinese as cowardly, sneaky, and unhygienic. Here again, a favored piece of Japanese doggerel translates roughly as "Chinka, chinka, chinka, you do stinka!" All of this was reinforced by the idea that age-old differences among cultures could never be bridged and each would always remain "other": "East is east and West is west and never the twain shall meet."

Imperialism and Nationalism in the Colonies

Ironically, the institutions, ideas, laws, and so on the imperial powers brought with them also contained the seeds of the destruction of their empires. That is, since all the colonies were ruled by tiny minorities of foreigners, a considerable degree of cooperation had to exist in order for such rule to continue. The key to this cooperation in many respects was that the vast degree of technological superiority enjoyed by the rulers convinced a portion of the ruled that the laws, institutions, philosophy, art, and so on of the rulers was similarly superior. In this sense, the British and French empires were built largely on bluff because tiny numbers of colonial troops and administrators were sufficient to convince potential rebels that overwhelming force would be brought against them if they attempted to resist. If, however, the colonial peoples could be persuaded to unite and not cooperate with the system, then the empires would become ungovernable. This, in a nutshell, was the strategy used by Mohandas Gandhi in the 1920's and 1930's: He was able to convince large numbers of Indians that they had more in common with each other than not, and that they did not need the British to govern them any more. A powerful factor in this process throughout the colonial world, and one that was just coming to the fore before World War I, was nationalism. Just as Europe was kept in ferment by the idea of the "nation" and the proper place of the nation to be governed by its own state, these ideas were soon exported abroad, where their attraction was equally potent. In some places the fit was a natural one: As an island society shaped by isolation to a considerable degree, the Japanese had long recognized themselves as one people governed by one state. Thus the attempts by the Meiji government to inculcate national sentiment through the schools and the military were comparatively easy. The Ottoman Empire and China, on the other hand, held nations within them. The Ottoman Empire struggled desperately to hang on to the Persians, Arabs, Azerbaijianis, Armenians, Turks, Serbs, Bulgarians, Croats, and others, each of whom sought statehood for themselves. Even after the Chinese revolution, the problem of defining "Chineseness" in purely national terms was problematic all through the post-World War I period. In Africa, the problem still exists, largely because the colonial borders that ultimately became independent countries had been drawn by the European powers for their own purposes, without any consideration of the ethnic or national makeup of particular regions. Thus, the goal of fighting for independence based on a shared national unity, and a desire to create a state for it, was to be a complex one throughout the twentieth century.

Practice Test Questions

1. A key difference between the New Imperialism and previous empire building was

   A. the thoroughness of the process.
   B. the huge edge in weaponry of the imperialists.
   C. the speed of the conquests.
   D. the ideology of Social Darwinism.
   E. all of the above.

2. An important factor in the confidence that technological superiority engenders in imperialism is

   A. it makes potential imperialists hesitant to enlarge their empires.
   B. it encourages an attitude of superiority.
   C. it confirms the conquered in the superiority of their own technology.
   D. it confirms for the conqueror that the religion and culture of the conquered are superior to their own.
   E. it leads to a wholesale questioning of European Values.

3. Japan was markedly successful in resisting imperial conquest because

   A. it created a unified government with a sound policy for modernization.
   B. the samurai and daimyo were the world's most formidable warriors.
   C. the Tokugawa Shogun was shrewd in giving concessions to the Chinese.
   D. it quickly conquered Korea in 1870.
   E. it had abundant natural resources.

4. The Sepoy Rebellion ultimately resulted in

   A. a new Mughal Dynasty and a united India.
   B. the creation of the East India Company.
   C. dissolving of the East India Company and direct British rule.
   D. an independent Pakistan.
   E. a union between India and Afghanistan.

5. Spectacular victories by indigenous forces over imperial armies took place at

   A. Islandwana and Adowa.
   B. Plassey and Omdurman.
   C. Khartoum and Nanking.
   D. Taiping and Cawnpore.
   E. Little Bighorn and Wounded Knee.

Answers and Explanations

1. E. All of these are hallmarks of the New Imperialism.

2. B. The remaining choices run counter to the evidence provided.

3. A. B might have been anecdotally true but had little immediate impact on the early unequal treaties imposed on Japan; the rest are all false.

4. C. A refers to the attempt by the rebels to unsuccessfully revive the Mughals; the rest are anachronistic and/or not directly related to the rebellion.

5. A. B and E list one defeat of indigenous forces; the others have a city name (Nanking) and the name of a group of rebels (Taiping).

Time, Structure, and Demographics Since 1914

How Does This Period Differ from the Previous Period and Why?

It has sometimes been said that the nineteenth century came to an end in 1914 with the outbreak of World War I. Though this comment refers to something very real (mainly the final end of the old monarchical and aristocratic order and the beginning of the end of the European empires), it suggests too much of a break with the past. Looking back over several hundred years, it is easier to see that many of the features of life after 1914 had been in development for some time.

The Great Transformation

By the twentieth century, what has been called the Great Transformation was more or less complete. This transformation, affecting Europe first and then the rest of the world, included the market revolution, the industrial revolution, urbanization, and the realignment of culture and society away from tradition and religion and toward science and technology.

Tradition consists of the beliefs, customs, ways of life, language, and world views inherited from the past and usually passed on by informal (usually oral) means. It is by tradition that we shake hands, wave, and tip our hats—there is no law or code that requires it. We learn tradition beginning at a very early age, and it becomes part of who we are. Collectively, it is a part of the life of communities and larger social groupings. Tradition tells us to do or think things, usually without giving clear cut reasons.

The market revolution affected the way in which most people effected their personal or family economy. In pre-market times, most families provided the three necessities—food, fiber (for clothing), and fuel—themselves, and they engaged in a very diversified agriculture on the lands they farmed to do this. In many places around the world, some of those necessities may have come from lands or other resources held in common with others in their region or local community. Firewood is a good example of this, but so are common pasture lands and fisheries.

If the family (as the principal unit of production) produced a surplus of any of the things they grew or made, they might sell that surplus in small local markets for consumption by the few who lived in towns and cities. With the money thus obtained, they might purchase items that they could not or did not wish to produce themselves—spices, cast iron goods, horseshoes, and the like. The important thing to remember is that the family's need for cash was minimal, and what they produced was mostly for their own consumption. They were, in fact, both producers and consumers.

The market revolution changed this traditional relationship between production and consumption. Farmers would now specialize in only a few (or even just one) crop, and this would be sold for money in the market. With the proceeds of these cash sales, farmers would now purchase the bulk of their needs instead of producing them directly.

With the growth of the market system came the growth of market towns and cities that served as nodes of commercial interaction. Those who made their living as merchants actually produced nothing at all, but instead took a portion of the proceeds of a sale as profit and used it to purchase necessities (and, increasingly, luxuries as well).

Since the market revolution happened at the same time as the Industrial Revolution, now factory production of cloth, wood, and metal goods was added to agricultural production, and this stimulated the development of market devices and institutions (such as bills of credit, bank notes, and other monetary arrangements). By the end of the nineteenth century in much of the Western world, production-for sale (of either agricultural or manufactures goods) had all-but replaced production-for-use as the center of the economy.

This revolution in the relationships of production and consumption had profound consequences. First of all, in the context of the Industrial Revolution, it made the population increasingly urban, and therefore more dependent than ever on market relationships (since you can't produce food, fiber, and fuel in town). Secondly, and just as significantly, the market revolution changed the way people thought about work. As the consumer of what he himself had produced, the worker *owned* both his labor and the fruits of his labor.

As an industrial worker, he no longer owned the products he made, and he sold his labor as just another commodity in the market. Even aside from the foul and nasty nature of industrial work in the nineteenth (and much of the twentieth) century, this meant the worker was no longer the master of his own work and time. He had been a free agent before, now he was a wage laborer. It was for this reason that in countries in which voting was important (such as Britain and the United States), there were strict property qualifications well into the twentieth century (earlier in the United States)—one had to own a certain amount of property to vote. It was assumed that if you didn't own property, you must have worked for wages, and if you worked for wages, you weren't "free"—only free people could vote.

The Great Transformation has not been universally accepted. There are small groups of people around the world who keep many aspects of post-Transformation life at arms length. One example is the Amish in the United States. Settled in small communities in Pennsylvania, Ohio, and other American states, the Amish deliberately avoid the use (and certainly the dependence) upon most modern technology. Subsistence farming (in which a family produces most or all of what they need themselves) is still the Amish ideal. They avoid the use of internal combustion engines, of the telephone, radio, and other electronic devices, and many do not even use electricity. By avoiding these technologies, the Amish believe they can readily sustain their faith and their communities in a World that has by and large lost both.

There are also surprisingly large groups of people around the world who, while cautiously embracing technology, use it in an attempt to sustain traditional culture. The best example in the early twenty-first century might be the various Muslim fundamentalist sects that keep the very modern ideal of social and gender equality at arms length.

Community or Society?

Early in the twentieth century, social commentators such as Max Weber, Ferdinand Tonnies, Henry Main, and others pointed out that a profound shift had taken place during the nineteenth century in the ways in which people interacted and conducted their mutual affairs. Tonnies noted that where once people had commonly associated as members of "communities" (*Gemeindschaft*), they now acted as members of "society" (*Gesselschaft*). The differences between these two were significant, each being deeply rooted not only in social norms and customs but also in the psyche of individuals.

According to Tonnies (and others who noted similar changes), *community* had been the classic form of human interaction during all of recorded history into the nineteenth century (italics used hereafter in this section to emphasize key terms and concepts). It is *local*, often consisting of extended or closely-related families, and the *way of life* within it was based on *tradition* and *custom*. In other words, individuals were deeply embedded and integrated within communities as *organic* associations.

Society, on the other hand, is not created by organic associations as much as it is by *mechanical* ones. Formal *institutions* such as church, government, corporations, and even private institutions form essential nodes of interaction without which many modern people would be isolated.

It is important to remember that these two modes are not mutually exclusive—they can and do exist at the same time and in the same place. There have always been (or at least very long been) institutions that served as focal points of interactivity. And, today's world still enjoys (or suffers, as the case might be) some forms of traditional community life. This is especially true where life is still rural and limited in its access to modern technology. In general, though, *society* dominates life in the modern world, while it is, for many, an increasingly distant (and romantic) ideal.

Secularization

The secularization of both personal mentality and public institutions that became virtually complete by the twentieth century began (in the Western world) during the Renaissance. With the recovery and widespread dissemination of the learning of the ancient Greeks and Romans—that is, the learning of non-Christian polytheists—the Church's role as the sole source of knowledge began to weaken. If ancient pagans had had the truth, then truth was not something that was "revealed" only to the faithful.

Enlightenment: the replacement of a world view that saw God as an almighty magician, making everything happen, with a view that, if it accepted God at all, saw him as the creator of a system, the features of which were thereafter fixed and "natural." The classic metaphor of the Enlightenment was the clock—the universe like a clock—a system of parts that interact in discoverable and predictable ways. God built the clock, but thereafter does not disturb or change the way it operates. What came to be known as "science" was simply a way of studying the clock to see how it works. Here's the key point—you could study the clock in order to gain insight into the mind and purposes of God, or you could just study the clock as an end in itself.

And, once you take God out of the day-to-day operation of the cosmos—whether or not you believe in an original creator—you take away the bulk of the motivation behind adherence to a religion: to be right with the world by being right with God as you see him (or her, or them).

By the nineteenth century, both science and the naturalistic world view had progressed so far that God's direct hand in life itself could be questioned and debated. Nothing addressed this question and advanced the debate more than Charles Darwin's *Origin of Species* (1859). Based on extensive and detailed evidence observed in the natural world, Darwin proposed a theory that explained how natural selection had resulted, not in the creation, but in the evolution of species from lower animals to vertebrates to primates and then, by implication, to humankind. And then, even the existence of God: "God is Dead."

Exceptions: fundamentalists of most kinds—Christians, Jews, Muslims. There are also shades of secularization. Some don't want the establishment of a national church with powers and privileges granted by the government, but they do want the government to print, "In God We Trust" on currency. In the American and Western European experience, until well into the twentieth century, issues of secularization had little to do with whether or not a person was "religious." Mostly at issue were the connections between particular denominations and the state. If the state privileged one denomination over another, that was bad. If the state vaguely supported (usually Christian) religion in general, that was okay.

What emerged in the nineteenth century to virtually rage during the twentieth was the efflorescence of politically-charged ideologies. Nationalism was probably the most powerful of these pseudo-religious ideologies, but Marxist Communism, dozens of kinds of socialisms, free-market capitalism, and feminism seem to hold the passions of their adherents every bit as much as religion had hold of their parents and grandparents. Among some, even science itself took on a ideological aspect upon the claim that its methods and procedures were the only valid way of knowing the truth. That's a dead give-away of an **ideology** (and of most religions)—the claim to the exclusive possession of truth.

An ideology is a system of ideas about various aspects of life or society, sometimes taking on many of the compelling features of religion. Examples of history-making ideologies during the nineteenth and twentieth centuries include Marxism, Feminism, and nationalism. The adherents to an ideology often zealously promote it to the exclusion of other ideologies or ways of thinking.

Bureaucratization

Historically, the management or administration of government or business functions was undertaken as a *personal* matter—a king and his household staff, for instance—rather than as a systematic process that is, by nature, *impersonal* and governed by rules.

Similarly, when even large industrial companies were still run by families, management was a family matter that may or may not have been systematically organized. Under the corporate organization of business, though, **bureaucracy** replaced family management, and managers at all levels in the corporation conducted their designated parts of the business according to written rules and procedures handed down and approved by higher-ups.

Bureaucracies are the system of procedures and rules, along with the organizational structure that employs them, for the detailed functioning of any organization—a government, a business, a church, and so on.

Although bureaucracies are frequently the butt of both complaints and jokes, they are a necessary part of both business and government in the modern age. The sheer volume of work done in a world of billions of people and trillions of dollars makes the personal approach of *pre-modern times* impossible. Also, the modern ideal of rule by law rather than by personal fiat makes the personal approach undesirable when it is not disciplined within a bureaucratic structure of some kind.

Bureaucracies came from a series of reform movements that attempted to either rationalize, systematize, and therefore make *scientific* the administration of both private and public institutions. "Efficiency" experts such as Frederick W. Taylor (author of *Principles of Scientific Management*, 1911) emerged along with many other professions in the second half of the nineteenth century. Engineers, accountants, managers, and most of the academic fields were "professionalized" during that era. Statistical control of management and industrial processes emerged as well—all as part of the drive to make life "scientific."

Bureaucratization would also serve the interests of those who wanted to clean up the corruption and dishonesty, that had always seemed to have gone hand-in-hand with more personal forms of administration. In one country after another all during the nineteenth and into the twentieth century, a professionalized civil service was established. In countries in which electoral processes have been important, to get enough votes to be elected to office has often meant putting together a "political machine" that could organize campaign efforts and even offer payment (or intimidation) to get the needed votes. In order to put together these organizations, local operatives had to be promised some kind of reward.

For a person elected to an executive position—governor or president—that person was in a good position to offer a government job to his friends, and (conversely) to threaten the government jobs of his enemies. In the so-called democratic countries, this had come to be known as the "spoils system" (from the phrase, "to the victors go the spoils").

In addition to the element of corruption that was built into the system, there was no guarantee (or even likelihood) that the person who was given a job would actually be qualified to do it. With the coming of civil service administration, one could be hired only on the basis of merit, often determined through a standardized examination, and one could be fired only for malfeasance or violation of regulations.

The ideal was not removing the human element, but rather limiting the human element to the rational. Since some proportion of what we call human is not rational (nor would we really want it to be), bureaus are not entirely compatible with people. And, since they usually represent very large (and even sovereign) institutions, their power can be immense.

In the minds of a great many critics, though, bureaucratization was just another aspect of the increasingly inhuman nature of human society.

Decolonization

The process that began after World War I of the breakup of the European overseas empires. Belgium, Britain, Denmark, France, Germany, Italy, and the Netherlands lost their colonies by revolution, confiscation, or by granting independence. In most cases, the former colonies established their own sovereign governments. Because of the nature of their former colonial relationship with their "mother" countries, most of the former colonies had not industrialized or otherwise developed stable economies. Most of the so-called "Third World" nations had been colonies of a European power.

The twentieth century would see the end (or near end) of closed mercantilist trading systems and competing trade empires. One after another, the great global empires of Britain, France, the Netherlands, Belgium, German, Italy, and Portugal fell apart, mostly of their own weight and mostly at the relief of those countries.

After 1914, overseas empires were understood by some to be too costly to maintain, but also at odds with the "liberal" ideologies of the West. Not only was free trade "in," but so was nationalism. This meant that intense pressures from trading interests pressing from one side and the desire of dozens of colonial peoples to be free of European domination pressing from the other.

Though colonial peoples were not always pleased with the pace at which the empires granted their former colonies their independence (which by and large took place only after World War II), unlike the colonial revolutions of the eighteenth and nineteenth centuries (in North and South America) in the twentieth century the process was mostly peaceful.

Also, though in most cases independence came peacefully, the aftermath of independence was sometimes violent as in the Congo, and between Hindus and Muslims in India and Pakistan. It is important to note that political independence was not the same thing as economic independence. The very nature of the colonial relationship between colony and "mother" country limited the development of a diversified economy in most colonies. Most of the former colonies were far behind Europe and the United States in industrial development, and they continued as suppliers of raw materials.

One consequence of decolonization is that competition for world trade would now be more between multinational corporations rather than between empires and their governments.

Globalization

The drive to open the world's markets and lower or eliminate the trade barriers characteristic of European mercantilism was begun by the United States through the so-called Open Door Notes. By the end of the nineteenth century, American industrial manufacturing had developed to such a point that domestic markets were glutted with all sorts of manufactured goods. In other words, Americans could produce more than Americans could buy; over-production is the result.

This was less of a problem for the manufacturers of Britain (or French, the Netherlands, etc.) because in India the rest of its far-flung empire the British had captured markets of very large numbers of people. For example, British imperial law prohibited the manufacture of cloth in India. Indians had to buy it from British mills. While it remained part of the Empire, India was trapped in the old mercantile formula: raw materials from the colonies (in India's case, cotton and indigo dye) to be exchanged for manufactured good from the "mother" country.

By 1900, American manufacturers desperately need overseas markets for the excess, but they possessed no captured markets in which to sell them. Additionally, free and open markets seemed naturally consistent with "free enterprise," and freedom in general. Long-standing American anti-imperialism now had a selfish component. Open trade doors were good for business and profits.

During the twentieth century, the increasingly open trade rules made for an environment in which multinational corporations could develop and flourish. Most of these corporations began in the United States, and they are one reason why the United States has been able to dominate world trade. Eventually, the ideal of free trade would call into being new global institutions to both act as deliberative bodies and to regulate (according to agreed-upon rules) how countries can or cannot regulate for themselves their own imports and exports. The most notable such institution is now called the World Trade Organization (WTO), founded in 1995.

The WTO is perhaps a natural development in an era that saw the creation of other global institutions such as the League of Nations, the United Nations, the International Monetary Fund, and the World Bank. These are (or were) institutions of collective security—military or economic. They are attempts to address the problems of global society and global economy in units larger than the sovereign nation-state or empire.

Another important aspect of globalization in the twentieth century was the diffusion of an international and global culture around the world. In large part, this also meant the Americanization of that culture. American sources of music, motion pictures, and television dominated in world markets, especially after World War II. Likewise, certain American consumer goods such as Coca Cola and Levis made deep cultural impressions around the world. American multi-nationals such as McDonalds and Starbucks have made significant inroads in promoting even American food ways and dietary choices. In many places, American English is freely mixed with the local language, to the chagrin of cultural purists (or even those with some sense of traditional culture).

Demographics: Is the World Full Enough?

More than any other era in human history, the period since 1914 has seen explosive population growth. The United Nations estimates that in 1900, world population was about 1.5 billion. By 2000, that figure had risen to just over six billion—a four-fold increase.

The previous century saw rapid growth as well—a near doubling between 1800 and 1900. Estimates for most centuries before 1800 show steady but modest growth, though some centuries would actually experience net declines, mostly due to disease and famine.

In terms of the phases of the demographic transition discussed in Chapter 19, where does the twentieth century fit in? You'll recall that Phase I of the transition is characterized by a high birth (HB) rate and a high death (HD) rate. A HB/HD phase usually results in little or no population growth. This phase characterizes most of the Middle Ages in Europe and around the world.

Phase II begins when birth rates are still high but when death rates decline (DD). In a population with HB/DD, population (and usually the economy) begins to grow and change. In Europe, this phase began during the sixteenth century and continued well into the nineteenth.

Phase III is characterized as HB/LD, and by rapid population growth. This was Europe and its "Frontier"—the United States and other European satellites--in the eighteenth and nineteenth centuries. Phase IV is best described as low birth and low death (LB/LD)—the industrialized world in the twentieth century.

What about the non-industrialized world and those countries that are in the process of "development" and industrialization? By and large, these countries are now in Phase III, with growth rates that are sometimes alarming. To put this into global perspective, here is a table of countries experiencing low and high rates of population growth:

Table 26.1 Selected Countries and Their Growth Rate (by natural increase)—2005			
Canada	0.3%	Bangladesh	2.1%
Denmark	0.1%	Indonesia	1.4%
Netherlands	0.2%	Kenya	2.5%
United States	0.6%	Nigeria	2.3%

Source: U.S. Census Bureau

You will notice that the countries on the left have low rates of growth, and those on the right have relatively high rates. The United States has the highest rate of those listed on the left (it is more diverse in terms of ethnicity and social class than the other three), but it is still less than one-quarter the rate of the highest on the right—Kenya. Compare Kenya's 2.5% annual growth by natural increase (birth rate minus deaths rate) with that of Denmark at 0.1%. It is more than twenty-five times greater!

You'll also notice from the table that the countries on the right are usually thought of as being part of the "Third World." Since these rates of growth will continue for most of the twenty-first century, many scholars believe that the still-rapid growth in the "underdeveloped" nations will shape much of global politics in the decades to come.

What are the factors that make for the difference in population growth rates in the twentieth century? The most important factor is the rate of live births. For a number of reasons, this rate is usually higher in developing countries with adequate food supplies and other security factors (such as the United States in the nineteenth century). The next most important factor is the death rate. Again, in countries with adequate food security, this rate could be low, especially if disease is not an important consideration.

Effecting the death rate is another demographic statistic: "life expectancy." As a calculated figure, life expectancy really means the average age at death, and it is sometimes effected as much by childhood death as it is death in old age. For this reason, "life expectancy" should not be understood as a figure related to "how long people lived" in the past eras.

However, as people began to live much longer than in previous ages because of better hygiene, sanitation, and medical practice (vaccines, antibiotics, corrective surgeries, and trauma interventions), the effective death rate goes down relative to the birth rate. The result: rapid (and sometimes explosive) growth in countries that still have high birth rates but now benefit from at least some of the positive factors indicated previously (such as better medical interventions).

What Causes Changes and Breaks within This Period?

In addition to the various trends and conjunctions discussed previously, specific and concrete historical events acted as fulcrums or hinge points of change during the twentieth century. These will be developed more fully in coming chapters, but these historical fulcrums were: the First World War, the Great Depression, the Second World War, and the Cold War.

Of all the wars of the twentieth century, the First World War is the most difficult to explain. One cannot point to specific or clear-cut aggression as the cause, as in most wars. Instead, the road to war began deep in the nineteenth century, as the stability created by the "Concert of Europe" after the Napoleonic era began to break down.

If World War I was the last war of the nineteenth century (as some have written), then World War II was wholly a twentieth century phenomenon. It rose as an expression of the persisting discontents of the First War, combined with a ferocious and radicalized nationalism on the part of the Germany, Italy, and Japan.

Both wars combined resulted in the death of over sixty million people and the shattering, not once but twice, of a fragile world order. In between the two wars was the Great Depression, an economic disaster of global proportions (in the age of globalism, all disasters are global). The second half of the century would be spent in putting the world back together through the creation and nurturing of a series of collective security arrangement, and in keeping it from blowing apart in a thermonuclear war during the Cold War.

Practice Test Questions

1. Among the changes that took place during the "Great Transformation" is the

   A. decolonization of European empires.
   B. slowing of population growth.
   C. market revolution.
   D. persistence of a mostly-rural population.
   E. All of the above.

2. Among the forces that contributed to secularization since the eighteenth century is

   A. efflorescence of nationalism.
   B. rise of Muslim fundamentalism.
   C. a series of agreements made between governments and various religious denominations.
   D. All of the above.
   E. None of the above.

3. Which of the following former colonies is an exception to the generalization that decolonization came about mostly by peaceful means?

   A. Australia
   B. Algeria
   C. Philippines
   D. Egypt
   E. All of the above.

4. Much of the pressure for free trade in the twentieth century was the result of

   A. the over-production of manufactured goods.
   B. an excess of workers on the world labor market.
   C. the success of Communist trade competition.
   D. poor management practices condemned by experts like F.W. Taylor.
   E. None of the above.

5. In international relations, one important difference between the twentieth century and previous centuries was the development of

   A. the H-Bomb.
   B. a universal diplomatic language.
   C. the organic state theory.
   D. mercantilism.
   E. collective security arrangements.

Answers and Explanations

1. **C.** Of the options given, only Option **C**, "the market revolution," is correct. Each of the other options, the "decolonization of European empires" (Option **A**), the "slowing of population growth" (Option **B**), and the persistence of a mostly-rural population (Option **D**) are pretty much exactly opposite of what took place during the Great Transformation. The empires reached their height during the Transformation, and population growth was very rapid and it was increasing urban.

2. **A.** Among the forces that contributed to secularization since the eighteenth century was the efflorescence of nationalism (Option **A**). The rise of Muslim fundamentalism, Option **B**, was exactly counter to secularization. Option **C**, "a series of agreements made between governments and various religious denominations," has no basis in reality. It is a nonsense option.

3. **B.** Of the former colonies listed as optional answers, only Algeria (Option **B**) is an exception to the generalization that decolonization came about mostly by peaceful means. Australia is still technically a part of the British "Commonwealth," though, like Canada and New Zealand, it has full autonomy. The Philippines, acquired by the United States after the Spanish-American War of 1898 was granted its independence in 1946 as part of a long-term plan (interrupted by World War II), rather than through agitation or revolution. Similarly, Egypt acquired its full independence without revolution. Of the three, only Algeria, a French North African possession until 1962, experienced significant armed conflict as part of it decolonization process.

4. **A.** Much of the pressure for free trade in the twentieth century was the result of the over-production of manu-factured goods (Option **A**). Very productive countries such as the United States could easily fill their domestic demand for goods, causing them to seek markets abroad. But without any significant overseas possession, the United States had no captured markets in which to sell excess goods. For the Americans, as for others, the only option was to apply pressure to open the markets of the European empires to "free trade." Though there is some reality to the existence of an excess of workers (Option **B**), this mostly effected wages (keeping them low) rather than forcing an opening of markets. Options **C** and **D** are nonsense answers.

5. **E.** In international relations, one important difference between the twentieth century and previous centuries was the development of collective security arrangements (Option **E**) such as the United Nations and NATO (see Chapter 30). The H-Bomb (Option **A**) certainly influenced foreign relations in the second half of the twentieth century, but it was one of the things that made collective security arrangements so important. In spite of the frequent use of English (again, especially, in the second half of the twentieth century), there never has been a truly universal diplomatic language (Option **B**). The "organic state theory" (Option **C**) and "mercantilism" (Option **D**) are nonsense answers.

World War I, World War II, the Holocaust, and the Cold War

For all of the "progress" that has been hailed as the glory of modern times, it would be hard to find a century so filled with death and destruction as the twentieth. To a certain extent, it was "progress" in the first place that would bring on on the terrors of total war, genocide, and the prospect of thermonuclear annihilation that gripped the World during the 1900s. "Advances" in technology, the unification of previously fragmented nationalities, and even the adoption of parliamentary democracy in countries previously ruled by absolute monarchs—all these were (and still are) "double-edged swords." Technology created to aid and extend life would be used to destroy life, and on a bigger scale than ever before. The self-determination and rationalism implied by national unification would be distorted and twisted into a raging force of exclusion and genocide. Through propaganda and party politics, even parliamentary democracy would be used for frightful ends by those who could have never acquired power in less liberal times.

This chapter deals with four of the most significant ways in which global progress went awry during the twentieth century: World War I, World War II, the Holocaust (and other genocides and "democides"), and the Cold War. As such, it is a chapter on the "dark side" of modern history. Happily, though, it ends on a good note with the peaceful breakup of what American President Ronald Reagan called the "evil empire" (the Soviet Union), bringing to a close the Cold War with its relentless threat of global destruction.

World War I

Of all the wars of the twentieth century, the First World War is the most difficult to explain. One cannot point to specific or clear-cut aggression as the cause, as in most wars. Instead, the road to war began deep in the nineteenth century, as the stability created by the "Concert of Europe" after the Napoleonic era began to break down. Whatever the causes, World War I would shake Europe and the World to its foundations. It has been said that the nineteenth century ended only in 1914 with the outbreak of the war. It was understood at the time as a great turning point in history. Some though of it as the "war to end all wars." Others (notably the Americans) saw it as a war to "make the World safe for democracy." A few saw the war a merely a continuation of what the nineteenth century Prussian General Von Clauswitz said all war was: politics by other means.

But if World War I was just business as usual, there was no mistaking the fact that the scale of the enterprise was, on account of technology and industrial growth, going to be immense compared to earlier conflicts. Its outcomes were similarly immense. Entire centuries-old empires were destroyed. Ancient monarchical regimes were dissolved, and in their places modern ideologies and obsessions sometimes reigned supreme. Spheres of Influence and Balances of Power were shifted and sometimes created anew, and the seeds were sown at the end of this "war to end all wars" that would grow into the Second World War—a conflagration even more deadly and destructive than the First.

Causes

Because the origins of World War I are so complex, it might be well to break them down into long-term, short-term, and "trigger" causes.

Long-Term Causes

Nationalism as a political force. Nationalism has been one of the most powerful forces unleashed on Europe as a result of the French Revolution and the Napoleonic Wars. In fractured Germany and Italy, there were powerful movements that promoted unification of all Germans within a single Germany, and all Italians into one Italy. Activists in both countries finally achieved this by the 1870s, but unification disrupted the old order dominated by a few major powers. In particular, Germany's victory over the French in the Franco-Prussian War of 1870-71 placed France in a new (and more nationalistic) position. Now, Germany and Italy, newly unified along nationalistic lines, would seek their own share of power in Europe and abroad.

Nationalism also worked against the stability and power of polyglot empires such as Austria, the successor of the old Holy Roman Empire. Though a German-speaking aristocracy and bureaucracy dominated the Austrian empire, it still included dozens of other European nationalities, including Poles, Hungarians, Czechs, Slovaks, Serbs, Bosnians, Italians, and many others. By the middle of the nineteenth century, many of these nationalities were agitating for autonomy or independence with the empire. The Hungarians succeeded in securing a special place within the empire, thereafter called the Austro-Hungarian Empire. Other subjugated nationalities continued their drive toward autonomy, thus seriously weakening the empire from within.

International instability in Europe. The unification of Germany and Italy disrupted old alliances and created the need for new ones. The German defeat of France in the Franco-Prussian war of 1870 created deep-seated animosities between the two powers. In order to protect itself, France made an alliance with Russia, also fearful of the new German power in the heart of Europe.

The Germans, now fearful of "encirclement" by their French and Russian enemies now sought close ties with Austria and Italy. All three sought to keep both the Russians and the British out of the Balkan Peninsula, and they formed the so-called Triple Alliance. By the turn of the century, the British had settled their long-standing colonial conflicts with the French, and both now joined with Russia in the so-called Triple Entent (triple friendship). These mutually exclusive alliances formed new and opposing power blocks that served to divide Europe into increasing well-armed camps.

International militarism. The creation of these new power blocks in Europe touched off an international arms race that continued unabated until 1914. The world's navies converted from wooden sailing vessels to all-steel steam-driven ones. Each new ship of larger displacement and greater armament called for the navies of the other nations to first match and then surpass and exceed the size of the latest naval "advance." Europe's armies amassed other armaments as well, such as those described in the Technology section below.

A series of international crises also accompanied this arms buildup during which animosities between the European powers were intensified. Between 1905 and 1911, France and Germany almost went to war twice over possession of Morocco in North Africa. In seeking control over Morocco, Germany sought to divide Britain and France and thus weaken the Triple Entente. Ultimately, the Moroccan Crises accomplished the opposite—they brought France and Britain into a closer alliance.

Technological developments. The arms race that had been under way since before the turn of the twentieth century had taken full advantage of the technology developed during the industrial and scientific revolutions of the nineteenth century. The muzzle-loading muskets used in the Crimean War of the 1850s and the American Civil War of the 1860s had now become breach- and cartridge-loaded repeating rifles, and by the turn of the century, inventors had perfected rapid-fire machine guns, capable of firing many rounds each second.

The following lists the most important developments in warfare available to world powers by 1914 (in alphabetical order): the airplane, aerial reconnaissance and bombardment, anti-submarine depth charges, big-bore, shell-loaded, long-range artillery, cartridge-loaded repeating rifles, hand grenades, industrial production and transport, land mines, poison gas, radio and telephone field communications, railroad and truck transport of troops and supplies, steam-driven, all-steel ships of immense displacement—the Dreadnaught Battleships, each with a dozen or more guns capable of firing a thousand-pound explosive shell ten or more miles at a barely-visible enemy ship, and, famously, submarines and submarine-launched torpedoes.

The principal significance of these developments was that warfare would be much deadlier than in earlier centuries. The deadliest war prior to the World War I had been the American Civil War, partly because some of this technology was available even then. That war has sometimes been called the first of the "modern wars" for this reason, though battlefield tactics and the deployment and movement of troops had been more or less unchanged since Napoleonic times. In particular, the use of frontal-assault "charges" against enemy implacements was shown in the American experience to be outmoded, given some of the new weaponry available in the Civil War.

Short-Term Causes

The short-term causes of World War I began with the Balkan conflicts of 1908 and 1912 and had much to do with Serbian territorial ambitions. As part of the settlement created at the Berlin Conference of 1878, the Turkish (Ottoman Empire) provinces of Bosnia and Herzegovina had been turned over to the control of the Austrian Empire, though they were to remain part of Turkey. The Kingdom of Serbia had long wanted both provinces, because they would have given Serbia an outlet to the Adriatic Sea. But fearing growing Serbian power, Austria annexed both provinces outright, in violation of the Berlin Treaty. An infuriated Serbia sought Russian intervention, but Russia's humiliating naval defeat at the hands of the Japanese in 1905 kept it out of the picture. However, with Russian support, Serbia, Bulgaria, Montenegro, and Greece formed the Balkan League to take Macedonia from the Ottoman Empire. Secret agreements among league members would have given Albania and large portions of Macedonia to Serbia. In 1912, the League invaded Macedonia and easily defeated the Turks. Again, fearing an enlarged Serbia, during negotiations to end the Balkan War of 1912 Austria was able to force the creation of an independent Albania, which would stand in the way of Serbian ambitions. Anti-Austrian sentiments were now at their peak in Serbia and the rest of the Balkans.

Trigger Causes

On June 28, 1914, a Bosnian radical named Gavrilo Princip assassinated the Austrian Archduke Franz Ferdinand, heir to the Habsburg throne of the Austro-Hungarian Empire, while the latter motored through the streets of Sarajevo. Because Princip was a member of a radical Serbian party known as the Black Hand, the Austrians believed that the assassination was part of a Serbian plot.

The Black Hand and other Serbian agitators wanted to prevent Franz Ferdinand from implementing his plan of "trialism"—dividing the empire again into a third autonomous region (as Hungary had been made years before) consisting of the Balkan provinces. Serbia and Bosnia opposed this plan because they wanted Austria to abandon the Balkans altogether, and they feared autonomy within the empire would have deflated pressures for total withdrawal.

After a delay of nearly a month, the Austrians issued an ultimatum insisting that Serbia act to suppress anti-Austrian activities with their country. When the Serbia refused to accede to the entirety of the Austrian demands, Austria severed diplomatic relations with Serbia and began to mobilize their army.

In the language of diplomacy of that era, the mobilization of troops was an act of war. Serbia understood this well enough—they had mobilized their own troops three hours before sending their reply to the Austrian ultimatum. The timing of these actions was symbolic of how the advanced technology of the day—in this case telegraphic communication—made otherwise serious situations potentially explosive.

The Russians, for instance, knew of the ultimatum the same day Austria issued it—July 23, 1914—since the Serbians were their clients and long-time allies. On July 24, Tsar Nicholas II's advisors had persuaded him to mobilize Russian troops. In response to both Serbia's refusal and Russia's mobilization, Austria declared war on Serbia on July 28.

The response on the part of the other European powers to this explosive situation was not predestined, but the previous emergence of power blocks (such as the Triple Alliance and the Triple Entente) and interlocking treaties of mutual security very strongly influenced how the powers would react. Germany, long-time ally of Austria, was committed, along with Italy, to the security of the Austrian Empire. On July 30, the German government sent its own ultimatum to the Russian foreign minister insisting that the Russian mobilization cease within twelve hours. The Russians refused, and Germany declared war on Russian on August 1.

Since France was Russia's ally and a traditional German enemy, Germany declared war on them on August 3. Britain, a French and Russian ally and also committed to the security of Belgium (across which the Germans would likely invade France), declared war on August 4. Montenegro, allied with Serbia, declared war against Austria and its allies.

A few weeks after this flurry of declarations, Japan declared war on Germany, in part because of its alliance with Britain, and in part to secure German possessions in the Pacific. Italy claimed that since no country had attacked Germany, that Italy had no obligation according to treaty to come to their aid. However, in May, Italy came into the war on the side of the British, French, and Russians.

America's Entry

At the beginning of the war, American sentiment backed neither the British nor the German sides. Traditionally anti-imperialist, many Americans saw the war as an inevitable fight between the Great Powers of Europe as they competed for overseas empires. Woodrow Wilson, the American president, believed that colonial possessions had corrupted the

European powers, and that the war might cleanse them of their evil ways. He called for Americans to be neutral "in both word and deed." Wilson also criticized Europe's entangled alliance system, especially the tendency for treaties to include portions kept secret from the rest of the World. The secret pacts, he believed, had helped to bring on the war.

However, two developments would bring about a transformation in American thinking on the war. The first was Germany's frequent use of submarine warfare, especially against private (non-naval) shipping. As neutrals, the United States claimed the right to ship goods to all sides in the war, but a British blockade effectively cut off trade with the Central Powers (Germany, Austria, and Turkey). The sinking of the British liner *Lusitania* was triply horrifying to Americans— it resulted in the death of 1,195 civilians (over a hundred of which were Americans), it threatened the sanctity of neutral shipping on the high seas, and it used what Americans thought was a barbaric (and sneaky) weapon to attack a civilian vessel without warning. The submarine was, after all, the first of the century's "stealth" weapons. The American outcry against unrestricted submarine warfare caused the Germans to curtail the practice by the summer of 1915.

The second development that helped to break American neutrality was the program of anti-German propaganda created by the British and the French as a means of turning public opinion against the Central Powers and toward the Western Allies (the British and the French). Additional annimosity against Germany came as a result of the so-called Zimmerman Affair—an ill-considered telegram from the German Foreign Minister to the German embassy in Mexico City (intercepted and made public by the British) exploring the idea that Germany might support Mexican efforts to reconquer the American Southwest in exchange for Mexican support of German war objectives (mainly to keep the Americans out of the war). This propaganda portrayed the German people as the descendants of the vicious and barbaric Huns of central Asia, whose medieval invasions of Europe, led by Attila and others, left a lasting and horrifying memory. Propagandists circulated in the American press stories of raped nuns, pitch-forked babies, and other atrocities.

Woodrow Wilson, who had offered to mediate a settlement based on his "Fourteen Points," and who had campaigned in 1916 on the slogan, "he kept us out of war," was now hard-pressed to resist public opinion calling for American entry. The German resumption of unrestricted submarine warfare early in 1914 left the president no choice but to ask Congress for a declaration of war in April of that year. It would be almost a year before large numbers of American troops arrived on the European fronts as the previously-neutral United States mobilized its social, economic, and enormous industrial energies to wage war.

Total War

One important difference between World War I and most previous wars was the degree to which the "homefront" was involved in war and warmaking. Hints of the mobilization of domestic economies and of the involvement of large numbers of civilians in direct contact with the war had come during the American Civil War, which was the world's first real taste of industrialized war.

In Britain, France, Germany, Russia, and the United States, nearly the entire civilian economy had to be reoriented, sometimes forcefully as even in the United States, toward mobilization for war. The scale of the war was so large, and the numbers of those mobilized were so great, that just supplying those in uniform with food and other necessities strained the capacities of the civilian economy to cope. Shortages of basic commodities and foodstuffs were common, as were government-mandated rationing programs.

Owing also to the large number of war casualties (upwards of thirty million dead and wounded on all sides), there were few families not directly touched in sometimes tragic ways by the war. Millions of civilians would suffer directly as shortages, famines, and disease took their toll. As it would turn out, civilian involvement during the First World War was only a taste of the vast suffering that would flood across the Globe during World War II.

Versailles Treaty

One must remember that Germany and the other Central Powers had not been defeated and therefore did not "lose" the war. Instead, the armistice of November 11, 1918 was simply an agreement to stop the fighting and to demobilize. It seems clear in retrospect that with American entry (and industrial support) that the Central Powers could not win a war of attrition. Since Germany had to accept Wilson's "Fourteen Points" before he would accept an armistice agreement, it was clear that Wilson and the Western Allies had Germany "against the wall." Nevertheless, it remained for later treaty negotiations to settle the question of a permanent peace. Since the abdication of the Kaiser and a brief socialist revolution had brought about radical changes in the German government by the time of the armistice, it was not at all clear that Germany would be abused by the coming treaty.

In this project, though, the Germans would be significantly mistreated. The Western Allies would claim that Germany had been the aggressor who had forced war on the otherwise innocent British, Belgians, and French, and now the Allies would punish the Germans for their barbarity. The Versailles Treaty forced Germany to pay reparations—money to cover the damage done by the war. They had to reduce their army and navy to a very small size, and they could have no air force. Under the terms of the Treaty, the League of Nations would parcel out all of Germany's former overseas empire among the other Great Powers through the so-called "mandate" system. The Treaty also stripped away parts of Germany itself to create the new nation-states of Poland and Czechoslovakia.

Another, and perhaps more important aspect of the Treaty of Versailles was the redrawing of the map of Europe, based loosely on Woodrow Wilson's concept of the "self-determination" of nations. Much of central and eastern Europe had been parts of the Austrian, the Russian, or the Turkish empires, and included dozens of national groups such as the Poles, the Czechs, and the Hungarians. As far as practical, the Treaty of Versailles sought to give each of these nationalities their own countries. Poland, Hungary, Bulgaria, and Austria represented independent national groups. The expert geographers advising the Western Allies made compromises and combinations in other cases, such as Czechoslovakia (combining Czechs with Slovaks) and Yugoslavia, combining all the southern (yugo) Slavic nationalities (Serbians, Bosnians, etc.) into a single country.

One aspect of the Treaty of Versailles that held great promise was its provision, forced in by Woodrow Wilson, for a League of Nations, the purpose of which was to provide a means of dealing with international tensions before they became armed conflicts. The League was to provide *collective security* to the nations of the World. Never before had such an international organization been created. Ultimately, neither the Treaty of Versailles nor the League of Nations delivered on their promise. With regard to the Treaty, historians generally agree that it caused far more problems in international relations than it solved. The failure of the American Senate to ratify the treaty meant that the United States would not be a direct participant in the League of Nations, dooming it to irrelevance and ineffectuality.

World War II

Though World War I had frequently been billed as the "war to end all wars," it of course did no such thing. Within the span of a single generation, war would again rage around the World, this time with a deadly intensity such as had not been seen before in world history. Between September, 1939 and August, 1945, the first truly global war would be waged on all the world's continents except Antarctica, and would result in the deaths of at least forty million people.

The war would see new and horrifying forms of "industrialized" killing of civilian populations in the attempted genocide of Jews and others minority groups, and in the liberal use of aerial "firebombing" of German and Japanese cities. The war came to an end only after the use of weapons of truly awsome power—the atomic bombs used on the Japanese cities of Hiroshima and Nagasaki.

Since World War I had ended with such hope for future peace, and since the partial disarmament of many of the world's powers during the interwar years had seemed to at least begin to make good that promise, how had such a brutal war happened again, and so soon?

Causes

Though the relationship between cause and effect is the great "if" in any historical question, the following five causes of World War II seem very sound.

The Failure of the Treaty of Versailles to Keep the Peace. The adoption of the Wilsonian principle of "self-determination," as forward-thinking as it seems, actually increased tensions in Europe when it was not possible to create a separate nation-state for every national minority on the continent. Groupings of nationalities that seemed superficially logical, nevertheless ignored other historical tensions and hatreds, as in Yugoslavia, where Christians and Muslims had long been at odds. Also, giving territory to one nationality in the name of "self-determination" meant taking it from another nation. The inclusion in a re-created Poland of traditional German territories opened wounds that are still fresh.

The Failure of the League of Nations to Contain Nationalistic Aggression. The League was supposed to act to prevent international conflicts from coming to war, and it was to serve as a guarantor of the peace if aggression did erupt. In neither expectation did the League deliver. Instead of acting as an overarching institution of collective security, the League failed to replace the old system of interlocking treaties which agreed, openly or secretly, to delineated "spheres of influence"—the "power politics" approach to international affairs that had led to World War I.

Global Economic Conditions. Though the 1920s was generally a prosperous decade for the Western capitalist powers (in the United States it was called the "Roaring Twenties"), for the Soviets and the Germans it was a decade of hardship and strife. By the beginning of the 1930s, the World's economy virtually collapsed. The investment "bubbles" of the 1920s in the United States brought about a wide-spread deflation and severe reduction in the demand for goods and services all around the World. The result was the Great Depression, the worst economic downturn in modern history. The widespread unemployment and discontent helped to intensify popular discontent.

Charismatic nationalist leaders such as Benito Mussolini and Adolph Hitler used the economic downturn as a means to sway public opinion and to justify huge government expenditures for their armies and navies. Rearmament would employ large numbers of otherwise unemployed workers.

Nationalism. This force had been at work in the history of the world since before the French Revolution. It had played an enormous role in the origins of the First World War. That war, often touted as the "war to end all wars," had done little to diminish nationalism and much to inflame it in the aftermath of the Versailles Treaty.

Nowhere else in the world did nationalism become a factor in national and international affairs more than in Germany, Italy, and Japan. The war, a truly global conflict, was the result of the expansionist policies and actions of Germany under **National Socialism,** of Italy under Fascism, and of Japan under right-wing militarism. In each case, those policies and actions were justified both domestically and internationally in terms of national honor, pride, and destiny.

Appeasement. The experience of World War I and its revolutionary aftermath had made many people around the world understandably reluctant to risk war in the future. Even small and seemingly localized conflicts could get out of control, as they did in 1914. So, when the Germans moved troops into the Rhineland and annexed Austria in the 1930s, both in violation of the Versailles Treaty, none of the European powers took decisive action.

Likewise, though the Italian invasion of Ethiopia brought letters of protest and speeches in the League of Nations condemning Italian aggression, neither the League or the Great Powers took any action to force Italy to withdraw. In the events leading up to the German invasion of Poland in 1939 (discussed below), Britain, France, and the other Western powers (including the United States) gave the aggressor nations a free hand in the hope they would be appeased and satisfied with their gains. From a later historical perspective, appeasement only led to more aggression as the aggressors logically concluded that they could get away with it.

National Socialism

National Socialism is a short term (in English) for the full name of what people commonly call the Nazi Party: the National Socialist German Workers Party. One must take care not to confuse National Socialism with any other party or movement using the word *socialism*. The Nazis were not socialist in any meaningful way, and were actually vigorously opposed to any of the left-wing socialisms of their time. Instead, National Socialism was aggressively right-wing, and it sought to replace liberal and representative democracy with an authoritarian regime governed by a single party: the Nazi Party.

National Socialism was one of the totalitarian regimes that emerged during the twentieth century and that drove much of its history. While such regimes are often nationalist, the Nazis were obsessively so, and pursued both domestic and foreign policies based on the mystical and supposedly superior virtues of the German *folk*.

In many ways, Germany was even riper for popular discontent than Italy. Oppressed by the terms of the Versailles Treaty, and deeply disillusioned by the weaknesses of the Weimar Republic that had replaced the imperial government of the Kaisers, many Germans yearned for a strong leader, a new Kaiser. As in Italy, unemployed veterans of the war formed groups known as *Freikorps* and threatened law and order. The German government was in shambles, and the burdens of reparation payments had ruined the German economy.

In this political turmoil, dozens of political parties vied for power in the fractured Reichstag (parliament). One party, formed with only a few members in 1919, called themselves the *Nationalsozialistische Deutsche Arbeiterpartei* (National Socialist German Worker's Party) or *Nazi* for short. Adolph Hitler, the son of a minor Austrian bureaucrat and recently a corporal in the German Imperial Army, rose quickly in party leadership owing to his charismatic style and his bold ideas.

In 1924 the Nazis staged an aborted coup in the German state of Bavaria. Hitler and other Nazi leaders were briefly imprisoned. While in prison, Hitler wrote (dictated, actually) *Mein Kampf* (My Struggle) in which he clearly laid out the agenda for the Nazi Party. In *Mein Kampf*, Hitler boldly proclaimed most of the characteristic Nazi ideas and beliefs that would drive party policy down to the end in 1945. The most obvious feature of that ideology was an intense racism, the belief in the superiority of the White, Germanic, Aryan, or Nordic "races." This meant that in addition to denigrating peoples of color, Whites not considered by the Nazis to be of their "race" were also denigrated, especially Jews and Slavs (Poles, Russians, etc.).

Nazi racism flowed naturally from their ultra-nationalism. The red and black of the Nazi flag symbolized German *Blut und Boden* (Blood and Soil). Nazism promoted traditional German culture and despised (though made effective use of) what they considered the degraded and decadent modern international culture of which Germany was only a part.

Partly because of their anti-Semitism and anti-Slavism, Nazis were also anti-Marxist, anti-Communist, and anti-Bolshevist. But their fierce opposition to left-wing politics related as well to their rejection of democracy, and an almost mystical attachment to the *Führerprinzip* (Leader Principle). Hitler himself came to be the personal embodiment of this idea, but the Leader Principle extended to the entire Party establishment. Consequently, on coming to power in 1933, the Nazis outlawed other political parties, labor unions, and the free press.

In foreign policy, all this added up to a very aggressive posture. By the time they came to power, Hitler and other Nazi leaders had long promoted the idea that Germany needed more *Lebenraum* ("living space," meaning national territory). According to Nazi propaganda, the Danube Valley of Europe, along with the vast stretches of fertile lands to the east as far as the Ural Mountains was Germany's *Schicksalraum*, or Land of Destiny. That Poles, Czechs, Slovaks, Hungarians, Bulgarians, Ukrainians, and Russians already occupied these lands meant that destiny had to wait upon a campaign of conquest and what the world now calls "ethnic cleansing."

Turning Points

The build-up to war in Europe began only a few years after the Nazis came to full power in Germany in 1934. In 1936, in violation of the Treaty of Versailles, Germany reoccupied the Rhineland with German troops. Technically, this was an act of war, but the Western allies did nothing other than send official letters of protest. In 1937, Nazis in both Germany and Austria brought about the *Anschluss*, the annexation and unification of Germany and Austria. Again, Britain and France did little but issue weak protests. In 1938, Germany occupied the western portion of Czechoslovakia, known as Sudetenland, claiming that the Czech government had mistreated ethnic Germans living in the region.

This encroachment brought about a more vigorous Western response, and English, French, and German leaders held a special conference in Munich in an attempt to settle the crisis. Adolph Hitler assured the Western Allies that the Sudetenland was his last territorial objective in Europe. With that assurance, British Prime Minister Neville Chamberlain and the French Premier Edouard Daladier agreed to the partition of Czechoslovakia as the Germans wished. No one had consulted the Czech government.

In spite of Hitler's assurances, later in 1938 the German army occupied all of Czechoslovakia, effectively dissolving Czech government. It was now clear that appeasing the Germans with concessions would not contain their territorial objectives. But instead of going to war over the Czech situation, the British and the French made assurances to the Polish government that they would counter an invasion by declarations of war against Germany.

The Polish situation had been on the Nazi agenda for some time. The Treaty of Versailles had taken large portions of eastern Germany to create the modern Polish state. There were still many German speakers living in what was now Poland. In their own version of "self-determination," Hitler and other Nazis claimed that all Germans living with Europe should be part of the Germany. In particular, the city of Danzig, situated on the Baltic coast, had been almost entirely German before the Treaty of Versailles "internationalized it so that Poland could have a seaport. "*Danzig ist Deutsch!*" (Danzig is German!) was a frequent rallying cry of the prewar years in Germany.

By 1939, the German army was under orders to plan for an invasion of Poland in the late summer of that year. In the meantime, Nazi officials made superficial efforts for the sake of show to settle differences with the Polish government regarding the treatment of ethnic Germans. Additionally, by the early summer of 1939 the Nazis negotiated a "Non-Aggression Pact" with their otherwise archenemy the Soviet Union. The secret pact called for the partition of Poland—Germany getting the Western half and the Soviet Union the eastern. Germany also gave assurances that it would not oppose Soviet attempts to annex the Baltic countries of Latvia, Lithuania, and Estonia.

The invasion campaign that army planners devised for Poland would introduce a new kind of warfare to world history, one carefully tailored to German economic and military realities. The Polish invasion would be a B*litzkrieg* or "lightning war" in which fast and heavy blows, carefully planned in advance, would bring about the rapid collapse of enemy resistance and quick victory. The Polish campaign would rely heavily on advances in military technology developed since the last war: the dive bomber, fast-moving, heavily armored and heavily-armed tanks, and other mechanized field artillery.

The economic and military realities the *Blitzkrieg* addresses had to do with Germany's geopolitical place in the world. Located in the heart of Europe, Germany had few outlets to international shipping, and few domestic resources in terms of oil, coal, metal ores, or other "strategic" supplies. It could not wage a lengthy war without running out of needed materials. Likewise, though Germany had a significant population, it could not sustain large numbers of military casualties when pressed upon by "encircling" enemies such as Britain, France, and the Soviet Union.

Nazi planners hoped that *Blitzkrieg* would provide one more benefit: a quick victory over Poland would soon be a *fait accompli,* an accomplished fact that British and French opposition could not undo. They gambled that the Western Allies would not go to war over Poland. Given Britain's and France's record of earlier appeasement, this was not an unrealistic assumption.

But the British and the French did declare war, four days after the invasion of Poland began on September 1, 1939. This is the date usually given for the beginning of World War II. In keeping with their guarantees to Poland, Britain and France declared war on Germany on September 3, but to no immediate effect: the Polish surrender came after only three weeks of *Blitzkrieg*. During the fall of 1939 and the winter of 1940 was the *Sitzkrieg* (literally, the "sitting war," but also a play on *Blitzkrieg*) or "Phony War." The Phony War came to an end in April when Germany invaded Denmark and Norway, mostly to gain strategic advantage and to open the Baltic and North Sea to German naval operations.

Hard on the heels of the invasion of Germany's neighbors to the north came their preemptive strike against France on May 10, 1940. Using the same strategy of invasion through Belgium and the Netherlands they had used in 1914, the German army and air force also used the *Blitzkrieg* tactics that had been so effective on Poland. Beginning May 26, both navy and private vessels, some capable of carrying only a few persons, ferried over two-hundred thousand British troops across the English Channel at Dunkirk avoid encirclement and capture. This left France to fight alone. France signed an armistice on June 22 and a pro-German puppet government was set up at Vichy. German forces would occupy northern France until after D-Day. Again, *Blitzkrieg* has been a brilliant success.

In September, Germany, Italy, and Japan signed the Tripartite Pact, creating the so-called "Axis." The Axis powers agreed to mutual support and cooperation. With this alliance in force, the Germans forced the puppet government of France to turn over their Indochinese possessions (Cambodia, Laos, and Vietnam) to the Japanese. Japan now had good supplies of rubber, tin, and rice within their Western Pacific sphere. For the time being, since Japan had not declared war on the British or the Dutch, they were careful to avoid interference with Singapore or Indonesia.

While the Battle of Britain raged on into 1941, Germany consolidated its alliances with Romania, Bulgaria, and Hungary. Italy invaded Greece and Yugoslavia in October, but quickly faltered, necessitating the diversion of German forces in April, 1941 to support the Italian conquest of the Balkans. This would not be the last time that Italian forces proved incapable.

In December, 1940, Hitler ordered plans drawn up for Operation Barbarosa, the invasion of the Soviet Union. After German troops had to be diverted to assist the Italians in North Africa and the Balkans, the Russian campaign was delayed until June of 1941. The American declaration of war on Japan on December 8, 1941, resulted, two days later, in the German and Italian declarations of war on the United States. Though neither the Germans nor the Italians had attacked the United States, the European Axis powers felt compelled to support their Japanese ally. Additionally, though the United States was officially neutral, the Lend-Lease Act of 1941 (allowing the transfer of American war materials to Britain), and other American activities, clearly supported the British side.

With the American entry in the war, the President Franklin Roosevelt and British Prime Minister Winston Churchill met in Washington to discuss a long-term strategy for victory. They decided that the defeat of Germany was more important in the short run than that of Japan. After the defeat of the European Axis powers, the allies could turn their entire attention to Japan. In the meantime, the war in the Pacific would continue since it was largely a naval operation.

American military planners pressed for an invasion against German-held Europe as soon as possible, perhaps even in 1942. The British opposed this, forcefully asserting that the allies were unprepared. In order to launch some kind of strike against the Axis, British and American forces landed in North Africa as part of Operation Torch. By May, 1943, British and American forces had routed both the Italians and the Germans from North Africa. Now the Western Allies turned their attention on striking across the Mediterranean at the "soft underbelly" of Europe—Sicily and Italy.

Combined American and British forces landed on Sicily July 10, 1943. This event led to the arrest of Mussolini on the orders of King Victor Emmanuel II and a new government established under Pietro Badoglio. The Badoglio government quickly offered unconditional surrender to the Allies, and Italy was out of the war. Anticipating Italian surrender, German forces quickly moved to occupy much of Italy, including Rome. Allied invasions at Anzio began in January, 1944, with Rome liberated from German control on June 4, two days before the Allied invasion of Normandy on D-Day

The D-Day invasion of June 6, 1944, Operation Overlord, was the largest amphibious landing in World history, involving more than 5,000 ships and more than 150,000 men. Since the Germans had years to prepare coastal defenses, early Allied loses were high, but after a beach hold was established, a steady stream of men and material resulted in a "breakout," a pushing past fixed German lines. Allied forces, including units of the Free French, liberated Paris on August 25.

With Allied forces approaching the Rhine River border between Germany and France, the Allied commanders were in disagreement about whether they should advance on Germany across a broad front or make a narrower thrust to penetrate German defenses and encircle the enemy. Operation Market Garden, under the command of British General Montgomery, sought to take key bridges across the Rhine and then pour across in large numbers. The plan collapsed when Allied forces were unable to take the needed bridgeheads.

The delay in the advance of Allied troops allowed the Germans to mount one final counter attack in December in Belgium known as the Battle of the Bulge, a kind of Market Garden in reverse. By this time, however, Allied forces were stronger than ever and the Soviet Army had already retaken Poland. The Allies now had Germany caught in the jaws of a vise. Defeat was only a matter of time.

The end came in early spring, 1945. The Soviet Red Army entered Berlin on April 23, and on April 30, Adolph Hitler committed suicide with his just-married wife, Eva Braun. On May 7, Germany surrendered unconditionally to Allied forces. The war in Europe was over.

Pearl Harbor

In pursuing their dream of an "East Asian Co-prosperity Sphere," the Japanese had ridden roughshod over the Koreans, the Manchurians, and the Chinese. American sentiment took a sharp turn against Japan with the Japanese invasion of mainland China in 1937. Though the United States would remain officially neutral, the American president, Franklin Roosevelt, began to pressure the Japanese to back off their expansionist goals. Given Japan's economic dependencies, Roosevelt had a potentially powerful argument to use: Unless the Japanese complied, the Americans could cut off the flow of steel, oil, and other commodities Japan needed.

Japan faced a situation the Germans faced in their strategic planning before the Polish invasion: neither could wage a war of attrition. Victory had to be rapid, decisive, and it had to bring about "accomplished facts" that no one could undo without immense efforts.

Hence, by the middle of 1941, as the Japanese war with China dragged on and as American opposition and economic pressure grew acute, Japan's policy makers decided that they had to eliminate the United States as a rival for power in the Pacific. This would not mean an all-out victory against the United States—even the most nationalist of Japans leaders understood that this was impossible, given America's resources and population. Instead, if Japan could delay or "sidetrack" American response to a planned "blitz"-like campaign of expansion in East Asia, Japan could consolidate its new empire before any other power could do anything about it. If Japanese gains in the Western Pacific and East Asia were significant enough, then the risk of a general war with the United States would be worth it.

Japanese naval planners decided that the best way to cripple any short-term American military opposition would be to destroy as much of the American Pacific Fleet as possible while it was at anchor at Pearl Harbor, Hawaii. This would be accomplished through the use of dive bombers and torpedo bombers launched from Japanese carriers several hundred miles from Hawaii. The attack was planned as an air-only assault—no other naval engagements of any significance were planned.

The attack on Pearl Harbor, when it was actually carried out on December 7, 1941, caught the American Navy completely by surprise. Bombers launched from the Japanese carriers managed to destroy or disable nineteen American ships, including five battleships. Ironically, the Japanese bombers found none of the American carriers at anchor—all were out to sea. For this reason, rather than risk detection and possible destruction, the Japanese carrier fleet withdrew without having launched a follow-up attack that would have finished of the American ships. In terms of the Japanese objective, then, the attack on Pearl Harbor was only partially successful since portions (and, given the new importance of naval air power, the most significant portions) of the American fleet were undamaged.

The Japanese attack on the American fleet at Pearl Harbor initiated a new kind of naval warfare in world history. Instead of great warships firing salvos at each other with cannon and great guns, the decisive naval battles of World War II in the Pacific were air engagements between aircraft carrier fleets that did not even come within visual contact of each other. Pearl Harbor had demonstrated that the older battleships were virtually "sitting ducks" to attack from the air, and that their previous importance in naval warfare was now superceded by the aircraft carrier.

The War in the Pacific

For the first six months of the war, though, the news was all bad for the Americans. Japan scored one victory after another, pursuing in a way a *Blitzkrieg*-like strategy of taking territory and other strategic targets quickly and relying on the fait accompli to hold on. The British Crown Colony of Hong Kong surrendered to the Japanese on Christmas Day, 1941. The British colony of Singapore capitulated on February 15, 1942, and in the final defeat, the combined American and Philipino forces surrendered to Japanese troops on May 6.

In spite of the severe blow suffered at Pearl Harbor, the American navy began to push back against the Japanese juggarnaut with the so-called Doolittle air raids of B-25 bombers launched from American air craft carriers in April, 1942. The Battle of Coral Sea stopped the advance of the Japanese war machine by forcing a Japanese abandonment of their plan to capture Port Moresby in New Guinea. This prevented any serious threat of the invasion of Australia. The Battle of Coral Sea also brought something new to modern warfare. For the first time in history, two fleets battled one another without ever coming within sight. Each launched attacks from aircraft carriers and fought the battle mostly with naval air power. Given the scattered nature of the islands and archipelagos of the Western Pacific, the United States and its allies would adopt a strategy of "island hopping"—taking one island with military or strategic significance and securing it before hopping to another island to do the same thing. Taking a single island on which to build an airstrip might mean command of the air in a radius of several hundred miles. Establishing supply depots, refueling ports, and other facilities while advancing north to the Japanese main islands might sometimes mean leaving isolated Japanese units in the rear to be "mopped up" later.

Somewhat stung with the New Guinea setback, the Japanese navy prepared to attack the Midway Island chain northeast of Hawaii in order to extend their defensive perimeter as far West as possible, and perhaps to draw the American navy into a decisive battle for the Pacific. Unknown in Japan, though, was that the Americans had cracked the Japanese code and knew about their Midway plans in advance.

The Battle of Midway in June, 1942, was a stunning American victory. The Japanese lost four aircraft carriers and the bulk of their experienced pilots. Still weak from the losses at Pearl Harbor, the American Navy nevertheless halted the expansion of Japan's "Co-prosperity Sphere" in the Western and South Pacific. The Americans now settled in for a protracted naval war based on the island hopping strategy. In August, 1942, combined navy and army operation began to loosen the Japanese hold in the Solomon Islands, with the island of Guadalcanal the key to the entire region.

Since Roosevelt and Churchill had decided that the defeat of the Nazis was the first priority of Allied efforts, the war against Japan moved at a slower pace than in Europe. A new Allied push came in June, 1944, with the American and Philipino invasion to liberate the Philippines. Though not strictly of strategic necessity, the retaking of the Philippines was a serious blow to the Japanese war effort.

The American navy now focused its attention on the chains of islands leading directly to the Japanese home islands. With the full-scale production of the B-29 long-range bomber, the strategy was to build airbases on liberated islands from which to launch firebombing raids on Japanese cities and force an end to the Pacific war. The Battles of Guam, Iwo Jima, Tinian, and Okinowa were for this purpose. With most of the Japanese naval offense capacity destroyed, with an American naval blockade to strangle Japan's economic lifeline overseas, and with the firebombing of dozens of Japanese cities, Japan's defeat was just a matter of time by the summer of 1945.

Hiroshima and Nagasaki

No aspect of the American involvement in World War II is as controversial as the use of atomic bombs on these two Japanese cities. That this was the first use of atomic energy for military purposes gives the question special significance. Many also see the number of deaths they brought about as giving the bombs a moral gravity not usually encountered in war. To a certain extent, this is true. But the reader should put the death toll from these two bombs into a larger perspective. In particular, they should be compared with the death toll from the "fire bombing" of both German and Japanese cities in the years and months leading up to August, 1945.

Firebombing was a method of mass bombing meant to create self-sustaining fire storms in their target cities. Instead of ordinary explosives, new materials such a napalm (a gelled form of gasoline) were dropped in massive numbers to set fires on such a large scale that they actually created their own winds as oxygen was drawn in from surrounding areas. These winds would push the firestorms into untouched areas of a city.

First attempted on the German port city of Hamburg in July, 1943, the fire bombing technique worked better than expected. Some 50,000 Hamburg civilians died. The British and American air forces used the firestorm technique on many other German cities, including those such as Dresden, which had no real military significance. It is clear that the strategic purpose of firebombing was to terrorize the population, thus weakening their ability and willingness to sustain the German war effort. Estimates vary, but it is clear that the fire bombings killed hundreds of thousands of German civilians.

When the island hopping-strategy employed in the Pacific had given the Americans possession of islands large enough and close enough to Japan for use as bases for long-range heavy bombers like the B-29, the American air force employed fire bombing on Japanese cities. By 1944, it was clear that World War II was a new kind of war, a war with new horrors. The death toll in the First World War had been great, but it was still mostly from military deaths. During World War II, civilian deaths would far outnumber military ones. This was "total war."

On August 6th, 1945, one atomic bomb utilizing enriched uranium dropped from a single B-29 bomber destroyed the Japanese city of Hiroshima. A second bomb, this time based on plutonium, destroyed Nagasaki on the 9th. Between the two bombs, in an unprecedented move, the Emperor Hirohito forced his government to capitulate. The formal Japanese acceptance of surrender terms came on September 2.

The Holocaust

The Holocaust was the genocide of millions of European Jews, Slavs, Gypsies, homosexuals, and political prisoners as part of the hyper-nationalist policy of Nazi Germany in the early 1940s. Between 1942 and 1945, systematic extermination was carried out in concentration camps in Germany and in Poland. Mostly focused on European Jews, the Holocaust (original dictionary definition: great fire or conflagration) was National Socialism's "final solution" to what would much later be called, "ethnic cleansing," but what the Nazis understood as "eugenics."

Though some commonly use **genocide** as a synonym for mass murder, its use should be limited to the attempted murder of entire identities of people: Jews, Gypsies, or other national or ethnic groups. The scale of such attempts (hundreds of thousands or millions of people) is such that genocide is usually the consequence of a government's policy, even when normal government functions have broken down, as in a civil war. The single most notorious genocidal episode in world history was the Holocaust—the attempted extermination of all the Jews of Europe. Estimates vary, but the government of Nazi Germany may have killed as many as six million persons of Jewish ancestry between 1941 and 1945.

Causes

The longest-term cause of the Holocaust was endemic anti-Semitism in Europe since the Middle Ages. Official anti-Jewish policies began to disappear throughout the nineteenth century, only to see a resurgence of anti-Semitism in the 1890s and beyond. In France, the Dreyfuss Affair brought many of the old hatreds to the surface, and the 1890s saw the birth of modern Zionism—the drive on the part of some Jews to reoccupy and settle in their historic homelands in Palestine.

The 1880s and 1890s also saw the renewal of pogroms (anti-Jewish riots and rampages, often supported by the government) in Russia since many, including the royal family, blamed Jews for the assassination of Tsar Alexander II. The new Tsar, Alexander III, put new restrictions on Russian Jews as a result. Similar pogroms took place in Romania, Poland, and in Ukraine. Historians estimate that by 1924, pogroms had killed some 500,000 eastern European Jews. Violent anti-Jewish sentiment in Europe resulted in a flood of immigration of Polish and Russian Jews into the United States until tight restrictions were imposed by the American Congress in the 1920s.

Added to long-standing European anti-Semitism were the various theories of race and eugenics that pseudo-science had popularized in the decades after the 1859 publication of Darwin's *Origin of Species*. In the pseudo-science of the late nineteenth and early twentieth centuries, Jews were members of a separate race, and a race that possessed certain characteristics and deficiencies. The theory of eugenics claimed that a race could improved by keeping it "pure," and by excluding "degrading" elements. Certainly from the European (and American) perspective, that meant any people of color, and for many Europeans (and some Americans), that meant Jews as well.

The hyper-nationalistic ideology of Nazi "thinkers" considered Jews to be among the most degraded of the "races" of Europe. They were not, however, the only ones so characterized. Nazi ideology also placed the Slavic peoples low on their scale of human evolution. It is clear from Hitler's writings that Russians, Ukrainians, Serbs, Poles, other Slavs, and Gypsies merited ultimate elimination.

Progression

Hitler and the Nazi Party lighted the fires of the Holocaust after they gained full control over the German government in 1934. In that year, using "emergency" powers granted by the German constitution, the Nazis barred Jews from government service, firing civil servants, school teachers, and university professors. Soon to follow were laws that limited the number of Jewish children who could attend public schools.

On May 10, 1934, the infamous book burning events staged around Germany destroyed books written by Jewish authors. Later that year, German schools were required to teach that "non-Aryans" were inferior to "Aryans," and Jewish children were prohibited from participating in "Aryan" sports clubs, school orchestras, and they were banned from playgrounds, swimming pools, and parks.

The Nuremberg Laws, announced by Hitler at the Nuremberg Party Rally in 1935, deprived all Jews of their civil rights, and the "Law for the Protection of German Blood and German Honor" made marriages and extra-marital sexual relationships between Jews and Germans punishable by imprisonment. Earlier that year, decrees banned Jews from service in the German armed forces.

In 1936, the German Ministry of Science and Education prohibited teaching by "non-Aryans" in public schools and even banned private instruction by Jewish teachers. Later that year, the government required Jews to carry identification cards.

In 1938, in supposed reprisal for the attempted assassination of a German diplomat in Paris by a Polish Jew, on the night of November 9 and 10, Nazis launched coordinated pogroms all over Germany that resulted in the burning of hundreds of synagogues; the looting and destruction of many Jewish homes, schools, the looting of 7,500 Jewish stores, and many other sorts of violent vandalism. The world now knows this night as *Kristallnacht*, the "Night of Broken Glass." Many Jews were beaten, and Nazi mobs killed more than ninety. Authorities arrested more than thirty-thousand Jewish men and sent them to concentration camps.

Over the next four weeks, official actions against German Jews came in a torrent. A few days after *Kristallnacht*, the government ordered German Jews to pay one billion Reich marks in reparations for damages of that evening of destruction.

On November 15, officials issued orders to expel all Jewish children from German public schools. On December 2, decrees banned Jews from public streets on certain days and forbade them from driving automobiles. On December 3, decrees ordered Jews to sell their businesses, real estate, and other valuable property to the government at very low prices.

After the outbreak of World War II on September 1st, 1939, the progress of the Holocaust picked up speed. By the time of Poland's capitulation later in September, Jews in Germany were required to turn in radios and cameras to local police. They also received fewer ration coupons than other Germans, and none at all for milk or meat. In Poland, the German occupiers forced Jews to wear a yellow Star of David on their chests or a blue-and-white Star of David armband. At the end of November, the first ghetto (enclosed section of a city) of Polish Jews was established.

In May, 1940, 164,000 Polish Jews were concentrated and imprisoned in the Lódz ghetto. That same month, the concentration camp at Auschwitz, Poland, took in its first prisoners. By November, the Warsaw ghetto had been closed off with more than a half million Jewish inhabitants.

In the meantime, in occupied France, the puppet government at Vichy passed a number of anti-Jewish laws and Romania, now an Axis ally along with Hungary and Slovakia, passed a law condemning adult Jews to forced labor. The pro-Nazi government would later take similar action in Hungary. Hatred of Jews was not unique to the Nazis or even the Germans, and other Europeans and Americans bear some responsibility for the Holocaust.

In June of 1941, Germany violated its "non-aggression" pact with the Soviet Union by invading in the largest land forces operation in history. From Hitler's and other Nazi writings, it was clear that the Soviet Union was the objective all along. It was less clear what would become of its people in the Nazi geopolitical scheme of things.

Clarity on that point came in the wake of the advancing German army as "special operations" units (*Einsatzgruppen*) of the elite Nazi SS army cleared towns and village of their population. The SS took special care to exterminate Jews, Gypsies, and Soviet officials, but the death squads killed many others as well.

The *Einsatzgruppen* were the first to experiment with "efficient" methods of mass murder. Throughout the summer and fall of 1941, they used the "trench and machine gun" method: groups of victims as many as two or three hundred at a time—men, women, and children—were lined along the edge of a trench that had been bulldozed to a depth of five or six feet and then sprayed with machine gun fire. Those shot would fall back into the trench. After all had been shot (though not necessarily killed), the trench was then bulldozed over, burying the victims. Reliable statistics do not exist on how many died this way. Official Soviet sources would claim as many as one million, and this figure may be close to accurate.

The problems encountered with Germany's early experiments with mass extermination led to an effort to find what Nazi planners would come to call the "final solution." To this end, some fifteen legal, logistic, and military experts— all hardcore Nazis—met in Wannsee, a suburb of Berlin, in January, 1942.

Adolph Eichmann, a colonel in the SS and aid to General Reinhard Heydrich, head of the Gestapo, prepared the minutes for this meeting. Historians now know Eichmann's minutes as the "Wannsee Protocol." Allied prosecutors used the protocol as key evidence at the Nuremburg War Crimes trials after the war.

Discussion at the meeting, which lasted only eighty-five minutes, focused on the expulsion of Jews from "every sphere of life of the German people and the expulsion of the Jews from the living space of the German people." The main logistical assumption of those present was that German Jews and the Jews in occupied countries and in other Axis allies would be collected and sent to labor camps in occupied Poland and the Soviet Union.

This would provide a large and skilled labor pool to aid the German war effort, and it would also ultimately eliminate a large number by "natural causes" (starvation and disease). The "final remnant will... have to be *treated accordingly* [emphasis added], because it... would, if released, act as the *seed of a new Jewish revival*" [emphasis added]. According to Eichmann's testimony at his Israeli trial in 1959, in preparing the protocol, he used euphemisms such as "treated accordingly" when the actual discussion dealt with various means of extermination such as mass firing squads and gas chambers.

According to their best statistical sources, Germany and their allies had to eliminate roughly eleven million Jews then thought to be still living in Europe. Always methodical and careful with detail, the Wannsee conferees considered issues such as the age and country of origin of those to be "evacuated." They also carefully discussed how people with "mixed blood" were to be treated.

After the Wannsee conference, Nazi planners gave the tentative and experimental measures taken so far firmer and more vigorous direction. Death camps located in occupied Poland at Auschwitz, Birkenau, Treblinka, Sobibor, Belzec, and Majdanek-Lublin begin mass murder of Jews in gas chambers. Nazi officials had determined that the firing squad methods were too inefficient and wasted ammunition needed for the war effort.

They also found that the squads took too great a psychological toll on the soldiers doing the shooting. Additional problems such as the contamination of ground water from decaying corpses added weight to the Nazi decision to employ gas chambers and crematoria in efficient death camps.

In order to forestall panic, SS guards took prisoners not suitable for use on labor projects directly from railroad cars to gas chambers disguised to look like showers and delousing stations. Guards ordered the victims to undress and, after other Jewish prisoners had collected clothing and other possessions, the airtight doors of the chambers were sealed and they were flooded with a gaseous insecticide known as Zyklon B.

At the most efficient camps, several thousand victims could be "processed" in a day. The operation of the death camps in Germany and Poland continued until April, 1945. Soviet troops liberated the Majdanek camp in Poland in July, 1944, and as the Red Army pushed west they liberated more camps, including the vast labor and death camp complex at Auschwitz-Birkenau in Poland.

For those not to be immediately exterminated, life was hellish, to say the least. In addition to the constant abuse inflicted by German SS guards conditioned to look upon Jews and other prisoners as "sub-human," prisoners were severely underfed and overworked. More horrific still, Nazi physicians such as Josef Mengele conducted all sorts of experiments on inmates in the interest of "science."

Mengele's experiments included placing subjects in extreme high- or low-pressure chambers, testing various drugs and lethal poisons on them, subjecting them to long periods in either ice water or extremely hot water, and many other fatal traumas. In addition to experiments having at least some faint connection with medical science, some were merely sadistic or frivolous, including attempts to change eye color by injecting chemicals into the eyes of children and other brutal surgeries.

The Cold War

After the end of World War Two, significant tensions developed between the former allies who had defeated the Axis powers of Germany, Italy, and Japan. The Soviet Union, perceived by the Western allies (dominated by the United States and Britain) to be opportunistically and aggressively expansionist, believed that the West had sought their destruction (or weakening) during the war by delaying the opening of a western front against Nazi Germany, essentially allowing the Germans to destroy as much of the USSR as possible before being pushed back and defeated. In the end, neither perception was accurate, though both were plausible.

After the American use of the atomic bombs in Japan, the Soviets were even more wary of western objectives since the Western Allies had neither informed them nor included them in the Manhattan project. Some historians have concluded that the last shots of World War Two (the two bombs on Hiroshima and Nagasaki) were also the first "shots" of the Cold War, so-called because no actual fighting between the Soviets and the western allies actually took place.

Causes

The most significant causes of the Cold War between the United States and its allies and the Soviet Union were ideological incompatibility and mutual distrust. The United States and the rest of the industrial capitalist World were not happy when Communists took power in Russia after the April Revolution of 1917. The United States did not even recognize the formation of the Union of Soviet Socialist Republics (completed in 1922) until 1933.

From the American perspective, the Soviet Union was a new Russian autocracy dominated by a "godless" ideology and ruled by a ruthless dictator: Joseph Stalin. From the Soviet perspective, the Americans and the other Western capitalists were unscrupulous imperialists who sought to rob the world and its workers of their just desserts—the capitalist attachment to "democracy" was a sham and a smoke screen, or so the Communists thought.

Against this background of distrust came World War II, with its unlikely though necessary alliance between Western capitalists and Soviet communists. By the end of the war, Stalin and other Soviets had come to believe that the Western Allies had given the Nazis a free hand on the Eastern Front in order to weaken the Soviets, thereby setting the stage for a postwar world completely dominated by capitalism.

For their part, by the end of the war the Americans and the British believed that the Soviets had taken advantage of their successful "liberation" of Eastern Europe as they pushed the Germans further and further west to expand the influence and dominance of Soviet Communism. After all, no one had forgotten the Non-Aggression Pact that Stalin had made with Hitler in 1939, thus giving Germany a free hand in western Poland in exchange for the Soviet possession of the three Baltic states and eastern Poland.

Progression

Specific grievances that led to growing conflict began shortly after the end of the war in Europe. At the Yalta Conference in February, 1945, and again at the Potsdam Conference in July of that year, Stalin had agreed that there would be free and open elections for new governments in those countries that had been occupied by the Germany but that had now been "liberated" by the Soviet Red Army—Poland, Czechoslovakia, Romania, Bulgaria, Hungary, and parts of Austria.

By the fall of 1945, it seemed clear that the Soviets had reneged on this promise and had staged rigged elections putting communist puppets in power in those countries. By 1946, the Soviets had come to so dominate eastern Europe that Winston Churchill, the British Prime Minister during the war, said that an "iron curtain had descended across Europe."

Tensions would be further heightened as the four allied powers—Britain, France, the Soviet Union, and the United States—continued to occupy and administer Germany and its capital, Berlin. Each of the victorious powers had its zone of occupation in Germany as a whole, and each had a separate portion of Berlin, otherwise wholly enclosed within the Soviet zone. The Soviets were to allow the other allies free and open access to Berlin. By the middle of 1946, the four-power agreement began to fall apart.

By 1948, the three western powers had agreed to unify their zones under one government and to support the industrial and economic recovery of that part of Germany. The Soviet Union held onto to its portion in the East. In retaliation for British, French, and American unification in western Germany, the Soviets closed off access to Berlin.

For fifteen months, the western allies flew in food, fuel, and other supplies to keep the non-Soviet portion of the city going. By this time, it was very clear: the Soviet Union and the American-dominated allies were virtual enemies. All that was missing was the "heat" of armed conflict.

From the Western perspective, the Soviet Union was using the late war and its decisive victory against the Nazis in the East to install one compliant "puppet" regime after another and thus expand both its strategic and ideological reach further into Europe's heartlands. Though the Soviets had agreed during the war to open and fair elections in those countries it occupied after the war, most of the elections were rigged or heavily influenced by the Soviet presence. To the extent that there were elements within Poland, Hungary, and other occupied countries in Eastern Europe that resisted Soviet domination, American and other Allied sentiment favored their support.

Made public in a speech before Congress in 1947, the Truman Doctrine declared that the United States would help "free peoples" resist communist infiltration or aggression. He was referring specifically to the situation in Greece and Turkey, but he and subsequent American presidents applied the policy until the end of the Cold War.

The Truman Doctrine was just one aspect of a larger American and Allied anti-Soviet and anti-Communist policy that would come to be known as "containment"—keep the Soviets from expanding beyond territory they already dominated at the end of the war in Europe.

An important aspect of this containment policy was the necessity of propping up anti-Communist governments in Western Europe, and this meant helping them to rebuild their economies after the devastation of the war. Weak economies meant strong communist movements, or so the common analysis of the times concluded. The so-called Marshall Plan would pour billions of American dollars into the rebuilding of the French, German, Italian, and other European economies. The American government also offered funding to the Soviet Union, but it refused.

The Marshall Plan, named after George C. Marshall, the American Secretary of State who proposed it, has often been called a selfless act on the part of the Americans, but its main purpose was to support pro-American governments in the West. So important was the rebuilding of Western Europe that President Harry Truman considered the Truman Doctrine and the Marshall Plan "two halves of the same walnut."

After the end of World War II, the long Chinese civil war between the so-called Chinese Nationalists and the Chinese Communists flared up again. In 1949, Communist forces pushed the Nationalists off the mainland and onto the island of Taiwan, and the communists declared a new Chinese government with Mao Zedong as its leader.

Though the connection between the Chinese communists and the Soviet regime in Moscow was only theoretical and for historical reasons weak, the "loss of China" looked like a victory for what many thought was an international communist conspiracy to take over the world. In the United States, it touched off a "Red Scare" that led to McCarthyism and other abuses of civil rights.

Further evidence of communist expansionism came when the Soviet satellite North Korea attacked South Korea in April, 1950 in a move to reunify Korea under communist rule. It was clear that the Americans had established a compliant and pro-Western regime in South Korea just as it and its allies had in West Germany. Later that year, the Chinese came into the conflict on the North Korean side, in part to support the communist regime in North Korea and in part to divert American attention away from the support of the Chinese "Nationalists" on Taiwan. Contained in Europe, it now looked as if communism was on the march in East Asia.

American led forces authorized by the United Nations fought to keep the North Koreans north of the thirty-eighth parallel line established at the end of World War II between the Soviet and American occupation zones on the Korean peninsula. Both American and United Nations policy was limited to this objective and did not include the defeat of either North Korea or China. Korea, then, represented the first of a new kind of war—a limited war, with narrowly-prescribed objectives in an attempt to prevent escalation. Behind this policy, of course, was the fear of touching off another general World War.

The other new element was the successful creation by the Russians of their own atomic bombs. If the Korean "police action" (as the American President Truman preferred to call it) got out of hand, it might lead to an atomic war with the Soviet Union. So when the American five-star general Douglas Macarthur tried to overstep the bounds placed on him by civilian authority, Truman dismissed him from command.

The threat of atomic and nuclear war would hang like a Sword of Damocles over the entire World for the remainder of the Cold War. Clearly, there was a new arms race in the running, and as if the earlier weapons were not fearsome enough, the new ones were positively apocalyptic. In 1953, the United States successfully tested a new kind of bomb based on the nuclear process of fusion (instead of the atomic process of fission used in the bombs dropped on Japan).

Also by the end of the decade of the fifties, both sides had developed reliable missiles that could deliver these super bombs halfway around the globe, actually entering space before dropping back to Earth on ballistic trajectories. By 1960, the old protective safety of two oceans (for the Americans) and of vast continental land masses (for the Soviets) had disappeared. No place was now safe from attack, and both Europe and East Asia were as likely to be targets as any other region. Adding to these new nuclear tensions was the development of H-bombs by the British, the French, and the Chinese.

In 1953, the Soviet dictator Joseph Stalin died. Over the next few years, the other senior leaders of the USSR jockeyed for position for the premiership. By 1956, the Soviet Communist Party had revised and reformed the system that Stalin had built up after he came to power upon the death of Lenin in 1924. One important feature of the new Soviet system was it distributed power into more hands than during Stalin's dictatorship. Never again would the Soviets suffer the power of an absolute ruler like Stalin.

That same year, a clear leader emerged in the person of Nikita Khrushchev, a short, sometimes bellicose, sometimes jolly survivor of Stalin's regime. He came to the leadership of the Communist Party in part by repudiating Stalin's brutality and other excesses. And, also unlike Stalin, he believed that an accommodation not only could be made with the Western capitalists, one had to be made to ensure the survival of Russia's "communist revolution."

In spite of a significant change in the Soviet regime, tension remained high in Europe. Khrushchev had to deal with hard-liners in his government who wanted to push harder for Soviet objectives. So, in 1956, when an anti-Soviet regime came to power in Hungary, Khrushchev sent in the Soviet army to put down the revolt. Hard liners pushed to suppress a similar movement in Czechoslovakia some years later.

Cold war tensions in Europe found no greater source than the ongoing conflicts over the continued division of Germany and of Berlin. In 1961, in response to an ongoing "brain drain" from East Germany and East Berlin, the Soviet-backed East German government erected barbed-wire fences along the dividing line between East and West Berlin. The government later built permanent concrete walls to replace the barbed wire.

In addition to the specific hardships this created for Berliners, to Americans and other Westerners, this was totalitarianism near its worst. In response, American President Kennedy increased the number of troops in Berlin, and American tanks faced Soviet tanks across the barbed wire at the Brandenburg Gate in Berlin. But neither the Americans nor the Soviets were willing to risk war over Berlin, so the situation remained a standoff.

1962 was also a bad year for the Cold War in the Western Hemisphere. American spy planes discovered in Cuba that Soviet technicians were in the process of installing medium range ballistic missile capable of carrying H-bomb warheads to two-thirds of the major cities in North and South America.

The Soviets were in Cuba to prop-up the pro-Soviet and anti-American regime established by Fidel Castro in 1959 after his successful revolution against the pro-American President Fulgencio Batista. Since declaring himself a communist, the presidential administrations of Eisenhower and Kennedy were intent on deposing Castro. The aborted invasion of an army composed of American-trained Cuban exiles at the Bay of Pigs in April, 1961, was open evidence of the American distaste for a pro-Soviet government ninety miles from Florida.

In large part, the Soviets installed missiles in Cuba to counter the American presence in Turkey and other NATO member countries that were just as close. After the Americans surrounded Cuba with a naval "quarantine," Khrushchev agreed to withdraw the missiles. But until that agreement, both sides were on full alert, and many around the world thought that nuclear war was imminent. Direct participants and historians alike agree that the Cuban Missile Crisis was as close as the world ever came to nuclear war.

After the Cuban crisis, both American and Soviet negotiators took the opportunity to back off a little from their hardline positions. To keep the lines of communication open, both governments installed a direct telephone line between the American White House and the Soviet Kremlin. In 1963, the Soviet Union, the United States, and a few dozen other nations signed the Nuclear Test Ban Treaty to halt testing of nuclear bombs in the open atmosphere.

In 1964, in a shake up of Soviet leadership, hard liners removed Khrushchev as premier and replaced him with a protégé, Leonid Brezhnev. Brezhnev would come to take a harder line than Khrushchev, and in some ways would roll back Khrushchev-era reforms. In 1968, Brezhnev sent Warsaw Pact troops and tanks into Czechoslovakia to put down an anti-Soviet movement under the Czech leader Alexander Dubchek known as the "Prague Spring." In spite of his hard line, Brezhnev was skilled in negotiations with Western powers since his personal style was more muted and less prone to bombast than Khrushchev's, though, like Khrushchev, he saw the need to get along with the Western powers.

A new era in the Cold War began in 1972 after the normalization of relations between the United States and China that followed President Richard Nixon's Chinese visit. In spite of sharing the Marxist ideology of communism, relations between China and the Soviet Union had never been very good, and since the late 1950s had been in sharp decline. By the early 1970s, war was as likely between the two as between either of them and the United States.

Nixon's masterstroke of diplomacy (with the advice of his National Security Advisor, Dr. Henry Kissinger) was in playing China off against the Soviet Union. By thawing relations with China, he forced the Soviets to seek a similar thawing in their relations with the United States. The result has come to be known as *détente*—the French word for "relaxation." Out of the era of détente came the SALT I (Strategic Arms Limitation Talks) and SALT II agreements, the ABM (Anti-Ballistic Missile) Treaty, and a general accommodation of interests. Trade also became more open between the three powerful nations.

Détente came to an end with the Soviet invasion of Afghanistan in 1979. Widely (though privately) criticized within the upper-Soviet leadership, Brezhnev decided to support the pro-Soviet regime of Nur Muhammad Taraki, premier of the Democratic Republic of Afghanistan. Anti-Soviet and pro-Islamic insurgents such as the *Mujahideen* fought Soviet forces, often with surprising success, with American-supplied weapons and advice.

The Cold War tables were now turned: the Soviets had supplied North Vietnamese and Vietcong insurgents against American forces, and now Americans were supporting the Mujahideen against the Soviets. After the death of Brezhnev and the coming of *Perestroika*, Michel Gorbachev withdrew Soviet troops from Afghanistan in 1989. The power vacuum they left behind ultimately resulted in the coming to power of the radical Islamic regime of the Taliban.

In other ways, the Soviet Bloc in Europe was coming apart. In 1980 a Polish dock worker named Lech Walesa organized an anti-communist and ant-Soviet trade union called Solidarity. By the end of 1981, the union had nine million members and included Catholics, workers, intellectuals, and others demanding a more open and democratic Poland, one free of Soviet domination. In December of that year, the Polish government moved to suppress Solidarity and briefly imprisoned its leaders. After that, the movement moved underground and continued to contribute to a climate of anti-communist and anti-Soviet sentiment in the Eastern Bloc.

Perestroika

By the middle of the 1980s, the Soviet Union experienced serious economic and political difficulties. Historians and other commentators have often compared the Soviet Union's long war against insurgents in Afghanistan with the American experience in Vietnam—the wrong war at the wrong time. At the same time, pressure from the hard-line presidential administration of Ronald Reagan (1981-1989) kept Soviet military spending at a higher rate than their otherwise weak economy could bear. The old adage that you can have "gun" or "butter" but not "guns and butter" held true for the Soviet Union in the 1980s, and increasing public discontent applied other pressures, this time within the USSR, for reform.

Fortuitously, in 1985 a new General Secretary and President of the Soviet Union, Michel Gorbachev, came to power with a program for what he called *Perestroika* (reform) and for *Glasnost* (openness). *Perestroika* had to do mainly with the centralized Soviet state system with its poorly-run and inefficient "command economy." By the time of the Soviet breakup in 1991, a new "union treaty" had been negotiated between the separate Soviet republics, more or less giving them greater autonomy within the USSR. Had the Soviet Union not come apart at it did, this new autonomy would probably have resulted in multi-party government and in the introduction of market-oriented economic reforms.

Glasnost had more to do with the relationship between the Soviet people and the Soviet government. Though much had changed since Stalin's death, the Soviet Union still tended toward the same kind of police-state totalitarianism that suppressed dissent, curtailed free expression of ideas, and limited the free movement of it people. Though always something of a vague "buzzword," Glasnost would come to symbolize a willingness on the part of the Soviet leadership to listen to and tolerate dissent and expression of political points of view.

Though not without internal opposition from hardliners, Gorbachev had a great deal of support from the Soviet people and from world opinion. In spite of the hard line of the American President Ronald Reagan, a new openness seemed to be in the making between the two Superpowers as well.

It is not clear whether or not *Perestroika* and *Glasnost* in the Soviet Union helped to create similar developments in the other countries of the Warsaw Pact, or that the movements in the Soviet Union were reflections of larger movements in Eastern Europe. In 1988, the communist regime in Poland restored the Solidarity movement to legal status.

In Germany, a reunification movement among students and intellectuals proved successful in 1989. The pro-Soviet communist government of the German Democratic Republic ("East Germany") seemed powerless to put down the movement. After more than twenty-eight years, jubilantly successful activists and students tore down the Berlin Wall. Similar developments took place in Czechoslovakia, Hungary, and Romania.

In the Soviet Union, an important turning point was Gorbachev's 1988 call for multi-party elections for the members of a new legislature, the Congress of People's Deputies. The elections duly took place in the spring of 1989 and they resulted in defeats for a number of many Communist Party officials and victories for candidate who had openly criticized Communist-Party leadership.

Among these critics was Boris Yeltsin, still formally a member of the Central Committee of the Communist Party, but otherwise an outspoken critic of party policy. As a result of these elections, it was clear that Glasnost had become Western-style freedom of speech and freedom of the press. Eager Soviet readers now purchase books long prohibited under the old regime. While an astounded World watched, the Soviet Union was becoming an open, participatory democracy.

Collapse of the USSR

But Glasnost and *Perestroika* did not necessarily mean the end of the Union of Soviet Socialist Republics. It did not even mean an end to Marxism in the Soviet Union. Gorbachev continued to maintain that he was a committed Marxist, and he argued that the Soviet Union should remain communist in its essence. It might add certain aspects of free-market capitalism, but not in such a way as to destroy the objectives of the "Revolution."

In this regard, the Soviets had plenty of examples even in Western Europe of mixed political economies, where capitalism blended easily with various sorts of socialism. To a certain extent, by the end of the twentieth century, every capitalist country had some elements of socialism deeply entwined with the "free market," even in the United States (though less in the United States than in Europe). Collectively, these socialistic elements are sometimes known as "welfare capitalism" and include government-sponsored health care, unemployment and disability compensation, protection for labor union activities, and even a certain degree of national state ownership of key industries—all overlying the so-called free-market capitalist economy. Some historians have suggested that this blending of capitalism with elements of socialism "saved" capitalism from revolution in the West by minimizing public discontent with the harshness of the pure *laissez faire* capitalism.

The trouble in the Soviet Union was that the economy was in deep trouble. Massive expenditures for military build-up forced through by hardliners in response to the Reagan-era hard line in the United States, had crippled the Soviet economy. At the same time, the "command economy" structures of centralized planning and control were becoming increasingly ineffective. Constant and sometimes acute shortages of basic necessities plagued the Soviet people, and this added to a deep-seated sense of discontent.

Accompanying all this political and economic movement was an associated rise in nationalism among the diverse peoples of Soviet Union and its satellite countries of Eastern Europe. Germans, Poles, Czechs, Slovaks, Estonians, Lithuanians, Latvians, Ukrainians, Byelorussians, Georgians, Serbians, Bulgarians, Chechnyans, and literally dozens of other nationalities began to press for either autonomy within the Soviet system or outright independence.

The final breakup of the Soviet Union came in 1991. Open elections had made Boris Yeltsin the Chairman of the Russian Supreme Soviet (the highest legislative body of the Russian Soviet Socialist Republic (R.S.S.R.—the largest of the "states" within the Soviet Union). In that role, he led a movement that demanded more Russian autonomy within the Soviet federal system. In June, 1991, Yeltsin became President of the R.S.S.R. and now demanded full Russian independence.

In order to keep the U.S.S.R. together, President Gorbachev negotiated a new "Union Treaty" or constitution that would redefine the relationship between the government of the Soviet Union and its constituent republics, one of which was Russia. The new Union would be a much looser confederation than the old centralized U.S.S.R.

On the day before the new Union Treaty was to be signed into effect, conservative hard-line Communists still in powerful positions in the Soviet government stage a coup d'etat against Gorbachev and his supporters. On August 18, the conspirators placed Gorbachev under house arrest in his vacation home in Crimea and they ordered units of the Soviet Army to move on key positions in Moscow and other cities.

This time, in defense of Gorbachev and the Union, Yeltsin rallied his supporters and dramatically faced-down Soviet tanks. In confusion and disarray, and genuinely impressed by both Gorbachev's and Yeltsin's popular support, the hardline leaders of the coup withdrew Soviet troops and returned power to Gorbachev on August 22.

Now, with enormous prestige and public support, Yeltsin abandoned his support for the new Union Treaty and pushed for full independence for Russia. Having more than two-thirds of the land area and population of the Soviet Union, a U.S.S.R. without Russia was not possible. At the same time, the other Soviet Republics, most notably Ukraine and Georgia, were pressing for independence as well.

In the months after the August coup attempt, the Soviet Union literally fell apart, with one republic after another either declaring or just acting as if they were independent. In a televised speech on Christmas Day, 1991, Gorbachev announced his resignation as President and the dissolution of the Soviet Union. That same day, the red "Hammer and Sickle" flag of the Soviet Union came down for the last time over the Kremlin in Moscow, and the Union of Soviet Socialist Republics was formally at an end.

Rise of International Organizations

The twentieth century saw a new thing in world history: "total war," the kind of warfare that involved entire national populations and that killed tens of millions, both soldier and civilian. Never before had war reached the scale it did in that century, the enormity of which had as much to do with technology as it had ideology or passionate national ambition. War had become such a dreadful enterprise that new institutions emerged to provide for "collective security" against aggression.

To a limited degree, collective security was the object of earlier systems of "mutual-defense" treaties that countries entered into against traditional enemies. The so-called Concert of Europe created at the Vienna Congress of 1815 was such a treaty system. The French Revolution and subsequent predations of Napoleon had turned Europe upside down, and the Great Powers would not allow such a thing ever to happen again. But the Concert created a system that relied upon individual treaties between traditional friends against traditional enemies, with sufficient overlap such that an attack against one country would bring on retaliation by several others.

It could be argued that the system worked, more or less, for the remainder of the nineteenth century. But because the Congress of Vienna did not create any overarching institution that would provide universal and concerted opposition to aggression, it failed to provide sustainable collective security. It indeed seems clear that the interlocking treaty system ultimately helped to bring on World War I.

After that war, proposed by Woodrow Wilson of the United States, and supported by vigorous public opinion around the World, the first institutional attempt at global collective security, the League of Nations, came into being in 1919.

The League of Nations

The League of Nations found its roots in the negotiations of the Paris Peace Conference in 1919. At the urging (and ultimately, the insistence) of the American President Woodrow Wilson, the Conference designed the League to promote international disarmament, provide "collective security" to each of the World's nations, settle disputes between those nations in the open forum of the league through negotiation and diplomacy, and in other ways promote global welfare.

On paper, the League was a "government of governments," and thus a departure from the old Concert of Europe approach which relied on the Great Powers and their shifting alliances to maintain a balance of power and along with it, peace. But in practice, since the League lacked an armed force of its own, it still depended on the voluntary cooperation of the Great Powers. Without the independent power to enforce its resolutions, the League could have little effect on the course of world history.

After a number of notable successes and some early failures, the League ultimately proved incapable of preventing aggression by the fascist Axis Powers in the 1930s. The onset of the Second World War made it clear that the League had failed in its primary purpose—to avoid any future World war. The United Nations effectively replaced it after World War II and inherited a number of agencies and organizations founded by the League.

One important flaw—some would say fatal—was the failure of the United States to ratify the Covenant (treaty) of the League of Nations. Though there was widespread majority support for the League in America, ratification required a two-thirds majority in the U.S. Senate. The final vote fell short by four senators, known ever since as the "irreconcilables." Without American participation and support, even the power of the League to impose trade sanctions meant very little since the United States was by then the greatest exporter and importer of goods on the world market and paid little heed to League resolutions.

United Nations

The Victorious Western Allies founded the United Nation on the failed ruins of the League of Nations. The founders of the UN had high hopes that it would act to prevent conflicts between nations and make future wars impossible, by fostering an ideal of collective security. The 1945 UN Charter envisaged a system of regulation that would ensure "the least diversion for armaments of the World's human and economic resources."

The UN Charter obliges all member nations to promote "universal respect for, and observance of, human rights" and to take "joint and separate action" to that end. The General Assembly adopted the "Universal Declaration of Human Rights" in 1948 and, though it is not legally binding, serves as a common standard of achievement for all.

Under Security Council resolutions, UN peacekeepers go to various regions where armed conflict has recently ceased, in order to enforce the terms of peace agreements and to discourage the combatants from resuming hostilities. Member states provide these forces since, like the League of Nations, the UN has no armed forces of its own.

UN General Assembly, UN Security Council, UN Economic and Social Council, UN Secretariat, International Court of Justice: Of these divisions within the United Nations, the Security Council holds the real power. There are five permanent members of the Council, each with the power the veto any resolution or action taken by the entire Council: China, France, Russia, the United Kingdom, and the United States. Under the Nuclear Non-Proliferation Treaty, these are the only members of the UN permitted to possess nuclear weapons, although it seems clear that others do as well. The General Assembly elects ten other nations every two years to serve as rotating members of the Security Council.

NATO and Warsaw Pact

Established by the North Atlantic Treaty signed into effect in April, 1949, the purpose of North Atlantic Treaty Organization (NATO) is no more clearly expressed than in the following passage from Article V of the treaty:

> "The Parties agree that an armed attack against one or more of them in Europe or North America shall be considered an attack against them all. Consequently they agree that, if such an armed attack occurs, each of them, in exercise of the right of individual or collective self-defense recognized by Article 51 of the Charter of the United Nations, will assist the Party or Parties so attacked by taking forthwith, individually and in concert with the other Parties, such action as it deems necessary, including the use of armed force, to restore and maintain the security of the North Atlantic area."

The drafters of the Treaty assumed the armed attack referred to in the treaty would come from the Soviet Union and its allies, but, perhaps in part because of NATO, no such attack ever came. For the only time in its history, though, a NATO member, the United States, invoked Article V on September 12, 2001, the day after the terrorist attacks on Washington and New York on September 11.

The original member nations of NATO were the United States and the countries of Western Europe. During the 1950s, Greece, Turkey, and West Germany joined the organization, and since the end of the Cold War, eleven other nations became NATO members. Most of these had been members of the Soviet-dominated Warsaw Pact (see below).

Though it has several political functions and agencies, NATO is essentially a military alliance and maintains a joint command structure with American officers dominating the upper-command levels. The "Supreme Allied Commander Europe," for instance, has always been an American. The NATO agreements also have allowed the United States to establish military bases within the borders of member nations. The United States does not similarly "host" the bases of other member countries.

The Warsaw Pact was the common term for the "Treaty of Friendship, Co-operation and Mutual Assistance" and it was for the Soviet Union and its allies what NATO was for the United States and its allies—a military alliance for mutual protection and defense. Organized by the emerging Soviet leadership of Nikita Khrushchev in 1955, the Warsaw Pact was a response to the remilitarization of West Germany and its membership in NATO.

Like NATO, the members of the Warsaw Pact agreed to defend each other if one or more of the members came under attack. Interestingly enough, the treaty also asserted principles of "mutual noninterference in internal affairs and respect for national sovereignty and independence." The Soviet Union itself violated these principles by their invasions of Hungary (in 1956) and Czechoslovakia (in 1968)—both member nations of the Warsaw Pact.

The Warsaw Pact came to an end on July 1, 1991, just a few months before the Soviet Union itself came to an end.

Non-Aligned Movement

The Non-Aligned Movement (NAM—formerly known as the Non-Aligned Nations) expressed the desire of its members not to become involved in the East–West ideological confrontation of the Cold War. Officially established in September, 1961, the Movement's original members included India, Egypt, Yugoslavia, and Indonesia, and dozens of other nations not connected with the great Superpowers of the Cold War.

The term "Non-Alignment" itself was coined by Jawaharlal Nehru, India's first Prime Minister, in 1954. Nehru defined the "five pillars" of international relations: respect for territorial integrity, mutual non-aggression, mutual non-interference in domestic affairs, equality and mutual benefit—that is, trade—and peaceful co-existence.

By 1964, NAM had forty-six member nations, among them some of the world's most populous, such as India and Indonesia. In 1973, a NAM created a permanent organization and bureaucracy to deal with the increasingly-complex issues involving trade and monetary relationships. Most of NAM's member countries are among the poorest half of the World nations, and economic development is key to their future.

As of this writing, NAM has over a hundred member nations representing more than half of the World's population and almost two-thirds of the member countries of the United Nations. Though the end of the Cold War had eliminated the necessity for "non-alignment," the economic and development needs of NAM members are a vital as ever.

Practice Test Questions

1. During the Balkan conflicts of 1908 and 1912, the Austrians

   A. helped negotiate settlements between the French and the Russians.

   B. were successful in stopping Serbian expansion.

   C. sided with Russia against Serbia.

   D. tried to stop German aggression against Bosnia.

   E. All of the above.

2. The most significant of the "trigger" causes of World War I was

   A. Russian plots to force Austria out of the Balkans.

   B. French guarantees of military aid to the Bosnians.

   C. Kaiser Wilhelm's Moroccan exploits.

   D. the assassination of Archduke Franz Ferdinand.

   E. the naval arms race of the previous two decades.

3. The main purpose of the "Blitzkrieg" strategy was to

   A. test new weapons and tactics.

   B. avoid attrition by striking fast for a quick victory.

   C. make use of virtually endless supplies and manpower.

   D. maximize pro-German sentiment by minimizing the duration of war.

   E. All of the above.

4. The Truman Doctrine declared that

   A. civilian leaders must limit the power of military commanders.

   B. recently-liberated countries had to repay reconstruction loans.

   C. European colonial powers had to give up their empires.

   D. the United States would help "free peoples" resist communist infiltration or aggression.

   E. None of the above.

5. Inspired by the leadership of Soviet Premier Gorbachov, "Perestroika" referred to the

   A. aggressive military policy of the U.S.S.R.

   B. reform and restructuring of the Soviet state system.

   C. abandonment of Marxism in Russia.

   D. All of the above.

   E. None of the above.

Answers and Explanations

1. **B.** The Balkan conflicts were among the short-term causes of World War I. In each cases, the key opponents were Austria and Serbia, as Serbia sought to expand westward to the Adriatic Sea and the Austrians sought to prevent them from doing so. Consequently, Option **B**, "[the Austrians] were successful in stopping Serbian expansion," is correct. Option **A** could not be correct because the French and the Russians were allies, as were the Russians and Serbia (Option **C**). The Germans (Option **D**) were not directly involved the Balkan conflicts, except as Austria's ally.

2. **D.** The "trigger" causes of World War I took place in the weeks leading up to the outbreak of the war. First and most significant among these trigger causes was the assassination of the Archduke Franz Ferdinand (Option **D**), the heir to the throne of the Austro-Hungarian Empire. Austria blamed Serbia for this crime. It is true that Russia wanted Austria out of the Balkans (Option **A**), but they were open in that desire and did not "plot" (nor was their opposition to Austria among the "trigger" causes). The French made no guarantees to Bosnia (Option **B**), and the Kaiser's exploits in Morocco were not directly involved in the events June, July, and August, 1914. Option **D**, "the naval arms race," must be seen as a long-term rather than trigger cause of the war.

3. **B.** The German "Blitzkrieg" strategy was devised to avoid a war of attrition (Option **B**)—which resource-poor Germany could not win—by striking fast for a quick victory. Option **A**, the testing of new weapons and tactics, has some validity, but it was a minor consideration. Options **C** and **D** are essentially nonsense answers: Germany didn't have endless supplies and manpower (Option **C**), and the best way to maximize pro-German sentiment (Option **D**) would have been by avoiding war altogether.

4. **D.** Made public in a speech before Congress in 1947, the Truman Doctrine declared that the United States would help "free peoples" resist communist infiltration or aggression (Option **D**). He was referring specifically to the situation in Greece and Turkey, but the policy was applied thereafter all through the Cold War. Options **A, B,** and **C** are mostly nonsense answers, though each one contains a small grain of truth—Truman would later limit the power of commanders in Korea (**A**), the Marshall Plan funds to rebuild Western Europe were technically loans (**B**), and the European colonial empires were well on their way to dissolution after the war (**C**).

5. **B.** Inspired by the leadership of Soviet Premier Gorbachov, "Perestroika" referred to the reform and restructuring of the Soviet state system (Option **B**), making it more open and less totalitarian. Gorbachov, though, was a committed communist and had no thought of abandoning Marxism (Option **C**). Though "Perestroika" dealt entirely with Soviet domestic issues, it had the effect of softening Soviet military policy (contrary to Option **A**) and of lessening tensions between the Soviet Union and the United States.

Patterns of Nationalism

Nationalism's Impact

The undersanding among a specific people that they are a *nation*—a people with a common language, culture, history and, frequently, destiny. In this context, *nation* should be understood as something apart from country or state (though we frequently use nation as a synonym for country). There are nations who possess no country (the Kurds, Palestinians, Navajo, and so on). When nationalism is strong enough, it has historical consequences, especially when a nation is under the power of another nation (as in the case of the Hungarians and Serbians in the nineteenth century Austrian Empire, or when a nation asserts a strong sense of identity and purpose (as in the case of German National Socialism in the 1930s and 1940s).

The Interwar Years

Nowhere else in the world did nationalism become a factor in national and international affairs than in Germany, Italy, and Japan. The war, a truly global conflict, was the result of the expansionist policies and actions of Germany under National Socialism, of Italy under Fascism, and of Japan under right-wing militarism. In each case, those policies and actions were justified both domestically and internationally in terms of national honor, pride, and destiny.

In *Mein Kampf*, Hitler boldly proclaimed most of the characteristic Nazi ideas and beliefs that would drive party policy down to the end in 1945. The most obvious feature of that ideology was an intense racism, the belief in the superiority of the white, Germanic, Aryan, or Nordic "races." This meant that in addition to denigrating peoples of color, whites not considered by the Nazis to be of their "race" were also denigrated, especially Jews and Slaves (Poles, Russians, etc.).

The Nazis were enthusiastic promoters of eugenics and ultimately they would pursue policies of "racial hygiene" to keep the non-Aryan elements out of what we would now call the "gene pool." These ideas, radicalized to a point that still seems incredible, led to the Holocaust in the 1940s. The desired goal was the creation of *a Herrenrasse,* a "Master Race."

In Japan, three generations of industrial and technological development had built a nation that had no peer in East Asia. In part because of the military tradition of its ruling class, and in part because of the economic need to develop foreign sources of raw materials, Japan embarked on a long-term program of expansion that reached its peak during the 1940s. To a very large extent, nationalist sentiments and forces within Japan were responsible for Japan's program of conquest and domination during the interwar years.

Genocide

The term **ethnic cleansing** (means) the policy, usually of a government, to forcibly remove people of specific ethnic groups from a country. The terms is sometimes used as being virtually synonymous with genocide. "Undesirable" peoples can be identified on the basis of religious or ethnic identity, or because of various political or ideological factors, or a combination of any of these. The term originally was used in connection with the program of the government of Serbia to remove, by whatever means required, non-Serbians from either Serbia or Serbia-claimed territory.

The preceding chapter dealt at some length with the single most notorious genocidal episode in world history—the Holocaust, the attempted extermination of all the Jews of Europe. Estimates vary, but the government of Nazi Germany may have killed as many as six million persons of Jewish ancestry between 1941 and 1945. The Holocaust was by no means the only such episode in the twentieth century, and some estimates put the death toll by genocide at nearly one hundred million all around the globe.

In 1948, the United Nations General Assembly adopted Resolution 260, "Convention on the Prevention and Punishment of the Crime of Genocide." In this convention, the UN defined genocide as any of the following acts committed with intent to destroy, in whole or in part, a national, ethnic, racial or religious group, including (a) killing members of the group (b) causing serious bodily or mental harm to members of the group (c) deliberately inflicting on the group conditions of life calculated to bring about its physical destruction in whole or in part (d) imposing measures intended to prevent births within the group (e) forcibly transferring children of the group to another group.

In the current chapter, it might be useful to broaden the scope of the discussion by including **democide** along with genocide and considering them together. If the ancient Greek roots of the word, genocide, means the killing of a type (*genus*) of people, then democide simply means the mass killing of "the people" (*demos*) in general (homicide is the word for the killing of a single person). Although usually undertaken by government regimes (from all actions, including war), democide can also refer to private actions on the part of ethnic or religious groups against other groups. An idea of the importance of democide in history can be had by considering that by conservative estimates, some 180 million people were killed in democidal actions in the twentieth century.

Table 28.1 Selected Democides of the Twentieth Century (Excluding the World Wars and the Holocaust)					
Democide	**Years**	**Estimated Deaths**	**Democide**	**Year(s)**	**Estimated Deaths**
Congo Free State	1886–1908	8 million	Bangladesh	1971	1.25 million
Mexican Revolution	1910–1920	1 million	Cambodian Khmer Rouge		1.65 million
Armenian Massacres	1915–1923	1.5 million	Mozambique	1975–1992	1 million
Nationalist China	1928–1937	3.1 million	Afghanistan	1979–2001	1.8 million
Korean War	1950–1953	2.8 million	Iran-Iraq War	1980–1988	1 million
Rwanda and Burundi	1959–1995	1.35 million	Sudan	1983–present	1.9 million
"Second" Vietnam War	1960–1975	3.5 million	Kinshasa Congo	1998–present	3.3 million
Ethiopia	1962–1992	1.4 million			
Nigeria	1966–1970	1 million			

It should be noted that though United Nations resolutions effectively criminalize genocidal and democidal actions, the experiences of the past few decades do not provide good examples of concerted action on the part of the nations of the world to halt mass killings. In the few cases in which the United Nations or single nations took direct action to stop or prevent government- or faction-sponsored democide (as the United States tried to do in Somalia in 1995), the efforts were halted when the "costs" of the interventions became too high. Those regimes and factions that are disposed to use mass killings as part of their political strategies know that the world will do very little to stop them.

Racism

One of the consequences of the rise of science, especially biological science, during the eighteenth and nineteenth centuries was the application of scientific study and theory on human beings. Hence, the mid-1800s saw the development of anthropology—the study of humans—and of Darwinism, with its theory of evolution and natural selection. The term, "survival of the fittest," was not used by Darwin himself, but it was one of the popular phrases taken from his theories. Darwinism worked its way into the study of humankind not so much by way of explaining human origins as by its influence of pseudo-scientific "theories" of human characteristic and capacities.

By 1900, reputable anthropologists, geographers, and physicians were promulgating theories that the evolution process was still at work on the human organism, and that some of the world's peoples were more "evolved" than others. Environmental conditions were usually given as the reason for differences between peoples. The peoples of Northwest Europe were claimed to be hardier, more intelligent, and more industrious because of the cold and hard environment of the North had not "softened" them as it had the peoples of the tropics (who, not coincidentally, were also "of color"). The same argument was even made regarding Southern Europeans—the Spanish and Italians.

During this period, the so-called science of eugenics came to the fore in an attempt to study ways in which the human "race" could be improved by selective breeding and, of course, by eliminating from the "gene pool" the weaker traits of humankind. Some eugenicists went so far as to suggest that sterilization and euthanasia was an appropriate method to be employed in weeding out the weakest elements (such as the mentally retarded and those with congenital birth defects).

A real watershed was reached with the rise Nazism and its vitriolic and racist hatreds of all peoples not Germanic. After the revelation of the horrors of the Holocaust, justified as it was by racist theories, racial theories had become anathema to mainstream scientists and scholars.

In the United States, racism had always (at least since the 1680s) been a matter of habit rather than of theory or thought. Contrary to popular notions, racism against black Africans did not really precede the Euro-American use of slavery as the basis for a large portion of its economy. Instead, it was created by institutional arrangements and by government policies that kept poor whites and black slaves from making common cause in rebelling against the ruling classes, mostly in the American South. Racism was the wedge that effectively kept dominated whites and enslaved blacks safely apart.

In a series of "Jim Crow" laws, Southern states would require a rigorously-strict segregation of black and white. When these laws were tested in court, as in the celebrated *Plessy v. Ferguson* case (1896), the courts ruled that segregation did not violate the civil rights of black citizens, and that "separate but equal" facilities were legally acceptable. Civil Rights activists would spend the next sixty years trying to get the Plessy decision overturned. Though some activists were hopeful that a loosening of Amerian racism would follow black involvement in World War I, no such reform took place.

The real turning point was World War II. This was for two important reasons. The first was that the United States and its allies had condemned the racist regimes of the Axis Powers, and they were engaged in a struggle to defeat them. This meant, to a certain extent, condemning and defeating racism. It was at least understood this way by American blacks and by many Peoples of Color around the world.

The second reason was that the needs of industry and war production during the war meant that long-standing policies that kept blacks out of good-paying industrial jobs had to be abandoned, and hundreds of thousands of Southern blacks made their way North (and West) to work in the war industries. The mixing of the previously-segregated races, along with the demonstration that black skills and capacities were the equal of whites, accomplished in a few years what generations had not—the old racist habits of thought began to weaken. Add to this the revelation of what evils racism could unleash on the world (in the Holocaust) and the time had come for change.

That change would come during the 1950s, 1960s, and 1970s. The landmark case of Brown v. Board of Education (1954) overturned the Plessy doctrine of "separate but equal." Between 1957 and 1971, the American Congress passed a series of new Civil Rights laws that outlawed segregation of any kind and that provided legal protections for voting and other civil rights.

One should carefully note that though there have been advances in both the United States and around the world in eliminating racism, it is still very much a part of that world in the twenty-first century. Racism and xenophobia (the fear and hatred of people unlike oneself) still account for not only personal attitudes and behavior, but also corporate and government policies around the globe.

Nationalism after World War II

Vietnam

Chapter 30 deals more thoroughly with Vietnam, but in the context of nationalism, a few comments are in order here. Vietnam was a good example of the rise of nationalist sentiment that flourished around the world after World War II and the defeat of Global fascism. On the day of Japan's official surrender in September, 1945, the provisional government of Vietnam was declared independent by the Viet Minh coalition led by Ho Chi Minh.

Ho (in Vietnam, as in China, the family name comoes first), born in a well-to-do Vietnamese family but educated in Paris (where he discovered and became a life-long adherent of Marxism), returned to Vietnam to organize opposition to

French rule. While in Chinese exile, he formed the League for the Independence of Vietnam (Vietminh), a coalition of various parties and factions, though heavily influenced by Marxists such as Ho.

It was this element of Marxism that obscured the true nature of Vietnamese nationalism well into the 1980s. During the Cold War, American analysts and policy makers could see developments in Vietnam in only one way—as en element in the global expansion of communism and part of what some (though not the most thoughtful) Americans called the "international communist conspiracy" to take over the world. In the mind of most in the West, communism was synonymous with totalitarianism, mostly because of the history of the repressive Stalinist regime of the Soviet Union.

The classic metaphor of the 1950s and 1960s was the "Domino Theory." If you allowed a country to fall to communism, its neighbors would fall as well, just as each of a row of dominoes set on edge fell, one after another. The Domino Theory blinded three American presidential administrations to what was really going on in Vietnam.

Pan-Arab Nationalism

A sense of Arab nationalism—that there was someone who could legitimately be called an "Arab" in spite of his country or citizenship—developed slowly during the middle to late nineteenth century. It emerged, in fact, at about the same time as Zionism—the nationalistic counterpart for those who thought of themselves as Jews as something separate from their adherence to the Jewish faith.

Like other nationalistic movements of that era, Arab Nationalism and it logical extension—Pan Arab Nationalism—developed in an imperial environment—mostly rule within the Ottoman Turk empire. The Ottoman empire had ruled most of the Arab lands for centuries and though by the end of the nineteenth century it was known as the "sick man" of Europe, Turkey nevertheless kept a tight grip on its Arab possessions.

Before World War II, Arab nationalists usually avoided using their Islamic religion as a feature of their political identity. In part, this was related to the broader movement toward secularization around the world. In part, it was also related to the lack of unity among the various Muslim sects. Moreover, their Turkish overlords were also Muslim, and the Turks had done more to expand the Muslim presence in Europe since the Middle Ages than any other Muslim regime.

Before World War I, Arab nationalists were generally moderate in their demands. What they wanted, most asserted, was the reform of and some autonomy within the Ottoman Empire. They also promoted the more widespread use of Arabic in schools.

After the collapse of the Ottoman Empire in 1918, however, nationalist sentiments became more prominent. During World War I the British had promoted Arab nationalist thought and ideology because doing so weakened their enemy (and Germany's ally) Turkey. After the war, the League of Nations turned most of the Arab lands over to Britain as a "mandate," a kind of trusteeship. Now Arab nationalism was targeted against the British colonial control, and Pan-Arab nationalism became an important force in the post-World War II decolonization movement.

Eager to shed the great expense of its once-mighty empire, Britain encouraged Egypt, Iraq, Lebanon, Saudi Arabia, Syria, Transjordan, and Yemen to form the Arab League. The purpose of the League was to coordinate policy and build useful mutual ties between the Arab states. Unfortunately, internal animosities and fear of territorial expansion (each thought the others were expansionist) soon caused the League to fall apart.

But as the Arab League disintegrated, there was new cause for at least some degree of Arab unity. Late in 1947, the United Nations General Assembly approved a plan which divided the British Mandate of Palestine into two states: one Jewish and one Arab. The ancient city of Jerusalem, claimed by three world religions (Christianity, Islam, and Judaism) as the geographic center of their faith, was to be an international city governed by the United Nations. Both Jews and Arabs criticized parts of the plan, but by and large Zionist Jews accepted the plan as the quickest road to a creation of a Jewish state—modern Israel. Also by and large, the plan was rejected by most Arabs—certainly those in Palestine, but also throughout the Arab World.

Between November of 1947 and July, 1949, the fledgling State of Israel and its Arab neighboring states fought a bitter war in which the Israelis generally prevailed. In May, 1948, the British mandate expired and Israel declared its independence. What the Israelis called the War for Independence waged for another year and a half, and ended with a negotiated settlement greatly in Israel's favor. Essentially defeated, the Arab nations would continue in their opposition to Israel and, though rarely united for the purpose, kept the pressure on.

In 1958, under the leadership of Egyptian President Gamal Abdul Nassar, a forceful and influencial advocate of Pan-Arab unity, Egypt and Syria joined to create a unified state, the United Arab Republic (UAR). Nassar wanted Yemen included as well, but a military coup in Syria dashed hopes for the survival of the UAR. Egypt continued to use the official name of United Arab Republic until Nassar's death in 1971.

The principal instrument of Pan-Arabism in the early 1960s and beyond was the Ba'ath party. The Ba'athists first came to power in Syria in 1963. That same year, they came to power in Iraq and remained influential until the American-engineered "regime change" of 2003.

The Arabic word Ba'ath means "resurrection." Ba'athist beliefs combine Arab Socialism, nationalism, and Pan-Arabism. Though most are nominally Muslim, most Ba'athists promote a secular ideology that often seems at odds with the Islamism and theocracy of other Muslim nations.

In the ideology of Arab Socialism, the ownership of the means of production was to be nationalized, but only allowing for the traditional values such of private property and inheritance. Out-of-date social structures such as feudalism, nomadism, tribalism, and religious factionalism were to be done away with eventually, but not at the cost of severing the community and family ties that had a central place in Arab identity. It seems clear now, in retrospect, that the Ba'athists in the Hussein regime in Iraq had done little to promote this kind of moderate and progressive socialism.

The defeat of the Arabs in the Arab-Israeli War of 1967 and the death of Nasser in 1970 was a blow to Pan-Arabism from which it has not yet recovered. Unified Arab action would have been a "dead letter" thereafter had it not been for the creation of the Organization of Petroleum Exporting Countries (OPEC) in 1960. Since the 1970s, OPEC, composed mostly of Arab countries, has exercised a great deal of influence in world affairs.

In response to their defeat in the 1973 Arab-Israeli War, the Arab members of OPEC embargoed oil shipments in an effort to pressure Europe and the United States into breaking their long-standing support of Israel. For a brief moment, there was cohesion among the Arab nations. This cohesion was destroyed by the signing of the Camp David accords between Egypt and Israel. Egyptian President Anwar Sadat, Nassar's hand-picked successor, made a separate peace with the Israelis and was thereafter a hated figure in the Arab World. He was assassinated by Pan-Arab extremists in 1979.

Practice Test Questions

1. A belief in the superiority of the "white" races was a significant aspect of

   A. Italian nationalism in the twentieth century.
   B. German nationalism in the 1930s.
   C. Japanese nationalism after World War I.
   D. Ukrainian nationalism after the collapse of the Soviet Union.
   E. None of the above.

2. In the United States, a prominent example of racist belief and practice was

   A. "Jim Crow" segregation.
   B. the "Separate but Equal" doctrine.
   C. popular resistance to school integration.
   D. All of the above.
   E. None of the above.

3. As an example of nationalism in the post-World War II era, Vietnam

   A. proved that the "domino theory" was correct.
   B. gained full "self-determination" after decades of struggle.
   C. rejected Chinese domination.
   D. Both A and B are correct.
   E. Both B and C are correct.

4. As a result of the collapse of the Soviet Union, the many peoples of Eastern Europe

   A. set aside their latent nationalism in the interests of unity.
   B. worked together in securing their "self-determination."
   C. sought to recover their national identities and autonomy.
   D. resisted attempts to reestablish Soviet power.
   E. All of the above.

5. The Egyptian President, Gamal Abdul Nasser, was an example of

   A. Pan-Arab leadership in the post-World War II era.
   B. pro-British cooperation in the Arab world.
   C. the early spirit of reconciliation between Arabs and Israelis.
   D. None of the above.
   E. All of the above.

Answers and Explanations

1. **B.** A belief in the superiority of the "white" races was a significant aspect of German nationalism in the 1930s, at least as it was expressed by the Nazi movement (Option **B**). Though Italian nationalism was often intense in the twentieth century (Option **A**), it did not emphasize race. On the other hand, Japanese nationalism after World War I (Option **C**) did tend to be racist with regard to even other East Asian peoples (such as the Koreans and Chinese), but it certainly did not see "white" peoples as superior in any way. Racism played almost no part in the rise of Ukrainian nationalism after the collapse of the Soviet Union (Option **D**).

2. **D.** In the United States, a prominent example of racist belief and practice was "Jim Crow" segregation (Option **A**), the "Separate but Equal" doctrine (Option **B**), and popular resistance to school integration (Option **C**). Option **D**, therefore, is the correct choice.

3. **E.** As an example of nationalism in the post-World War II era, Vietnam gained full self-determination after decades of struggle (Option **B**) and it rejected Chinese domination (Option **C**). The correct choice, then, is Option **E**.

4. **C.** As a result of the collapse of the Soviet Union, the many peoples of Eastern Europe sought to recover their national identities and autonomy (Option **C**). They certainly did not set aside their latent nationalism in the interests of unity (Option **A**), nor did they work together in securing their "self-determination" (Option **B**). Option **D** is a nonsense answer: after the collapse of the Soviet Union, there was no Soviet Union to reestablish its power.

5. **A.** The Egyptian President, Gamal Abdul Nasser, was an example of Pan-Arab leadership in the post-World War II era (Option **A**). Contrary to the sense of Option **B**, Nassar was a frequent thorn in Britain's side, especially during the so-called Suez Crisis. And, more than other Arab leaders of that era, Nassar helped to organize a coherent military opposition to the Israelis.

The Global Economy

Technology's Impact on Globalization

It is safe to say that in the absence of modern technology, globalization could not have taken place. Before rapid trans-oceanic shipping and air travel, before the telegraph, teletype, radio, television, Internet, and satellite communication, and before computer automation of complex international transactions, the globalization as we understand it today would not be possible.

This is not to argue that the roots of globalization cannot be found in a time of relatively crude technology—in the world-wide trade relations that emerged within and between the great European Empires. The "sun never set" on the British Empire in the nineteenth century with only sailing ships and hand-carried mail to tie it together. But by and large, empires to the contrary notwithstanding, economies around the world still remained small and local, and, with a few important exceptions (such as the African Diaspora in the seventeenth and eighteenth centuries), the impact on culture and ways of life was small.

But in addition to the communications technologies mentioned previously, others have made a significant impact as well, especially in the decades after World War II. There was, for instance, the development of "containerized" and "intermodal" shipping beginning in the 1950s. A shipping container of standardized design and dimensions (typically forty feet long, ten feet high, and ten feet wide) can be loaded at a factory (or, if refrigerated, in the farm field) with goods, placed on a flatbed truck-trailer, transferred by efficient crane facilities to railroad flatcars, and then loaded on board the deck of a ship by dockside cranes. At the destination port, the process is then reversed.

By minimizing the handling the goods, standardizing the unit to be loaded (thus maximizing cargo space aboard ship), by mechanizing (and even computerizing) the loading processes as much as possible, and by computerizing the tracking of the shipment and its contents, enormous reductions in what economists call "transaction costs" can be realized.

Transaction costs include the expenses of transportation, finance, contract negotiation, warehousing, and inventory control. Each of these expenses has been greatly reduced by the application of technology. Transportation cost has been reduced as described previously. The costs of credit transfers, banking deposits and bank-draft processing, and all the associated communication required to make all that happen have plummeted with the introduction of technology (in the beginning) even as simple as the telegraph. By the end of the twentieth century, computerized banking and finance by means of the global internet have reduced the costs to a very low point.

By the 1970s, warehousing and "drayage" of goods in transit, once a significant expense when shipments had to be transferred from one mode of transportation to another (such as at a port or railroad yard), had been virtually eliminated by intermodal shipping. Similarly, another traditional and significant expense of both merchandising and manufacturing has been control and monitoring of inventory. Before the introduction of computerized systems, barcode scanners, and embedded identification "chips" (the last two since the 1980s), inventory had to be counted and tracked by hand, and though clerical and bureaucratic procedure (themselves forms of technology—of "techniques") could do this with some degree of efficiency, costs were high and control was limited.

One effect of poor inventory control was the need for merchandisers and manufacturers to keep a bigger inventory than absolutely necessary since the consequences of inadvertently running out of stock were more serious than those of keeping a large inventory. But there were still costs associated with it. Every dollar (or Yen or Franc, and so on) that was unnecessarily tied up in inventory was a dollar that could not be deployed elsewhere, such as in enlarging the company's productive capacity. Because of this, in recent years business managers have adopted "just-in-time" inventory and management systems that carefully align sales or manufacturing operations with inventory in stock. This kind of precision is absolutely dependent on advanced technology in transportation, manufacturing, and accounting control. Powerful computers and a distributed computing network (the global "Internet") are necessary.

Other technological developments have been (and will be) a factor in globalization as well. The development of effective pesticides and other agricultural chemicals beginning just before World War II has been combined in more recent decades with the introduction of new strains of wheat, rice, soybeans, and other farm products. Since the 1980s, some of these strains have been "genetically engineered" beyond the (almost) natural processes of hybridization.

With advances in genetic knowledge and technology touched off by the 1953 discovery of the chemical structure of DNA, by the 1980s it was possible to "splice" genes (strings of DNA with specific biological information encoded in the molecule pattern) into, say, soybean DNA in order to produce an economically-useful result such as resistance to disease or tolerance of draught. In some cases, the "donor" genes are not even from the same species family as the "target," and sometimes not even of plant "kingdom."

The use of genetic engineering in food production (or for any other purpose) has become in recent years a very controversial subject around the world. "GMOs"—genetically-modified organisms—are illegal for food purposes within the European Union. In many other places around the world, including the United States, concern is high as well. Critics fear the unintended consequences of this technology, and that it is taking science and technology into realms that many still think more appropriate for deity.

Technology's Impact on National Economies

Without question, technology has revolutionized the economies of the so-called "Third World" by reducing the transactions costs once associated with doing business. In particular, as information and technology have become more important in the already developed world, the old industrial centered have moved industrial production "off-shore" to countries with labor surpluses and low wages.

To a large extent, though, this movement had been hampered until after World War II by the still-high trade barriers around the world. If a particular product was manufactured in, say, Mexico, even if it was made for an American company it was still considered a Mexican product and therefore subject to import duties. International trade agreements such as the North American Free Trade Agreement (NAFTA) have either significantly lowered or eliminated these duties, and products manufactured by cheaper labor in nations such as Mexico can be imported into the United States profitably. The reverse is also true, of course. Americans can export goods to Mexico duty-free.

One effect of technology has been that the natural protection that some countries have enjoyed through history because of distance or other barriers is now virtually gone. Because of technological advances, international competition is now felt everywhere and sometimes intensely. This can be a benefit to small and underdeveloped countries if they can find a niche in the global market for either their goods or their services. Because industrial plants can be operated virtually any place close to transportation facilities, the old problem of industrial development, especially during the colonial era, may have been overcome. In the relatively-recent environment of free-trade agreements, if a country has a labor surplus, odds are that it will attract industry.

This is not exactly the same thing as industrial development in the past, which was more or less nation-based and which therefore helped to build a national economy. Due in part to advances in technology, this is no longer the case. Branch plants of transnational manufacturing corporations might very well bring employment to a country, but that country will not thereby be building its own industrial base. It will instead be merely supplying workers for essentially foreign companies.

Technology's Impact on Leisure

As with family life, technology has transformed leisure time. First of all, because of technology and the industrialization and affluence it brought, in general there has been a great increase in the amount of time devoted to leisure activities. In the nineteenth century and into the twentieth, twelve or fourteen-hour work days for six days a week were common in the factories of the industrial revolution. In the 1880s a labor protest song became popular in the United States and Britain with the refrain, "Eight hours for work, eight hours for rest, [and] eight hours for what we will."

By the 1930s in most of the industrialized world, working eight hours per day for five days a week had become the stable norm. In the 1980s and 1990, a few European countries limited work hours to only 35 per week. Added to this limit were annual vacation periods of one to several weeks, usually negotiated by contract with employees or their unions. Collectively, leisure time had become significant, especially during good economic periods.

The beneficiaries of leisure in the industrialized countries have used that time in travel, in recreation, in "hobbies," and (increasingly since the advent of television) in the passive receipt of mediated entertainment. To a great extent, the travel use of leisure has itself been made possible by technology. Whether by train, automobile, or airplane, long-distance travel has been common for "vacation" leisure. In the United States, the family automobile vacation has become much more intense, with the daily travel of hundreds of miles, and the pressure to collect vacation destinations (and souvenirs) along the way. Before well-engineered and paved roads and before large and comfortable (and often air conditioned) automobiles, family vacations in America were often limited to en extended stay at a "resort," often at the seashore, beside a lake, or in the mountains, and compete with tennis courts, boating and fishing experiences, and pseudo-camping accommodations. Since World War II, vacations by airplane have been more and more common, including those requiring intercontinental travel.

The vaction behavior of Europeans and others around the world tends to be more international than that of most Americans, owing in part to the small but very diverse nature of European national geography. It is not at all uncommon, for instance, for a German to vaction in the south of France, or for the British to vacation in Italy. One consequence of this is that many Europeans have frequent leisured contact with people of other cultures, and consequently tend to see World affairs in a more international light than is typical of most Americans.

For day-to-day and "weekend" leisure, various recreation activities have become common throughout the industrialized world. Amateur teams sports has been among the most popular, as has excursions to local hiking, fishing, and boating destinations. Particularly in the United States, a country still in possession of large areas of mountainous and forested landscape, the "sports" of fishing and hunting are very common. In the 1990s, by one estimate, nearly twenty percent of the American population regularly engaged in one or the other.

The coming of leisure time to the industrial world also brought something fairly new in world history: "hobbies." A hobby is a leisure-time activity that focuses on a narrow interest: pursuits such a stamp collecting, butterfly collecting (collecting of just about anything, in fact), gardening, woodworking, photography, sewing, model building, "crafts" of all kinds, and literally thousands of other "pastimes." Many of these pursuits rely directly on advanced technology and ready-made manufactured products and materials, each that were made possible by technology.

Since the 1960s, some observers in the United States and Western Europe have noted a decline in the interest in hobbies, and that this decline has been accompanied by a significant increase in the amount of time spent as a passive recipient of mediated entertainment, including radio or television broadcasts of sporting events. The advent of inexpensive video recording and playback technology in the 1980s, and the subsequent development of the "digital video disk" (DVD) has meant that individuals can pretty much watch what they want and when they want, a trend that began in the 1970s in the United States, Europe, and Japan with the introduction of cable-delivered television.

Similarly, the introduction of small and personalized music playback devices in the late 1970s (the Sony Walkman, for instance) and the public release in the 1980s of optical recordings on "compact disks" (CDs), also available in a form easily carried on the person, and in recent years the popularization of Internet devices such as the iPod—all this fairly-new technology has made it possible for one to enclose oneself with music and sounds of one's own choosing, simultaneously cutting off contact with others in the process.

Because of cheap and widely available technology, it is now possible for people to be constantly accompanied by music—indeed, with piped in music in business establishments, on the telephone while "on hold," and in other public settings, it is almost impossible to avoid (someone else's) music. Because of technology, the leisure-time activity of listening to music is frequently thoroughly mixed with non-leisure activities—even in the classroom. Acquiring the skills and developing the talents of *making* music is pursued less and less. *Making* something is the activity of a producer, not of a consumer, and in the post-industrial world, there are not nearly as many producers now as in the past.

The Pacific Rim and the Global Economy

The **Pacific Rim** designates the countries on the edges of the Pacific Ocean as well as the various island nations within the region. Tokyo is the most important commercial and cultural capital of the region. The Pacific Rim includes countries and people of great diversity: the economic vibrancy of Hong Kong and Taiwan, the high technology in Japan, Korea, and the Western United States, the natural resources of Australia, Canada, and the Russian Pacific region, the labor resources of China and Indonesia, and the agricultural productivity of Chile, New Zealand, and the United States.

In 1889, later-Secretary of State John Hay wrote that the Mediterranean was the "ocean" of the past, the Atlantic the ocean of the present, and the Pacific the ocean of the future. To a large, though not exclusive extent, Americans have always looked across the Atlantic to it European roots, even while extending its reach to the Pacific. By 1848, the United States had built a transcontinental land empire, with fine Pacific ports and potential to make inroads into East Asian trade that, at the time, was the exclusive preserve of the European powers. To underscore the new potential, the American navy under Commodore Perry threatened Japan in the 1850s if it failed to open its markets to the outside world.

With the American acquisition of Pacific ports, of the Hawaiian Islands, and of the Philippine archipelago by the end of the nineteenth century, the United States was in the best position among the Western powers to dominate Pacific affairs. The rapid and even astonishing rise of Japan to the status of world industrial and military power (Japan defeated the Russian navy in 1905) challenged American primacy in the Pacific Rim, and in part the outbreak of war between them in 1941 was the result of this competition.

During the postwar decades, though the United States was in a secure position of military power (the Cold War notwithstanding), Japan and other Western Pacific economies would quickly build industrial capacities that would soon challenge American economic primacy. By the 1970s, the United States trade balance shifted from the Atlantic to the Pacific.

Statistics for the period 1970-1982 show United States trade with major West European countries increased four hundred percent while trade with Pacific Rim countries increased eight hundred percent during that twelve-year period. Trade deficits (an excess of imports relative to exports) was a growing concern in the United States. Instead of wealth flowing in to America from the Pacific Rim, it was now starting to leak out.

Much of the shift to the Pacific Rim has to do with the high technology and consumer electronics sector. Japan, Taiwan, and to a lesser extent Korea and other East Asian nations have led the world in the production of inexpensive consumer technology. Though most of the science and design of microelectronic "chips" is done in the United States, actual manufacturing and assembly of the parts is much cheaper in Pacific Rim countries. Japanese-based companies such as Sony likewise contributed to the rise of the Pacific Rim "tech sector."

The shift in the Pacific Rim trade balances relate as well to the very successful—some have said "catastrophic"—incursion of Japanese and Korean automobile manufactures into the United States and global markets. In the early 1970s, when OPEC oil embargoes and the rising cost of fuel, and with widespread concerns with auto-generated air pollution, the Japanese companies of Toyota, Honda, Datsun (now Nissan), and others were able to immediately market small, "compact" cars with fuel efficiencies at least twice that of what had become traditional for at least the American market. Some inroads were made as well by European auto manufacturers in this regard (such as Volkswagen, Volvo, and BMW—autos were smaller and otherwise more modest in Europe as well), but none could match the efficiency and overall reliability of Japanese-made vehicles.

Similarly, transportation in the Pacific Rim become so systematized and so cheap during the last decades of the twentieth century that even high bulk and low value commodities like wheat, apples, and table grapes could be shipped profitably from growers in Chile and New Zealand (and other Pacific Rim countries) to northern markets. The inclusion of Southern Hemisphere agricultural producers in the much larger Northern Hemisphere markets has helped (along with mechanical cold-storage and long-keeping produce varieties) to de-seasonalize the diets of the Pacific Rim and other regions of the world since the two hemispheres have opposite seasons. It has also increased competition for such produce to the point that smaller farmers are threatened with flooded markets. The internationalization of food production has resulted in the decline of local food production, and from a food security standpoint, many of concerned.

In addition to shift in industrial and agricultural production around the Pacific Rim, economic interactions are multiplying in international finance. Money markets, stock and bond markets, and various commodity markets operate in Japan and other Pacific Rim centers even while Americans sleep. In the financial markets, the major Pacific Rim nations (including the PRC) are in a position to purchase or sell large amounts of American securities such as Treasury bonds, and in the process have a significant effect on market factors in the United States. Of course, American investors and institutions have the same ability to influence markets in Japan, Korea, Taiwan, and the rest of the Pacific Rim.

In general (and so far), economic relations around the Pacific Rim have been mutually beneficial. In the post-World War II years, the United States engendered good political relations with many nations of the Asian Pacific by encouraging and contributing to their economic development. In no country was this truer than Japan, defeated and occupied at the end of war, but largely rebuilt with American aid and Japanese industriousness. Americans have also contributed technology, capital, and equipment while purchasing the relatively-cheap manufactured goods produced in the Western and Southern Pacific Rim. To a large extent, American relationships with the other nations of the Pacific Rim have been emblematic of a global shift of industrial manufacturing away from its historic sources in Western Europe and the United States and toward the developing nations of the Third World. Japan and Taiwan could hardly be described as the "Third World," but neither are they Euro-American.

However, relationships around the Pacific Rim have not always been easy. The American presence in the Pacific has raised questions about nuclear power. In 1985, New Zealand would not permit the U.S.S. Buchanan to visit because the Americans refused to state whether or not the ship was carrying nuclear weapons. The United States government has a long-standing policy of neither confirming nor denying such requests for information. Compliance with this request would have set a precedent and perhaps jeopardized United States bases in other countries. In August 1986, the United States suspended its military commitment to defend New Zealand under the ANZUS pact.

A potential or very serious conflict exists with regard to the relationship between China, Taiwan, and the rest of the world. At the end of the Chinese Civil War in 1949, the Chinese Nationalist government fled to the island of Taiwan, long a part of China proper. There, it maintained a separate Chinese "government" and for many years actually represented China in the United Nations. In 1971, the People's Republic of China (PRC) replaced the Taiwanese government as the representative of the world's most populous country. International recognition of "Red China" was enhanced in 1972 when the United States formally extended diplomatic recognition to the PRC.

At this point, the fate of Taiwan was thrown into question. As a Pacific Rim country firmly within the economic orbit of the capitalist nations of the region (United States and Japan the two largest), in the last decades of the twentieth century Taiwan became an important source of high tech and other manufactured goods—essentially a full partner in the Pacific Rim community.

However, the PRC adamantly maintains that Taiwan is an inseparable part of China, and that it will not tolerate any assertions of independence on the part of the Taiwanese. That Taiwan has been *de facto* independent for decades seems not to matter. On their part, the Taiwanese have been just as adamant in maintaining their autonomy. A reunion of the two Chinas is not out of the question, and as the PRC moves closer and closer to free-market capitalism, unification would be more likely. For the time being, though, China has all but promised military action if the face of a declared Taiwanese independence. For their part, the United States and other Pacific Rim nations have assured Taiwan of their military support if necessary. Time will tell.

The last but not the least point to consider is migration within the Pacific Rim region. During the postwar years, the United States has been the largest recipient of Pacific Rim migrants. During the 1970s, political refugees from Vietnam taxed the ability of American immigration resources, but most were soon settled and as a group have prospered. Koreans, Taiwanese, and Philippinos constitute significant sources of trans-Pacific migration as well. By the end of the twentieth century Australia and British Columbia had surpassed the United States as a destination of choice, though it is still fashionable (though certainly not necessary) for Japanese families to send their children to the United States for a college education. A certain percentage of these student remain in the United States, or move back and forth as agents of trans-Pacific interrelations.

This circulation around and between Pacific Rim countries has had (and will have) significant cultural consequences. Migrants practice a wide variety of religions: Buddhism, Shintoism, Islam, Christianity, and others. Ways of life range from the highly urban experiences of Tokyo, Singapore, and Hong Kong to rural places without much technology or even running water.

The much longer national histories and cultural traditions of many Asian nations has much to offer the Euro-American mind. An infusion of East Asian culture could engender a longer range view, delayed gratification in the interests of future security and happiness, and longer-range thinks in general.

The Emergence of the Third World

Discussion of the so-called "Third World" and its significance in the modern world has found its way so far into Chapters 26, 27, 28 of this guide, and you will find more discussion when you get to Chapter 32. In addition to these materials, the following review and supplement will be useful.

It is important to note that political independence was not the same thing as economic independence. The very nature of the colonial relationship between colony and "mother" country limited the development of a diversified economy in most colonies. Most of the former colonies were far behind Europe and the United States in industrial development, and they continued as suppliers of raw materials.

One very serious problem that has plagued the economies of Third World countries since the end of World War II has been foreign debt. Debts owed by most of the world's poorest nations grew dramatically during the 1970s, and both the governments of the developed nations and private bankers saw loans to developing countries as good foreign policy and good business.

By the 1980s, though, after years of global inflation accompanied (oddly enough) by high interest rates, the loan pyramid collapsed in 1982 when Mexico was unable to refinance or service (make the payments on) its privately-held debts (those held by private banks). Soon thereafter, dozens of other countries also faced the same situation and they sought relief and the "forgiving" of their loans.

Many Third World debtor nations, particularly in Latin America, object at being asked to pay down their large debts, at least at rates thought satisfactory by the banks and by the governments who extended the loans to begin with. From the Third World perspective, the debt is strangling their economies and high loan payments are draining away resources desperately needed to finance growth or even to pay for a decent level of government services, such as education and health care.

An additional complicating factor is that high levels of debt in the Third World can have significant environmental consequences by placing an extra burden on natural resources. Debt pressure has brought about increases in export-oriented mining and logging in developing countries. Some studies have found that a statistical link exists between high debt burdens and deforestation.

The Impact of Multinational Corporations

A **multinational corporation** is a corporation whose sales or business in other countries is at least 25 percent of that of its home country. Multinationals have branch plants and offices in the countries in which they do business, even if their planning and business strategies are conducted from their home offices. Since the end of World War II, the economic significance and influence of multinational corporations has been growing, some say to alarming levels.

As very large organizations, the multinational corporation has had many of the same impacts during the twentieth century as any large corporation, just on an international scale. *Scale* is an important word in this context. Any large operation benefits from what economists call, *economies of scale*—the bigger the operation, the more it can produce for less cost. Costs go down and efficiencies can go up when size increases. One large factory can usually produce more for less than two smaller factories combined. When the combination of corporate resources spans national borders, then economies-of-scale can be enormous.

Enormous economies and efficiencies mean that a large multinational corporation is in a better competitive position than a smaller one, and certainly more competitive than a merely local firm. Since this is so, a large multinational can easily capture entire markets and force smaller competitors out. The result is fewer opportunities for enterprise, and more centralized control that is less responsive to either customer demands or social needs or policies.

Moreover, because multinational corporations can command vast resources (sometimes exceeding the national budget of many countries), they can exert powerful influence on media, on government officials, and on legal processes. It is widely claimed that multinationals exert all but command influence on powerful institutions such as the World Trade Organization (WTO), a global legislative and judicial body created by the United States and other developed nations to devise global trade rules and then enforce them through trade sanctions. Fear of multination-corporation influence is all the greater since the WTO conducts most of its business behind closed doors.

With the increased growth of multinational corporations since the end of World War II, some old concepts and norms are necessarily giving way. First of all, the terms "import" and "export" no longer retain their standard definitions in the face of global manufacturing, assembling, and originating patterns. Many United States firms have operations based in the Pacific Rim, while nations such as Korea and Japan continue to open plants in the United States.

Likewise, old tax rules and accounting methods become difficult when the operations of a single corporation take place around the world. What portion of its income is taxed by which nations? The trend has been that the difficulty of this question has worked in the favor of the corporations, as had national laws related to labor relations, wage and hour laws, and similar questions of national sovereignty.

Practice Test Questions

1. Among the benefits of technology to global trade has been

    A. the elimination of waste in manufacturing.
    B. longer work hours for increasingly-healthy employees.
    C. a great reduction in transaction costs.
    D. All of the above.
    E. None of the above.

2. NAFTA has made trade between the United States and Mexico

    A. cheaper, but still difficult.
    B. duty-free.
    C. beneficial to the United States only.
    D. All of the above.
    E. None of the above.

3. Between 1970 and 1982, American trade with Pacific Rim countries grew at a rate

    A. twice that of trade with Western Europe.
    B. half that of trade with Western Europe.
    C. the same as with Western Europe.
    D. All of the above.
    E. None of the above.

4. In the face of continued Taiwanese autonomy, the PRC had promised

    A. open trade agreements upon Taiwanese independence.
    B. to forgive loans made for economic development.
    C. technology transfers in genetic engineering and manufacturing.
    D. All of the above.
    E. None of the above.

5. High levels of debt among many Third World nations has

    A. brought about rampant corruption among First World bankers.
    B. benefited Western banks through foreclosure on Third World assets.
    C. placed heavy burdens on natural resources in Third World countries.
    D. All of the above.
    E. None of the above.

Answers and Explanations

1. **C.** Among the benefits of technology to global trade has been a great reduction in transaction costs (Option **C**). The elimination of waste in manufacturing (Option **A**) might benefit from technology, but its not directly related to global trade. Option **B**, "longer work hours for increasingly-healthy employees," is a non-sense question since work hours have, in general, decreased historically.

2. **B.** NAFTA has made trade between the United States and Mexico duty-free (Option **B**). Option **A**, "cheaper, but still difficult," is wrong by degrees, but still wrong. Option **C**, "beneficial to the United States only," has been claimed by some, but most of them are not Mexicans.

3. **A.** Between 1970 and 1982, American trade with Pacific Rim countries grew at a rate twice that of trade with Western Europe (Option **A**). Options **B** and **C** are simply wrong.

4. E. In the face of continued Taiwanese autonomy, the PRC had promised to take firm military action if Taiwan actually declared its independence. Options **A** ("open trade agreements upon Taiwanese independence"), **B** ("to forgive loans made for economic development"), and **C** ("technology transfers in genetic engineering and manufacturing") have no basis in reality. Option **E**, "None of the above are correct," is the right answer.

5. C. High levels of debt among many Third World nations has placed heavy burdens on natural resources in Third World countries (**C**). Option **A**, "brought about rampant corruption among First World bankers" is a nonsense answer (however tempting), and Option **B**, "benefited Western banks through foreclosure on Third World assets," might sound correct, except that there is no way that foreclosure could have taken place if the government of the Third World country did not want it to.

New Forms of Social Struggle and Revolution

Guerilla Struggles

Guerrilla warfare is generally understood as the use of small marginally trained groups conducting mobile military actions against targets often associated with the functioning of the government or economy. It is a form of warfare expressly avoiding direct conflicts with an opposing military force. While this type of warfare can be traced back to ancient history, guerrilla warfare in the twentieth century became a common form of resistance to the declining European colonial empires throughout the world. After the end of the Second World War, individuals, including Ho Chi Minh in Indochina and Che Guevara in Latin America, were inspired by nationalism and a desire for political independence. By the 1990s, guerilla warfare advocates, including Osama bin Laden, drew their strength from religious rather than secular ideologies but retained an almost romantic attachment to individual leaders.

Cuba

Until 1958, Cuba's Batista openly corrupt dictatorship retained the active support of the United States. By the early 1950s, a Cuban resistance movement began to form outside Cuba around the person of Fidel Castro. Beginning in 1953, however, **Castro's revolutionaries** in Miami and Mexico City launched the 26 July Movement. In December 1956, Castro's supporters landed in Cuba and incited revolts in Sierra Maestra and Santiago. Employing what is best defined as a form of guerilla warfare, popular support for the revolutionaries grew. Within two years, the revolts extended at all Cuba's major cities and even enjoyed the support of the American press. Within the United States, Castro's reputation declined in 1959 when he assumed a pro-Soviet stance and declared that Cuba would adopt a socialist style of government. As Castro formalized relations with the Soviet Union in 1960 and nationalized foreign firms, relations with the United States steadily declined until President Kennedy broke relations with the Cuban government in 1961. In 1961, the Kennedy administration sanctioned the invasion of Cuba by Cuban refugees trained in the United States. The invasion failed as quickly as it began in Cuba's the Bay of Pigs in early 1961. After this attempt by the American government to overthrown the Cuban government, Castro assumed a more open and aggressive support for Marxism-Leninism in exchange for Soviet aid and arms. These events set the stage for the Soviet-American clash over the placement of Soviet missiles in Cuba, better known as the Cuban Missile Crisis.

Numerous efforts were made to export the Cuban revolution to Africa and Latin America over the course of the 1960s. Applying the model of guerilla warfare as the key to political success, Che Guevara assisted Marxist forces in Congo and Bolivia until his death in 1967. Guevara rested his hopes largely on his reputation as a successful Cuban revolutionary. As revealed in his writings, Guevara also believed that active participation in guerilla warfare would elevate a sense of social justice and an understanding of the Marxist cause. Guevara's hopes of growing popular support for his revolutionary bands did not materialize.

Cuban support for Marxist revolutionaries continued into 1970s and 1980s. Rather than rely upon the support of the indigenous population, Castro attempted to export revolution with the assistance of large numbers of Cuban troops and Soviet military aid. Over the course of these two decades, Castro sent almost 100,000 Cuban troops into Angola, Ethiopia, and Nicaragua. In these cases, however, pro-Soviet Marxist groups were already well established. With the decline of the Soviet Union in the 1990s, Soviet aid to Cuba ended. Cuban foreign policy shifted from exporting revolution to providing revolutionaries/terrorists with a place of refuge, including known Basque, Colombian, Chilean, and Irish terrorists. Since the attacks on the World Trade Center on September 11, 2001, Castro has criticized the American war on **terrorism** in traditional Marxist terms while choosing, nevertheless, to give Cuban support for the United Nations' own campaign against terrorism.

Terrorism differs from guerilla warfare primarily in its emphasis on inspiring fear in a target population. State-sponsored terrorism has been associated with Iran, Syria, and Lybia, and has served as an alternative to traditional foreign policy. The United States has defined terrorism as planned violence directed against civilians by politically motivated groups.

However, "terrorist" groups have increasingly identified with radical religious circles rather than the secular ideologies of the early twentieth century, namely Marxism, fascism, and nationalism.

Vietnam

Vietnam has had a long history of cultural and political influence from outside its borders. While China proved the dominant influence early on, French colonial aspirations guided much of Vietnamese history in the nineteenth and twentieth centuries. Beginning in the 1850s, French control over Vietnam expanded and by 1867 included southern Vietnam; subsequently known as Cochinchina. Interested in Vietnam's natural resources, the French built the transportation system necessary to move raw materials from the interior to the ports. Vietnamese nationalists quickly discovered that French authorities would not tolerate any challenge to their political authority and forced Vietnamese nationalists into exile or imprisonment. Vietnamese nationalists, most notably Ho Chi Minh (1890-1969), interpreted French colonial policy as a consequence of western capitalism. As a participant in the founding of the French Communist Party, Ho went to study in Moscow and work with the Comintern, which actively supported pro-Soviet Marxist groups. While the Marxist-Leninist doctrine served to explain French colonial policy as a stage of capitalism, it also emphasized the need for a cadre of professional revolutionaries to incite popular revolt. In 1930 Ho formed an Indochinese Communist party. French authorities tolerated the new party and other opposition elements until 1938.

France's defeat in 1940 by Nazi Germany during the Second World War encouraged another outside power, Japan, to assume the role of colonial overlord. Anticipating the end of the war, Ho's Communists organized the broad Vietminh Front to secure Vietnam's independence. Ho's vision of the future Vietnamese state, however, was guided less by revolutionary Communist principles and more by a call for a nationalist agenda of limited political reform.

France's political revival in early 1945 and Japan's surrender in August 1945 set France on a collision course with the newly declared independent republic in Hanoi. Determined to reassert themselves in Vietnam, French forces began pushing the Vietminh into the northern territories. By late 1946, efforts at a diplomatic solution had failed and both sides prepared for war. Over the coming decade, Ho's nationalists successfully conducted a guerilla war against French forces. Despite increased American aid for the French, the French will to remain in Indochina broke with the fall of Dien Bien Phu in May 1954. Subsequent negotiations conducted in Geneva, Switzerland resulted in the creation of Laos, Cambodia, and Vietnam. Vietnam, however, was divided along the 17th parallel with elections slated for 1956 to determine Vietnam's political future. Apprehensive about Vietnam's drift into the Communist camp, the United States extended its support to the stanch Catholic anti-Communist Ngo Dinh Diem (1901–1963). Deim proved to be an uncontrollable and oppressive ruler imprisoning roughly 100,000 individuals he believed to be political opponents. Lacking popular support, it came as little surprise that Diem refused to honor the decision made in Geneva to hold elections in 1956. War with Ho's Viet Minh was only a matter of time.

As a second period of warfare running from 1959 to 1975, the United States escalated its military presence and by 1965 assumed the primary military responsibility for defending the Diem government. North Vietnam did not engage in typical military operations against South Vietnam. Rather, it orchestrated the guerrilla campaign of the National Liberation Front (Viet Cong) against South Vietnamese troops. By 1969, American anti-war sentiment led President Richard Nixon to seek a way out of Indochina. After the withdrawal of American troops, North Vietnamese troops increased pressure on South Vietnam, which was completely overrun by early 1975.

Reflecting back on Vietnam's path to unity and independence, guerilla warfare played a central role in Vietnamese success against France and the United States. Motivated by nationalist desires for an independent state and a generic understanding of the world through a Marxist point-of-view, the Vietnamese fought an anti-colonial war from 1946 to 1954. Within the context of the growing Cold War between the United States and the Soviet Union, American foreign policy by the early 1950s focused on containing the spread of Communism. Concern for the general populace or support for a more democratic process commonly gave way to support for regional strongmen willing to openly align their state with United States. During the 1960's, South Vietnam's Diem government enjoyed the extensive American military and financial support against the North Vietnamese sponsored Viet Cong guerrillas. This second war from 1959 to 1975 represented a continuation of the guerilla warfare conducted against the French. This second war, however, also demonstrated that America's technological edge could not overcome the damage done by a corrupt South Vietnamese government or the difficult jungle terrain where most of the fighting would take place.

237

Guerilla Struggles and the Emergence of the Religious State

The religious state has existed throughout human history when religious doctrine served as the social and legal foundation of the state. Classic examples of the religious state would include the Achaemenid and Ottoman Empires. Contemporary religious states, most notably Iran, are often Islamic. Contrary to a theocracy controlled by religious leaders, the modern religious state is a complicated merger of religious and secular groups. However, social and political issues are usually decided by either the leader of a religious state, for example Iran's Ruhollah Khomeini, or his immediate supporters. Minorities must act cautiously to avoid mistreatment. Similarly, foreign policy tends to be guided by religious interests before more secular concerns.

Afghanistan

Afghanistan's recent history begins with the Soviet Union invasion in 1979. Resistance to the Soviet presence was led by anti-Communist mujahidin forces, representing a merger of international Islamic and regional tribal interests. The Soviet-supported regime Communist regime finally collapsed in 1992. Despite the efforts of guerrilla leader Gulbuddin Hekmatyar to unify the factions, Afghanistan remained divided until late 1994 with the emergence of the Taliban, initially a Islamic fundamentalist militia. In 1996, Taliban first sought a working arrangement with Hekmatyar. By late 1996, however, Taliban forces controlled most of Afghanistan, including Kabul. Once in power, the Taliban created the religious state of the Islamic Emirate of Afghanistan. Between 1998 and 2000, the Taliban extended its control to virtually all regions except those controlled by the Northern Alliance, which had the support of the United States and the United Nations. Religious and ethnic division complicated cooperation between the factions even further. On the one hand, the Taliban identified with the Islam's mainstream Sunni tradition but are also strongly linked with the Pashtuns, a collection of roughly 60 tribes inhabiting the region between Afghanistan and Pakistan. In contrast, the Northern Alliance is more ethnically and religiously diverse, including followers of the Sunni and Shi'ite traditions, for example, the Hazara, and representatives of the major Turkic speaking peoples of Central Asia, namely, Tadjiks, Turkmen, and Uzbeks.

Politically, Taliban authorities strained relations with the United State further by refusing to turn over Osama bin Laden as well as tolerating his terrorist training base outside Kabul. Typical of an increasingly radicalized religious state, Taliban authorities ordered the destruction of all figures, ancient and modern. The most notable losses came in 2001 with the destruction of the two massive Buddhas (175 and 120 feet high) carved out of solid rock in Bamian, located on central northern Afghanistan inhabited by the Hazara. Dating back possibly as far as the seventh century, these Buddhas recalled earlier centuries when caravans crossed the region bringing both Chinese Buddhism and Buddhist monks. Taliban authorities also sought to reform Afghan society based upon their radicalized vision of Islam. As a result, Afghan women were denied basic civil rights, legal equality, as well as access to a basic education.

The September 11, 2001, terrorist attacks against the World Trade Center orchestrated by Osama bin Ladin and his organization, al Qaeda, resulted in joint military action on the part of the United States and the Northern Alliance. As the Taliban quickly collapsed, concerted efforts were made to track down Osama bin Ladin and those associated with al Qaeda. As an organization engaged in guerilla warfare, al Qaeda's loss of its training facilities accompanied the capture of leadership and rank-in-file elements. Beginning in January 2002, these individuals were transferred to the United States military prison at Guantanamo on the island of Cuba. The approximately 600 prisoners in question came from 43 different countries. While a great deal of controversy exists over the legal status of these individuals, their individual histories have revealed a loose-knit collection of terrorist organizations and affiliated groups. These groups are unified behind a veneer of fundamentalist Islamic values, staunchly anti-Western beliefs, and an intent to change the policies of the non-Islamic world through acts of terrorism. Concurrently, Afghanistan's political reconstruction began in Bonn, Germany, with a meeting of various Afghan leaders. By October 2004, Afghanistan had a democratic constitution and a democratically elected president in Hamid Karzai.

Iran

The Iranian plateau had been the home of the the Sasanid Empire until the seventh century when Arab power swept through the region. Prior to that time, Sasanid society adhered to the religious and political doctrines of Zoroastrianism, the official state religion. Better known in the twentieth century as Persia, Iran remained a monarchy under Shah Mohammed Reza Pahlevi until January 16, 1979, when he was forced into exile. Long before he went into exile beginning in the 1950s, his government became well known for the brutality of its internal security forces but also for a foreign and domestic policy pushing the westernization of Iranian society. In the preceding months his exile, violent clashes between the shah's security forces and anti-shah demonstrators eroded what support remained for the monarchy. Opposition to the shah found expression in popular support for Ayatollah Ruholla Khomeini's Muslim traditionalist movement, operating from exile in France. Under his leadership, Iran became Islamic republic in 1979.

Khomeini's traditionalist movement established a religious state where political authority rested heavily on the religious leader himself, namely, Ayatollah Ruholla Khomeini. The seizure of the American embassy in Tehran in November 1979 by Iranian students (but with the tacit approval of the new government) severely strained relations between the United States and Iran. The hostage crisis which ensued would not be resolved until January 1981, following the election of Ronald Reagan over Jimmy Carter as United States President. Further clashes with the United States occurred during the final years of the Iran-Iraq war in the Persian Gulf in 1987–1988.

Iranian government agencies, namely, Iran's Islamic Revolutionary Guard Corps and Ministry of Intelligence and Security, have been active sponsors of a variety of terrorist groups and activities. With the election of the more moderate President Mohammad Khatami in 1997, Iran foreign policy softened its hard stance towards the United States and condemned attacks by Algerian and Egyptian terrorist groups. Anti-American political statements aside, Iranian leaders do not appear to have played any role in the attacks on the World Trade Center in 2001. On the other hand, Iranian supported the Palestinian up-risings against Israel and Palestinian terrorist groups, most especially HAMAS, Hezballah, the Popular Front For The Liberation Of Palestine-General Command, and the Palestine Islamic Jihad, all of which focus their energies on the destruction of the state of Israel and its replacement with an Islamic Palestinian state. There is also significant evidence that Iran has implemented a policy of assassinating dissidents abroad, including, Khomeini's condemnation of Salman Rusdie's *Satanic Verses* (1988) and fatwa (or legal pronouncement) for the his death.

Israelis versus Palestinians

Israelis and Palestinians constitute two very diverse groups in the modern Middle East. Israelis represent a new nationality composed of European and American Jews assimilated into the existing Arab-Jewish population inhabiting Palestine. Israelis identify Biblical Israel and Jerusalem, in particular, as the historical territories of the Jewish state, and generally speak Hebrew. Theodor Herzl, founder of the Zionist movement, first called for the creation of a Jewish state in 1896. Inspired by ideas of European nationalism and rising Antisemitism in France, Zionism also appealed to Russian Jews (many of whom lived in the territories identified today as Poland), who were regular victims of pogroms. Zionists believed that the settlement of as many Jews as possible in Palestine would create the foundations for the future creation of an independent Jewish state. The Palestinian people, in contrast to Israelis, speak a form of Arabic, practice Sunnite Islam, and trace their origins to the Palestine itself. Of the roughly two million Palestinians, the majority reside in territories under Israeli occupation, the West Bank, and Gaza.

Israel's unique origins reveal the origins of many of the problems faced in the Middle East today. Israel's remote origins begin with the decline of the Ottoman Empire and the emergence of modern day Turkey, on the one hand, and the emergence of the Zionist movement, on the other. Under the Paris Peace Settlement concluding the First World War, the defeated Turks watched as portions of the former Ottoman Empire were awarded by the League of Nations to Britain and France. The British mandate included Palestine. The Zionist movement traced its origins to the efforts of Theodor Herzl. While Jewish interest in Palestine has deep historical roots, Antisemitism in Russia and France encouraged Jewish leaders in 1880s-1890s to organize the movement of Jews to Palestine to avoid persecution. Encouraged by the Britain's Balfour Declaration of 1917, European Jewish leaders felt they had support for the creation of a homeland for Jews in Palestine, assuming Britain and her Allies won the war. When Britain assumed control over Palestine after the war under the mandate given them by the League of Nations, however, British authorities limited Jewish immigration to Palestine and plans for a Jewish homeland were put on hold.

Jewish settlements in Palestine rose rapidly from 80,000 in 1919 to almost a half million two decades later. Jewish immigration to Palestine increased significantly after 1933 with Hitler's rise to power in Germany. Concurrently, Arab mistrust of British authorities and resistance to further Jewish immigration reached violent proportions in the early 1920s and later in 1929 and 1936. British proposals to partition Palestine in 1937 into separate Jewish and Palestinian areas found little support among either Jews or Palestinians.

The Second World War and the Holocaust fundamentally changed Jewish attitudes and plans regarding a future independent state for the Jews. During the war, the British army trained a small number of Palestinians Jews as a defensive force against a possible German invasion. Some gained additional military experience during Allied efforts to take Italy from the Germans in 1944. Concurrently, news about Holocaust spread through Zionist circles. Zionist nationalism combined with the events of the Holocaust radicalized Jewish demands for a separate state for the Jews.

While Britain, the United States, and the United Nations conducted hearings and proposed studies on Palestine problem in 1946–1947, Jewish terrorist groups, namely, the Irgun, Stern, and Haganah, escalated their attacks against the British as they sought to move as many Jews as possible to Palestine. Attempting to stem the tide of Arab-Jewish tension, British policy aggressively limited further immigration. By 1948, the British government lost faith in its ability to control the situation and declared their intention to evacuate Palestine on May 15, 1948. On May 14, Jewish Provisional State Council proclaimed in Tel Aviv the existence of the State of Israel, with Chaim Weizmann (1874–1952) as Israel's first president, David Ben-Gurion as prime minister. The former underground Jewish army (and terrorist group in British circles), the Haganah, became the new army of Israel. On May 15, every Islamic state bordering the new state of Israel as well as Iraq, specifically, Egypt, Lebanon, Syria, and Transjordan (now Jordan) declared their support for Arab/Palestinian guerillas in their fight against the Jews. Israel, on the other hand, was quickly recognized only a few days later as a legitimate state by both the United States and Soviet Union.

The Middle East has been the scene of a series of clashes between Israel and the Arab world since 1948. The first Arab-Israeli war (also known as the Israeli War of Independence) lasted from 1948 into 1949. Although trained in part by the British, Arab military forces proved no match to their Israeli counterparts. The Suez War in 1956 resulted in Israel's momentary occupation of Egypt's Sinai Peninsula. Over the course of the 1960s, Israel also confronted the Palestine Liberation Organization (PLO), led by Yassir Arafat until his death, which employed a combination of guerilla warfare and terrorist attacks. The Six-Day War in 1967 included Israel's seizure of the West Bank, Sinai, and Golan Heights. The Yom Kippur War of 1973 caught Israeli forces off guard in a surprise attack by Egypt and Syria but failed to defeat Israel. Since 1973, Israel has taken a more proactive stand to protect itself. In 1982, Israel invaded of Lebanon in an effort to destroy the PLO. The Israeli occupation of southern Lebanon lasted until 2000 as Israel sought the creation of a buffer zone between itself and the rest of Lebanon. Beginning in late 2000 and lasting until early 2004, the so-called "Al-Aqsa" Intifada unleashed another round of guerrilla warfare between Israel and Palestinian groups resulting in thousands of deaths.

One Land/Two Histories

Israel and Palestine represent two histories competing for one land. Each claims a unique history and culture. Israeli nationalism, that is, Zionism, took advantage of the political uncertainty of the British mandate over Palestine and international sympathy generated by revelations of Hitler's policy of genocide towards the Jews. In contrast, the Palestinian sense of identity remained divided between several components, namely, as members of a greater Arabic and Islamic community, on the one hand, and as current or former inhabitants of the territory of Palestine.

Israel

Since the 1991 Madrid Conference, Israeli policy towards the Palestinians has softened. In an attempt to initiate a reconciliation of outstanding differences, Israel agreed in September 1993 in principle to Palestinian self-rule. In October 1994, Israel-Jordan Treaty of Peace ended decades of territorial disputes. In May 2000, Israel ended its occupation of southern Lebanon. In June 2002, the United States endorsed the objective of a two-state solution.

Palestine

As a territory from 1918 to 1948, the British mandate of Palestine included the Israel, Jordan, Gaza, and the West Bank. Politically, the Palestinians became a refugee people with an uncertain future living in territories under Israeli occupation. Arabic states supporting the Palestinian cause did not welcome the presence of large numbers of Palestinian refugees. These conflicting images may account for the immense frustration felt on the part of Palestinians and their leaders. It may also explain the regular outbreak of apparent spontansous violence against Israel. With the death of the Yasser Arafat in 2004, the PLO must elevate a new generation of leaders who may be better prepared to accept a negotiated solution with Israel. It remains to be seen if Palestinians and their leaders are ready to endorse a two-state solution.

There is a major difference between these exceptional cases in the context of Israeli politics (which even include a few orthodox Jews promoting the dissolution of the state of Israel as well as more terroristic elements) and Palestinian groups who uniformly promote the dissolution of the state of Israel as well as the implicit sanctioning of the killing of Jews. Furthermore, Israel is democratically governed, has a court system, and other legal checks-and-balances. Typical of any democracy, the system doesn't work perfectly and not all groups are satisfied with the results—but the political opposition is not in danger of losing its life or income. Within the Palestinian camp, however, there was no political unity at any level and no effort at a system governed by the rule of law until very recently—and there is still a serious debate as to the level of success of this effort.

It is a different argument, however, to ask if Palestinians deserve this fate or if other parties—Arab and Israeli alike— could not have taken more aggressive measures to address the welfare of the Palestinian people. The Palestinians have been caught as a people and as a political tool. In the beginning, Arab leaders encouraged Palestinians to engage in acts of violence against Israel while early Israeli leaders provided Palestinians with little reason to assume that the new Jewish state would adequately protect their economic, religious, and social interests. The decades since the 1940s have not yielded a significant change in Arab or Israeli policy towards the Palestinians.

Terrorism

Terrorism has a legal concept has eluded a precise definition. Islamic theologians gathering in Mecca in 2003 proved no more successful than western specialists in international law. Terrorism, in the most general sense, has been and remains part of the history of every region of the world. By the end of the 20th century, terrorism conceptually represented a fundamental change in attitude by official authorities towards states and groups employing violence to alter the political and social status quo. Specifically, it refocused public attention on violence directed against civilian rather than government targets. American involvement escalated existing anti-terrorist measures from largely international police actions to almost unilateral acts of military intervention. Conceptually, American policy constituted an extension of the Monroe Doctrine onto a global scale.

9/11

September 11, 2001, moved Americans to reevaluate the process of globalization and America's role in it. Prior to the attacks on the World Trade Center, Americans passively accepted history as justifying the cause of western-styled democracy. Francis Fukuyama's *The End of History and the Last Man* (1992) popularly received work argued that liberal democracy had proven itself to be the final stage of humanity's political evolution. The attacks on September 11 forced Americans to confront the problems of globalization and their own growing susceptibility to events unfolding on a global stage. Specifically, American involvement in Afghanistan and Iraq changed American perceptions of the world towards a more active role in influencing the course of world affairs.

September 11 must also be understood within the context of political Islamism. Contrary to Asia and Latin America, Marxist and Socialist doctrines found little support in traditionally Islamic regions. On the other hand, the West's vision of a secular liberal democracy also failed to attract significant support. As a reform movement, political Islamism seeks to bridge the gap between a religious ideal of proper government and the dynamics of fractions within government. Islamic fundamentalists, however, would be inclined to reject any compromise on religious principles. Frustration with a lack of progress towards the creating of the ideal Islamic state and a strong belief in the social justice of their cause have led some within the Islamic world to see terrorism as their only recourse, including Osama bin Ladin.

Iraq

Although part of the Ottoman Empire in modern times, Iraq fell to British force during the World War I and became a British mandate under the League of Nations in 1920. Iraqi nationalists operating out of Syria took various approaches to forcing a British withdrawal. Popular revolts against the British presence spread throughout Iraq with the exception of major cities control by British military forces, namely, Baghdad, Basra, and Mosul. Although British authorities successfully suppressed the revolts, Britain conceded to Iraqi nationalist aspirations in 1929 and declared the mandate would be terminated in 1932. The new monarchical government, however, never enjoyed popular support. Led by reform-minded young officers, a "republic" replaced the monarchy with a republic in 1958. This first republic endured until 1968 when the Ba'ath Party, counting Saddam Hussein among its key leaders, and Iraqi military overthrew the presidency of 'Abd ar-Rahman 'Arif in a bloodless coup. Despite the image of republican government, Iraqi politics was dominated by a series of military strongmen, including Saddam Hussein, who assumed power in 1979.

Taking advantage of the apparent confusion associated with Iran's revolution, Saddam Hussein led Iraq in 1980 into a brutal and costly war with Iran that was heavily subsidized by the United States. After eight years of fighting, a United Nations proposed cease-fire was accepted by both sides 1988. Exhausted by the war with Iran, Hussein pressured Kuwait, which had extended substantial loans to Iraq to finance the war, to cancel the debt. While Kuwait's immense oil resources were one factor in Iraqi thinking, Kuwait's refusal to cancel the Iraqi debt resulted in the August 1990 Iraqi invasion of Kuwait. The Iraqi military quickly overran Kuwait and its capital city, Kuwait City, in a matter of hours. The international community, including the Arab world, condemned the invasion and supported an American-led coalition of United Nations forces to liberate Kuwait. Kuwait's liberation arrived in January-February 1991; now referred to as the Gulf War. Although portions of the military campaign took place on Iraqi territory, its purpose remained limited to the removal of Iraqi military forces from Kuwait but not the removal the Saddam Hussein and his supporters from power. During the war, Hussein appealed to the greater Arabic and Islamic community for support. To that end, he attempted unsuccessfully to provoke Israeli involvement in the war by launching a series of missiles towards Israel. In the wake of Iraq's military defeat, Iraq would be required by the United Nations Security Council eliminate its weapons of mass destruction, including long-range missiles, its capacity to produce these weapons, and allow UN-directed inspections top verify that these measures had been implemented.

After a brief period of cooperation with United Nations inspectors, Iraqi authorities chose not to cooperate but increasingly evade verification efforts by the United Nations. During this same period, Iraq actively supported a number of well-known terrorist groups and provided bases to several terrorist groups including the Mujahedin-e-Khalq (also known as the National Liberation Army of Iran), the Kurdistan Workers' Party (PKK), whose operations are largely directed against Turkey, as well as anti-Israeli terrorist groups, including Palestine Liberation Front (centered in Lebanon), Popular Front for the Liberation of Palestine (operating from Lebanon and SyriA. and the Abu Nidal organization, whose leadership moved to Baghdad in 1998. (The Abu Nidal organization split off from the Palestinian Liberation Organization in 1974 and received financial support from Libya, Syria (until 1987), and Iraq.) Although Iraqi foreign policy clearly included support for terrorist groups throughout the 1980s–1990s, it did not represent the export of a revolutionary message typical of Cuban revolutionaries. Contrary to figures like Che Guevara and Ho Chi Minh, Saddam Hussein did not become the rallying-point for any of these groups nor were Iraqi troops sent in to provide support. Additionally, Iraq directed its statements primarily towards the Arab world in support for an anti-Israeli and Anti-American course of action. Rather, there appears to have been a collusion of interests, which were tapped by Iraqi authorities for their own regional purposes.

The American-led invasion of Iraq in March 2003 traced its origins to Iraqi resistance to United Nationals resolutions extending back to the first Gulf War in 1990. Concern centered over Iraq's alleged development of weapons of mass destruction, including chemical, biological, and possibly nuclear weapons. Iraqi authorities denied United Nations inspectors access to facilities and documentation to confirm Iraq's claim that it had destroyed all such facilities after the Gulf War. Frustrated with the apparent inability of the United Nations to force Iraqi compliance, the United States chose unilaterally to invade Iraq. The invasion proved militarily successful and quickly toppled the regime of Saddam Hussein. The failure to find weapons of mass destruction, however, proved a political embarrassment. Nevertheless, political reconstruction began in June 2004 when the Coalition Provisional Authority transferred sovereignty to the Iraqi Interim Government. In January 2005 Iraqis took part in national elections for the Transitional National Assembly, which would assume the responsibility of drafting a permanent constitution. It is believed that popular support for the insurgency will subside with the completion of the new constitution.

Practice Test Questions

1. Guerilla warfare is best defined as

   A. a direct confrontation with an opposing military force.
   B. a political movement.
   C. a small group tactic.
   D. All of the above.

2. Terrorism is perhaps best understood as

   A. directed against civilians to inspire fear.
   B. motivated by Islamic beliefs.
   C. inherently anti-West.
   D. All of the above.

3. Afghanistan recent history included all of the following *except*

   A. a drawn out struggle against the Soviet military.
   B. a return to monarchical rule.
   C. the introduction of a more democratic form of government.
   D. All of the above.

4. Palestinians can be characterized as all of the following *except*

   A. were welcomed into other Islamic countries as victims of Israeli policy.
   B. are Arabic-speaking.
   C. identify with Sunnite Islam.
   D. All of the above.

5. Political Islamism represents a very recent attempt to

   A. provide Islamic (as opposed to western) solutions to governing the state.
   B. secure a more secular way of life.
   C. recruit younger Arabs for military service.
   D. All of the above.

Answers and Explanations

1. **C.** While the term may make us think of Cuban revolutionaries, it has a much broader application applicable to many examples in history; thus, it is better understood as a small group tactic.

2. **A.** Terrorism has been practiced by groups from both political extremes of the right and left as well as served as a tool for religious extremists. It differs from guerilla warfare primarily in its targeting of civilians for the expressed purpose of inspiring fear. Terrorism is not unique to Islam and all terrorists are not necessarily anti-West.

3. **B.** Afghanistan was ruled by a monarch for most of it history. Recent history, however, drove Afghanistan into the ranks of religious states.

4. **A.** Much the contrary, Islamic states (especially Jordan) have proven to be unsympathetic to the Palestinian cause. Although the official press may strongly suggest otherwise, Palestinians residing outside territories occupied by Israel have proven dangerous and poverty-stricken. Southern Lebanon would be one region. In 1971, there was an open clash between Palestinians and Jordan's king, also known as Black September.

5. **A.** Typical of political terminology, this very general label covers a wide range of states. As a new movement, it fills a cultural gap caused by discredited European influence, the rise of regional nationalisms, and the rise of Islamic reform movements.

Social Reforms and Social Revolutions

Feminism and Changing Gender Roles

Feminism is the idea and ideology that, contrary to tradition, women should have and enjoy equal rights in law, the political arena, as well as in business and the professions. Additionally, in the area of reproduction, feminists argue that women should have control over their own bodies and have the power to decide for themselves whether or not they will bear children and when. In the western world, though feminism emerged in the early nineteenth century as one of the consequences of Enlightenment thinking and the revolutionary fervor, the implications (such as reproduction rights) of early feminist thinking were not fully developed until after World War II.

The West

In many western countries, the nineteenth century saw a slow drift toward greater rights and roles for women. Property ownership laws were liberalized to allow for greater rights for women as individuals (rather than as wives), as were laws in the United States, Britain, and other western European countries, which loosened restrictions of divorce.

After almost a century of protest and agitation, most of these countries had extended the voting franchise to women by the 1920s. Although there were still some die-hard beliefs that women did not possess the hard-headed mentality necessary for political thought, that was not the reason why the franchise was withheld into the twentieth century.

In the United States, though some states had extended the vote to women as early as the 1870s (mostly western states), there was not a national requirement until the ratification of the Nineteenth Amendment in 1920. In most American states, there was no "secret ballot" until the early twentieth century. A person's vote was either cast publicly or it was a matter of public record.

This meant that a woman's vote, if allowed, would be known to her husband, and the cultural norm was that husbands dominated their wives. If you gave the vote to women, so the objection went, you would be giving her husband two votes—his and hers. With the universal adoption of the secret ballot, this last objection to women voting fell away and it was only a matter of a few years before Progressives were able to push through an amendment. Similar movements had been underway in England and other western European countries as well.

Some Europeans extended the vote to women relatively early. Finland did so in 1906 and Norway followed suit in 1913. After the Russian Revolution, the Bolshevik government enfranchised women in 1917. In France, though, equal suffrage did not come until the end of World War II. Belgium followed in 1946. In Switzerland, women were denied the vote in federal elections until 1971. Among the British Commonwealth nations, New Zealand granted suffrage in 1893, Australia in 1902, and Canada in 1917 (except in Quebec, where it was postponed until 1940). In Latin American countries, the franchise was extended to women in Brazil in 1934, El Salvador in 1939, the Dominican Republic in 1942, Guatemala in 1945, and Argentina and Mexico both in 1946. In East Asia, Philippine women have voted since 1937, Japanese women since 1945, in the People's Republic of China since 1949.

The French experience with voting rights for women was an interesting twist of twentieth century politics. Women had been important players in the French Revolution, the creation of the French Republic of 1848, and in the uprisings of the Paris Commune in the 1870s. Oddly enough, a female suffrage movement did not develop until the end of the nineteenth century. Opposition to women suffrage came from both the Left and the Right. Leftists feared that women would vote for conservatives and thus endanger their power. Conservative Catholics opposed the vote for women because their leaders believed that suffrage would help bring about the breakup of the family.

It was perhaps out of this French experience that feminism as such emerged in post-war Europe. One influencial French feminist, Simone de Beauvoir, saw the condition of women in the modern world in "existential" terms (she was the wife of the French Existentialist Jean Paul Sartre. In her landmark book, *The Second Sex* (1949), Beauvoir argued that one may be born female, but one *becomes* a woman through socialization a acculturation. Part of that cultural process was, she argued, to conceptualize women as "The Other"—that is, the non-male. This conceptualization, Beauvoir argued, was fundamental to women's oppression.

By the 1960s, the modern "women's movement" emerged as a mostly middle-class phenomenon, but by the 1970s it was global and included Third World countries and women of the working classes. By this time, a woman's position in society had changed a great deal since the nineteenth century. The old idea that a woman's place was in the home was now being challenged on two essential grounds. The first was that many women had to work in order to support themselves and their families, either as single-parents or as one of two breadwinners. This condition was especially true of women in the lower classes. At various times, governments had even called upon women to enter the workforce, as during World War I and World War II.

The other basis for challenging the traditional "housewife" role was that many women were no longer satisfied with such a limited and narrow challenge. Along with this went the widespread availability and acceptance of contraception in many western countries which meant that women had more choice—that biology did not mean destiny. Women could have fewer children, or they could have them at times they chose instead of only when "nature took its course." In some countries still dominated by Catholic majorities (such as Ireland), easy and legal access to contraception came as late as the the 1990s.

As good example of feminist activism can be found in the story of the American feminist, Betty Freidan. In 1963, Freidan published her landmark book, *The Feminine Mystic.* In 1957 Freidan surveyed her fellow Smith College alumnae and found that a large number of them felt as she did—suffocated and unfulfilled. The challenges of domestic life came no where near utilizing their potential as intelligent and very-well-educated women. As a result of her survey, Freidan researched and wrote *The Feminine Mystic.* The book was a best-seller, and it spurred others to address many of the same issues. In 1966, Freidan and other feminist activists organized the National Organization for Women (NOW). As active in the political arena as in its efforts at cultural reform, NOW would press for legislation to end discrimination against women in the workplace, to legalize abortion, and to obtain government funding for child-care centers.

In 1973, feminist activists celebrated the landmark Supreme Court decision in the case of *Roe v. Wade,* which outlawed any legislation to forbid abortion during the first trimester of pregnancy. The court based its decision on what it argued was the Constitutionally-protected right of privacy, that the decision to obtain an abortion was a matter of private concern to a woman and not a public matter. Feminists saw this a powerful statement endorsing the idea that women "own" their own bodies and have full control over them.

In many other western countries, by the 1960s and 1970s, laws were enacted to promote equal access to employment, and equal pay for equal work. In the United States, the Affirmative Action program was expanded to include women as a "protected category."

But even as women were more and more accepted in what were once thought to be "male-only" professions, the statistics could often be disheartening. Even by the turn of the twentieth century, on average, women were paid less for the same work as men, and in some professions and line of work still faced various forms of discrimination and exclusion.

In many cases, there still exists what some have called the "glass ceiling"—one could climb the corporate ladder, for instance, and see no obstacles above as one climbed, but then bump hard into the glass ceiling, a barrier for women that otherwise was invisible. One need only look at statistics on the numbers of women in high corporate office to see that something is going on. By one recent count, only about one percent of the world's corporations are headed by a woman CEO.

East Asian Societies

From its beginnings, the Chinese Communist Party aggressively criticized traditionally rigid Confucian gender roles, making women's equality a major part of their program. After their 1949 victory, the Communists pushed women into the workplace, outlawed foot-binding and prostitution, and portrayed women as "comrades" who, with men, were advancing the "revolution." The typical image in films and other media productions was of the brave woman soldier, farmer, or worker. The party encouraged women to build their character and contribution to society rather than to focus on their looks and their families. This idea was advanced ferociously during the so-called "Cultural Revolution" in the 1960s.

Since the slow liberalization of Chinese society began in the 1980s, and with the introduction of capitalist elements into the Chinese economy, some observers note that many of the gains made by women during the "Revolution" have been lost. Some have argued that as market forces and western goods and ideas infiltrate Chinese society that the norm increasingly is that men as seen as the most appropriate wage-earners, and that women should be domestic care-givers and sexual objects.

Similar changes have taken place in Japan, though for very different reasons. After the Meiji Restoration and the extremely-rapid industrialization of Japanese society began in the second half of the nineteenth century, women became one of the keys to the country's economic success. In spite of rapid change and social upheaval, women were to be the moral foundation of Japanese life. The Japanese government even promoted the idea that women should build the nation by having more children.

This does not mean, however, that women were to remain only at home. Women would work in large numbers in the textile mills of Japan and in so doing contribute to Japan's economic rise. By the turn of the twentieth century, women accounted for almost two-thirds of the industrial labor force. Most were paid very low wages and worked in conditions similar to exploited labor elsewhere—that is, very poor conditions.

In the decades that led up to the Second World War, the position of women in Japan changed little, though some educators and government leaders sometimes engaged in politcal rhetoric that spoke of equality for women as a aspect of the class equality that was the official (though never the actual) policy of the japanese government. Women could not votes, they could not divorce their husbands, though they were subject to easy divorce by their husbands.

During World War II the role of women in Japan changed, as it did in most of the beligerant countries. With so many millions of men removed from industry in the armed forces, women found themselves working in coal mines, steel mills, and arms factories. With their husbands gone, wives were now in complete control of the home.

In the aftermath of the war, the Americans occupiers forced a number of reforms on Japanese society. Though otherwise known for his conservatism, the Allied Supreme Commander, Gen. Douglas MacArthur, insisted on extending equal rights for women in Japanese life. The vote had been given to women in 1946, and the labor law of 1947 required equal pay for equal work. As in many other countries, these laws have often not been strong enough to end inequality and other abuses in many cases.

During the postwar decades, many observers have noted a shift in power within the Japanese family, as wives and mothers would see to the daily operation and economy of the family and the husbands and fathers would be absent for long hours working, and long hours communiting to and from work. Similarly, though women are underrepresented in government office, Japanese women commonly exercise significant political power at the "grass roots" level, particularly with regard to consumer and environmental affairs.

In these way, the situtation for women in modern-day Japan can be compared to that in Britain, the United States, and other western countries—equality and equal access on paper, inequality and the expectation of traditional women's roles as mother and homemaker still predominantly the reality.

Religious States

Over the decades since 1914, in countries where religion played a large role in the formulation of government policies—most of the Islamic and some of the Catholic countries—changes in gender-defined roles have a spotty record. In fairly secularized Islamic countries such as Egypt and Turkey, women acquired more and more freedoms over the decades than in more conservative countries such as Afghanistan, Iran, and Saudi Arabia, and regime changes in some of these countries has resulted in either significant advances for women (as in Afghanistan after the fall of the Taliban regime in 2001) or in declines (as in Iran after the 1979 revolution that deposed the secular regime of the Shah).

It should be noted that in a few respects, Islamic law has for centuries been more liberal than in Christian countries with regard to two issues: the separate (separate from their husbands) ownership of property and the freedom to divorce without the consent of the husband.

Nevertheless, in some Islamic countries women are greatly restricted in public. They are not allowed to be seen unless fully covered by the burka (including their faces), and they must be accompanied by men in public places. In some countries, employment outside the home is prohibited, and "morals police" can arrest women for violations of the laws.

In some predominantly Catholic countries such as Ireland and Portugal, women enjoy more or less the same freedoms and rights as in other western nations, except that access to abortion and contraception is more difficult. The Roman Catholic Church is opposed to the use of contraception and strongly condemns abortion. In addition to Ireland and Portugal, the mostly Catholic countries of Malta, Poland, Slovakia, and Spain either greatly restrict abortion or ban it altogether. All of these countries are representative democracies, but the majority of voters have repeatedly rejected referendums that significantly liberalized anti-abortion laws. Often this means that women seeking abortions must travel to neighboring countries with more liberal laws.

The Family Structure

By the twentieth century, much had changed in family life around the world. The centrality of urbanized industry had replaced family-centered production on farms as the basis for the social order in most of the western world. This meant that one or more "breadwinners" had to leave the family home to "bring home the bacon" from outside employment. As mothers were still seen as the primary child care provider for the family, this usually meant that fathers left the home and worked long hours out of contact with his wife and children.

Paradoxically, though officially women had acquired nearly equal civil and legal rights by the middle of the century, at home their rights and influence were generally in decline. At issue was the distribution of power within the marriage unit. When the family was understood to be the unit of production, and when the labor of production was shared by both husbands and wives, and to whatever extent possible by the children, there was no basis other than "patriarchic" tradition for male dominance.

When production was family-centered, this tradition was tempered by shared labor to provide necessities and wants for the family. In the industrial age, there was no similar tempering of tradition, and the valuation exclusively of men's work enhanced his power in the home.

It should be noted that much of the foregoing explanation is a generalization, and that families are far more complex and have to do with much more than just relationships of production. Nevertheless, the impacts of the "Great Transformation" on family life cannot be ignored. It should also be noted that in those countries around the world where there was still significant family-centered production, the same dynamic was not at work.

The loosening of social restrictions and mores than accompanied the transformations of the twentieth century had a number of important effects of the family, especially in the West and in those part of the world that were increasingly influenced by western economies and ways of life (such as Japan and Indonesia). One of these effects was a general (and sometimes alarming) increase in rates of divorce.

Before the twentieth century, divorce was usually very difficult to obtain, even for kings such as Henry VIII. Since the Koran made provisions for relatively-easy divorce, the changes of the twentieth century had little effect on Islamic countries, but this was not true of Judeo-Christian, Hindu, or Buddhist countries. For them, secularization meant a greater number of divorces.

Increased divorce resulted in an increase in the number of single-parent families, though remarriage is almost as frequent as divorce so often the single-parent condition is only temporary. Some have argued, in fact, that divorce rates seem worse than they are (in the United States, for instance, half of all marriages end in divorce) because they are inflated by multiple marriage and divorce—one person marrying *and* divorcing more than once.

In demographic terms, the family underwent great changes during the twentieth century, and not just in the so-called "developed" nations. By and large, the demographic transition as discussed in Chapters 19 and 29 continued to operate into the twentieth century. By the end of twentieth century, the industrialized and "post-industrial" countries (those whose economies are no longer dominated by industry but instead by "service" and "information" sectors) were in Phase I—best described as low birth and low death (LB/LD) rates with the resulting very slow or even negative natural growth (excluding growth by immigration). In these countries, families are small and childless marriages are much more common than in past eras. In some Western countries this point was reached just after World War II. In the United States, there was a short-lived growth in the birth rate known popularly as the baby boom that lasted between 1945 and 1964.

But what then of the non-industrialized world and those countries that are in the process of "development" and industrialization during these decades? By and large, after World War II these countries had entered Phase III of the transition, a phase of high birth rates and low or declining death rates. Population growth by natural means took on in the countries of Africa, Southern America, and Southeast Asia, with growth rates that were sometimes alarming (see Chapter 29 for an more detailed description). Birth control, education, and even the AIDS pandemic do not seem to have had much effect on this rapid growth. What then of families in these countries. Time will tell, but thus far a lifetime of poverty seems most likely. Additionally, as population and economic conditions force more and more families into the already bulging cities, extended family ties in local traditional communities will either be severely stretch, or will be severed outright, forcing nuclear families to face their many challenges without traditional support networks.

Some countries that have experienced rapid and alarming population growth have taken measures to curb their birth rates. The most notable example is China's one-child policy adopted in 1979. The policy limited couples living in urban areas to a single child. Fines, various official pressures to abort a second pregnancy, and in some cases forced sterilization have resulted from enforcement of the policy. As heavy-handed as it is, the one-child law has reduced population growth in China (with an estimated 2005 population of 1.25 *billion*) by some 300 million people since it was implemented.

The one-child policy was had a very serious effect on family lives and relationships. Traditionally, male children had always been preferred in China—partly because sons were later obligated to take care their parents in old age, an obligation not incumbent (or even possible) for daughters. Now, if a couple could have only one child, they preferred that child be a boy. The traditional disdain for girls has been greatly intensified, and high rates of do-it-yourself abortions, abandonment, and even infanticide (not otherwise uncommon in China) have happened as a result to female infants. Further the unfortunate impacts on family life, estimates are that in 2005, there is now a ratio of 118 males for every 100 females of childbearing years. The unavoidable consequence of this is that almost one out of every five men will not be able to marry. And what are the social and familial consequences of that?

International Marxism

As a mode of historical analysis, **Marxism** assumes that society is founded on the "relations of production"—those who own the "means of production" (land, animals, machinery, and so on) are in a position to control those who do not, and to "expropriate" the largest share of the fruits of production—which should go to those who actual perform production labor (the "workers") for themselves.

Marxism also assumes a progression in history regarding the relationships of production, and this leads to its political and revolutionary implications. Just as the bourgeoisie (the commercial and industrial middle classes—not workers) had overthrown the power of the aristocracy by the nineteenth century, so would the proletariat (the workers) overthrow the middle class and form a society in which the means of production were owned by society as a whole, for the benefit of all.

As a political ideology, Marxism in the twentieth century was focused on replacing free-market capitalism with communism, through revolutionary means if necessary. Since the publication of Karl Marx's landmark book, *Capital* and his death in 1883, various socialist-oriented movements around the world have looked to Marxism as both a mode of historical and economic analysis, but also as an ideological basis for their political programs and platforms.

It is important to note that there have been since the nineteenth century and there still is a side array of left-oriented "socialisms" that were either developed before Marxism or that had little to do with Marxist analysis and politics. And even with the Marxist branch of socialism, there have been significant differences of opinion. Some Marxists have argued who argued that the transition to socialism should take place within the "liberal" parliamentary structures that have existed in Europe and the United States for a long time.

Other Marxists believed that change could come only though revolutionary means—that the capitalist middle classes would never voluntarily reform itself in the direction of socialism. The Marxists who took the revolutionary stance came to be known generally as Communists, and all others were often known generically as socialists (though during the Cold War in the United States, any one with left-of-center ideas was apt to be called a Communist).

Marx himself thought that socialism would come incrementally, just as capitalism had emerged bit-by-bit out of feudalism and aristocracy. Capitalism, which he admitted was an improvement over feudalism, would eventually evolve into a class-less society in which the state "withers away" as unnecessary. The means of production (factories, utilities, transportation facilities, and large farms would be owned collectively, and society would no longer be divided into workers and owners.

It probably should go without saying that such a society never emerged in an the so-called communist countries, and to the extent that they still exist, it has not occurred yet. The reason why seems clear: the authoritarian regimes established in the wake of the communist revolutions were simply unwillingness to give up the power they seized in the first place.

Instead the communist regimes establish one-party rule and tried then tried to force a Marxist model on peoples who, by and large, had not yet even entered the industrial capitalist phase of their historical development. Marx himself commented in his writings that the least likely choices for communist development in the foreseeable future were exactly those countries were Communist revolution were later successful in seizing power: Russia and China.

"Communist" and "Marxist" are fairly problematic terms for countries that were (or still are) governed by a single political party which only says it bases its policies on Marxism. The problem essentially is that though the objective of a supposedly-Marxist is a classless and stateless society, the revolutionary Marxists considered the state—and a powerful one— necessary in to bring out the utopians ends of their ideology. In practice, this meant the central direction of what is sometimes called a "command economy"—one in which market forces play little or no role, but only government plan and directives matter. The experience of every so-called Marxist country in the twentieth century can only lead one to the conclusion that command economies don't work, and that what could be called "command Marxism" had been a total failure.

Historically, most of the Communist countries of the twentieth century were formed in the aftermath of World War II in Eastern Europe. Most had been "liberated" from Nazi occupation by the advancing Soviet Armies in 1944 and 1945, though in Yugoslavia Communist-led insurgents drove out the Nazis out and took power themselves. With most of Eastern Europe occupied by the Red Army, it was not particularly difficult to establish Communist governments in Bulgaria, Czechoslovakia, East Germany, Hungary, Poland, and Romania. In East Asia, the Soviet Union joined the war against Japan (between the dropping of the atomic bomb on Hiroshima and the one dropped on Nagasaki) and established a Communist government in North Korea, its "zone" of postwar occupation.

A few years later, with Soviet military aid, Mao Zedong's Communist Party defeated the so-called Nationalists under Chiang Kai-shek and established the People's Republic of China in 1949. Like the Soviet Union, China was largely a country of rural peasants and not of industrial workers. In fact, China hardly had any industry at all. China still considers itself to be a Marxist state, but it seems clear that it is now moving in the direction of free-market capitalism.

After the establishment of the PRC, Communists governments came to power in Vietnam (1954 in the North and 1975 throughout the country), also in Laos and Cambodia (also in1975). In 1959, the on-again-off-again Cuban Revolution resulted in the first Communist state in the Western Hemisphere. In 1969, civil war led to the establishment of the People's Democratic Republic of Yemen in southern Yemen (on the Arabian Peninsula).

Though they claimed to espouse and represent the same progressive ideology, there have been several wars or other conflicts between Communist states over the decades since the end of World War II. There was the 1956 invasion of Hungary by the Soviet Army to squash an anti-Communist movement, and a similar invasion of Czechoslovakia in 1968. In Asia there was the long-standing conflicts between the Soviets and the Chinese (that the American President Richard Nixon skillfully exploited diplomatically), the Cambodian-Vietnamese War of 1978, the Chinese-Vietnamese War of 1979, and the Soviet invasion of Afghanistan (also in 1979—later to be known, interestingly enough, as the Soviet Union's "Vietnam").

Practice Test Questions

1. In the 1960s, the American feminist Betty Freidan

    A. helped to found the National Organization for Women (NOW).
    B. argued against the need for an Equal Rights Amendment.
    C. pressed for strictly limited abortion rights.
    D. traditional ideas of male and female roles.
    E. None of the above.

2. After their victory in 1949, the Chinese Communists portrayed woman as

    A. strictly limited to the domestic sphere.
    B. needed in the revolution, but otherwise limited to child rearing.
    C. heroes of the revolution and comrades-in-arms.
    D. Both B and C are correct.
    E. None of the above.

3. One family consequence of increased divorce rates is

    A. the likelihood that children of divorced parents will not marry.
    B. the increase in abortion rates.
    C. the frequency of single-parent families.
    D. All of the above.
    E. Only B and C.

4. In China, the "one-child" policy has resulted in

    A. increased infanticide of the females.
    B. significantly-decreased population growth.
    C. an imbalance between the numbers of males compared to females.
    D. All of the above.
    E. None of the above.

5. According to Marxist theory, Communism would ultimately result in

    A. the "greatest good for the greatest number."
    B. a centralized "command economy" run by a one-party government.
    C. democracy and free enterprise after an initial period of "command Marxism."
    D. a society without social classes and without the need for government.
    E. All of the above.

Answers and Explanations

1. **A.** In the 1960s, the American feminist Betty Freidan helped to found the National Organization for Women (Option **A**). As a committed feminist, she would not have argued against the need for an Equal Rights Amendment (Option **B**), nor argued for limited abortion rights (Option **C**). Replacing traditional ideas of male and female roles (Option **D**) with new ones was what feminism was all about.

2. **C.** After their victory in 1949, the Chinese Communists portrayed woman as heroes of the revolution and comrades-in-arms (Option **C**). At no time did they suggest that women should be strictly limited to the domestic sphere (Option **A**), nor did they hedge their perspectives with qualifications, as in Option **B**, "needed in the revolution, but otherwise limited to child rearing."

3. **C.** One family consequence of increased divorce rates is the frequency of single-parent families (Option **C**). Option **A**, "the likelihood that children of divorced parents will not marry," seems not to be the case. Option **B**, "an increase in abortions rates" really makes very little sense.

4. D. In China, the "one-child" policy has resulted in increased infanticide of females (Option **A**), significantly-decreased population growth (Option **B**), and an imbalance between the numbers of males compared to females (Option **C**). Option **D**, "All of the above," is the right answer.

5. D. According to Marxist theory, Communism would ultimately result in a society without social classes and without the need for government (Option **D**). Option **A**, "the greatest good for the greatest number," is a phrase much used by capitalist theorist. A Marxist would not be content with the "greatest number." The avowed object of Marxism would be expressed this way: "the greatest good for ALL." Option **B**, "a centralized "command economy" run by a one-party government," was not the end goal of Communism but rather was supposed to be a means to an end—a classless and stateless society. In Option **C**, only the "democracy" reference in "democracy and free enterprise after an initial period of "command Marxism" is consistent with Marxist thinking.

Globalization of Technology and Culture

Technology on a Global Scale

As discussed in Chapters 27 and 29, and elsewhere in this study guide, technology is really an important key for understanding the developments of the twentieth century. In large part, the horrors of World War I and its unprecedented battlefield death tolls came as a result of using nineteenth-century tactics with twentieth-century weaponry. World War II was an even clearer example of the deadly combination of science and technology. Likewise, it is safe to say that virtually all of the transformations that have taken place in the world since then either had their genesis in technology, or would have been impossible without it.

Terrorism will likely be in the twenty-first century what Total War was in the twentieth—the biggest threat to World peace. But even though some terrorist methods are seemingly "low-tech" (such as those employed by suicide bombers) most have been dependent on high technology for its sometimes ferocious impacts. The suicide attacks on New York and Washington, D.C., of September 11, 2001, were made possible by sophisticated airliners with computerized "fly-by-wire" systems that allowed only partly trained terrorists to fly into the Pentagon building in Washington, D.C., and into the twin towers of the World Trade Center in New York City. In these attacks, both the weapons (the jet airliner as human-guided missile) and the targets-of-choice were symbolic and emblematic of science and technology on a global scale. But even the lone suicide bomber with high explosive strapped to his body had been involved in a network of electronically-linked activist and terrorist "cells," dependent as well on modern transportation, manufacturing, and communications.

Some might disagree, but one could argue that the most significant of the technologies developed in the twentieth century—at least in terms of globalization—has been in communication. At the beginning of this period (1914), intercontinental communications were still limited to telegraphy, whether by wire or wireless (radio) means. Voice communication by radio was not developed until the 1920s. As early as 1865, reliable telegraphy by trans-Atlantic cable connected the United States and Britain. The telephone was put into widespread use on a local and small regional scale in the 1880s, but the first trans-Atlantic telephone cable was not laid until 1956.

Closely related to telegraphy was the teletype technology that emerged in the 1920s. A tele-typewriter was like a kind of automated typewriter that received five-bit digital signals (timed sequences of on-and-off impulses) and then typed each character as it was received. Teletype transmissions could be sent over the then-elaborate telegraph networks, or by the growing telephone and data radio networks developed by the early multinational corporations such as International Telephone and Telegraph and Western Union.

The elaboration of telegraph and teletype networks between North America and Europe, and between North America and Asia, revolutionized business, diplomatic, military, and journalistic communication, although with capacities and efficiencies far below communication technology at the end of the century. A famous example of inefficiency was the delay in transmission of the last of a fourteen-part communiqué sent from Tokyo to the Japanese embassy in Washington, D.C. The communiqué contained a formal declaration of war between Japan and the United States. It was to be delivered to the American government just before the attack on Pearl Harbor in 1941 but was not available until a few hours after. Thereafter, Japan was accused of having launched a sneak attack in the absence of a formal declaration.

Even though teletype and other early textual transmission systems proved to be a remarkable advance over earlier communication methods, they remained expensive well into the 1970s, just before the Internet began as a consortium of research universities and military agencies. By the late 1980s, Bitnet and other computer networks that used **TCP** (Transmission Connect Protocol) and **IP** (interconnect protocol) over either commercial telephone line or dedicated transmission line had linked the computer networks of hundreds of universities and research institutes. At the same time, a number of technologies—network services, actually—sprang up to take advantage of the new connectivity—email, gopher (*go for* a particular document), newsgroups, chat groups, and the hyper-text driven functions of the World Wide Web. By the middle of the 1990s, these and other Internet methods and services had become globally commercialized and constituted a vast and as yet still developing market of global information, advertising, media, music, and research technology.

Some have argued that the World Wide Web is revolutionizing the world by breaking down information and news barriers that were once commonly employed by nondemocratic regimes to filter out subversive information and communication. Optimists see the Web as a great democratizing force in a global world. Others worry that it has been thoroughly co-opted by commercial interests and that the commercial and advertising content constitutes significant **noise** and obstruction to substantive communication and information exchange.

Other technological developments have also been important in globalization. In 1957, Soviet scientists were successful in placing the first artificial Earth satellite, Sputnik, into orbit with radio communications gear aboard. The United States followed suit early in 1958. By the early 1960s, satellites were being used for global weather imaging, television broadcasts, and space surveillance of Cold War enemies.

Similarly, during the 1970s and early 1980s, manufacturers were producing inexpensive facsimile-transmission machines that utilized new microcircuit digital imaging. These fax machines added further efficiencies in commercial, government, and military communication. During the events of 1990 and 1991 in Russia and the Soviet Union, when activists and Russian officials were pressing for the dissolution of the Soviet Union, the fax machine was credited with keeping an underground news and information service going, which was completely immune from government interference.

The internationalization of communication and of commerce has resulted in globalized **technology transfers.** In a very real way, the proliferation of computer, medical, manufacturing, agricultural, and media technology around the world has only increased the market for more transfers as well as the overall flows of world trade.

Globalizing Art and Culture

One very important outcome of the globalization of technology, especially communications technology, has been the growing globalization of fine art and culture. **Fine art**, as opposed to **pop** (or popular) art and culture, refers to such art forms as painting, printmaking in all its various forms, sculpture, and the relatively new form of installation art. Where once it was possible to discern national or ethnic characteristics in many art forms (such as with Japanese wood-block prints), national distinctions have faded significantly in the face of instantaneous image transmission and the relative ease with which an exhibit of art can be shipped to museums or other venues around the world.

At the same time, there has been an international professionalization of functions in the art world, from museum curators, to art dealers, and auction firm art specialists. Similarly, globalization has taken place among the major museums around the world as they have tried to reach audiences much broader than their own city and even the country. Museums such as the Guggenheim in New York City, the Louvre in Paris, and the Hermitage in St. Petersburg, Russia, are establishing branches around the world.

Some art critics see this as a positive development, a step toward the democratization of art, and also as a means of better educating mass tastes by providing more alternatives to commercial and popularized culture products. Others worry that the internationalization of art will become just another mode of Americanization—the vigorous and aggressive spreading of the popular culture of the United States that began in the decades after World War II. Globalized media, direct contact with millions of American servicemen during the war, and the flood of American export goods transformed popular culture around the world. One particularly pervasive fear is that the diversity of cultural expression once found in the world will decay into a "stultifying sameness" driven mostly by mediating technologies.

Global Popular Culture

The **diffusion**—the spreading out and gradual transmission of ideas, literatures, music, philosophies, religions, and languages as one culture comes into contact with another—of popular culture across frontiers and boundaries has been taking place for thousands of years. Even so, the globalization of popular culture during the twentieth century was more extensive, more pervasive, and harder to escape (if that was one's desire) than during previous eras. Today, the same music can be heard in Zimbabwe as in Oregon. Madonna and Michael Jackson paraphernalia, hip-hop pants, and Rasta dreadlocks are now global, worn and otherwise adopted as somehow emblematic of peoples all over the world.

The nineteenth and twentieth centuries were periods of the development of extensive interconnections between the world's peoples that paradoxically could not have been developed (at least as quickly) without imperialism, war, and globalized trade. For better or for worse, these brought more peoples into new relationships—economic, political, and social. In the nineteenth century, the development of mass media—mostly made possible for the industrial mechanization of printed materials—made a global diffusion possible for the literate. In the twentieth century, the radio, motion picture, and television would do what the mechanized printing had done in the nineteenth.

In music, technology has played an extremely important role. When the gramophone was invented in 1877, it was possible to record and distribute music and song anywhere in the world. In fact, the academic field of ethnomusicology explicitly sought to collect and catalog the world's music. The invention of the easier-to-use tape recording technology that became commercialized after World War II was both a more efficient means of collection but also—in the 1970s and beyond—one of the most popular forms of distribution of commercialized music.

One style of global music that can stand as an example of many others is Reggae. Reggae had its roots in the slave music of British Jamaica as well as the Pan-African ideology that began to emerge after World War I in the United States and elsewhere. An aspect of the ideology sought to focus on Africa as both cultural center and potential source of a kind of cultural (if not political) salvation for those whose ancestors had been scattered in the African Diaspora (see Chapter 19).

In the 1930s, some Jamaicans believed that the Ethiopian emperor Haile Selassie, whose real name was Ras Tafari, was the Messiah spoken of in Jewish and Muslim scriptures. Out of this belief came **Rastafarianism**—an international religious movement that had its origins in 1930s Africa and the Africanized islands of the West Indies. In music, art, dance, and literature, Rastafarianism is a mix of African, Native American, Spanish, French, Catholic, and Muslim elements. In the 1960s, American musical styles—especially R&B and Soul—were blended with those indigenous to Jamaica. The result was Reggae. Its most widely-known artist—really the global popularizer of the form—was Bob Marley, a Jamaican adherent of Rastafarianism whose band, The Wailers, blended the international sounds of Reggae with the spiritual message of Rastafarianism, along with a message of political resistance.

Another **syncretic** form of global music is Worldbeat. This is not a single style of music but rather a related set of styles that combines many Africanized forms such as hip-hop, funk, Reggae, and Highlife, the latter being a combination of musical forms that came out of West African interaction with European merchants and colonial officials.

For all of the twentieth century, the world headquarters of motion picture production was located in Hollywood, California, where, by the end of the century, huge media conglomerates dominated production and mediated cinematic tastes. Although there were other important centers of film production and independent film makers not directly connected with the mega corporations, none of them could match Hollywood for output volume or the pervasiveness of the product, especially after the established motion picture companies had taken over most television programming production by the 1960s.

Far from promoting art in any "fine" sense, Hollywood productions have usually focused on large popular audiences, which they were able to both create and exploit through the use of formulaic and stereotyped images and themes—Cowboys and Indians, tap-dancing dandies in top hats and tails, and an endless stream of happy-ending love stories.

To a certain extent, popular culture was also the dominant product of film making in other countries such as India. There, during the last decades of the twentieth century, the light-hearted musical became very popular; one such production after another came out of the Indian studios in Mumbai, often known collectively as **Bollywood.**

There have been notable international productions of more serious cinematic endeavors. The films of Swedish director Ingmar Bergman and the Japanese film maker Kurosawa have helped to make the foreign film a special category among motion picture aficionados worldwide. In spite of the usual necessity and bother of English subtitles, many films produced around the world have found large audiences in America.

In addition to communications, music, and cinema, sports—especially team sports—also has had a significant global dimension. With no sport is this truer than with football, what Americans call soccer. Football came out of the British working classes in the nineteenth century, and due to British imperialism was soon spread around the world with the British Empire and British commerce. As a means of what many have called cultural imperialism, missionaries, colonial officials, and British settlers encouraged the adoption of football among native peoples. (Cricket, a more orderly and sedate game, was reserved mostly for the British.)

During their independence movements, colonial nationalists encouraged their peoples to play football since the competitiveness of the game helped to foster a sense of national identity among both players and fans. After football had become global, national styles began to emerge as in Brazil, where improvisation on the playing field began to replace more formal strategies for victory.

Practice Test Questions

1. The development of teletype technology

   A. was no real improvement over earlier forms of telegraphy.
   B. was slow in making an impact due to its high cost.
   C. revolutionized commercial and military communications.
   D. All of the above are correct.
   E. None of the above is correct.

2. The Russian-launched Sputnik craft was the first

   A. man-made Earth satellite.
   B. successful spy satellite.
   C. orbiting H-bomb.
   D. All of the above are correct.
   E. None of the above is correct.

3. One of the most revolutionary technologies of the last century, the Internet was

   A. developed first to reduce "transaction costs" in global trade.
   B. created by publicly-funded research universities.
   C. originally a secret military logistics system.
   D. All of the above are correct.
   E. None of the above is correct.

4. Museums have helped to globalize fine art by

   A. expanding their operations around the world.
   B. limiting the display of national art.
   C. commissioning global works of art.
   D. All of the above are correct.
   E. None of the above is correct.

5. Although a global movement, Rastafarianism originally emerged from the

   A. hip-hop culture of the 1990s.
   B. Pan-African Movement.
   C. WorldBeat musical styles of West Africa.
   D. All of the above are correct.
   E. None of the above is correct.

Answers and Explanations

1. **C.** The development of teletype technology revolutionized commercial and military communications. Teletype was a significant improvement over earlier forms of telegraphy (Choice **A**). It also lowered the costs of transmitting messages (Choice **B**).

2. **A.** The Russian–launched Sputnik craft was the first man-made Earth satellite. It carried only a beacon radio and had no spy equipment (Choice **B**). Although a fear of some Americans, it did not carry an H-Bomb (Choice **C**).

3. **B.** One of the most revolutionary technologies of the last century, the Internet was created by publicly-funded research universities, and it was created neither for commercial purposes (Choice **A**) nor for military ones (Choice **C**).

4. **A.** Museums have helped to globalize fine art by expanding their operations around the world. Except by the space taken by occasional displays of explicitly-global art, no attempt has been made to limit the display of national art (Choice **B**). Museums rarely commission works of art (Choice **C**).

5. **B.** Although a global movement, Rastafarianism originally emerged from the Pan-African Movement. Although there are connections between Reggae and both hip-hop (Choice **A**) and WorldBeat (Choice **C**), Reggae was an earlier development.

Demographic Changes and the Environment in the Wake of Globalization

Modern Migrations

In the aftermath of World War II, Europe was in shambles. In those zones occupied by the Western Allies (many more than those occupied by Soviet forces) early postwar immigration brought about a remarkable economic recovery in Germany, in France, in Italy, and in Belgium and the Netherlands. Moreover, the influx of millions of immigrants, refugees, asylees, and migrant workers profoundly and permanently altered the social and cultural bases of Western European societies. In fact, migration has become one of the key social phenomena reshaping Europe since 1945.

Over 30 million people had been forcibly moved or scattered by the Nazis. During the occupation of Europe that followed the war, some ten million ethnic Germans and those of German descent were forced out of Poland and other places in Eastern Europe, many from land they had lived on for generations. As after World War I, the map of Europe was redrawn, and the bulk of this German relocation was due to the elimination of East Prussia and the renewed (and enlarged) creation of Poland. Likewise, German-speakers were forced out of the Baltic states, Czechoslovakia, Romania, and Hungary.

These would not be the last forced or coerced migrations of the remainder of the twentieth century. Beginning in 1947, the partitioning of India and Pakistan upon their independence from the British Empire uprooted more than 18 million. The partitioning plan was based on religion: Where there was a Hindu majority, that would be India. Areas with a Muslim majority would become Pakistan. As it turned out, there were Muslim majorities on both sides of the Indian subcontinent and the resulting Pakistan had two regions separated by hundreds of miles. Those who found themselves among a minority in the wrong country were forced to cross in both directions to escape the bloody riots occurring among religious groups. Armed conflict also broke out over rival claims to the princely states of Jammu and Kashmir.

Similarly, with the United Nations creation of the state of Israel, about one million Muslim refugees were all but forced outside the borders of Israel. At the end of and after the Vietnam War in 1975, more than 600,000 left the country to either avoid reprisals or political persecution. Many of these went in boats of varying size and seaworthiness—these were the "boat people." In South Africa during the "apartheid" period, Blacks were forced to live in designated "homelands" from 1959 to 1994. The Soviet invasion of Afghanistan in 1979 led to the forced migration of millions of Afghans to Pakistan and Iran.

In the 1980s and 1990s, war and civil war resulted in large numbers of refugee migration around the world. In Somalia and Ethiopia, civil war combined with long-term drought to force hundreds of thousands into refugee camps. Likewise, hundreds of thousands of Kurdish refugees migrated from Iraq to Turkey and Iran during the civil war that followed the Persian Gulf War in 1991. The breakup of Yugoslavia in the 1990s caused the dislocation of Bosnians, Croats, and Serbs. In Burundi and Rwanda, millions of Tutsis escaped ethnic civil war mid-1990s. Some of them crossed into Congo and faced similar threats there.

Naturally, not all migration in the last half of the twentieth century was under involuntary or even unpleasant circumstances. Partly as a result of decolonization, there were significant streams of migrants who were allowed to migrate to the "mother" country. Immigrants from India, Pakistan, and the former British colonies in Africa were favored by British immigrations laws, as were Algerians (and other peoples from Francophone colonies) by the French. In 1962, there were about 350,000 so-called "French Muslims" in France. That number rose to 470,000 in 1968 and to 800,000 in 1982. By that time, though, the liberal immigration policies once favoring colonial peoples had been significantly curtailed in response to political backlash and rising racial tensions.

In the age of globalizing markets, the market for labor would become international as well, and this would be the cause of a significant amount of migration, much of it of a temporary nature. Relatively cheap transportation and modern communications has helped to create this international market for labor since the risks—the costs involved, or the isolation from family and home—are minimized. Some countries such as Germany have special immigration programs to recruit *Gastarbeiteren* (guest workers) who are allowed to live in Germany while they contribute to the German economy.

Between other countries, labor migration is often both informal and illegal, but in many cases makes up a significant source of valuable labor in "labor shortage" countries, and a significant benefit for "labor surplus" ones. The best example at hand of this kind of migration is the prevalence of so-called "illegal aliens"—mostly from Mexico—among the migrant farm-labor force in the United States, particularly in California and the West.

Shifts in Global Birthrates

By and large, the demographic transition as discussed in Chapters 19 and 29 continued to operate into the twentieth century. By the end of twentieth century, the industrialized and "post-industrial" countries (those whose economies are no longer dominated by industry but instead by "service" and "information" sectors) were in Phase I—best described as low birth and low death (LB/LD) rates with the resulting very slow or even negative natural growth (excluding growth by immigration). In these countries, families are small and childless marriages are much more common than in past eras. In some Western countries this point was reached just after World War II. In the United States, there was a short-lived growth in the birth rate known popularly as the baby boom that lasted between 1945 and 1964.

By the middle of the twentieth century, the non-industrialized world and those countries that were in the process of "development" and industrialization had entered Phase III of the transition, a phase of high birth rates and low or declining death rates. Population growth by natural means took off in the countries of Africa, Southern America, and Southeast Asia, with growth rates that were sometimes alarming (see Chapter 29 for a more detailed discussion). Birth control, education, and even the AIDS pandemic do not seem to have had much effect on this rapid growth.

Some countries that have experienced rapid and alarming population growth have taken measures to curb their birth rates. The most notable example is China's one-child policy adopted in 1979.

Like China, India has been experiencing very high birth rates since the middle of the twentieth century. In 1999, India became the second of the world's countries to reach the one-billion population mark—in a county with one third the land area of the United States (with just over 280 million population). The heavy-handed answer to rapid population growth as employed in China would be impossible within India's more liberal political culture, but the Indian government has made serious efforts to address the problem.

But India's policies in this regard since the 1960s have been heavily criticized for their narrow focus on contraception and female sterilization rather than other social and economic factors related to fertility and birth rates. The policies and education programs, critics assert, place the greatest burden on women to take responsibility for "family planning," and too little burden on men. Moreover, in ignoring the socio-economics of fertility, they fail to address some of the greatest factors in lowering birth rates and population growth. The very low birth rates in the industrial (or "post-industrial") and affluent countries suggest that there is a link between social and economic well-being and the birth rate.

In Mexico, the situation looks more hopeful. Though the country's population has quintupled since 1940, and though it will continue to rise by about a million per year for some time, many forecasters predict that the now-lower fertility rates will bring Mexico's growth to a stand-still by 2045.

This is a result of a significant drop in the female fertility from an average of seven children per woman in 1965 to just 2.5 today. A number of factors have contributed to this decline, the most significant of which are the slowly-improving standard of living for certain segments of the Mexican middle class and the twenty-year and government-sponsored media campaign to encourage family planning. As in many other predominantly-Catholic countries, this campaign has had to overcome church teachings against *artificial* contraceptive practices (such as the use of birth-control pills and condoms), but it has managed to do so with a considerable degree of success.

But in Russia the demographic outlook is very bleak indeed. The high growth rates of past decades have gone the other way. In 1960, Russia's birth rate was relatively high and its death rate was low—a classic "Phase III" condition. Russia was still in a period of expansive industrial growth and development. But from that point, the birth rate dropped precipitously in the 1960s, seeing some gains in the 1970s and 1980s, only then to nosedive beginning during the *Glasnost* and *Perostroika* period of late-Soviet history (just before the collapse of the U.S.S.R.—see Chapter 30 for a full discussion).

At the same time, the death rate began to climb, from a very low level in 1960 to a point where it actually exceeded the birth rate—sometime in the early 1990s. Since then, both the birth and the death rates have continued their trends—the birth rate continues to drop and the death rate continues to rise. Observers, both Russian and outsiders, believe the high death rate is the result of widespread alcoholism. "Life expectancy"—the average age at death—especially among working-age men, has dropped significantly.

Russia's abortion rate is the highest in the world at 225 abortions per 100 births, much higher than the second highest rate—Romania's (formerly a "satellite" of the now-defunct Soviet Union) 157 per 100 births. Abortion is Russia's main method of birth control. They are easily obtained without cost, while contraceptives have inexplicably become either very expensive or hard to find.

As a result, for the first time in Russian history, the annual number of deaths has exceeded the number of births. Compounding these challenges, the population is aging rapidly—meaning that the percentage of older people is increasing relative to that of younger people. This is a trend that is expected to accelerate over the next several decades and not to happy effect.

Shape and Impact of Urbanization

Since the end of World War II, the world has seen a new urban phenomenon: the "megacity"—a city with more than ten million inhabitants. Since the end of the war, 21 megacities have emerged. Among the most populous of these are Tokyo, Mexico City, São Paulo, New York City, Mumbai, Jakarta, and Teheran. To a certain extent, urban growth in general and Megacities in particular have resulted from continuing declines in rural economies and communities as a consequence of industrialization and the globalization even of food production. But explosive urban growth has also resulted from new communication and transportation technology that make centralization of commerce and trade easier within the intense environment of huge cities.

Another cause of Megacities is history and tradition. Though it is true that technology could be used as an instrument of centralization (and this has happened to a small extent in economic sectors that specialize in the creation and transmission of information), in most cases this has not happened. Instead, cities long established and recognized as national or regional centers have simply attracted more and more people. Such places are known by geographers as *primate cities* and examples include New York, Paris, London, Mexico City, and Beijing. The "pull" of such cities is often stronger than the "push" (the undesirability) of their great size and attending urban problems.

Another urban phenomenon seen in the last decades of the twentieth century was the "megalopolis"—the "conurban" smearing together, as it were, of several large cities into an urban aggregation that can be seen and identified from space. Examples of these conurban areas are "Bowash"—the megalopolis of Boston—New York—Newark-Philadelphia—Baltimore—and Washington, D.C. Other examples (also American) are the Los Angeles-to-San Diego corridor, the San Francisco Bay Area (San Francisco, Oakland, San Jose, and soon maybe Sacramento), and the Everett-Seattle-Tacoma corridor. Global examples include the Tokyo-Kawasaki-Yokohama megalopolis, and Johannesburg and Pretoria in South Africa.

Just as there has been conurban growth in the twentieth century, so has there been "suburban" development. In the years after World War II, in the United States and in many of the other developed nations, there was a "flight" of well-to-do and middle class professionals from the inner cities into outlying areas near enough to commute into town for employment, but also far enough away that the pressures, noise, and smell of dense city life could be avoided.

The suburbanization of American cities actually began around the turn of the twentieth century as commuter and interurban rail service became cheap, fast, and reliable. Suburbanization was given a tremendous boost by the perfection of automobile technology and by the development of good, paved roads in the 1920s and beyond. In the minds of many, though, the postwar years were the years of the automobile, and with families owning multiple autos, suburbanization farther and farther away from cities became (technologically, at least) more attractive and feasible.

To a small extent, a phenomenon opposite to suburbanization has been taking place in some cities in the United States and Europe. In a process sometimes known as "gentrification," previously run-down or decayed parts of cities have been "reclaimed" and reoccupied by well-off members of the middle classes—the "gentry." Though many parts of a city's decayed core have been improved by gentrification, the effect on the poor living in those neighborhoods has not always been good as rising property values and rents force them into even poorer circumstances.

Environmental Activism

Many date the rise of global environmentalism from the publication of Rachel Carson's *Silent Spring*. Published in 1962, the book details the ways in which the "miracle" pesticide, DDT, had poisoned the ecosystem of many places to the extent that wildlife was affected. Carson found that one of the effects of DDT on bird reproduction was that it caused birds to lay eggs with very thin or poorly-cemented shells, and this resulted in a profound reduction of birdlife in some areas where DDT use was widespread. As a result of her investigations, DDT was eventually banned for use in the United States and most other Western nations.

By the 1960s, there were already latent discontents and concerns about the environmental effects of industrialization, chemical pollution, and nuclear contamination. So when *Silent Spring* became a best seller, the impact on public opinion was electric, and to the list of causes that captured the imagination of progressive activists was added "environmentalism" and "ecology" (the study of natural and interrelated systems). Activists promoted the idea of the commons—the resources owned and used in common by all the globe's inhabitants—water, air, the oceans, fisheries, and other natural resources.

Activist groups such as Greenpeace and even "eco-terrorists" such as Earth First! work globally to coax sometimes reluctant governments to take actions designed to at least regulate environment-damaging activity. By the 1980s, most of the world's governments had ministries or agencies for environmental affairs or protection, and in Western Europe especially, entire political parties such as the Grunen (the Green Party) have made significant legislative inroads.

Deforestation

Deforestation is the permanent conversion of forest lands for other uses, including other agricultural ones. Deforestation has been taking place for several thousands of years. Ancient Greek and Chinese commentators wrote of deforestation in their times, and most of the natural forests of Europe and the bulk of those in North America have been clearing to create farm lands. In the twentieth century, with its mechanized processes and its global markets, deforestation has reached a new plateau.

The greatest damage since the 1960s has been done to the tropical "rain" forests. In South America and Africa, these forests are the last great expanses of forest lands left on the planet. Environmental commentators worry that their loss would have significant consequences, from the reduction of bio-diversity and oxygen production, to the increase in the atmosphere of the greenhouse gas carbon dioxide.

Deforestation in the tropics has occurred over the decades for many reasons. Most of the clearing is done for agricultural purposes—grazing cattle, planting crops. Farmers—mostly poor ones—will clear a few acres at a time by "slash-and-burn" methods and then either farm the land or graze it. Larger concerns and corporations are more apt to use heavy machinery and to clear hundreds or even thousands of acres at a time. Large cattle pastures, then, often replace the rain forest to grow beef for the global marketplace. There are other reasons for deforestation, such as to construct towns or dams which flood large areas. Yet, these latter cases constitute only a very small part of the total deforestation.

Critics of deforestation in the developed countries of the world often fail to notice the economic reasons why conversion of forest lands is such an attractive prospect for some developing countries. For the peasants on up to national government and banking officials, forests are an economic resource that can help break the endemic poverty and debt of their countries. Many say they are doing in their countries in recent decades what the already developed countries did in the nineteenth century and earlier decades of the twentieth—exploiting natural resources for profits and national wealth. What could be wrong with that?

Global Warming

Concerns about the possibility that the average temperature of Earth and Earth's atmosphere might be rising due to *anthropogenic* (human) causes began to emerge in the 1960s. Concerns are based on the nature of certain gases in the atmosphere that allow short-infrared radiation to strike the Earth's surface, but will not pass the long-infrared that is re-radiated from the Earth. This is the effect that builders of greenhouses create with glass or plastic glazing—it passes solar heat in, but won't allow nearly as much radiant heat to escape.

For this reason, gases such as methane and carbon dioxide—both extremely common in the natural environment (in fact, both are vital to the functioning of almost all of the biological world)—are sometimes called "greenhouse gases." The theory of man-made global warming is that by increasing the output of greenhouse gases through combustion (internal or otherwise) and through deforestation (which releases the trapped carbon in wood into the atmosphere and depletes the world's inventory of carbon-dioxide breathing trees and plants), the world is growing steadily warmer with not completely known but nevertheless ominous consequences.

Scientists are divided on this issue, but many of the most committed activists who campaign for concerted and global government action are themselves scientists. Groups such as the Union of Concerned Scientists have made strenuous calls for action. In 1997, world leaders met in Kyoto, Japan for talks to amend the "United Nations Framework Convention on Climate Change" with new guidelines. The convention had been negotiated in the early 1990s in response to global calls to government action. Out of the 1997 talks came the "Kyoto Protocol"—a statement that set guidelines for the timetable for global action. By 2012, greenhouse gas emissions are to be cut five percent globally. Countries can engage in "emissions trading" if they maintain or increase emissions of these gases. Certain developing countries would be exempt from the program for an undefined amount of time in order to accommodate industrial development and parity with the developed nations.

By 2005, there were 56 countries that had ratified the Kyoto Protocol. Among the hold-outs is the United States, fearful that exemptions for the developing nations will put it at a disadvantage in the world market.

Food Security

The term "Green Revolution" was coined in the 1960s when improved varieties of wheat seemed to greatly increase yields in Mexico and other countries. These varieties, mostly hybridized versions of traditional strains, produced more than traditional varieties because they were more responsive to controlled irrigation and to artificial chemical fertilizers. New varieties of maize (corn) and rice were soon developed as well.

By the 1970s the new seeds, accompanied by chemical fertilizers, pesticides, and, for the most part, irrigation, had replaced the traditional farming practices of millions of farmers in developing countries. By the 1990s, almost 75 percent of the area under rice cultivation in Asia was growing these new varieties. The same was true for almost half of the wheat planted in Africa and more than half of that in Latin America and Asia, and more than 50% of the world's corn as well. Overall, a very large percentage of farmers in the developing world were using Green Revolution seeds, with the greatest use found in Asia, followed by Latin America.

The effect of these improvements was hard to deny, and they greatly relieved the problems of food security in developing countries. In India as in other places, memories of crop failures and famine were close at hand. As late as 1943 there was a severe famine in Bengal, then part of British India. Observers estimated that as many as four million people died as a result.

As impressive as the Green Revolution has been since the 1960s, it has also created a number of problems, mostly with regard to negative impacts on the environment. The increasing use of herbicides and pesticides has many people worried, and few forget about the death of some twenty-five thousand inhabitants of Bhopal, India in 1984 due to the accidental release of forty metric tons of methyl isocyanate—a pesticide—from a Union Carbide pesticide plant in the city.

Likewise, the effect on soils and other aspects of the environment of irrigation, double-cropping, and chemical-based fertilizers have even more people worried. If the natural system that supports agriculture—even "scientific" agriculture—breaks down, food security will be at great risk.

Practice Test Questions

1. Among those forcibly uprooted in the aftermath of World War II were

    A. Japanese settlers living in New Zealand.
    B. Zionist settlers in Palestine.
    C. ethnic Germans living in Eastern Europe.
    D. Both A and C are correct.
    E. None of the above.

2. After the partitioning of Pakistan and India at the time of their independence from the British Empire

    A. populations remained fairly stable.
    B. millions of Hindus and Muslims were uprooted.
    C. Hindus were forced to relocate to East Pakistan.
    D. All of the above.
    E. None of the above.

3. In the United States, the biggest source of domestic migration was

    A. the South.
    B. New England.
    C. the "Sunbelt."
    D. the "Rustbelt."
    E. None of the above.

4. In the United Nations Framework Convention on Climate Change (as amended in Kyoto in 1997), more than 50 nations agreed to

    A. limit the emission of "greenhouse" gases in developing countries.
    B. wait for more scientific evidence before acting.
    C. prohibit the trading of emissions "credits" among industrialized nations.
    D. reduce greenhouse emissions by five percent by 2012.
    E. All of the above.

5. The "Green Revolution" increased food security around the world by

    A. encouraging new developments in crop breeding and the use of chemical inputs.
    B. preventing corporations from owning farm land.
    C. encouraging small farm practices, including farmer co-ops.
    D. improving the health and tilth of farm soils.
    E. All of the above.

Answers and Explanations

1. **C.** Among those forcibly uprooted in the aftermath of World War II were ethnic Germans living in Eastern Europe (Option **C**). Option **A**, "Japanese settlers living in New Zealand," was not discussed in the chapter and, in any event, the few Japanese who had settled there before the war were not forced to leave. Option **B**, "Zionist settlers in Palestine," were not forced out—in fact, there was something of a mass migration of Jews dislocated by the war arriving in Palestine, in spite of official opposition.

2. **B.** After the partitioning of Pakistan and India at the time of their independence from the British Empire millions of Hindus and Muslims were uprooted (Option **B**). Because the partitioning followed the lines of religious majorities, and because there were Muslim majorities on two sides of the Indian subcontinent, populations could hardly have remained stable (Option **A**). Option **C**, "Hindus were forced to relocate to East Pakistan," is a nonsense answer since Pakistan was a Muslim country.

3. D. In the United States, the biggest source of domestic migration since 1945 was the "Rustbelt" (Option **D**). The South (Option **A**) was actually the eastern end of the Sunbelt and was, therefore, not a significant source of migration in the postwar decades (unlike those of the prewar years). New England (Option **B**) might seem like a good answer, since parts of it make up the eastern end of the Rustbelt, but for that reason it is not the "best" answer. The "Sunbelt" (Option **C**) was actually the destination for most in the internal migration since 1945.

4. D. In the United Nations Framework Convention on Climate Change (as amended in Kyoto in 1997), more than 50 nations agreed to reduce greenhouse emissions by five percent by 2012 (Option **D**). Option **A**, "limit the emission of "greenhouse" gases in developing countries" is to some extent valid, but the Protocol gave developing countries leeway to actually increase emissions if necessary to affect development. Option **B**, "wait for more scientific evidence before acting" was not part of the agreement, but it was part of the policy adopted by the G.W. Bush administration when it decided not to seek U.S. Senate ratification of the UNFCCC treaty. Option **C**, "prohibit the trading of emissions "credits" among industrialized nations," is also incorrect since the Protocol explicitly allows such trades.

5. A. The "Green Revolution" increased food security around the world by encouraging new developments in crop breeding and the use of chemical inputs (Option **A**). Almost without exception, corporations were not prevented from owning and using farm land (Option **B**). Though some small farmers (Option **C**) utilized some of the methods promoted during the Green Revolution, by-and-large, the Revolution encouraged the aggregation of small farms into bigger units in the interests of "efficiency." Among the many criticisms of the Green Revolution has been that the cropping methods and that chemical inputs damaged the health and tilth (Option **D**) of farm lands (and the health of people as well).

PART II

THREE FULL-LENGTH PRACTICE TESTS

Practice Test 1

Practice Test 2

Practice Test 3

Although the actual AP World History multiple-choice section of the exam has five choices, the purpose of the following tests is to help you review and evaluate your progress and readiness to take the actual exam. We have provided four choices to make your test-taking review faster and easier.

Practice Test 1

Multiple-Choice Questions

Instructions: Each question below is followed by four possible answers. Choose the one that best answers the question.

1. Which of the following was the primary purpose of Columbus' first voyage?

   A. Conversion of native peoples to Catholicism
   B. Foundation of colonies
   C. Position as governor in the New World
   D. Discovery of a Western trade route to the East Indies

2. How was Hinduism able to prevail over Buddhism in India as the predominant faith?

   A. The great diversity available in Hindu worship incorporated all social classes.
   B. The Brahman class successfully forced the worship of Hinduism on society.
   C. The Vedas scriptures were translated into several different dialects.
   D. Indian society more readily accepted the tenets of Hinduism as they are not as complex as Buddhist traditions.

3. In the fifth-century Athenian democracy, who had the right to vote?

   A. Males residing within the polis
   B. Male and female citizens
   C. Male citizens
   D. Land-owning males

4. All of the following were considered humanists except

   A. Thomas More.
   B. Desiderius Erasmus.
   C. Francis Bacon.
   D. Pico della Mirandola.

5. By what means did Martin Luther believe one could gain salvation?

   A. Faith
   B. Faith and good works
   C. Predestination
   D. Good works

6. As a result of the Dreyfus Affair in France

   A. the socialist movement in France slowly lost power and influence.
   B. the salaries of Catholic clerics were subsidized by the French government.
   C. the state sided with the military against the influence of the Catholic church in France.
   D. at the initiative of the government, there was a formalized separation of church and state.

7. In the 1890s, Japan chose an authoritarian constitution as the model for the new state based on the governmental structure of which European nation?

   A. Germany
   B. England
   C. France
   D. Italy

8. The Egyptian pharaoh Amenhotep IV (1379–1362 BCE) chose to worship which god above all others?

   A. Amen-Re
   B. Aton
   C. Horus
   D. Osiris

9. How does Aristotle explain the human perception of reality?

   A. Reality is experienced through sense-perception.
   B. The soul is able to perceive reality through meditation.
   C. Humans cannot understand or see reality, only shadows of reality.
   D. Only males can comprehend reality.

GO ON TO THE NEXT PAGE

10. Which two empires ruled comparable populations and territories during the first century CE?

   A. Rome and Egypt
   B. Rome and China
   C. Greece and Egypt
   D. China and India

11. What event directly contributed to the Creoles in South America declaring independence from Spain in the early nineteenth century?

   A. The Spanish garrisons were weakened by prolonged warfare providing opportunity for revolt.
   B. A slave rebellion incited revolt amongst the Creoles who declared New Granada's independence from Spain in 1808.
   C. The Creoles knew that Spain, distracted by frequent military conflicts with the French, would not oppose New Granada's declaration of independence.
   D. Napoleon deposed the king of Spain, resulting in the formation of an elected congress in New Granada that declared independence.

12. Which of the following statements best explains the core of Adam Smith's economic theory?

   A. The government must not interfere in the economic market in order to increase production.
   B. Wages cannot be regulated by legislation.
   C. The value of production derives from the amount of required labor.
   D. A decrease in the required labor force leads to an increase in profit.

13. Which scientist/mathematician was the first to describe a heliocentric universe?

   A. Johannes Kepler
   B. Galileo Galilei
   C. Tycho Brahe
   D. Nicolaus Copernicus

14. Which of the following statements best describes the central similarity between Buddhist nuns and Christian nuns during the early Middle Ages?

   A. Buddhist and Christian religious women were unable to function in their religious duties independent of the supervision of a male clerical intermediary.
   B. Female nuns in both Christian and Buddhist society were cloistered.
   C. Both Buddhist and Christian male clerics encouraged women desiring to adopt a religious life to become nuns.
   D. Christian and Buddhist nuns were easily integrated into the existing ecclesiastical structures.

15. All of the following innovations appear in the archaeological record of early Sumerian society except

   A. the plow.
   B. the wheel.
   C. iron metallurgy.
   D. written language.

16. Who controlled trade in the Eastern Mediterranean in the late sixteenth century?

   A. Dutch
   B. Portuguese
   C. Turks
   D. British

17. Japanese and European feudalism shared all of the following characteristics except

   A. loyalty to a lord.
   B. a contractual relationship between the lord and each individual retainer.
   C. hereditary possession of lands acquired by retainers from the lord.
   D. the retainers collected fees from all persons residing on their lands.

18. What event first set in motion the revolt that eventually led to Haiti's independence?

   A. The French Assembly denied free individuals of African descent citizen-status in French colonies.

   B. French planters refused to enforce the French Assembly's decree that slaves were to be considered French citizens.

   C. The chaos of the Revolution prevented the interim government in France from assisting white planters in controlling minor slave revolts in French colonies.

   D. The revolutionary government in France strictly regulated trade and commerce between France and its colonies, thereby creating internal conflicts in the Caribbean colonies and opening the door for revolution.

19. According to his writings, Karl Marx believed industrialization would change women's roles in the household in what way?

   A. He denied the value of female labor outside the household and maintained that women should remain domestic laborers only.

   B. While their husbands were away from the home in factories, women would manage the household.

   C. Marx advocated a familial structure in which women were not subordinate to their husbands.

   D. A woman's role in the household would correspond to her social class.

20. Japanese society in the sixteenth century was divided into which of the following social hierarchies?

   A. Nobles, merchants, Samurai, peasants
   B. Samurai, nobles, artisans, peasants
   C. Nobles, Samurai, merchants, peasants
   D. Samurai, merchants, artisans, peasants

21. After the fall of the Mongol empire, who had a monopoly on land trade routes to Asia in the fifteenth century?

   A. Ottomans
   B. Venetians
   C. Portuguese
   D. Genoese

22. Which best describes the state of the Maya at the time Spanish explorers first reached Central America?

   A. The Maya resided in small villages tied to a central city governed by a powerful class of priests.

   B. They lived in several small city-states comprising a unified empire.

   C. The Maya had retreated to small villages lacking in political unity and organization.

   D. They were a militaristic society ruled by a warrior class and living in villages.

23. In the twentieth century, a new form of dictatorship referred to as *totalitarianism* emerged and typically included all of the following characteristics except

   A. control over all media communications.

   B. set policies that determined the dictatorship to be totalitarian.

   C. forcible dominance.

   D. a government-regulated economy.

24. How was land tenured in the Mughal Empire?

   A. Land was owned by the state and technically leased by the people from whom revenues were indirectly collected by the state.

   B. The state distributed land to peasant farmers for an initial relief tax followed by a yearly rent.

   C. Citizens of the Empire had a right to petition for land-use rights that would be granted to persons able to pay all associated fees.

   D. The state endowed officials of the government with parcels of land, which the officials would preside over as lords over a territory.

25. Within an Absolutist state, the monarch is

   A. subject to the same laws as the general populace.

   B. capable of enacting legislation independently.

   C. answerable to a parliament or other representative body.

   D. able to break the law at his or her discretion.

GO ON TO THE NEXT PAGE

26. What was Peter the Great's primary goal in reforming Russia?

    A. Imitating Western policies and ideas to be accepted by Western societies

    B. Modernization and strengthening of the military

    C. Improving Russia's education system

    D. Organizing his administration into specialized divisions

27. What was the response of the Tokugawa Shoguns to foreign missionaries in the seventeenth century?

    A. Christian missionaries were seen as a serious threat to the Tokugawa Shogunate.

    B. The Tokugawa regime sought to regulate contact with missionaries, but was largely unsuccessful.

    C. The Tokugawa Shoguns embraced Christian missionaries.

    D. Christian missionaries were expelled from Japan.

28. Which of the following was a major source of weakness in the Ottoman Empire in the seventeenth and eighteenth centuries?

    A. There was a lack of nationalist sentiment causing fissures within the infrastructure of the Empire.

    B. Peasant farmers discontented by their economic situation frequently revolted against wealthy land owners.

    C. Muslim rulers refused to extend freedom of worship to Jews and Christians, inciting resentment.

    D. The standing military was completely dependent on the sultan and not given sufficient power to enforce order.

29. Which statement best summarizes Confucius' educational objectives?

    A. Confucius encouraged his students to challenge classical Chinese philosophical thought.

    B. He was a radical who incited his students toward rebellion.

    C. As a conservative educator Confucius upheld tradition and sought to preserve ancient Chinese culture.

    D. He taught a few select disciples with the intention that they would eventually travel and disseminate his teachings.

30. Before the Mongol invasion, the ideal model of the Chinese family for all social classes

    A. included an extensive network of kin groups living together in a community of goods.

    B. required women and men to share responsibilities working alongside one another.

    C. should have extended family members of different generations living together in the same household.

    D. limited the household to parents and their children only.

31. During and immediately after World War I, all of the following occurred in various European countries except

    A. women tended to dress conservatively and adopted behavior encouraged by moralists as a response to their new role in the work force.

    B. the suffrage movement gained momentum after the war and the vote was granted to women in many European countries.

    C. debate began surrounding a woman's right to equal wages and the possibility of women replacing men in several positions.

    D. many women acquired a greater degree of independence.

32. What was one of the most controversial issues discussed at the Yalta Conference in 1945?

    A. Russian military presence in Poland

    B. The occupation of Germany

    C. Stalin's refusal to declare war on Japan

    D. The removal of the Vichy government in occupied France

33. According to the tenets of Islam, who is the last prophet?

    A. Abraham

    B. Gabriel

    C. Jesus

    D. Muhammad

34. How did Charlemagne regard religious worship within his empire?

   A. He granted freedom of religion to all persons residing in his empire.
   B. Charlemagne himself practiced a pagan Germanic religion and forcefully compelled his subjects to reject Christianity and remain pagan.
   C. He often threatened death to those who would not reject paganism and embrace Christianity.
   D. Although a Christian, Charlemagne's long conflict with the pope caused him to reject Christianity and he encouraged his people to do the same.

35. What group invaded Rome in 410 BCE and sacked the city?

   A. Huns
   B. Visigoths
   C. Gauls
   D. Ostrogoths

36. Which best describes the form of government established in the early years of the Han Dynasty?

   A. A form of feudalism combined with a centralized autocracy.
   B. The Han dynasty was one of three competing kingdoms in China, each with an emperor.
   C. The Han emperor divided China into fiefs with local lords governing their respective regions.
   D. The autonomous emperor maintained complete control over his empire independent of a bureaucratic structure.

37. During the sixth century, Western Christianity and Buddhism shared which of the following characteristics?

   A. The belief that the status of one's rebirth depends on the merits and demerits of his or her previous existence.
   B. Only monks were thought capable of achieving salvation.
   C. Salvation could be gained through the realization that there is no human soul.
   D. The reverence of saints.

38. Before the seventh century the majority of the population of Egypt, Nubia, and Ethiopia primarily practiced a form of

   A. Paganism.
   B. Christianity.
   C. Islam.
   D. Zoroastrianism.

39. Who settled in the Indus Valley as the Harappan Civilization entered into a period of decline around 1500 BCE?

   A. Egyptians
   B. Aryans
   C. Mesopotamians
   D. Hittites

40. All of the following statements are true regarding Aztec religion except

   A. Aztecs worshipped one central deity.
   B. Aztecs practiced polytheism.
   C. human sacrifice was central to Aztec religious practice.
   D. Aztec rulers relied on religion to legitimize warfare.

41. In Shang China, the economy depended primarily on

   A. animal husbandry.
   B. trade.
   C. farming.
   D. hunting and gathering.

42. Which ruler was responsible for the *Corpus Iuris Civilis* (Body of Civil Law) codifying Roman law?

   A. Constantine
   B. Theodosius
   C. Theodoric
   D. Justinian

GO ON TO THE NEXT PAGE

43. In the late nineteenth century John Hay, Secretary of State for the United States, proposed to all occupying foreign powers in China an Open Door policy that would

  A. turn over the arbitration of trade agreements between foreign powers to the United States.

  B. guarantee the same trading privileges in China to all foreign nations.

  C. provide uninhibited use of trading ports amongst all foreign nations occupying China excluding Russia.

  D. serve to effectively end all conflicts between the Chinese and Japanese.

44. All of the following factors contributed to the rise of the trans-Saharan slave trade in the eighth and ninth centuries except

  A. Islamic conquest.

  B. the ascension of a prosperous ruling class.

  C. commercial success of the merchant class.

  D. the existence of an already large slave population of sub-Saharan Africans.

45. During the early decades of the nineteenth century, what was the wealthiest colony in the Hispanic world?

  A. Peru

  B. Venezuela

  C. México

  D. Chile

46. How were the Mongols able to create their extensive empire?

  A. The majority of the areas they conquered were disunited and lacked central leadership.

  B. The Mongol population exceeded that of the Chinese.

  C. Their violent perseverance toward the ultimate goal was to establish a vast empire.

  D. Asian populations were already dependent on Mongol trade goods.

47. The scientific principles proposed by Charles Darwin that infiltrated social theory as social Darwinism can be best described as

  A. limiting the natural selection process to social classes alone.

  B. determining social dominance through the survival of the fittest.

  C. proposing socialism in order to equalize gender, race, and class.

  D. intended to reinforce nationalism.

48. In which former Spanish colony was the practice of slavery not abolished but actually reinforced after the gaining of political independence?

  A. Columbia

  B. Bolivia

  C. Peru

  D. Brazil

49. All of the following features were common to the early Greek Orthodox and Roman Catholic Churches except

  A. missionaries.

  B. belief in the Trinity.

  C. Latin as the only language used in the liturgy.

  D. bishops had to remain celibate.

50. A definition of the term *imperialism* included all of the following in the late nineteenth century except

  A. a European nation's domination and control over areas outside of Europe.

  B. European intervention solely in the economic affairs of non-European nations.

  C. European ethnocentrism toward outside peoples and cultures.

  D. imperialism is an extension of social Darwinism.

51. Which Asian nation was able to avoid European domination in the late nineteenth century and maintain its independence?

  A. Siam

  B. Burma

  C. India

  D. Afghanistan

52. What was one of the consequences for women resulting from Stalin's first Five-Year Plan to industrialize in Russia?

A. Women were generally discouraged from taking industrial jobs in order to fulfill their household responsibilities.

B. Women and children were occasionally employed in industrial jobs, but unlike adult males were not required to work a continuous work week.

C. The State forbade women from working in any field outside of health care and education.

D. The state encouraged women to enter into the industrial workforce.

53. How was the Yugoslavian government structured in 1945, after World War II had ended?

A. The country became communist and a Soviet puppet regime.

B. Yugoslavia became communist and operated independent of Soviet interference.

C. After the national elections, the communist party was shut out of the republican government.

D. After the communist party in Yugoslavia staged a coup, the United States and Britain intervened and eventually helped to establish a democratic government.

54. Which two nations supported Ho Chi Minh's regime in Vietnam?

A. France and the United States
B. France and Britain
C. China and the Soviet Union
D. China and Japan

55. Which event directly led to the invasion of Egypt by French, British, and Israeli forces?

A. Gamal Abdel Nasser attacked British troops occupying Egypt.
B. Nasser nationalized the Suez Canal.
C. Egypt allied itself with the U.S.S.R.
D. Egypt encouraged Algerian independence from France.

56. In medieval Europe, master artisans and merchants attempted to create product and service monopolies in order to serve their interests by forming organizations known as

A. Consuls.
B. Corporations.
C. Guilds.
D. Federations.

57. How did the founder of the Ming dynasty in China reorganize society?

A. The emperor decided to continue the practice of slavery to benefit farmers and middle class families.

B. He subjected the poorer classes to high tax rates whereas the aristocracy was exempt from taxes.

C. The emperor granted members of his bureaucracy large endowments of land displacing peasant farmers.

D. The dynasty enacted new policies designed to favor the poor to the detriment of the wealthier members of society.

58. Which modern art movement centered on geometric shapes, skewed lines, and planes superimposed on one another?

A. Cubism
B. Expressionism
C. Surrealism
D. Postimpressionism

59. During the Cuban Missile Crisis, what was the Soviet Union's relationship with China?

A. As its closest ally, China strongly supported the Soviet Union during the Crisis.

B. At the time of the Crisis, the relationship between China and the Soviet Union was seriously strained.

C. China rejected its former allegiance to the Soviet Union and sided with the United States.

D. China remained a loyal ally of the U.S.S.R., but stayed neutral concerning the situation in Cuba.

GO ON TO THE NEXT PAGE

60. The majority of Trans-Sahara trade merchants adhered to what form of religion worship?

    A. Christian
    B. Sudanic
    C. Muslim
    D. Judaic

61. What was the primary difference in the organization of the Aztec and Incan Empires?

    A. The Incan Empire was divided into city-states whereas the Aztec Empire revolved around a central capital.
    B. The Aztecs and the Incas both had city-states, but the Aztec city-states did not govern themselves independent of the capital.
    C. The capital of the Incas was the foci of the empire, but the Aztec Empire was organized into city-states.
    D. The Aztec Empire was organized into provinces reporting to the capital, but the Incan Empire had self-governing provinces.

62. Which former Portuguese colony in Africa was engaged in a civil war in which the United States and the Soviet Union became involved on opposing sides?

    A. Angola
    B. Ghana
    C. Libya
    D. Algeria

63. Which social group comprised the majority of members in the communist party in China in the late 1930s?

    A. Middle-class industrial laborers
    B. Upper-class business owners
    C. Wealthy farmers
    D. Peasants

64. Which Eastern religion is based on the teachings of the Way?

    A. Confucianism
    B. Daoism
    C. Hinduism
    D. Buddhism

65. According to the Qur'an, how were Muslims to deal with Christians and Jews in their empire?

    A. Christians and Jews were to be converted by whatever means necessary, including force.
    B. Muslims did not have to convert Christians and Jews because they share the same God as Muslims and will therefore receive salvation.
    C. Jews and Christians were not to be converted by forceful means.
    D. Christians and Jews should be allowed complete freedom of worship and were to be subject to the same rights and privileges of the Muslims.

66. During which dynasty did Buddhism reach its zenith in China in terms of popularity?

    A. Song
    B. Ming
    C. Han
    D. Tang

67. The rulers of the Mughal Empire practiced what religion?

    A. Islam
    B. Buddhism
    C. Hinduism
    D. Judaism

68. All of the following were contributing factors that led to the Taiping Rebellion of 1850 in China except

    A. the population increased more rapidly than the food supply.
    B. the unmitigated control of a powerful government oppressed the population and incited rebellion.
    C. a displaced, poor, and unemployed social class emerged for the first time in China's history.
    D. the overall standard of living deteriorated.

69. How did the Japanese empire in the seventh and eighth centuries incorporate the Chinese bureaucratic model into its own government?

A. Similar to the Tang bureaucracy, the Japanese government was controlled by an educated scholarly class.

B. The previous importance placed on clan descent in choosing civil servants was rejected.

C. As was the case in Tang China, the Japanese intended for a single emperor to be the supreme head of the government.

D. The state was governed by provincial magistrates reporting directly to the emperor.

70. Which of the following played a role in the rise of the Women's Movement in the 1970s?

A. Feminist literature criticizing gender relations

B. The rising number of unemployed married women

C. More women were working out of the home

D. The increase in the birthrate

Free-Response Questions

Document-Based Essay Question

Did ancient marriage practices and laws afford women opportunities for subversion, or were women continually denied agency in marital relationships? Did women ever hold control over their male counterparts, or were men ultimately dominant? Utilize the following documents to recognize either subversive or submissive behavior in order to evaluate the role of ancient women as wives.

Document 1

Source: The Code of Hammurabi; Hammurabi (r.1792–1750 BCE) was a Mesopotamian king who is credited with this law code.

128. If a man has married a woman but has not drawn up a contract, that woman is not his wife.

131. If a husband has accused his wife and she has not been found lying with another man, she will swear by god and go back to her house.

132. If a wife is accused because of another man but she has not been found lying with another man, on behalf of her husband she will throw herself into the holy river.

134. If a man has been captured and taken prisoner and there is no food in his house, and his wife has gone into the house of another, that woman carries no blame.

137. If a man has cast off his concubine who has borne his children or his wife who has given him children, to that woman he will return her dowry and will grant her half of the field, orchard, and goods, and she will raise the children. At the point her children are grown, out of whatever is granted to her children they will share with her a portion equal to that of one son, and she will marry whomsoever she chooses.

138. If a man has cast off his bride who has not borne him children, he will pay back her dowry and the marriage portion which she brought with her from the house of her father, and he will divorce her.

Document 2

Source: Xenophon, *Discourse on the Skill of Estate Management*, treatise written in dialectic by a male philosopher in Athens, Greece, fifth century BCE. Xenophon was a student of Socrates, which is probably why he chose to use his name as a character in the dialogue.

Socrates: Whenever a sheep is in a bad way, we usually blame the shepherd, and whenever a horse is unruly, we usually find fault with its rider. As for a wife, if she manages poorly although she was taught what is right by her husband, perhaps it would be right to blame her. But if he does not teach her what is right and good and then discovers that she has no knowledge of these qualities, would it not be proper to fault the husband? Anyhow, Critobulus, you must tell us the truth, for we are all friends here. Is there anyone to whom you entrust a greater number of serious matters than to your wife?

Critobulus: No one.

Socrates: Is there anyone with whom you have fewer conversations than with your wife?

Critobulus: No one, or at least not many.

Socrates: Would it not be more extraordinary if she had any knowledge whatsoever about what she ought to say or do than if she made mistakes?

GO ON TO THE NEXT PAGE

Critobulus: What about those who you say have good wives, Socrates? Did they educate themselves?

Socrates: There is nothing like a personal inquiry. I will introduce Aspasia to you; she is far more knowledgeable in this matter than I am and she will show you all this far more expertly than I should. I think that a wife who is a good partner in the estate carries just as much influence as her husband in attaining prosperity. Property generally comes into the house through the exertions of the husband, but it is mostly distributed through the housekeeping of the wife. If these duties are performed well, estates increase, but if they are managed clumsily, estates diminish. And I think I could also point out men who practice each of the other branches of knowledge in a competent way, if you think you need any further demonstration.

Document 3

Source: Ban Zhao (c. 45–116 CE), *Lessons for Women*, a text written by a woman Confucian in Han China. Zhao was the sister of the imperial court historian and after the death of her brother became court historian herself.

Husband and Wife

The Way of the husband and the wife is closely linked to the *Yin* and *Yang*, and connects the individual with gods and ancestors. Truly it is the great principle of Heaven and Earth, and the great foundation of human relationships. Thus, *The Classic of Rights* [a collection of formal procedures] honor the union of male and female; and in *The Classic of Odes* [a compilation of Confucian poetry] the "First Ode" presents the principle of marriage.

For these reasons, the relationships cannot but be important. If a husband is unworthy, then he has nothing by which to control his wife.

If a wife is unworthy, then she possesses nothing with which to serve her husband. If a husband does not control his wife, then the rules of conduct producing his authority are abandoned and broken. If a wife does not serve her husband, then the proper relationship between male and female and the natural order of things are neglected and destroyed. As a matter of fact the purpose of these two is the same.

Now examine contemporary man. They only know that wives must be controlled, and that the husband's rules of conduct producing his authority must be established. They therefore teach their boys to read books and study histories. But they do not in the least understand that husbands and masters must also be served, and that the proper relationship and the rites should be maintained. Yet only to teach men and not to teach women; is that not ignoring the essential relationship between them?

Document 4

Source: Laws of Manu (c. first century BCE–second or third century CE), the Sacred Law of dharma, an Indian law code. *Manu* is the father of human-kind in Hindu mythology and, according to the Vedas, the first teacher of dharma.

The Nature of Women

It is the nature of women to seduce men in this world; thus, the wise are never unguarded in the company of females... For women no rite is performed with sacred texts, therefore the law is settled; women who are destitute of strength and of the knowledge of the Vedic texts are as impure as falsehood itself; that is a fixed rule.

Betrothal

No father who knows the law must take even the smallest gratuity for his daughter. For a man who takes a gratuity through greed is a seller of his child...

Three years let a woman wait, though she may be marriageable, but after that time let her choose for herself a bridegroom of equal caste and rank. If, being not given in marriage, she herself seeks a husband, she incurs no guilt, nor does he whom she weds.

Marriage and Its Duties

Women were created to be mothers, and men to be fathers. Therefore, religious rites are ordained in the Vedas to be performed by the husband together with the wife...

By violating her duty towards her husband, a wife is disgraced in this world, after death she enters the womb of a jackal, and is tormented by diseases as punishment for her sin...

Let the husband utilize his wife in the acquisition and expenditure of his wealth, in keeping everything clean, in the fulfillment of religious duties, in the preparation of his food, and in looking after the household utensils...

Let man and woman, united in marriage, continually strive so that they may not be disunited and may not violate their mutual fidelity.

Document 5

Source: The Institutes of Gaius, a second-century CE commentary on marital law during the reign of the Roman Emperor Augustus (r. 27 BCE–14 CE). Augustus' original marriage laws do not survive.

Parents are permitted to appoint guardians...for male children under the age of puberty and for females who are beyond it, even if they are married, because the ancients thought it right that women should be under guardianship, even when of full age, because of their fickleness of mind. Thus, if anyone appoints a guardian for his son and daughter and both reach the age of puberty, the son will cease to have a guardian but the daughter will still be under guardianship because according to the Julian and Pappian Laws [Augustus' marital legislation] women are freed from guardianship only by the birth of children...There does not seem to be any good reason why women of full age should be under guardianship, the typical thought is that, because of their fickleness of mind, they are easily misled and so it is only fair that they be under the authority of their guardians, it seems more unfounded than real. For women of full age manage their own business affairs. In some cases the guardian interposes his authority merely as a matter of form; and he is not infrequently compelled to do so by the praetor [Roman political office] even though he may be unwilling.

Change-Over-Time Essay Question

Examine the effects of Western intrusion on native populations in ONE of the following regions from 1450–1914. Be sure to consider the economic and social consequences and discuss topics such as slavery, trade, and religion. Lastly, describe the result of Western conquest and abuse of native peoples on global relations and the world market.

    Africa
    Japan
    Latin America
    India

Comparative Essay Question

During the twentieth century, several world nations adopted communism as a form of government. Compare the various conditions that allowed for a triumph of communism in two of the following nations from 1914–present.

    China
    Cuba
    Russia
    Vietnam

Answers and Explanations for Practice Test 1

1. **D.** Columbus entered into a partnership with Ferdinand and Isabella in which the monarchs funded Columbus' voyage in exchange for his command of the voyage. The arrangement was a strict business agreement with the primary goal of economic gain through the discovery of a Western route to the East Indies. The monarchs hoped to establish a profitable trade route to Asia; conversion of the natives to Christianity was not their concern, neither was the establishment of colonies. After the discovery of the New World, colonization was a goal of future voyages, but it was not the purpose of the first voyage. Columbus assumed he was traveling to Asia and therefore did not expect a position as governor in the New World. However, the business arrangement did give Columbus a position as governor over whatever new lands were discovered, but this was not the primary purpose of the first voyage.

2. **A.** Hinduism has no set form of worship and therefore the possibility for variety in worship incorporated all social classes. The faith was readily embraced by many and the Brahmans had no need to force the faith on society. The Brahman texts, the Vedas, were not required reading to understand Hinduism, despite the fact that Hinduism is extraordinarily complex.

3. **C.** In fifth-century Athens, only male citizens had the right to vote. Thus, the term "democracy" refers to a small portion of the population. Women and slaves were not permitted to vote, neither were foreign occupants of the polis.

4. **C.** Pico della Mirandola was an Italian humanist active in the late fifteenth century, and both Thomas More and Desiderius Erasmus wrote humanist treatises in the sixteenth century in Western Europe. Francis Bacon behaved more as an advocate for science than a scientist himself during the Scientific Revolution in the seventeenth century. He disdained humanists and humanism and was not part of the humanist movement.

5. **A.** Martin Luther was forced to make a formal break with the Roman Church based in large part on his assertion that salvation was achieved by faith alone. Conversely, Catholic doctrine dictates that salvation is achieved through faith and good works.

6. **D.** Captain Alfred Dreyfus was falsely accused of treason based on evidence that anti-Semitic individuals in the French army fabricated against him (because Dreyfus was Jewish). The concocted charge and Dreyfus' subsequent conviction sparked a controversy in France and divided the nation. The conflict eventually led to Dreyfus being absolved of the alleged charges. Catholic authorities in France opposed this end result and maintained Dreyfus was guilty, thereby stimulating anti-Catholic sentiment, which gradually resulted in the state taking action to separate church and state. For example, the state no longer subsidized Catholic schools or the salaries of Catholic clerics.

7. **A.** Japan wanted a strong political structure and likened its state's government after Germany's constitutional regime. A strong emperor and ministry were preferred over a democracy in both nations; Germany had a central government with a chancellor and a parliament (the *Reichstag*) and Japan imitated this form of leadership.

8. **B.** Amenhotep IV opposed the worship of Amen-Re in favor of the aton, the disk of the sun, as the primary god in Egyptian polytheism. The pharaoh later changed his name to Akhnaton to reflect his devotion to aton and moved his capital from Thebes to an isolated city in the desert he called Akhetaton, where a temple was erected in honor of the deity. Conservative priests were not prepared to abandon the worship of Amen-Re and Akhnaton's new cult died with the pharaoh.

9. **A.** Whereas Plato rejected the notion that the human senses can correctly perceive and understand reality, Aristotle advocated an empirical approach to experiencing reality. Through sensual experience, it is possible to discern real forms accurately; true wisdom derives from practice.

10. **B.** During the first century CE, following the rule of Augustus, the Roman Empire had successfully expanded within Europe and into Eurasia. Likewise, in the first century, the Han Dynasty in China expanded the Chinese empire into Central Asia and into present-day Korea and Vietnam. Both the Chinese and Roman Empires had similar population numbers and ruled a comparable land area, over which both Empires were completely dominant.

11. **D.** In 1808, the Creoles formed an elected congress that declared independence from Spain resulting in war with the Spanish who occupied present-day Venezuela, Columbia, and Ecuador. Spain eventually reclaimed their rule over these areas of South America, known as New Granada, around 1816. After intermittent campaigns against

the Spanish, the Creoles were finally successful in gaining their independence when the Spanish were defeated in 1819.

12. **A.** In *The Wealth of Nations*, Adam Smith's central argument surrounds the notion of a free-market economy; namely, the government must not regulate a market economy so as to restrict production, which would subsequently hinder opportunities for profit. David Ricardo, a contemporary of Smith's, argued that the worth of a product could be calculated based on the labor needed for its production, and that wages were ultimately not subject to legislation because the "iron law of wages" naturally regulated the rate of wages.

13. **D.** Nicolaus Copernicus rejected the ancient theory of a geocentric universe, in which all planetary bodies revolve around the earth, because it conflicted with the perceived motion of the planets and defied mathematical explanation. Although Tycho Brahe, his student Johannes Kepler, and Galileo Galilei eventually built upon Copernicus' theories, they were not the original proponents of the notion of a heliocentric system; specifically, the planets, including the earth, revolve around the sun.

14. **A.** Both Christian and Buddhist nuns were initially viewed as problematic by male clerical authorities. Buddha was reluctant to allow women to lead lives as mendicant nuns. Despite the fact that he eventually conceded to his aunt's proposal to permit women, like their male counterparts, to give up their property in favor of a mendicant lifestyle, female nuns were subject to the discipline of monks and were required to provide monks with the utmost respect. Similarly, Christian ecclesiastics believed that women needed guidance. In particular, nuns were to be under the supervision of a bishop or abbot, and not merely an abbess. Moreover, Christian nuns could not receive the sacraments independent of a male priest.

15. **C.** The advent of the plow was one of the most significant advancements in Mesopotamian society in terms of agricultural production. No less important were the use of cuneiform writing and the implementation of the wheel. Metallurgy was also a critical development; however, early Sumerians practiced bronze metallurgy. Iron metallurgy began around 1200 BCE, and Sumerian bronze metallurgy was at its height centuries before.

16. **C.** Turkish naval power gradually came to dominate trade in the Eastern Mediterranean in the late sixteenth century after a long conflict with the various European countries. Muslim Turks also dominated trade in the Indian Ocean, until the beginning of the seventeenth century when the Dutch and the English began to encroach upon the formerly Turkish-controlled seas.

17. **B.** Unlike European feudalism, in Japan the Samurai were organized into clans whereas in Europe, vassals swore individual oaths of homage and fealty to a lord thus sealing the contractual and reciprocal relationship between the two parties.

18. **A.** White planters and merchants in the French Caribbean colonies persuaded the French Assembly to deny citizenship to free-persons of African descent in the late eighteenth century. The planters and merchants believed that slavery in the colonies depended on the subordination of all individuals of African descent, including free-persons. As a result of the French Assembly complying with this racist view, these free-persons revolted, thus directly contributing to a slave rebellion led by Toussaint-L'Ouverture against white planters. The colony in which this rebellion took place was declared the independent nation of Haiti, and France abolished slavery in its colonies.

19. **C.** Karl Marx felt that when women began to work for wages, their status as subordinate to their husbands would change and they would begin to function as equals. As a result, family life in general would improve. Patriarchy, according to Marx, was as oppressive as capitalism; capitalism, in fact, directly contributed to patriarchy because husbands viewed their wives as nothing other than a means of production.

20. **D.** Japanese society in the sixteenth century can be divided into four classes: The warrior class, the *Samurai*, who were governed by the *daimyo* (their feudal lords), who were in turn controlled by the Shogun. The next level in the hierarchy was the merchant class followed by the artisan, or working, class. Lastly, the peasant farmers and laborers represented the lowest level of the Japanese social strata.

21. **B.** In the fifteenth century, the Venetians successfully negotiated with the Ottoman Empire for a monopoly over land trade routes to Asia. Under Mongol rule, trade routes to Asia had become safe highways for travelers whose safety was guaranteed. After these routes were seized by Ottoman Turks, travelers were no longer safe and trade became difficult, thus prompting sea exploration in search of alternative passages to Asia. The Italian city-state of Venice held a monopoly over the formerly safe and accessible

trade routes and acted as an intermediary for all Europeans desiring to trade with Asian merchants. During the *Pax Mongolica*, Venice had previously held trade monopolies in Egypt and Palestine, and nearby Genoa had a monopoly over trade in the areas surrounding the Black Sea.

22. **C.** Despite the fact that archaeological evidence indicates that the Maya once lived in a vast empire, occasionally under militaristic rule combined with priestly control, at the time the Spanish entered into Central America, Mayan farmers had removed themselves from city centers, such as temples, and retreated into small, disconnected villages. The Maya did not reside in a unified empire at this time.

23. **B.** Totalitarian regimes are not based on governmental policies, but rather on tactics. Totalitarian dictators advocate oppression and utilize fear in order to maintain hegemony. Force is often employed in order to assure dominance, and the government controls all media and the economy to further prevent citizen resistance.

24. **A.** Land tenure under the Mughal government was anomalous to most contemporary Western structures in that land was not rented; subjects of the Empire had hereditary rights to the land they held, although they had to compensate the government for possession of the land. Land revenues comprised a significant portion of the state's revenues, but some revenues were directed to officials who received these funds in place of wages.

25. **D.** An Absolutist monarch is not answerable to a representative body in theory. Moreover, under a system of Absolutism, the monarch is free to break laws at will; the monarch is above the law.

26. **B.** In spite of Peter's use of Western models in his administration, the primary purpose of his reforms was to build a strong military through modernization in Russia. Western models made this possible, but Peter did not intend to mirror the West as much as to challenge Western armies with his own powerful military.

27. **D.** Missionaries were never a serious threat to the Tokugawa Shogunate; however, the militaristic regime did not welcome Christian missionaries and chose to expel all foreign missionaries in the seventeenth century. It also regulated Japanese contact with all foreigners, including trade merchants.

28. **A.** The Ottoman Empire ruled over numerous peoples and cultures, but participation in the administration of the Empire required knowledge of the Turkish language, thereby excluding a large percentage of the population who did not speak Turkish from involvement in the government, thus discouraging Turkish nationalism and weakening the Empire. The Ottoman Muslims did not forbid freedom of worship to Christians or Jews, but non-Muslims practicing their respective faiths were subject to taxation that Muslims were not required to pay. The standing army was powerful independent of the sultan and not reliant upon his power.

29. **C.** Confucius was a tradition thinker who did not challenge classical Chinese ideals but rather sought to reinforce well-established social mores. Although he did have disciples, he taught a great number of students (versus a few individuals) at one time and traveled with them throughout parts of China. He did not encourage rebellion in his teaching; on the contrary, Confucius wanted his students both to serve the state to the best of their ability and to become valued members of society.

30. **C.** The ideal model of the Chinese family during the Sung period prior to the Mongol invasion (mid-tenth century to the late thirteenth century CE) included multiple generations living together within the same household in a hierarchical structure with the younger generations subordinate to their elders. Consistent with the overarching culture, in this structure women and men were not supposed to work together. In general, they were expected to spend little time with one another and therefore ideally they would not work together in household tasks.

31. **A.** During World War I, women supported their respective nations through their role in the work force. Women replaced men engaged in warfare in a variety of positions. Consequently, women generally became more independent. In addition, women's involvement in the workplace incited debate over whether or not they should be receiving pay equal to that of a man. There was also a concern that women would permanently replace men in the work force. These issues overlapped with the question of granting the vote to women. A few nations had already given women the right to vote prior to the war, but during and after the war many more nations followed suit. Another change was a shift in the moral code for both women and men. Women in particular started to wear more risqué clothing and to behave contrary to the standards of contemporary moralists.

32. B. When the Allied leaders of the United States, the Soviet Union, and Great Britain met at Yalta, one of the most heated discussions took place over the occupation of Germany. The U.S.S.R. was initially opposed to the proposal made by the U.S. and Britain to divide Germany into zones occupied by the Allied forces including France. France had become independent of the Vichy by this time and Charles De Gaulle had become president. The central problem with the occupation of Germany, however, was not the inclusion of the French. Rather, it was a concern among the Western nations that the Soviet Union would dominate Eastern Europe. For this reason, the United States and Britain were wary of the U.S.S.R. participating in talks regarding the establishment of governments for newly liberated nations, for there was a risk of these governments becoming communist. The U.S.S.R. freely agreed to declare war on Japan, in exchange for land that had been lost to Japan in the early twentieth century. Stalin was unopposed in his treatment of Poland; Allied leaders did not interfere with his control there.

33. D. Muhammad, born circa 570 CE, was the last prophet of Islam. He heard the angel Gabriel speak to him and he received revelations, which were recorded in the Koran. Muslims also consider Abraham and Jesus to have been prophets, but Muhammad was the final prophet.

34. C. Charlemagne was Christian and a loyal ally to the pope, whom he served on a number of occasions when he fought the Lombards as well as various other groups opposed to the pope in Rome. After defeating the Saxons, he forcefully converted them to Christianity under the threat of death.

35. B. Although the Visigoths eventually moved into Gaul, they were not originally from there. After the Visigoths left Rome, the Ostrogoths took their place but were not the first group to sack the city, and neither were the Huns.

36. A. After the Chi'in's harsh laws sparked a civil war, the Han dynasty was established in the third century BCE. and ruled effectively into the third century CE. Under Han rule, China saw a revival of feudalism combined with a centralized autocracy. There was an emperor and a centralized bureaucracy, but the regime did distribute hereditary fiefs in parts of the empire. Later, the central government of the Han dynasty degenerated into three kingdoms ruled by warlords, resulting in the end of a unified China.

37. D. Orthodox Christian tradition never supported the notion of karma (or reincarnation), whereas this idea is a central tenet in Buddhism. Furthermore, in the sixth century Western Christianity was Catholicism, the doctrine of which states that salvation is achieved through faith and good works. Monks are not the only persons capable of receiving salvation in Christianity, and only specific Buddhist schools of thought such as Theravada emphasized this idea. Both Buddhism and Christianity, however, do share the belief in a cult of saints. Saints exist and are to be revered in both faiths, although the reasons why and the practice of reverence differ.

38. B. Egypt and its southern neighbors Nubia and Ethiopia had all adopted Christianity by around the fourth century CE, although Ethiopia gradually came to practice a form of Christianity called *Monophysitism* that focuses on Jesus' divine nature rather than his humanity. Both the Eastern and Western Christian Churches denounced this belief as heretical in the fifth century leaving Ethiopia disconnected from these Christian centers. In the seventh century, Egypt was conquered by Muslims and the kingdom began practicing Islam while Christians became the minority. Islam took much longer to infiltrate Nubia and Ethiopia.

39. B. Aryans, nomadic warriors, entered the Indus Valley Civilization (also referred to as the Harappan Civilization) around 1500 BCE. It is unclear whether or not the Aryans arrived peacefully or chose to violently overthrow the present weakening regime. Either way, the Aryans adopted farming in place of their former nomadic lifestyle and established themselves in the Indus Valley as the Vedic culture, integrating aspects of Harappan culture into this new cultural identity.

40. A. Aztecs practiced a form of polytheism with various diverse gods, primarily anthropomorphic, who frequently required a blood sacrifice. The need for human victims for religious sacrifice was cited as a justification for rulers to expand the empire through conquest.

41. C. The Shang economy did not rely on hunting or foraging; rather, agriculture was of primary importance. Animal husbandry was not as predominant as farming and relatively insignificant. Trade was important, but not the backbone of the economy.

42. D. Constantine and Theodosius ruled the Roman Empire centuries before Justinian. Justinian was the first emperor, albeit of the Eastern Empire in Byzantium, to organize an effort to codify Roman law into a law code known as both the *Corpus Iuris Civilis* and Justinian's Code. Both Church and commercial law were based on this code that persevered for centuries during the Middle Ages. Theodoric was an Ostrogoth ruler in the city of Rome and a contemporary of Justinian.

43. B. In 1899 John Hay sent correspondence to the foreign powers occupying China; namely, Japan, Russia, Great Britain, France, and Italy. Hay asked that each nation allow for free trade within their respective territories in China, and each responded stating that they would comply with the policy provided the remaining nations did the same. In spite of this elusive reply, Hay announced that every nation had accepted the Open Door policy. Only Japan and Russia opposed his announcement, although both had been included in the initial agreement. The U.S. did not hold a sphere of influence in China, but Hay believed that the implementation of the Open Door policy was essential to ensure U.S. trade activities.

44. D. The rise of the first Islamic empire resulted in many changes for Africa, one of which was the trans-Saharan slave trade. The slave trade resulted primarily from Islamic conquest; Muslims ruled over many lands with existing slave populations. However, before the Muslim invasions, relatively few sub-Saharan Africans were enslaved. As the Islamic empire became more powerful and wealthy, a ruling elite class emerged that required significant slave labor. Likewise, along with the commercial success of the merchants came a demand for slaves.

45. C. At the start of the nineteenth century, México had the largest population and most wealth of all Spanish colonies. Venezuela and Cuba, once marginal areas of the empire, began to develop very quickly during this period; however, México had grown economically long before these colonies. Peru was immediately behind México in terms of wealth at this time, but it was also in competition with the emerging economic powers of colonized territories such as Cuba and Venezuela.

46. A. The Mongols were nomadic peoples with no initial desire to conquer vast territory and rule an empire. As a result of their nomadic lifestyle, they were unable to carry surplus products or livestock and therefore depended on others (the Chinese, for example) to furnish them with supplies; Asian populations were not dependent on the Mongols for trade goods; the reality was the reverse. In

addition, the Mongols had a relatively small population especially compared to that of the Chinese, which makes their conquests even more remarkable. Among the many factors that allowed for these tribes of nomadic warriors to rule over an empire was the state of Asia at the time. China and parts of Russia and the Middle East were disunited or in a state of political decline during the Mongol invasions, thereby enabling the recently united Mongol tribes to take over in place of the former weakened governments.

47. B. Social Darwinists did not accurately apply Darwin's evolutionary theory to society, and their ideas were not part of Darwin's original theory. They did not take into account the extensive amount of time involved in the process of evolution. Moreover, they used Darwin's notion of species variation in reference to the diversity in social classes, culture, and nations. The theory was not limited to describing the relationship between social classes alone, and although social Darwinism was used to reinforce nationalism, that was not the original goal or intention in developing the theory. The core of the theory was the belief that inferior human beings in society would be dominated by select individuals as determined through the survival of the fittest in that society.

48. D. In the nineteenth century, most former Spanish colonies abolished slavery within ten years after gaining political independence. As a result, production in the mines of Bolivia and Peru declined, as did agricultural production in Columbia. However, Brazil's participation in the slave trade only increased after independence allowing for increased production on coffee plantations.

49. C. One of the largest differences between the Eastern Orthodox and Western Catholic Churches was that the Western Church used Latin in the liturgy, whereas the Eastern Church permitted vernacular languages in the liturgy. Both churches believed in the Trinity, although the Roman Catholic Church maintained that the Holy Spirit proceeds from the Father and the Son. The Eastern Church rejected this idea, favoring the idea that the Holy Spirit proceeds from the Father alone. The Eastern and Western churches had missionaries, which often led to conflict when the two were conducting missionary work in the same area. Celibacy among bishops was common to both churches, but in the Eastern Church, married men could be ordained as priests.

50. B. A general definition of nineteenth-century imperialism is the interference of European powers in foreign lands (outside of Europe) resulting in complete dominion over those lands. This definition would include European intervention in the economic policies of marginalized areas; however, economic domination is associated primarily with the later twentieth century imperialism, which does not necessarily include intervention in political affairs. Nineteenth-century imperialism did include continued political domination, and not solely economic control. Social Darwinism was an important theory used by imperialists and their supporters to legitimize the ethnocentric behavior of European nations directed toward peoples in Africa and Asia, for example.

51. **A.** Siam (Thailand) was able to remain independent in the wake of nineteenth-century European imperialism partly due to its openness to incorporate European culture into its own, and partly because the European nations occupying various areas of Southeast Asia hindered one another from taking control in Siam. These nations were busy competing for other territories in Asia while trying to hold on to those possessions they had already obtained. As a result of these factors, Siam maintained its independence. India and Burma, on the other hand, were British possessions, and Afghanistan was within the realm of British control.

52. **D.** Under the first Five-Year Plan, Stalin's regime urged women to enter into the industrial workforce to increase production. In addition, the state required workers, including women, to work a continuous work week in order to meet the demands of industrialization.

53. **B.** The situation is Yugoslavia after the end of World War II was unique. In 1945, communist Marshal Tito defeated his opponents in the national elections and became Prime Minister; Tito would also eventually become President in the early 1950s. The government of Yugoslavia became communist under Tito and remained so for several decades. Tito ruled as a dictator, but unlike his fellow communist rulers, he did not come to be dominated by Soviet intervention in his domestic policies. He challenged Stalin and refused to become subordinate to him. Tito's actions resulted in a serious rift between Yugoslavia and the Soviet Union.

54. **C.** Communist Ho Chi Minh was responsible for the unification of Vietnam. After the nation was unified under his leadership, the U.S. urged the French to try and remove him from power despite the fact that France had recognized the independence of Vietnam years earlier. The French gained little from the war attempting to defeat Ho

Chi Minh and they eventually withdrew from Vietnam. Since Ho Chi Minh and his regime were communist, he drew support from two very powerful communist countries, the Soviet Union and China.

55. **B.** When Gamal Abdel Nasser decided to nationalize the Suez Canal, which was the property of a British company, Britain reacted by first attempting to reach a compromise with Nasser and then invading Egypt along with the French and the Israelis after no compromise could be reached. Although Nasser's encouragement of Egyptian nationalism and acceptance of aid from communist countries made the United States distrust his government, the U.S. and the Soviet Union opposed the invasion and worked with the United Nations to arrange the withdrawal of all foreign troops. Algerian Arab nationalists were later encouraged by the Western failure to remove Nasser from power, and gained their independence from France in 1962, years after the nationalization of the Suez Canal.

56. **C.** During the Middle Ages, merchants and artisans in towns organized themselves into unions called guilds (either known as or called). Each guild developed standards of production in order to guarantee the quality of their work. These standards ensured the guild members would maintain a monopoly over their respective craft because any artisan or merchant working independent of a guild would not be able to provide the same guarantee to customers regarding the quality of their product or service. Guild members would elect officials annually known as consuls or wardens. Among their many duties, these individuals would be responsible for verifying that products and services of guild members had met the standards set by that guild.

57. **D.** The founder of the Ming dynasty, T'ai-tsu (also known as Chu Yüan-chang or Hung-Wu), was born to farmers in the fourteenth century. He later became a Buddhist monk and then a warlord who proclaimed himself emperor and then expelled the Mongols from Northern China. As the son of commoners, T'ai-tsu implemented programs to benefit the poorer classes. For example, he imposed high taxes on the wealthy, abolished slavery, took possession of large properties and redistributed some such properties for rent to persons without land.

58. **A.** Postimpressionists and expressionists strove to present visions of reality beyond the visible world; they wanted to communicate their personal

impressions of various scenes taken from real life, but filtered through their mind's eye. Although Cubism is also highly expressive, unlike postimpressionism and expressionism, it was a movement devoted to geometric forms and sharp angles. Surrealism developed after Cubism but often fused with it in paintings of such artists as Pablo Picasso. Surrealist painters sought to make a statement about the state of the world around them, and therefore did not rely on traditional painting styles but rather developed innovative approaches to convey their vision of reality.

59. **B.** In 1961, before the Cuban Missile Crisis, relations between China and the Soviet Union were rapidly breaking down. As a result, Nikita Khrushchev was more inclined to reach a compromise with the United States over the Crisis in 1962. Despite the strained relationship between the two communist superpowers, China did not ally itself with the U.S.

60. **C.** By the twelfth century, Islam was the primary religion practiced by African merchants, but it was by no means the dominant faith held by the majority of persons living in the Sudan outside the realm of commerce. After North African merchants first adopted Islam in the seventh and eighth centuries, they spread the faith while traveling on the Trans-Sahara trade routes. When they came into contact with merchants from other areas of Africa, they spread Islam and gradually the merchant class became predominantly Muslim.

61. **C.** The Aztec Empire was organized into city-states that served the population as the political and religious center of the community and outlying areas, independent of a central capital. Conversely, the Incan Empire was organized around a centralized capital, Cuzco, and further divided into a pyramid system of regions and descending units within a chain of command ultimately reporting to the emperor.

62. **A.** By the mid-twentieth century, most European colonies in Africa had gained their independence. Algeria became independent from France in 1962, Ghana from Britain in 1957, and Libya from Italy in 1951. Angola's struggle for independence from Portugal began in the early 1960s, but after finally gaining independence in the 1970s, civil war erupted in the former colony. Both the Soviet Union and the United States became involved in the conflict, each supporting one side and thus indirectly engaging each other.

63. **D.** In the late 1930s, membership in the Chinese communist party swelled, in large part because of the war against Japan. Peasants were particularly attracted to the party, and were responsible for the increase in the membership rate. The most attractive feature of communism to the poorer classes, and to women as well, was that they would no longer be considered marginalized members of society as they had been before; the peasant population was recognized as equal to other more prominent social classes. Economic reform accompanying Mao's communist policies was often deficient, and therefore the appeal of the party was primarily social recognition.

64. **B.** The word *Dao* means "the Way" and is by nature paradoxical; the Way can be taught but at the same time cannot be fully understood. According to the Daoist text written by Laotzi in the sixth century BCE, *The Classic of the Way and Virtue*, the Dao rules over everything but does not control its subjects. Similarly, although the Dao (Way) is unchanging and creates all things, it refuses to possess anything it produces.

65. **C.** Despite some evidence of forceful conversions, Islamic conquerors did not generally seek to convert Jews and Christians. Regardless of the actions of these conquerors, the Qur'an itself forbids Muslims from forcefully converting Christians or Jews, and Muhammad supported this tenet. Jews and Christians were free to worship; however, Jewish and Christian subjects of the empire did have to pay a tax to symbolize their complete obedience to Muslim authorities. Muslim subjects were not required to pay such a tax. In addition, although Muslims, Jews, and Christians share the same God, the Qur'an stipulates that all persons refusing to become Muslim will not achieve salvation.

66. **D.** Buddhism first reached China through the Silk Road trade routes from India during the Han Dynasty. However, some Buddhist tenets fundamentally violated traditional Chinese culture, thus preventing the faith from immediately gaining a secure foothold. Gradually, Buddhism became a permanent fixture in China but it was not until the Tang Dynasty that Buddhism began to have a significant influence over the population. There was an increase in Buddhist monasteries and devotees, and the Tang imperial court would frequently patronize these new monasteries. Nevertheless, much of China remained rooted in Confucian values that contradicted Buddhist doctrine, therefore religious conflict did not end during the Tang Dynasty.

67. A. The founder of the Mughal Empire was an Islamic conqueror, Babur. The Mughal emperors brought the faith of Islam to India, and it had a great influence; nonetheless, Hinduism was an integral part of Indian society and eventually overcame Islam as the predominant faith in India.

68. B. The government was in a weakened state at the time of the Taiping Rebellion. Far from having the capability to oppress the people, the state barely managed to quell small uprisings. Prior to the Rebellion, these smaller revolts had broken out due in large part to the increase in population and subsequent decrease in the food supply, which had led to a decline in the standard of living. Corruption in the government added to the situation; the people had no faith in the state, and revolt was inevitable under these conditions.

69. C. Japanese officials traveled to China during the Tang Dynasty to observe Chinese government and culture, but upon their return they sparingly incorporated Chinese ways into their own culture. The most significant similarity between the two governments is the emperor, who should theoretically be in complete control. However, feudal lords in Japan tended to dominate the countryside as local magistrates. Despite his divine heritage, the emperor had difficulty controlling these individuals often leaving Japan bereft of central leadership. These feudal, hereditary aristocrats ruled Japan whereas in China a scholarly class controlled the government.

70. A. Women were motivated to challenge their present status in society by feminist writers and intellectuals who began to address the inequality between genders in the 1970s. In addition, by this time more married women than ever before were being employed in the work force, prompting a desire for equal rights and equal pay. From the early twentieth century onward it had become increasingly difficult for women to work from home, and less financially advantageous for their families. The increase of working married women led to a decrease in the birthrate in the U.S., parts of Europe, and the U.S.S.R.

Document-Based Essay

Overall Approach

1. Organize your essay around a thesis and use the documents to support that thesis.
2. Use all but one of the documents.
3. Thoroughly explain how your evidence proves your argument.
4. Do not ignore any portion of the question.
5. Analyze the documents as they relate to your thesis; do not summarize their content.
6. Consider the sources of the documents (biases of the authors and historical context).
7. Be aware that your argument is based on only small excerpts of much more extensive documents.
8. Discuss the nature of the various documents. To what extent do documents such as law codes and commentaries reflect reality?
9. Think about the audience. To whom were these documents directed? To all social classes, or to a select few?

Key Points to Include

- The most important thing to avoid is a thesis that argues that women were oppressed. Not only is that thesis too general, it tends to be more based on a modern assessment. Be more specific in your thesis. Consider whether or not women were oppressed in the context of their own society, or if they were ever awarded opportunities for power or even subversion.

- Your essay must connect the documents in a unifying thesis. Recognize similar features of marriage within the various societies. For example, in most cultures the dowry and marital property were significant aspects of a marriage. Other similar features include the raising of children, an idealized relationship between husband and wife, laws concerning divorce and adultery, and the management and delegation of household duties.

- Marriage for some cultures is a spiritual union, for others it is a legal one. Marriage can also be both spiritual and legal. The classification of marriage defines the role of a woman as wife. Specifically, she could be a partner, or an asset like any other form of property.

- In ancient Mesopotamian, Hammurabi's law code defined marriage as contractual with consequences on both sides for failure to meet with the terms of the contract. Law 128 states that a man cannot hold a wife without a contract, and law 137 states that a man who rejects his wife because she has not born him children will forfeit her dowry. However, the essay should mention that law codes do not necessarily reflect social reality. It would be relevant to comment on this fact.

- Xenophon's text also illustrates another point about the difficulties in defining social reality. The characters in his dialogue are not only imaginary they are also male, as is the author. Xenophon is expressing a woman's role through male eyes; this is an idealized view of a how a wife should behave. Therefore, it is difficult to see opportunities for agency. However, Xenophon argues through dialectic that a woman is capable of managing the household independent of her husband provided she has received the proper instruction. Although wives are ultimately dependent on their husbands for their education, they can perform specific tasks on their own.

- An overarching theme becomes clear in Ban Zhao's *Lessons for Women*, which was written from a female perspective. In ancient Mesopotamia, Greece, and Han China, women were ideally servants to men. They were to bear their husbands children (Hammurabi's Code) and manage the household successfully (Xenophon), and a wife was to always serve her husband (Zhao).

- Another theme appears in the *Laws of Manu*; namely, women are weak-willed and thus require male supervision and control. Again, this is not a text that is reporting on social reality. According to this text, women should be mothers and men should be fathers, but women are to be employed by the husband to benefit him and his holdings. A woman is also to manage household duties, as was the case in Xenophon's text.

- The last two documents also discuss marital law, but not in terms of religion as in the case of Zhao (Confucianism) or the *Laws of Manu* (Hinduism). Again, these texts may or may not accurately indicate the relationship between husband and wife. In *The Institutes of Gaius*, women are labeled as unable to function independent of a guardian, similar to a few of the aforementioned texts. However, Gaius judges that practice as applied to married women as ridiculous.

- It is important not to take for granted the rights available to women, and the question asks you to discuss how these rights might have led to female

power in marriage. Therefore, you must recognize trends between the documents that may have either afforded women rights or denied them privileges. You must also account for differences in marital rights, which are often based on historical context.

- Lastly, you should mention that in order to better answer this question, additional documentation discussing actual marriages would be useful. The law codes and tracts here represent idealized relationships and therefore do not adequately reflect social reality.

Change-Over-Time Essay

Overall Approach

1. Organize your essay around a thesis and provide points to support that thesis.

2. Use accurate historical evidence to support your points.

3. Thoroughly explain how your evidence proves your argument.

4. Do not ignore any portion of the question.

5. Use historical context to demonstrate change over time and recognize continuities as well.

Key Points to Include

- A discussion of Western conquest should mention the primary motivation. In the case of Latin America, after the initial discovery of the New World, Spanish and Portuguese explorers intended to glean a profit by stripping conquered territories of their natural resources and by founding colonies to establish trade networks.

- Reflect upon the nature of the relationship between the West and the specific region under examination. While some regions were colonized, others were subject to imperialism. Moreover, policies toward specific regions changed over time. For example, early explorers did not focus their efforts on Africa, but by the nineteenth century European powers struggled for control throughout the continent.

- It is important to mention any reverberating effects of European presence in Latin America; namely, the spread of disease, the subsequent annihilation of native populations, the enslavement of native peoples, and the spread of Christianity.

- Changes in trade over time will be an important part of this essay in terms of its effect on native populations. Trade allows for you to discuss the impact of the subjugation of native peoples into slavery on the global market. Slaves, both native and African, were vital for the production for both domestic and exported goods. Latin American trade and the domestic economy would not have succeeded to the extent it did without slave labor.

- Address changes in social issues; examine changes in class structures and gender relations over time as it pertains to native groups. For example, dramatic demographic changes took place during the colonial period. The rise in biracial births led to several racial identifications and associated stigmatization; as the population of racially-mixed individuals rose, social changes occurred.

- Consider the changing impact of Christianity and Western missionaries in Latin America. Conversion of native peoples to Christianity was the goal of Jesuit missionaries in the region, for example. These missionaries also sought to bring education and literacy to the New World.

- It is important to examine the effects of independence movements because they involved European intervention directed against a colonial population that differed dramatically from previous populations; biracial individuals had influence in society as well.

- During the early nineteenth century, Latin American wars of independence affected both political structures and the economy. In terms of this question, focus on the impact of these wars on native groups. For example, several Latin American nations abolished slavery following independence, a decision with enormous social and economic repercussions.

- Essay responses will vary depending on the chosen region; therefore, do not assume the outline above for Latin America will be consistent with that of India, for example. Nevertheless, the basic formula should remain intact. Specifically, for all societies, examine trade networks and their impact on the native populations and the global market, the marginalization of native peoples (whether or not this included enslavement), and the impact of Western religions.

- Remember that the arrival of Westerners in some regions was not initially rooted in conquest; some areas maintained successful trade negotiations with Westerners for some time while other areas managed to partially repel Westerners for years (Japan).

- Most importantly, consider how and why the role of Western intrusion changed over time, which requires accurate knowledge of historical context.

Comparative Essay

Overall Approach

1. Organize your essay around a thesis and provide points to support that thesis.

2. Use accurate historical evidence to support your points.

3. Thoroughly explain how your evidence proves your argument.

4. Do not ignore any portion of the question.

5. Use historical context to account for differences and similarities.

6. Do not simply list facts for each society.

7. Clearly indicate how and why the two societies are similar and different.

Key Points to Include

- The essay requires an answer to the question of how communism rose in two nations through a comparison of the conditions present in each nation prior to the adoption of communism; thus, the thesis should be an answer to this question in the form of an argument supported by historical evidence.

- In discussing Soviet and Chinese communism, consider the respective conditions that enabled the rise of communism. In Russia, the failures of the government began to severely affect the economy around the same time that World War I broke out in Europe. There was inflation, food shortages, and consequently, worker and peasant uprisings. Explain how economic issues inspired political movements; consider the role of Russian workers as instigators in the Revolution.

- China was in a similar situation during the twentieth century. The empire ended in 1912 and was replaced briefly by a republic, which also failed and became a dictatorship. The nation then grew splintered and the centralized government disintegrated into a system of fragmented parcels of land ruled by various overlords. Therefore, prior to the rise of communism, both China and Russia were in a state of chaos and lacked a centralized government; China was divided, and the czar abdicated in Russia allowing for an unstable provisional socialist government.

- It is important to note in the essay that although the communist party in China rose during this period of chaos, by the late 1920s a non-communist centralized regime known as Guo Min Dang was established and governed the majority of China; nonetheless, the nation was not unified in support of the Guo Min Dang because of the growing influence of the communist party on the peasant population, which comprised the majority of the total population.

- In China and Russia, one individual managed to rise to power to further propel the communist party forward and eventually establish a stable regime; namely, V.I. Lenin in Russia and Mao Zedong in China. Compare the role each leader played in his respective nation's political struggles. For example, Lenin and Mao were both successful in organizing their followers, and both took advantage of current wars to seize power. In Lenin's case, he persuaded Germany to help smuggle him into Russia during World War I with the hope that he would undermine the Russian war effort.

- Similarly, Mao recognized the Japanese invasion of China as an opportunity to cooperate with the existing Guo Min Dang leadership. However, the communist party gained a significant following of guerilla peasant fighters among the peasantry in outlying areas not controlled by Guo Min Dang forces. These peasants not only aided in expelling the Japanese, but later also managed to destroy the Guo Min Dang army after relations between the Red Army and the Guo Dang Min had deteriorated. The Red Army drove the Guo Dang Min to Taiwan and succeeded in placing Mao in control of the new communist state.

- The fact that a peasant revolution enabled the establishment of communism in China was a new concept and represents one of the major differences between the rise of communism in Russia and China. This point relates to historical context.

- In Russia, Lenin viewed the communist party as one led by industrial workers. These workers would help to industrialize Russia and establish communism.

- Conversely, in China the peasants comprised the majority of the communist party and Mao sought to industrialize China and establish communism by means of the peasant class.

- The question does not mention Karl Marx, but as part of your comparison it may be relevant to note that neither Soviet nor Chinese communism adhered to original Marxist theory, which stipulated that only after industrialization would the working class bring about communist revolution as a response to capitalist oppression.

- Consider relations between these regions and the West and how those relations affected the spread of communism or efforts to impede upon that spread. In reference to this point, think about Vietnam and Cuba in particular.

Practice Test 2

Multiple-Choice Questions

Instructions: Each question below is followed by four possible answers. Choose the one that best answers the question.

1. Egypt is best described as

   A. the land between the rivers.
   B. the river between the lands.
   C. the world's oldest civilization.
   D. a civilization based on the Mediterranean.

2. Who was the first true emperor of China, the man who imposed strong centralized government and brought the country out of the Warring States Period?

   A. K'ung Fu-Tzu
   B. Liu Bang
   C. Qin Shihuangdi
   D. Wang Mang

3. Mediterranean is a Greek word. It means

   A. the Balkan Peninsula.
   B. the sea in the middle of the world.
   C. the center of the planet.
   D. welcome to Athens.

4. When Alexander the Great set out to conquer Persia, he was opposed by the Persian King

   A. Cyrus the Shepherd.
   B. Darius I.
   C. Darius III.
   D. Xerxes.

5. The first civilization in India was located in

   A. Delhi.
   B. Ganges River Valley.
   C. Indus River Valley.
   D. Sogdiana.

6. The most important Indian civilization was

   A. Aryan.
   B. Harappan.
   C. Olmec.
   D. Vedic-Aryan.

7. The major missing piece in our understanding of the Indus River Valley Civilization is

   A. stories about their gods.
   B. lack of writing.
   C. our inability to decipher their writing.
   D. when they existed.

8. The Greeks were successful during the Persian War primarily because of their victory at the battle of

   A. Artemisium.
   B. Platea.
   C. Salamis.
   D. Thermopalae.

9. The Persian War is best described in the works of

   A. Aeschlyus.
   B. Aristophanes.
   C. Euripides.
   D. Sophocles.

10. The most perfect building in the ancient Greek world was the

   A. Agora.
   B. Erecthion.
   C. Parthenon.
   D. Temple of Apollo.

GO ON TO THE NEXT PAGE

11. Homer's *Iliad* recounts the

    A. Jason's War against the Argonauts.
    B. Peloponessian War.
    C. Persian War.
    D. Trojan War.

12. The Greek tragic writers *exclude*

    A. Aeschlyus.
    B. Aristophanes.
    C. Euripides.
    D. Sophocles.

13. Alexander the Great was the son of

    A. Apollo and Diana.
    B. Hera and Zeus.
    C. Olympus and Zeus.
    D. Philip and Olympias.

14. Alexander the Great conquered the known world. This *excluded*

    A. Sogdiana.
    B. Bactria.
    C. Macedonia.
    D. China.

15. The Romans date their founding to the year

    A. 753 BCE.
    B. 509.
    C. 44.
    D. 31.

16. What answer best describes Roman religion?

    A. Monotheism
    B. Henotheism
    C. 12 gods and goddesses on Mount Olympus
    D. More gods than citizens

17. The First Triumvirate consisted of

    A. Jupiter, Ares, and Neptune.
    B. Julius Caesar, Pompey, and Catiline.
    C. Catullus, Cicero, and Romulus.
    D. Livy, Ovid, and Vergil.

18. The Second Triumvirate consisted of

    A. Octavian, Marc Antony, and Lepidus.
    B. Brutus, Cassius, and Tiberius.
    C. Delphi, Julius Caesar, and Nero.
    D. Claudius, Nerva, and Trajan.

19. Octavian defeated Marc Antony in 31 BCE at

    A. Actium.
    B. Philippi.
    C. Rome.
    D. Rubicon.

20. The most basic Christian tenet is

    A. love thy neighbor.
    B. feed the hungry, clothe the naked, comfort the sick.
    C. go to church on Sunday.
    D. praise the Lord.

21. All of the following are Fathers of the Christian Church *except*

    A. Arian.
    B. Augustine.
    C. Jerome.
    D. Origen.

22. The five good emperors (96–180) include everyone *except*

    A. Antonius Pius.
    B. Commodus.
    C. Hadrian.
    D. Nerva.

23. The first persecutor of Christians was the Roman Emperor

    A. Claudius.
    B. Nero.
    C. Tiberius.
    D. Vespasian.

24. How many Roman Emperors were there between 235 and 284?

    A. 5
    B. 7
    C. 26
    D. 2

25. Diocletian's reforms

   A. saved the Western Roman Empire.
   B. saved the Eastern Roman Empire.
   C. did nothing.
   D. allowed for the conquest of Persia.

26. Constantine is *most* important for

   A. his victory at the Milvian Bridge.
   B. the Council of Nicea.
   C. becoming the first Christian Emperor.
   D. constructing three basilicas in Rome.

27. The *least* important reason given for the decline and fall of the Western Roman Empire would be

   A. Christianity.
   B. the move of the capital to the East.
   C. lead poisoning.
   D. economic decline.

28. The East German tribes are, in part, responsible for the decline of the Western Roman Empire. They include

   A. Goths, Huns, and Visigoths.
   B. Goths, Vandals, and Germans.
   C. Visigoths, Vandals, and Ostrogoths.
   D. Visigoths, Persians, and Byzantines.

29. The West German tribes picked up the pieces after the fall of the Western Roman Empire. They include

   A. Franks, Angles, and Goths.
   B. Franks, Angles, and Saxons.
   C. Franks, Lombards, and Avars.
   D. Jutes, Lombards, and Vikings.

30. Charlemagne is most important because of his

   A. conquest of the Saxons.
   B. visit to Rome in 800.
   C. support of education and the Carolingian Renaissance.
   D. support of his family at Aachen (Aix-la-Chapelle).

31. "Islam" is Arabic for

   A. submission.
   B. recitation.
   C. substitute.
   D. umma.

32. Which is *not* one of the Five Pillars of Islam?

   A. If at all possible, make a pilgrimage to Mecca at least once.
   B. Fast during the daylight hours of the holy month of Ramadan.
   C. Give alms (money) to the poor.
   D. Jihad

33. The most advanced dynasty in China before the year 1000 would be the

   A. Qin.
   B. Han.
   C. Ming.
   D. Tang.

34. All of the following are major political-military leaders in sixteenth-century Japan *except*

   A. Oda Nobunaga.
   B. Toyotomi Hideyoshi.
   C. Kublai Khan.
   D. Tokugawa Ieyasu.

35. Which Pope called the First Crusade?

   A. Alexander III
   B. Gregory VII
   C. Innocent III
   D. Urban II

36. The home of the Italian renaissance was the city of

   A. Florence.
   B. Milan.
   C. Naples.
   D. Rome.

37. All of the following were early Protestants *except*

   A. Johann Tetzel.
   B. John Calvin.
   C. Martin Luther.
   D. Ulrich Zwingli.

38. All of the following were major explorers following Christopher Columbus *except*

   A. Cabot.
   B. Vasco da Gama.
   C. Prince Henry the Navigator.
   D. Verrazaño.

GO ON TO THE NEXT PAGE

39. The dominant family in late-fifteenth-century Florence was the

    A. Habsburgs.
    B. Hohenstauffens.
    C. Machiavellis.
    D. Medicis.

40. The dominant family in Central Europe between 1430 and 1930 was the

    A. Bourbons.
    B. Habsburgs.
    C. Hanoverians.
    D. Medicis.

41. The greatest seventeenth-century English poet was

    A. Thomas Carew.
    B. John Dryden.
    C. Andrew Marvel.
    D. John Milton.

42. Voltaire's greatest satire was

    A. Candide.
    B. On Toleration.
    C. The Social Contract.
    D. Zadig.

43. The most important pamphlet of 1789 was written by

    A. Tom Paine.
    B. The Abbé Emmanuel Sieyès.
    C. Immanuel Kant.
    D. Jacques-Louis David.

44. All of the following are Enlightenment philosophers *except*

    A. Denis Diderot.
    B. François Marie Arouet.
    C. Jean-Jacques Rousseau.
    D. Frederick the Great.

45. The leader of the radical Jacobins was

    A. Brissot.
    B. Danton.
    C. Robespierre.
    D. Saint Just.

46. The Thermidorian Reaction of 1794 refers to the

    A. overthrow of Robespierre and the Jacobins.
    B. Levee en Masse.
    C. Marsaillies.
    D. Law of 22 Prairial.

47. The Coup of 18 Brumaire 1799 consisted of the

    A. overthrow of the Directory.
    B. end of the Great Terror.
    C. end of the French Revolution.
    D. overthrow of the legislative Assembly.

48. Napoleon's greatest victory was at

    A. Aüsterlitz.
    B. Borodino.
    C. Jena.
    D. Ulm.

49. Napoleon's greatest achievement was

    A. the Napoleonic Code.
    B. expansion of the French state.
    C. invasion of Russia.
    D. Italian Campaign of 1796–1797.

50. All of the following help explain why Great Britain was the First Industrial Nation *except*

    A. water power.
    B. political stability.
    C. government planning.
    D. religious toleration.

51. All of the following were successful reactions to industrialization *except*

    A. Benthamites.
    B. Luddites.
    C. Marxists.
    D. Socialists.

52. The greatest problem of the Industrial Revolution was

    A. child labor.
    B. unemployment.
    C. no insurance.
    D. pollution.

53. The key question for Karl Marx was:

   A. Who owns the means of production?
   B. How can we create capital?
   C. What is to be done?
   D. What is the Third Estate?

54. Karl Marx was ultimately in error because he discounted the force of

   A. the Bourgeoisie.
   B. nationalism.
   C. the Proletariat.
   D. government programs.

55. The unification of Germany was due primarily to

   A. Alfred von Tirpitz.
   B. Bernhard von Bülow.
   C. Wilhelm II.
   D. Otto von Bismarck.

56. Imperialism included

   A. the Scramble for Africa.
   B. the Carving up of the Chinese Melon.
   C. the American conquest of the Philippines.
   D. All of the above.

57. The leader of the Bolsheviks was

   A. Karl Marx.
   B. Josef Stalin.
   C. Vladimir Lenin.
   D. Leon Trotsky.

58. The Treaty of Versailles was

   A. too soft.
   B. too harsh.
   C. just right.
   D. well-intentioned, but unworkable.

59. The main reason for the rise of Fascism in Italy was

   A. the retreat of liberal democratic institutions.
   B. the charisma of Benito Mussolini.
   C. the Great Depression.
   D. unemployment.

60. The main reason for the rise of the Nazis in Germany was

   A. Adolph Hitler.
   B. the Great Depression.
   C. the Treaty of Versailles.
   D. the breakdown of parliamentary democracy.

61. During the interwar years (1919–1939), the United States was

   A. an active member of the League of Nations.
   B. isolationist.
   C. supportive of Germany.
   D. anti-Russian.

62. The turning point in the European Theater of World War II was the battle of

   A. Moscow.
   B. El Alaimain.
   C. Stalingrad.
   D. Berlin.

63. The turning point in the Pacific Theater of World War II was the battle of

   A. Midway.
   B. Coral Sea.
   C. Leyte Gulf.
   D. Okinawa.

64. The Cold War is *best* exemplified by the

   A. Korean War, 1950–1953.
   B. Vietnam War, 1945–1975.
   C. Berlin Wall, 1961–1989.
   D. Killing Fields in Cambodia, 1972–1987.

65. The Cold War peaked during the

   A. construction of the Berlin Wall.
   B. Cuban Missile Crisis.
   C. Bay of Pigs invasion of Cuba.
   D. Korean War.

66. American policy towards Vietnam was largely defined by President

   A. Harry S Truman.
   B. John Fitzgerald Kennedy.
   C. Lyndon Baines Johnson.
   D. Richard Millhouse Nixon.

GO ON TO THE NEXT PAGE

67. The Cold War ended in 1991 because

- **A.** Leonid Brezhnev surrendered.
- **B.** the United States launched a pre-emptive attack against the U.S.S.R.
- **C.** a coup d'état removed Mikhail Gorbachev from power.
- **D.** the Soviet Union, led by Mikhail Gorbachev, dissolved into its constituent parts.

68. The person most responsible for the end of Apartheid ("apartness," or strict racial separation) was

- **A.** Steven Biko.
- **B.** P. W. Botha.
- **C.** F. W. de Klerk.
- **D.** Nelson Mandela.

69. The United States and the United Kingdom invaded Iraq in March 2003 because of

- **A.** weapons of Mass Destruction.
- **B.** their desire to introduce democracy there.
- **C.** their desire to remove Saddam Hussein.
- **D.** oil.

70. What country is most likely to both rapidly expand economically and require more natural resources for this expansion by 2025?

- **A.** China
- **B.** India
- **C.** Japan
- **D.** United States

Free-Response Questions

Compare and Contrast Essay Question

Analyze Christianity and Islam. Do not try to convert me and do not favor one over the other. Out of what milieu did each arise? How did they differ from other religions we have seen in this course? What are their elementary beliefs, and who are the key figures? To whom did they appeal, and why? What was their early development like? What are the differences between them?

Change-Over-Time Essay Question

In the tenth century Western Europe was one of the most backward portions of the Eurasian landmass. By 1648 this same area had produced a civilization, which was reaching out to many parts of the planet and was beginning to assume global leadership. In a thoughtful historical essay examine at least **four (4)** ways in which the Christian Church contributed to the rise and expansion of western civilization during these seven centuries.

Specific Essay Question

Why did Germany lose the Great War? Could they have won, or was victory never a possibility? Assess the settlement of Versailles. What were its benefits to Europe and the world, and what were its drawbacks? Was the settlement too harsh or too conciliatory? Could it have secured lasting peace in Europe and the world? How might it have been improved?

Answers and Explanations for Practice Test 2

1. **B.** The river between the land refers to Egypt, as the Nile makes life possible in the country. The land between the rivers refers to Mesopotamia, to the Tigris and Euphrates. China is the world's oldest *continuous* civilization, and both China and Mesopotamia are older than Egypt. A civilization based on the Mediterranean is too vague.

2. **C.** Qin Shihuangdi was the first emperor, 220–206, the man who imposed strong centralized government and brought the country out of the Warring States Period. K'ung Fu-Tzu is the Chinese spelling of Confucius. Liu Bang was the founder of the Han Dynasty in 206 BCE. Wang Mang was the "Socialist Emperor," an interregnum between the Early Han and the Later Han, 6–25 CE.

3. **B.** The sea in the middle of the world is a literal translation from the Greek. Greece is a part of the Balkan Peninsula. The "center of the planet" and "Welcome to Athens" are too vague.

4. **C.** Darius III (336–330) was the Persian ruler who opposed Alexander. Cyrus (originally called the Shepherd) founded the Persian state and the Achaemenid Dynasty, 557–530. Darius I was an important Persian ruler, 521–486, responsible for conquest but especially for administration. Xerxes was the Persian ruler during the Persian War (versus the Greeks), 486–465.

5. **C.** The Indus River Valley represents the first Indian civilization, c.2200–1800 BCE. Delhi is an eastern city built much later. The Ganges is the eastern river valley, populated much later. Sogdiana is north and west of the Indian subcontinent.

6. **D.** Vedic-Aryan was the second civilization in India, c.1800 BCE to 200 CE, one that influenced all later developments, although without writing and urban centers. The Aryan race was an invention of Adolph Hitler in the 1920s. Harappan, also known as the Indus River Valley civilization, was India's first civilization (2250–1850) but its script has yet to be deciphered. The Olmecs were the earliest civilization in Mesoamerica, 1200–100.

7. **C.** Our inability to decipher their writing is correct. There are a number of languages we have been unable to decipher, most notably Etruscan and the people of Easter Island. Keep in mind that it has been estimated that the number of literate people in pre-classical societies numbered one-third of those attending a college football game today, or under 40,000. Although we do not know a great deal about their gods, this is not the missing piece. They had writing; we just can't decipher it. We know when they existed, c.220–1800.

8. **C.** Salamis was the major Greek victory during the Persian War; Xerxes returned to Persia after it to quell possible uprisings. Artemisium and Thermopalae were complimentary. Cape Artemisium a naval battle won by the Greeks and Thermopalae a land battle won by the Persians after killing the 300 Spartans under King Leonidas. Platea was a Greek victory in Asia Minor in 479.

9. **A.** Aeschylus was a participant, a hoplite (infantry soldier) who wrote about his experiences in his plays. Aristophanes was a comic writer of the 420s and 410s, best known for *Frogs* and *Lysistrata*. Euripides was a dramatist who included women more frequently and sympathetically than other tragedians, and was a great influence on later tragic writers. Sophocles is best known for his three-play *Oedipus* cycle.

10. **C.** The Parthenon is considered to be the most perfect building in the ancient world. It looks perfectly symmetrical from a distance. In fact it is not, but the Greeks had the ability to have it appear to be. The Agora was the cultural, religious, social, and economic center of Greek life. The Erecthion is a nice temple to Athena that combines monumental architecture and monumental sculpture, although asymmetrical. The Temple of Apollo was at Basai and is the best-preserved temple to incorporate all three orders. Doric outside, Ionic inside, and one Corinthian column at the back of the Temple. Same architect as the Parthenon.

11. **D.** Homer's *Iliad* recounts the story of the end of the Trojan War, from the pouting to the wrath of Achilles. Jason's War against the Argonauts is a Greek myth. The Peloponessian War was between Sparta and Athens, won by Sparta, 431–404. The Persian War was between Greece and Persia, 492–479.

12. **B.** Aristophanes was a comic writer of the late fifth century BCE. Aeschlyus, Euripides, and Sophocles are the great tragic writers of the fifth century BCE.

13. **D.** Alexander was the son of Philip of Macedonia and Olympias. Apollo and Diana are a Greek god and goddess. Olympus is the mountain where the major deities lived and Zeus is the chief god.

14. D. Although he may have wanted to go to China, Alexander's troops rebelled at the Indus River and he turned homeward. Sogdiana Bactria are located south of Afghanistan and west of India. Macedonia was Alexander's homeland.

15. A. 753 BCE is the mythical date Romulus and Remus founded the city of Rome. 509 was the date the last Etruscan king was expelled, and the Roman Republic established. 44 was the year Julius Caesar was assassinated. 31 was the year of Octavian's victory over Mark Antony at Actium.

16. D. More gods than citizens most accurately reflects the Roman practice. Although they adopted the 12 major Greek gods and goddesses, there were many household gods, and emperors were deified after death. Monotheism describes Judaism, Christianity, and Islam. In Henotheism there are many gods, but eventually one emerges as the most important. Twelve gods and goddesses on Mount Olympus represents the Greek view.

17. B. The First Triumvirate ("tri," three, so three joint rulers) consisted of Julius Caesar, Pompey, and Catiline. Julius Caesar was the most important, Pompey second, and Catiline the least, 58–44. Jupiter, Ares, and Neptune are three Roman gods. Caullus was a Roman poet; Cicero the ancient world's greatest orator and rhetorician who tried to bring the Senate back to power; and Romulus was the supposed founder of Rome. Livy was the historian, Ovid the erotic poet, and Vergil the epic author of ancient Rome.

18. A. The Second Triumvirate consisted of Octavian, Marc Antony, and Lepidus, 44–31. Mark Antony was the most important initially, later displaced by Octavian, Caesar Augustus; Lepidus was the weakest of the three. Brutus and Cassius were the main assassins of Julius Caesar, while Tiberius was the stepson of Octavian. Delphi was the location of a Greek Temple and Oracle; Nero was a later emperor 54–68. Claudius was one of the best, a great justice, 41–54. Nerva was the first (96–98) and Trajan the second (98–117) of the Five Good Emperors (96–180).

19. A. Octavian defeated Marc Antony at the Battle of Actium, 31 BCE, off the western Greek coast. Philippi was where the Second Triumvirate defeated and killed Brutus and Cassius. Rome was the capital of the Roman world. The Rubicon was the river Julius Caesar crossed in 49 BCE with his army, a violation of Roman practice and a step toward dictatorial control.

20. A. Love God and love thy neighbor as thyself is the most basic Christian belief. Feed the hungry, clothe the naked, comfort the sick represents "Practical Christianity" from the Book of *James*. Go to church on Sunday was added many years later by the Roman Catholic Church. Praise the Lord is from the 95th *Psalm*.

21. A. Arian was a priest later declared to be a heretic, and certainly not a Church Father. Of these five Church Fathers (Clement of Alexandria and Ambrose are the other two), Augustine was the most influential; Jerome translated the Bible from Greek to Latin, the "Latin Vulgate;" and Origen was an earlier (third century) figure.

22. B. Commodus was the son of Marcus Aurelius, who attempted to establish a dynasty; incompetent as a ruler. Nerva established the "Five Good Emperors," 96–180. The idea was *not* to create a dynasty, but to find a competent general and administrator and bring them along as an "emperor in training." Antonius Pius was the fourth of the five, 138-161. Hadrian was a great justice, emperor 117–138. Nerva was the first of the good emperors, 96–98.

23. B. The Roman Emperor Nero, 54–68, ordered the first persecution of Christians between 64 and 66. Nero was behind the great fire of 64, which destroyed about 25 percent of Rome. He was a cruel and probably insane ruler who wanted to build more palaces and stables. To counter the rumor that he had "fiddled while Rome burned," he claimed it was the Christians' fault. All of the others were Roman emperors. Claudius was a great justice, 41–54, and Nero's stepfather, executed by Nero's orders. Tiberius, 14–37, was the stepson of Octavian. Vespasian, 69–79, brought stability out of the civil wars caused by Nero's death.

24. C. 235–284 was a very turbulent time in the empire, with 26 emperors in 50 years, only one of whom died peacefully. The five good emperors governed between 96 and 180. There were seven emperors between Octavian and Nerva, 14–96. There were only two emperors between 284 and 337, Diocletian (284–305) and Constantine (306–337).

25. B. Diocletian's reforms saved the Eastern Empire and allowed it to continue until 1453. He successfully reformed the army and civilian administration; less so taxation, labor, and the coinage. His reforms eventually caused the Western Empire to collapse in 476. All of his reforms had some impact, and Rome never conquered Persia.

26. **C.** Constantine is most important for converting to Christianity. The emperor has gone from a heathen persecutor to, in theory at least, "your brother in Christ." Constantine's victory over Maxentius in October 312 at the Milvian Bridge led to the Edict of Milan ("Edict of Toleration"), issued in 313. The Council of Nicea, May-June 325, was the first great council of the Christian Church, called and presided over by Constantine. The construction of three basilicas (great churches) in Rome was a nice touch, but Constantine then left Rome for Constantinople, never to return

27. **C.** The *least* important reason for the Decline of the Western Roman Empire would be lead poisoning. Supposedly the Roman aristocracy kept their wine in lead containers, thus leading to lead poisoning; not a deciding element. The argument of Edward Gibbon in *The Decline and Fall of the Roman Empire* (1776) was that Christianity was the main cause of the fall. While having some merit, Christianity softened the fall of the Western Empire. Economic decline is one of the more important reasons given, as is the move of the capital to the east. In reality, it was the combination of a number of reasons.

28. **C.** The East German tribes who were, in part, responsible for the decline of the Western Roman Empire include the Ostrogoths, who were struck by the Huns in 375. Eventually all three tribes migrated through the Western Roman Empire during the fifth century, eventually settling in Visigothic Spain, the Vandals in North Africa and some Mediterranean islands, and Ostrogothic Italy, the most 'successful' of these three tribes. The Goths were a Germanic tribe; the Huns are from the central Asian steppes and *caused* the movement of the East Germanic tribes; "Germans" is too general. The Vandals were an East Germanic tribe. Persia had their own problems with the Huns, but never migrated west; the Eastern Roman Empire is also referred to as the Byzantine Empire.

29. **B.** The West German tribes that picked up the pieces after the fall of the Western Roman Empire include the Franks, who established Frankland (France), the Angles, who established Angle-Land (England), and the Saxons, who also went to England (the Anglo-Saxon settlements and language). See the previous question for the Goths. The Lombards were found in northern Italy and were the least Romanized of the tribes; the Avars were in northern Germany. Jutes went to England, but in smaller numbers; Vikings were later, and from Scandinavia.

30. **C.** Charlemagne (sole King of the Franks 774-814) is most important because of his support of education and the Carolingian Renaissance. This represents his greatest legacy. The conquest of the Saxons was a perennial (yearly) experience for much of his reign, to the north and east. Charlemagne was crowned (Holy) Roman Emperor by Pope Leo III on Christmas Day. Although this was a looking back, and claimed that the Franks were now the legitimate successors of the Romans, it was not as long lasting or important as the Carolingian Renaissance. He did support his family at Aachen (Aix-la-Chapelle), giving his daughters land so that they would be independent of their brother, Louis the Pious, but this is not one of his major accomplishments.

31. **A.** "Islam" is Arabic for submission to the will of Allah (Arabic for "Lord"). Recitation, or the *Qur'an (Koran),* is the sacred text of Islam, the revelation of Allah to Mohammed. Caliph is Arabic for "substitute." The caliph was the ruler of the Islamic world, considered to be Mohammed's substitute. Compare with the pope as the "Vicar (or substitute)of Christ." Umma is Arabic for the "community of Islam."

32. **D.** The concept of jihad was used to forcibly convert people to Islam; most modern Muslims now view it as an internal struggle to remain faithful to Allah. At best this is considered to be the *sixth* pillar. The Five Pillars are "There is no God but Allah and Mohammed is His prophet;" prayer at five prescribed times a day, facing Mecca; if at all possible, make a pilgrimage to Mecca (the "Haji") at least once during your lifetime; fast during the daylight hours of the holy month of Ramadan; and give alms (money) to the poor.

33. **D.** The most advanced Chinese dynasty before 1000 CE was the Tang Dynasty (618–907). The most important early figure was Tang Taizong (627–649). Culturally and politically very advanced; Japan adopted many Tang structures and ideas, including their numbers. The Qin Dynasty was the first dynasty to incorporate strong, centralized government throughout China. Founded by Qin Shihuangdi, the "first emperor," it lasted from 221 to 210. The Han was founded by Liu Bang and named after his home province; this dynasty picked up the pieces from the Qin's fall. Han Wudi, the "Martial Emperor," 141–87, was an important figure. The Early Han date from 206 BCE

to CE 9; the Later Han, 25–220. The Ming was the greatest modern dynasty, 1368–1644. Founded by Hongwu (1368–1398), China recovered from the Mongol invasions and foreign rule. Voyages of discovery, the construction of the Forbidden Palace in Beijing (and the completion of the Great Wall), and Ming porcelain are their great triumphs.

34. C. Kublai Khan was the Mongol khan (ruler) who conquered the Song Dynasty of China in 1279. He attempted to invade Japan in 1274 and 1281, but failed. Marco Polo visited his court in the 1280s. Japan was engulfed by civil war for most of the time between 1450 and 1560. By 1560 three individuals stood out in civil-war Japan. Oda Nobunaga, Toyotomi Hideyoshi, and Tokugawa Ieyasu. There is a saying in Japan: "Nobunaga mixed the cake, Hideyoshi baked it, and Ieyasu ate it," indicating the role each played in giving Japan a political order it had never before possessed. Their dates are Nobunaga (1560–1584), Hideyoshi (1584–1598), and Ieyasu (1598–1623). Success in the Battle at Sekigahara in 1600 led to the Tokugawa Settlement and the Tokugawa Shogunate, where the shogun (the real power in Japan) was a member of the Tokugawa family until their abdication in 1867.

35. D. Urban II called the First Crusade at Clermont, France in November 1095. Alexander III was pope 1159–1181. The rise of Canon Law, the law of the Catholic Church, and "lawyer popes," led to disputes with Frederick I Barbarossa ("red beard"), German Emperor 1152–1190. Gregory VII (Hildebrand) is the first of three great Medieval popes, important for the Investiture Controversy, Winter 1075–1076, with the German Emperor Henry IV, and later for a papal wish list, the *Dictate Papes. Innocent* III (1198–1216) was born Lothar dei Conti of Segni in 1160/1161. The most powerful and influential figure in Western Christendom, spiritual and temporal, the greatest Western ruler of his time. Elected unanimously at age 37. Successful in disputes with the rulers of England, France, and Germany (the Empire). Called the Fourth Crusade in 1202 and the Fourth Lateran Council in 1215.

36. A. Florence was the home of the Renaissance. Milan, Naples, Rome, and Venice all shared in its glories, but Florence, on the river Arno, in Tuscany (central Italy) was its home.

37. A. Johann Tetzel was a Dominican priest who arguably *caused* the Protestant Reformation by selling Indulgences in Germany and certainly did not protest about the abuses of the Catholic Church. John Calvin (1509–1564) was born in Noyon, France in 1509 and broke from the Catholic Church. He believed in Predestination, the idea that God had decided whether people were going to Heaven or Hell (elect and reprobates) before birth. There was nothing you could do about it. Established his ideas in Geneva. Wrote the *Institutes of the Christian Religion* in 1559. His followers are know as Huguenots and Presbyterians. Popular in France, Scotland, England, and among the Dutch. Martin Luther (1483–1546), the "first successful heretic." Posted his 95 Thesis on the door of Wittenberg cathedral on 31 October 1517. Supported and protected by Frederick the Wise, Elector of Saxony. Later married a former nun, Katherine von Bora. Ulrich Zwingli (1484–1531) was a moderate Protestant who initially followed Luther. Killed at the battle of Keppel in 1531.

38. C. Prince Henry the Navigator was a member of the Portuguese royal family who established a "school" at Sagritz for sailors to learn the latest developments. Columbus and da Gama "studied" there. The prince never went to sea himself. John and Sebastian Cabot explored the eastern coast of North America for Henry VII and Henry VIII of England. Vasco da Gama was a Portuguese explorer who sailed around Africa to India in 1497–1498. Verrazaño explored the North American coast for François I of France in the 1520s and 1530s.

39. D. The de Medicis dominated Florence during the fifteenth and sixteenth centuries. They made their initial money from the wool trade, then became bankers. The most powerful was Lorenzo de Medici ("Il Magnifico") who dominated politics between 1478 and 1492. Two sons became cardinals and one Pope Leo X, who declared Martin Luther a heretic. A granddaughter, Catherine, married Henri II of France (1547–1559). The Habsburgs (Haspburgs) were the dominant family in Central Europe, 1437-1919, when a Habsburg was first Holy Roman Emperor and, after 1806, Emperor of Austria-Hungary. There was a Spanish branch under Charles V, who divided his empire when he abdicated in 1556 between his son Philip II and his brother Ferdinand II. The Spanish Habsburgs died out in 1700. The Hohenstauffens ruled Medieval Germany/the Empire 1152–1250 and the Kingdom of the Two Sicilies 1190–1250. They were brought down by the Papacy, and Germany would not be reunited again until 1870. Niccolò Machiavelli (1469–1527) wrote *The Prince* for the children of Lorenzo de Medici.

40. B. The Habsburgs dominated Central Europe, 1437–1919. See answer #39. The Bourbons were the last French dynasty, 1589-1793 and 1814–1848. The Hanoverians controlled Hanover, a province of northern Germany. George Ernest became an Elector, one of those who (in theory, at least) elected the Holy Roman Emperor in 1692. His son, George August, became King of Great Britain in 1715, where their descendants rule today. For the de Medicis see answer #39.

41. D. John Milton was the greatest seventeenth-century English poet, author of the great poems *Paradise Lost, Paradise Regained,* and *Samson Agonistes.* Thomas Carew and Andrew Marvel were second-class (but still important) seventeenth-century poets. John Dryden was a Catholic and poet laureate of England in the 1680s, author of a version of *Absalom and Achitohel.*

42. A. Voltaire's *Candide* is one of the greatest satires of all time. *On Toleration* was a pamphlet by Voltaire advocating religious toleration. *The Social Contract* was written by Jean-Jacques Rousseau and argues for a social contract among the people, not the divine right of kings and the rule of monarchs. *Zadig* was a lesser satire by Voltaire.

43. B. The Abbé Emmanuel Sieyès wrote *What is the Third Estate* in January 1789. He argued that the First and Second Estates (Nobility and Clergy) were blood-sucking leeches, and that the Third Estate was nothing but should be everything. Very influential in the early stages of the French Revolution. Tom Paine authored *Common Sense* in January 1776 in the American colonies. The more radical *The Rights of Man* appeared in two parts in 1792–1793. Immanuel Kant was a German philosopher, best known for the phrase *Sapere Aude,* "Dare to know!" Jacques-Louis David chronicled the Revolution and Napoleonic Europe, but as a painter.

44. D. Frederick the Great of Prussia (r.1740–1786) was an enlightened despot who entertained Voltaire, but was excessively militaristic, and not an Enlightenment philosopher. Denis Diderot (1713–1784) edited the *Encyclopadie,* a collection of Enlightenment articles, forerunner of our modern encyclopedias. François Marie Arouet (1694–1778) is better known as Voltaire. Jean-Jacques Rousseau (1712–1778) wrote *The Social Contract* and *Émile, or on Education.*

45. C. Maximilian Robespierre led the Jacobins and the Committee of Public Safety during the Revolution. He was responsible for the Terror and Great Terror of 1793–1794, and the hundreds of thousands of deaths they entailed. He was executed on 10 Thermidor (28 July) 1794 because his opponents feared yet another of the National Convention and acted before Robespierre could. Brissot was the leader of the moderate Girondins. Danton was an important political figure in revolutionary France, 1792–1794, but was less radical and never led a group. Executed by Robespierre in April 1794. Saint Just was a Jacobin and member of the Committee of Public Safety.

46. A. The Thermidorean Reaction refers to the overthrow of Robespierre and the Jacobins in July 1794. It also refers to a less radical phase of a political revolution (Russian, Chinese, Iranian, etc.). The Levée en Masse was the first modern draft, detailing the conscription of young men and the role of other groups in society. *Le Marsaillies* was a rather bloody song composed by Captain Rouget d'Lisle from Marseilles that became the French national anthem. The Law of 22 Prairial (10 June) 1794 or the Law of Suspects, allowed people to be arrested for simple facial expressions taken to be against the Jacobins. They were sent to trial very quickly, without a lawyer, and they could call no witnesses. They were either guilty and immediately executed, or acquitted and freed.

47. A. The Coup of 18 Brumaire (9 November) 1799 consisted of the overthrow of the Directory, which had governed France since 1795. Napoleon would then outmaneuver Sieyès and become First Consul. The Great Terror wound down after the execution of Robespierre in July 1794. The Revolution ended with a combination of the Papal Concordat (1801) and the Peace of Amiens (25 March 1802). The overthrow of the Legislative Assembly occurred in September 1792.

48. A. Napoleon's greatest victory was at Austerlitz in December 1805. It made him master of southern Germany. Borodino was a Phrryic victory in Russia in September 1812. Phrrys was a Greek general who "won" a battle in the third century BCE, but his casualties were so high that he had to retreat; one more victory like that and he would have lost the war. Jena was a Napoleonic victory in 1806 over Prussia that made him master of northern Germany. Ulm was where Napoleon forced an Austrian force under Karl Mack to surrender on 20 October 1805.

49. A. The Napoleonic Code, somewhat harsh and authoritarian, was Napoleon's greatest achievement. It forms the basis for modern French law. The expansion of the French state was ephemeral, it did not last all that long. The invasion of Russia was a disaster. The Italian Campaign of 1796–1797 was professional in every sense of the word, but not his greatest achievement.

50. **C.** Government planning played no part in the Industrial Revolution. It was all done by entrepreneurs. *Laissez Faire* economics was the norm, essentially "government hands off." Water Power, political stability, religious toleration, the Royal Navy, deposits of coal, colonies and trade, an available workforce, entrepreneurs, and a climate fostering investment are all reasons why Great Britain became the First Industrial Nation.

51. **B.** Luddites, or "rage against the machine," were a failed response to industrialization. They believed that the machine had taken their job away, and if they destroyed the machine they would get their job back. Factory owners, however, were making too much profit, and hired unemployed soldiers to guard the factories and prevent such actions. Jeremy Bentham and his followers believed in Utilitarianism, "the greatest good for the greatest number." The problem is, who decides the answers to these questions? Karl Marx provided a rigorous intellectual critique of industrialization, but it has proved to be impractical. Robert Owen's socialism, "to each according to their needs, from each according to their abilities," was the most successful response to industrial capitalism. Sometimes called "capitalism with a human face".

52. **A.** Child labor was the greatest problem and threat to industrialization. If all children (as young as six) did was work, they gained no skills, and were possibly doomed to be a permanent underclass. Unemployment was a problem for those unemployed, although as David Ricardo stated in his Iron Law of Wages, subsistence wages were all that workers (hands) could expect. No insurance (health, worker's compensation, etc.) was a problem, one addressed by factory owners beginning in the 1870s. Air and water pollution was, and still is, a serious byproduct of industrialization.

53. **A.** The central question for Marx was "who owns the means of production?" He was not opposed to industrial capitalism, just the exploitation of the workers. "How can we create capital?" was not a question asked by Marx, although his mother once said, "If only Karl had *made* capital instead of writing about it. . . ." *What is to be Done?* was a pamphlet written by the Bolshevik (Marxist) V. I. Lenin in 1905. *What is the Third Estate?* was written during the French Revolution.

54. **B.** Karl Marx was ultimately in error because he discounted the force of Nationalism. Marx believed that French, German, British, Russian, et. al., workers would unite as workers. The bonds of modern nationalism proved far stronger. The bourgeoisie are Marx's middle class and the proletariat his working class. Although not as important as nationalism, government programs (plus factory owners cleaning up industrialism's worst excesses) were important reasons as to why workers did not revolt en masse (in large numbers), as Marx predicted.

55. **D.** The unification of Germany was due primarily to Otto von Bismarck, the "Iron Chancellor" of Prussia and a unified Germany, 1862–1890. Alfred von Tirpitz was Admiral and leader of the Reichsmarineamt (the Navy) and Wilhelm II's closest adviser, 1898–1918. Bernhard von Bülow was Foreign Minister 1898–1902. Gave the "Hammer or Anvil" speech on 11 December 1899 ("In the coming century Germany must be either the hammer [that which acts] or the anvil [that which is acted upon]"). Wilhelm was the Kaiser ("Caesar"), 1888–1918; dismissed Bismarck in March 1890.

56. **D.** Imperialism included all of the above. The "Scramble for Africa;" in 1875 Europeans controlled only 11% of Africa. By 1902 they controlled 90 percent and only two countries, Liberia and Abyssinia, remained independent. "Carving up the Chinese Melon" refers to the Great Powers dividing China into Spheres of Influence in the mid- to late-nineteenth century. The American conquest of the Philippines was important because the United States, itself an ex-colony, became a colonial power.

57. **C.** Vladimir I. Lenin (Vladimir Ilyich Ulyanov, 1870–1924) was the leader of the Bolsheviks, even in exile. He revised Marx's thought, hence Marxism-Leninism. Karl Marx wrote the *Communist Manifesto,* the blueprint for Communism. Josef Stalin (Josif Vissarionovich Dzhugashvili, 1879–1953), the "man of steel," was the number two man in the Communist Party under Lenin and would lead the Union of Soviet Socialist Republics (U.S.S.R.) 1928–1953. Leon Trotsky (Lev Davidovich Bronstein, 1879-1940,) was the leader of the Red Army under Lenin. Lost the power struggle to Stalin and exiled. Assassinated by Stalin's agents in Mexico.

58. **B.** The Treaty of Versailles was too harsh, and too vindictive. It divided Germany and placed very heavy reparations on them. No attempt was made

by the victors (especially France) to reintegrate Germany into the European or world economy or to the League of Nations. The Treaty of Versailles was certainly not too soft or just right. Well intentioned but unworkable describe President Woodrow Wilson's idealistic 14 Points, which lay behind the treaty.

59. **A.** The *main* reason for the rise of Italian Fascism was the retreat of liberal democratic institutions throughout Europe, but first in Italy. The charisma of Benito Mussolini and unemployment both played a role, but the liberal democratic government collapsed after the March on Rome on 28 October 1922.

60. **B.** The main reason for the rise of Fascism in Germany was the Great Depression, beginning in October 1929. The isolationist United States turned even further inward, and the shock to the world economy was severe. Germany was unable to meet their reparations payments and became open to the radical right with their black and white answers. Germans did become more open to Hitler, but only after the Crash. The Treaty of Versailles was extremely unpopular in Germany, and gained political capital by ignoring it, but again, after October 1929. The German parliamentary system broke down in 1932; Hitler was appointed Chancellor in January 1933 and given unlimited powers two months later.

61. **B.** The Treaty of Versailles was written for the United States, as the Allies realized they would have lost the war without them. The U.S. Senate failed to ratify the treaty, and the United States did not join the League of Nations, preferring to return to isolationism. The U.S. did nothing more than lend Germany money to help them make their reparations payments to France. The U.S. participated in the war against the Bolsheviks in 1919–1920, but then moved to isolationism. In 1933 diplomatic recognition was extended to the U.S.S.R.

62. **C.** Stalingrad was the turning point of the European Theater. One would expect the Russians to fight for a city their leader named after himself, but it was also a strategic location. It was the westernmost point on the Volga River—if the Germans controlled it, they could cross the Volga at will, control traffic up and down the river valley (cutting off key supplies, particularly petroleum, which were reaching Russian armies from the Persian Gulf and Iran), and strike into the Russian heartland east of Moscow. The Soviets were so determined to hold it, and the Germans so determined to take it, that their struggle became probably the most bitter and brutal battle in

human history, with each side taking about a quarter of a million casualties over seven months. The Soviets defended the city street by street and house by house. By late Fall 1942 they controlled only a few blocks on the west bank of the river. Every day, they would hold off German attacks, usually taking nearly one hundred percent casualties—every night, they would send troops across the river in small boats to replace those lost the day before.

The Germans were so deeply committed in the battle, and so over-extended in the vast reaches of the southern Soviet Union, that they had to use Rumanian troops to cover their flanks north and south of Stalingrad. In November, with the ground and river frozen, the Soviets counterattacked against those inferior units, broke through, and surrounded the German Third Army. Hitler refused to authorize a retreat and, by January, Germany had lost more soldiers and equipment and, above all, more highly skilled commissioned and non-commissioned officers than it could ever hope to replace. From that point on, Germany was in constant retreat in the East. Even if Britain and the United States had simply given up fighting in early 1943, Germany would almost certainly still have been crushed. The Battle of Moscow was important, as it was the capital, but not decisive. El Alamein was an Allied victory in North Africa under Field Marshal Bernard Law Montgomery (1887–1976). Berlin was not conquered (and by the Red Army) until Spring 1945.

63. **A.** Midway, 4 June 1942, was the turning point in the Pacific Theater, as four Japanese aircraft carriers, as well as their most experienced pilots, were lost in a matter of minutes. The Battle of the Coral Sea, 7–9 May 1942, was only five months after the attack on Pearl Harbor. The first naval battle where the opposing ships never saw each other. The Battle of Leyte Gulf, 24–26 October 1944, was a part of the reconquest of the Philippines. The Battle of Okinawa, April 1945, was especially costly in American lives, indicative of Japanese resistance close to the home islands.

64. **C.** The Cold War was primarily ideological, and the most appropriate symbol was the Berlin Wall, August 1961 to November 1989, a wall built to keep people *in*. Also spies were more important than soldiers, and Berlin not only had its share, but many valuable spies were 'traded' at Berlin. The Korean War of 1950–1953 was a Soviet probe to gain South Korea. It failed. The Vietnam War of 1945-1975 consisted of two phases. The French attempt to reconquer Indochina (Vietnam,

Cambodia, and Laos), 1945–1954, was supported by the United States. The American phase, 1956–1975, was an attempt to make South Vietnam a democracy and keep the North Vietnamese from conquering the south. Both failed, and the United States withdrew. A bloodbath followed American withdrawal. Pol Pot and the Khmer Rouge took over Cambodia in the 1970s and established a state modeled on Mao Zedong's Communist China. Some 25 percent of the population were killed (hence the "Killing Fields") until they were overthrown by the North Vietnamese in 1987.

65. **B.** The Thirteen Days of the Cuban Missile Crisis in October 1962 was the closest the world came to nuclear war during the Cold War. At the end the Soviets backed down and did not try to cross the American quarantine line. The Berlin Wall was a flash point, and many East Berliners lost their lives or were wounded trying to escape, but it never threatened a nuclear war. The Bay of Pigs/invasion of Cuba by American-trained Cuban nationals in April 1961 failed because the U.S. did not give them air and naval support. Although the U.S.S.R. did not intervene, this led to the Cuban Missile Crisis 18 months later. The Korean War could have become a major conflict had the Allies invaded or bombed China in 1950 or later. As it was China intervened, but the war then settled into a stalemate, ultimately resolved by President Eisenhower after the death of Stalin.

66. **C.** Lyndon Baines Johnson (1963–1969) defined American policy towards Vietnam by dramatically increasing American forces there beginning in 1965. Escalation involving all of the armed forces in an attempt to defeat the North Vietnamese. American power did just that, but lost the war on the home front and ultimately withdrew. Harry S Truman (1945–1953) was president when the Cold War began. He supported the French attempt to reconquer Indochina. John Fitzgerald Kennedy (1961–1936) continued the Eisenhower Administration's (1953–1961) policy of support for South Vietnam, although primarily through advisers. Richard Millhouse Nixon (1969–1974) sought to decrease American casualties and turn more of the effort over to the South Vietnamese ("Vietnamization").

67. **D.** The Soviet Union, under Mikhail Gorbachev, was unable to sustain its economy, political, and military structure, and collapsed into its constituent parts, the various Republics. Leonid Brezhnev (1964–1982) most certainly did not surrender. Fortunately nuclear bombs were not used, although the threat was always there. A coup d'état was certainly *attempted* against Gorbachev in August 1991, but it failed, as did Communism.

68. **D.** Nelson Mandela (b. 1918, imprisoned in 1964 and released in 1991) was the driving force to end apartheid ("apartness," or racial segregation) in South Africa. First president of a united, one-man one-vote election in April 1994, and served until 1999. Thabo Mbeki is currently in his second term. Stephen Biko was a black nationalist killed by police in 1977. P. W. Botha was a white Prime Minister who strongly supported the police state and apartheid. F. W. de Klerk was a white Prime Minister who, although he advanced through the apartheid system, had second thoughts, released Mandela, and eventually lost the 1994 election to him.

69. **A.** Anglo-American forces invaded Iraq in March 2003 because of the threat of Weapons of Mass Destruction (WMDs). That was the reason given by the G. W. Bush administration to the United Nations. They have since announced that none have been found and that they did not exist. March was the date determined to invade because temperatures regularly reach 125 degrees Fahrenheit by June. The introduction of democracy and the removal of Saddam Hussein were offered much later, after no WMDs were found. Oil has been offered by critics of the invasion as the real reason to go in.

70. **A.** China has experienced continued growth since the 1980s, close to double-digit growth for the past five years, and is projected to do so for the immediate future. India is experiencing growth and resource demand, but not as much as China. Japan is experiencing growth that is nowhere near as rapid as India's or China's. The United States has experienced little growth and has a large debt.

Compare and Contrast Essay

Overall Approach

1. Most history essay questions ask you to *analyze* the subject matter. Make sure you understand what analysis is all about, as opposed to *narrative*.

2. You are to write an *essay*. An essay consists of an *introduction*, in which you essentially restate the question, followed by a *body*, in which you provide specific examples to support your position or argument, and a *conclusion*, which sums up your main points and explains why all of this is important.

3. All history is based on evidence; all evidence is based on testimony; and all testimony is biased. How might you incorporate this into your essay?

4. You may include primary sources as you remember them to support your position.

5. Do *not* go off on tangents—address the question and sub-questions as provided.

6. Provide a time frame to the best of your ability.

7. Include only material you are *certain* about—leave out what you are unsure of.

8. Make sure you follow through on all of the separate questions.

Key Points to Include

- Milieu is French (literally "place") for context. The context for both religions is polytheism, "many gods." For Christianity that meant the Roman Empire, in which there were literally more gods than citizens. It was believed that the emperor would become a god upon his death, and you would worship (drink wine, offer incense to) his image. Islam came about in Arabia, a desert. In the early seventh century of the Common Era they practiced Animism, in which natural elements are worshipped as gods or spirits.

- Both also came out of Jewish monotheism, with Christ representing the promised Messiah or a great prophet.

- Elaborate on the basic Christian beliefs (love God, love your neighbor, feed the hungry, comfort the sick, clothe the naked, and so on).

- Elaborate on the Five Pillars of Islam.

- Introduce and discuss the teachings of Jesus and at least Peter and Paul.

- Introduce and discuss the life of Mohammed, Khadija, and Abu Bakr. Include the Hegira, the return to Mecca, and Mohammed's death in 632 CE (10 AH).

- Discuss their sacred texts, and other writings.

- Remember that we have nothing directly from Jesus or Mohammed.

- Remember also that Paul's *Epistles* are the earliest Christian writings; the gospels came later. The same applies to the Hadiths and Sharia.

- Discuss the early reaction to these faiths and their persecutions.

- Discuss their days of worship and dietary restrictions, and their views on slavery.

- Appeal and why. For Christianity, consider "the first shall be last and the last shall be first." Also, who were the downtrodden at the time? The "unfree," so perhaps women and slaves. For Islam, consider who Mohammed told about his revelations—his family and his clan. They were, therefore, if you will, the chosen, as opposed to the wicked idolators who made up the Meccan élite. (Also more involved).

- Compare the slow expansion of Christianity to the rapid movement of Islam. Why did Christianity expand so slowly between 50 and 400? Could it be the use and threat of persecution. Diocletian's persecution of c.305 was the last major one, but it was not until Constantine (306, really 324–337) that the emperor became, in theory, your "brother in Christ," and not until Theodosius I the Great (378–395, February 380) that Christianity became the ONLY religion of the Roman Empire.

The expansion of Islam, especially 632–732, is more involved, as that often involved and required forced conversion. However, the "People of the Book" (Christians and Jews) were usually forbidden to convert but were taxed for "religious freedom."

Change-Over-Time Essay

Overall Approach

1. Thoroughly explain how your evidence supports your argument.

2. Include a time frame to the best of your ability.

3. Do not simply list facts, *unless in an outline for your use only*. Facts are, in and of themselves, inert. It is what you *do* with the facts that matters.

4. Make sure you follow through on all of the separate questions.

5. Include only material you are *certain* about—leave out what you are unsure of.

Key Points to Include

- In 1000 Western Europe was reeling under invasions from Vikings, Magyars, and Muslims.

- In 1648 Western civilization had discovered North and South America, begun to explore these continents, and also to populate them with colonists.

- Remember that Columbus and da Gama were looking for a shorter route to India, China, and Japan. Westerners strongly desired increased trade with these areas.

- By 1750 the West dominated India, by 1840 China, and by 1880 Sub-Saharan Africa.

- The Church was responsible for much of the Twelfth-Century Renaissance, Gothic Cathedrals, and so on.

- The Church called the Crusades, which sent Western knights to the Middle East, where they acquired knowledge.

- The Church, under the Imperial Papacy (Gregory VII, Innocent III, and Boniface VIII) led to the rise of secular power (by papal oppression).

- Sponsorship of voyages of exploration and discovery (which leads to mass conversions in some parts of the world and, thus, a solidification of Western Europe's and the church's political and ecclesiastical power).

- The Protestant Reformation unleashed great energy in Europe and the New World.

- New orders (that is, Franciscans and Dominicans) and the Catholic and Protestant efforts to spread the good news of the gospels.

Specific Essay

Overall Approach

1. Make a distinction between the *why* and *how* parts of the question.

2. Take a position but be sure to support it with evidence.

3. Analyze both the Great War and the Treaty of Versailles.

4. Include a time frame to the best of your ability.

5. Make sure you follow through on all of the separate questions.

Key Points to Include

- It was called the Great War because it was so much greater than anything that had been experienced before. Also, you need a World War II before you can have a World War I.

- Germany and the Central Powers (Austria-Hungary and the Ottoman Empire—later Bulgaria) started the war.

- They were opposed by the Triple Alliance of Great Britain, France, and Russia (later Italy and the United States).

- The United States tilted the balance in the Allies' favor.

- Germany came very close to defeating the original Triple Alliance.

- Most of the battles resulted in very high casualties on both sides; a "Lost Generation."

- The Treaty was too harsh and vindictive, imposed by the threat of force. It did produce the League of Nations, but the keystone, the United States, neither ratified the Treaty nor joined the League.

- It could have been improved, but only if France did not insist on crippling reparations *and* the United States had been active within the League.

- As it was the United States reverted to their isolationist past, and Europeans indulged in pipedreams (for example, the Locarno Treaty and the Kellogg-Briand pact).

- You should also consider not simply the military implications, but also politics, society and culture, ideology, music, art, propaganda, and so on.

Practice Test 3

Multiple-Choice Questions

Instructions: Each question below is followed by four possible answers. Choose the one that best answers the question.

1. Which of the following best describes the development of Roman government?

   A. As a result of pressure from civil wars and political instability, Roman government changed from a republic to an imperial military dictatorship in the first century BCE.

   B. The republican form of government remained stable until mounting pressure from barbarian invaders brought about the end of Roman rule in the west during the fourth century CE.

   C. Roman government was constitutionally changed from a monarchy to an empire during the late first century CE.

   D. The collapse of the western half of the Roman empire convinced leading citizens in the surviving eastern half to abandon imperial government and form a Byzantine republic.

2. The earliest civilizations generally emerged in

   A. protected plateaus ringed by mountains.
   B. fertile river valleys.
   C. islands with harbors suitable for inter-regional trade.
   D. wide grasslands.

3. Identify the statement that does NOT accurately describe the Hellenistic era.

   A. The cultures of Greece, Persia, and other eastern societies mixed.
   B. Latin became the dominant *lingua franca* of the Hellenistic world.
   C. Egyptian merchants learned to use monsoon winds to facilitate trade with India.
   D. The old city-states of Greece were overshadowed by large, dynastic kingdoms.

4. Which religion no longer dominates its homeland?

   A. Islam
   B. Judaism
   C. Buddhism
   D. Hinduism

5. In what way were the fates of the (western) Roman and the Han empires tied together?

   A. Constant warfare with Sassanid Persia was the most critical factor leading to the collapse of both Rome and Han China.

   B. Despite their great distance from each other, both empires were at least partly weakened by attacks from barbarian groups connected with the steppes of central Asia.

   C. The closing of the Silk Road by bandit tribes in central Asia during the fourth century CE led to the economic collapse of both empires.

   D. Both empires carried out extensive persecutions of Christians and Jews in the latter stages of their collapse.

6. Which of the following is true of Alexander's empire, the Roman empire, and the Mughal empire of India?

   A. The societies that founded these empires absorbed significant elements of conquered cultures into their own.

   B. Each of these empires maintained diplomatic relations with each other during times of peace.

   C. Polytheism was the dominant religion among the initial founders of each empire.

   D. The dominant religion of each empire was marked by missionary movements.

GO ON TO THE NEXT PAGE

7. Although definitions of civilization vary, the following were common to all ancient civilizations, EXCEPT

A. agriculture and food production.
B. complex social structure.
C. the wheel.
D. writing.

8. When discussing the development of metallurgy, scholars assign Ages or phases of development to certain periods in ancient societies. Which of the following metals is NOT identified with such an Age?

A. Bronze
B. Steel
C. Iron
D. Copper

9. The classical civilizations of Mesoamerica

A. cultivated rice as their staple crop.
B. practiced religions involving, among other things, human sacrifice and astronomic observations.
C. were significantly influenced by regular contacts via trans-Pacific global trade routes.
D. built pyramid-shaped temples reflecting the cultural influence of the ancient Egyptian empire.

10. The Neolithic Revolution involved

A. the violent rejection of tribal despotism and the formation of more egalitarian social structures.
B. the first discovery of stone-shaping techniques, allowing the production of early flint tools and weapons.
C. incorporation of village communities, the domestication of animals, and farming.
D. the development of writing systems.

11. The civilizations of Mesopotamia and Egypt shared all of the following EXCEPT

A. rulers seen as priest-kings and intermediaries to the gods.
B. reliance on rivers to support irrigation and farming.
C. political unity as a typical state of affairs across each cultural area.
D. the development of the world's earliest writing systems.

12. This religious system was patronized by Chinese rulers and emphasized conservative rituals, the worship of traditional deities, and proper behavior based on a social hierarchy.

A. Confucianism
B. Taoism
C. Buddhism
D. Shinto

13. This form of social inequality was not widely practiced in the ancient Mediterranean world.

A. Slavery
B. Repression of women
C. Serfdom
D. All three were common around the ancient Mediterranean.

14. Which of the following statements concerning the Mongol empires is NOT accurate?

A. Internal political concerns caused the Mongols to cease pushing westward into Europe.
B. Collectively, Mongol armies conquered more territory than any other pre-Modern people.
C. European superiority in weaponry and tactics halted the Mongols' westward advance during the 1200s CE.
D. After initial conquests, "Silk Road" trade routes across central Asia were protected by Mongol rulers until their disruption during the fourteenth century CE.

15. It is often said that western Medieval European society was built on a foundation of three survivals from the ancient world. Which of the following is not one of those three?

A. Christianity and the Church
B. Roman institutions
C. Germanic institutions
D. Greek democratic political forms

16. Feudalism, as practiced in western Europe, did NOT

A. involve exchanges of land for loyal service.
B. require vassals to provide specified amounts of military service to lords.
C. apply to relations between peasants and nobles.
D. partly reflect the Roman custom of patronage and the traditions of Germanic warbands.

17. Early in its history, Islam experienced a significant division in these two rival sects:

    A. Sunni and Shi'ite
    B. Sunni and Salafist
    C. Sufi and Shi'ite
    D. Wahhabi and Sunni

18. For the period 450–800 CE, what differences contrasted the western (Roman/"Catholic") and eastern (Greek/"Orthodox") branches of Christianity?

    A. The eastern church was torn by controversy over the acceptability of doctrines introduced by the rise of Islam, whereas the western church did not have cause to address this issue.
    B. The eastern church supported missionary activities to northern barbarian areas; the western church did not.
    C. During this period, only the western church led crusades to retake the Holy Land from Muslim conquerors.
    D. In the east, the church remained under the influence of the Byzantine emperors, whereas in the west, the church became a more politically independent force of its own which helped stabilize society after the collapse of the western Roman empire.

19. The plague pandemics of the fourteenth century in Europe caused all of the following, EXCEPT

    A. merchants, now aware of the risks to society posed by commerce-spread epidemics, gave up long-term interest in trade with Asia.
    B. the severe population reduction, especially in the numbers of available peasant laborers, led in some areas to increased social mobility and loosening of the restrictions of serfdom.
    C. political instability following the death of rulers.
    D. scapegoating and persecution of Jews, who were sometimes blamed for the plague.

20. The advent of gunpowder weaponry in the late Medieval period

    A. made possible the defeat of armored knights, which no previous weapons had been able to do.
    B. made traditional fortifications obsolete.
    C. decreased the amount of warfare in society.
    D. brought about the end of Viking raids in Europe.

21. In its earliest, traditional forms, government in the Islamic Caliphate was marked by

    A. clear division between officials holding political and religious authority, to prevent corruption of doctrines for political reasons.
    B. no division between political and religious authority.
    C. separation between political and religious authorities, with religious authorities controlling the military to ensure their dominance.
    D. separation between political and religious authorities, although political authorities maintained dominance through control of the military.

22. The period of China's Sung Dynasty (960–1279 CE) saw significant political, economic, and intellectual changes. These included all of the following, EXCEPT

    A. the imperial bureaucracy came to rely on highly skilled officials who had passed the civil service exam, rather than aristocrats.
    B. a Confucianist revival occurred among political elites.
    C. tribes north of the empire were integrated into China's economic system, making the era one of relative freedom from "barbarian" attacks.
    D. growth and commercialization of urban centers made China's cities the largest and busiest at that time in the world.

23. The success of Ghana and other Medieval kingdoms of west Africa was PRIMARILY due to

    A. the arrival of Islam, which provided a unifying cultural force among previously scattered tribes.
    B. technological innovations in weaponry which allowed Ghana to resist northern and southern conquerors.
    C. the refusal of west African rulers to integrate into the Islamic world, preventing the imposition of tribute.
    D. their strategic position relative to the trans-Saharan caravan trade in gold, ivory, and slaves.

GO ON TO THE NEXT PAGE

24. The arrival of this formerly nomadic Muslim people-group in the Middle East was part of the motivation for Europeans to launch the Crusades.

   A. Mongols
   B. Turks
   C. Viking mercenaries
   D. Bantu

25. The Vikings' impact DID NOT include

   A. temporary settlements in North America.
   B. significant role in the formation of Kievan Russia.
   C. frequent direct trade with Chinese markets.
   D. destabilizing raids on western Europe.

26. The following statements compare urbanization in different societies during the period 600–1000 CE. Identify the INCORRECT statement.

   A. The Maya built elaborate cities primarily for religious and ritual purposes; rural agriculture provided the base for regular Maya society.
   B. The center of society in Sung China shifted from the country to the cities, which became commercial centers.
   C. Still in recovery from the collapse of Rome, Europe (with the exception of Constantinople) was left without major cities which could compare with those of the Islamic or Chinese world.
   D. Although small trading depots were numerous, the political division in the Islamic world prevented the rise of truly flourishing cities there during this time period.

27. Which statement accurately compares the status of women in traditional Mongol society to that of women in Medieval Europe and (pre-Mongol) China?

   A. As part of a nomadic society, gender relations among the Mongols were typically more egalitarian.
   B. As members of a nomadic society, Mongol women generally did not receive as much freedom or respect as their contemporaries in Europe and China.
   C. While Medieval European women benefited from far more social freedom than Mongol women, Mongol women held more freedoms than Chinese women.
   D. Not enough information is available to historians to reconstruct an adequate picture of medieval European social life; thus, this comparison can not yet be made.

28. The intellectual and artistic flowering known as the Italian Renaissance, and the ensuing cultural revolution in Europe, was made possible, at least in part, by

   A. the preservation of much classical learning during the Medieval period by Arab scholars.
   B. Christopher Columbus' discovery of the Americas.
   C. the literary example set by playwright William Shakespeare.
   D. the inspiration of art objects imported from Persia.

29. The spread of the printing press using moveable type in fifteenth century Europe had all of the following effects on society there, EXCEPT

   A. printing made books more available to non-noble, poorer members of society, since earlier handwritten manuscripts had been very costly.
   B. secular domination of the printing industry made printed books an easy vehicle for the spread of ideas subversive to the point of view of the Catholic Church, which had dominated much of the production of hand-written books.
   C. the mass-production of printed matter made the spread of new ideas faster in Europe.
   D. the ease of reproducing images using the printing press, in contrast to the laborious methods required to produce paintings or sculpture, led to the discrediting of artists in non-print media as a profession in society.

30. The family that controlled Spain, much of Germany and the Netherlands, and vast areas in the New World, making it a global power in the sixteenth century CE, was the

A. Hohenzollerns.
B. Habsburgs.
C. Tudors.
D. Trastamaras.

31. The Protestant Reformation in Europe DID NOT

A. provide opportunities for rulers in England and Germany to gain new political independence from the Roman church.
B. cause the emergence of numerous new Protestant confessions or denominations.
C. lead to a doctrinal reconciliation with Eastern (Orthodox) churches.
D. benefit from the printing press, which allowed new writings and ideas to spread rapidly.

32. Absolutist rulers in Europe

A. relied on alliances with powerful noble families, and avoided employing skilled non-noble officials.
B. failed to achieve much prominence except in highly troubled areas, such as Constantinople and the Italian states.
C. represented the outdated but intact survival of feudal government into the period 1450–1700 CE.
D. argued that they ruled through divine will.

33. The European pursuit of new trade routes to Asia via the Atlantic or around Africa was caused by

A. the closing of overland Silk Road routes by Mongol invaders.
B. the Mughal monopoly over Chinese silk.
C. the closing of Egypt's Red Sea ports and other routes by the rising Ottoman Empire.
D. the destruction of Italy's Mediterranean trading fleets in a series of storms.

34. The following statements attempt to describe relationships between gender and politics in several societies during the era 1450–1750 CE. Identify the CORRECT statement.

A. In western Europe, women were successfully barred from monarchic rule due to the retention of late Medieval misogyny.
B. In the Ottoman Empire, royal women were sequestered in harems, yet played critical roles behind the scenes in politics and court intrigues nonetheless.
C. In South America, the Spanish conquest significantly improved the social-political opportunities of most native women.
D. Three female empresses played a significant role as rivals to the Shoguns of Tokugawa Japan.

35. Which of the following statements DOES NOT accurately describe institutions of slavery and servitude in different societies between 1450–1750 CE?

A. Despite being enslaved from their childhood, Janissaries were trained as soldiers and played an important part in the political history of the Ottoman Empire.
B. Operators of the trade in African slaves shipped to the Americas included Europeans, Arabs, and native Africans.
C. In Russia, peasants were emancipated from serfdom in the early 1700s, setting an example followed by other European governments thereafter.
D. The trade in African slaves to provide labor for European colonies in the Americas was a radical new hallmark of this period; earlier, slavery had mostly faded away as an institution in Europe.

36. Muslim and Hindu subjects and institutions mixed heavily in this empire:

A. Persian
B. Mughal
C. Gupta
D. Ottoman

GO ON TO THE NEXT PAGE

37. Scientists engaged in the Scientific Revolution stressed that

    A. scholars should rely on the conclusions of ancient scientists, not medieval theologians.

    B. science needed to rely on new, objective forms of reasoning and research.

    C. religion and faith lacked value in the face of new scientific discoveries.

    D. extant political systems were detrimental to scientific progress and thus needed to be replaced.

38. European commercial activity in Japan was severely limited after 1600 CE, because

    A. most European nations had decided that Japan lacked enough resources and markets to make heavy trade worthwhile.

    B. in the 1599 Treaty of Sinkiang, the Portuguese and Dutch agreed to focus their efforts on China instead of other east Asian countries in return for favorable tariff rates from the Chinese emperor.

    C. the Tokugawa rulers of Japan adopted an isolationist policy and strictly limited European access to Japan for centuries.

    D. as a result of political instability and civil war, piracy flourished on the western coast of Japan, driving away foreign traders, until the unification of Japan under the Meiji in the 1800s CE.

39. What do the concepts Columbian Exchange and Triangular Trade have most in common?

    A. Each concept focuses on the continuity of commercial ties between Canada, Latin America, and the United States in the early 20th Century.

    B. The two concepts refer to economic plans developed during the heyday of Britain's overseas empire to allow the lucrative production of opium and other drugs to spread from China to Latin America and the Indian subcontinent.

    C. Both concepts deal with the complicated mercantile arrangements made between early explorers, such as Christopher Columbus, and the Spanish and Portuguese governments about the division of profits from exploratory trading voyages.

    D. Both concepts point out that trans-Atlantic activity between Europe, Africa, and the colonial and post-colonial Americas involved interdependent connections on both sides of the ocean; the maritime nations along the Atlantic were tied together in an interdependent transfer of ideas, people, trade goods, and other items.

40. How did the Portuguese and Spanish overseas empires differ?

    A. Portugal formed a naval-based mercantile empire mostly consisting of trading posts; Spain seized large amounts of territory for active colonization.

    B. Portugal's empire became strongest to the west of the Treaty of Tordesillas demarcation line, Spain's to the east.

    C. Portuguese forces avoided violence in their rise to global power, whereas the Spanish empire was founded almost entirely on conquest.

    D. In the Americas, Portugal did not use slave labor, whereas the Spanish made heavy use of it.

41. Which of the following did NOT characterize the Incan empire?

   A. Rule by kings allegedly descended from the Sun god.
   B. Government by a centralized administrative bureaucracy.
   C. Avoidance of militaristic expansionism.
   D. Government distribution of physical resources from diverse ecological niches.

42. What was common to the medieval kingdom of Ethiopia and the sixteenth century CE kingdom of Kongo?

   A. Rulers of both kingdoms accepted and patronized Christianity.
   B. Rulers of both kingdoms accepted and patronized Islam.
   C. Rulers of both kingdoms refused to allow European traders to influence their society.
   D. Rulers of both kingdoms conquered territories outside of Africa.

43. This non-European power launched major long-distance commercial voyages in the Pacific and Indian Oceans during the fifteenth century CE, but later abandoned the idea of additional voyages for internal cultural/political reasons.

   A. Japan
   B. China
   C. The Maori kingdom of New Zealand
   D. Delhi Sultanate

44. Political revolutionaries of Europe and the Americas in the late eighteenth and early nineteenth centuries CE, with ideologies shaped by belief in natural law, the equality and rights of man, and the need for representative government, were influenced most by what type of political thought?

   A. Absolutist
   B. Enlightenment
   C. Renaissance Humanist
   D. Marxist

45. The reign of the French ruler Napoleon Bonaparte affected Europe, and the world, in many ways. Identify the INCORRECT Napoleonic influence.

   A. The system of laws codified by Bonaparte proved influential in the legal systems of many later nations.
   B. Bonaparte's need for money to pursue his war aims made possible the United States' territorial expansion westward into North America through the Louisiana Purchase.
   C. Napoleon fought a series of bloody wars with the other powers of Europe, affecting Europe, north Africa, and other regions.
   D. As a champion of the ideals of the French Revolution, Napoleon proved a sympathetic supporter of early Communist philosophers in territories conquered by his armies, opening the way for later Communist influence across Europe.

46. The full opening of Japan's and China's markets to trade with (and on the terms of) western powers in the nineteenth and very early twentieth century CE was due to

   A. military pressure from European nations and the United States.
   B. western promises to ship opium to China and Japan, providing a way for rulers of those nations to pacify their discontent citizens, in return for granting trade rights to the West.
   C. the desire of east Asian rulers—wary of Mughal India's last wave of expansion—to obtain the trade patronage of western powers in order to receive their military protection.
   D. Japanese and Chinese markets did not open to western trade until the end of the Second World War, in the twentieth century CE.

47. Which of the following inventions or discoveries had the greatest impact on global passenger transportation during the period 1800–1900?

   A. Aviation
   B. The steam engine
   C. Telegraph
   D. Exploitation of monsoon wind patterns in the Indian Ocean

GO ON TO THE NEXT PAGE

48. Global religious diffusion during the nineteenth century was affected most significantly by

- **A.** a surge in global missionary activity among Christians native to North America and western Europe.
- **B.** the conquest of many Mediterranean ports by the Muslim Ottoman Turks, leading to the spread of Islam along trade routes associated with those ports.
- **C.** western imperialism, since most European governments discouraged missionary activity in foreign colonies for fear that it might alienate native allies, who were important for the control of economic resources.
- **D.** widespread conversions to Hinduism in Africa and Latin America following proselytism by Indian workers shipped to those regions to provide cheap labor.

49. Which of the following did NOT practice imperialism during the nineteenth century CE?

- **A.** The United States
- **B.** Belgium
- **C.** Germany
- **D.** All of the above practiced imperialism.

50. Of the following, identify the nineteenth-century ideology that MOST DIRECTLY promoted imperialism.

- **A.** Marxism
- **B.** Women's Suffrage movement
- **C.** Social Darwinism
- **D.** Luddite movement

51. Which of the following is most closely associated with westernizing the nation in which it occurred?

- **A.** The Boxer Rebellion
- **B.** The Bolshevik Revolution in Russia
- **C.** The Meiji Restoration
- **D.** The formation of the League of Nations

52. From the following, identify what nineteenth-century Egypt under Mohammed Ali, and the Zulu people in the last half of the nineteenth century, had in common:

- **A.** Both successfully prevented European nations from imposing colonial rule on their territory.
- **B.** Both championed Islam as an alternative to European cultural influence.
- **C.** Both were heavily involved in the shipping of African slaves to the United States of America.
- **D.** Both sought to build empires in Africa through conquest.

53. Independence movements in nineteenth century Latin America were generally spearheaded by

- **A.** well-to-do aristocrats.
- **B.** peasant workers.
- **C.** Indian/Native groups.
- **D.** exiled European revolutionaries seeking to spread their ideals.

54. How did the object of European nations participating in global trade in the late nineteenth century differ from that of centuries before?

- **A.** The object of trade did not change significantly; however, European nations seized firm control of the overseas markets in which they had previously competed.
- **B.** Previously, Europeans overseas had mostly sought gold or luxury goods which could be sold at great profit back home in Europe. In the late nineteenth century, the focus of global trade changed; now, European nations sought resources and raw materials for industry.
- **C.** With the advent of the Industrial Revolution, import/export patterns changed; in the late nineteenth century, European nations began to mostly export finished products to non-European nations, while now importing few materials from outside Europe.
- **D.** In the late ninteenth century, European nations focused trade patterns in ways that would economically cripple rising rivals such as China and the emerging Latin American nations.

55. Nineteenth century CE nationalist movements in Europe generally appealed most to which segment of society?

 A. The upper classes
 B. The middle classes
 C. Peasants and the poor
 D. Nationalist appeal was not strongest among any social class

56. Karl Marx argued that

 A. human progress has been held back across all of history by capitalism, and socialist economics are the best way to correct the damage that has resulted.
 B. human society has advanced through a series of socio-economic "modes of production," such as feudalism and capitalism, towards an eventual communist mode of production.
 C. violent revolutions in support of communist ideas would be most effective in Europe's overseas colonial holdings.
 D. human society can only be stabilized through governmental protection of the private ownership of wealth.

57. Which of the following was NOT a key factor in the onset of the First World War?

 A. The activation of a series of defense alliances between various European powers.
 B. Ideological differences between major European powers.
 C. Pent-up nationalist rivalry between competing colonial powers.
 D. Underestimation of the likely extent and duration of a European war.

58. The First World War, or events that occurred during or a few years after that war, brought an end to all of these political structures EXCEPT

 A. Ottoman empire.
 B. Austro-Hungarian empire.
 C. British empire.
 D. Tsarist Russia.

59. Nuclear weapons have been deployed against wartime enemies

 A. once, by the United States.
 B. twice, by the United States.
 C. twice, once by the United States and once by the U.S.S.R.
 D. twice, once by the United States and once by Germany.

60. Economic conditions and production slumps brought on by the Great Depression during the 1930s DID NOT

 A. contribute to political extremism in Germany.
 B. influence nations outside the U.S.A./Western Europe industrial zone.
 C. fully "bounce back" until the Second World War.
 D. lead to significant inflation and unemployment in many countries.

61. The following statements list consequences of the Second World War. Identify the INCORRECT statement.

 A. Europe lost its dominant position in geopolitics.
 B. As European colonial powers retreated from empire, most national borders in the Middle East were redrawn to reflect more stable hereditary tribal boundaries, reducing tension in the region.
 C. The United States and the Soviet Union emerged as rivals for global supremacy.
 D. The Holocaust in Europe was put to an end.

62. Generally, which of the following was NOT characteristic of both fascist and communist regimes of the twentieth century, but rather only characteristic of one of these types?

 A. Tight governmental control over national economies.
 B. The avowed goal of worldwide revolution.
 C. Totalitarian approaches to government.
 D. Militarism and mass murder.

GO ON TO THE NEXT PAGE

63. In twentieth-century geopolitics, the term Domino Effect referred to

    A. the string of pro-democracy movements which swept Eastern Europe at the close of the Soviet era.

    B. the rapid pace of globalization/internationalization of world culture during the late twentieth century.

    C. concerns that Communism could rapidly spread throughout the world, prompting the United States' "containment" strategy.

    D. the diffusion of wealth from wealthy industrialized nations to poor developing nations.

64. The division of the Indian subcontinent into three nations—India, Pakistan, and later, Bangladesh—in the second half of the twentieth century was due, in part, to which process?

    A. The nuclear arms race

    B. Decolonization

    C. Globalization

    D. The spread of Communism

65. Over the course of the twentieth century, which of the following international organizations proved LEAST influential in world affairs?

    A. The League of Nations

    B. The United Nations

    C. The Organization of Petroleum-Exporting Countries (OPEC)

    D. North Atlantic Treaty Organization (NATO)

66. In the second half of the twentieth century, there were numerous military conflicts between powerful nations, such as the United States, the Soviet Union, and Great Britain, and comparatively weak opponents in the developing world. What military strategy, when adopted by these weak opponents, historically proved most troublesome for powerful nations to combat?

    A. Conventional warfare focusing on tanks and air combat

    B. The use of nuclear weapons

    C. Guerrilla warfare

    D. Hiring better-equipped foreign mercenaries

67. A wave of nationalist independence movements in the 1990s led to the establishment of numerous new nation-states in Europe and Asia. Most of these movements were made possible by

    A. United Nations military intervention on behalf of international consensus.

    B. regional economic growth fostered by multinational corporations.

    C. the collapse of the communist Soviet Union.

    D. the world's major powers were preoccupied by the increasing rivalry between the United States and the U.S.S.R., which allowed many small nations to take an unprecedented free hand in driving regional political developments.

68. Which factor contributed most to significant political instability in the Middle East during the second half of the twentieth century?

    A. The lack of economic growth in the region, due to a lack of natural resources.

    B. The Arab-Israeli conflict.

    C. Soviet attempts to pressure Turkey to leave the NATO alliance during the Cold War.

    D. Opposition to the controversial spread of Christianity in several rural areas throughout the region.

69. In the last decades of the twentieth century, many identified a new socio-economic division of the world into two separate blocs. Looking at the world as a global economic system, identify the most significant socio-economic global division at the close of the century.

    A. A wealthy, industrialized North and a poor, developing South

    B. Islamic nations and non-Islamic nations

    C. Democratic nations and Communist nations

    D. The United States and the United Nations

70. Which of the following is NOT CORRECT for Latin America since 1930?

    A. Most nations in the region quickly developed the economic strength to remain independent of foreign economic influence.

    B. Politically, the region has experienced numerous revolutions and periods of unrest.

    C. Most nations in the region remained neutral during the Second World War.

    D. The environmental consequences of growth, production, and industry in the region have became a major concern to "green" and environmental groups.

Free-Response Questions

A Document-Based Question (DBQ)

Based on the following documents, discuss the cultural influence between the Romans, and their subjects and neighbors, in areas conquered by or near to the Roman Republic/Empire. Are the patterns revealed in these documents best described in terms of one-sided cultural imposition, or multi-directional cultural exchange? What additional type(s) of documentation might help one better assess these issues?

Document 1

Source: Plutarch, *Life of Marcus Cato.* From a biography of a Roman statesman during the Roman Republic [prior to the rise of emperors to power]. Cato lived in the third and second centuries BCE, the time when Rome expanded to control much of the Mediterranean world, including Greece.

Translated by J. Dryden, revised by A. H. Clough.

He was now grown old, when Carneades the Academic, and Diogenes the Stoic, came as deputies from Athens to Rome, praying for release from a penalty of five hundred talents laid on the Athenians, in a suit, to which they did not appear, in which the Oropians were plaintiffs, and Sicyonians judges. All the most studious youth immediately waited on these philosophers, and frequently, with admiration, heard them speak. But the gracefulness of Carneades's oratory, whose ability was really greatest, and his reputation equal to it, gathered large and favorable audiences, and ere long filled, like a wind, all the city with the sound of it. So that it soon began to be told, that a Greek, famous even to admiration, winning and carrying all before him, had impressed so strange a love upon the young men, that quitting all their pleasures and pastimes, they ran mad, as it were, after philosophy; which indeed much pleased the Romans in general; nor could they but with much pleasure see the youth receive so welcomely the Greek literature, and frequent the company of learned men. But Cato, on the other side, seeing this passion for words flowing into the city, from the beginning, took it ill, fearing lest the youth should be diverted that way, and so should prefer the glory of speaking well before that of arms, and doing well. And when the fame of the philosophers increased in the city, and Caius Acilius, a person of distinction, at his own request, became their interpreter to the senate at their first audience, Cato resolved, under some specious presence, to have all philosophers cleared out of the city; and, coming into the senate, blamed the magistrates for letting these deputies stay so long a time without being dispatched, though they were persons that could easily persuade the people to what they pleased; that therefore in all haste something should be determined

about their petition, that so they might go home again to their own schools, and declaim to the Greek children, and leave the Roman youth, to be obedient, as hitherto, to their own laws and governors.

Yet he did this not out of any anger, as some think, to Carneades; but because he wholly despised philosophy, and out of a kind of pride, scoffed at the Greek studies and literature; as, for example, he would say, that Socrates was a prating seditious fellow, who did his best to tyrannize over his country, to undermine the ancient customs, and to entice and withdraw the citizens to opinions contrary to the laws. Ridiculing the school of Isocrates, he would add, that his scholars grew old men before they had done learning with him, as if they were to use their art and plead causes in the court of Minos in the next world. And to frighten his son from anything that was Greek, in a more vehement tone than became one of his age, he pronounced, as it were, with the voice of an oracle, that the Romans would certainly be destroyed when they began once to be infected with Greek literature; though time indeed has shown the vanity of this his prophecy; as, in truth, the city of Rome has risen to its highest fortune, while entertaining Grecian learning.

Document 2

Source: Procopius, *Buildings.* From a description of part of the frontier between Persia and the eastern Roman empire during the sixth century CE, by which time the Roman empire had fallen in the west, but held on in the eastern Mediterranean (sometimes referred to as the Byzantine empire).

Translated by H. B. Dewing.

As one goes from Citharizôn to Theodosiopolis and the other Armenia, the land is called Chorzane; it extends for a distance of about three days' journey, not being marked off from the Persian territory by the water of any lake or by any river's stream or by a wall of mountains which pinch the road into a narrow pass, but the two frontiers are indistinct. So the inhabitants of this region, whether subjects of the Romans or of the Persians, have no fear of each other, nor do they give one another any occasion to apprehend an attack, but they even intermarry

GO ON TO THE NEXT PAGE

and hold a common market for their produce and together share the labours of farming. And if the commanders on either side ever make an expedition against the others, when they are ordered to do so by their sovereign, they always find their neighbours unprotected. Their very populous towns are close to each other, yet from ancient times no stronghold existed on either side.

Document 3

Source: Tacitus, *Agricola.* From a biography of a Roman general and governor of Britain during the late first century CE, describing his activities to pacify that troubled province. Britain had only been conquered by Rome for several decades by the time of the events recorded here, and many Britons had not yet come to terms with Roman rule by the time of Agricola's administration.

Translated by A. J. Church and W. J. Brodribb.

The following winter passed without disturbance, and was employed in salutary measures. For, to accustom to rest and repose through the charms of luxury a population scattered and barbarous and therefore inclined to war, Agricola gave private encouragement and public aid to the building of temples, courts of justice and dwelling-houses, praising the energetic, and reproving the indolent. Thus an honourable rivalry took the place of compulsion. He likewise provided a liberal education for the sons of the chiefs, and showed such a preference for the natural powers of the Britons over the industry of the Gauls that they who lately disdained the tongue of Rome now coveted its eloquence. Hence, too, a liking sprang up for our style of dress, and the "toga" became fashionable. Step by step they were led to things which dispose to vice, the lounge, the bath, the elegant banquet. All this in their ignorance they called civilisation, when it was but a part of their servitude.

Document 4

Source: Suetonius, *Life of Claudius.* From a biography of a Roman emperor written during the second century CE (the events described took place during the mid-first century CE).

Translated by J.C. Rolfe.

He allowed the envoys of the Germans to sit in the orchestra, led by their naïve self-confidence; for when they had been taken to the seats occupied by the common people and saw the Parthian and Armenian envoys sitting with the senate, they moved of their own accord to the same part of the theatre, protesting that their merits and rank were no whit inferior. He utterly abolished the cruel and inhuman religion of the Druids* among the Gauls, which under Augustus had merely been prohibited to Roman citizens; on the other hand he even attempted to transfer the Eleusinian rites from Attica** to Rome, and had the temple of Venus Erycina in Sicily, which had fallen to ruin through age, restored at the expense of the treasury of the Roman people.

*Druidic religion, practiced by Celts conquered by Rome, involved human sacrifice, and was thus banned by the emperor.

**In Greece.

Document 5

Source: Minucius Felix, *Octavius.* From an approximately second century CE debate on the relative merits of Christianity and paganism (the overall work was written in favor of Christianity, although the speaker quoted in this passage is advocating Rome's traditional paganism).

Translated by A. Roberts & J. Donaldson.

Thence, therefore, we see through all empires, and provinces, and cities, that each people has its national rites of worship, and adores its local gods: as the Eleusinians worship Ceres; the Phrygians, Mater; the Epidaurians, Aesculapius; the Chaldaeans, Belus; the Syrians, Astarte; the Taurians, Diana; the Gauls, Mercurius; the Romans, all divinities. Thus their power and authority has occupied the circuit of the whole world: thus it has propagated its empire beyond the paths of the sun, and the bounds of the ocean itself; in that in their arms they practise a religious valour; in that they fortify their city with the religions of sacred rites, with chaste virgins, with many honours, and the names of priests; . . . while in the city of an enemy, when taken while still in the fury of victory, they venerate the conquered deities; while in all directions they seek for the gods of the strangers, and make them their own; while they build altars even to unknown divinities, and to the Manes [Spirits]. Thus, in that they acknowledge the sacred institutions of all nations, they have also deserved their dominion. Hence the perpetual course of their veneration has continued, which is not weakened by the long lapse of time, but increased, because antiquity has been accustomed to attribute to ceremonies and temples so much of sanctity as it has ascribed of age.

Change-Over-Time Essay Question

Discuss the development of methods, forms, and objectives of warfare between nation-states, 1800–1950 CE. Identify the reasons for major breaks or changes in the nature of organized warfare and comment on the impact of those changes on war-fighting societies. Your essay might focus on the Western/European way of war for the period 1800–1900, but should consider global patterns of modern warfare for the period thereafter. [Because this question focuses on organized warfare between nation-states, analysis of the many European "small wars" of colonial imperialism is not necessary].

Comparative Essay Question

Compare and contrast the medieval Islamic to the medieval Western European/Christian approaches to the ideal relationship between government and religion—that is, the relationship between secular and spiritual authority.

GO ON TO THE NEXT PAGE

Answers and Explanations for Practice Test 3

1. **A.** The division between Republic and Empire, occurring in the first century BCE, is one of the key divisions in Roman history along with the change from a monarch to a republic centuries earlier. Following a series of civil wars, Octavian (later named Augustus) seized power and became the first emperor. Answer D is wrong because, although Rome did collapse in the west, imperial government was retained in the eastern (Byzantine) remnant of Roman territory; republican government was not instituted there.

2. **B.** Fertile river valleys were home to the world's earliest civilizations—Mesopotamia, Egypt, Harappan/Indus valley civilization. These areas allowed widespread agriculture and facilitated communications, essential for societies to begin supporting large cities and central governments.

3. **B.** Greek, not Latin, was the *lingua franca*, the commonly understood language of trade and diplomacy, of the ancient Hellenistic world. Even after the Romans conquered the eastern Mediterranean, Greek maintained its position of dominance over Latin in the area except in certain military and governmental roles.

4. **C.** Although Buddism's origins were in India, that religion eventually lost most of its adherents there; instead, it flourished in China, Japan, and southeast Asia. Hinduism won back most of the ground lost to Buddism in India. The other religions mentioned—Islam, Judaism, and Hinduism—all remain dominant religions in their homelands (Saudi Arabia, Israel, and India).

5. **B.** Both the Roman and Han empires were struck by barbarian invaders associated with the steppes of central Asia—the Huns against Rome and the Hsiung-Nu against China. Some scholars have argued that both groups might have been related or moving in response to the same large series of migrations; presently, such definite connections between the two are unclear, but the fact remains that central Asian steppe invaders did loom large in the later history of both Rome and Han China. Although barbarian invasions should not be seen as the sole cause of the collapse of these empires, they certainly played a role. Warfare with Persia was problematic for the Romans but did not, alone, destabilize their empire. D is not applicable—Christianity was not a major concern in Han society, and by the time of the late Roman empire, the faith had been accepted as the state religion.

6. **A.** These three empires did not coexist at the same time, making choice B impossible. Alexander's and Rome's empires were both dominated by polytheist religions (until the Christianization of the Roman world), and the Mughal empire was formed by Muslim conquerors (although some non-Islamic Indian concepts eventually influenced Mughal rulers). A, however, is correct; as with many empires of conquest, each of these three empires saw conquered cultures being aborbed into the ruling society (deliberately, in Alexander's case—via Hellenism—and somewhat deliberately, but just as effectively, in the melting-pot of the Roman empire). The syncretism seen in the later Mughal state might have been distasteful to its founders but it occurred nonetheless. This assimilation of conquered cultures is typical of frontier areas or conqueror-conquered relations.

7. **C.** The wheel is not necessary for a society to develop civilization. The Mayas, Incas, and Aztecs of central and South America developed flourishing civilizations even though the wheel was not introduced to the Americas before the arrival of the Europeans.

8. **B.** Steel is iron that has undergone special metallurgical treatment, but the use of steel does not sufficiently differentiate societies from those that have developed ironworking to merit a separate age of its own. Bronze is copper mixed with tin; the use of bronze marks a significant step forward in the development of prehistoric and/or ancient societies. Copper, Bronze, and Iron are all ages assigned to some ancient cultures.

9. **B.** Only B is correct. Maize, not rice, was the staple crop of ancient Mesoamerica; and the region's civilizations appear to have developed fairly independently (from societies outside the Americas, although they certainly were in contact with each other). Although pyramid-shaped temples were common to many Mesoamerican sites, there is not believed to have been any regular contact with societies in the Old World.

10. **C.** The Neolithic Revolution and the Agricultural Revolution are roughly equivalent. Although benefiting from important social developments, Neolithic villages were not free from inequality. The beginning of stone-shaping techniques and tool-making, referred to in Choice B, belongs in earlier phases of the Stone Age—the Neolithic is the final phase after the Paleolithic and Mesolithic.

Writing, too, does not coincide with the Neolithic Revolution but later, with the rise of civilizations.

11. **C.** All choices except C were common to both Mesopotamia and Egypt. Egypt was typically ruled as a cohesive political and cultural unit—one kingdom and one society under one ruler, except for scattered periods of unrest. Mesopotamia, however, often saw several rival powers ruling different areas of the region; Mesopotamia was not a cohesive political/cultural unit in the same way that the kingdom of Egypt was.

12. **A.** Although Confucianism, Taoism, and Buddhism were all patronized by Chinese rulers—in fact, the three together are considered the three key religions of China—only Confucianism fits the description of emphasizing conservative rituals, the worship of traditional deities, and proper behavior dependent on one's place in the social hierarchy.

13. **C.** Both slavery and the repression of women were common in the ancient world. Serfdom, however, belongs to the medieval and early modern period, although its roots may be traced to the socio-economic conditions under the late Roman empire. It is not considered a common practice in the ancient Mediterranean world.

14. **C.** The Mongols were able to inflict crushing defeat on European armies who had little experience in dealing with standard Mongol tactics, which involved waves of light horse-archers firing at opponents while using their mobility to always stay just out of reach of a counter-attack. In fact, Mongol armies halted their westward advance due to internal political concerns - but for a time, it appeared that eastern Europe might be overrun by these invaders. With reference to answer choice **D**, the Mongol empires, once conquered, were famed for their trade routes and road systems; Mongol governments strictly enforced the law and protected travellers crossing central Asia, a great boon to trade between Europe and east Asia.

15. **D.** German society, Roman institutions, and Christianity are the three ancient pillars upon which western medieval Europe stood. Greek democratic ideas did not play a significant role in most medieval thought; democracy as a concept was disliked by most upper-class Romans and was not a key part of the Roman heritage passed on to the west. It was not until the Enlightenment that Greek democratic ideals would again become truly influential.

16. **C.** In medieval Europe, feudalism did not apply to relations between nobles and peasant serfs; feudal relationships involved warriors—one stronger, one weaker—agreeing to trade land, protection, and other support in exchange for military service. Since serfs were not in a position to provide or bargain for quality military support (heavily armed and armored knights) they did not get involved in feudal relationships—they simply worked for whichever feudal vassal had been given the land on which they lived.

17. **A.** Sunni and Shi'ite Muslims represent the two most significant branches of Islam. The difference between them is centered on the question of succession to the Caliphate—who should be the heir of Mohammed? Shi'ite Muslims favored selecting only heirs of Ali, Mohammed's son-in-law, whereas the majority Sunnite branch chose to accept other candidates for the Caliphate. None of the other Islamic sects and movements mentioned as answer choices are as early or significant (nor are they paired correctly as rivals).

18. **D.** Although the rise of Islam eventually resulted in major losses in territory for the Byzantine empire, reducing the influence of the Orthodox church, Islamic doctrines were not merged with Orthodox thought. The true major controversy in Orthodox doctrine in the early medieval period involved the use and veneration of icons—sculptures, paintings, and other physical images of Christ and saints. Bitter disputes occurred in the Byzantine world over whether or not the use of icons in religious practice was appropriate. Both the western and eastern churches supported missionaries to northern regions. The call for the Crusades did not occur until the late 1000s CE. Only **D** is correct.

19. **A.** Despite the dangers involved, Europeans did not abandon their interests in trade after the Black Death. Indeed, the century and a half following the plague pandemic saw the birth of European overseas exploration.

20. **B.** Although gunpowder did eventually make armor obsolete, it was not the first tool or weapon to threaten the supremacy of mounted knights. Several times in the Hundred Years' War, English archers destroyed armies of knights using powerful bows. Gunpowder artillery did soon make traditional castles and fortifications obsolete, however; earlier designs could be quickly demolished using cannons. Society remained

violent and filled with war after the arrival of this powerful weapon. The Viking raids occurred centuries before the advent of gunpowder in Europe.

21. **B.** Traditional Islam does not recognize a true division between church and state. Authority in both spheres was held by the Caliph, who was theoretically responsible to guide the world of Islam both in spiritual pursuits and in military and governmental affairs.

22. **C.** Although a time of dramatic changes in society and economics, the Sung Dynasty did not eliminate the threat from northern tribes. In fact, northern tribes eventually overran much of Sung China. Before this occurred, the processes discussed in answer Choices **A, B,** and **D** all occurred.

23. **D.** Ghana's success was primarily due to the trans-Saharan trade routes. As these routes began to flourish under Arab and Berber traders, several west African states emerged, centered around depots for the desert crossings. Islam did not have uniform success in the region; initially, some states accepted Islam and others rejected it.

24. **B.** The Turks were initially a nomadic people who moved into the Middle East out of central Asia. Two Turkish groups—first the Seljuk and then the Ottomans—overcame Byzantine resistance and stripped much (and finally all, under the Ottomans) of their territory away. The Seljuk onslaught motivated the Byzantine emperor to ask the Pope for military aid from Western Europe—leading to the first of many Crusades. Thus, it was not only Arabs but Turks that fought the Crusaders. The Mongols did invade the Middle East but were not (initially) Muslims; the Bantu were in Africa; Viking mercenaries fought on behalf of the Byzantines, but were not a significant factor in the Crusades (and were not allied with the Muslims).

25. **C.** Although they were famous and widespread traders (as well as raiders), even the Vikings did not normally carry goods along the entire length of the trade routes with China. Goods shipped to and from the east were generally carried by a series of middlemen. Nevertheless, the Vikings had access to trade goods from the far east; they did not personally trade in east Asian markets, however. All of the other choices describe accomplishments of the Vikings.

26. **D.** During the early medieval period, Islamic cities such as Baghdad flourished, even with the breakup of the single Islamic Caliphate into rival political entities. Urbanized society became

especially influential in shaping Islamic civilization despite the nomadic roots of many of its original champions.

27. **A.** Generally, nomadic societies offer somewhat higher levels of social status to women than do sedentary societies. Thus, Mongol women generally enjoyed greater status and freedoms than in either contemporary European or Chinese society.

28. **A.** Much ancient learning was retained by medieval Arab scholars, then slowly returned to Europe through a series of translations. As a result, Humanist scholars of the Renaissance had access to much of the classical learning that had perished in western Europe during the medieval era.

29. **D.** Choices **A–C** describe actual elements of social change after the development of printing in Europe in the mid-fifteenth century. However, the visual arts continued to be heavily patronized in Europe after this time, playing a largely different role than printing, which benefited the spread of information.

30. **B.** The Habsburgs were key actors in most of Catholic-controlled Europe during the sixteenth and seventeenth centuries CE, as the territory gathered by conquest and marriage into the hands of the family was quite extensive. Habsburgs such as Charles V, both Holy Roman Emperor of Germany and King of Spain (and thus of the Spanish Americas), were among the most politically powerful persons on earth during their time.

31. **C.** The Protestant Reformation represented a break from Roman Catholic tradition. Although the Eastern, Orthodox church was also opposed to the Roman Catholic Church, Orthodox opposition was for different reasons than those which motivated the Reformation. There was no large merger or doctrinal reconciliation between Protestant and Orthodox churches during the era of the Reformation.

32. **D.** Divine will was often cited as the reason absolutist kings ruled and required obedience. Options **A** and **C** both suggest a connection between absolutism and medieval political structures, namely a powerful nobility and feudal institutions. This is misleading, however. Absolutist rule, adopted in a number of powerful European nations, represented a break from the traditions of medieval government, which had often limited monarchical power. Absolutist rulers sought to curb the power of traditional noble families and recruited bureaucratic officials from emerging, lesser classes such as the gentry to help run the government.

33. C. The Ottoman Turks, growing toward dominance of the eastern Mediterranean and controlling Egypt and the Red Sea ports, shut off Europe from easy access to eastern trade. This prompted Portuguese and Spanish voyages seeking new routes to Asia— leading to Columbus' discovery of the Americas. Option **A**, blaming the Mongols, may seem appealing; however, Mongol rule was actually very conducive to overland trade in central Asia, because they maintained an excellent and safe system of roads through their territories.

34. B. Only **B** is correct. Female English queens such as Mary and Elizabeth I disprove option A. In the Spanish Americas, native men and women alike generally did not fare well at the hands of their new conquerors; enslavement and forced labor were typical. The Spanish conquest was not related to a significant improvement in the lives of women. The Emperors of Japan—let alone their Empresses—were completely overshadowed by the Shoguns (military dictators) during the Tokugawa era; they were not serious rivals for power, but figureheads. Not until the time of the Meiji Restoration did the Emperor again become a dominant factor in Japanese government.

35. C. Rather than leading the way, Russia dragged its feet and did not emancipate its serfs until the mid-1800s CE.

36. B. The Mughal empire controlled much of India, with masses of Hindu subjects, but its initial conquerors had been Muslims from the north. Over the course of Mughal history, Islamic and Hindu (along with other Indian) traditions blended into a unique society. The Gupta empire, another option for this question, was also influenced heavily by Hinduism but predates the Islamic invasions of India.

37. B. Scholars pushing forward the Scientific Revolution generally called for new, objective means of inquiry into scientific questions. These scientists, despite the Renaissance craze for ancient scholarship, did not uncritically prefer classical scholarship to new ideas, but often corrected the work of ancient thinkers. Neither was disproving or attacking religious belief the goal of this new science; a number of scientists were themselves churchmen, who sought to correct erroneous theological intepretations which misinterpreted both nature and the Christian scriptures. Finally, the Scientific Revolution did not inherently involve political protest; it was the thinkers of the Enlightenment who would later

begin to fully question extant political systems, with revolutionary results.

38. C. After 1600 CE, the Tokugawa Shoguns controlled Japan. Although Europeans (especially Dutch and Portuguese traders, as well as Jesuit missionaries) had already begun to interact with Japanese society, the Tokugawa rulers sealed most of Japan from outside influence, banning Christianity and forbidding foreign trade apart from a few government-controlled venues. This policy of isolation remained in effect for centuries until western military superiority was able to force Japan's markets open.

39. D. The concept of the Columbian Exchange describes the multi-directional transfer of people, goods, ideas, diseases, and so on, by which Europe and Africa not only affected the New World during the colonial era, but were also affected by the Americas. The Triangular Trade refers to the three-sided system of which the shipping of slaves to the Americas was only one side; slaves went to the Americas, resources went from there to Europe, and European manufactured goods were finally shipped to Africa in exchange for further slaves, renewing the process. Thus, both concepts treat Atlantic nations as economically and culturally interdependent.

40. A. Both Portugal and Spain employed violence and slavery to further their overseas empires. However, Portugal (which received territory to the *east* of the Treaty of Tordesillas line, not west) did concentrate more on the establishment of scattered trading ports, whereas Spain primarily seized vast tracts of territory for active colonization.

41. C. Like most empire-builders, the Incas were military expansionists, who used force to build their empire. They also maintained a central government bureaucracy which worked to coordinate resource distribution across the empire.

42. A. Both Ethiopia and sixteenth-century Kongo had Christian rulers. Kongo actively traded with the Portuguese.

43. B. China sent out large commercial fleets on expeditions in the fifteenth century, but later voyages by these fleets were cancelled. It is possible that, had China not abandoned these voyages and greater involvement overseas, it might have played a greater role as a rival of European merchants across the Pacific and Indian Oceans in the coming centuries.

44. **B.** The beliefs described belong to Enlightenment thinkers, whose ideas were radically opposed to advocates of an Absolutist government—where a king's decree was binding by divine decree. Marxist philosophies developed in the nineteenth and twentieth centuries; Renaissance Humanism, although a fore-runner of the Enlightenment, occurred much earlier and emphasized different ideas.

45. **D.** A–C all describe actual Napoleonic influences; the Napoleonic wars were fought in Europe, in Egypt, and on the high seas. **D** is the correct choice; Marxism post-dates Napoleon and hardly agrees with his elevation as Emperor of France.

46. **A.** Commercial access to Japanese and Chinese markets was indeed brought about via military force—so called *gunboat diplomacy* such as the Opium Wars and the Perry expedition to Japan. The opium trade was opposed by the Chinese Imperial government but was forcibly continued by Western pressure.

47. **B.** The steam engine, which made travel by railroad and steamship possible, revolutionized passenger (and cargo) transport, significantly shortening travel times. Travel by airplane did not develop until the twentieth century. The telegraph revolutionized communication, but did not transport passengers; monsoon winds had been exploited for centuries before the nineteenth century.

48. **A.** A missionary movement among western Christians resulted in numerous Christian missions across the world, and a major number of worldwide conversions to Christianity during the nineteenth century. Such missions were often favored by colonial powers, because they also often spread acceptance of western culture and laws. The aims of governments and missionaries, however, were not always the same.

49. **D.** Germany and Belgium both seized colonies in Africa, and the United States seized territory in the Pacific and Latin America during the nineteenth century.

50. **C.** Social Darwinism is an idea, linked by some to Charles Darwin's theory of biological natural selection, which states that over time, an elite of those most fit for survival will, and should, dominate those who lack the attributes necessary for survival. On a social/political level, this philosophy was believed to allow rich and powerful individuals or nations to conquer, exploit, or abuse less wealthy or powerful individuals and nations; this idea is often seen as a racist viewpoint which

encouraged some Westerners to advocate foreign imperialism during the nineteenth century. Generally, Marxism claims to be opposed to imperialism (in theory); the Luddite movement was an anti-technological movement.

51. **C.** The Meiji Restoration ended centuries of Japanese isolation, restored the power of the Emperor (instead of the Shogun/dictator), and led to conscious attempts to rapidly Westernize Japanese society. The Boxer Rebellion, which failed, was meant as a challenge to Western influence in China. The Bolshevik Revolution turned Russia away from other Western powers, eventually hiding Russia behind the communist Iron Curtain. The League of Nations was itself largely a Western-dominated (and short-lived) idea meant primarily not to produce Westernizing cultural change, but to promote peace and security among member nations.

52. **D.** Both Mohammed Ali's Egypt and the Zulu people used military force to carve out African empires during the nineteenth century. Although the Zulus are known as opponents of British imperialism in Africa, one should not forget that peoples inhabiting European-colonized areas were often just as active in seeking increased territory or political advantage as the more technologically advanced European imperialists. The Zulus were not a Muslim people, invalidating Choice **B**. The slave trade to the United States had ceased by the era of the Zulu Wars, in the second half of the nineteenth century.

53. **A.** Although later, twentieth century movements often championed lower-class or indigenous causes, most nineteenth century Latin American independence movements were led by upper-class persons wishing to retain control over society but achieve independence from Spanish colonial control.

54. **B.** To feed European industry, late nineteenth century trade shifted to focus on the importation of large amounts of natural resources and materials to be processed in European factories.

55. **B.** The middle class spearheaded nineteenth century nationalist revolutionary movements in Europe. Members of upper classes saw little reason to change the status quo through revolution, since they were in power; society's poorest were generally out of touch of the ideological concerns of the more privileged middle class.

56. **B.** Marx argued that history is driven by socio-economic factors which have created different

stages of modes of production. Since Capitalism is only one of these modes of production, A can not be correct. Marx's Communist philosophy argues against private ownership of wealth, which discounts choice D.

57. **B.** The causes of the First World War were not marked by significant ideological differences, but rather by geopolitical concerns over the balance of power in Europe, and extreme nationalist competition between countries. A common misperception at the beginning of the war was that it would "all be over by Christmas"—the horrific four-year war which ensued was largely unexpected.

58. **C.** The Ottoman and Austro-Hungarian empires were dissolved at the end of World War One (WWI) or shortly thereafter; Tsarist Russia fell to internal revolution as the Great War (WWI) drew to a close. The British Empire, however, did not finally unravel until after the end of the Second World War.

59. **B.** The only two uses of nuclear weapons against wartime enemies to date have been the bombings of Hiroshima and Nagasaki by the United States in the final days of the Second World War.

60. **C.** Until the war effort associated with the Second World War gave a boost to industry, the Great Depression sapped the economic strength of most regions of the world. The desperate economic conditions produced by the Depression helped fuel support for radical groups such as Hitler's Nazi party in Germany, which many believed would restore the nation's strength.

61. **B.** Exhausted by the long struggle of the Second World War, the European powers generally lost most of their remaining colonial possessions in the decades after the war, whereas a strong United States and Soviet Union became the new dominant powers in geopolitics. In the Middle East, national borders (many of which were drawn at the end of the First World War, not the Second) often represented arbitrary European impositions rather than traditional regional borders. Additionally, the establishment of an independent Israeli state during the late 1940s led to further tension in the region.

62. **A.** Both fascist and communist regimes often threatened their neighbors with military expansion, tightly controlled their national economies, and oppressed their subjects with authoritarian practices. However, communist ideology (when it was consistent with Marxist-Leninist philosophy) generally called for a global communist revolution to sweep the world, installing communist regimes in all nations and ultimately leading (it was argued) to a dissolution of nation-state entities into a global, classless society. Fascism, on the other hand, did not involve an ideology seeking pan-global unity, but rather an ideology of force and power that was focused by local nationalism. The dissolution of the State, as an avowed ultimate goal of communism, was anathema to fascist thinking.

63. **C.** The Domino Effect was the idea that Communism, if left unchecked by the United States and its allies, would rapidly spread from country to country across Europe and Asia. This fear prompted the U.S. strategy of containing Communism, motivating the United States to oppose Communist regimes in Korea and Vietnam.

64. **B.** The partition of the Indian subcontinent reflects the process of decolonization. In achieving independence, those in the region—formerly under colonial British rule—were now more free to explore local agendas. The post-colonial period saw the establishment of an Islamic state (Pakistan) and mostly Hindu India; Bangladesh later split off from Pakistan. Tensions, whether those partially suppressed under colonial rule or those which emerged as part of the decolonization process, continue to destabilize the region.

65. **A.** The League of Nations proved short-lived and failed to achieve the hopes of its founders to ensure peace and international cooperation in the post-World War I era. However, in the second half of the twentieth century, the United Nations has proven much more active as a forum for world opinion and a provider of economic, social, and sometimes military influence; NATO, the multi-national treaty organization opposed to the Soviet Union's Warsaw Pact, played a key role in strategic geopolitics during the Cold War and continues to operate; and OPEC has proven itself influential in its ability to manipulate global oil prices, causing a significant economic impact on superpowers such as the United States.

66. **C.** Insurgent groups and other weak opponents of powerful nations learned in the twentieth century that guerrilla warfare (a prolonged war of escalating ambushes and raids from hidden bases, often relying on some level of support, supply, and concealment among the civilian populace) was the most effective way to combat superpowers. Guerrilla tactics were used, for example, against the Soviet Union in Afghanistan, against the United States in Vietnam, and against Britain in Aden. Attempts to combat major nations using conventional field armies often

resulted in disastrous defeat—as Argentina learned in its defeat by Britain during the Falklands war. Nuclear weapons have never been used in combat since the Second World War.

67. C. The Soviet Union collapsed during the 1990s, breaking up into a number of smaller nations in Europe and Asia.

68. B. With two parties bitterly contesting ownership of the same territory, in a context complicated by ethnic and religious opposition, the Arab-Israeli conflict has been the most disruptive of the factors mentioned (militant opposition to Israel's existence has been common and widespread throughout the Middle East, and has led to multiple wars with Israel). The region does have potential to exploit natural resources—most significantly oil—which has led to major economic growth in the oil-rich states bordering the Persian Gulf.

69. A. The world of the late twentieth/early twenty-first century is often seen as divided into northern and southern socio-economic blocs; the north consisting of those developed, industrialized nations, mostly in North America, Europe, and Asia (such as the United States, Great Britain, Japan—and Australia), while the south is the "Third World of poor and developing nations", mostly in South America, Africa, and south/south-east Asia.

70. A. Most twentieth-century Latin American nations remained heavily influenced, socially and economically, by foreign economic involvement; weaker economies have produced dependence in some areas on foreign corporate investment or foreign employment of cheap labor.

Document-Based Essay

Overall Approach

1. Organize your essay around a clear thesis statement, which should summarize your answer to the question, and use the documents to support that thesis.

2. Use all but one of the documents.

3. Thoroughly explain how your evidence proves your argument.

4. Do not ignore any portion of the question.

5. Analyze the documents as they relate to your thesis; do not summarize their content.

6. Consider the sources of the documents (biases of the authors and historical context).

Key Points to Include

- It is clear from several of the documents that Rome worked deliberately to influence the culture of subject peoples. (Suetonius), in discussing Claudius' banning of the Druids' cult, shows the willingness of the Roman government to override pre-existing religious and cultural norms in conquered Celtic territories, although, here, in relation to a rather extreme practice; human sacrifice. (Tacitus), in *Agricola*, shows us that Romans consciously imposed their culture on conquered persons to make them more amenable to Roman political rule.

- The other documents indicate that beyond influencing subject or neighboring peoples, Roman culture was itself modified by interaction with those peoples. (Procopius) indicates that, on at least part of Rome's eastern frontier with Persia, there were few regular barriers to the movement of people and ideas into the Empire. (Plutarch) shows that many Romans, even in the days of the Republic, admired and sought to absorb elements of Greek culture, such as Greek philosophy and learning—even though Rome had come to politically dominate Greece and despite the suspicions of Roman traditionalists such as Cato the Elder. (Minucius Felix) expresses the extent to which Roman religious practices had absorbed foreign cults, and tells us that the Romans consciously followed a policy of assimilating the religious practices of nations they conquered, contributing to the overall stability and unity of the empire.

- Surveying these documents, the student should conclude that cultural influence in and around the Roman empire was multi-directional; elements of traditional Roman culture did influence conquered and neighboring people-groups, but also, Roman society absorbed a large amount of religious and cultural material from other groups, even peoples considered enemies at some point by Rome. The documents show that Rome's borders were not so tight as to prevent cultural exchange with neighbors, and that the culture of people-groups brought within the empire by conquest also continued to influence Roman society.

- A student might note that a better analysis would include additional documentation of the nature of Rome's frontiers in areas beside those mentioned in the texts, and documents written from the perspective of non-Roman cultures, whether those of conquered or neighboring peoples.

Change-Over-Time Essay

Overall Approach

1. Organize your essay around a clear thesis statement summarizing your arguments. Be sure to back up your argument with historical examples and evidence relevant to your thesis.

2. Keep in mind that the question asks you to discuss wars fought between nation-states, which often had a very different character from wars fought between or against other types of political groups.

3. Fully answer the question: note that the question asks you to focus on key breaks or changes in how wars were fought during the period, as well as on the social consequences for nation-states engaged in warfare during the period.

4. Since this is a change-over-time essay, organizing your comments in chronological order is appropriate.

Key Points to Include

- A good response would begin by describing the nature of warfare at the beginning of the period under consideration (1800), noting that war, as typified by the Napoleonic wars in Europe, focused on the pursuit of decisive victory through formal land battles between large field armies including infantry, horse-mounted cavalry, and artillery. Naval power (relying on wooden, wind-driven sailing ships) was important as a means of transport and influence on economic shipping routes but was not generally seen as the key to winning wars.

- After defining this initial status, a good response would turn to changes seen as the period progressed, noting the importance of advances in technology in changing the nature of warfare and the impact of those changes on society.

- By the second half of the nineteenth century, warfare had begun to change significantly as a result of the industrialization of society: The railroad and steam engine now allowed much more rapid deployment of troops and resources and the telegraph was making communication much more efficient in wartime. Furthermore, the intense production of war material by industrialized societies became key to winning wars; the object of war began to switch from seeking decisive victory on the battlefield to a "total war" of attrition (of resources and manpower), which aimed at the capture or destruction of the enemy's (civilian) industrial centers as well as his armies.

- Moving into the early twentieth century, the student should note the revolutionary new battlefield technologies revealed during WWI: armor (tanks), air warfare, and "weapons of mass destruction" such as chemical weapons, as well as the extent to which warfare had become crucially dependent on "home front" industrial production and the struggle to deliver produced resources safely to the battlefront. In addition to increased industrial production, "home fronts" now began to see a new level of almost total control of many areas of life, influenced by government propaganda, the organization of labor, rationing, and other measures in support of war efforts. As a result, civilians "back home" began to feel the effects of war to a degree not experienced in previous eras.

- By the Second World War, these trends had continued, and now highly mobile mechanized warfare became critical to quickly seize key enemy areas. Air power was becoming perhaps the most critical element in warfare, used to destroy enemy centers of production and entire cities in addition to supporting ground troops. Naval power, too, began to rely on air power launched from aircraft carriers.

- The trend toward air power met with further technological development in the beginning of the nuclear age, with the atomic bombings of two Japanese cities at the close of the Second World War. When the world's major superpowers began, by the close of the period under study (1950), to stockpile nuclear bombs for potential use against each other, warfare took on distinctions in form between conventional—using non-nuclear armies fighting traditional land, air, and sea battles, and unconventional—carrying the possible threat of the utter eradication of a nation state by nuclear fire. The desire to avoid this possibility would lead to new strategic challenges—and would, at times, lead to the intentional limiting of battlefield successes to prevent enemies from becoming concerned enough to resort to nuclear warfare.

- As the period closed, other strategies also became more prevalent. Although usually directed against nation-states rather than between them, guerrilla warfare—which had already been practiced at the beginning of the century by Boer fighters against the British in South Africa—emerged as a major type of warfare. The forms of some modern nation-states, such as Vietnam, were determined through guerrilla conflicts with their roots in struggles related to decolonization at the end of the period.

Comparative Essay

Overall Approach

1. Organize your essay around a clear thesis statement summarizing your arguments. Be sure to back up your argument with historical examples and evidence relevant to your thesis.

2. Since you are comparing how two different systems dealt with the same issue, be sure that you focus on similarities and dissimilarities between those systems; do not simply describe each system separately without contrasting the two. Use historical examples as evidence to illustrate and support your argument. Show balance in the amount of attention you devote to each society.

Key Points to Include

- Looking at the Islamic world, the student should note that classical Islamic teaching did not call for any division between secular and spiritual authority, but rather placed both types of authority in the hand of a single ruler, a Caliph. In the formative days of Islam after the death of Mohammed, this ruler bore responsibility for the political and religious wellbeing of the entire community. In this way, the Islamic community was ideally a community unified under the authority of a single leader representing the continuing legacy of the prophet Mohammed's leadership, although the reality of Islamic politics became much more diverse and disunified than this ideal represents. For example, the great split between the Shi'a and Sunni sects produced not only two rival religious groups within Islam, but also rival political groups defined by religious difference.

- In practice, caliphs after Islam's first century, focusing more on political and military issues, delegated much of their religious authority to jurists and teachers of Islamic law, but the religion generally still recognized no need for a conscious split between religious and political authority.

- In Western Europe, the medieval period saw tension between two poles of authority, king and church; these two centers of power, one secular, the other religious, often cooperated (as was the case with the crowning of Charlemagne by the Pope) and often clashed as rivals (for example, a German king was excommunicated by the Pope during the Investiture Crisis). Medieval Western European teachings often held that God had granted authority over men's spiritual lives to the Christian Church, and authority over their political lives to secular monarchs; tension ensued when either party attempted to infringe on the authority of the other, with cooperation in their mutual roles forming the "ideal"—kings working to ensure justice and stability in the earthly kingdom, churchmen working to teach eternal salvation in the heavenly kingdom.

- In addition to describing the contrasts above, you might also place the question in a broader context by noting that the medieval European view represented a significant addition to the much more apolitical form which Christianity took in its original nature, whereas the secular/religious relationship discussed for Islam was a part of that religion from its beginning. As a similarity between the two political-religious systems, the student might note that rulers in both systems often presented themselves using religious imagery and language; despite the separation of the secular/spiritual poles in Europe, religion remained a powerful issue for secular figures to deal with and framed many public and private identities. Similarly, Muslim rulers, by necessity, generally presented themselves partly in terms of religious authority even when many of their efforts were being directed toward the secular sphere. Overall, however, the most significant area of contrast is, as noted, that Muslim rulers were expected to wield both spiritual and secular power without conflict, while European Christian rulers were expected to wield secular power in cooperation with the Church's spiritual authority.